Interventions

Support for Individual Students With Behavior Challenges

THIRD EDITION

Randy Sprick
Cristy Coughlin
Mickey Garrison
Jessica Sprick

With Contributions by:
Geoff Colvin
Barbara Gueldner
Kenneth W. Merrell

© 2019 Ancora Publishing, Inc.

Reproduction of the downloadable materials is granted to a single school-based professional (principal, school psychologist, teacher, special education teacher, school counselor, or behavior specialist) to assist in designing behavior interventions for individual students. Except as expressly permitted above and under the United States Copyright Act of 1976, no materials in this work may be used, reproduced, or distributed in any form or by any means, electronic or mechanical, without the prior written permission of the publisher.

Published in the United States by
Ancora Publishing
21 West 6th Avenue
Eugene, Oregon 97401
ancorapublishing.com

ISBN: 978-1-59909-105-1

Cover by Abby Park
Book design and layout by Natalie Conaway

Any resources and website addresses are provided for reader convenience and were current at the time of publication. Report broken links to info@ancorapublishing.com.

DOWNLOAD REPRODUCIBLE MATERIALS
Go to download.ancorapublishing.com and enter access code 978-1-59909-105-1

TABLE OF CONTENTS

Strategies vi
About the Authors vii
Preface ix
Acknowledgments xi

INTRODUCTION The Importance of Behavior Intervention 1

What Is Behavior Intervention? 1
Individual Intervention Within a Multi-Tiered System of Support
  for Behavior (MTSS-B) 4
  Changing the Culture 5
  Creating a Continuum of Supports 7
    Tier 1. Universal Supports for All Students 8
    Tier 2. Targeted Supports for Some Students 9
    Tier 3. Intensive Supports for a Few Students 10

Book Organization 13
References 17

SECTION 1 Establishing a System for Individualized Intervention 19

Task 1. Assess the organization and efficacy of staff and teams working on the
  behavioral aspects of MTSS 20
    Step 1. Assess the current status of your building's universal behavior support practices 20
    Step 2. Clarify the organizational framework and purpose of existing MTSS-B teams 21

Task 2. Establish one or more teams to engage in problem-solving for individual students . . . 30
    *Step 1. Identify the interventionists and behavior problem-solving teams that already exist
      within your building 31*
    Step 2. Specify how your problem-solving team should function 32
    Step 3. Set a meeting schedule for each problem-solving team 36
    Step 4. Write job descriptions for all interventionists and teams 36

Task 3. Develop processes for identifying students in need of additional behavior support . . . 37
    Step 1. Identify a set of red-flag indicators 37
    Step 2. Develop a process for teachers to request assistance 40
    Step 3. Consider implementing universal behavior risk screening 40
    *Step 4. Establish a process for regularly reviewing red-flag indicators and
      teacher referrals 44*

Task 4. Develop a support coordinator program 45
    *Step 1. Identify staff members in your school who can serve as support coordinators for
      identified students 45*
    Step 2. Create a process for assigning support coordinators to identified students 46
    Step 3. Outline the specific responsibilities of a support coordinator 46
    *Step 4. Plan to meet with support coordinators regularly and keep clear, detailed records of
      all students 48*

Task 5. Develop a menu of ready-to-use interventions 49
    Step 1. Identify the ready-to-use interventions already in place within your building and select new interventions to develop or adopt   *50*
    Step 2. Identify staff who will coordinate ready-to-use interventions, and outline their responsibilities for implementation   *53*

Task 6. Establish processes for responding to Code Red situations 54
    Step 1. Adopt policies for documenting Code Red situations   *54*
    Step 2. Develop policies for responding to unsafe or severely disruptive behavior   *55*
    Step 3. Develop policies regarding threats of targeted violence in schools   *57*
    Step 4. Establish a threat assessment team   *60*
    Step 5. Clarify procedures for systematically responding to threats   *67*
    Step 6. Create a plan to conduct threat awareness sessions for staff and students   *73*

Task 7. Coordinate training and ongoing professional development support for interventionists 75

Task 8. Plan to monitor implementation fidelity of your building's classroom management practices, early-stage intervention strategies, and menu of ready-to-use interventions 80
    Step 1. Select a method of assessing fidelity   *81*
    Step 2. Using measurable terms, define what "good" fidelity means   *81*
    Step 3. Create a schedule for monitoring fidelity   *82*
    Step 4. Make a plan to provide fidelity support as needed   *83*

Task 9. Assess system outcomes and continuously look for opportunities to improve 84
    Step 1. Plan to assess intervention participation and outcomes   *84*
    Step 2. Continuously identify opportunities to better meet the needs of your students   *84*

Section Summary 88
References 102

SECTION 2   Embedding a Problem-Solving Model into Each Tier of Support   105

A Consistent Problem-Solving Framework 106
Applying the Problem-Solving Model Across All Tiers of Support 109
Initiating Individual Problem-Solving Efforts 111
    Assigning a Support Coordinator 111
    Stage 1 Problem-Solving 112
        Coordinating Enrollment in Existing, Ready-to-Use Interventions   *112*
        Summary of Stage 1 Problem-Solving   *114*
    Stage 2 and Stage 3 Problem-Solving 115
        The Teacher Interview   *115*
        Summary of the Teacher Interview   *147*
        The 25-Minute Planning Process   *157*
        Summary of the 25-Minute Planning Process   *180*
        The Multidisciplinary Team Planning Process   *191*
        Summary of the Multidisciplinary Team Planning Process   *215*

Section Summary 216
References 231

SECTION 3 Designing an Effective Behavior Intervention Plan   233

What Are the Components of a Behavior Intervention Plan? 234
How to Build a Behavior Intervention Plan 236
Task 1. Clearly define target behaviors and goals in objective, measurable terms 238

Step 1. Objectively describe problematic behavior 238
Step 2. Objectively describe appropriate/replacement behaviors 244
Step 3. Specify measurable goals for both the problematic and the appropriate /replacement behaviors 247

Task 2. Select antecedent intervention strategies 248
Task 3. Identify teaching intervention strategies 252
Task 4. Identify positive consequence intervention strategies 257
Task 5. Identify corrective consequence intervention strategies 261

Step 1. Categorize problem behaviors and define limits 261
Step 2. Select corrective consequence intervention strategies 264

Task 6. Identify interactional strategies 276

Step 1. Determine baseline ratio of positive to corrective interactions (optional) 277
Step 2. Select strategies to increase noncontingent positive interactions and school connectedness 282

Task 7. Describe other group interventions, academic supports, accommodations,
 or specialized intervention strategies to include in the student's plan 287
Task 8. Specify procedures for collecting data and monitoring progress 289

Step 1. Select a data collection method 289
Step 2. Determine how to summarize and interpret data 298

Task 9. Make a plan to monitor and ensure implementation fidelity of the plan 303

Step 1. Identify a method for monitoring and evaluating implementation fidelity 303
Step 2. Make a plan to encourage good implementation and provide follow-up support as needed 305

Section Summary 310
References 316

SECTION 4 Specialized Intervention Strategies   321

Behavioral Contracting 322
Structured Reinforcement 344
Self-Monitoring and Self-Evaluation 373
Behavior Emergency Planning 406
Managing Emotional Escalation 433
Supporting Students with Internalizing Challenges 469

APPENDIX A Trauma-Sensitive Practices   541
APPENDIX B Reinforcer Checklist for Elementary and Secondary Students   551

STRATEGIES

Foundational Intervention Strategies

Antecedent strategies — *248*
    A. Change assigned seating. — 248
    B. Change work requirements. — 249
    C. Provide breaks. — 249
    D. Change expectations or procedures. — 250
    E. Offer viable choices. — 250
    F. Use precorrections. — 250
    G. Increase opportunities to respond. — 251
    H. Increase monitoring and supervision. — 251

Teaching strategies — *252*
    I. Re-teach classroom expectations. — 253
    J. Provide demonstrations and modeling. — 254
    K. Provide positive practice and feedback. — 254
    L. Provide opportunities for verbal practice. — 255

Positive consequence strategies — *257*
    M. Deliver praise and specific feedback. — 257
    N. Offer rewards. — 258
    O. Send positive news home. — 258

Corrective consequence strategies — *261*
    P. Ignore misbehavior. — 264
    Q. Reduce peer attention. — 266
    R. Use gentle verbal reprimands or warnings. — 266
    S. Assign time owed. — 267
    T. Assign in-class timeout. — 267
    U. Assign out-of-class timeout. — 268
    V. Revoke a privilege. — 270

Interactional strategies — *276*
    W. Increase the frequency of noncontingent positive attention. — 282
    X. Assign a meaningful duty or responsibility at school. — 283
    Y. Encourage and facilitate the student's participation in clubs, after-school activities, and other school events. — 283
    Z. Connect the student with an adult or peer mentor at school. — 283

Specialized Intervention Strategies

    1. Behavioral Contracting — 322
    2. Structured Reinforcement — 344
    3. Self-Monitoring and Self-Evaluation — 373
    4. Behavior Emergency Planning — 406
    5. Managing Emotional Escalation — 433
    6. Supporting Students With Internalizing Challenges — 469

ABOUT THE AUTHORS

RANDY SPRICK, Ph.D., has worked as a paraprofessional, teacher, and teacher trainer at the elementary and secondary levels. Author of a number of widely read books on behavior and classroom management, Dr. Sprick is director of Safe & Civil Schools, a consulting company that provides inservice programs throughout the country. He and his trainers work with numerous large and small school districts on longitudinal projects to improve student behavior and motivation. Efficacy of that work is documented in peer-reviewed research, and Safe & Civil Schools materials are listed on the National Registry of Evidence-Based Programs and Practices (NREPP). Dr. Sprick was the recipient of the 2007 Council for Exceptional Children (CEC) Wallin Lifetime Achievement Award.

CRISTY COUGHLIN holds a Ph.D. in school psychology from the University of Oregon and an undergraduate degree in psychology from Western Michigan University. Dr. Coughlin has worked as a school-based behavioral consultant and program evaluator for educational projects in the United States, Australia, and Africa. Her areas of expertise are oriented around educational assessment, applied behavior analysis, and translating educational research to practice.

MICKEY GARRISON, Ph.D., has been a teacher, administrator, and consultant. As a principal, her school was awarded national recognition and received attention from the George Lucas Foundation, which created a documentary about the school's accomplishments in mathematics (see www.glef.org/magic-of-math). She is currently the school improvement director for a joint venture among the Oregon Department of Education, Oregon's Education Service Districts, Oregon's K–12 system, and higher education. Under Dr. Garrison's leadership, districts are advancing school improvement from being an event to becoming an integral part of how their schools operate. As a consultant, Dr. Garrison specializes in training school teams to increase student achievement and improve behavior.

JESSICA SPRICK, M.S. in Special Education, is a consultant and presenter for Safe & Civil Schools and a writer for Ancora Publishing. Ms. Sprick has been a special education teacher for students with behavioral needs and Dean of Students at the middle school level. Her practical experience working with special and general education students and staff, along with strong training in positive behavior support techniques, drives her passion to help school personnel develop and implement effective behavior management plans.

Contributors

GEOFF COLVIN, Ph.D., draws on his experiences as a teacher (both in special education and in general education), school administrator, and research associate at the University of Oregon. Dr. Colvin is a nationally recognized educational consultant who has assisted personnel in more than 200 school districts and agencies manage problem behavior, teach challenging students, and plan for school safety. He has authored more than 80 publications, including books, book chapters, articles, and video programs, on teaching and managing students who exhibit the full range of problem behavior. His video program Defusing Anger and Aggression received national recognition by winning the 2000 Telly Award and Communicator Award of Distinction. As an administrator, he directed a juvenile detention school for 5 years and was the principal for a countywide school for seriously emotionally disturbed youth for 5 years. He also served for several years as a supervisor of special programs with Bethel School District in Oregon.

BARBARA GUELDNER, Ph.D., MSE is a licensed psychologist and Nationally Certified School Psychologist (NCSP) who has worked with youth, families, and community partners for 25 years. Her clinical work has spanned a diverse array of settings, including public and private schools, a university-based child and family clinic, pediatric primary care, inpatient medical and psychiatric units at Children's Hospital Colorado, and private practice. Her research, publications, and trainings focus on social and emotional learning (SEL); childhood mental health prevention, treatment and resilience; internalizing problems, school-based mindfulness practices; and working with adults to facilitate children's emotional development. Dr. Gueldner is coauthor of the book, *Social and Emotional Learning in the Classroom* (2nd edition due for release in 2019), and the SEL curricula *Merrell's Strong Kids and Merrell's Strong Teens*, now in their second edition. She lives in Steamboat Springs, Colorado.

KENNETH W. MERRELL, Ph.D., until his death in 2011, was Professor of School Psychology and Director of the Oregon Resiliency Project at the University of Oregon. For 25 years, Dr. Merrell's influential teaching and research focused on social–emotional assessment and intervention for at-risk children and adolescents and social–emotional learning in schools. He published more than 90 peer-reviewed journal articles, several books and nationally normed assessment instruments, and the Strong Kids programs, a comprehensive social and emotional learning curriculum. Dr. Merrell was a Fellow of the Division of School Psychology (Division 16) and the Society for Clinical Child and Adolescent Psychology (Division 53) of the American Psychological Association. He received the Senior Scientist Award from Division 16, the Division's highest honor for excellence in science.

PREFACE

This book was originally published in 1993. Since that time, research has continued to confirm that the proactive, positive, and instructional approaches suggested in the original edition are far more effective in managing and motivating students than traditional authoritarian and punitive approaches. From the literature on schoolwide behavior support, classroom management, and interventions with individual students, we know at a minimum that students are most likely to thrive with educators who:

- Maintain and communicate high expectations for student success
- Build positive relationships with students
- Teach students how to behave successfully
- Create consistent, predictable classroom routines
- Provide consistent monitoring and supervision
- Provide frequent positive feedback
- Correct misbehavior in a calm, consistent, and logical manner

This third edition of *Interventions* translates these broad ideas about behavior management and interventions into specific actions you can take to improve the behavior of individual students.

This revision includes information on schoolwide coordination for delivery of intervention services that first appeared in *Behavioral Response to Intervention* (B-RTI): *A Schoolwide Approach* (Section 1). This is the background information administrators and school leaders need to set up a system for individualized intervention. It offers guidance on how to organize resources within a school to ensure that no students fall through the cracks and that students and teachers receive the support they need. In addition, this revision presents detailed direction and tools for applying a consistent approach to problem-solving across tiers of support (Section 2). Finally, we present step-by-step instructions for designing an effective behavior intervention plan (Section 3) and for planning and implementing selected specialized interventions (Section 4).

This book fits into a continuum of behavior support products in the Safe & Civil Schools Series, a comprehensive set of resources designed to help school personnel make all school settings physically and emotionally safe for all students. In implementation projects throughout the country, we and our colleagues have learned that when expectations are clear and directly taught to students, much as you would teach writing skills, the vast majority of students will strive to be cooperative and meet those expectations. By implementing the preventive aspects of the Safe & Civil Schools Series, teachers can spend less time dealing with disruption and resistance and more time teaching.

However, some students will need more. Sometimes you will have to initiate problem-solving efforts and provide additional targeted (Tier 2) or individualized (Tier 3) supports to meet a student's needs. This book is intended to furnish everything necessary to design and implement intervention strategies that can be used at both of these tiers.

ACKNOWLEDGMENTS

We would like to give special thanks to the authors of specific chapters and sections. Their names also appear on the respective chapters or material they contributed to, and we wish to recognize their efforts and thank them for their time and expertise.

- Mike Booher for his contributions on suicide threat assessment included in Section 1
- Geoff Colvin: Author of Managing Emotional Escalation in Section 4
- Barbara Gueldner and Ken Merrell: Authors of Supporting Students With Internalizing Challenges in Section 4
- Shawn Reaves for his contributions on managing physically dangerous behavior, specifically Managing Threats in Section 1

We would also like to thank Sara Ferris, Natalie Conaway, Marilyn Sprick, Matt Sprick, Faye Venteicher, Nic Roy, Jake Clifton, Jackie Hefner, Jen Colley, Carole Mangels, and Caroline DeVorss at Ancora Publishing.

INTRODUCTION

The Importance of Behavior Intervention

Student misbehavior is one of the leading frustrations of educators. Any major misbehavior that students engage in chronically—insubordination, disruption, disrespect, or refusal to do work—can make even highly skilled teachers feel helpless, frustrated, and angry. This book gives teachers and all educators more tools to correct any and all chronic problems—overt misbehavior, lack of motivation, anger and hostility, and even chronic internalizing behaviors such as shyness, depression, and anxiety. This book is built on the understanding, well founded in the research literature of the last 70 years, that behavior can be changed. Positive and respectful intervention procedures can shape and modify problem behavior to become productive behavior. One important and unavoidable job of educators is to use these procedures to help students learn to be successful students and, eventually, successful and productive citizens.

What Is Behavior Intervention?

Behavior intervention is the term educators have devised for a planned response to a behavior (or set of behaviors) that is interfering with a student's success in school. To go a little deeper, Tilly & Flugum's (1995, p. 485) definition aligns well with the processes and goals of intervention as presented in this book. They define *intervention* as "a planned modification of the environment made for the purpose of altering behavior in a pre-specified way." Three key phrases in this definition call attention to the following features of behavior interventions:

> An intervention is *planned* ahead of time, providing an important roadmap for addressing misbehavior by clarifying the specific actions that will take place and the responsibilities of people involved in its implementation.
>
> An intervention seeks to *alter behavior in a pre-specified way*, meaning that it's goal directed, with desired outcomes outlined prior to implementation.
>
> An intervention is focused on *modifying the environment* rather than the individual—identifying those variables that can be changed to encourage appropriate behavior and discourage misbehavior.

The basis for this book is a set of well-researched behavioral principles:

1. **Behavior has a purpose.** Problem behavior exists because it serves some useful purpose for the student (Carr, 1977; O'Neill, Albin, Storey, Horner, & Sprague, 2015). Acknowledging that there is an underlying reason for behavior requires you to ask: What is the student achieving with this misbehavior? A student may be trying to get something, such as attention from teachers or peers, or avoid something, such as an embarrassing or stressful situation. Behavior that seems illogical, mean-spirited, and unproductive from the teacher's point of view may seem logical, reasonable, and even smart from the student's perspective, which is made up of past experience and current perceptions. In some situations, misbehavior may be the only behavior in the student's repertoire that results in the desired outcome. For other students, misbehavior may just be more efficient or effective than more socially appropriate ways of achieving an outcome. Understanding what motivates problematic behavior is the first key to finding an appropriate approach to intervention.

2. **Behavior is related to the environment in which it occurs.** Behavior is influenced by the events that happen before (i.e., antecedent and setting events) and the consequences, both positive and negative, that follow (Foster-Johnson & Dunlap, 1993; Iwata, Dorset, Slifer, Bauman, & Richman, 1982). To understand the purpose of behavior, you must first determine the relationship between problem behavior and the environment in which it occurs. By identifying antecedent events that trigger problem behavior and consequences that typically follow it, you can develop a *functional hypothesis*, or a prediction about the purpose, or function, that the problem behavior is serving for the student.

3. **Lasting behavior change is more likely with positive, rather than punitive, techniques.** While a behavior intervention will typically need to specify reactive strategies (e.g., redirection, de-escalation, clearly outlined consequences, crisis management procedures), the goal of intervention is not just the absence of misbehavior. Positive, proactive intervention plans emphasize strategies that prevent problem behavior and explicitly teach and reinforce alternative desired behaviors (Carr et al., 2002). Compared with reactive interventions that rely on punitive consequences alone, proactive interventions are more likely to produce lasting behavior change (Carr, Robinson, & Palumbo, 1990).

4. **No student should be intentionally or unintentionally humiliated or belittled.** The only absolute rule about behavior management is that belittlement of students has no place in any educational setting—all behavior interventions must treat students with dignity and respect. To have a positive and lasting impact, interventions must attempt to build up student strengths and expand their skills for replacing problem behavior, rather than simply squelching or containing problem behavior (Kincaid, 1996; Wehmeyer, 1999).

5. **Behavior can be changed through environmental redesign.** All students can learn to exhibit appropriate behavior. By considering how the environment supports misbehavior and doesn't support more socially appropriate behaviors, you can identify environmental variables to change that will make problem behavior irrelevant (i.e., making access to desired outcomes easier or more frequent so the student no longer needs to use misbehavior), inefficient (i.e., teaching an alternative, more socially appropriate behavior that leads to the outcome previously reached

All behavior interventions must treat students with dignity and respect.

through problem behavior), and/or ineffective (i.e., ensuring that problem behavior is no longer rewarded [Dunlap & Fox, 2011; O'Neill et al., 2015]) . By focusing on the environmental factors that contribute to problematic behavior patterns, you can harness educators' greatest power to motivate students to change their behavior—through structuring for success, teaching expectations, observing and monitoring student behavior, interacting positively, and correcting fluently.

As vast as the body of research literature regarding behavior change is, its key findings can be encapsulated in five broad categories of environmental variables that have proven effective in changing behavior, especially when used in combination: prevention, teaching, monitoring, encouragement, and correction. To more easily remember the variables, use the acronym STOIC, where each letter in the acronym represents one category.

Structure for Success: Changing the *structure* of the setting can impact the events that happen before behavior (i.e., antecedents and setting events). Modifying features of the schedule, physical arrangement of the classroom, instructional procedures, and other structural elements known to trigger a student's problem behavior can eliminate or reduce the impact of these antecedent and setting events on behavior.

Teaching Replacement Behaviors: By *teaching* expectations, appropriate behaviors, and coping and self-control strategies, you help the student develop or strengthen behaviors that are alternatives to misbehavior. Identify a plan to teach students to function successfully in the structure you have created.

Observe and Monitor: The simple act of active observation goes a long way to curtail behavior. Incorporating strategies to increase monitoring, such as continuously circulating throughout the room and scanning during challenging times, can help prevent misbehavior from occurring as well as ensure that you provide appropriate redirections when misbehavior does happen.

Interact Positively: Interacting positively involves two connected efforts: 1) providing frequent positive feedback when the student demonstrates appropriate behavior, such as meeting expectations, using replacement behaviors, and responding appropriately to requests and directions, and 2) building positive, rewarding relationships with students by greeting and showing an interest in them.

Correct Misbehavior Fluently: When misbehavior occurs, it's important for all staff to know how to respond calmly, briefly, consistently, and immediately. Corrections should minimize distraction from the instructional activity and redirect the student to engage in appropriate behavior.

ABC ANALYSIS

Those with training in behavior analysis will recognize an *Antecedent-Behavior-Consequence* (ABC) analysis of behavior embedded in the STOIC acronym. With ABC analysis, any behavior can be viewed as a function of the antecedents (those stimuli that precede a behavior) and the consequences that naturally follow from the behavior—simply meaning that people learn from their environment.

Positive interactions and encouragement reinforce desirable behavior, and corrections calmly discourage problem behavior. This increases the likelihood that students will choose to engage in positive behaviors in the future.

STOIC is a way of thinking about intervention that encompasses the essential ingredients of every successful behavior intervention plan. It is the perfect definition of educators who understand behavior intervention practice: They are relentless in striving to find interventions that will help troubled students, and they continually demonstrate high positive regard for all students. They do not "tolerate" misbehavior, but are endlessly patient in experimenting with different interventions until they find some combination of strategies to help their students become successful.

> **stoic** /sto·ic/ adj.
>
> 1. Tending to remain unemotional, especially showing an admirable patience and endurance in the face of adversity.
>
> 2. Unruffled, calm, and firmly restrained in response to pain or distress.

Individual Intervention Within a Multi-Tiered System of Support for Behavior (MTSS-B)

While individualized interventions are necessary, they are much easier to carry out in a school with a well-designed and fully implemented schoolwide behavior plan. Although this book will be helpful to an individual teacher, it works best when implemented schoolwide as part of a *Multi-Tiered System of Support for Behavior* (MTSS-B) approach. Multi-tiered systems of support for behavior integrate positive behavior support practices and a response-to-intervention framework:

Positive Behavior Supports

Warger (1999, p. 2) defines positive behavior support as a long-term, long-view process:

> *Unlike traditional behavioral management, which views the individual as the problem and seeks to "fix" him or her by quickly eliminating the challenging behavior, positive behavioral support and functional analysis view systems, settings, and lack of skill as parts of the "problem" and work to change those. As such, these approaches are characterized as long-term strategies to reduce inappropriate behavior, teach more appropriate behavior, and provide contextual supports necessary for successful outcomes.*

The objective of PBS is to place more time, effort, staff development, and financial resources on proactive, positive, and instructional approaches rather than on reactive and exclusionary approaches (Sprick, Knight, Reinke, Skyles, & Barnes, 2010).

Response to Intervention

Batsche et al. (2005, p. 3) defines response to intervention as:

> *The practice of providing high-quality instruction and interventions matched to student need, monitoring progress frequently to make decisions about changes in instruction or goals, and applying child response data to important educational decisions.*

Put in simple terms, this means always trying the easiest and cheapest thing first and moving to more intensive intervention only when those easier, cheaper interventions were implemented well but did not help improve the student's behavior.

In sum, MTSS-B merges these simple concepts:

- Prior to using more complicated and costly interventions, you should try the easiest, cheapest, and least time-consuming intervention that has a reasonable chance of success.
- You cannot know that a simple intervention will not work unless you try it and implement it well.

While individualized interventions are necessary, they are much easier to carry out in a school with a well-designed and fully implemented schoolwide behavior plan.

- If a student with a behavior problem is resistant to simple interventions, progressively more detailed and intensive interventions should be attempted until the problem is resolved.
- To be considered, an intervention should have a long track record of success—evidence and research literature documenting its effectiveness in a variety of settings, with varied student populations, and without being coercive or humiliating to the student.

MTSS-B involves changing the system to meet the needs of the student while also helping the student fit successfully into the system. At the broadest level, this means that schools need to become places where students want to be. Creating a safe, positive, and inviting school climate is one important part of successful MTSS-B implementation (Carr et al., 2002; Sprick, Booher, Isaacs, Sprick, & Rich, 2014).

> **RESOURCE: EFFECTIVE BUILDING- AND DISTRICT-LEVEL POLICIES**
>
> *Foundations: A Proactive and Positive Behavior Support System* provides a broader overview of effective policies at the building and district level that can help ensure that:
>
> - School is a physically and emotionally safe place for students and staff.
> - Policies and procedures are clear, reasonable, and equitably enforced.
> - Staff actively strive to build relationships with students that inspire them to do their best.
>
> If your school does not have a proactive and positive schoolwide approach, we urge you to involve the whole staff in a continuous effort to implement and sustain such policies. There is no more effective way to reduce the need for individual interventions.

The principles underlying MTSS-B and behavior intervention are simple and based on common sense as well as a sound theoretical foundation and research base.

Changing the Culture

As is often the case when considering a system to support positive behavior, there is good news and bad news.

Good news: The principles underlying MTSS-B and behavior intervention are simple and based on common sense as well as a sound theoretical foundation and research base. They boil down to this: Keep adjusting the variables in a student's situation until something starts to work. The best behavior managers in schools aren't necessarily those who know the most, but rather those who don't give up—those staff members who are relentless in their quest to get the best from their students. These teachers say, "I am going to keep manipulating your environment until I find a way to help you unlock your success."

Bad news: Although the principles are simple, most schools and teachers are not applying them. Why? The reason is just as simple. Student behavior problems drive teachers crazy. A lot of emotional baggage comes into play with many teacher-student interactions. Teachers are under tremendous pressure; they are held accountable for their students' academic success or failure. When a student is disruptive, noncompliant, passive, resistant, or exhibiting any other of myriad potential behavior problems, the student poses a direct and immediate threat to the teacher's authority.

In addition, many, if not most, schools operate under a culture of control. It is all too easy for teachers to get into a power struggle with a misbehaving student by trying to *make* the student behave appropriately. It's the human reaction to threatening situations: fight or flight. Teachers can't run screaming from the classroom (as much as they might like to sometimes), so the fight reaction kicks in. If this pattern continues, by the time the teacher asks for assistance or the student's behavior needs rise to the attention of the administrator, school counselor, school psychologist, or other problem-solving professional, the teacher does not want help for the student—rather, the teacher wants someone else to manage the student (think about repeated referrals to the office) or wants the student placed in a different setting. Problem-solving professionals, a role we call *interventionists*, commonly hear, "I've tried everything for this student. He needs to be placed in a special education setting."

Administrators, school psychologists, school social workers, and school counselors (when in the role of interventionists) must take this pressure into account when they try to create better behavioral practices in schools. It's not just a matter of sharing all the right information with staff. You also have to proactively change teachers' mindsets about student behavior problems and, in turn, change their behavior by getting them to implement evidence-based behavior management practices, thus reducing the frequency of power struggles, negativity, and frustration. To bring about this cultural change, administrators and members of your behavior leadership team must infuse the following assumptions of MTSS-B into your building's culture of behavior support.

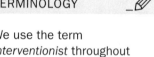

TERMINOLOGY

We use the term *interventionist* throughout this book to mean anyone who is involved in planning an intervention. An interventionist can be a teacher, school counselor, behavioral specialist, special education teacher or consultant, or administrator. All interventionists should be trained in the full range of interventions that your school or district has in place.

1. **All staff have a role in behavior support.** When a student is exhibiting academic or social behavior difficulties, all teachers understand that they must play an active role, in fact a pivotal role, in preventing the development of problems and in problem-solving to support the student's needs. Simply handing the problem off to a different adult or moving the student to a different setting is no longer a viable option—too many students need help.

2. **Behavior is highly malleable, and behavioral skills must be taught.** Starting with the concept that behavior can be changed gives educators great confidence. The best problem-solvers are those who recognize that, despite what a student's behavior looks like right now, it can improve dramatically with the right intervention plan. No matter how difficult or problematic a student's behavior may be, there is some combination of variables that can be changed in such a way that the student will make meaningful progress toward more responsible behavior. If teachers do not understand and operate from the belief that behavior can be changed, they are more likely to view any intervention as doomed to failure (e.g., "That is just the way this student is!"). Behavior is learned and can be changed through careful consideration and manipulation of the environmental factors that may be contributing to problematic behavior patterns. When educators fully understand this concept, they are well on their way to becoming active problem-solvers, not passive problem-admirers.

3. **Problem-solving processes should focus on variables that can be changed.** Spending too much time discussing concerns about a student's home life or attributing problematic behavior to static characteristics of a student (e.g., a label of ADHD, a "bad attitude") places blame on the student and can derail teams from fully exploring possible ways the problem can be solved (Walker, 1995). Rather than attributing problem behavior to variables that cannot be easily changed, an effective problem-solving process targets variables within the student's environment that are amenable to change (e.g., modifying the classroom environment to make problem behavior less relevant, teaching and reinforcing appropriate behavior, and altering adult responses to problem behavior so that it no longer leads to a desired outcome for the student).

Every adult in the school must become part of the solution, working collaboratively to ensure that no student falls through cracks (or chasms) in the behavior support systems within the school.

Creating a Continuum of Supports

Service delivery is how adults and systems in the school work together to ensure that all students' behavioral and emotional needs are met. Behavior support service delivery includes both the problem-solving strategies used to assess the situation and the resulting intervention plan created from these efforts.

Most educators are familiar with the triangle (Figure A) used by public health (Commission on Chronic Illness, 1957) that has universal prevention and intervention at the bottom, selected or targeted services in the middle, and intensive services at the top.

Every adult in the school must become part of the solution, working collaboratively to ensure that no student falls through cracks in the behavior support systems.

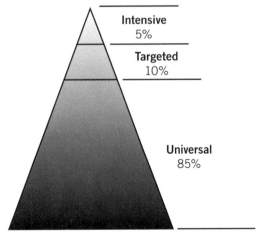

FIGURE A *Public Health Triangle*

Our model of service delivery turns this triangle upside down (see Figure B on the next page). In our model, universal services move to the top to represent the broadest level of services for the broadest group of students. The purpose behind inverting the triangle is to highlight the importance of spending the most time, energy, and money on universal, Tier 1 interventions, those services applied by all staff members and directed at all students. Students whose needs are not met by the wide net cast at the top of the triangle fall into the safety net of the next tiers: targeted (Tier 2) and intensive (Tier 3). In essence, the MTSS-B model functions like a sifting process. Only the 10%–15% of students who don't benefit from universal efforts need services at other levels.

FIGURE B *Safe & Civil Schools MTSS Model of Service*

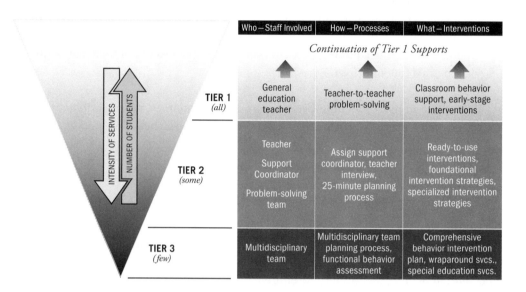

Tier 1 includes not only universal policies, but also a layer of effective classroom management practices and a set of early-stage interventions for common behavior problems.

Tier 1: Universal Supports for All Students

Tier 1 supports are designed to prevent problem behavior from occurring. Effective Tier 1 systems should address the behavior of most students (80%–90%) and *reduce the number of students w*ho need more expensive and time-consuming resources at Tiers 2 and 3. Multi-tiered systems of support can be structured in different ways. In some models, Tier 1 is concerned only with universal prevention efforts. In our model, Tier 1 includes not only universal policies, but also a layer of effective classroom management practices and a set of early-stage interventions for common behavior problems (Sprick, Booher, Isaacs, Sprick, & Rich, 2014).

At Tier 1, the primary interventionist is the teacher. We suggest that all teachers be trained to implement a set of basic interventions before they ask for collaborative assistance. These early-stage interventions are easy and unobtrusive, and require minimal paperwork and administration involvement. They should always be tried before initiating more time-intensive or resource-heavy interventions. For most students, these efforts can adequately address problems in the early stages.

Examples of Tier 1 supports include:

- Use of evidence-based classroom management practices
- Teacher-to-teacher problem-solving
- Prereferral, early-stage, teacher-led interventions, such goal setting or planned discussion with the student

Tier 2: Targeted Supports for Some Students

Tier 2 supports are designed to reduce current incidents of problem behavior for students who continue to experience behavior problems despite implementation of Tier 1 supports (5%–10%). For students who are identified as at-risk through school screening processes, Tier 2 supports offer additional behavior support strategies in addition to the universal supports already in place within the classroom. Tier 2 interventions do not replace Tier 1 interventions; rather, they are supplemental to continuing universal efforts (Brown-Chidsey & Bickford, 2015).

At this level, problem-solving becomes *collaborative,* involving other professionals in addition to the teacher. These professionals might be another teacher, a school counselor, a school psychologist, a school social worker, an assistant principal, or a highly trained behavior specialist. While Tier 2 interventions are planned in conjunction with a building-based interventionist or problem-solving team, they are implemented by typical school personnel, most commonly the classroom teacher or an intervention coordinator.

Tier 2 supports that are put in place within the classroom should require minimal time commitment from classroom teachers and fit within existing classroom routines. In addition, skill sets required for implementing the intervention should already be a part of the teacher's repertoire or be easy to learn (Newcomer, Reeman, & Barrett, 2013). For some group supports, a staff member may be designated to serve as the intervention coordinator to oversee and monitor implementation of an intervention for a group of students.

The process for accessing Tier 2 supports should be efficient to ensure that students are matched with an appropriate intervention within a few days of an identified need. Tier 2 interventions should be continually implemented across the school year so that students can be added to the intervention at any time (OSEP Technical Assistance Center on PBIS, 2015). Procedures for implementing Tier 2 supports should also be consistent across students but allow minor modifications to increase the effectiveness of the intervention. Significant modifications to or individualization of Tier 2 interventions for a student may be more characteristic of Tier 3 support (Anderson & Borgmeier, 2010).

At Tier 2, problem-solving becomes collaborative, involving other professionals in addition to the teacher.

Examples of Tier 2 supports include:

- Participation in small group anger management lessons
- Assignment to an adult mentor
- Use of a daily behavior report card

MTSS FRAMEWORK

An MTSS-B framework is never about the process—getting a particular student through a series of interventions until the student reaches the one the teacher wants. Many teachers view interventions as simply a hoop-jumping process they must go through before they can refer a student to a special education program or an alternative placement. This approach is rooted in "not-my-problem" thinking and needs to be part of the cultural change. Effective problem-solving is about making a good-faith effort to find a solution that will help a student behave more responsibly and, accordingly, become a better student. It is always about achieving the intended end result and is never about the steps taken along the way.

Tier 3: Intensive Supports for a Few Students

Intensive Tier 3 supports are reserved for the small group of students (1%–5%) who don't respond to Tier 1 and Tier 2 services or need specialized support. A problem may be considered intensive because of its severity, immediacy, or resistance to other interventions. This level involves a more comprehensive, resource-intensive approach. A much more detailed level of problem-solving is required, and the most highly skilled personnel in the building participate. Problem-solving efforts may involve any or all of the following:

- Observations of the student in multiple settings
- Systematic records review
- Interviews with the student, all staff who work with the student, and family members
- Completion of a comprehensive functional behavior assessment (FBA)
- Coordination with other community or family agencies

Resulting interventions will be individualized and involve multiple components (Crone & Horner, 2003; Eber et al., 2009).

Note that in the case of high-intensity behaviors, such as a threat by a student to self-harm or harm someone else, the situation demands an immediate jump to a Tier 3 level of intensive problem-solving. MTSS-B is not an inflexible set of hoops wherein every situation must progress through Tier 1 and Tier 2 before Tier 3 problem-solving efforts are initiated. Crisis situations must be addressed immediately without any delay related to referral processes, paperwork considerations, or rigid definitions of tiered services.

A problem may be considered intensive (Tier 3) because of its severity, immediacy, or resistance to other interventions.

Examples of Tier 3 supports include:

- An individualized behavior intervention plan based on the results of a comprehensive FBA
- Wraparound coordination of school, family, and community agencies
- Mental health counseling or family therapy

DIFFERENCES AMONG MTSS MODELS

The language used here to describe a three-tier model may not fit the language in your school, district, or state. Our MTSS model is intentionally designed to be applied flexibly across your school's definition of Tier 1, Tier 2, and Tier 3 supports, and is independent of a school district's process for referring students to special education programs. This model can operate in parallel to your school or district framework, but we do not suggest any specific point at which a student is referred. We are mainly advocating for a framework for service delivery wherein most energy goes into universal prevention, but there are services that meet individual student needs in a manner that matches the intensity of resources to the intensity of student needs.

The goal of designing effective behavior interventions within a multi-tiered system of support is to meet student needs in the most efficient manner possible. More time- and resource-intensive processes or interventions aren't used unless previous efforts have been unsuccessful or the intensity of the problem warrants a greater level of support. If you treat all students with highly structured, multipersonnel problem analysis and intervention, there will most likely be an implementation delay, and resources that could have been used on a more serious case will have been wasted (Walker & Shinn, 2002). Further, a system that does not try simple, easy-to-implement analysis and intervention first may actually compound a problem and make things worse. For example, if waiting lists for students to get assistance from a school psychologist are long, a minor, easily treated problem may go on for so long that it becomes resistant to a simple intervention. In addition, a student who has deep-seated problems is on the same waiting list. That student's access to a multifaceted analysis and intervention may be delayed as the school psychologist spends time on problems that never needed help from someone with that level of skill and training.

In this third edition, we have attempted to clarify the two major aspects of helping students with chronic or severe behavior challenges within an MTSS-B framework. The first aspect involves the problem-solving processes that will be used to describe and analyze the context of the problem. The second aspect involves the intervention design processes that will guide development of a behavior intervention plan. While these are interrelated, both should match the intensity of the student's need. That is, the more intensive the need, the more intensive the problem-solving process should be, including the number of professionals involved, the time required to analyze the problem and develop a plan, and the quality of data collected and used to develop functional hypotheses about the nature of the problem. Likewise, the intensity of the resulting behavior plan should match the intensity of student need, including the number of professionals involved, the time required of the teacher and others to implement the plan, the quality of data collected to monitor the plan's efficacy, and the quality of processes to monitor implementation fidelity. One of the goals of this resource is to help school personnel create a continuum (from easiest and cheapest to very intensive) of both problem-solving processes and evidence-based behavior intervention plans.

One way to implement supports on a continuum is to follow a structured process to guide problem-solving and intervention design at different stages of a problem. As shown in Figure C (p. 12), we suggest adopting a range of options, moving from the type of problem-solving done by a general education teacher in a few minutes after school to more collaborative and time-consuming problem-solving processes to a full and complete functional behavior assessment guided by the most highly trained behavior analyst available to the district.

The vertical arrow in Figure C points both up and down. The down portion of the arrow is intuitively obvious. If a process and set of interventions are unsuccessful (i.e., the student's problems do not respond to intervention at that level), the problem-solving process will take on a greater degree of structure, as will the intervention strategies that result from that process. However, the arrow also points up, meaning that when a student's difficulties respond positively to the current intervention, a move to less-structured interventions should occur if there is a reasonable chance of continued success when you modify or fade the previously implemented supports.

The goals of MTSS-B are to create a range of collaborative problem-solving structures, establish a continuum of behavior interventions, and identify a variety of personnel who can assist with problem-solving and intervention design.

INTERVENTIONS: SUPPORT FOR INDIVIDUAL STUDENTS WITH BEHAVIOR CHALLENGES

FIGURE C *Continuum of Problem-Solving Processes and Intervention*

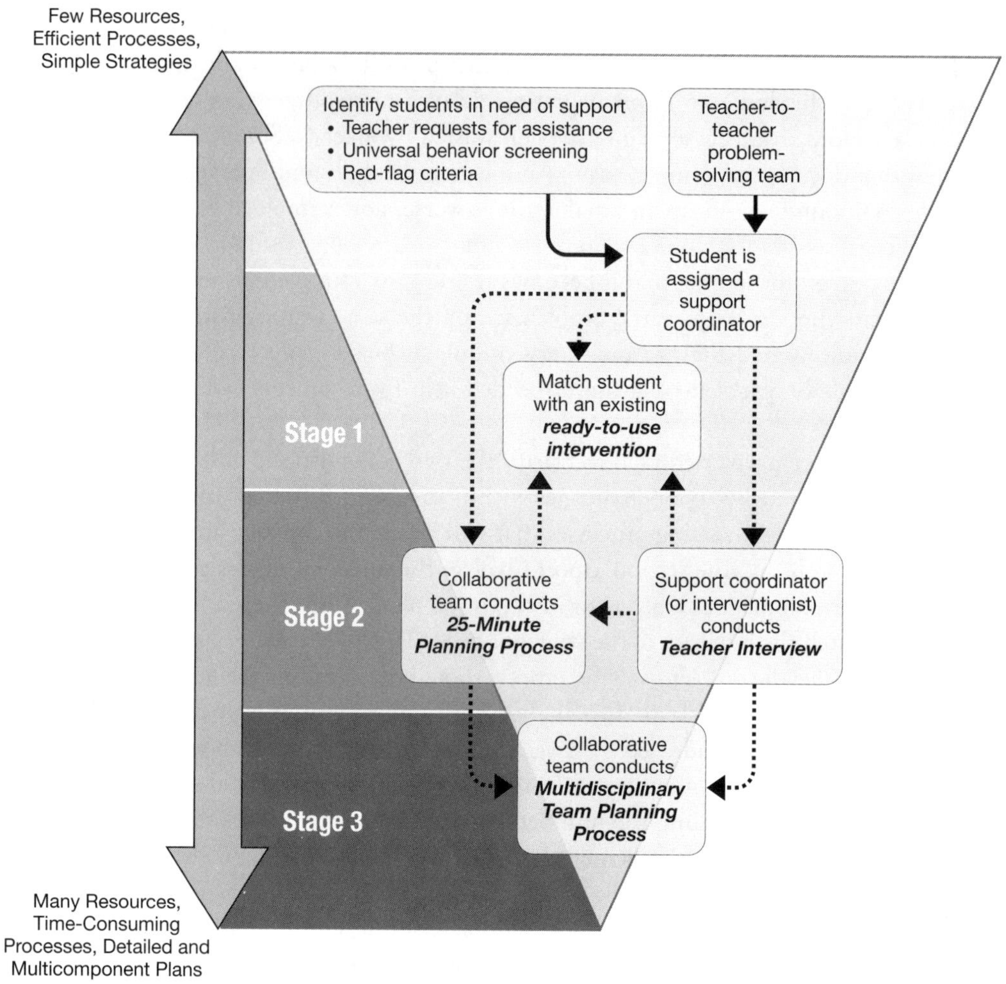

Few Resources, Efficient Processes, Simple Strategies

Identify students in need of support
- Teacher requests for assistance
- Universal behavior screening
- Red-flag criteria

Teacher-to-teacher problem-solving team

Student is assigned a support coordinator

Stage 1

Match student with an existing *ready-to-use intervention*

Stage 2

Collaborative team conducts *25-Minute Planning Process*

Support coordinator (or interventionist) conducts *Teacher Interview*

Stage 3

Collaborative team conducts *Multidisciplinary Team Planning Process*

Many Resources, Time-Consuming Processes, Detailed and Multicomponent Plans

Example: Continuum of Behavior Interventions

Schoolwide positive behavior support procedures and classroom management plans

Early-stage interventions

Menu of ready-to-use interventions
- Connections
- Meaningful Work
- Structured Recess

Foundational intervention strategies
- Deliver precorrections and reminders
- Model and practice behavior skills
- Increase behavior-specific praise
- Increase rate of positive interactions
- Correct behavior fluently

Specialized intervention strategies
- Behavioral Contracting
- Structured Reinforcement
- Self-Monitoring and Self-Evaluation
- Behavior Emergency Planning
- Managing Emotional Escalation
- Supporting Students With Internalizing Challenges

Comprehensive wraparound services
- Detailed behavior support planning based on results of a functional behavior assessment
- Coordination of school, family, and community agencies

This book is about designing and implementing layers of problem-solving and intervention efforts to most efficiently meet the needs of all students. As you read these suggestions, analyze the current organization and use of resources within your building and set up a plan for filling in any gaps in service delivery. It is our hope that this book will encourage building-based behavior leadership teams and district-level personnel to examine their current problem-solving processes and the types of interventions staff have been trained to implement. The goal is to determine strengths and areas for improvement in your current service delivery relative to the social, emotional, and behavioral needs of your students.

Book Organization

This book focuses on problem-solving and intervention for students who don't respond to Tier 1 supports—or those students who require the higher levels of support, more resources, and greater expertise that are characteristic of Tier 2 or Tier 3 supports. This book is divided into four sections.

Section 1: Establishing a System for Individualized Intervention

This first section presents information on schoolwide coordination for delivery of intervention services. This section is intended for an audience of administrators and school leaders responsible for building or districtwide behavior support efforts, including members of your school's behavior leadership team. These are the background tasks that must be completed in order to establish a system for individualized intervention. This section provides guidance on how to:

- Develop processes for identifying students in need of additional support (e.g., using red-flag indicators, universal behavior screening, and teacher requests for assistance)
- Create a menu of ready-to-use behavior interventions that will quickly and easily accommodate students identified as needing extra support
- Develop a support coordinator program that enlists staff members to ensure that at-risk students do not fall through the cracks of your system
- Organize interventionists and teams within your school to engage in individual problem-solving and intervention design
- Establish policies and processes for responding to Code Red situations that involve unsafe or severely disruptive behavior, as well as procedures for responding to threats
- Create a staff development plan that helps ensure strong implementation of interventions and problem-solving processes
- Develop a plan to monitor and ensure implementation fidelity of your building's individualized behavior support practices

TERMINOLOGY

More students than ever live in one-parent households, in foster care, with grandparents, and in other circumstances. It is often inaccurate to refer to "the student's parents," and it is cumbersome to continually refer to "the student's parent(s), grandparent(s), or guardian(s)." Therefore, in most cases the term "student's family" will be used when referring to a student's primary caregivers.

Section 2: Embedding a Problem-Solving Model Into Each Tier of Support

This section of the book describes how to use an evidence-based model to guide effective and efficient problem-solving and intervention design at the individual student level. This section is intended for anyone who will be involved in planning an intervention, which may include school psychologists, school counselors, behavior specialists, and members of existing problem-solving teams, as well as administrators and members of your behavior leadership team. In this book, we advocate for the use of a consistent problem-solving framework for addressing the needs of individual students across all tiers of support. This framework reflects the scientific method of defining and describing a problem, generating possible solutions, and implementing, monitoring, and evaluating the effectiveness of a selected solution.

Applying Tilly's (2008) description of problem-solving within a three-tiered model of support, we provide guidance in using the following five-step model to describe, understand, and solve problems across all tiers of support:

Step 1: Define the problem — *What is the problem?*
Step 2: Analyze the problem — *Why is the problem happening?*
Step 3: Consider possible solutions and select an intervention — *What solutions might improve the problem?*
Step 4: Collect data to monitor progress — *How can we measure whether improvements are occurring?*
Step 5: Evaluate whether supports are working — *Did our plan work to adequately address the problem?*

We advocate for the use of a consistent problem-solving framework for addressing the needs of individual students across all tiers of support.

This section also offers step-by-step instructions for using the following problem-solving processes and associated tools:

- *Teacher Interview*, a time- and resource-efficient tool that guides the teacher and an interventionist through developing a potentially effective initial intervention
- *25-Minute Planning Process*, a process designed to guide a problem-solving team through developing a worthwhile plan of action in less than half an hour
- *Multidisciplinary Team Planning Process*, the most intensive problem-solving process that occurs on the continuum, takes place when initial efforts have proven to be ineffective or more expertise, additional data, and comprehensive intervention supports are required to remedy the problem

Section 3: Designing an Effective Behavior Intervention Plan

The third section discusses the type of intervention plan that will result from problem-solving efforts, regardless of the setting the student is in. That is, who will work with the student, and what interventions will be implemented? This section presents a framework for building behavior interventions and can be used for any stage of a problem. Less severe problems may be addressed within this framework, but strategies used should require fewer resources, staffing, expertise, etc. than strategies used for more severe problems.

Step-by-step directions explain how to build an individual behavior intervention, with guidance on:

- How to clearly define target behaviors and goals in objective, measurable terms
- How to develop a plan for collecting data, monitoring student progress, and determining the effectiveness of the intervention plan
- How to create a plan for monitoring and ensuring fidelity of the intervention plan

In addition, this section introduces a list of *foundational intervention strategies* from five categories:

- *Antecedent strategies* to address events and conditions (e.g., times, places, people, activities) that occur before the student's misbehavior
- *Teaching strategies* that provide the student with positive replacement behaviors for misbehavior
- *Positive consequence strategies* that outline rewards and responses from staff that are intended encourage appropriate behavior and discourage misbehavior
- *Corrective consequence strategies* that are designed to increase the consistency and efficacy of corrective consequences that are implemented when misbehavior occurs.
- *Interactional strategies* that are designed to provide students with a high rate of positive interactions and help them feel connected to school.

These foundational intervention strategies form the basis of any intervention plan. For minor problems, you might need to include strategies from only one or two categories. For more severe or chronic problems, you'll likely need to address all categories in your intervention plan.

Foundational intervention strategies form the basis of any intervention plan.

Section 4: Specialized Intervention Strategies

The final section of the book contains six chapters that describe procedures for planning and implementing *specialized intervention strategies*. These intervention strategies are a powerful group of tools that may be more time intensive to plan and more time consuming to implement. They expand on the foundational intervention strategies presented in Section 3. Specialized intervention strategies will apply only to certain types of situations or intervention goals.

The following specialized intervention strategies are included in this section:

- *Behavioral Contracting.* Behavioral Contracting is a collaborative method of defining behavioral expectations, setting goals, specifying rewards, and clarifying consequences in writing. Developed through negotiation with the student, behavioral contracting can increase student motivation and investment in changing behavior.
- *Structured Reinforcement.* A Structured Reinforcement system motivates students to break deeply ingrained cycles of inappropriate behavior by offering external rewards for behavior improvements. When problems have been resistant to change or when a student needs additional encouragement to demonstrate desired behavior, a structured system for rewarding increased positive behavior or decreased rates of inappropriate behavior can provide an extra boost of motivation and help make success a reality for a student.
- *Self-Monitoring and Self-Evaluation.* Self-Monitoring and Self-Evaluation helps students become more aware, responsible, and in control of their own behavior. In

self-monitoring, the student observes and records the occurrence or nonoccurrence of certain behaviors. *Self-evaluation* is a modified form of self-monitoring in which the student evaluates and records the quality of some aspect of a behavior. Both strategies are designed to help students better understand their own behavior and use this information to change behavior over time.

- *Behavior Emergency Planning.* A Behavior Emergency Plan skips over preventive strategies and moves directly to specifying the protocol for responding immediately to behaviors that have escalated into a Code Red situation. It is appropriate when the student has exhibited one or more Code Red behaviors in the past or misbehavior has escalated or the possibility of a Code Red situation is likely. Code Red situations involve behaviors that are either so dangerous or so disruptive that classes cannot continue. These include behaviors such as:

  - Overt aggressive behavior toward others (e.g., kicking, hitting, fighting)
  - Threats of targeted violence toward others
  - Brandishing items that could be used as weapons
  - Carrying weapons
  - Self-injurious behavior
  - Vandalism or property destruction
  - Sexual assault
  - Clear signs of using controlled substances (drugs and alcohol)
  - Running away from school property
  - Sustained confrontational or defiant behavior resulting in refusal to follow immediate, reasonable adult directions

- *Managing Emotional Escalation.* Managing Emotional Escalation is designed to help defuse and resolve any behaviors that are the result of emotional escalation. This strategy can help prevent and control escalated behaviors, such as tantrums, volatile or explosive behavior, and sustained disruptions. It is applicable when misbehavior tends to escalate as the student becomes more agitated or the teacher and student engage in frequent power struggles. It can also be used as a long-term intervention for students whose chronic disruptive or dangerous behavior warrants a Behavior Emergency Plan.

- *Supporting Students with Internalizing Challenges.* This chapter is designed to assist students with symptoms associated with depression and anxiety. This chapter provides an overview of the nature of internalizing problems and includes detailed descriptions of strategies, considerations for using them effectively, and troubleshooting when students need more assistance.

In some cases, a general education teacher with responsibilities for teaching many children may find these interventions more involved or complicated than is possible or realistic to implement without some assistance. Specialized intervention strategies are well worth knowing and understanding, but the assumption is that intervention design and implementation will be a collaborative endeavor among teams of school professionals. In this way, school resources are directed to the students who need the most intensive interventions and will benefit from them the most.

School resources are directed to the students who need the most intensive interventions and will benefit from them the most.

References

Anderson, C. M., & Borgmeier, C. (2010). Tier II interventions within the framework of school-wide positive behavior support: Essential features for design, implementation, and maintenance. *Behavior Analysis in Practice, 3*(1), 33–45.

Batsche, G., Elliott, J., Graden, J. L., Grimes, J., Kovaleski, J. F., & Prasse, D. (2005). *Response to intervention: Policy considerations and implementation.* Alexandria, VA: National Association of State Directors of Special Education.

Brown-Chidsey, R., & Bickford, R. (2015). *Practical handbook of multi-tiered systems of support: Building academic and behavioral success in schools.* New York, NY: Guilford Press.

Carr, E. G. (1977). The motivation of self-injurious behavior: A review of some hypotheses. *Psychological Bulletin, 84,* 800–816.

Carr, E. G., Dunlap, G., Horner, R. H., Koegel, R. L., Turnbull, A. P., Sailor, W., . . . Fox, L. (2002). Positive behavior support: Evolution of an applied science. *Journal of Positive Behavior Interventions, 4,* 4–16.

Carr, E. G., Robinson, S., & Palumbo, L. W. (1990). The wrong issue: Aversive versus nonaversive treatment. The right issue: Functional versus nonfunctional treatment. In A. C. Repp & N. N. Singh (Eds.), *Perspectives on the use of nonaversive and aversive interventions for people with developmental disabilities.* Sycamore, IL: Sycamore Publishing.

Commission on Chronic Illness. (1957). *Chronic illness in the United States: Prevention of chronic illness* (Vol. 1). Cambridge, MA: Harvard University Press.

Crone, D. A., & Horner, R. H. (2003). *Building positive behavior support systems in schools: Functional behavioral assessment.* New York, NY: Guilford Press.

Dunlap, G., & Fox, L. (2011). Function-based interventions for children with challenging behavior. *Journal of Early Intervention, 33*(4), 333–343.

Eber, L., Hyde, K., Rose, J., Breen, K., McDonald, D., & Lewandowski, H. (2009). Completing the continuum of schoolwide positive behavior support: Wraparound as a tertiary-level intervention. In W. Sailor, G. Dunlap, G. Sugai, & R. H. Horner (Eds.), *Handbook of positive behavior support* (pp. 671–703). New York, NY: Springer.

Foster-Johnson, L., & Dunlap, G. (1993). Using functional assessment to develop effective, individualized interventions. *Teaching Exceptional Children, 25,* 44–50.

Iwata, B. A., Dorsey, M. F., Slifer, K. J., Bauman, K. E., & Richman, G. S. (1982). Toward a functional analysis of self injury. *Analysis and Intervention in Developmental Disabilities, 2,* 3–20

Kincaid, D. (1996). Person-centered planning. In L. K. Koegel, R. L. Koegel, & G. Dunlap (Eds.), *Positive behavioral support.* Baltimore, MD: Brookes.

Newcomer, L. L., Freeman, R., & Barrett, S. (2013). Essential systems for sustainable implementation of Tier 2 supports. *Journal of Applied School Psychology, 29*(2), 126–147.

O'Neill, R. E., Albin, R. W., Storey, K., Horner, R. H., & Sprague, J. R.(2015). *Functional assessment and program development for problem behavior: A practical handbook.* (3rd ed.), Stamford, CT: Cengage Learning.

OSEP Technical Assistance Center on Positive Behavioral Interventions and Supports (October 2015). *Positive behavioral interventions and supports (PBIS) implementation blueprint: Part 1—Foundations and supporting information.* Eugene, OR: University of Oregon. Retrieved from www.pbis.org.

Sprick, R. S., Booher, M., Isaacs, S. J., Sprick, J., & Rich, P. (2014). *Foundations: A proactive and positive behavior support system* [Modules A–F]. Eugene, OR: Ancora Publishing.

Sprick, R. S., Knight, J., Reinke, W., Skyles, T., & Barnes, L. (2010). *Coaching classroom management: Strategies and tools for administrators and coaches* (2nd ed). Eugene, OR: Ancora Publishing.

Tilly, W. D., III (2008). The evolution of school psychology to science-based practice: Problem solving and the three-tiered model. In A. Thomas & J. Grimes (Eds.), *Best practices in school psychology IV* (pp. 17–36). Bethesda, MD: National Association of School Psychologists.

Tilly, W. D., III, & Flugum, K. R. (1995). Ensuring quality interventions. In A. Thomas & J. Grimes (Eds.), *Best practices in school psychology III* (pp. 485–500). Washington, DC: National Association of School Psychologists.

Walker, H. M. (1995). *Antisocial behavior in school: Strategies and best practices.* Pacific Grove, CA: Brooks/Cole Publishing Co.

Walker, H. M., & Shinn, M. R. (2002). Structuring school-based interventions to achieve integrated primary, secondary, and tertiary prevention goals for safe and effective schools. In M. R. Shinn, H. M. Walker, & G. Stoner (Eds.), *Interventions for academic and behavior problems II: Preventive and remedial approaches* (pp. 1–25). Washington, DC: U.S. National Association of School Psychologists.

Warger, C. (1999). *Positive behavior support and functional assessment.* Arlington, VA: Council for Exceptional Children. (ERIC Clearinghouse on Disabilities and Gifted Education, ERIC/OSEP Digest E580, No. ED434437)

Wehmeyer, M. L. (1999). A functional model of self-determination: Describing development and implementing instruction. *Focus on Autism and Other Developmental Disabilities, 14*(1), 53–61.

SECTION ONE

Establishing a System for Individualized Intervention

Providing support for students with behavioral and motivational challenges will be most effective when there is a strong multi-tiered framework to support and coordinate the work of teachers, administrators, and interventionists. That framework should ensure that allocation of resources—personnel, time, financial resources—matches the intensity of resources to the intensity of student need. Because resources are limited, the easiest and cheapest intervention that might be successful should be implemented with fidelity to see if it can help the student learn new, more prosocial behaviors that will contribute to school success, thus saving more intensive resources for students with more intensive challenges.

This section is designed to help school and district-based leaders—members of a problem-solving team, administrators, teacher leaders, and interventionists—evaluate and improve the current framework to ensure an efficient and effective MTSS support system. This section is organized around nine tasks, each of which describes an essential aspect of such a framework. Work through each task to evaluate current efficacy within your school or district and make any changes that may improve service delivery to help students, families, and staff work together to meet the behavioral and motivational needs of individual students.

If you are an individual interventionist but not in a leadership position that allows you to shape service delivery, either skim or skip this section. Sections 2, 3, and 4 present information about the problem-solving process and designing interventions that you, individually, may be able to apply within the current structures of your school and district.

TASK 1 Assess the organization and efficacy of staff and teams working on the behavioral aspects of MTSS.

This task provides checklists and guided reflection about the current state of your school's Tier 1 behavior supports. The hope is that continuous improvement of Tier 1 is operating in tandem with efforts to improve and expand on Tier 2 and Tier 3 supports for individual students.

STEP 1 Assess the current status of your building's universal behavior support practices.

Although this resource is geared toward assisting interventionists and members of problem-solving teams, for the reasons described previously it is essential that school personnel continue and deepen their work on universal aspects of climate, safety, and discipline, both at the schoolwide level and in every classroom. Consider evaluating the effectiveness of your practices across four major categories that should be the responsibility of a schoolwide positive behavior interventions and supports (PBIS) team. The four categories and key indicators of effectiveness are:

It is essential that school personnel continue and deepen their work on universal aspects of climate, safety, and discipline.

1. **Schoolwide processes**

   - A team represents and involves the entire staff.
   - Multiple data sources are used to set priorities and assess progress.
   - Staff are committed to continuous improvement—part of School Improvement Goals.
   - Policies and practices are archived.
   - The team and school improvement processes are sustainable from year to year and across changes in personnel.

2. **Schoolwide strategies for shaping climate, safety, and discipline**

   - Common areas (halls, cafeteria, arrival/dismissal, and so on) are safe and orderly.
   - Common policies (dress code, electronics, profanity, and so on) are implemented consistently.
   - Conscious creation of a positive, inviting climate is a priority.
   - Procedures are in place to encourage attendance.
   - Procedures are in place to manage conflict and prevent bullying and cliques.

3. **Classroom-level behavior support**

   - An evidence-based model for classroom management has been adopted by the school/district.
   - Professional development opportunities are available to all staff.
   - Staff know the "look-fors" that administrators use during walk-through visits and formal evaluations.
   - Teacher self-evaluation and peer coaching are supported and encouraged.
   - Nonevaluative coaching support is available to teachers who request it.

4. **Classroom-based early-stage interventions**
   - A district-based protocol of early-stage interventions has been adopted.
   - Staff development has been provided to teachers on how to implement the protocol.
   - Implementation of early-stage interventions is documented before any referral to problem-solving teams or specialists.

Reproducible 1.1 (pp. 22–25) is a checklist based on Safe & Civil Schools approach to Tier 1 universal prevention and intervention. This checklist is intended to help assess how your building's organizational framework supports MTSS-B implementation.

STEP 2   Clarify the organizational framework and purpose of existing MTSS-B teams.

An effective organizational framework is one in which everyone has clear roles and everyone's role is supportive of others. Your building's organizational framework should clearly outline the relationship between universal prevention efforts and problem-solving processes for individual students.

Universal prevention efforts are led by a *behavior leadership team*, which coordinates the implementation and continuous refinement of behavior support procedures. This leadership team is responsible for:

- *Designing and managing the universal practices and support structures in the building.* Universal practices are broad-based policies and procedures that change or structure the system so that it meets the behavioral and emotional needs of most students. These policies are preventive in nature and should address school safety, civility, motivation, behavior, discipline, and climate. From a staff development standpoint, universal behavior practices address every aspect of school that is not academic, including parent and community involvement.
- *Ensuring that schoolwide expectations are translated to effective practices that carry into each classroom.* This may involve adopting a schoolwide classroom management model, clarifying expectations for good student behavior in the classroom, creating collaborative structures to ensure that teachers are successful and feel supported, and coaching teachers in how to implement evidence-based classroom management practices.
- *Creating unity among the staff for implementing evidence-based practices related to safety, discipline, motivation, climate, and so on.* For universal practices to be effective, the leadership team must work with the staff to design policies that teachers are willing to adopt and implement. Without teacher support, the practice part of universal practices will never be a reality—you'll have universal theories instead.
- *Creating and maintaining a cycle of continuous improvement.* Once policies and practices are in place, the leadership team must review and revise these polices regularly. This continuous improvement cycle begins with collecting and analyzing data about how practices and support structures are working within the building. Specifically, this involves reviewing meaningful data about safety, discipline, and climate to determine both strengths of current practices and gaps or weaknesses that need to be addressed.

An effective organizational framework is one in which everyone has clear roles and everyone's role is supportive of others.

REPRODUCIBLE 1.1 *Checklist: Universal Prevention and Early Intervention (1 of 4)*

Checklist: Universal Prevention and Early Intervention

Date _____

NA = Not applicable
0 = Not present in our school
1 = Partially in place, but not fully consistent or effective
2 = Fully in place and effective
3 = Fully in place and archived to ensure continuity across personnel changes

1. Process of Continuous Improvement

- Foundations (PBIS) Team directly represents all faculty and staff groups. _____
- Foundations Team meets regularly and uses surveys, observations of common areas, attendance data, and disciplinary referral data to identify strengths and areas of improvement related to safety, climate, and discipline. _____
- Foundations Team members communicate with the entire staff at least once per month. _____
- Foundations Team is known by all staff and is highly involved in all aspects of climate, safety, behavior, motivation, and student connectedness. _____
- Foundations Team engages all staff to actively participate in setting priorities, developing revisions, adopting new policies and procedures, and implementing all aspects of school climate, behavior, and discipline. _____
- Foundations Team has established and maintains an archive of all behavior support policies, procedures, lessons, presentations, and communications (e.g., letters to families). _____

2. For Every Common Area and All Schoolwide Policies

- Current structures and procedures have been evaluated and protected, modified, or eliminated. _____
- Lesson plans have been developed, taught, practiced, and re-taught, when necessary. _____
- Common area supervisory procedures are communicated to staff and monitored for implementation. _____
- All staff have been informed of their role in supporting and enforcing schoolwide policies such as dress code. _____

3. Positive Climate

- Guidelines for Success are posted, reviewed regularly, and embedded into the culture. They are part of the common language of the school. _____
- Ratios of Interactions: Observation data show that most staff at most times strive to interact with students at least three times more often when students are behaving responsibly than when they are misbehaving. As needed, this concept is reviewed with staff. _____
- Attendance: All students with chronic absenteeism (absent 10% or more of school days) are identified at least quarterly; Foundations Team determines whether universal intervention is warranted. _____

REPRODUCIBLE 1.1 *Checklist: Universal Prevention and Early Intervention (2 of 4)*

Checklist: Universal Prevention and Early Intervention

NA = Not applicable
0 = Not present in our school
1 = Partially in place, but not fully consistent or effective
2 = Fully in place and effective
3 = Fully in place and archived to ensure continuity across personnel changes

3. Positive Climate (continued)

- Programs to meet students' basic needs are in place and analyzed at least once per year to determine their effectiveness and assess whether the needs of all student groups are being met. _____

- Foundations Team has analyzed procedures and suggested improvements for welcoming and orienting new students and families at the beginning of the school year. (New students include both those in a new grade-level cohort [e.g., ninth graders in high school] and those who are new but not part of that cohort.) _____

4. Correcting Misbehavior

- Foundations Team has created lessons for students on how to interact appropriately with adults. These lessons are implemented at least annually. _____

- Foundations Team has identified common misbehaviors that get students into trouble and has created procedures and lessons for students to reduce the future occurrence of these behaviors. _____

- Staff understand the potential limitations of office referral as a corrective procedure and avoid using it whenever possible. _____

- Staff have been made aware of the limited benefits and potential drawbacks (including disparate impact) of out-of-school suspension (OSS) as a corrective consequence. _____

- Staff avoid pressuring administrators to use OSS. Staff perceptions of consistency and administrative support for disciplinary actions are documented in staff survey results. _____

- Annually, staff discuss and agree on what behavior must be sent to the administrator, what can be sent to the administrator, and what should be handled in the setting in which the infraction occurred (3-level system for responding to misbehavior). _____

5. Safety, Conflict, Bullying

- Staff are aware of the importance of a comprehensive view of safety that includes preparing for outside attackers as well as the more common occurrences of playground injuries, student fights, bullying, and so on. _____

- Foundations Team has assessed problems with safety, conflict, and bullying within the last 3 years. If a problem exists, a plan for addressing the problem, including student lessons, has been developed. _____

REPRODUCIBLE 1.1   *Checklist: Universal Prevention and Early Intervention (3 of 4)*

Checklist: Universal Prevention and Early Intervention

NA = Not applicable
0 = Not present in our school
1 = Partially in place, but not fully consistent or effective
2 = Fully in place and effective
3 = Fully in place and archived to ensure continuity across personnel changes

6. Classroom management: Expectations for teachers, administrators, and staff coaches

Adapted with permission from *Coaching Classroom Management*, by R. Sprick, J. Knight, W. Reinke, T. Skyles, & L. Barnes, 2010. Eugene, OR: Ancora Publishing. © 2010 Ancora Publishing.

- A schoolwide or districtwide model for classroom management has been adopted that creates a common language to connect professional development, procedures, and problem-solving among teachers, coaches, and administrative staff. The only absolute rule within that adopted model (e.g., CHAMPS) is that all people should be treated with respect. Belittlement of students has no place in any teacher's repertoire. ____

- Staff understand that managing a classroom is part art and part science, conceptually simple enough to reduce to a handful of critical variables yet so intricate and complex that it is a lifelong learning task. Even the best and most experienced teachers must continually refine their classroom management plans. ____

- Staff also understand that the goal of effective classroom management is not creating "perfect" children, but rather providing the perfect environment for enhancing the growth of all students toward increasingly responsible and motivated behavior. ____

- Administrators make clear what they expect to see when visiting classrooms, specifically that students are (a) meeting the teacher's procedural and behavioral (CHAMPS) expectations, (b) academically engaged in meaningful learning tasks, and (c) interacting respectfully with one another and with the teacher. ____

- Administrators provide clear expectations that all staff will strive to maintain a 3:1 ratio of attention to positive behavior compared with corrective feedback. ____

- Skilled and respected staff members have been designated as classroom management coaches. In most cases, these will be instructional coaches who assist with classroom management as part of their efforts to help teachers implement effective instructional practices. Ideally, their role should be nonevaluative and their work with teachers confidential. ____

- When observations or collected data reveal that a teacher needs to improve essential classroom management outcomes, the teacher is made aware of the options for help available in the school and encouraged to seek assistance from a coach. ____

- Coaches work within a systematized framework to ensure that reliable data are collected within and across classrooms, and they should be well equipped with assessment aids and interventions—classroom ecology checklists, teacher interview questions, observation and feedback forms, data collection instruments, and charts and graphs for interpreting data. Coaches know how to communicate effectively, what to look for when observing classrooms, and how to provide meaningful, ongoing support and follow-up. ____

- Classroom management coaches meet regularly for ongoing professional development and support, continually engaging in dialogue, self-reflection, and praxis to refine their craft. ____

REPRODUCIBLE 1.1 *Checklist: Universal Prevention and Early Intervention (4 of 4)*

Checklist: Universal Prevention and Early Intervention

NA = Not applicable
0 = Not present in our school
1 = Partially in place, but not fully consistent or effective
2 = Fully in place and effective
3 = Fully in place and archived to ensure continuity across personnel changes

7. Early-stage interventions

- All teachers and support staff have been trained on a protocol of early-stage interventions. For example:
    — Planned Discussion
    — Academic Assessment (Is it a "cannot" or a "will not" problem?)
    — Goal Setting
    — Data Collection and Debriefing
    — Cueing/Precorrecting
    — "Connectedness" for the Student
    — Function-Based Behavior Plan

- All teachers have been trained how and why to keep records of each intervention.

- Data Collection and Debriefing (or an equivalent) is adopted as a required intervention for most chronic behavior problems. Data must be charted before assistance is requested from support staff or problem-solving teams.

- *Encouraging parental involvement in the school and building a partnership between staff and parents.* This requires consciously constructing a school environment that is inviting and inclusive of families. The team should also guide the staff in how to increase the school's connection with the community. A school should not be separate from the neighborhood and businesses, but rather a central part of that broader community.

NOTE: This task description provides a condensed version of information that appears in *Foundations: A Proactive and Positive Behavior Support System* (Sprick et al., 2014) and *CHAMPS: A Proactive and Positive Approach to Classroom Management* (Sprick, 2009). For comprehensive guidance in creating an effective leadership team as well as descriptions of the many responsibilities of the leadership team, consult these resources for more information.

CHECKLIST FORM

To help the leadership team stay organized and meet regularly, we developed a nine-point Schoolwide Behavior Leadership Checklist (Reproducible 1.2, pp. 28–29). The checklist outlines critical features that characterize effective leadership teams, such as meeting on a regular basis, keeping minutes, and assigning tasks. The checklist also outlines the broad areas of the team's responsibilities, such as reviewing data, developing schoolwide expectations, providing classroom management support, and more.

Such a monumental set of responsibilities requires a building-based leadership team to take responsibility for shaping and overseeing these practices. To be most effective, this leadership team will consist of six to nine staff members, including a school-based administrator and representatives of the entire staff. In all but very small schools (say, fewer than 300 students), this team should focus exclusively on implementation of behavior support processes, not on case management of individual students. The leadership team monitors all programs and processes to ensure seamless implementation. The team should have a deep understanding of how your schoolwide and classroom universal supports integrate with targeted and intensive problem-solving and intervention supports for individual students.

In contrast, *problem-solving teams* focus on identifying supports for individual students. Although this team may be called different things in different districts (TAT, CARE, SST, etc.), it is a group that meets regularly to conduct problem-solving for the behavior issues of individual students.

Problem-solving teams are responsible for:

- *Identifying students who need additional support.* Students come to the attention of the problem-solving team through teacher referral, universal behavior screening, or red-flag alerts embedded in your building's data collection processes (see Task 3).
- *Describing and analyzing the context of the problem.* The team gathers information about the problem and the context in which it is occurring, and generates a hypothesis about variables in the student's environment that may be contributing to the problem.
- *Identifying appropriate supports.* The team creates an intervention plan that matches the severity of the problem, aligns with the function (or purpose) of the student's misbehavior, and helps meet the student's needs. For this team to be maximally effective, all team members should be familiar with the range of intervention supports available within the building or district.
- *Monitoring the effectiveness of individual supports.* After putting an intervention plan into effect, the team reviews ongoing progress-monitoring data to determine whether the plan is effectively changing student behavior.

One problem-solving team that most schools already have in place is a permanent or ad hoc multidisciplinary team. This team deals with students whose needs have not responded to earlier intervention, and its work will probably overlap into special education referral and all other special education processes. This team should include regular or ad hoc participation of wraparound community-based resources such as special education services, mental health resources, physical health resources, law enforcement, and so on. However, unless the school is very small, MTSS implementation requires earlier and less intensive collaborative problem-solving efforts.

Below is a sample of what universal and individual problem-solving team structures might look like in an elementary school of 500 students:

- *Academic MTSS and School Improvement Team:* Mainly focused on universal prevention for academics
- *Behavioral MTSS and School Improvement Team:* Mainly focused on universal prevention for behavior
- *Teacher-to-Teacher Problem-Solving Team:* Grade-level teams of teachers meet to discuss behavioral and academic issues
- *Tier 2 Behavior Problem-Solving Team:* Collaborative team of teachers and specialists within the building addresses ongoing behavior issues
- *Tier 2 Academic Problem-Solving Team:* Collaborative team of teachers and specialists within the building addresses ongoing academic issues
- *Multidisciplinary Team:* Collaborative team of teachers and specialists within the building or district meets to conduct detailed problem-solving and design appropriate academic or behavior support plans

Note that one of the bulleted items above is a teacher-to-teacher problem-solving team. This group could meet regularly to implement the *25-Minute Problem-Solving Process* described later in this book. In this proposed schema, before involving specialists, teachers share expertise and ideas on interventions, which, if effective, will remove the need to involve specialists.

Because each team's purpose varies, most schools will include different staff members on the different types of teams. Some staff members in the building might be on several, but probably not all, of the teams described in the example above. The universal team should have a very high representation of general education teachers, whereas problem-solving teams will have some teacher representation, but also a heavy representation of specialists—counselor, psychologist, social work, nurse.

The types of problem-solving team processes will be influenced by the size of the school and the personnel available to assist with those processes. If Middle School A with 1,200 students in grades 6–8 has the exact same team structures as Middle School B with 300 students, a student needing support is four times more likely to get support if he attends School B. Where a student goes to school should not dictate whether social/emotional/behavioral needs are noticed and attended to. Therefore, School B will need different processes than School A. For example, School A may choose to have a problem-solving team at each of the three grade levels, while School B has one team that serves all three grade levels. The next task presents more options and considerations for creating different types of problem-solving teams based on the resources and needs of your school.

The types of problem-solving team processes will be influenced by the size of the school and the personnel available to assist with those processes.

REPRODUCIBLE 1.2 *Schoolwide Behavior Leadership Checklist (1 of 2)*

Schoolwide Behavior Leadership Checklist

Item	Component or Process	In place?	Actions
1	A behavior leadership team, including active involvement of the building principal, represents the entire staff.		
2	The team meets on a regular basis and uses its time efficiently—starting and ending on time, keeping minutes, assigning tasks, etc.		
3	The team involves the staff in a continuous cycle of improvement that includes: a) collecting data, b) setting priorities, c) revising existing practices, d) adopting new policies or procedures, and e) ensuring implementation by staff.		
4	The team reviews meaningful data to identify strengths of current behavior support practices and areas that need improvement.		
	4a. Annually, the team guides the staff in collecting and analyzing staff, student, and parent perceptions of existing policies and practices as well as overall school climate.		
	4b. Annually, the team (with help from staff and students) conducts observations of all common areas.		
	4c. The administrator provides quarterly summaries of disciplinary referrals so the team can analyze trends based on location, type of offense, time, date, and so on.		
5	These data are used to identify new priorities for improvements and assess the efficacy of current and past priorities.		

REPRODUCIBLE 1.2 *Schoolwide Behavior Leadership Checklist (2 of 2)*

Schoolwide Behavior Leadership Checklist

Item	Component or Process	In place?	Actions
6	For any given priority, revision proposals are developed for new policies and procedures. Any revision proposals are presented for feedback to the entire staff.		
	6a. Guidelines for Success (or equivalent) have been developed and are used as the basis for rules, procedures, and lessons.		
	6b. Common areas have been assessed with regard to safety, civility, and efficacy and improved as needed. In secondary schools, particular attention is paid to hallway/passing time issues.		
	6c. Procedures for coordination among administrative, counseling, and teaching staff regarding severe misbehavior have been assessed and improved as needed.		
	6d. An analysis has been conducted to determine gaps in the school's efforts to create school connectedness and to meet all students' basic needs.		
7	Any revision proposal will be implemented only after being adopted by the staff.		
8	The team will monitor implementation of new policies and practices, refining implementation until a subsequent review of data indicates that specific priority issue has been largely resolved.		
9	A classroom management model has been adopted, training and coaching provided, and reasonable accountability created.		

Adapted with permission from *Foundations: A Proactive and Positive Behavior Support System* (Sprick, Booher, Isaacs, Sprick, & Rich, 2014). © 2014 Ancora Publishing.

In order for your MTSS-B framework to function effectively, everyone on staff must understand the relationship between universal prevention and targeted/intensive individual support. Additionally, all staff members must understand their role on the team or teams that offer a full continuum of problem-solving and intervention supports. It is essential that your school and district give careful thought to the configuration and logistics of collaborative problem-solving processes.

> ### TASK 1 SUMMARY
>
> In this task, you:
> - ☑ Assessed the current status of your building's universal behavior support practices.
> - ☑ Clarified the organizational framework and purpose of existing MTSS-B teams, differentiating between the role of your building's behavior leadership team and the purpose of problem-solving teams for individual students.

Now that you have a clear idea of the organizational framework and existing universal practices that support your school's MTSS-B implementation, you can establish or assess the status of individual problem-solving teams within your building.

In order for your MTSS-B framework to function effectively, everyone on staff must understand the relationship between universal prevention and targeted/intensive individual support.

TASK 2: Establish one or more teams to engage in problem-solving for individual students.

Your school may already have one or more teams in place that are responsible for behavior problem-solving at the individual student level. These teams are known by many names—School Assistance Team (SAT), Student/Staff Support Team (SST), Problem-Solving Team (PST), Behavior Team, etc. If your school does not already have a collaborative team in place, it is important to create one. As two heads are usually better than one, team intervention planning is inherently more effective than individual problem-solving. Just as a physician who is puzzled by a medical problem is expected to collaborate with others to diagnose and treat the patient, teachers who have tried a few interventions on their own should work with others to tackle chronic behavior issues. In addition, because everyone has specific blinders in the way they approach behavior interventions, collaborative problem-solving can be particularly useful. Working with others who are not constrained by the same blinders can lead to better understanding of a problem and a wider range of possible solutions. Finally, a team-based approach improves consistency in the supports that a building provides its students and increases accountability for actually following through with efforts to solve problems.

NOTE: For clarity, we refer to any staff member involved in the problem-solving process as an interventionist and to any group of interventionists as a problem-solving team.

STEP 1 Identify the interventionists and behavior problem-solving teams that already exist within your building.

Identify and document the resources (individuals, teams, and organizations) available in your school or district to offer problem-solving and intervention services. In other words, who are the interventionists who can provide the collaborative problem-solving processes that are discussed throughout this book? These resources may include grade-level colleagues, small learning communities, intervention planning team members, school counselors, behavior specialists, literacy coaches, speech/language specialists, school psychologists, county mental health experts, child protective services, and others. While the names of these positions may vary from district to district and state to state, the goal is to build a menu of people and teams who are available to provide support for problem analysis, intervention design, implementation, and follow-up.

We recommend including the following staff members on your problem-solving teams:

- Assistant principal
- General education teacher
- Special education teacher or supervisor
- Counselor
- School psychologist
- School social worker or community liaison
- School nurse

However, staff membership on each problem-solving team will vary depending on the staffing of the school, district, and state. For example, in the 2018–2019 school year, as this third edition goes to publication, staffing of nurses is wildly different from one state to the next. Though a ratio of one school nurse to 750 students has been widely recommended (American Academy of Pediatrics, 2008; U.S. Department of Health and Human Services 2014), these recommendations don't always translate to practice. For example, in Vermont, the nurse-to-student ratio is 1:275; in Utah, the ratio is 1:4,893 (National Education Association, n.d.). Given this variability, participation by the school nurse will vary from state to state. In Vermont, it may be possible, and undoubtedly useful, for a school nurse to serve on the problem-solving team for each grade level. However, in Utah, a school nurse would likely be unable to participate on any problem-solving team in the schools attended by the 4,893 students who the nurse serves. Instead, a nurse in Utah is likely to be called in to serve on a problem-solving team when the specific case has some health aspects and the problem has not been solved by earlier intervention. Likewise, whether a problem-solving team includes a social worker, psychologist, or counselor depends greatly on staffing patterns.

Ideally, a problem-solving team should contain four to seven permanent members, with each member adding to the balance of expertise and experience. We recommend that a team have no more than eight members. However, your team should always be open to the option of adding adjunct members for a referred student based on the student's unique needs and characteristics. For example, it would be appropriate to invite a speech/language specialist to join the team when the referred student has or is suspected to have a communication disorder.

The goal is to build a menu of people and teams who are available to provide support for problem analysis, intervention design, implementation, and follow-up.

Also try to include a range of people who can function as interventionists so that your team can maintain flexibility in delegating tasks and reduce the likelihood that cases will be delayed when the only person serving as an interventionist is out with an illness. In addition, with a range of interventionists, you can better match the style and expertise of the interventionist to a particular case or provide teachers with a choice of who they want to work with in supporting a student.

STEP 2 Specify how your problem-solving team should function.

The general purpose of any problem-solving team is to:

1. Identify the problem and clarify a student's needs.
2. Develop an intervention plan.
3. Monitor and evaluate how the plan is working in supporting the student.

Again, while we highly recommend differentiating between your behavior leadership team (which focuses on universal prevention) and your problem-solving team or teams (which focus on the needs of individual students who may have targeted or intensive needs), the organization of your problem-solving team should be tailored to align with the resources and structure of your school. Teams can be organized in a variety of ways, such as:

- In a small school, one team provides problem-solving support for all students.
- In another school, a teacher-to-teacher problem solving team meets regularly to discuss the needs of students who could benefit from more attention in the classroom but don't yet require more individualized supports, and a multidisciplinary problem-solving team addresses problems that are moderate to severe enough to warrant targeted, structured intervention.
- In a third school, grade-level teams meet to identify strategies for supporting individual students within the classroom; a problem-solving team is responsible for coordinating, implementing, and monitoring ready-to-use interventions; and a multidisciplinary team develops and evaluates individualized behavior plans for students with intensive needs.

When identifying or creating a problem-solving team or teams, consider the following:

- Who should be involved in the planning team?
- What expertise is required to participate in the problem-solving team?
- How will referrals be brought to the team?

Following are possible options for organizing different types of problem-solving teams within your building.

Teacher-to-Teacher Problem-Solving Team

In this structure, teachers are grouped together by grade level or by a small learning community. This structure is especially powerful when you have scheduled early-release days

The organization of your problem-solving team should be tailored to align with the resources and structure of your school.

every week or every other week for planning purposes. Depending on the time allotted for planning, the team might alternate the focus of meetings from week to week. For example, one week the team meets to discuss grade-level curriculum planning, and the next week they meet to discuss classroom management practices and conduct problem-solving for an individual student.

In a grade-level team arrangement, individual problem-solving involves having all the seventh-grade faculty focus on the behavior problems of one seventh-grade student, all the eighth-grade faculty focus on one eighth-grade student, and so on. By using grade-level organization, all teachers participate. During every meeting or every other meeting, one identified student from each grade gets the undivided attention of all grade-level staff.

If you don't have an early-release structure in place, asking every teacher to meet weekly to discuss an individual student may be too burdensome. Instead, you might organize a representative team of teachers to meet every week. In an elementary school, the team might consist of a primary-grade teacher, an intermediate-grade teacher, a special education teacher, a paraprofessional, and a counselor. The disadvantage of this approach is that fewer general education teachers are involved. The advantage is that the process is less burdensome on all teachers. As compensation for their time, consider relieving team members of a school duty such as bus supervision.

A teacher-to-teacher problem-solving team may meet to:

- Discuss behavior issues of individual students who are experiencing difficulties in the classroom.
- Identify classroom management strategies and early-stage interventions that may help address behavior problems.
- Collaborate on resources, ideas, and strategies for supporting individual students in the classroom.
- Develop common lesson plans for teaching and reinforcing behavior expectations.
- Set goals, review progress, and analyze student outcomes.
- Refer students to more intensive problem-solving processes.

Teacher-to-teacher problem-solving teams can be trained to use the 25-Minute Planning Process, which is discussed in detail in Section 2.

Intervention Planning Team

Although this team may be called different things in different districts (e.g., TAT, CARE, SST), it is a group that meets regularly to conduct problem-solving for behavior issues for individual students. This team includes teachers but also involves a few expert participants, such as a school counselor, school nurse, administrator, or school social worker. For this team to be maximally effective, all team members should have some training in basic problem-solving, behavior functions, and a range of research-based interventions, with some team members having more specialized skills or in-depth knowledge (Benazzi, Horner, & Good, 2006).

One identified student from each grade gets the undivided attention of all grade-level staff.

This team may meet to:

- Discuss progress of students participating in ready-to-use interventions
- Collect additional data about a student's behavior to better understand the problem and its context.
- Make modifications to existing supports or identify additional support strategies.
- Initiate or refer a student to more intensive problem-solving processes.
- Maintain accountability for monitoring implementation fidelity of ready-to-use interventions in place within the building.

This type of team could benefit from training in the Teacher Interview and 25-Minute Planning Process presented in detail in Section 2.

Multidisciplinary Problem-Solving Team

This team is made up predominantly of experts such as special education teachers, school psychologists, school counselors, administrators, school social workers, and, when appropriate, players from other agencies such as mental health, juvenile justice, and district-level truancy offices. Because the problem has been resistant to simpler, easier solutions, this team can develop a more comprehensive, community-based view of the problem to better support the student. However, even on an expert team like this, including one or two highly experienced and respected general education teachers is an excellent way to increase the team's credibility with the rest of the teaching staff.

This team may meet to:

- Discuss progress of students who haven't responded to initial and modified supports that have been attempted.
- Conduct more in-depth problem analysis to better understand the problem and its context (e.g., observe the student in multiple settings; systematically review student records; conduct interviews with the student, staff who work with the student, and family members; complete a comprehensive functional behavior assessment).
- Develop an individualized behavior intervention plan (BIP).
- Monitor BIP implementation, reviewing progress and making modifications as needed.
- Coordinate with other agencies that may help the student and family.

This type of team can be trained to use the Multidisciplinary Team Planning Process presented in detail in Section 2.

Core and Ancillary Teams

Another possible structure is to have a core team that meets on a regular basis across all tiers of support and a team of ancillary members that meets at the request of the core team when problem-solving for a particular student. This core team may comprise several individuals who are representative of the school staff and have a range of experience and skills to contribute to the problem-solving process. For example, your core team that

> **NOTE ABOUT SPECIAL EDUCATION**
>
> As a reminder, we are not taking a position on when, where, or how these problem-solving processes relate to special education issues of setting and type of intervention. Although what we describe as multidisciplinary problem-solving may overlap with your building or district process for considering special education eligibility, it is our hope that the process will become fluid enough to accommodate different scenarios, such as:
>
> - A special education student would benefit from attention during a teacher-to-teacher problem-solving meeting, but the team will avoid changing the student's placement or making major instructional changes that would interfere with the student's IEP.
> - A student who is not identified as special education but who exhibits high-intensity crisis behaviors would immediately rise to the attention of a crisis or threat assessment team.
> - A student who is receiving special education services for speech/language issues and begins to exhibit behavior problems would first be matched with a ready-to-use intervention before waiting for the problem to be addressed by an entire multidisciplinary team.

meets regularly might include two general education teachers, a special education teacher, a school counselor, and your school's check-and-connect program coordinator. Ancillary members are support personnel whose training and experience bring a level of expertise to the team that can better help meet a particular student's needs. For example, you might recruit administrators, the school psychologist, school nurse, school social worker, or district behavior specialist to serve as ancillary members.

This type of team can be trained to use the Teacher Interview, 25-Minute Planning Process, and Multidisciplinary Team Planning Process presented in detail in Section 2.

Crisis/Threat Assessment Team

As part of your MTSS system, your school should adopt a set of policies, procedures, and record-keeping standards related to threats or incidences of violence. Those policies should include a building-based team that can convene immediately whenever there is a threat. This team's job is to determine whether the threat is a transient or substantive threat. A *transient* threat is one in which there is no sustained intent to cause harm beyond the current situation. While still serious in nature and requiring a response from school staff, transient threats are often impulsive, said in a moment of anger or in a joking or sarcastic manner. A *substantive* threat is one in which there is ongoing intent to cause harm beyond the situation at hand. Substantive threats are often premeditated or thought out in advance, have a greater level of detail in the plan, and involve threats, or variations of threats, that are repeated over time. For any substantive threat, this team will involve either a district-level crisis team or relevant authorities. Task 6 offers more guidance on establishing policies and processes for preventing and responding to threats and crisis situations.

As part of your MTSS system, your school should adopt a set of policies, procedures, and record-keeping standards related to threats or incidences of violence.

> IMPORTANT NOTE: Because of the intensity of behaviors such as a threat by a student to self-harm or harm someone else, this type of situation demands an immediate jump to intensive problem-solving. An effective multi-tiered system of supports is not a rigid set of hoops wherein every situation goes through the first stages of problem-solving before getting to later stages. Crisis situations must be addressed immediately without any delay related to referral processes, defined tiers, or paperwork considerations.

STEP 3 Set a meeting schedule for each problem-solving team.

For each of your problem-solving teams, establish a schedule of regular meetings for the entire school year. Share this schedule with all team members at the beginning of the school year and communicate the importance of regular attendance at these meetings. Also consider setting time limits on meetings. Section 2 introduces the 25-Minute Planning Process that teams can use as an efficient team-based problem-solving structure to eliminate some of the drawbacks of lengthy meetings. If plans from this efficient meeting prove to be ineffective at solving the problem, a longer and more intensive process can be used. However, if all problems were to be worked on with a high level of intensity, there would likely be long lists of problems waiting to be addressed.

STEP 4 Write job descriptions for all interventionists and teams.

All interventionists should write a brief job description to clarify for support coordinators, teachers, and other interventionists how their role fits within the process of supporting the needs of students and staff. The job description should outline services that the interventionist can provide as well as how to access these services.

For example, the following job description for a school psychologist articulates how teachers and other staff can enlist the skills and expertise of the school psychologist in any given situation:

> If teachers are struggling with a student and early-stage interventions have not been sufficient, I can potentially collaborate with you through a structured interview process to develop a function-based intervention.

In addition, creating job descriptions for existing building- or district-based teams of interventionists that engage in problem-solving processes can help make support coordinators and teachers aware of how to access their services. For example:

> The Student Support Team meets twice a month to review teacher requests for assistance and red-flag alerts. We work together to develop a plan for following up and supporting all students and teachers who come to our attention.

> The Multidisciplinary Team convenes monthly to conduct in-depth problem-solving for students with intensive or urgent needs or chronic behavioral problems that haven't responded to initial support efforts. We develop comprehensive behavior support plans for students who require a higher level of support.

> **TASK 2 SUMMARY**
>
> In this task, you:
> - ☑ Identified the interventionists and behavior problem-solving teams that already exist within your building.
> - ☑ Specified how problem-solving teams should function.
> - ☑ Created a meeting schedule for each problem-solving team.
> - ☑ Developed job descriptions for all interventionists and teams.

Once your school has organized interventionists into one or more functioning problem-solving teams, you can start identifying students who may benefit from additional support from these teams.

TASK 3: Develop processes for identifying students in need of additional behavior support.

You will have students who need more support than is provided in Tier 1, no matter how well universal supports and early-stage interventions are implemented. These needs may be temporary, as in the case of a student having a tough time adjusting to a new school, or they may be long term, as in the case of a student with severe attention deficit disorder challenges. The most important task in this process is to identify those situations that should alert your MTSS system that a student has a significant need and that work needs to be done immediately. In other words, schools should identify the student-based conditions that indicate a need for the system to launch one or more of the collaborative problem-solving processes. The following steps can help to make sure no student falls through the cracks in your system.

Red-flag indicators are data that signal when a student needs to be watched more carefully and might benefit from additional supports.

STEP 1 Identify a set of red-flag indicators.

Red-flag indicators are data that signal when a student needs to be watched more carefully and might benefit from additional supports.

Red-flag indicators are basically decision rules that you apply to information that your school already collects. For example, most schools already have a system for collecting and monitoring attendance, academic failure, and office disciplinary data. Identifying a red-flag indicator simply means determining where to set the threshold that indicates a cause for concern and signals the need to initiate problem-solving efforts. Red flags can cover a wide range of potential problems, but their primary function should be to act as a systemwide alert to the academic failings and disciplinary problems of any individual student (Irvin, Tobin, Sprague, Sugai, & Vincent, 2004; Lane, Oakes, & Menzies, 2010).

Consider establishing red-flag indicators for the following categories.

- *Academic failure.* Students who experience ongoing academic failure are at an increased risk for dropping out of school (Christle, Jolivette, & Nelson, 2007; Fan

& Wolters, 2014; Griffin, 2002; Perez-Johnson & Maynard, 2007). Identifying red-flag criteria related to academics can help prevent the long-term academic failures that keep students from graduating from high school. For example, you may elect to monitor semester grades and flag any student who fails two classes in a semester. Failing several classes can soon become failing a whole grade level. Better yet, use a more proactive approach: Before the end of the quarter, ask teachers to identify students who are at risk for failing a class. This way, you may be able to provide supports to help these students get on track for academic success before they receive a failing grade.

In addition to failing grades, any other academic indicators in place in your district can and should be used as red flags that initiate collaborative support efforts. For example, if your district conducts regular progress monitoring of oral reading fluency using curriculum-based assessment measures (e.g., DIBELS, AIMSweb), you can use built-in risk levels to indicate a need for problem-solving (Kaminski, Cummings, Powell-Smith, & Good, 2004).

- *Disciplinary referrals.* When a student receives repeated disciplinary referrals in a short period of time (e.g., a 9-week quarter or semester), it should be a warning sign that the student may not view referrals in a negative way or that referrals alone are not a sufficient consequence to motivate a change in behavior. Determine the number of disciplinary referrals that signals a need for proactive planning. Every school or district can choose its own threshold number and time period (such as during one month or one semester), but we recommend using three disciplinary referrals in a single semester to signal that a student needs a targeted or comprehensive intervention. Three disciplinary referrals in a semester indicate that disciplinary action is not enough to correct whatever is going on with that student. Once launched, the collaborative problem-solving process can design interventions that include alternatives to corrective action alone. Such interventions may prove more successful in reducing the student's problem behavior and future office referrals.

- *Out-of-class consequences or detention referrals.* If your school assigns lunchtime or after-school detention, consider flagging when a student hits a certain number of detentions. For example, if a student has been in detention six times during the semester, you know that detention by itself will not work to change the student's behavior and that other strategies should be tried. This flagging system can also be relevant if teachers often use out-of-class consequences, such as sending a student to the office or another class for timeout, or remove privileges for misbehavior, such as taking away recess or lunch. If a student is regularly assigned out-of-class consequences or is frequently losing recess or lunch privileges, it is safe to conclude that these consequences aren't effective in changing the student's behavior. Again, the school or district can choose the number that sets off the alert.

- *Chronic absenteeism.* Another red flag that can be embedded in your system is an alert for absenteeism. Once a student has been absent for a specific, predetermined number of days during a semester, the response should be automatic, and a team should move into action. Students who drop out of school don't reach that point overnight; they often practice not coming to school for months or years first (Christle et al., 2007). A preset alert in the attendance database can be the first step toward preventing that student from becoming a statistical casualty. Don't wait until the end of the year to analyze attendance and absence rates. We recommend flagging any student who is absent more than 10% of school days. Begin your review of attendance data after the first month of school or 20 days of instruction. Students with two or more absences at that time have missed at least 10% of school days. Continue to monitor attendance data on a monthly basis, noting which students have missed 10% of school days to date and which students show major changes in their attendance patterns within the last month.

- *One or more grade levels behind chronological peers.* Research findings have revealed that grade retention is a powerful predictor of later high school dropout (Jimerson, Anderson, & Whipple, 2002). Roderick (1994) found that, of students who were retained once in kindergarten through eighth grade, more than 69% dropped out of high school. Students who are 2 years behind chronological peers are even more likely to drop out; more than 93% of students who were retained two or more times in kindergarten through eighth grade dropped out of school. To increase the likelihood of graduation, make note of any students who are one or more grade levels behind their chronological peers and consider whether they are at risk and might benefit from additional supports to stay on track for graduation.
- *Visits to the nurses or counselor's office.* Students who frequently visit the school nurse or counselor may be experiencing physical health or mental health issues that affect their experience at school. While frequent visits to the nurse or counselor may not necessarily indicate a need for additional problem-solving efforts, it is important to be aware of these visits, monitor the situation, and offer additional follow-up support if needed. For example, compare Student A, who visits the school nurse twice in 2 weeks, but is well-connected to the school community and performs well in class, with Student B, who visits the school nurse that same number of times, but who appears withdrawn in class, doesn't seem to have many friends at school, and is barely passing math and science classes. Red-flag criteria alert the system to both of these students, but a follow-up investigation shows that Student B is more at-risk and may benefit from additional supports, while Student A is just experiencing seasonal allergies.
- *Social network analysis.* Another option for identifying students who may need additional support is to gather data about school connectedness. The Centers for Disease Control and Prevention (2009) defines school connectedness as "the belief by students that adults and peers in the school care about their learning as well as about them as individuals." Students who don't feel connected to school are at increased risk for school failure and negative behavior outcomes (Catalano, Haggerty, Oesterie, Fleming, & Hawkins, 2004). To proactively identify these students, make a list of all students in the building and have staff in the school put their initials next to any student that they feel confident having a conversation with. Follow up on any student without initials—have staff work to increase positive interactions with the student and determine whether other supports should be put into place to increase the student's feelings of connectedness to school.

Students who don't feel connected to school are at increased risk for school failure and negative behavior outcomes.

STEP 2 Develop a process for teachers to request assistance.

Red-flag indicators are designed to ensure that student needs are met. This second step is designed to ensure that the MTSS system is fully ready to help and support teachers, whether or not a student's problems have risen to red-flag status. The team's priority should be to make it easy for busy teachers to request and receive the assistance they need—without creating a cumbersome bureaucracy that hinders the process.

Two forms that teachers can use to ask for help are shown as models: an informal request for assistance (Reproducible 1.3, p. 42) and a more formal request (Reproducible 1.4, p. 43).

Include these resources in your school handbook along with a statement that highlights the collaborative nature of your staff. The statement could say something like, "We are a collaborative staff who work together as professionals." Teachers need to know that if the first person they turn to is not the correct one to assist them, that professional will recommend another professional. This collaborative nature, and the documentation of it, reinforces for the staff that asking for help and using resources are not considered weaknesses but instead are signs of teaching strength. When you create a culture of teamwork and collaboration among school personnel, the combined knowledge results in increased problem-solving efficiency (Feldman & Kratochwill, 2003).

Also consider establishing a clear process for students and parents to request assistance. Schools should do more to advertise to students that direct assistance is available to them as well. Students should know that they can ask for help when they don't feel safe (e.g., bullying, weapons), when they don't feel connected to the school, when they have trouble passing classes, or simply when they need assistance getting to school on time. It's important for the behavior leadership team to remind staff to encourage students to seek help from adults within the building when they need it.

The details of how your problem-solving systems work—including who collects the forms and how they come to the attention of the leadership team—may already be established by your district. However, if systems are not in place, see Section 2 for guidance in constructing clear and consistent processes to ensure that the needs of staff, students, and parents are met within your systems for problem-solving and intervention design and implementation.

ADVERTISE RESOURCES

Create opportunities throughout the year to communicate and advertise the resources available in your building. One way to accomplish this is to send out an invitation at the beginning of the school year that notifies teachers, students, and parents about school or district resources and outlines the brief process for requesting assistance: what forms to use, where to locate them, and who to give the completed forms to.

STEP 3 Consider implementing universal behavior risk screening.

Universal behavior screening assessments are brief measures conducted for all students in the school to predict which students might be at-risk for long-term behavior problems and poor outcomes. Research has found that between 9% and 13% of students have some kind of emotional-behavioral problems (Walker, Severson, & Feil, 2014). Left untreated, these students are more likely to drop out of school and experience low grades, troubled peer relationships, long-term unemployment, incarceration, substance abuse, and even suicide (Walker et al., 2014). Schools generally don't do a good enough job of finding those students early enough, before behavior patterns become so firmly established that they are less responsive to intervention. Teachers tend to refer only those students who severely disrupt the classroom or are atypical learners. Universal screening gives each student an equal chance to be assessed and identified for serious behavior adjustment problems that can contribute to academic failure, poor peer relations, or school dropout. Screening procedures can be conducted 1–3 times per year to identify students whose behavior might be problematic enough to warrant additional support.

Consider using a universal screener in conjunction with your red-flag indicators and process for teacher referrals to reduce the likelihood of at-risk students falling through the cracks of your system. See "Universal Behavior Screening Tools" below for a list of universal behavior screening tools to consider.

UNIVERSAL BEHAVIOR SCREENING TOOLS

Systematic Screening for Behavior Disorders, 2nd ed. (SSBD; Walker, Severson, & Feil, 2014) is considered by many to be the gold standard of universal screeners for behavior (Lane et al., 2012). SSBD was first published in 1992, and online and print versions with updated norms were released in 2014. SSBD uses a two-stage process for screening. It is designed to detect both externalizing behavior patterns (behavior that is directed outward toward the social environment and involves behavior excesses that are usually maladaptive and aversive to others, such as aggression or noncompliance) and internalizing behavior patterns (behavior that is directed inward, away from the social environment, and often involves behavior deficits or problems with self, such as shyness, withdrawn behavior, depression, or school phobia). In Stage 1 of the screening process, the classroom teacher identifies a small group of students who demonstrate the most risk for externalizing or internalizing problems. In Stage 2, the classroom teacher evaluates these students' behavior in more detail, using checklists and rating scales to verify or confirm their risk status. SSBD has been normed for use with students in pre-K through grade 9 and requires only about an hour to screen an entire class. Learn more: ancorapublishing.com/product/ssbd-portfolio/

BASC-3 Behavioral and Emotional Screening System (BASC-3 BESS; Kamphaus & Reynolds, 2015) is a one-stage screener that uses a multidimensional approach to conducting screening, using input from teachers, parents, and student self-reports. Three separate rating scales are included and can be used with students in preschool through grade 12. Learn more: pearsonclinical.com

Student Risk Screening Scale (SRSS; Drummond, 1994) is a one-stage universal screening tool for grades K–6. It is simple, reliable, and valid. Screening with SRSS takes about the same amount of time as with SSBD, but does not provide detailed information that may help in designing individualized interventions. Learn more: pbis.org

Strengths and Difficulties Questionnaire (SDQ; Goodman, 1997) is a one-stage screener for students ages 3–16. Teachers, parents, and students (age 11 and up) provide input. Learn more: sdqinfo.com

State tools: Some states provide screening tools. Check with your state department of education.

REPRODUCIBLE 1.3 *Informal Request for Assistance*

Informal Request for Assistance

Date _____

To _____

From _____

Position _____

Re: _____

Brief description of the problem:

☐ This is an informal request for assistance. (I'd just like some ideas at this point.)
☐ This is a request for formal assistance. (The problem may be serious enough for a structured intervention plan.)

Interventions © 2019 Ancora Publishing

REPRODUCIBLE 1.3

REPRODUCIBLE 1.4 *Formal Request for Assistance*

Formal Request for Assistance

Referring person _____ Position _____ Date _____

Student _____ Grade _____ DOB _____ Sex: M F

Check the type of problem behavior.

Academic	Social	Communication	Self-Help	Health
☐ Reading ☐ Spelling ☐ Writing ☐ Study Skills ☐ Other: _____ _____	☐ Aggression ☐ Noncompliance ☐ Truancy ☐ Tardiness ☐ Withdrawal ☐ Disruptions ☐ Social Skills ☐ Self-Management ☐ Other: _____ _____	☐ Language ☐ Fluency ☐ Articulation ☐ Voice ☐ Other: _____ _____	☐ Dressing ☐ Hygiene ☐ Other: _____ _____	☐ Vision ☐ Hearing ☐ Physical ☐ Other: _____ _____

Provide a specific and observable description of the problem:

Provide a specific description of the problem context:

    Where:

    When:

    With Whom:

    Other:

Provide a list of previous remediation attempts (if any):

    1.

    2.

    3.

Interventions © 2019 Ancora Publishing

STEP 4 Establish a process for regularly reviewing red-flag indicators and teacher referrals.

Once you select a set of red-flag indicators and develop a process for teachers to request assistance, make sure that flags and referrals are monitored on a regular basis.

We suggest that you keep records for red-flag indicators in a database. In many cases, this allows red-flag criteria to be integrated directly into your data collection system. You may be able to automate some red-flag alerts by embedding thresholds within the database systems your school uses. For example, you could design your attendance system to automatically flag students who have missed more than 10% of school days to date. Or you could arrange for your office disciplinary referral record system to deliver an alert when a student receives three referrals within a semester. If you can't customize your database or need to keep paper-based records, staff members can manually review records and identify students whose data exceed the red-flag threshold. Regardless of whether you automate red-flag alerts or generate them manually, it is crucial to review the alerts regularly to initiate timely intervention or problem-solving.

As you develop a plan to review red-flag criteria, make sure to:

- Schedule regular reviews throughout the year (e.g., red-flag alerts will be compiled monthly, teacher referrals will be reviewed weekly by an administrator).
- Assign responsibility to one or more staff members for reviewing data (e.g., each member of the behavior leadership team will review one source of monthly data).
- Clearly outline the process for accessing data (e.g., a behavior leadership team member is appointed Data/Evaluation Coordinator, with responsibility for gathering and sending data to other members at the end of each month).
- Specify a timeline for completing each data review (e.g., a list of at-risk students will be created within 2 weeks).
- Define the desired outcomes of the data review process (e.g., a list of students, ordered by grade level and homeroom teacher, who exceed the red-flag threshold for failing grades, chronic absenteeism, or discipline referrals).
- Clarify the process for following up on identified students (e.g., red-flag reviewers will report findings back to the Data/Evaluation Coordinator, who will then share results with the school's problem-solving team).

By compiling red-flag alerts at least monthly, the team can promptly discuss newly flagged students at the next problem-solving meeting to determine whether to collect additional information or start to plan intervention supports.

Finally, it is also important to regularly monitor and follow up on teacher referrals and requests for assistance. At least weekly, assign someone to review, document, and relay new referrals to the appropriate staff member or team responsible for following up on requests for assistance. With a weekly review, your teachers can be confident that the system will work for them.

By using red-flag alerts, streamlining procedures for teachers to request assistance, and regularly compiling and reviewing this information, you will create multiple avenues for efficiently identifying students in need of support.

It is crucial to review the alerts regularly to initiate timely intervention or problem-solving.

TASK 3 SUMMARY

In this task, you:

- ☑ Identified a set of red-flag indicators to signal when a student might benefit from additional supports.
- ☑ Developed a process for teachers to request assistance.
- ☑ Considered universal behavior risk screening.
- ☑ Established a process for regularly reviewing red-flag indicators and teacher referrals.

TASK 4 Develop a support coordinator program.

Some schools do a great job of identifying student needs through universal screening or by regularly reviewing red flags and requests for assistance, but then don't follow through with using those data to determine how to better support individual students. Because of that gap, students' needs aren't being met. To ensure that this gap doesn't occur in your school, we recommend that you develop a support coordinator program.

Support coordinators are staff members enlisted to make sure that at-risk students do not fall through the cracks of the system. Support coordinators should know the full range of support available in the school, including programs, personnel, and procedures for initiating supports, and be able to link potentially at-risk students to appropriate resources. Each staff member acting as a support coordinator will monitor the student closely, assess whether the school is doing everything possible to meet the student's needs, make sure that the teacher feels supported, and initiate additional actions necessary to support the student at school.

> **TERMINOLOGY**
>
> We use the term *support coordinator* throughout this book, but feel free to select any term that will be received with positive associations. Other options include school-based student advocate, case manager, student champion, or Tier 2 support person.

STEP 1 Identify staff members in your school who can serve as support coordinators for identified students.

Consider the following professional-level people to serve as support coordinators:

- Administrator
- Dean
- Nurse
- Social worker
- School resource officer
- School psychologist
- Counselor
- Parent liaison
- Behavior specialist

Teachers will probably not have enough time to serve as support coordinators unless they're on special assignment or they teach half time and spend their remaining time in a coaching or supervisory role.

NOTE: *Support coordinator* is a term we use for anyone on the team who advocates for the student. It is not a job title, but rather a role that everyone on the problem-solving team has for particular students.

STEP 2 Create a process for assigning support coordinators to identified students.

Once you compile a list of support coordinators, determine how and when to assign support coordinators to students. For example, you might assign support coordinators to students who are identified through universal screening procedures or during your end-of-quarter review of red-flag alerts, and to new students who come to the attention of your problem-solving team through staff referrals. You may assign more students to some support coordinators than to others, depending on the support coordinator's availability and position in the school. For example, a school nurse might have only 2–3 students, while a school counselor might be assigned 10–11 students. You might plan to assign students to support coordinators in rotation—the dean is assigned a student, the nurse is assigned the next student, the social worker is assigned the next, and so on.

Early in the process, don't worry too much about ensuring a perfect match between student and support coordinator. The most important priority is the timely assignment of someone who will take responsibility for ensuring that the school meets the student's needs. Later, if necessary, you can change support coordinators if someone else is better suited to communicating and working with the student and family. For example, "I am currently Rachel's support coordinator, but since the new report says there are some complex medical issues, I wonder if Keiko (school nurse) would be better as Rachel's coordinator."

The overarching responsibility of a support coordinator is to investigate the problem and advocate for the student, family, and student's teachers until an intervention is successful.

STEP 3 Outline the specific responsibilities of a support coordinator.

The overarching responsibility of a support coordinator is to investigate the problem and advocate for a student, the family, and the student's teachers until an intervention is successful or until it's determined that a different staff member should be the support coordinator. In some cases, the support coordinator might conclude that even though the student was red-flagged as needing support, the student has no need for support at this time.

Determine specific responsibilities the support coordinators will agree to take on in supporting their assigned students. Consider giving support coordinators these responsibilities:

- Participate in problem-solving team meetings that discuss the student's needs. For example, "I am the support coordinator for Fareed and think he would benefit from more positive attention from staff."
- Explain to the student and family how the student was identified through universal screening, your red-flag alert system, or other means as needing extra support from the school.
- Review the student's records and talk with teachers to get their perceptions of what action, if any, may be most beneficial for the student.
- Identify existing ready-to-use interventions that may be a good fit for the student.
- Monitor the student's progress and review academic and behavioral data on a regular basis.
- Talk with the student's teachers and build relationships.
- Check in with the student on a regular basis and serve as the liaison between home and school.
- Alert the problem-solving team to any barriers to implementation or concerns from the teacher, student, or parents.

The student should continue to have a support coordinator until one of these three situations occurs:

- Behavior has improved and the student no longer needs support.
- A different school-based professional becomes the support coordinator.
- The student is no longer enrolled in the school.
  NOTE: If the student is moving to another school, the support coordinator should contact the new school to see if a new support coordinator can be assigned to watch over the student. Examples of this situation include a fifth-grade student who is moving up to the middle school and a third-grade student who is moving across town to a different elementary school.

CONFIDENTIALITY

Support coordinators are responsible for maintaining confidentiality. They will need to strike a balance between protecting the student's privacy and exploring avenues for supporting the student. Limit discussion of potentially sensitive information, such as health or psychological diagnoses, assessment results, and involvement in the legal system, to team meetings, and share relevant information only with parties who have legitimate educational interest (i.e., individuals in the building or district who need to know information in the student's education record in order to perform their professional responsibilities). When establishing a support coordinator program, make sure that the support coordinators access and use student records and sensitive information in accordance with your school or district policies on student confidentiality.

STEP 4 Plan to meet with support coordinators regularly and keep clear, detailed records of all students.

Your support coordinator program will function more effectively by holding regular meetings and keeping detailed records. Records should include a list of all students who have been assigned support coordinators and who their support coordinators are. Support coordinators should meet at least once a month and give brief reports about how each of their students is doing, including a quick review of any data they've collected. For students who aren't making progress, the group can discuss appropriate next steps.

It's also beneficial for support coordinators to meet as needed to conduct a post hoc analysis of any system failure. Any time a student is expelled, drops out, or commits a violent act, we suggest that the support coordinators meet to analyze what happened. Without blaming anyone, consider: Could the system be structured more effectively? Do we have gaps in our system? Did we provide the best quality of care that we could? By addressing those questions, you may improve the outcomes for students in similar situations in the future.

Support coordinators serve an important role in following up on students who need more support than is provided in Tier 1, acting as a liaison between the student, the teacher, and the school's problem-solving structures. By knowing the support resources available in their schools and initiating additional problem-solving efforts as needed, support coordinators take ownership for making the system work for each student they are assigned.

NOTE: Avoid placing support coordinators in an evaluative role. For example, perhaps a team thinks that a classroom teacher might benefit from additional support around classroom management practices. In some situations, a support coordinator may be the appropriate person to provide coaching to the teacher (e.g., the support coordinator is the building's behavior coach). However, unless this role has been determined ahead of time, be cautious about asking support coordinators to provide coaching or evaluate a teacher's practices. The support coordinator's main responsibility is to investigate the problem, advocate for the student, and develop a positive relationship with the student's teachers. If support coordinators take an evaluative approach to working with teachers, they may jeopardize this goal.

TASK 4 SUMMARY

In this task, you:
- ☑ Identified staff members in your school who can serve as support coordinators for identified students.
- ☑ Created a process for assigning support coordinators to identified students.
- ☑ Clarified the specific responsibilities of a support coordinator.
- ☑ Made a plan for support coordinators to meet regularly, and ensured that clear, detailed records of all students will be maintained.

SECTION 1: ESTABLISHING A SYSTEM FOR INDIVIDUALIZED INTERVENTION

TASK 5 Develop a menu of ready-to-use interventions.

A menu describes the various programs and interventions you already have in place as part of your framework for supporting students identified by your system as needing additional support. Creating a menu of interventions offers several advantages. First, it allows your behavior leadership team to clearly identify, document, and manage the breadth of intervention practices and support structures in the building. By building a bridge between students and the structures created for them, a menu of existing interventions can help expedite connecting students with the supports they need. Second, a menu of existing interventions can guide decisions around staff training, professional development, and resource allocation. It can also increase implementation fidelity and ensure that schoolwide expectations translate to effective practices that carry into each classroom.

Good interventions to include in your menu have the following features (Anderson & Borgmeier, 2010):

- *Ready to use.* Ready-to-use interventions can quickly and easily accommodate new students at any time during the year. The process for accessing supports should allow students to be matched with an appropriate intervention within a few days of an identified need. The interventions should also be continually implemented across the school year so that students can be added at any time. Ready-to-use interventions are advantageous because schools can try one or more interventions instead of delaying support until comprehensive problem-solving and intervention design processes can take place.
- *Standard procedures.* Procedures for implementing supports should be consistent across students, but allow minor modifications as needed to increase the effectiveness of the intervention. For example, behavior goals addressed within a mentoring relationship should be tailored for the individual student, but the process for matching students to mentors, the mentoring schedule, and activity options may be already established. Significant modifications to these interventions may be appropriate if a student doesn't respond to initial efforts or if the problem-solving team determines that a greater level of individualization is required. However, schools should develop a written procedures manual for all interventions included on their menu and adhere to those procedures for most students.
- *Minimal time commitment from teachers.* Supports included in your menu should require minimal time commitment from classroom teachers and fit into existing classroom routines. Skill sets required for implementing the intervention should already be a part of the teacher's repertoire or be easy to learn. For some group supports, a staff member may be designated to serve as intervention coordinator to oversee and monitor implementation of the intervention for a group of students.
- *Matched to the needs of students.* When selecting an appropriate intervention, schools should examine what seems to be driving the student's misbehavior (i.e., the function of the behavior, or what the student is gaining from misbehaving) and consider how the intervention will help meet different needs of the student (e.g., attention, acknowledgment, belonging, nurturing, competence, etc.). For example, for a student who engages in frequent arguments with teachers and seems to enjoy the adult attention that such arguments offer, an intervention such

A FLEXIBLE MODEL

Our MTSS model is intentionally designed to be flexibly applied across your school or district's definition of Tier 1, Tier 2, and Tier 3 supports. In many schools, the list of ready-to-use interventions described here is considered a menu of Tier 2 supports.

as Connections would allow the student to receive adult attention on a regular basis. In contrast, a student who argues to avoid completing work and participating in class might need a different type of intervention. When establishing a menu of interventions, consider the spectrum of needs that characterize your student body and select a range of interventions that will fit these needs.

- *Instruction in prosocial behavior, frequent feedback, and ongoing data collection are embedded in intervention procedures.* Interventions included in your menu should incorporate proactive strategies to help students learn and be motivated to behave appropriately. In addition, all interventions should include a process for collecting objective data and monitoring progress to help schools determine how the intervention is working for each student.

Creating a menu of ready-to-use interventions that share the features described above will help your school maximize efficiency in responding to the needs of students in your building.

STEP 1   Identify the ready-to-use interventions already in place within your building and select new interventions to develop or adopt.

Listed below are brief descriptions of interventions to consider for your menu. Some of these structures may already be in place in your school or district. Most of the supports described below are explained in more detail in other resources, so consult those sources if your needs go beyond the scope of what this book offers. (See "Ready-to-Use Programs" on the next page for resources.)

- *Check-and-connect program (elementary and secondary levels):* Students check in with a program coordinator each morning and receive a daily monitoring card that they carry with them throughout the day. Teachers rate students on specific behaviors (e.g., "following directions," "keeping hands, feet, and objects to self," accepting feedback without argument") several times during the day. Students then take the monitoring card home for parents to review and sign. The coordinator meets with students the next morning, provides feedback and reinforcement, and gives them a new monitoring card for the day. Later, the coordinator compiles the data and monitors the students' progress. Students may be enrolled in the program for a few weeks, a few months, or even a few years—until their ratings are consistently high enough that they can move to self-monitoring or graduate from the program.
- *Meaningful work (elementary level):* Meaningful work is a very powerful program based on the idea that students thrive on feeling useful, needed, and important. Staff develop school-based jobs that can be assigned to students, and individual students are offered or apply for the positions. You can structure the program to meet the needs of individual students for acknowledgment, attention, belonging, competence, nurturing, purpose, recognition, and stimulation and change by engaging them in meaningful jobs that contribute to the school. For example, a student who just needs to move for a while each day could spend 15 minutes each afternoon visiting all the classrooms and collecting empty coffee cups.

- *Special attention for targeted students (elementary and secondary levels):* During a staff meeting, the support coordinator shows the staff a picture of the student, talks a little about the student's interests, and asks everyone to make overt efforts to greet, interact with, and praise the student. If many staff members consciously make an effort to engage the student, it is more likely that the student's needs for attention, acknowledgment, belonging, nurturing, and competence will be met. This, in turn, can help reduce the student's need to misbehave to get these needs met.

READY-TO-USE PROGRAMS

Check and Connect Program

Connections (Garrison, 2013) streamlines the check-and-connect system and enables staff to connect with, monitor, and provide effective feedback to students who demonstrate chronic challenging behaviors. Using scanning technology and automated reporting, *Connections* maximizes the ease and efficiency of daily report card intervention implementation.

School Jobs Program

Meaningful Work (Wise, Marcum, Haykin, Sprick, and Sprick, 2011) provides ideas for student jobs and more details about how to implement this intervention strategy.

Social Skills Programs

SMART Kids (Mulkey & Sprick, 2010) provides young children with instruction in social grace, respectful talk, and good old-fashioned manners. Lessons are designed specifically to meet the needs of young children—complete with direct instruction and age-appropriate activities and games.

Superheroes Social Skills (Jenson et al., 2011) is an evidence-based program that enhances the social competence of elementary students with autism spectrum disorders (ASD), behavior disorders, or developmental delays. *Superheroes* was specifically designed to improve the social skills of high-functioning children with ASD, but is also appropriate for any student who needs to learn to interact appropriately with peers and adults.

The Tough Kid Social Skills Book (Sheridan, 2010) teaches students in grades 3–7 the learned behaviors they need to get along successfully in most social situations. Skills include joining in, playing cooperatively, solving problems, dealing with teasing, and accepting "No." The book also includes assessment and data collection tools for identifying students in need of social skills training.

To learn more about any of these programs, visit ancorapublishing.com.

- *Involve students in clubs (secondary level):* Ensure that your school is providing a range of clubs, after-school activities, and other events that interest your students. If a support coordinator finds out that a student is interested in an activity—photography, for example—the support coordinator can tell the student about the club, introduce the staff member who advises the club, and help with the process of joining.
- *Structured recess (elementary):* A PE teacher and several classified staff teach students how to play a few whole-group games such as ultimate Frisbee. During recess, selected students are required to pick one of three structured games that the whole group will play. Because all of the selected students participate under adult supervision, there are very few of the extraneous negative behaviors that you often see on playgrounds. Students who need to build peer relationships or learn anger management can be plugged into structured play with adult supervision for a week or two, then move back to free play during recess.
- *Social skills training classes (elementary):* For students who have skill deficits, teaching them the social skills they lack can be an effective means of changing behavior. The biggest drawbacks to these programs are that they often take time away from academic instruction and that they are not likely to be effective if not carefully designed and implemented based on student skill needs (Gresham, 2002).
- *Leadership class (secondary level):* Each semester, the school counselor (or another appropriate, available staff member) teaches a for-credit elective class to a group of approximately 20 students. Class content includes communication skills, leadership skills, confidence-building activities, and so on. The students in the class complete two major projects: planning and implementing a community service project and organizing a school dance. What makes this program different from most leadership classes is that staff members nominate students based on their lack of involvement in the school. This class is not for students who are already established as school leaders in some way.
- *Problem-solving task force (secondary level):* This program is appropriate for a schoolwide problem, such as tardiness, vandalism, harassment, or increased numbers of students not completing work. The principal and the counselor convene a task force of students to evaluate the problem, propose solutions, implement a plan, and evaluate the plan's effectiveness. For example, a high school's problem-solving task force might focus on a different problem every semester (e.g., absenteeism in the fall, cliques in the winter, and a specific community service project in the spring). By knowing the upcoming focus, you can consider whether any students might benefit from serving on the next task force. The goal is to actively involve students in resolving school problems. Their participation can give them a sense of belonging and purpose and increase their pride in and willingness to take care of their school. A support coordinator who thinks that a student might benefit from helping to solve a problem in the school can get the student involved in the task force.
- *Mentorship (elementary and secondary levels):* Adult volunteers are paired with individual students who would benefit from a friendly, nurturing, one-on-one relationship with an adult. Mentors meet with students on school grounds and during school hours at least once a week. Activities can include, but are not limited to,

eating lunch together, playing a game, participating with the student in class activities or projects, or just taking a walk. Students who do not have nurturing home situations (and even some students who do) often benefit from a relationship with a caring adult who consistently meets with and shows an interest in them.

When choosing interventions to include in your menu, remember to:

- Consider the needs and characteristics of your students and include a range of options that will help meet these needs.
- Make sure that support coordinators can quickly and easily arrange for an identified student to get involved in any intervention you include on the menu.

STEP 2 Identify staff who will coordinate ready-to-use interventions, and outline their responsibilities for implementation.

For each ready-to-use intervention you place on your menu, identify a staff member responsible for overseeing implementation and outline their responsibilities. Responsibilities will vary depending on the intervention and how you choose to set up staffing and resources, but all intervention coordinators should be well versed in the intervention's procedures, prepared to support other staff involved in the intervention, and willing to take responsibility for ensuring that the intervention is continuously implemented as intended.

Intervention coordinators may also be responsible for:

- Overseeing enrollment in the intervention
- Managing resource and staffing needs
- Monitoring and aggregating data for students participating in the intervention
- Supervising or training staff, students, and families involved in the intervention

This menu of ready-to-use interventions helps students in need of additional support get involved in an existing program quickly, rather than waiting for a team to design an individual response for every student whose needs aren't being met. If no ready-to-use intervention fits a student's needs, you can work with the problem-solving team to build an individual intervention tailored to the specific needs of the student. However, individual interventions are time consuming and resource heavy, so if a ready-to-use intervention will suffice, that's better.

TASK 5 SUMMARY

In this task, you:
- ☑ Created a menu of ready-to-use interventions, including interventions already in place in your building and new interventions that you plan to develop or adopt.
- ☑ Identified staff who will be responsible for coordinating each intervention offered on your menu.

INTERVENTIONS: SUPPORT FOR INDIVIDUAL STUDENTS WITH BEHAVIOR CHALLENGES

TASK 6 Establish processes for responding to Code Red situations.

Code Red situations involve behaviors that are either unsafe or so disruptive that classes cannot continue. These include behaviors such as:

- Overt aggressive behavior toward others (e.g., kicking, hitting, fighting)
- Brandishing items that can be used as weapons
- Carrying weapons
- Self-injurious behavior
- Vandalism or property destruction
- Sexual assault
- Clear signs of using controlled substances (drugs and alcohol)
- Running away from school property
- Sustained confrontational or defiant behavior resulting in refusal to follow immediate, reasonable adult directions.
- Threats of targeted violence toward others.

If a student's behavior is considered a Code Red situation, you will skip simple intervention strategies and move directly to implementing the protocol that your district has in place for handling severely disruptive or unsafe behavior.

If a student's behavior is considered a Code Red situation, you will skip simple intervention strategies and move directly to implementing the protocol that your district has in place for handling severely disruptive or unsafe behavior. Once procedures for responding to Code Red situations have been put into place, you can return to identifying appropriate ready-to-use interventions or developing a long-term intervention plan to help the student learn appropriate behavior.

This task presents guidance in developing policies related to Code Red situations that involve unsafe or severely disruptive behavior, as well as developing procedures for responding to threats.

STEP 1 Adopt policies for documenting Code Red situations.

First, develop a plan for keeping systematic and detailed records of Code Red incidents at the individual, school, and district levels:

1. **Student-level records.** First, determine what information, if any, will be maintained in a student's cumulative records. This decision should not be made lightly. The goal for the permanent records of all students should be to provide a valid representation of their behavior in order for their needs to be met in current and future educational settings. That said, it is essential that students not be labeled as "threats" simply because they made an inappropriate remark in a moment of anger, frustration, or joking.
2. **Building-level records.** Schools will also need to determine how to maintain internal records at the school level. Typically, administrators will keep ongoing files or logs of all incidents that occurred in the building. Schools will need to determine how these records will be stored, transferred, and destroyed, and should plan for record-keeping procedures that withstand the passage of time and potential changes in administrative staff.

54

3. **District-level records.** A final level of documentation that you need to address is at the district level. Depending on the size of your district, you will need to consider specific information to keep in an electronic database or other central record-keeping system.

In specifying documentation procedures for Code Red incidents at the student, building, and district level, you will also need to stipulate who will have access to those records. Principals have a legitimate "need to know" status because they will be dealing with potential threats within their school. They should have some level of access to a student's prior records, whether from an earlier grade or a prior school placement. Other staff who may be given access include school psychologists, school resource officers, and designated district-level staff, such as the PBIS coordinator or director of student services.

It is critical to restrict access to a very limited number of people. No district should allow unlimited access to sensitive records of prior misbehavior, and any use of such information should be with the intent of helping to meet the needs of the student while maintaining school safety.

One approach to documenting Code Red situations is to create a centralized electronic database that allows designated individuals to access the information. For example, after threat assessments that are classified as serious and substantive, the principal and/or school psychologist would be expected to enter basic demographic information about the student and a brief summary of the incident. The complete file would be maintained in accordance with district policies regarding student records (e.g., maintained at the school level, the district level, or both). After the database is established, designated personnel can access these records as needed to address possible future incidents of dangerous or threatening behavior.

Conduct a thorough review of district policy, as well as state and local laws, and consult with professional legal counsel before implementing any changes to documentation methods at the student, school, or district level. Schools must constantly balance the privacy rights of students with the "need to know" of faculty and staff working with students.

STEP 2 Develop policies for responding to unsafe or severely disruptive behavior.

If your district or building does not already have a policy for responding quickly and safely to unsafe or severely disruptive behavior, plan to develop one.

Unsafe behaviors pose a threat to the student's own safety or the safety of others. These behaviors include:

- Overt aggressive behavior toward others (e.g., kicking, hitting, fighting)
- Brandishing items that could be used as weapons
- Carrying weapons
- Self-injurious behavior
- Sexual assault
- Clear signs of using controlled substances (drugs and alcohol)
- Running away from school property

Severely disruptive behaviors make continuing normal class routines impossible and may include any of the following:

- Severe disruption to the classroom (e.g., screaming, tantruming)
- Significant vandalism or property destruction
- Refusal to follow a reasonable, immediate adult direction (see "Refusal to Follow Direction" below)

When students engage in dangerous or severely disruptive acts, adults who haven't been briefed on how to respond are at a disadvantage. Building and district administrators (or site-based teams) should establish policy guidelines that address as many contingencies as possible, and staff should be trained to implement the policies swiftly and effectively. Of particular importance are clear guidelines for if and when staff members should implement a room clear, attempt physical restraint, call for help, and notify police.

By knowing and adhering to a consistent schoolwide policy, staff can respond efficiently even in unpredictable emergency situations. There are no right or wrong answers, but here are some general guidelines:

- Restraint should be avoided if at all possible. If used, restraint should be used only to eliminate the immediate threat of physical injury, and only after the student or students involved have ignored verbal warnings or directions. (See "Guidelines for Using Physical Restraint" on p. 58 for more considerations.)
- If room clears are recommended, the policy should address how to handle possible property damage by students and when and how staff members are expected to

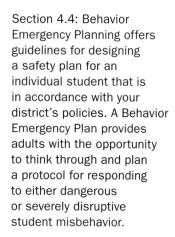

SAFETY PLAN

Section 4.4: Behavior Emergency Planning offers guidelines for designing a safety plan for an individual student that is in accordance with your district's policies. A Behavior Emergency Plan provides adults with the opportunity to think through and plan a protocol for responding to either dangerous or severely disruptive student misbehavior.

REFUSAL TO FOLLOW DIRECTION

Noncompliance with adult directions should be considered a Code Red situation only when the student overtly and immediately refuses to comply with a reasonable adult direction, and the student's behavior is so severe that it poses a threat to the student or others, or makes continuing class impossible. Staff might have difficulty defining where to draw the line between typical defiance and extreme insubordination—sometimes it's a judgment call. Because these concepts are so broad and open to interpretation, its best to avoid labeling behavior as *defiant* or *insubordinate*. As an alternative, *refusal to follow reasonable, immediate adult direction* offers an observable definition of the misbehavior, where:

Reasonable means that the direction is clear and observable. Clear directions are "Sit down at your desk" and "Raise your hand if you want to say something." Unclear and unobservable directions include "Change your attitude" and "Shape up."

Immediate means that the direction needs to be carried out in the next minute or so. If a teacher instructs a student to bring her homework the next day and she doesn't, that incident should not be viewed as refusal to follow a reasonable direction. However, failing to comply with an immediate direction, such as "get down from that desk right now," can be viewed as refusal to follow a direction.

prevent such damage. Procedures might include requiring the violent student to repair or replace damaged property. Any student who is unable to repair or replace damaged items might be required to work before or after school at a reasonable hourly rate to compensate for the damage.
- The policy should provide staff with guidance to determine what situations are severe enough to involve the police. For example, the line between hitting and assault should be predetermined.
- The policy should guide the reactions of all staff members in responding to and managing physically dangerous behavior in order to reduce the chance of inconsistency from situation to situation.

Using this information, the history of violent situations in the school, and any other relevant information, the policy-making group should develop recommendations to fit the needs of the school. Recommendations should be reviewed to ensure that they comply with board policy and state and federal statutes. The proposed policy should then be presented to the entire staff and revised if necessary. Once a written policy is accepted and finalized, staff must be trained on how to implement each of the identified procedures.

STEP 3 Develop policies regarding threats of targeted violence in schools.

Over the past two decades, many highly publicized acts of targeted violence have taken place in educational institutions. Although our collective awareness of possible violence has risen, many schools find themselves ill-prepared to respond when warning signs are observed. Unfortunately, the public outcry for "something to be done" to address school violence has led many districts to engage in misguided efforts to create profiles or checklists to identify potential school shooters, only to find that no such profile exists.

Although there are no simple profiles or checklists to guide responses to threats of targeted violence, there are effective strategies you can use to better recognize and respond to situations where students may pose a threat to others at school. Effective interventions for managing threats of targeted violence should follow a sequence of five major steps that focus on preparation, response, and recovery, as shown in Figure 1.1 below.

Although there are no simple profiles or checklists to guide responses to threats of targeted violence, there are effective strategies you can use to better recognize and respond to situations where students may pose a threat to others at school.

FIGURE 1.1 *Steps for Managing Threats of Targeted Violence*

Step 1	Adopt schoolwide policies, procedures, and standards for record-keeping. (Preparedness)
Step 2	Conduct training for threat assessment teams and awareness sessions for staff and students. (Preparedness)
Step 3	Immediately implement procedures to respond to possible threats and ensure everyone's safety. (Response)
Step 4	Involve parents and community agencies as appropriate. (Response)
Step 5	Restore a sense of safety and security. (Recovery)

GUIDELINES FOR USING PHYSICAL RESTRAINT

1. **Remove other students from the area.** In the classroom, use a room clear; outside, students may be sent to another part of the playground. Use a firm voice to direct students to another location. "Everyone needs to move immediately to the other side of the blacktop. Jackson, Alissa, Sandra, Tom, move now!"

2. **Always try verbal interventions before resorting to any procedures.** Avoid shouting, but use a firm and loud command. "Jeremy, stop pounding on that window and move to this side of the room—now!" Using a student's name increases the likelihood that the student will respond to the verbal instruction. If more than one student is involved, direct each student to a different location. "Rico, move over to the doorway! Zach, move over to the lockers!"

3. **If at all possible, signal or call for help before beginning any sort of restraint.** To avoid possible concerns regarding the use of undue force or even abuse during restraint, the adult involved should always summon assistance. The act of calling for help indicates that the presence of another adult was requested as quickly as possible and that the adult has made no attempt to engage in inappropriate physical contact. If the school staff does not currently have routines for signaling for adult assistance, such procedures should be devised for every school location, including all classrooms, hallways, playgrounds, cafeterias, bus waiting areas, and so on.

4. **Decide whether restraint is necessary and helpful.** If the student does not stop the dangerous behavior after a staff member issues verbal instructions, the staff member must use professional judgment regarding whether to intervene physically before assistance arrives or wait until help comes. No set rule can be used for making this decision. However, staff should understand that they are not required to put themselves in direct physical jeopardy. Staff members may mistakenly believe that they will be negligent if they do not intervene physically in a fight. However, staff should behave in a reasonably prudent manner to keep everyone physically safe, including themselves. What is reasonable and prudent may depend on several factors:

- Number of students involved
- Size of the student or students involved
- Size and strength of the adult
- Degree of violence taking place
- Presence of any weapons or potential weapons
- Staff training in the use of nonviolent restraint methods

If a small child is pounding on a window, it would be reasonable and prudent to remove that student. However, if the student is large and strong and the teacher is small, it would be neither reasonable nor prudent for the teacher to attempt restraint. The teacher should address the student calmly and wait for help to arrive so the student can be safely restrained.

When two or more students are fighting physically, take into account that attempting to break up the fight by pulling one student off may actually increase the risk of injury for everyone involved. If you grab the arms of one of the combatants, you make that student more vulnerable to direct blows from the other. Unless both students are very small, you should probably wait for assistance before trying to physically break up an altercation.

The less training staff have received in the use of physical restraint, the more cautious they should be in using restraint. If staff are not sure whether they can successfully restrain a student without injury, they should avoid attempting to do so. At a school where violent incidents occur frequently, staff should be well trained in methods of restraint and students should be regularly instructed in nonviolent conflict resolution.

Training in uses and methods of physical restraint requires demonstrations, practice, and rehearsal. It is beyond the scope of this book to provide detailed guidelines. Local law enforcement, mental health organizations, state agencies, and schools with successful violence prevention programs in place may be good resources for strategies and recommendations.

NOTE: If a student of any size has a weapon, staff members should not to try to disarm the student. The police should be called, and all adults and children should be kept as far from the crisis situation as possible.

A *threat* is defined as any expression of intent to harm another person. Threatening communications may come to schools in the form of writings, drawings, verbal statements, postings on Internet sites, and a host of other communication technologies.

Examples in which concern about a student's future behavior may come to the attention of school personnel include:

- A student writes a story for an English class in which one student shoots another student at school.
- A student uses a personal Web page to sympathize with others who have engaged in school shootings and to fantasize about mimicking that behavior.
- A principal receives an e-mail from a recently suspended student stating, "It's time for you to die!"

Reports from others may also reveal these concerns, such as:

- A student shows the principal what appears to be a hit list written by a peer.
- A mother calls to report that her teenage son is ruminating over a breakup with his girlfriend and is preoccupied with violence, death, weapons, and revenge.
- A student reports that he saw what he believed was a switchblade in another student's backpack.

A third way that possible threats may come to the attention of school authorities is through anonymous communication. Some communities have anonymous tip lines operated by local schools, districts, or law enforcement agencies. Schools may also receive anonymous calls, letters, or e-mails with messages such as "Judgment Day is Here" or "This school is going down in flames!"

If schools can learn to identify and address warning signs and threatening communications in the early stages, they may prevent a student's violent thoughts or behaviors from turning into physical violence and also greatly increase the general sense of safety and security in the school. Your school or district's policies on threats create the foundation for effective threat prevention and response. Develop policies about threats of targeted violence in schools that include the following:

- A clear statement that threatening communication of any kind is not appropriate or acceptable on school property or at school functions
- A list of types of communication that are unacceptable, such as verbal threats, written threats, gestures that indicate intent to cause harm to others, creation of hit lists, bomb threats, and threats made through electronic communications
- Procedures for investigating and responding to potential threats of violence, such as conferencing with the principal; threat assessment; interviews with the school psychologist, counselor, or other mental health professional; notification of law enforcement; and notification of parents
- Procedures for removing a student from a classroom or district transportation system
- Procedures for possible disciplinary action, such as suspension, expulsion, and alternative placement
- Procedures for possible legal action

If schools can learn to identify and address warning signs and threatening communications in the early stages, they may prevent a student's violent thoughts or behaviors from turning into physical violence.

Figure 1.2, shown on the next page, is a sample of policies and procedures for dealing with assault and threats of violence.

Following adoption of effective policies and procedures to address threats of violence, the school or district should make the information available to the public, including students, parents, the community, and the media. By sharing district policies on threatening communications and by teaching students the expectations about what is and is not acceptable on school grounds and school functions, schools can significantly reduce the number of incidents of inappropriate joking, sarcasm, and figures of speech. Clear policies and procedures also increase the likelihood that threats will be reported to school personnel.

STEP 4 Establish a threat assessment team.

Every school should have a designated team of professionals who can respond effectively when a threat of targeted violence is brought to the attention of school personnel (Jimerson & Brock, 2004). The purpose of the team is to lead the threat assessment process when the need arises. A building administrator should chair the threat assessment team because that position is responsible for overall operations, safety, and security in the school.

Threat assessment teams help schools distinguish between two types of situations:

1. Students who may have communicated a threat but have no actual or sustained intent to cause harm to others (i.e., transient threat)
2. Students who have made threatening communications and actually pose a threat to others (i.e., substantive threat)

To help clarify these two situations, we will use the terms *transient threat* and *substantive threat*. A transient threat is one in which there is no sustained intent to cause harm beyond the current situation. Transient threats are often impulsive acts, said in a moment of anger or in a joking or sarcastic manner. Though these circumstances do not excuse threatening language, such situations should be handled differently from more serious threats.

In contrast, a substantive threat is one in which there is ongoing intent to cause harm beyond the situation at hand. Substantive threats are typically more premeditated and thought out in advance of any communications or attempts to engage in a violent attack.

Finally, although not a distinct category, in some situations a student's behavior raises concerns, but on investigation the concerns turn out to be misunderstandings or false reports. A threat assessment team should be able to distinguish between the two types of threats and determine procedures for responding to them. See "The Difference Between Transient and Substantive Threats" on pages 62–63 for more in-depth information.

While schools must acknowledge and address all threatening communications, distinguishing between transient and substantive threats is essential in determining appropriate responses to less serious versus more serious circumstances.

In terms of effectively managing staff resources, it is impractical and inadvisable to conduct a formal full-scale threat assessment for every situation that could remotely be considered a threat. Those situations with low need should receive a low-level response, and those with high need should get a greater allocation of resources. Use the descriptions above for transient and substantive threats to make a judgment about whether a higher-level assessment is necessary. When in doubt, ask for input from other professionals (administrators, psychologists). If the situation is still uncertain, refer for a higher-level threat assessment.

> *Every school should have a designated team of professionals who can respond effectively when a threat of targeted violence is brought to the attention of school personnel.*

FIGURE 1.2 *Sample Policy on Assault and Threats of Violence*

Policy on Assault and Threats of Violence

STUDENTS

Any student who threatens, assaults, batters, or abuses another student shall be subject to appropriate disciplinary action, including suspension or expulsion.

SCHOOL PERSONNEL

Any student who threatens, assaults, batters, or physically or verbally abuses a teacher or other school personnel shall be subject to appropriate disciplinary action, up to and including expulsion from school and/or legal action.

REMOVAL OF STUDENTS

School administrators, teachers, or other school personnel may immediately remove or cause to be removed threatening or violent students from a classroom setting or from the District's transportation system pending any further disciplinary action that may occur. Threatening or violent behavior shall include, but not be limited to:

1. Verbal or written statements or gestures by students indicating intent to harm themselves, others, or property.

2. Physical attack by students with the intent to inflict harm to themselves, others, or property.

   - The Principal shall be notified immediately of such removal.
   - Removal of students from a bus shall be made in compliance with state statutes.
   - Each school shall designate the site(s) to which employees may remove students from a classroom setting and the employee(s) who will supervise the student at the site.
   - When teachers or other personnel remove a student, they shall complete and submit a form to document the removal and the causes of the removal as soon as practicable. The Principal shall review the removal as soon as possible to determine if further disciplinary action is warranted or if the student is to be returned to the classroom.

REPORT TO LAW ENFORCEMENT AGENCY

When they have reasonable belief that a law has been violated, the Principal or building administrator shall immediately report the violation to law enforcement officials when the following conditions are met: 1) an act has occurred on school property or at a school-sponsored function; and 2) the act involves assault resulting in serious physical injury, a sexual offense, or kidnapping; or 3) the incident of assault involves the use of a weapon.

NOTIFICATION

Any District employee assigned to work directly with, or who comes in contact with, a student with a documented history of weapons violations and/or physical abuse of a school employee or of carrying a concealed weapon on school property or at a school function shall be notified in writing of the student's history by the Principal or designee, guidance counselor, or other school official who has knowledge of the student's behavior prior to the assignment or contact.

Adapted from Fayette County Public Schools, Lexington, KY. Used with permission.

THE DIFFERENCE BETWEEN TRANSIENT AND SUBSTANTIVE THREATS

Not all threats are created equal; therefore, not all responses to threats should be equal. While some threats clearly communicate a serious and plausible intent to cause harm, others clearly do not. Following is a more detailed description of transient versus substantive threats and the implications for threat assessment teams in real-world applications.

Transient Threats

Transient threats are communications that do not convey a real or lasting intent to cause harm to another person. Such statements are often made impulsively and may include angry outbursts, inappropriate jokes, insults, and figures of speech. Several examples follow, adapted from actual cases, with a brief explanation of the actual intent:

- A kindergarten student says, "If you don't let me on that swing, I'm gonna kill you!" In reality, this student has no actual intent to cause harm to the other student; rather, his statement demonstrates his poor frustration tolerance.
- Following a particularly frustrating class, a middle school student uses the word "kill" as a figure of speech, as in "That teacher made me so mad I could have killed her." There is no actual threat and no intent to harm the teacher currently or in the future.
- Following the death of a teacher in an auto accident, a high school student insensitively jokes, "Let's take a poll to see which teacher we hope somebody will knock off next." The reality is that the student simply made a tasteless joke at the expense of teachers, but has no intent to cause physical harm.
- During a physical fight, one high school student yells to another, "After we get out of here, I'm gonna run your car off the road and wrap you around a tree!" Although this clearly *is* a threat, after his anger dissipated, the student showed significant remorse and regret, and apologized for his actions. During an interview, he said he was just trying to save face in front of peers and had no real intent to cause harm.

The most important characteristic of transient threats is that there is no sustained intent to cause harm beyond the current situation. That said, a clarifying explanation does not make such threats acceptable in a school setting. For example, even though the high school student in the example above apologized and acknowledged why he made the threat, the fact remains that he made a threat and therefore may be subject to administrative or legal consequences.

If there is any doubt about whether a reported behavior represents a transient threat, it should be addressed as a *possible* substantive threat and the threat assessment process should begin.

Substantive Threats

Substantive threats differ from transient threats in that there is an actual and sustained intent to cause harm beyond the current situation. Such actions are typically the end result of a series of thoughts and behaviors related to strong unresolved feelings, which may include social humiliation and torment, feelings of perceived injustice, inability to cope with significant losses, feelings of personal failure, etc.

Examples, adapted from actual threat assessment scenarios, include:

- An elementary school fifth grader asks, "Which one of these cars is Miss Miller's? When she gets in it, I'm going to drop a match in her gas tank." The student was found to have both matches and a lighter in his possession, and he repeatedly stated that he was going to carry out his plan "no matter what" anyone else did to him and even if he blew himself up in the process.
- A series of writings titled "Time for Them to Die" is found in a middle school student's English journal. A paragraph expresses rage at "years of torment" and details how she plans to push another girl in front of their school bus and to make sure it "looks like an accident."
- An Internet site is reported to school officials and law enforcement; it lists the following specific sequence of events:

    Tic 5—Get Josh to drive me to school, then kill him so he doesn't have to see what I'm going to do.
    Toc 4—Leave bag outside science lab window.
    Tic 3—Walk in that f***ing school like everything's normal.
    Toc 2—4th hour retrieve gun from bag.
    Tic 1—Blast my way into the office to render MY Final Solution!
    Toc 0—Die! Die!! Die!!!

Clearly the three substantive situations described above represent an entirely different level of concern than the examples of transient threats presented earlier. The main defining characteristic of substantive threats is the intent to cause harm beyond the current situation. Substantive threats also typically feature a greater level of detail in the plan, such as time, place, identified targets, and means of violence. In addition, threats are often repeated over time, and often others are recruited as accomplices or to serve as an audience to the unfolding plan. Finally, with substantive threats there is often physical evidence of efforts to carry out the plan, such as detailed writings, acquisition of weapons or weapon-making materials, or a list of intended victims.

Many schools that have implemented zero-tolerance policies require automatic responses to any and all behavior that could be considered a threat. This one-size-fits-all approach tends to be problematic because it does not allow for professional judgment or interpretation of behavior in context, and it often mandates specific consequences (such as suspension or expulsion) regardless of whether an individual actually posed a threat. In addition, schools that attempt to use student profiles or checklists have found two substantial deficits or concerns. First, the vast majority of students who meet established criteria for "school shooters" will never actually make or pose a threat of targeted violence (i.e., false positives). Second, some students who do pose a threat of targeted violence will not be identified by profiles because they share no, or very few, characteristics of prior school shooters (i.e., false negatives).

By contrast, a threat assessment approach is an inquisitive process in which a team reviews behaviors and facts on an individual basis to determine if a student appears to be on a path of violence. The team determines what may be done to provide support to that student and protect the safety of others. A threat assessment focuses on behaviors, evidence, and facts rather than traits or characteristics, which often do not provide an accurate view of the situation (Fein et al., 2002). Those in charge of examining behaviors of concern when responding to a threat (administrators or threat assessment team members) will make judgments based on the individual student rather than using blanket assessments and consequences. A team process is recommended for conducting threat assessments to ensure that different perspectives are considered and that no one person has responsibility for responding to possible threats of violence.

To further understand threat assessment, Figure 1.3 presents six fundamental principles of the threat assessment process as presented by the U.S. Department of Education and the U.S. Secret Service (2004). The Safe Schools Initiative was a project to study the "thinking, planning, and other pre-attack behaviors" of students who engaged in school shooting. The six principles provide a good starting point regarding effective threat assessment.

Whenever a threat assessment is necessary, the threat assessment team will gather the information needed to determine the nature and consequences of the potential threat. In broad terms, the basic purpose of a threat assessment is twofold:

1. To develop a plan to manage possible threats of targeted violence
2. To respond to and manage incidents of possible threats of targeted violence when the need arises

Depending on your school's staffing practices, threat assessment teams might include the following representatives:

- Seasoned principal or building administrator
- School psychologist or other mental health professional
- School resource officer (SRO) or other police officer assigned to the school
- School counselor
- School social worker or resource center coordinator
- Behavior specialist
- Special education specialist

Many schools that have implemented zero-tolerance policies require automatic responses to any and all behavior that could be considered a threat. This one-size-fits-all approach tends to be problematic because it does not allow for professional judgment or interpretation.

FIGURE 1.3 *Principles of Threat Assessment Process*

Six Principles of the Threat Assessment Process

1. Targeted violence is the end result of an understandable, and oftentimes discernible, process of thinking and behavior.

2. Targeted violence stems from an interaction among the individual, the situation, the setting, and the target.

3. An investigative, skeptical, inquisitive mindset is critical to successful threat assessment.

4. Effective threat assessment is based on facts, rather than on characteristics or traits.

5. An integrated systems approach should guide threat assessment inquiries and investigations.

6. The central question in a threat assessment inquiry or investigation is whether a student poses a threat, not whether the student has made a threat.

From *Threat Assessment in Schools: A Guide to Managing Threatening Situations and Creating Safe School Climates,* U.S. Secret Service and U.S. Department of Education, 2002)

To achieve maximum effectiveness, threat assessment teams should clarify their purpose as a team as well as their individual roles and responsibilities.

Though the entire team is concerned with providing for the safety and well-being of all students, the different members will bring their own expertise to the threat assessment process. Multidisciplinary training allows professionals to understand and learn from the unique perspective of their counterparts on the team. Mental health professionals, for example, are concerned not only with possible threats, but also with antecedent events, social contexts, risk factors, and precipitating events. Administrators, on the other hand, must focus on maintaining safe and orderly operations of the entire school, whether school rules or board polices have been violated, and whether a student should be removed from school grounds. Finally, school resource officers are concerned with whether a crime has been committed, if an imminent danger is present, and if a perimeter needs to be established to protect a school campus.

To achieve maximum effectiveness, threat assessment teams should clarify their purpose as a team as well as their individual roles and responsibilities in preparing for and responding to possible threats of targeted violence. Recognizing the wide variation in job titles and roles across schools and districts, Figure 1.4, shown on the next page, presents broad categories of how threat assessment roles may be defined and outlines a nonexhaustive list of responsibilities associated with each role. You are encouraged to adapt these roles and responsibilities for the unique positions you have in your district as well as the expertise of the individuals in those roles.

FIGURE 1.4 *Examples of Threat Assessment Team Roles*

Building Principal
- Lead the threat assessment process (both planning and response).
- Serve as initial contact for all referrals of potential threats of violence.
- Determine if there is imminent risk, and respond accordingly.
- Verify information by talking with the individual who reported the possible threat and the student of concern, as well as consulting with faculty, staff, and parents as indicated.
- Determine whether the behavior should be considered a transient or substantive threat, and address as warranted.
- Prepare and deliver communications to students, staff, parents, and media as warranted.
- Document actions taken.

School Psychologist, School Counselor, School Social Worker
- Assist the principal in directing the efforts of the threat assessment team.
- Conduct a mental health interview with the student.
- Gather information from records, parents, teachers, students, and others as needed.
- Serve as a liaison between school and community agencies, such as mental health centers, psychiatric hospitals, and child welfare.
- Assist in responding to the immediate situation at hand (short-term needs).
- Participate in safety planning meetings and implementation of safety plan (long-term needs).
- Document actions taken (forms, writings, drawings).

School Resource Officer (school based)
- In cases of imminent risk, provide immediate assistance to the school in response to threats of targeted violence in order to secure the facility.
- For non-imminent risk, collaborate with the threat assessment team to determine the nature of a potential threat, whether a crime has been committed, and possible legal actions to take.
- Serve as liaison with local law enforcement agencies, juvenile court, etc.
- Participate in safety planning meetings (short term) and implementation of a safety plan (long term).

Other Threat Assessment Team Members
- Assist and participate with team to assess and respond to the immediate situation at hand and follow-up safety planning meetings as needed.
- Assist with implementation of safety plan, monitoring, and follow-up activities as needed.

STEP 5 Clarify procedures for systematically responding to threats.

The model Threat Assessment Flowchart in Figure 1.5 on page 68 can help you conceptualize the threat assessment process. You may modify the model as needed to suit the unique needs of your school. In the first step of any flowchart, school personnel become aware of a possible threat of violence and report that information to the principal. Administrator notification ensures that the individual who is ultimately responsible for the safety and security of the building is aware of what is going on and therefore able to activate the threat assessment process and district resources as needed.

1. Determine whether or not there is an imminent risk.

Once notified of threatening behavior, the principal will determine if there is an imminent risk to anyone's safety. For purposes of this discussion, imminent risk is narrowly defined as when an individual is actively attempting to carry out a lethal threat of violence and has the means to do so. In other words, imminent risk goes beyond such acts as fighting, severe disruptive behaviors, and destruction of property. In the context of threats of targeted violence, an example of imminent risk would be a student brandishing a gun or knife and using it, or threatening to do so.

For imminent risk, the principal does not go through the relatively time-intensive threat assessment process, but instead takes immediate action to ensure everyone's safety. Actions may include calling 911, initiating lockdown procedures, and securing or isolating the student who is attempting to engage in violence.

For nonemergency situations, the principal will verify the report and gather additional information from the student of concern, consult other support staff, interview possible witnesses, and contact parents. If, following this initial inquiry, the principal is confident that the reported behavior is not a threat or is a transient threat, the principal addresses it as appropriate through disciplinary action, referral to the school's intervention team, or clarifying and re-teaching expectations. Although this places broad authority and discretion with the principal, this is consistent with the decisions and responsibilities principals face daily regarding student discipline and building safety and security.

SELF-HARM AND SUICIDAL IDEATION

If your threat assessment team will be responsible for assessing and responding to threats of self-harm and suicidal ideation, see "Assessing and Responding to Threats of Self-Harm and Suicidal Ideation" on pages 70–71.

2. Convene the threat assessment team.

If, after interviewing the student and consulting with others as warranted, the principal determines the behavior should not be addressed as a transient threat, the principal will notify and convene appropriate members of the school's threat assessment team. Team members will meet to discuss relevant behaviors and facts that are known up to this point and then determine a course of action, which may include any or all of the following:

- Conducting a structured clinical interview with the student
- Conducting interviews with other students, teachers, and others who may have pertinent information
- Contacting the student's parents
- Reviewing school records
- Conducting a criminal background check (school resource officer)
- Collaborating with community agencies

INTERVENTIONS: SUPPORT FOR INDIVIDUAL STUDENTS WITH BEHAVIOR CHALLENGES

FIGURE 1.5 *Threat Assessment Flowchart*

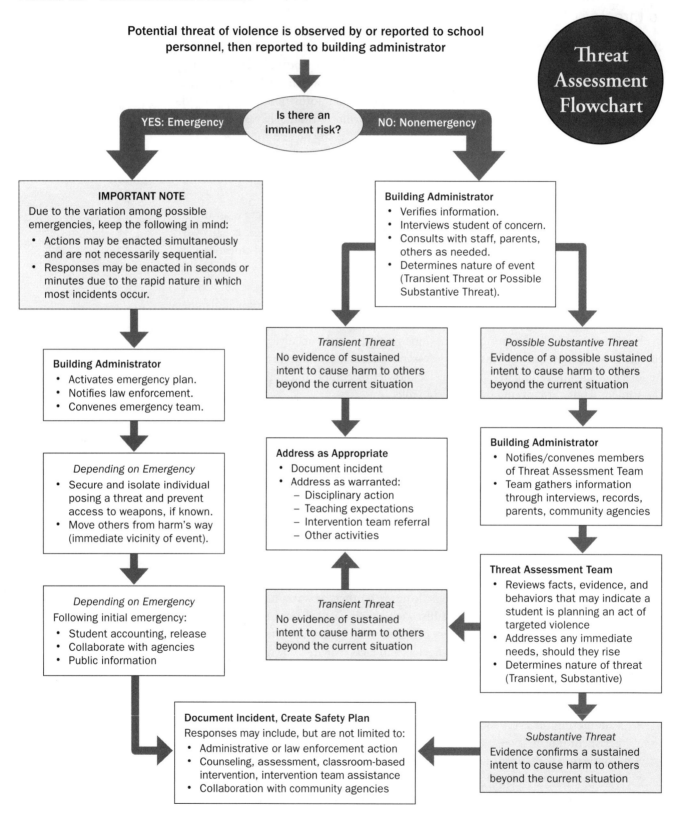

Adapted from Fayette County Public Schools, Lexington, KY. Used with permission.

During the initial threat assessment briefing, designate who will be responsible for each action in order to ensure that all areas of need are addressed and that services are not duplicated. At the end of the meeting, arrange specific next steps and determine when the group will reconvene.

3. Address short-term and long-term planning needs.

At the designated time, the threat assessment team should meet again to review various findings and then address the immediate short-term needs of the student and the school. As outlined on the Threat Assessment Flowchart, after conducting a more thorough investigation the team may determine that the behavior is simply a transient threat. If this is the case, the incident will be addressed through disciplinary action, referrals for school-based services, clarifying expectations, the Student Code of Conduct, and other relatively low-level responses.

If, however, the threat assessment team determines that the threat is substantive, short-term planning will focus on containing the situation, providing support to identified targets, and taking action to reduce the possibility that a threat will be carried out. Depending on the severity of the situation and the results of the threat assessment, short-term planning may involve referrals for mental health evaluation, coordination of services with juvenile court or child welfare workers, or school-based counseling and support.

Long-term planning means taking measures to minimize the likelihood that the student who posed a threat will engage in threats of targeted violence in the future. Such measures vary widely from situation to situation, ranging from the extremely intensive approach of searching a student's backpack every day and escorting the student from class to class to informal mentoring and relationship building. Long-term measures to ensure safety may focus on the individual student who caused concern or may address broader matters such as bullying prevention, effective supervision, and schoolwide discipline and classroom management.

It is in your school's best interest to establish positive working relationships with parents before, during, and after any possible emergency situation.

4. Involve parents as much as possible.

It is in your school's best interest to establish positive working relationships with parents before, during, and after any possible emergency situation. When a critical situation is at hand, your school will be better able to respond when there are open lines of communication, mutual levels of respect, and a climate of collaboration.

Whenever a student is suspected of expressing a threat of violence, the school must notify and involve parents as quickly as possible. That said, in some circumstances time is of the essence and rapid decision-making is required. Clearly, in serious situations (such as a student threatening to get a gun from his locker), the school should not wait to take action until staff can contact parents. The school should prevent access to the weapon and strive to protect everyone's safety.

While responding to possible threats of targeted violence can be an emotional and draining experience for school employees, it is even more traumatic for parents. Schools are encouraged to work to develop positive relationships with all parents throughout the school year as part of an overall effort to establish a collaborative tone. When you must interact with parents because their student may have made a threat of targeted violence,

ASSESSING AND RESPONDING TO THREATS OF SELF-HARM AND SUICIDAL IDEATION

While a threat assessment team is typically tasked with the responsibility for assessing and responding to threats of targeted violence toward others, with adequate training this team may also assess and respond to threats of self-harm and suicidal ideation.

Suicidal ideation or threats typically occur each year in every high school and middle school and surprisingly even in elementary schools. Suicide is the second leading cause of death for children ages 10–18 (Centers for Disease Control and Prevention [CDC], 2017). Although the number of completed suicides among elementary students is low (CDC counted 1,300 suicides among children ages 5 to 12 between 1999 and 2015), the CDC reports that the rate has risen in recent years, especially among 11- and 12-year-olds.

However, there are many more suicidal ideations and presentations than actual suicides. CDC's *Youth Risk Behavior Survey* (Kann et al., 2018) in 2017 surveyed high school students and found that in the past 12 months:

- 17.2% seriously considered attempting suicide
- 13.6% made a suicide plan
- 7.4% attempted suicide one or more times
- 2.4% made an attempt that had to be treated by a doctor or nurse

The Substance Abuse and Mental Health Services Administration (2012) recommends that schools develop protocols that specify the staff members who will be called to action in the event of suicide risk, suicide attempt, or completed suicide. This protocol should include details about:

- Essential documentation requirements (for incidents, assessments, referrals, and follow-up recommendations)
- Risk assessment procedures and tools, including identification of staff members within the building or district who are equipped to conduct suicide risk assessments
- Parental notification requirements, including mandatory reporting obligations and educational resources to share with families
- Follow-up support after convening a risk assessment, including an up-to-date list of community mental health resources to use as referrals and procedures for providing school-based support
- Resources and handouts, such as forms for parents and staff regarding risk factors and signs of suicide (Lieberman, Poland & Kornfeld, 2008)

Whether you choose to use your threat assessment team or other school-based crisis teams and personnel within your school or district to assess and respond to threats of self-harm, it is imperative to involve at least one staff member who is properly trained in assessing a student's suicide risk. School counselors, school social workers, and school psychologists are often in the best position to conduct risk assessments, but other staff members with adequate training may be a good fit for this role.

Knowing how to properly conduct a risk assessment and respond appropriately based on the student's level of risk are cornerstones of effectively addressing a threat to self-harm. Use the following guidelines when assessing a student's suicide risk:

- Demonstrate empathy, support, and trust.
- Remain nonjudgmental and refrain from minimizing the student's problems.
- Be direct in questioning the student. Ask if the student is thinking about or has ever thought about suicide, or has ever attempted suicide before. If the student says yes, seek details by asking why, when, how, where, and who else knows. Also ask if the student knows anyone else who has attempted or completed suicide. If the student says yes, ask for more details about who, when, how, and where.
- Don't promise confidentiality, but inform the student of actions that will be taken in disclosing information to ensure the student's safety.
- Develop a safety plan, including compiling a list of coping strategies and sources of support that the student can turn to when experiencing thoughts of suicide (Poland, 1995).

Based on Pena & Caine's (2006) review of suicide screening assessments, the following are among the most commonly used validated tools for conducting suicide risk assessments:

- *Suicidal Ideation Questionnaire* (SIQ; Reynolds, 1987): The SIQ was developed for use with students in grades 10–12; the SIQ-JR is available for students in grades 7–9. Thirty items are included in the SIQ and 15 in the SIQ-JR, all focusing on suicidal ideation.
- *Columbia Suicide Screen* (Posner et al, 2011): This tool was developed as a free, publicly available questionnaire to identify high school students at risk for suicide.
- *Suicide Risk Screen* (Halfors et al., 2006): This screening is administered as part of a larger High School Questionnaire to assess suicidal behaviors and depression.

Finally, consider the following recommendations when developing a school or district protocol for the risk assessment of a referred student:

- Conduct an interview with the referred student on the day of the referral, regardless of when the referral is made. If necessary, keep the student after school to complete the risk assessment. Always treat each referral as potentially high risk.
- Always inform the principal of the pending interview.
- Ideally, arrange for two licensed or certified staff members to conduct the interview. Having two staff members allows one staff member to leave the interview to get additional help without leaving the student alone. If possible, one of the interviewers should have a positive relationship with the referred student.
- Notify the student's parents/guardian of the risk assessment on the day of the interview. For liability reasons, two staff members should witness the notification of the parent. Furthermore, the interviewed student should be allowed to leave school (e.g., ride the bus, walk home, drive home, or go with another student or adult) only after the parent or guardian is notified about the interview. The reason for holding the student is that the parent may share relevant information about the student during the notification that could change the school's risk assessment. If the school's risk assessment suggests a high risk of self-harm, the student must be released physically to the parent.

- Based on the school's population, develop protocols for responding to the following situations:
  - The referred students or parents have limited proficiency in English
  - Students who are in the custody of the state
  - Referrals made after school day when the student is no longer on campus
  - Students who express thoughts or threats of self-harm while being seen by an administrator or school resource officer for disciplinary reasons
  - Responding to a student who has been referred and assessed repeatedly over the previous weeks or months
  - When a student with a history of suicidal ideation, threats, or attempts moves either to another school in the district or out of the district
  - A suicide pact involves two or more students at the school or at other schools

Additional resources to consult for developing effective suicide risk assessment and intervention efforts within your school include:

- American Foundation for Suicide Prevention, & Suicide Prevention Resource Center. (2018). *After a suicide: A toolkit for schools* (2nd ed.). Waltham, MA: Education Development Center. Learn more: www.sprc.org/resources-programs/after-suicide-toolkit-schools
- Boccio, D. E. (2015). A school-based Suicide Risk Assessment Protocol. *Journal of Applied School Psychology, 31*(1), 31–62.
- Lieberman, R., Poland, S., & Kornfeld, C. (2008). Best practices in suicide intervention. In P. Harrison & A. Thomas (Eds.), *Best practices in school psychology: Systems-level services* (pp. 273–289). Bethesda, MD, National Association of School Psychologists.
- Singer, J. B., Erbacher, T. A., & Rosen, P. (2018). School-based suicide prevention: A framework for evidence-based practice. *School Mental Health, 10*, 1–18. doi: 10.1007/s12310-018-9245-8
- Substance Abuse and Mental Health Services Administration (2012). *Preventing suicide: A toolkit for high schools*. HHS Publication No. SMA-12-4669. Rockville, MD: Author. Learn more: store.samhsa.gov/product/Preventing-Suicide-A-Toolkit-for-High-Schools/SMA12-4669

you should always strive to reassure them that you are not working against them, but with them on behalf of their child. However, we strongly recommend that your school actively work to establish proactive working relationships with parents so your first interaction with them is not to report a serious incident.

SHARING INFORMATION

In far too many incidents of school violence, numerous agencies that serve children have found themselves with significant records that indicate a student involved was experiencing serious difficulties, but those records were never shared with others. Though it would be inappropriate and most likely in violation of federal laws to recommend a wholesale exchange of sensitive information across agencies, schools *are* advised to establish formal and informal relationships with their counterparts in juvenile justice, child welfare, mental health, and similar agencies. Clearly, important restrictions limit the disclosure of information without obtaining signed releases; however, in certain instances such disclosures are allowed. Before sharing any student records, make sure to consult district, state, and current federal policies (e.g., Family Educational Rights and Privacy Act [FERPA]).

---

5. Restore a sense of safety and security.

While Step 4 deals with how to work with students, parents, and community agencies in *responding* to a potential threat, this step focuses on how to restore a sense of safety and security in the immediate and longer-term aftermath of the event.

To put it bluntly, threats of targeted violence, or even rumors thereof, have the potential to cause fear and panic in students, parents, staff, and the larger community. In this age of cell phones, e-mail, instant messaging, and a seemingly insatiable hunger for sensational "news," school districts must be prepared to deal with concerns as they arise. If a threatening incident happens on your campus, the news *will* get out, and you *will* have to address it. Therefore, it will be helpful to create guidelines for communication with students, parents, and the larger community during and following reported concerns.

Depending on the nature of the incident, information may change minute to minute and hour to hour. Principals should provide clear, concise, and prompt communications to appropriate internal and external audiences following a threat that affects the school community. Receiving direct information from the principal often reassures the staff and external community and prevents rumors from circulating.

Schools should be prepared to provide factual information to the parties who need it, while recognizing that different parties have different needs. Whether speaking to students, parents, concerned citizens, or the media, you should keep the following guidelines in mind.

You will essentially address three topics:

- Here is what happened.
- Here is what we are doing about it.
- Here is what we will do to see that it doesn't happen again.

In answering questions:

- Be brief and to the point when explaining what happened.
- Correct inaccuracies.
- Use clear, simple terms.
- Reassure children and adults that their safety is the primary concern of the principals, school staff, and district staff.
- Discuss what is being done to keep people safe.
- Name a contact person if interested parties have questions.
- Send home a backpack letter with students affected by the situation.

Students, parents, teachers, and community members all have legitimate concerns and needs for information about possible threats of violence on school grounds. Taking proactive steps to familiarize yourself with the recommendations above can assist you in being better prepared to speak to the unique needs of these constituents.

STEP 6   Create a plan to conduct threat awareness sessions for staff and students.

While establishing a threat assessment team and clarifying procedures for responding to threats are essential, also provide awareness training for all faculty and staff.

Staff training should raise awareness and instill confidence in responding to potential threats, but should not create undue fears. Assure all staff that despite recent highly publicized events, incidents of targeted violence in schools remain very rare. However, staff should also recognize that their efforts may make the difference in preventing threats from escalating to violence.

Staff orientation should address:

- School and district policy regarding threatening communications
- Student Code of Conduct regarding threatening communications
- How to recognize direct threats and behavioral signs of violence
- How to actively respond to direct observation or reports of threats
- How to conduct lessons for students on school policies and procedures regarding threatening communications

It may be effective to have one or more members of the school's threat assessment team conduct the general staff training by developing a brief presentation for a faculty meeting. The training session should address practical matters such as how to make a referral and when to seek immediate assistance. The primary focus of the training should be on the fact that the school is taking active steps to prevent school violence and preparing to respond should the need arise. If possible, highlight existing prevention efforts, such as social competency training and bullying prevention programs, in addition to addressing how to respond to possible threats.

In addition, you will also need to teach students the school's expectations regarding threatening communications. Such awareness training should be presented to the entire student body. Countless students have found themselves facing administrative or legal consequences because they did not understand or appreciate the magnitude of a certain behavior, such as a joking, sarcastic, or "in the moment" threat. Many of these situations could have been avoided had students been taught clear expectations regarding what constitutes threatening communication.

Plan to deliver awareness training in small classroom settings rather than in large assemblies (in which students may be more likely to zone out or otherwise miss the information).

Student orientation lessons should include:

- Age-appropriate descriptions of behavior that will be considered threatening
- A clear description of the actions that the school will take in response to threats of any nature
- What students should do if they observe a threat
- A review of other relevant information from your Student Code of Conduct

SUICIDE PREVENTION TRAINING

We recommend that threat awareness training also address threats of self-harm and suicidal ideation. This training may include presenting the warning signs of suicide, discussing what students can do if they or a friend is feeling suicidal, and presenting facts and resources about depression and suicide. Annually train all staff members (e.g., teachers, support staff, paraprofessionals, itinerant staff, school resource officer, etc.) on the warning signs of suicide and the process for referring a student showing any warning signs to appropriate personnel. Convey to the staff that they should never assume someone else will refer the student or that the situation is not serious.

Resources

- *Making Educators Partners in Youth Suicide Prevention: ACT on FACTS* is a free, online training program designed to helps educators and school staff understand their role in suicide prevention. Learn more: sptsuniversity.org
- *The SOS Signs of Suicide Prevention Program.* This is a universal, evidence-based depression awareness and suicide prevention program designed for middle-school (ages 11–13) or high-school (ages 13–17) students. Learn more: mentalhealthscreening.org/programs/sos-signs-of-suicide/training
- Suicide Prevention Resource Center: sprc.org/settings/schools
- American Foundation for Suicide Prevention: afsp.org/our-work/advocacy/public-policy-priorities/suicide-prevention-in-schools/

Sample lesson plans and student code of conduct language are shown in Figures 1.6 through 1.8 on pages 76–78, respectively, and may be adapted to meet the needs of different grade levels. Note that Figure 1.6 is a sample lesson plan for teaching the school threat policies shown in Figure 1.7, the Sample Policy on Verbal Threats.

Schools often do themselves a disservice by not being as clear as possible regarding policies and procedures that address threats of violence. Standard practices of conducting annual lessons may eliminate a significant number of incidents, especially those involving jokes, figures of speech, and remarks made impulsively in anger.

> **TASK 6 SUMMARY**
>
> In this task, you:
> - ☑ Adopted policies for documenting Code Red situations.
> - ☑ Developed policies for responding to unsafe or severely disruptive behavior.
> - ☑ Developed policies regarding threats of targeted violence in schools.
> - ☑ Established a threat assessment team.
> - ☑ Clarified procedures for systematically responding to threats.
> - ☑ Created a plan to conduct threat awareness sessions for staff and students.

Students who present a physical danger to themselves or others or engage in severely disruptive behavior require time-consuming and intensive help. Preparing to respond to these Code Red situations can be an emotion-filled, high-profile task. For school administrators and support staff, it can be frustrating, confusing, and even anxiety provoking to make sense of the myriad recommendations regarding how to respond to threatening, dangerous, or severely disruptive behavior. However, by taking action at the district, school, teacher, and student level, you can facilitate a sense of preparedness that will ease anxiety and help staff feel empowered to respond, even in the event of a possible threat of violence.

TASK 7 — Coordinate training and ongoing professional development support for interventionists.

A staff development plan helps ensure strong implementation of interventions and problem-solving processes. You will be more likely to experience success when you provide staff members with protocols, training, and a common language they'll need to accomplish the goals they've agreed to meet (Sheridan & Kratochwill, 1992).

In your staff development plan, include all interventionists who play a role in your school's multi-tiered system of support. This means developing staff development plans to train teachers, intervention coordinators, and problem-solving teams.

FIGURE 1.6 *Sample Lesson Plan on Verbal Threats*

Lesson 1:
Verbal threats will be taken seriously

TELL PHASE

- Give each student a copy of a document similar to the sample "Policy on Verbal Threats" found on the following page.
- Present and describe the concept that the rules and expectations regarding threats of violence have changed. (Section 1 of the sample "Policy on Verbal Threats" document.)
- Present and describe the types of statements that could be interpreted as threats. (Section 2 of the sample "Policy on Verbal Threats" document.)
- Present and describe the range of possible outcomes and consequences that could be imposed for making a threat. (Section 3 of the sample "Policy on Verbal Threats" document.)
- Make sure that students understand that the policy is nonnegotiable—all threats will be taken seriously.

DISCUSSION PHASE

- Allow questions and discussion on the policy.
- Ensure that students clearly understand all the components of the policy (i.e., threats are no joking matter, what constitutes a threat, and what the potential consequences are).
- Depending on individual preference, discuss issues such as:
    - The relationship of free speech to making threats
    - If the students were school administrators, what types of threats or situations would lead them to contact police or other law enforcement agencies
    - What students should do if they witness someone making a threat against someone else
    - What students should do if they are personally threatened; what they should do if there are no other witnesses to the threat

ASSIGNMENT

- Have students take the "Policy on Verbal Threats" document home. Tell them to discuss the document with a parent/guardian and have their parent/guardian sign the document.
- Tell students when they will be expected to return the signed document.

Reprinted with permission from *Foundations: A Proactive and Positive Behavior Support System,* Sprick, R.S., Booher, M., Isaacs, S. J., Sprick, J., & Rich, P. © 2014 Ancora Publishing.

FIGURE 1.7 *Sample Policy on Verbal Threats*

Policy on Verbal Threats

In the interest of ensuring that _____ School is a safe place for everyone, all threats will be taken seriously. Please read and discuss the information on this page with your student. Then sign the document and have your student return it _____. If you have any questions or concerns about this policy, feel free to contact a school administrator.

1. **The rules have changed. Threats are no joking matter!**

   The rules and expectations regarding language related to threats of violence have changed.

   In the past, if someone said something like, "I am going to shoot those teachers and students who gave me a hard time," it may have been treated as a joke or idle threat. Due to violent incidents that have taken place in schools, any statement of this type now will be taken seriously.

   "I was only joking" is not a reasonable explanation or defense. This type of comment will be treated as seriously in our school as it would be in an airport.

2. **The types of behavior that will be considered threatening include:**
   - Stating that you have a weapon or bomb in your possession at school
   - Stating that you plan to bring a weapon or bomb to school
   - Stating that you plan to cause physical harm to a student or staff member
   - Making a false statement that there is a bomb or other destructive device at school
   - Any written or verbal indication that you intend damage to any person or property

3. **In addition to parental notification, outcomes and consequences that may be imposed for making a threat include:**
   - Further investigation by school personnel
   - Detention
   - Suspension
   - Expulsion
   - Further investigation by law enforcement
   - Prosecution for disorderly conduct, criminal mischief, or menacing

We have read and discussed the information in the "Policy on Verbal Threats."

_____   _____
Parent/Guardian Signature   Date

_____   _____
Student Signature   Date

SAMPLE DOCUMENT
A document similar to this should be developed by staff ahead of time. Assistance with the specific content should be sought from the school district's attorney or legal department.

Reprinted with permission from *Foundations: A Proactive and Positive Behavior Support System,* Sprick, R.S., Booher, M., Isaacs, S. J., Sprick, J., & Rich, P. © 2014 Ancora Publishing.

FIGURE 1.8 *Sample Student Code of Conduct on Threats of Violence, Assaults, and Terroristic Threatening*

Student Code of Conduct: Threats of Violence, Assaults, and Terroristic Threatening

The Board of Education has adopted policies to ensure that students, teachers, and other school personnel are not subjected to assaultive or threatening behavior from other students. Any student who threatens, assaults, batters, or abuses another student shall be subject to appropriate disciplinary action, which may include suspension or expulsion from school and/or legal action.

Conduct and actions prohibited under this policy include, but are not limited to:

1. Verbal or written statements or gestures by students indicating intent to harm themselves, others, or property.

2. Physical attack by students intended to inflict harm to themselves, others, or property.

3. The act of threatening force or violence toward another person.

4. Making a threat that a bomb or chemical, biological, or nuclear weapon has been placed in or is about to explode in a school building, on school grounds, in a school bus, at a bus stop, or at any school-sponsored activity.

5. Creating a "hit list."

When a student is believed to have made a threat of harm toward another student, a teacher, or other school personnel, the school shall take appropriate steps to investigate the alleged incident and enact appropriate disciplinary and/or legal action. Procedures for investigating and responding to potential threats of harm may include, but are not limited to:

1. Removal of the student from the classroom setting or from the district's transportation system pending further disciplinary action that may occur.

2. Investigation of the alleged incident by the principal or designee.

3. Threat Assessment, as detailed in the district's "Threat of Harm" protocol. The Threat Assessment may include the student being interviewed by the school psychologist, school counselor, other qualified school personnel, and/or district personnel as needed.

4. Notification of and possible further investigation by law enforcement.

Adapted from Fayette County Public Schools, Lexington, KY. Used with permission.

- *Teachers.* As teachers are the foundation of your universal tier of support, it is critical to provide them with adequate professional development support. In addition to knowing how to use effective classroom management practices, all teachers should be familiar with a basic problem-solving process and a set of early interventions for common behavior problems. Develop a plan for supporting teachers in using effective classroom management practices, implementing early stage interventions, and utilizing a basic problem-solving model.
- *Intervention coordinators.* Interventionists responsible for coordinating ready-to-use interventions (e.g., your school's Connections program coordinator) or facilitating individualized interventions (e.g., the school counselor who will work one-on-one with a student to teach anger management skills) should be well versed in the procedures for implementing these interventions. Develop a plan for training coordinators to effectively implement, coordinate, and troubleshoot these interventions.
- *Problem-solving teams.* All problem-solving team members should be trained and experienced in behavior consultation and the entire range of behavior intervention strategies available in your building, including classroom management strategies and early-stage, ready-to-use, and individualized intervention strategies from this book. Develop a plan for training teams to use problem-solving tools (Section 2), and designing effective interventions (Section 3).
- *Threat assessment teams.* Rather than assume that individuals should simply know how to respond to threats of violence due to their profession or experience, schools should ensure that their teams have specialized training in threat assessment procedures. Ideally, the entire threat assessment team will participate in training together in order to form helpful working relationships and to clarify roles and responsibilities. Effective threat assessment team training should include content in understanding warning signs, risk factors, precipitating events, and stabilizing factors of threats of targeted violence. *What-if* scenarios (also known as tabletop exercises) will allow team members to gain experience interpreting and responding to unfolding threats of violence.

As your leadership team establishes a staff development plan, consider these questions:

- Which staff members will get which training?
- Who will provide training?
- When will training sessions be scheduled?

Staff development should include ongoing support beyond the initial training (Kratochwill, Volpiansky, Clements, & Ball, 2007; Oakes, Lane, & Germer, 2014). This follow-up support might include refresher training sessions, periodic memos to teachers about resources and support available, and scheduled meetings with individual staff or teams to give them an opportunity to communicate their support needs. In addition, as part of the staff development plan, the team must determine which staff members will receive training on which interventions. Consider the background of your interventionists, assess the level of training they already have in implementing interventions, and then determine how much more they need and who will provide it. Also plan to provide training to new interventionists who join your building or problem-solving team. If you plan to use the intervention strategies included in Sections 3 and 4, implementation guidelines are provided for the purpose of training staff members assigned responsibility for implementation.

> ### TASK 7 SUMMARY
>
> In this task, you:
>
> ☑ Developed a staff development plan to train teachers, intervention coordinators, and problem-solving teams.

Providing initial training and ongoing professional development to all staff involved in problem-solving and intervention implementation will help maximize the quality of support that your MTSS system offers.

TASK 8: Plan to monitor implementation fidelity of your building's classroom management practices, early-stage intervention strategies, and menu of ready-to-use interventions.

Implementation fidelity refers to the degree to which an intervention is implemented as it was intended. Without established procedures for monitoring and ensuring fidelity of implementation, it is likely that interventions will not be implemented as well as they could be.

There are many reasons why fidelity can suffer, such as (Gresham, MacMillan, Beebe-Frankenberger, & Bocian, 2000):

- *Lack of training:* Interventionists are not adequately trained in delivering intervention procedures or are unable to troubleshoot implementation problems when they arise.
- *Lack of oversight:* Nobody is monitoring whether plans are implemented, or follow-up doesn't occur.
- *A gap in the efficient delivery of services:* Plans are defined, but the required resources or staffing have not been secured.
- *Poor contextual fit:* The intervention design process was not collaborative, failed to consider contextual aspects of the problem or the classroom, or didn't have adequate buy-in from staff or the student.

For your building's universal, early-stage, and menu of ready-to-use supports, select a method of assessing fidelity, define what "good" fidelity means, create a monitoring schedule, and describe follow-up protocols for improving fidelity.

> ### IMPLEMENTATION FIDELITY
>
> A study conducted by Wickstrom, Jones, LaFleur, & Witt (1998) analyzed several behavior intervention plans that were written through a problem-solving process. When surveyed by researchers, almost half—46%—of the teachers admitted that they were *not* implementing the plans. Follow-up observations found that only 4% of the behavior intervention plans were being implemented with *fidelity*—that is, with tangible evidence that the plan was being implemented as it was designed. These findings clearly indicate that it is not enough to just write a behavior intervention plan—you also have to ensure that it is actually being implemented.

STEP 1 Select a method of assessing fidelity.

You can assess implementation fidelity in a number of ways, including:

- *Direct observation:* A third party observes the teacher or interventionist during implementation and records whether critical components of the intervention were implemented as intended. For example, your administrator might conduct quarterly classroom observations to assess whether certain classroom management practices are being used in all classrooms.
- *Permanent products:* Daily report cards, student self-monitoring sheets, and reward charts can tell a story about how, when, and if intervention strategies were implemented. If these products are created as part of your universal, early-stage, or ready-to-use interventions, you may consider reviewing them as a way to assess implementation fidelity.
- *Teacher or interventionist self-monitoring:* The person responsible for implementing the interventions uses a checklist to record whether essential components of an intervention have been implemented as planned. For example, the playground supervisor may conduct monthly fidelity checks to document whether essential components of the structured recess program are in place.

NOTE: For universal and classroom management practices, you might opt to use the fidelity checklist provided in Task 1 (pp. 22–25).

STEP 2 Using measurable terms, define what "good" fidelity means.

Consider the goals of each universal, early-stage, and ready-to-use intervention that you will be monitoring and define what "good" fidelity means. The research literature defines five major dimensions of implementation fidelity to consider (e.g., Durlak & DuPre, 2008; Dusenbury, Brannigan, Falco, & Hansen, 2003).

- *Adherence:* How well did we stick to the plan? What components of the plan were delivered as prescribed?
- *Exposure:* How often and how long did the student participate in the intervention?
- *Quality of delivery:* How well was the intervention delivered? How prepared, enthusiastic, communicative, etc., was the interventionist?
- *Student engagement:* How engaged and involved in the intervention were students?
- *Program differentiation:* How different are the critical components of the intervention from other interventions offered in your building?

Consider which of the above dimensions are most important to a plan's implementation and most likely to have an impact on student outcomes. Then define what "good" fidelity means by specifying measurable criteria as a threshold. For example, an intervention coordinator self-monitors fidelity by checking off essential components of each weekly anger management lesson he conducts with a group of students. "Good" fidelity for this intervention is defined as an average of 90% of lesson components checked off.

As another example, an administrator observes each teacher on a quarterly basis and collects data on the teacher's ratio of positive to corrective interactions, as well as the proportion of time the class is on task and engaged in instruction. Good fidelity in using classroom management practices is defined as: a) the teacher maintains a ratio of at least 3:1 positive to corrective interactions throughout the observation period, and b) students are on task and engaged in instruction for at least 85% of the time.

STEP 3 Create a schedule for monitoring fidelity.

At the minimum, compile and examine fidelity data after 2 weeks of first implementing a new intervention to promptly address any problems. If implementation levels are high, you can monitor fidelity on a monthly basis moving forward. However, more frequent monitoring and evaluation should take place when:

- Teachers or other staff members are initially learning how to implement an intervention strategy.
- Progress-monitoring data indicate little or no progress, or student behavior is deteriorating.
- Previous fidelity checks revealed implementation levels below your defined threshold.

In these cases, we recommend monitoring fidelity on a weekly basis until implementation levels are consistently meeting the threshold for good fidelity.

When developing a schedule, also identify who will be primarily responsible for conducting fidelity checks, collecting and summarizing fidelity data, scheduling check-ins and meetings, and providing follow-up support when implementation levels are low.

STEP 4 Make a plan to provide fidelity support as needed.

If fidelity monitoring indicates problems with implementation, it is important to address these issues in a timely manner. Identify the resources within your building that you can leverage to help support and improve fidelity of your classroom management practices, early-stage intervention strategies, and menu of ready-to-use interventions. Resources include staff members (e.g., coaches, behavior specialists, experienced teachers on special assignment), training materials (e.g., intervention manuals, training PowerPoint presentations), and fidelity-monitoring materials (e.g., fidelity checklists that come with programs).

Also identify follow-up actions that will be taken to increase fidelity. These may include:

- *Provide additional training or coaching to the teacher or interventionist.* If a teacher is not adequately trained in implementing classroom management strategies or an intervention coordinator struggles with troubleshooting implementation problems when they arise, additional training and coaching may be necessary to increase fidelity.
- *Increase the frequency of check-ins and collaborative meetings.* Scheduling regular check-ins and meetings with teachers or intervention coordinators communicates the availability of ongoing support, increases accountability, and offers a regular opportunity to address questions and concerns.

Reassess the contextual fit of intervention strategies. If your classroom management model or menu of ready-to-use interventions was chosen without careful consideration of the school's context or without buy-in and support from staff, you may need to reassess your plan. Use the continuous cycle of improvement presented in Task 9 to revise existing policy or practices to better fit the needs and limitations of your building and staff community.

If fidelity monitoring indicates problems with implementation, it is important to address these issues in a timely manner.

TASK 8 SUMMARY

In this task, you:
- ☑ Identified a method for monitoring implementation fidelity of your building's classroom management practices, early-stage intervention strategies, and menu of ready-to-use interventions.
- ☑ Defined what "good" fidelity means in measurable terms.
- ☑ Created a schedule for monitoring fidelity.
- ☑ Identified possible resources and follow-up actions to increase fidelity.

By creating a plan to actively monitor the fidelity of your building's universal, early stage, and ready-to-use interventions, you will increase staff accountability, maximize the effectiveness of behavior support practices, and create a structure for identifying and addressing fidelity-related barriers that may interfere with the success of your building's multi-tiered system of support.

Assess system outcomes and continuously look for opportunities to improve.

Once your support structures are in place, regularly monitoring how practices and support structures are working within the building will encourage a cycle of continuous improvement. In a school's dynamic environment, there is no such thing as maintaining—if you're not moving forward, you're losing ground.

STEP 1 Plan to assess intervention participation and outcomes.

At least annually, aggregate and review data on how your interventions and problem-solving processes are operating in your building. These data can help you assess staffing needs, evaluate how well your school is meeting the needs of students, and identify areas that might benefit from additional monitoring, resources, or training support. Some questions to consider investigating include:

- What proportion of our population are we serving with supports that go beyond what is provided at Tier 1?
- How many new students were identified as needing additional support from red-flag indicators, universal screening procedures, and teacher referrals?
- What proportion of students are we serving with our menu of ready-to-use interventions?
- How many students have an individual behavior intervention plan?
- From the point of identification, how long does it take to assign students a support coordinator?
- What additional training do teachers, interventionists, and problem-solving team members need?
- How has red-flag data changed from last year?
- How do staff members perceive the quality of our building's problem-solving services? Consider distributing a confidential survey during a staff meeting to gather this information. Reproducible 1.5 on the next page is provided as a sample.

At the end of each school year, gather data from sources that will help you answer these questions and others. If your school uses the Safe & Civil Schools Foundations approach, your behavior leadership team may use the End-of-Year Game Plan (Reproducible 1.6, pp. 89–101) to assess work to date and plan for renewed implementation at the beginning of the new year.

STEP 2 Continuously identify opportunities to better meet the needs of your students.

Regularly review policies, practices, and problem-solving processes to ensure that they continue to be effective in supporting staff, students, and families.

REPRODUCIBLE 1.5 *Sample Problem-Solving Team Survey*

Sample Problem-Solving Team Survey

Dear Staff:

Please take a minute or two to respond to the survey below. Your responses will be anonymous. Your honest opinions will assist us as we continue to develop collaborative problem-solving relationships.

* * * * *

1. Have you received assistance with a student this year? ☐ Yes ☐ No
   (If you answered Yes, please continue with Items 3–10. If you answered No, complete Item 2 only.)

2. Why haven't you received assistance with a student this year?
   ☐ I did not have any students with severe problems.
   ☐ I did not know consultation services were available.
   ☐ I prefer to handle things on my own.
   ☐ I do not feel comfortable with _____, but did seek assistance from someone else in the school.

Indicate your degree of agreement with each item below.	Not at all 1	Somewhat 2	Generally 3	Very much so 4
3. The problem-solving team was quick to respond to my concerns.	☐	☐	☐	☐
4. The problem-solving team was sensitive to my concerns.	☐	☐	☐	☐
5. The problem-solving team was easy to work with and listened to my ideas about how to solve the problem.	☐	☐	☐	☐
6. Working with the problem-solving team was time efficient.	☐	☐	☐	☐
7. The plan that was developed was organized and had clearly defined roles and timelines.	☐	☐	☐	☐
8. The plan that was developed was practical (e.g., the amount of teacher time required was realistic).	☐	☐	☐	☐
9. Adequate follow-up and support (e.g., modeling and coaching) were provided after the plan was developed.	☐	☐	☐	☐
10. The plan developed was effective (e.g., student behavior improved).	☐	☐	☐	☐

Interventions © 2019 Ancora Publishing

When you are not achieving desired outcomes, consider ways to revise or replace policies, practices, and processes that aren't working. Your team can enact this continuous cycle of improvement through the following five steps:

1. **Collect and review data.** The improvement cycle begins with the collection and review of meaningful data about the problem-solving processes and support structures in place within your school to determine both strengths of current practices and gaps or weaknesses that need to be addressed. Specifically, this involves reviewing data to identify the major discrepancies between how you want your system to function and how it is actually working. Your team might consider reviewing disciplinary referral patterns, conducting direct observations of common areas, or administering staff, student, and parent surveys. This compiled data will help the leadership team develop a hypothesis to explain why problems may be occurring, what factors are contributing to the problem, and how the problem may be addressed by revising policies or introducing new practices.

2. **Use data to prioritize a manageable number of things to improve.** The next stage of the improvement cycle is to use the collected data to get staff agreement on problems or concerns that need to be addressed and to put those concerns into some sort of hierarchy from most to least urgent. This means that the team's job is to unify the staff in defining the school's behavior support priorities for the year. What areas of improvement are the staff ready and willing to work toward addressing? If you've put together a great leadership team, its members will be enthusiastic and may even rally the staff to want to fix everything at once. Having 18 goals for the year, however, isn't realistic. Instead, the team should use data in guiding staff to agree on the most pressing priorities for a defined period of time (e.g., a semester, a school year). Choosing two or three main areas to focus on at any one time is a practical approach that will more likely produce improvement.

3. **For any given priority, develop a proposal to revise existing policy or practices.** This proposed revision will involve policies and procedures that are different from what staff have done in the past, because, as the old adage says: If we keep doing what we have always done, we will keep getting what we have always gotten. Because both data and agreement from staff show that the problem needs to be addressed, the staff must also be willing to explore what they can do differently to facilitate improvement in student behavior.

4. **Continue to revise based on staff feedback until staff are ready to adopt the new policies or practices.** Once a proposal has been created for any given priority, it is imperative to present the proposal to relevant staff for their approval. This is the adoption stage of the improvement cycle. Without staff support, new practices and policies, no matter how carefully designed, are not likely to succeed.

5. **Once new policies are adopted, ensure that all staff implement them.** Experience has taught us that in most schools, some small percentage of the staff may passively resist new policies and procedures. Even if the proposal is adopted, the leadership team must work to pump up support for implementation. Staff enthusiasm is key to making new practices effective. If even one staff member fails to implement policies, that nonsupport can derail the proposal. It is better to

have no policy at all (e.g., no dress code) than to have one that only seven out of ten teachers enforce. Inconsistency of implementation communicates very unclear information to the students about what is truly acceptable and unacceptable in the school.

Figure 1.9 provides a graphic representation of the improvement cycle. Institutionalize this cycle into the culture of the school to continuously identify opportunities to better meet the needs of your students.

FIGURE 1.9   *The Improvement Cycle*

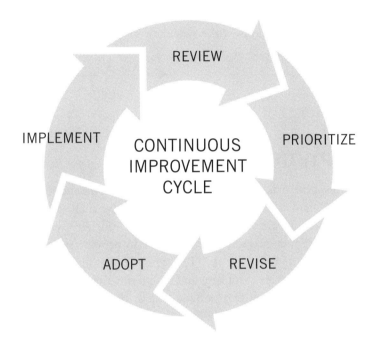

UNIVERSAL PREVENTION

Any time the number of students flagged as needing collaborative services begins to overwhelm the system, more work needs to be done on improving universal prevention. For example, if so many students in a high school fail two or more classes in the first quarter that there are not enough interventionists (school counselor, school psychologist, problem-solving team, etc.) to provide collaborative assistance, this is clear indication that you need to make schoolwide improvements to increase academic success. Whenever too many students hit a red-flag alert for individual intervention, you should assume that your entire system needs work in that particular area.

NOTE: This task provides abbreviated content from *Foundations: A Proactive and Positive Behavior Support System*. See Module A: Foundations of Behavior Support—A Continuous Improvement Process for more guidance on creating and maintaining a cycle of continuous improvement.

TASK 9 SUMMARY

In this task, you:

☑ Created a plan to assess intervention participation and outcomes.
☑ Committed to continuous work to identify opportunities to better meet the needs of your students.

Section Summary

Working through the nine tasks in this section takes time—changing any system is almost always laborious and difficult. Over time, implementing each of these tasks (those not currently in place in your system), should enhance the efficiency, coordination, and effectiveness of teachers' and interventionists' efforts to provide support to students. Concurrent with the work to improve your MTSS system, individual interventionists and problem-solving teams will analyze problems and design function-based interventions for any individual student whose needs are not being met by the school's universal behavior support processes. The remainder of this book is designed to assist with that work.

REPRODUCIBLE 1.6 *End-of-Year Game Plan (1 of 13)*

End-of-Year Game Plan

Date _____

Select dates to work on the End-of-Year Game Plan.

_____ Date the Data/Evaluation Coordinator and administrator will begin assembling data

_____ Date of team meeting to celebrate accomplishments and work through the form (about 4 weeks before the end of the year)

Assemble data for the end-of-year meeting.

1. Before the meeting, assemble the most recent data on the following:

    Incident referrals (i.e., infractions that resulted in the student being sent to the office): Generate year-to-date reports by total numbers, grade, type of infraction, location, gender, race/ethnicity, and special education status.

    Suspensions (out-of-school and in-school): Generate reports by total numbers, grade, gender, special education status, race/ethnicity, and frequent flyers (individual students with two or more suspensions).

    Detentions: Generate reports by total numbers, type, grade, gender, special education status, race/ethnicity, and frequent flyers (individual students who receive many detentions).

    Staff, student, and parent surveys (Safe & Civil Schools Climate & Safety Survey reports, for example)
    - Even if you administered surveys in the fall or winter, the information is still useful. If you've addressed some survey items, discuss addressing the items that are next on the list.
    - See Section 1C of this form for instructions for summarizing the data.

    Common area and schoolwide policy observations (from Foundations Common Area Observation forms, for example): Our general suggestion is to conduct observations a couple of times per year—once during the fall and once in midwinter to evaluate the efficacy of revised policies and procedures. If you can, also conduct end-of-year observations on one common area you revised during the year and one you are considering revising next year.

    Other data sources, such as:
    - Average daily attendance and absence rates
    - Tardiness rates
    - Expulsions and referrals to alternative education placements
    - Referrals to special education
    - Number of students referred to special education who did not qualify
    - Instances of vandalism and graffiti
    - Instances of other illegal activities
    - Injury reports (differentiate between playground injuries and other common area injuries)
    - Feedback from staff
    - Student focus groups
    - Social-emotional support (information from school social workers, counselors, and school psychologists)
    - Summary of students identified with red flags
    - Summary of universal screening

2. Complete a Data Summary form for the end-of-year data (the Data Summary form is available on the Module F CD or streaming video site and explained in Module A, Presentation 4, Task 1).

3. Complete a Data Summary form for comparable end-of-year data from the previous year (if you didn't do so last year).

4. Complete a Foundations Implementation Rubric or the Foundations Implementation Checklist for the modules you have implemented.

Steps 2–4 can be completed by the team during the meeting.

REPRODUCIBLE 1.6 *End-of-Year Game Plan (2 of 13)*

End-of-Year Game Plan

Meet to complete Game Plan.

Date _____

Team members present _____

_____

_____

> Other documents needed:
> - Common Area Observation form (F-30)
> - Data Summary form (F-31)
> - Foundations Implementation Rubric (F-01) or Checklists (F-02)
>
> Plan to bring the following items to the meeting:
> - Foundations Archive (current policies)
> - Foundations Process Notebook
> - Staff Handbook (all staff should bring their copies)
> - Student and Parent Handbook

SECTION 1: DATA

A. <u>INCIDENT REFERRALS (REGARDLESS OF DISCIPLINARY ACTION)</u>

Current year

Number of incident referrals ☐

Previous Year

Number of incident referrals ☐

Discussion Questions:

- Is the current year's total number of incident referrals lower, similar to, or higher than the previous year's total?

- What might you attribute the differences to?

Current year

Grade level with the most incident referrals ☐

Grade level with the second most incident referrals ☐

Previous Year

Grade level with the most incident referrals ☐

Grade level with the second most incident referrals ☐

Discussion Questions:

- Do the grade levels surprise you? Why? Is the same trend apparent in the data for the previous year?

- Why might these grade levels have the highest number of incident referrals?

- What can you do to address this trend next year? For example, do you need to increase supervision or tweak the student behavior expectations outside the classroom? If so, in which common areas or with which schoolwide policies?

REPRODUCIBLE 1.6 *End-of-Year Game Plan (3 of 13)*

End-of-Year Game Plan

Current year

a. Most frequent infraction _____
b. Second most frequent infraction _____
c. Third most frequent infraction _____
d. Top two locations for the above infractions
  1) _____
  2) _____
e. Top two grade levels for the above infractions
  1) _____ 2) _____

Previous Year

Most frequent infraction _____
Second most frequent infraction _____
Third most frequent infraction _____
Top two locations for the above infractions
  1) _____
  2) _____
Top two grade levels for the above infractions
  1) _____ 2) _____

Discussion Questions:

- Do the top three infractions surprise you? Why? How do they compare to the top three infractions for the previous year?

- In which two locations (e.g., classroom, hallway, cafeteria, playground, restroom) did the three most frequent infractions occur most often?
- What factors or variables in these two locations contributed to the frequency of the top three infractions?

- Do you have policies and procedures in place for these two locations? If yes, how do the student behavioral expectations specifically relate to the top three infractions?

- Which two grade levels were responsible for most of the top three infractions?
- What can you do to reduce the number of infractions next year? For example, do you need to increase supervision, clarify behavior expectations, or teach students how to respond to corrections by staff members?

- Do you see any other trends (by gender, race/ethnicity, special education status, for example) in the incident referral data that should be addressed? If yes, describe:

- What are the successes that you can celebrate?

REPRODUCIBLE 1.6 *End-of-Year Game Plan (4 of 13)*

End-of-Year Game Plan

B. <u>SUSPENSIONS (OUT-OF-SCHOOL AND IN-SCHOOL) AND DETENTIONS</u>

<u>Current year</u>

Number of suspensions ☐ OSS ____ ISS ____

Number of detentions ☐

<u>Previous Year</u>

Number of suspensions ☐ OSS ____ ISS ____

Number of detentions ☐

Discussion Questions:

- Is the current year's total number of suspensions lower, similar to, or higher than the previous year's total? _____
- What might you attribute the differences to?

- Is the current year's total number of detentions lower, similar to, or higher than the previous year's total? _____
- What might you attribute the differences to?

<u>Current year</u>

a. Two grade levels with most suspensions _____
b. Gender with the most suspensions _____
c. Percentage of suspensions that involved SPED students _____
d. Percentage of suspensions that involved repeat offenders _____

<u>Previous Year</u>

Two grade levels with most suspensions _____
Gender with the most suspensions _____
Percentage of suspensions that involved SPED students _____
Percentage of suspensions that involved repeat offenders _____

Discussion Questions:

- Do the grade level or gender data surprise you? Why? Are the same trends apparent in the data for the previous year?

- What percentage of the suspensions involved a student who qualified for special education? _____
  What percentages of those students were LD, ED, OHI, etc.? _____
- What percentage of the suspension incidents involved a repeat offender (i.e., a student with three or more suspensions)? _____
- What programs or policies has the school initiated to intervene proactively with repeat offenders?

- Do you see any other trends (by race/ethnicity, for example) in the suspension or detention data that should be addressed? If yes, describe:

- What can you do to reduce the number of suspensions and detentions next year?

Interventions © 2019 Ancora Publishing

REPRODUCIBLE 1.6

REPRODUCIBLE 1.6 *End-of-Year Game Plan (5 of 13)*

End-of-Year Game Plan

C. STAFF, STUDENT, AND PARENT SURVEY RESULTS

In the Surveys Rank Order Report for the Safe & Civil Schools Climate & Safety Surveys, sort the Staff % Agree column from most to least. (Check "Exclude No Opinion responses from results" if you don't want to consider how many survey takers answered No Opinion.) Then click Export Grid to create a PDF. On the PDF, highlight the groups of Excellent, Effective, Adequate, and Inadequate responses. (See the example in Presentation 7, Task 2 in the Module F book.)

Distribute the marked-up PDF to the team at the meeting or project it for all to see. Repeat the process with the Student % Agree column and Parent % Agree column.

Excellent: ≥ 90% agreement. "It ain't broke, so don't try to fix it!" Celebrate instead!
Effective: 70%–89% agreement. Minor fine-tuning is needed, but it is a lower priority.
Adequate: 51%–69% agreement. Improvements are needed but are not the highest priority if there are results in the Inadequate range.
Inadequate: ≤ 50% agreement. Major problems exist and immediate improvements are needed.

NOTE: We do not recommend interpreting the Possible Problems survey results in the way we describe for agree/disagree survey items. The problems range from relatively mild, such as inappropriate student language, to very serious, such as weapons, and it is not reasonable to rank order such a wide range of possible problems.

If you are using other surveys, determine your options for analysis and identify overall strengths and challenges as well as what has been done to address challenging areas. You might use the form below (or create a similar one that works for your survey) to summarize the results. Write a question tag (a brief version of the survey question) and the % Agree in the appropriate row. For example, for the item "Students feel safe in the restrooms," write "Safe restroom 77%" in the EFFECTIVE row.

Percentage of Agreement	STAFF Surveys Percentage & Question Tag	STUDENT Surveys Percentage & Question Tag	PARENT Surveys Percentage & Question Tag
Excellent (≥ 90% agreement)			
Effective (70%-89% agreement)			
Adequate (51%-69% agreement)			
Inadequate (≤ 50% agreement)			

Have the team discuss using these results to set priorities for what to work on and what to protect and celebrate. Even if you administered surveys in the fall or winter, the information is still useful. If you've addressed some of the most pressing survey items, discuss addressing the items that are next on the list in the fall.

Interventions © 2019 Ancora Publishing

REPRODUCIBLE 1.6 *End-of-Year Game Plan (6 of 13)*

End-of-Year Game Plan

D. <u>COMMON AREA AND SCHOOLWIDE POLICY OBSERVATIONS (e.g., from Common Area Observation forms)</u>
Discuss and analyze the observation data.
- Identify policies and procedures that are working well and plan to celebrate these successes with staff and students.

- Identify policies and procedures that are adequate, but portions need to be re-taught to the staff or students. Decide how and when the re-teaching will take place and who will re-teach.

- Identify policies and procedures that need major revision and plan to work through the Revise, Adopt, and Implement steps of the Improvement Cycle.

E. <u>OTHER DATA SOURCES</u>
Discuss these data and identify any concerns. *Remember that safety is always the top priority.*
- Average daily attendance and absence rates
- Tardiness rates
- Expulsions and referrals to alternative education placements
- Referrals to special education
- Numbers of students referred to special education who did not qualify
- Instances of vandalism and graffiti
- Instances of other illegal activities
- Injury reports (differentiate between playground injuries and other common area injuries)
- Feedback from staff
- Student focus groups
- Social-emotional support (information from school social workers, counselors, and school psychologists)
- Summary of students identified with red flags
- Summary of universal screening

F. <u>DATA SUMMARY FORMS</u>
- Complete a Data Summary form for the end-of-year data (the Data Summary form [F-31] is available on the Module F CD or streaming video website and explained in Module A, Presentation 4, Task 1).

- Assemble comparable end-of-year data from the previous year and complete a Data Summary form for that year (if you didn't do so last year).

REPRODUCIBLE 1.6 *End-of-Year Game Plan (7 of 13)*

End-of-Year Game Plan

G. ACTIONS TO TAKE BASED ON DATA ANALYSIS

☐ OPTION 1: If the policies and procedures are working well, inform the staff and students. Identify ways to celebrate your success.

Policies and procedures to celebrate:

☐ OPTION 2: If the team decides that the policies and procedures are working, but portions need to be re-taught to the staff or students, decide how and when the re-teaching will take place and who will re-teach.

Common Area or Schoolwide Policy	Plan for Re-Teaching	Target Date

☐ OPTION 3: If the team decides that a policy needs revising, decide:

- When to write the revisions.

- How and when to seek feedback from the staff about the revisions before finalizing them.

Common Area or Schoolwide Policy	First Draft Revision Due	Target Date

- How and when to seek feedback from the staff about the revisions before finalizing them.

- **OPTIONAL:** Seek student feedback by conducting a mini-survey, asking teachers to hold a class discussion, or conducting focus groups.

- Determine when to present the revised policy to the staff. Plan for a 5–10 minute discussion with voting. Identify the percentage of support needed for adoption and the voting procedure you will use. Remember, staff need to approve any changes in policy before they are implemented.

Plan to teach the revised policy:

- Decide whether staff or students need to be taught the revised policies and procedures. Students need to be taught a revised policy if expectations for their behavior have changed.

- If you need to teach the revised policies and procedures, decide how and when (e.g., date and time of day, whether new lessons plans are needed), and who will teach.

- Identify when to review policies and procedures during the upcoming school year (e.g., after winter and spring breaks, before and after state testing).

Interventions © 2019 Ancora Publishing

REPRODUCIBLE 1.6 *End-of-Year Game Plan (8 of 13)*

End-of-Year Game Plan

H. <u>COMPLETE THE FOUNDATIONS IMPLEMENTATION RUBRIC OR FOUNDATIONS IMPLEMENTATION CHECKLISTS FOR THE MODULES YOU HAVE IMPLEMENTED</u>

Identify one or two Foundations priorities for improvement to work on next year:

1)

2)

Identify steps and items needed to accomplish the improvements:

- Establish a task force to work on the priority.

- Create and teach lessons on expectations for students.

- Create staff training materials.

- Create forms or written information.

- Other.

I. <u>MAJOR CHANGES IN THE COMING YEAR</u>

What major changes will occur in school next fall? How can you proactively address the changes in student and staff behavior that might result from the changes?

REPRODUCIBLE 1.6 *End-of-Year Game Plan (9 of 13)*

End-of-Year Game Plan

SECTION 2: CRITICAL TEAM ISSUES AND DECISIONS

A. TEAM EFFECTIVENESS AND MEMBERSHIP

- Has the Foundations Team been effective this year? Do you need more or fewer members? Do you need a more diverse membership?

- Do you need to replace or add new members to the Foundations Team? If so, which grade or level needs to be represented, and how should staff members be approached and recruited? Do new members need any training or orientation to Foundations? (For example, they might view or read Modules A and B.) If so, how should the training be provided? Jot down your recommendations and decisions below:

- When should new team members begin serving on the team? Consider having them join before the end of the current school year so they have time and support to become familiar with how the team functions.

- What is your team name? Don't have one? Pick one! A unique team name can enhance your visibility and prominence in the school and emphasize the purpose of the team.

B. TEAM ROLES

Review team roles and ensure that all roles are filled for the coming year. Ask for volunteers or nominations for any roles that need to be filled. Consider adding or eliminating roles, depending on your experiences with team meetings during the year.

Role	Staff Member
Chair Creates and manages agendas, keeps people and discussion on task during meetings, leads the team; consider having cochairs.	
Recorder Keeps minutes of all meetings and monitors all tasks and timelines.	
Data/Evaluation Coordinator Manages data collection and analysis and presents data to staff.	
Materials Manager Maintains the Process Notebook, Foundations Archives, resources for team members to use, handouts that need to be copied, etc.	
Keeper of the List Maintains a reminder file of future topics for the team to address. May be combined with Recorder.	
Staff Liaison Ensures all staff are consistently informed about and involved in team activities. Also periodically monitors staff members' perceptions of the team and the MTSS process.	
Equity and Student Liaison Analyzes data for inequities and discrepancies between groups of students and serves as an advocate for students. For example, survey results may reveal that African American students experience more bullying than Asian American students. The liaison should lead an exploration of this issue, perhaps convening a focus group of students to talk about it.	
Family Engagement Coordinator Oversees programs and incentives that encourage positive family interactions with staff and family participation in students' school experiences. (This role is probably not necessary if the school has a Family Engagement Team that is as influential as the Foundations Team in the MTSS processes.)	

REPRODUCIBLE 1.6 *End-of-Year Game Plan (10 of 13)*

End-of-Year Game Plan

C. <u>STAFF REPRESENTATION</u>

Identify the team members who get feedback and input from each group listed.

- Grade(s) _____ _____
- Grade(s) _____ _____
- Grade(s) _____ _____
- Grade(s) _____ _____
- Paraprofessionals on staff _____
- Specialists, Special Ed, counselor, social worker _____
- Special education faculty _____
- School counselors _____
- School social workers _____
- School psychologist _____
- Administration _____
- Office support team _____
- Parent advisory groups, PTA _____
- Student council, other student groups _____
- Custodial staff _____
- Food service staff _____
- Campus security _____
- Nursing _____
- School volunteers _____

D. <u>RULES FOR TEAM MEETINGS</u>

Review and renew your ground rules for team meetings in the coming year. (Did your team have ground rules? If not, below are some sample ground rules to consider.)

- An established minimum number of members must be present.
- Meetings will start and end on time.
- No side conversations during the meeting.
- All team discussions and disagreements will be respectful.
- Before speaking, team members will paraphrase what the previous speaker said.
- A cochair will serve as the "on-task and on-time nag."
- Meeting minutes will identify specific tasks to be accomplished along with responsible staff and timelines.
- Decisions will be made by majority vote.
- The ground rules will be clarified and communicated to all team members.
- Minutes will be kept for all meetings and will be distributed to the team and all staff.

REPRODUCIBLE 1.6 *End-of-Year Game Plan (11 of 13)*

End-of-Year Game Plan

E. MEETING SCHEDULE

Determine a tentative Foundations Team meeting schedule for the next school year or at least for the first semester. We recommend a minimum of 4 hours per quarter. Schedule options (we recommend the more frequent meeting options for new teams):

- Meet weekly for 30 minutes before or after school.
- Meet twice a month for 1 hour before or after school.
- Meet once a month for a half day.
- Schedule a combination of 30- to 60-minute regular meetings plus half-day meetings as needed to develop and revise policies and work on other Foundations initiatives.
- Meet once a quarter for a full day (very experienced teams can consider this option).

SECTION 3: PLANNING YOUR FOUNDATIONS KICKOFF FOR THE NEW SCHOOL YEAR

Decide when and how to conduct the Foundations kickoff for the faculty during the August workdays before students report to school. Also decide whether to plan and provide a separate orientation for new staff members so they understand the Foundations concepts and know their responsibilities for implementation and sustainability. The kickoff might last 30–60 minutes, depending on what your team has shared about Foundations during previous years. Write down what your team needs to do regarding the following topics for your staff kickoff:

A. OVERVIEW

Provide a brief overview of Foundations (program components, goals, beliefs, implemented policies, and so on) to give new and returning staff an understanding of the process and the stage of Foundations your school is currently at (use the Foundations Implementation Rubric as a guide).:

- How much time is needed for the kickoff?
- How much staff time (before students report to school) is available for the kickoff?
- What topics need to be covered?
- Who from the team will present?
- Who will make copies of materials (e.g., lesson plans, handouts, schedule) for the faculty?
- Determine deadlines for preparing and copying the materials.

B. PREVIOUSLY IMPLEMENTED POLICIES

Review all previously implemented common area and schoolwide policies and the specific student and staff expectations for them.

Policies to review: _____

- How much time is needed for this presentation?
- Which team member will be responsible for coordinating this presentation?
- Will this person also be the primary presenter?
- Is a copresenter needed? If so, who?
- Who will make copies of any needed materials for the faculty?

REPRODUCIBLE 1.6 *End-of-Year Game Plan (12 of 13)*

End-of-Year Game Plan

C. <u>NEW POLICIES</u>

Describe how new common area and schoolwide policies will be implemented.

New policies: _____

- How much time is needed for this presentation?
- Which team member will be responsible for coordinating this presentation?
- Will this person also be the primary presenter?
- Is a copresenter needed? If so, who?
- Who will make copies of any needed materials for the faculty?

D. <u>TEACHING EXPECTATIONS</u>

Share with the entire faculty how to teach all adopted common area and schoolwide policies to the students during the first week of school.

- How much time is needed for this presentation?
- Who on the team will be responsible for coordinating this presentation?
- Will this person also be the primary presenter?
- Is a copresenter needed? If so, who?
- Would handouts be helpful? If so, who develops them and what's in them?
- Determine deadlines for preparing and copying the materials.
- Are new lesson plans needed, or can you recycle last year's lesson plans? If new lesson plans are needed, who will develop them?
- Show the teachers how to use the lesson plans and share the materials the teachers will need to teach the lesson plans (e.g., PowerPoint presentations, overhead transparencies, videos, forms).
- Share a teaching schedule of when the lesson plans will be taught to the students during the first week of school.

E. <u>SUPERVISORY SKILLS</u>

Teach or review effective supervisory skills—Foundations Module B, Presentations 4 and 5 for supervisory staff and Presentation 6 for faculty. Decide how to conduct the training and who from the team will present.

- How much time is needed for this presentation?
- Which team member will be responsible for coordinating this presentation?
- Will this person also be the primary presenter?
- Is a copresenter needed? If so, who?
- Would handouts be helpful? If so, who develops them and what's in them?
- Which staff members need to attend? (Best practice is to train the entire staff, including office support, teachers, custodian, etc.)

REPRODUCIBLE 1.6 *End-of-Year Game Plan (13 of 13)*

End-of-Year Game Plan

F. <u>OFFICE REFERRALS</u>

Review the behavior infractions that should result in office referral and the procedures staff should follow, including how to complete incident referral forms.

- How much time is needed for this presentation?
- Which team member will be responsible for coordinating this presentation?
- Will this person also be the primary presenter?
- Is a copresenter needed? If so, who?
- Would handouts be helpful? If so, who develops them and what's in them?

G. <u>OTHER TOPICS</u>

Are there any other Foundations topics to discuss or share at the kickoff? For example, the team might need to cover student incentives, staff buy-in activities, Guidelines for Success, three levels of misbehavior, CHAMPS or DSC expectations for implementation, planned professional development activities, or staff incentive programs.

- How much time is needed for this presentation?
- Which team member will be responsible for coordinating this presentation?
- Will this person also be the primary presenter?
- Is a copresenter needed? If so, who?
- Would handouts be helpful? If so, who develops them and what's in them?

H. <u>CELEBRATE</u>

Arrange to celebrate with staff the behavioral and academic accomplishments from the school year that is ending. Also share your Foundations goals for the new year.

References

American Academy of Pediatrics (AAP). (2008). The role of the school nurse. *Pediatrics, 121*(5), 1052–1056.

Anderson, C. M., & Borgmeier, C. (2010). Tier II interventions within the framework of school-wide positive behavior support: Essential features for design, implementation, and maintenance. *Behavior Analysis in Practice, 3*(1), 33–45.

Benazzi, L., Horner, R. H., & Good, R. H. (2006). Effects of behavior support team composition on the technical adequacy and contextual fit of behavior support plans. *Journal of Special Education, 40*(3), 160–170.

Catalano, R. F., Haggerty, K. P., Oesterie, S., Fleming, C. B., & Hawkins, J. D. (2004). The importance of bonding to schools for healthy development: Findings from the social development research group. *Journal of School Health, 74*(7), 252–262.

Centers for Disease Control and Prevention. (2009). *School connectedness: Strategies for increasing protective factors among youth.* Atlanta, GA: U.S. Department of Health and Human Services.

Centers for Disease Control and Prevention. (2017). *Web-based injury statistics query and reporting system (WISQARS)* (Fatal Injury Reports, 1999–2016, for national, regional, and states). Retrieved from https://webappa.cdc.gov/sasweb/ncipc/mortrate.html

Christle, C. A., Jolivette, K., & Nelson, M. (2007). School characteristics related to high school dropout rates. *Remedial and Special Education, 28,* 325–329.

Drummond, T. (1994). *The Student Risk Screening Scale (SRSS).* Grants Pass, OR: Josephine County Mental Health Program.

Durlak, J. A., & DuPre, E. P. (2008). Implementation matters: A review of research on the influence of implementation on program outcomes and the factors affecting implementation. *American Journal of Community Psychology, 41*(3–4), 327.

Dusenbury, L., Brannigan, R., Falco, M., & Hansen, W. B. (2003). A review of research on fidelity of implementation: implications for drug abuse prevention in school settings. *Health Education Research, 18*(2), 237–256.

Fan, W., & Wolters, C. A. (2014). School motivation and high school dropout: The mediating role of educational expectation. *British Journal of Educational Psychology, 84*(1), 22–39.

Feldman, E. S., & Kratochwill, T. R. (2003). Problem solving consultation in schools: Past, present, and future directions. *Behavior Analyst Today, 4*(3), 318–330.

Fein, R. A., Vossekuil, B., Pollack, W. S., Borum, R., Modzeleski, W., & Reddy, M. (2002). *Threat assessment in schools: A guide to managing threatening situations and to creating safe school climates.* Washington, DC: U.S. Secret Service and U.S. Department of Education. Retrieved from: http://www.ustreas.gov/usss/ntac/ssi_guide.pdf

Garrison, M. (2013). *Connections* [Web-based application]. Eugene, OR: Ancora Publishing.

Goodman, R. (1997). The Strengths and Difficulties Questionnaire: A research note. *Journal of Child Psychology and Psychiatry, 38,* 581–586.

Gresham, F. M. (2002). Best practices in social skills training. In A. Thomas & J. Grimes (Eds.), *Best practices in school psychology IV* (pp. 1029–1040). Bethesda, MD: National Association of School Psychologists.

Gresham, F. M., MacMillan, D. L., Beebe-Frankenberger, M. E., & Bocian, K. M. (2000). Treatment integrity in learning disabilities intervention research: Do we really know how treatments are implemented? *Learning Disabilities Research & Practice, 15*(4), 198–205.

Griffin, B. W. (2002). Academic disidentification, race, and high school dropouts. *High School Journal, 85*(4), 71–81.

Hallfors, D., Brodish, P. H., Khatapoush, S., Sanchez, V., Cho, H., & Steckler, A. (2006). Feasibility of screening adolescents for suicide risk in "real-world" high school settings. *American Journal of Public Health, 96*(2), 282–287.

Irvin, L. K., Tobin, T. J., Sprague, J. R., Sugai, G., & Vincent, C. G. (2004). Validity of office discipline referral measures as indices of school-wide behavioral status and effects of school-wide behavioral interventions. *Journal of Positive Behavior Interventions, 6*(3), 131–147.

Jenson, W. R., Bowen, J., Clark, E., Block, H., Gabrielsen, T., Hood, J., Radley, K., & Springer, B. (2011). *Superheroes Social Skills.* Eugene, OR: Ancora Publishing.

Jimerson, S. R., Anderson, G. E., & Whipple, A. D. (2002). Winning the battle and losing the war: Examining the relation between grade retention and dropping out of high school. *Psychology in the Schools, 39*(4), 441–457.

Jimerson, S. R., & Brock, S. E. (2004). Threat assessment, school crisis preparation, and school crisis response. In M. J. Furlong, M. P. Bates, D. C. Smith, & P. M. Kingery (Eds.), *Appraisal and prediction of school violence: Context, issues, and methods.* Hauppauge, NY: Nova Science.

Kaminski, R., Cummings, K. D., Powell-Smith, K. A., & Good, R. H. (2008). Best practices in using dynamic indicators of basic early literacy skills for formative assessment and evaluation. In A. Thomas and J. Grimes (Eds.), *Best practices in school psychology V* (pp. 1181–1204). Bethesda, MD: National Association of School Psychologists.

Kamphaus, R. W., & Reynolds, C. R. (2015). *BASC-3, Behavioral and Emotional Screening System.* San Antonio, TX: Pearson.

Kann, L., McManus, T., Harris, W. A., Shanklin, S. L., Flint, K. H, Queen, B., . . . Ethier, K. A. (2018). Youth Risk Behavior Surveillance—United States, 2017. *MMWR Surveillance Summaries, 67*(8), 24–28).

Kratochwill, T. R., Volpiansky, P., Clements, M., & Ball, C. (2007). Professional development in implementing and sustaining multitier prevention models: Implications for response to intervention. *School Psychology Review, 36*(4), 618–631.

Lane, K. L., Oakes, W., & Menzies, H. (2010). Systematic screenings to prevent the development of learning and behavior problems: Considerations for practitioners, researchers, and policy makers. *Journal of Disability Policy Studies, 21*(3), 160–172.

Lieberman, R., Poland, S., & Kornfeld, C. (2008). Best practices in suicide intervention. In P. Harrison & A. Thomas (Eds.), *Best practices in school psychology: Systems-level services* (pp. 273–289). Bethesda, MD, National Association of School Psychologists

Mulkey, S., & Sprick, M. S. (2010). *SMART kids: Social grace, manners, and respectful talk.* Eugene, OR: Ancora Publishing.

National Education Association. (n.d.). *A national look at the school nurse shortage.* Retrieved from http://www.nea.org/home/35691.htm

Oakes, W. P., Lane, K. L., & Germer, K. A. (2014). Developing the capacity to implement tier 2 and tier 3 supports: How do we support our faculty and staff in preparing for sustainability?. *Preventing School Failure: Alternative Education for Children and Youth, 58*(3), 183–190.

Pena, J. B., & Caine, E. D. (2006). Screening as an approach for adolescent suicide prevention. *Suicide and Life-Threatening Behavior, 36*(6), 614–637.

Perez-Johnson, I., & Maynard, R. (2007). The case for early, targeted interventions to prevent academic failure. *Peabody Journal of Education, 82*(4), 587–616.

Poland, S. (1995). Best practices in suicide intervention. In A. Thomas & J. Grimes (Eds.), *Best practices in school psychology III* (pp. 155–166). Washington, DC: National Association of School Psychologists.

Posner, K., Brown, G. K., Stanley, B., Brent, D. A., Yershova, K. V., Oquendo, M. A., . . . Mann, J. J. (2011). The Columbia–Suicide Severity Rating Scale: Initial validity and internal consistency findings from three multisite studies with adolescents and adults. *American Journal of Psychiatry, 168*(12), 1266–1277.

Reynolds, W. M. (1987). *Suicidal ideation questionnaire (SIQ).* Odessa, FL: Psychological Assessment Resources.

Roderick, M. (1994). Grade retention and school dropout: Investigating the association. *American Educational Research Journal, 31*(4), 729–759.

Sheridan, S. M. (2010). *The Tough Kid social skills book.* Eugene, OR: Ancora Publishing.

Sheridan, S. M., & Kratochwill, T. R. (1992). Behavioral parent-teacher consultation: Conceptual and research considerations. *Journal of School Psychology, 30,* 117–139.

Sprick, R. S. (2009). *CHAMPS: A proactive and positive approach to classroom management.* Eugene, OR: Ancora Publishing.

Sprick, R. S., Booher, M., Isaacs, S., Sprick, J., & Rich, P. (2014). *Foundations: A proactive and positive behavior support system* (3rd ed., Modules A–F0. [DVD program]. Eugene, OR: Ancora Publishing.

Substance Abuse and Mental Health Services Administration (2012). *Preventing suicide: A toolkit for high schools* [HHS Publication No. SMA-12-4669]. Rockville, MD: Author.

U.S. Department of Health and Human Services (USDHHS). (2014). *Healthy people 2020, educational and community-based programs.* Retrieved from http://healthypeople.gov/2020/topicsobjectives2020/objectiveslist.aspx?topicId=11

U.S. Secret Service & U.S. Department of Education (2004). *Threat assessment in schools: A guide to managing threatening situations and to creating safe school climates.* Washington, DC: Authors.

Walker, H. M., Severson, H. H., & Feil, E. F. (2014). Systematic screening for behavior disorders (2nd ed.). Eugene, OR: Ancora Publishing.

Wickstrom, K. F., Jones, K. M., LaFleur, L. H., & Witt, J. C. (1998). An analysis of treatment integrity in school-based behavioral consultation. *School Psychology Quarterly, 13*(2), 141.

Wise, B. J., Marcum, K., Haykin, M., Sprick, R., and Sprick, M. (2011). *Meaningful work.* Eugene, OR: Ancora Publishing.

SECTION TWO

Embedding a Problem-Solving Model Into Each Tier of Support

A multi-tiered system of support (MTSS) should encompass a range of processes—from low cost and time efficient to very high cost and time consuming—so that the intensity of the process matches the intensity of the need. Consider a medical metaphor. The first time you experience a headache, you might do some problem-solving and decide on a simple intervention such as taking a couple of aspirin. This process involves only one person who decides on a simple treatment plan, which, if effective, solves the problem. Contrast this with the person who consults a neurologist to assist with solving the headache problem. The neurologist may use data from CAT scans, MRIs, complex lab tests, and collaboration with a neurosurgeon. The first problem-solving process takes minutes and costs almost nothing. The other process may take weeks or months of problem identification and analysis before an intervention plan is determined, with associated costs that probably run into six figures. One process is not better than the other—the different processes, we hope, match the intensity of the need.

We suggest using a similar continuum to problem-solve individual behavior issues at school. An effective problem-solving framework achieves two goals:

1. It helps all students learn to function successfully in school in a manner that maximizes their ability to learn.
2. It accomplishes this success in the most efficient manner possible.

In other words, try the easiest solution first—it just might work. If your initial effort is effective, you've spent very few of your school's precious, limited resources. If schools had unlimited resources, you could assign a highly skilled teacher and fully trained school psychologist to every student who has any level of difficulty. But that would be like sending everyone with a headache to a neurosurgeon—an absurd waste of precious medical resources.

A Consistent Problem-Solving Framework

In this book, we advocate for the use of a consistent problem-solving framework for addressing the needs of individual students across all tiers of support. This will give your school or district the preparedness and flexibility to respond to a variety of student needs.

This problem-solving approach is guided by the following questions (Tilly, 2008):

- What is the problem?
- Why is the problem happening?
- What solutions might improve the problem?
- How can we measure whether improvements are occurring?
- Did our plan work to adequately address the problem?

Using these questions to build a framework for problem-solving, we propose the use of this five-step model:

Step 1: Define the problem.

What is the problem? First, objectively define what the problem is and analyze why it might be occurring. In doing this, you will describe both the problematic behavior as well as the context in which it is occurring. Consider questions such as the following:

- What does the problematic behavior look like?
- What is the student expected to do, and what is the student actually doing?
- Where, when, and how often does the behavior occur?

For example, Jason, a sixth grader, often refuses to follow directions in Ms. Lopez's math class. Instead, she reports that he'll talk back in a sarcastic tone, ignore her directions, and wander around the classroom talking to other students when they are working. Because he does this, he fails to complete his assignments by the end of the period and is at risk for failing math. Consulting her grade book, Ms. Lopez determines that for the first 4 weeks of the school year, Jason has turned in only 20% of his assignments. She also reports that he seems to be testing her more. Last week, she changed seating arrangements, but Jason refused to comply with his new seat assignment, saying, "If you want me to move, you'll have to make me." In this instance, she allowed him to keep his old seat in order to continue the class without a major disruption, but she says that she's concerned that he is looking for new opportunities to be defiant in class. When asked to estimate how often Jason ignores or refuses to comply with her directions, Ms. Lopez said that it happens about 2–3 times per day.

Step 2: Analyze the problem.

Why is the problem happening? In this step, you seek to explain why the problem behavior is occurring. Effective problem analysis links observed behaviors to hypothesized causes. The purpose of this step is to develop a hypothesis about why the student exhibits the behavior, then tailor the intervention to the hypothesis.

> *In this book, we advocate for the use of a consistent problem-solving framework for addressing the needs of individual students across all tiers of support.*

Questions such as the following will help you develop a hypothesis:

- Is the behavior a skill problem (can't do) or a performance problem (won't do)?
- Is the problem more likely to occur in particular situations or with certain people?
- What purpose (i.e., function) is the behavior serving for the student?

The resources and time needed to accurately explain why a problem is happening will vary depending on the severity and complexity of the problem, as well as on any efforts that have already been attempted to remediate the problem. Problems that have just risen to the attention of a teacher may require only a simple analysis, whereas chronic problems that have been resistant to previous intervention efforts will require a more in-depth, comprehensive analysis.

Ms. Lopez hypothesizes that Jason is trying to engage her in power struggles and also enjoys the attention that he gets from peers when he refuses to follow directions. Jason is in Ms. Lopez's advanced math class and, for the most part, his peers work hard, pay attention, and follow directions. When Jason acts out, it causes a break in the continuity of otherwise smooth instruction—and his peers notice, often responding by snickering or whispering to each other. Ms. Lopez admits to sometimes feeling angry and raising her voice in an attempt to get Jason to comply with directions, but she notes that her emotional response only seems to encourage his defiance.

Step 3: Consider possible solutions and select intervention strategies.

What solutions might improve the problem? Once you have an adequate description of misbehavior and a hypothesis for why it might be occurring, the next step is to generate a list of possible solutions and select one or two to try. Consider which variables in the environment can be manipulated to encourage the student to change their behavior. While it's impossible to force a child to behave appropriately, we can change the student's environment in a way that encourages appropriate behavior and discourages misbehavior, over time helping the student adopt more adaptive behavior patterns.

In considering possible variables to address within the student's environment, you'll ask questions such as:

- What changes can be made in the classroom environment to help prevent the problem from occurring?
- What skills can be taught to the student to help replace the problem behavior with a positive alternative behavior?
- What consequences, if any, can be put in place to reduce the occurrence of the problem behavior?

The problem-solving team discusses options for supporting Ms. Lopez and redirecting Jason's pattern of escalating misbehavior. Ms. Lopez agrees to first talking to Jason one-on-one to see if anything is going on in his life and to explain her concerns, including how his missed assignments are affecting his grade. The team suggests that she can also work on increasing the rate of positive attention she provides to Jason. By looking for positive behaviors to praise, chatting to him about his weekend, or saying hello when he enters the classroom, she may find that this positive attention fulfills the same need as the negative attention Jason recruits when he acts out. The team also develops a procedure for Ms. Lopez to use when Jason refuses to follow a direction. If he refuses to follow a direction, Ms. Lopez will repeat the direction and a negative consequence as a decision for Jason to make: "Jason, you can move to your assigned seat or you can stay after class with me and talk to the assistant principal."

Step 4: Collect data to monitor progress.

How can we measure whether improvements are occurring? To determine whether interventions are working to improve the problem, you must accurately assess change over time. This requires answers to the following questions:

- What specific, observable behavior are we targeting for change?
- How will we measure this behavior?
- What is the goal for improvement?

Often, the behavior used to define the presence and magnitude of the problem can also be used as an indicator of progress. In our example, Ms. Lopez plans to keep a simple tally of the number of times that Jason refuses to follow a direction from her. Because her original estimate indicated that Jason ignores directions about 2–3 times per day, the team proposes a goal of no more than one instance each day. She'll also continue to monitor the percentage of completed daily assignments that Jason turns in each week. Since Jason started the school year by completing only 20% of assignments, she talks with him and proposes the goal of turning in 80% of assignments going forward. Each week, she'll review her grade book and determine whether Jason met this goal.

Step 5: Evaluate whether supports are working.

Did our plan work to adequately address the problem? The final step of the problem-solving process is to assess whether efforts have influenced the magnitude of the problem. At this point, you will have collected some form of data to help make this judgment. Ask questions such as:

- Has behavior changed since the intervention started?
- If so, are changes adequate?
- What is the discrepancy between what the student is doing now and what the student is expected to do?

If the student hasn't made adequate improvements, you'll continue the problem-solving cycle. This might involve defining the problem in more detail, collecting additional information about why the problem is happening, considering other intervention strategies to try, and collaboratively working with others with more expertise.

Ms. Lopez agrees to put this plan into place for 2 weeks. In the meantime, she will collect data on the daily frequency of Jason's refusal to follow directions and the weekly average of assignments he turns in. The team sets a date in 2 weeks to review these data and determine whether the plan is working or if it needs any adjustments.

Applying the Problem-Solving Model Across All Tiers of Support

The problem-solving model is, at its core, about service delivery. Rather than follow a specific set of steps that say, "Take this action at this time," the model guides you to ask questions that consider the individual student's behavior and needs, the unique context in which the problem is occurring, and the available resources within your school. Because of this focus on service delivery, the problem-solving framework can be applied and reapplied across all tiers of support.

Problem-solving at Tier 1. Problem-solving at the individual level should start simply, with interventions that are easy, unobtrusive, and capable of being implemented in general education and special education classrooms. With this in mind, all teachers should be familiar with early-stage interventions, those simple yet promising interventions that require a minimum of paperwork and administration and should always be tried first. For most students, these efforts can solve early-stage problems in the early stages. To follow the medical analogy, it's similar to a standard action when you first get a headache — taking a couple of aspirin. For most students, the early intervention will do the job.

Problem-solving at Tier 2. For individual students whose problems are more significant than a simple headache — those who slip through the net of universal and early-stage intervention efforts — the next level of response should be *collaborative*. As two heads are better than one, it's important to get other professionals besides the teacher involved. The other person can be another teacher, a school counselor, a school psychologist, a school social worker, an assistant principal, or a highly trained behavior specialist. These interventionists fit into your MTSS service delivery model as collaborative providers of targeted interventions. In the health model, the interventionist is parallel to the general practitioners, nurses, and nutritionists a headache patient might see before being referred to a neurosurgeon.

Problem-solving at Tier 3. If the first two planning structures are ineffective, the third level involves a more comprehensive, resource-intensive approach. This approach is a much more detailed level of problem-solving and may call for observing the student in multiple settings, reviewing the student's school records, interviewing the parents, administering behavior assessments, and so forth. In the medical analogy, this is the point when, if a patient still has a headache that has not responded to early intervention or to multiple targeted interventions, it's time to call in the neurosurgeon.

We propose a process that your school can use to move through the different stages of problem-solving. Figure 2.1 on the next page displays this process in a flowchart to illustrate the tools and interventionists that can be used to help students at every stage of need.

- *Stage 1.* The first action after you've identified a student as needing extra support is to assign the student to a school-based support coordinator who will be responsible for ensuring that the student's needs are met through additional supports and problem-solving efforts. At this point, the support coordinator may try to match the student with an existing ready-to-use intervention, such as a mentor or a meaningful school-based job, that seems appropriate for the student. However, if additional data are needed, or if it is clear that the student will require more

The problem-solving model is, at its core, about service delivery. Rather than follow a specific set of steps, the model guides you to ask questions that consider the student's behavior and needs, the context in which the problem is occurring, and the available resources within your school.

intensive supports, a teacher interview or team-based problem-solving effort may be necessary.

- *Stage 2.* The second stage of problem-solving is initiated when a ready-to-use intervention wasn't able to remedy the problem, an appropriate support is not available, or more information is needed about the student. At this point, the support coordinator or other interventionist may conduct an interview with the teacher, or a team of interventionists may convene to conduct a brief planning meeting to further define the problem, analyze why it might be occurring, and develop an intervention plan.
- *Stage 3.* The third stage of problem-solving is initiated when previous intervention efforts were not successful or when the problem is complex and requires more extensive problem analysis and/or specialized input into intervention design. At this point, a multidisciplinary team of interventionists works on designing, implementing, and monitoring fidelity of a much more intensive intervention.

FIGURE 2.1 *Process for Problem-Solving at Different Stages*

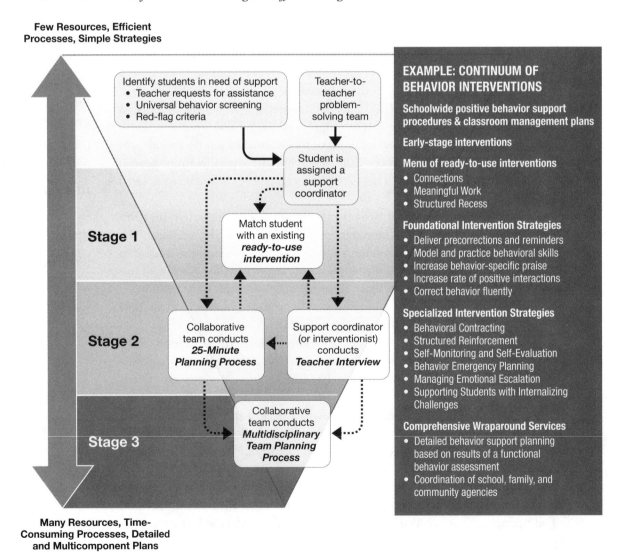

Initiating Individual Problem-Solving Efforts

Individual problem-solving is initiated when a student is identified as needing additional behavior support by your red-flag system, in universal screening procedures, or through teacher referral.

Assigning a Support Coordinator

Before beginning any problem-solving efforts, we recommend assigning the student to a support coordinator. Support coordinators are staff members who are enlisted to ensure that at-risk students do not fall through the cracks of the system. By taking a degree of ownership for making the system work for each student assigned to them, support coordinators monitor the student's progress at school and initiate additional actions necessary to make sure that the school is doing everything possible to meet the student's needs.

A support coordinator program offers a structure for following up on students who need more support than is provided in Tier 1. When creating your support coordinator program, you will outline specific responsibilities that support coordinators will agree to take on in supporting their assigned students. See Section 1, Task 4 on page 45 for more information about how to set up a support coordinator program. In most schools, the support coordinator will be responsible for coordinating initial supports for the student.

The remainder of Section 2 describes how to apply the five-step problem-solving framework to each of the three stages shown in Figure 2.1.

FLEXIBLE MODEL

Our MTSS model is intentionally designed to be flexibly applied across your school or district's definition of Tier 1, Tier 2, and Tier 3 supports, and is independent of a school district's process for referring students to special education programs. This model can operate parallel to your school or district framework, but we do not advocate for any specific point at which a student is referred.

PARENT CONTACT AND CONSENT

Parents have a right, both legally and ethically, to know when their child is having a problem. Further, it is well known that children whose parents are involved consistently do better in school (e.g., Henderson & Mapp, 2002). Contact with parents will let them know that staff are concerned enough to initiate intervention planning and may result in interventions that are more effective than those developed without input from parents (Esler, Godber, & Christenson, 2002). You may be working with families who can't or won't function as partners, but they need to be invited nonetheless.

We strongly encourage initiating parental contact at the point when a student is identified needing additional behavior support, whether by your red-flag system, universal screening procedures, or teacher referral. Check with your district or central office to determine what type of parent/family consent is needed or recommended for further assessment and intervention planning. See the sample Parent Permission Form (Reproducible 2.3) on page 181. Requirements can vary depending on the student's IEP status. Further, some families may be reluctant to participate or to have their child participate because of moral, religious, or other reasons. Ensure that all staff are sensitive to these concerns.

Stage 1 Problem-Solving

At this stage, the problem-solving process usually involves coordinating enrollment into one or more ready-to-use interventions already in place within the school that may help to address the student's needs. However, it may be necessary to move directly to Stage 2 problem-solving processes in the following cases:

- If completing Step 1 or Step 2 of the problem-solving process below proves difficult, or you need to collect additional information about the student and the context of the problem before selecting interventions.
- If no suitable ready-to-use interventions are in place within your building, or the problem is complex enough to require a more detailed intervention plan that incorporates strategies outside of your menu of ready-to-use interventions.
- If a ready-to-use intervention has been attempted and the problem has not improved.

Coordinating Enrollment in Existing Ready-to-Use Interventions

Most highly skilled professionals, such as school psychologists, behavior specialists, and school counselors, have long waiting lists of students who have been referred to them. Some of those students don't need complex interventions. For example, a student who needs only more adult attention can benefit greatly from a relatively simple intervention such as a school job where he regularly interacts with school staff. That student should not have to wait for help. Systems should be in place to allow school-based support coordinators to connect students with simple, established proactive programs *before* the student is placed on a waiting list for more intense interventions.

The support coordinator can use the five-step problem-solving model to identify and coordinate appropriate enrollment in existing, ready-to-use interventions as follows:

Step 1: Define the problem.

When defining the problem, the support coordinator should be able to answer the following questions.

- *What does the problem behavior look like?* In order to select an appropriate intervention, the support coordinator should have a sense of what the problem behavior looks like. Is the student receiving referrals for throwing tantrums? Is the student failing classes because of incomplete work? Did universal screening results suggest that the student may be struggling with an internalizing problem, such as depression or anxiety? Identify the main behavior of concern. Use the information provided by red-flag indicators, universal screening, and/or teacher referrals that alerted your system to the student's need. The data source may provide adequate information about the problem (e.g., a school attendance red-flag system will obviously identify an absenteeism problem). Teacher referrals should include a short description of the problem and reason that the student is being referred.
- *What is the general goal or desired outcome of additional supports?* Once you select an appropriate intervention, you'll more specifically define the goal of the

> **TERMINOLOGY**
>
> For clarity, we refer to the people in problem-solving roles as *interventionists*. People in positions such as school psychologist, behavior specialist, social worker, school resource officer, counselor, nurse, dean, and administrator typically fill the role of interventionist.

intervention. At this point, you just want to determine the purpose of initiating additional support. Is it to increase attendance? Reduce the frequency of tantrums? Increase the student's feeling of connectedness with the school?

- *Code Red Situations: Is the student's behavior unsafe or severely disruptive to the classroom?* Code Red situations involve behaviors that are either so dangerous or so disruptive that classes cannot continue. If the reasons a for referral could be considered a Code Red circumstance, you should move immediately to implementing the protocol that your district has in place for handling severely disruptive or dangerous behavior. See Section 1, Task 6: Establish Processes for Responding to Code Red Situations (p. 54) for a description of how to set up schoolwide policies, and Section 4.4: Behavior Emergency Planning for guidelines on creating a safety plan for an individual student. Once procedures for responding to Code Red situations are in place, you can return to identifying appropriate interventions. Under such circumstances, you will likely move to Stage 2 of problem-solving to ensure that the problem is adequately analyzed and addressed through a more detailed intervention plan rather than simply enrolling the student in an existing intervention.

Step 2: Analyze the problem.

Again, consult the data sources that have identified a cause for concern. At this stage of problem-solving, you may not need a comprehensive hypothesis for why the behavior is occurring. However, you should have some information about what might be contributing to the problem. If referrals provide a description of the incident, look for trends. Consider:

- *Where do the problems tend to occur?* For example, does the student usually receive referrals on the playground, at lunch time, or on the bus? Is the student typically tardy to some classes more than others?
- *When do the problems tend to occur?* Does the student seem to receive more referrals in the morning before school starts or toward the end of the day? Do problems tend to occur more often on certain days?
- *Do any situations seem to set off the problem behavior?* For example, do referrals suggest that the student usually gets in trouble when around certain peers? What events or activities are typically going on when the student gets in trouble?
- *What does the student seem to achieve through the behavior?* Chronic repetitive behavior usually serves a purpose, or *function,* for the individual exhibiting it. Does the student lack the ability or awareness to exhibit the expected behavior? Is the student trying to get something? Is the student trying to avoid or escape something? "Developing a Functional Hypothesis" on pages 130–133 provides a more in-depth discussion of the possible functions that misbehavior might serve for a student.

If there isn't sufficient information to create an initial hypothesis about why a problem is occurring, gather additional information about the student and the context of the problem. This could occur by either informally checking in with the student's teacher, reviewing the student's records, or moving to Stage 2 problem-solving processes.

CODE RED SITUATIONS

Code Red situations involve behaviors that are either unsafe or so disruptive that classes cannot continue. These include behaviors such as:

- Overt aggressive behavior toward others (e.g., kicking, hitting, fighting)
- Threats of targeted violence toward others
- Brandishing items that could be used as weapons
- Carrying weapons
- Self-injurious behavior
- Vandalism or property destruction
- Sexual assault
- Clear signs of using controlled substances (drugs and alcohol)
- Running away from school property
- Sustained confrontational or defiant behavior resulting in refusal to follow immediate, reasonable adult directions.

Step 3: Consider possible solutions and select intervention strategies.

Refer to the menu of existing ready-to-use interventions in place within your school. (See Section 1, Task 5 on p. 49 for more information about setting up a menu of ready-to-use interventions.) Identify supports that may be a good fit for the student and select one or more to implement. When selecting interventions to implement, make sure the intervention plan is related to the general goal of initiating initial supports. What are you trying to achieve through intervention? How will this intervention strategy help achieve this goal? If none of the existing ready-to-use interventions in your building seem like a good fit for the student, move to Stage 2 to broaden the scope of possible intervention strategies to implement.

Step 4: Collect data to monitor progress.

All of the available ready-to-use intervention programs in your school should have procedures for monitoring student progress built into them. If these are not in place, work with the intervention coordinator or implementer to determine how data will be collected and recorded to track the intervention's progress. Objective data collection might include frequency, duration, or latency data, rating scales, work products, self-monitoring data, data from a reinforcement system intervention, or audio and video records. Section 3, Task 8 (p. 289) offers more detailed descriptions of possible data collection methods.

READY-TO-USE INTERVENTIONS

Selecting appropriate and effective interventions requires a thorough knowledge of the interventions. Support coordinators should have knowledge about each of the ready-to-use interventions in place within your school in order to appropriately place students.

Step 5: Evaluate whether supports are working.

The support coordinator has the responsibility to follow up and monitor whether the student is improving as a result of participation in the selected ready-to-use intervention. Follow-up may involve checking in with the intervention coordinator, meeting regularly with the student's teachers, or periodically asking the student how they are doing. The support coordinator should also review any data being collected to determine if the situation is getting better, staying the same, or getting worse. If supports have not adequately improved the problem, it is time to initiate more in-depth problem-solving processes, as described in the next sections.

Summary of Stage 1 Problem-Solving

The support coordinator serves an important role in initiating additional supports for students in need. As the primary staff member responsible for coordinating initial problem-solving efforts, the support coordinator is knowledgeable about resources available to students, able to use the problem-solving model to find an appropriate intervention for the student, and responsive to student needs, ensuring that no students fall through the cracks of the system. With one or more ready-to-use interventions established in your school, a support coordinator can easily plug a student into the intervention and avoid more laborious problem-solving efforts that need to take place before supports can begin. In the case that no appropriate ready-to-use interventions align with the student's needs, or when interventions are not successful in remedying the problem, the support coordinator turns to the system's more intensive intervention and problem-solving resources.

Stage 2 and Stage 3 Problem-Solving

If you have worked through Stage 1 problem-solving processes and implemented interventions without success, it's time to move onto Stage 2 and/or Stage 3 problem-solving. We discuss three processes—the Teacher Interview, the 25-Minute Planning Process, and the Multidisciplinary Team Planning Process—for working through the tiers of intervention.

> Each problem-solving process—
> The Teacher Interview, 25-Minute Planning Process, and Multidisciplinary Team Planning Process is facilitated by a corresponding reproducible form.

The Teacher Interview

The Teacher Interview is designed to a) gather information from the student's teacher or teachers in order to better understand the history and context of the problem, b) identify appropriate intervention strategies to try, and c) convey support and set the stage for ongoing problem-solving collaboration by hearing, valuing, and including the teacher's perspective in the problem-solving process.

Use of the Teacher Interview may be appropriate under the following conditions:

- The support coordinator determines that additional information is needed about the student and the context of the problem in order to proceed with identifying appropriate supports.
- The support coordinator determines that no appropriate ready-to-use interventions are available in your building or that the problem is complex enough to warrant a more detailed intervention plan that incorporates strategies outside of your menu of ready-to-use interventions.
- Ready-to-use interventions have been in place for 2 weeks or more, but the student has not shown sufficient improvement.

Either the support coordinator or another interventionist in your school can conduct the Teacher Interview. Simply by bringing two heads together to discuss the situation, the Teacher Interview assures that the outcome will be better than if the teacher or the support coordinator/interventionist acted alone. In addition, the teacher, who works with the student every day, is often the best source of information about the student and can offer insights into the student's behavior and motivation.

The Teacher Interview is time and resource efficient. When this protocol is followed, the Teacher Interview serves as a rudimentary functional behavior assessment (FBA) that offers a foundation for developing a potentially effective first-step intervention. If the teacher and support coordinator/interventionist can plan an effective and easy-to-implement intervention, more extensive processes—such as direct observation, records review, and collaborative intervention design—can be skipped or saved for later, if needed. Further, the teacher interview takes care of collecting most of the background information needed for other problem-solving processes, including the first two steps of the 25-Minute Planning Process. Information gathered from the Teacher Interview may be used:

- *To match the student with a ready-to-use intervention:* By identifying situations that predict when the problem behavior will occur and generating an initial hypothesis about why the behavior is occurring, the teacher and support coordinator/interventionist can identify an existing ready-to-use intervention that may be a good fit for the student.

- *To identify intervention strategies that the teacher can implement in the classroom:* If existing ready-to-use interventions are not a good fit for the student, the support coordinator/interventionist and teacher can work together to identify one or two simple intervention strategies to put into place.
- *In conjunction with the 25-Minute Planning Process:* The Teacher Interview can be used for Steps 1–2 of the problem-solving model to gather information about the student and the problem, and the 25-Minute Planning Process can be used for Steps 3–5 to guide team-based intervention design and planning.

INVITING STAFF MEMBERS TO PARTICIPATE IN THE PROBLEM-SOLVING PROCESS

You may need to conduct multiple interviews in secondary school settings or when the student exhibits misbehavior across settings. If you know the problem happens only during one class or in a specific school setting, conduct the Teacher Interview with the class teacher or staff member in charge of supervising the targeted setting. If you are unsure about whether the problem occurs across periods or settings, distribute the Student Status Report (Reproducible 2.1) to all of the student's teachers. Use this information to determine if the intervention will involve one or more teachers and require multiple interviews.

While it is important to gather sufficient information to understand the scope of the problem, at this stage of problem-solving it may be most feasible to start an intervention plan in only one or two classes. Tackling too many settings may be overwhelming for the student and can create a large burden for the student's support coordinator to monitor and evaluate the plan's implementation. Instead, prioritize including those teachers who are most affected by the student's behavior and who report the greatest concerns about the student's performance in class.

Guidelines for Conducting the Teacher Interview

The person conducting the Teacher Interview should keep following considerations in mind throughout the meeting.

Be transparent about the purpose and process of the meeting. Before beginning the interview, describe the purpose of the interview, the types of questions you will ask, and the outcomes and support that the teacher can expect from the process. If the Teacher Interview will be conducted in conjunction with the 25-Minute Planning Process, familiarize the teacher with this problem-solving process and explain that the background information gathered in the interview will inform decisions made in the planning team meeting. This will help the teacher see that the planning team will attempt to choose interventions that fit the nature of the problem, the teacher's abilities and style, and any other factors that may be relevant.

All interventionists should know whether they are expected to report to the principal or district administrators about cases they are working on. If the principal expects you

REPRODUCIBLE 2.1 *Student Status Report*

Student Status Report

Student _____ Grade/Class _____

Staff member requesting information _____ Date _____

Directions: Please complete performance ratings for this student. The information you provide will be used to help develop an individualized plan of assistance and match the student with appropriate interventions.

Student Performance KEY: 5 = Always 4 = Usually 3 = Sometimes 2 = Rarely 1 = Never N/A = Not applicable	Period or Subject Area					
Academic standing (List student's current grade using the values listed on the report card [letter grades, ✓ /+/-, etc.].)						
Attends class regularly						
Punctual						
Cooperative						
Participates in class activities						
Stays on task						
Completes in-class assignments						
Completes homework						
Quality of work is satisfactory						
Passes tests						

Student strengths (list at least three):

List areas of concern:

NOTE: Please attach a representative sample of student work.

Interventions © 2019 Ancora Publishing   REPRODUCIBLE 2.1

to report your work with a teacher, make sure to let the teacher know in advance. It is very damaging to a collaborative relationship when teachers assume they are telling you things in confidence only to learn later that you are reporting to the principal about the collaboration. Some interventionists may have a job role in which the collaborative relationship allows confidentiality, such as a school counselor, whereas another job role, such as a school psychologist, may be required to report to the administrator. Clear, honest, before-the-relationship-begins communication is essential.

Make the classroom teacher feel welcome. It is essential to remember that teachers of at-risk students are frequently dealing with high levels of stress and anxiety. During this meeting, actively work to put the teacher at ease. Help the teacher realize that you are there in an effort to collaboratively find a solution, not to judge. Research has shown that establishing a supportive, encouraging relationship with the teacher can go a long way in positively affecting the outcomes of consultation (e.g., Gutkin & Curtis, 1999). Focus on establishing an atmosphere of support and advocacy for the student. Sit next to, not across from, the teacher. This takes away certain intimidation factors and removes the sense that the meeting is an interrogation. You are simply taking notes, not writing anything that is a secret. Allow the teacher to see the interview form so that the teacher can go back and ask questions or clarify the process. Ask a teacher who seems uncomfortable with the process to record the information—this offers a sense of participation and control.

Demonstrate active listening skills. During the interview, you will do much more listening than talking, so it's important to use active listening skills. Active listening is focused on building rapport, maximizing understanding, and creating a climate of trust and collaboration (Lasky, 2000; O'Shea, Algozzine, Hammittee, & O'Shea, 2000). Following are active listening skills you may wish to use:

- Pay attention to the teacher's tone of voice and body language. Does body language suggest that the teacher is uncomfortable, distracted, nervous, etc.?
- Restate and paraphrase what the teacher has just said to clarify understanding and to demonstrate that you are listening. When you paraphrase effectively, the teacher should want to tell you more.
- Ask open-ended questions that prompt the teacher to expand the discussion.
- Acknowledge and validate the teacher's feelings: *I appreciate your willingness to spend your planning period discussing Marco with me. You must be exhausted from the incident earlier today. I'm optimistic that we can work toward finding a solution to better support Marco at school.*
- Listen without judgment, and avoid jumping to conclusions. Seek to understand the context of the problem and the experience of the teacher. One of the primary roles of the interventionist is to help reduce teacher isolation and encourage collaboration. When dealing with challenging situations, teachers need an opportunity to talk to someone who is nonjudgmental. The interventionist needs to ask, *How else can I help you?*
- Present yourself as a collaborator rather than an expert. Ask questions and offer suggestions, but as much as possible, avoid telling people what they ought to do. Act as a resource, indicating that you are available to provide support, assistance, and guidance to teachers, students, and/or families as they design intervention plans. Make an effort to communicate a spirit of humility and service—that you are there to help, not to be directive and not to judge the teacher. Also

Make an effort to communicate a spirit of humility and service—that you are there to help, not to be directive and not to judge the teacher.

communicate that whatever intervention is subsequently developed will be an experiment, not something that is guaranteed to work. In other words, you are not such an expert that you know the solution to this challenging situation, but by working together you and the teacher can construct something that may improve the situation.

Use everyday language to discuss problems and share perceptions. Be careful to use language that staff, parents, and students are comfortable with. Technical jargon or confusing language may create barriers to collaboration (Allen & Graden, 2002). For example, someone with a school psychology background may be tempted to use phrases such as *intermittent reinforcement* and *antecedent event*. This vocabulary reflects useful concepts from the science of behaviorism, but these same ideas can be described in everyday language. Contrast the following two statements:

Interventionist 1: If you watch Norm carefully, the antecedent event to his agitation seems to be Mrs. Harper approaching him. I wonder if we can figure out why.

Interventionist 2: If you watch Norm carefully, he seems to get agitated whenever Mrs. Harper approaches him. I wonder if we can figure out why.

A teacher listening to Interventionist 1 might think, "Figure out what? I have no idea what he's talking about!" On the other hand, a teacher working with Interventionist 2 is more likely to respond, "That's interesting. Do you suppose that Norm just doesn't trust adults?"

Discuss problems and share perceptions in a value-free manner. Language that conveys particular biases or philosophies may hinder effective communication (Kratochwill, Elliott, & Callan-Stoiber, 2002). Value-laden terminology can inadvertently create barriers that are difficult to tear down. It's important to use neutral, objective language and to talk about directly observable behaviors. A discussion that is focused specifically on the needs of the student is more likely to engage the teacher. Contrast the following two comments:

Interventionist 1: Karla needs a developmentally appropriate environment. She needs to be able to stretch and move physically.

Interventionist 2: I wonder if Karla is just one of those kids who have a difficult time staying still. Do you think we could structure her workspace so she can move but not bother the other children?

The first interventionist has risked putting the teacher on the defensive. The term "developmentally appropriate" is potentially divisive or may seem judgmental. The teacher might wonder, "It feels like the interventionist is saying that my classroom is not developmentally appropriate. I think it's developmentally appropriate to teach children to stay on task and not prevent others from working." In future discussions, the teacher may feel the interventionist is judging her against the unknown standards of developmentally appropriate practice. On the other hand, by keeping the conversation focused on the needs of the student and the situation, the second interventionist can involve the teacher in problem-solving: "We could create a space for Karla to move about while she is working and also teach her not to bother other students."

The interview shouldn't take so long that it drags on, but it should take long enough to gather needed information and develop a sound intervention plan that the teacher is willing to implement.

Try to achieve a balance between giving the teacher room to vent and discouraging unproductive cycling on the problem. Because the Teacher Interview provides structure but no time limit, the interventionist must skillfully guide the process. The interview shouldn't take so long that it drags on, but it should take long enough to gather needed information and develop a sound intervention plan that the teacher is willing to implement. The more information the interventionist or team has and the more clearly the problem is defined (using the objective language of behaviors rather than child-deficit language), the greater the likelihood that the interventionist and the teacher can develop an intervention plan that is responsive to the needs of the student (Rosenfield, 2008; Tryon & Winograd, 2011). Ensure that the teacher has the opportunity to describe the full range of the problem and concerns about the student without getting mired in uncontrollable aspects of the problem. It is a challenging balance—the interventionist needs to move things along while recognizing that a teacher who feels rushed or dismissed is less likely to view the interventionist as an ally. Teachers often feel that they aren't listened to by interventionists, who may attempt to immediately identify and address the most critical problem. It will be far more productive in the early parts of the interview to be a good listener and acknowledge the range of problems associated with the student. This can further set the stage for collaboration, helping you and the teacher identify categories of problem behavior for a later stage of planning. If it seems that the conversation is circling back to the same concerns and turning into venting about the problem, try to wrap up this part of the interview by summarizing: "Let me see if I have a sense of the situation and all the things that concern you about the student's behavior."

Address conflicts of interest by focusing on the intervention plan. In some cases, the teacher may resist participating in problem-solving efforts or insist that the school move the student to another classroom or setting. In these situations, remain focused on the intervention plan. For example, if a teacher wants a disruptive child to be removed from the classroom, but the interventionist thinks that in-class interventions have a fair chance of helping the student, the interventionist might handle it as follows:

Teacher:	I really can't tolerate Jeffrey any more. He has disrupted my class more times than I care to remember. He's disrespectful and obnoxious, and I don't want him returned.
Interventionist:	I know that Jeffrey has really caused problems. I am sorry we were not there to help sooner.
Teacher:	I don't think it would have done any good. I've tried everything with that kid. Nothing works.
Interventionist:	I'm sure you have. What I'd like to do with you today is work through a plan for what types of misbehaviors should result in sending Jeffrey to the office and what types should be handled in the classroom. I know the vice-principal wants to have as much handled in the classroom as possible so students don't miss out on instruction. Let's talk through a plan, then run it by Mr. Corderra to see if you and he are on the same page about when and when not to send the student to the office. Does that sound OK to you? Then part of the plan will be to consider a special education referral, but we also need to figure out a plan to keep your classroom livable while we are doing that.

Step-by-Step Directions for Conducting the Teacher Interview

The Teacher Interview is organized around the five-step problem-solving model described at the beginning of this section. Each section included on the Teacher Interview form (Reproducible 2.2) includes specific questions to help the interviewer gather information for all steps of the problem-solving model. See the full form on pages 148–156.

Step 1: Define the problem.

The first couple of questions on the interview should be viewed as an opportunity to allow the teacher to explain any and every problem that is occurring with the student. Although the intervention plan will later be narrowed to address only the one or two behaviors of most concern, it is essential to determine the breadth of the student's problems.

> *Step 1. Define the problem.*   *excerpt p. 1 of 9*
>
> 1. Describe the problem or reason for referral:
>
> 2. How often do the problems occur? How long does the behavior last? How intense is the problem?
>
> 3. **Code Red Situations:** Is the student's behavior unsafe or severely disruptive to the classroom? Yes / No
>   If yes, consult your school's protocol for handling severely disruptive or dangerous behavior.
>
> 4. What are the student's strengths?
>
> 5. List interventions tried in the Intervention History table on the next two pages.

*The steps and items shown here directly correspond to the **Teacher Interview form** (Reproducible 2.2, pp. 148–156).*

    Item 1: Describe the problem or reason for referral. Ask the teacher to tell you anything and everything about the situation that resulted in the request for help. To prompt the discussion, ask questions such as: What does the student do? What frustrates you?

    Item 2: How often do the problems occur? How long does the behavior last? How intense is the problem? Knowing the frequency and duration of problems can be critical information when planning interventions. If a young student throws tantrums once or twice a week, the problem may not be severe. However, if the tantrums last for 60–90 minutes each, the student may need an intensive intervention plan. Other information that may be worth considering is the intensity of the behavior: Is it sometimes more intense than other times, and has the teacher noticed any trends or patterns? If the problem involves not following directions, ask the teacher to estimate how much time it takes from when a direction is given to when the student fully complies with it.

    Item 3: Code Red Situations: Is the student's behavior unsafe or severely disruptive to the classroom? Explicitly ask the teacher whether the student's behavior is currently, or may eventually be, unsafe or severely disruptive. If this question is not directly asked, you run the risk of missing warning signs about such behavior, in which case the teacher may be unprepared to handle a volatile situation. Code Red situations involve behaviors that are either so dangerous or so disruptive that classes cannot continue. Under Code Red circumstances, you will skip simple intervention strategies and move directly to the protocol that your district has in place for handling severely disruptive or dangerous behavior. If your district does not have such a policy, or if the policy is vague and does not define specific procedural actions, see Section 1, Task 6: Establish Processes for Responding to Code Red Situations for a description of how to set up schoolwide policies. For specific guidelines on creating a safety plan for an individual student, see Behavior Emergency Planning. Once temporary procedures are put in place for defusing or responding to Code Red situations, you can return to developing a long-term intervention plan that will help the student learn appropriate behavior.

Item 4: What are the student's strengths? Ask the teacher to identify 2–3 positive features or strengths that the student brings to the classroom. What academic areas does the student do well in? Does the student play any sports or have any talents that the teacher is aware of? What positive characteristics does the student show at school? A good intervention plan will build from the strengths the student already demonstrates. An additional goal of this part of the interview is to encourage the teacher to see the student as far more than the sum of the problems. If the teacher has become frustrated with the student, talking about strengths may give the teacher a greater sense of compassion and investment in the student's success.

Item 5: List interventions tried in the Intervention History table. Identify interventions and strategies that the teacher or other school staff have already tried in responding to the problem. Describe the intervention or strategy, how long it was implemented, and

Intervention History

Intervention/Strategy	Were data collected?	How effective was the intervention/strategy at addressing problem behavior?
	☐ Yes / ☐ No Describe:	☐ Not at all / ☐ Somewhat / ☐ Very Notes:
	☐ Yes / ☐ No Describe:	☐ Not at all / ☐ Somewhat / ☐ Very Notes:
	☐ Yes / ☐ No Describe:	☐ Not at all / ☐ Somewhat / ☐ Very Notes:

excerpt pp. 2–3 of 9

whether data were collected. If any interventions have been attempted with the student, ask to look at all records, contracts, and other data or forms collected during the intervention. Ask the teacher how effective the intervention or strategy was in addressing the problem.

As you move through this section, actively work to prevent teachers from feeling defensive or alienated. If no action was taken previously, make it clear to the teacher that this is OK and that information from this interview will help determine where to start. It may be useful to contact the student's previous teachers to find out whether they had success with any interventions.

Record any additional notes to help fully document the efforts and outcomes of each intervention or strategy. This list of interventions can be archived, expanded, and used in subsequent problem-solving meetings.

Item 6: Prioritize 1–2 major behaviors that are most problematic or urgent. Once the teacher has presented the full scope of the student's problems, guide the teacher in identifying 1–2 major behaviors or categories to address first with intervention. If the teacher wants to change too many of the student's behaviors, you may need to help narrow the scope of the initial intervention. If you are dealing with a student who has many problems, where do you start? It is important to identify objectives that allow the student to focus on one or two areas of improvement. Often, improving one pivotal behavior has a positive effect on several other problem areas.

To identify priorities for the initial intervention, ask the following questions:

- *Which behavior changes will help the student feel successful in the shortest period of time?* Select behaviors that have the highest probability of success in the least amount of time. Once the student experiences success, many secondary problems resolve themselves and the positive momentum makes other problems more amenable to future intervention efforts.
- *Which behavior changes will help the teacher see improvements in the shortest period of time?* Any intervention must focus not only on improving student behavior but also on addressing any misbehaviors that the teacher cannot tolerate. Although the objectives may need to be adjusted later to ensure they are observable, obtainable goals, it is important to get the teacher's perspective on the behaviors that are most disruptive and impossible to live with.

---

6. Prioritize 1–2 major behaviors that are most problematic or urgent:

☐ Physical aggression ☐ Anxiety ☐ Off task
☐ Self-injury ☐ Disruption ☐ Depression, withdrawal
☐ Peer conflict ☐ Absenteeism ☐ Inappropriate language
☐ Damage to property ☐ Bullying others ☐ Tardiness
☐ Noncompliance ☐ Other: _____ ☐ Other: _____

7. Narrow the scope of the problem and identify a goal for improvement.

excerpt p. 1 of 9

Item 7. Narrow the scope of the problem and identify a goal for improvement. What is the teacher's goal or desired outcome? The purpose of this item is to clarify what the teacher hopes to accomplish through the intervention. This is a pivotal point in the intervention planning process. The focus shifts from what is known about the past up to this point to what the teacher wants things to be like in the future.

Carefully guide the teacher toward developing a clear, reasonable, and achievable goal for the student's behavior by doing the following.

- *Select observable behavior.* When the behaviors to be changed can be narrowed and specified as much as possible in this stage of planning, it makes the next steps significantly easier. The goal of the intervention must be a specific observable behavior, such as "Help Mark learn to stay in his seat during class," and not a general label or conclusion, such as "Stop Mark from being so fidgety." Stating the goal of the intervention in observable and measurable terms establishes criteria that the interventionist and teacher can use to determine the success or failure of the intervention (Alberto & Troutman, 2012).

  Encourage the teacher to use objective descriptions of the student's situation and to avoid generalizations. If the goal can't be counted or measured somehow, it may be too broad or subjective. In this case, guide the teacher in redefining the goal for the student's behavior. By moving from subjective conclusions to objective descriptions of the problem, logical objective goals are more likely to emerge. Following are specific examples of each.

SETTING A GOAL FOR INTERVENTION

Establishing the goal of the intervention will be a cooperative process that at this stage is largely determined by the teacher. Because any intervention that has teacher support will have a greater likelihood of success, encourage the teacher to be a bit selfish in this stage of planning. What do you need to get out of the intervention? Determine not only what the teacher hopes to accomplish but also what the teacher can't live with any longer. Listen carefully to find out what the teacher wants. When a teacher feels cut off, the collaborative nature of planning may be damaged.

Conclusion	Objective Description	Goal of Intervention
Sara is really lazy.	Sara has completed only one of eight assignments and has not turned in any homework.	Sara will complete in-class assignments and homework.
James is totally out of control at recess.	James runs through the games other students are playing. He pushes others, and he will not follow directions from the playground assistants.	James will follow directions from the playground assistants, and for 2 weeks during recess he will be assigned to a specific game that one of the assistants will monitor closely.
Mariah doesn't seem to have any confidence.	Mariah does not ever talk with other students, and talks with adults only when they initiate the contact.	Mariah will learn social skills that will result in her initiating interactions with both students and adults.

- *Identify a positively stated goal.* Regardless of whether the goal is to reduce a negative behavior or increase a positive one, it's important to state the goal in positive terms. While most intervention plans will be created to address problematic behaviors, positively stated goals allow students to take pride in their accomplishments and convey a sense of progress. For example, "learning to respect the property of others" is a worthwhile goal, but "learning not to be destructive" is demeaning.
- *Include numbers and timelines.* The use of numbers is objective and can help define the goal of the intervention. Stating timelines and degrees of goal accomplishment is also useful. Collaborate with the teacher to incorporate numbers and timelines into your goals. For example, "Within 4 weeks, Ava will be able to complete at least 80% of her classwork every day."
- *Chose ambitious but obtainable objectives.* Overly ambitious goals might be revised to reflect more intermediary goals. For example, if a student has fits of anger and tantrums 10–15 times a day, it would be unrealistic to try to eliminate all outbursts within a week. Success would be impossible. Instead, the goal might be to reduce the average number of tantrums each week for the remainder of the year.

Step 2: Analyze the problem.

The next questions guide you and the classroom teacher to look for trends in the student's behavior by determining the *when*, *where*, and *how* of the most urgent problem behavior you identified in Item 6. When you look at situations that may set off or maintain the student's problem behavior, the function of or reason for the misbehavior may emerge (Gresham, Watson, & Skinner, 2001). These behavior trends will also help in later planning stages with tasks such as determining when to use intervention procedures and how often to monitor behavior.

It's important to work through each of the questions in this section. Ensure that the teacher knows that it's useful to think through each question even though there may not be enough information to answer it.

NOTE: In most situations, you should have narrowed the scope of the problem so that this step can be completed with one major category or set of related behaviors in mind. In some instances, you may need to address a set of unrelated problem behaviors at the same time. If this is the case, answer Items 8 and 9 separately for each behavior category.

At this stage, it will be helpful to gently ask the teacher for any data that might show trends in the student's behavior. Monitoring forms, frequency data, and any other collected information will be extremely useful in this stage of intervention planning. Use these collected data as you work through the following questions to analyze trends in the student's behavior. If the teacher does not have any data, proceed to the next steps to gather the teacher's subjective perceptions of patterns in the student's behavior.

Step 2. Analyze the problem.   5 minutes

8. Identify relevant triggers (antecedents) and conditions (setting events) that predict when behavior is likely to occur. Are there specific situations that seem to set off the problem behavior?

   excerpt p. 4 of 9

   Where do the problems tend to occur?

   When do the problems tend to occur?

   Possible Antecedents and Setting Events:
   - ☐ Unstructured time
   - ☐ Whole group instruction
   - ☐ Small group activities
   - ☐ Independent work
   - ☐ Transitions
   - ☐ Change in routine
   - ☐ Specific tasks: _____
   - ☐ Peers present
   - ☐ Peer conflict
   - ☐ After adult correction or reprimands
   - ☐ Corrective consequence or loss of privilege
   - ☐ Other: _____
   - ☐ Hunger
   - ☐ Conflict or stressors at home
   - ☐ Illness, pain, discomfort
   - ☐ Missed medications
   - ☐ Lack of sleep

Item 8: Identify relevant triggers (antecedents) and conditions (setting events) that predict when behavior is likely to occur. Focus the discussion on the student's main problems and ask the teacher to consider whether these behaviors are set off by certain precipitating or escalating events. If a teacher can identify such triggers, your intervention plan can be designed to anticipate and help prevent problem behaviors.

Ask the following questions:

- *Are there specific situations that seem to set off the problem behavior?* If the student fights with peers, what sort of interactions precipitate a fight? If the student is overly defiant of authority, what events occur before the insubordinate acts? When you can identify specific triggers, the intervention can be focused on teaching the student to manage their behavior under those conditions or to avoid situations that result in problems.
- *Where do the problems tend to occur?* Try to determine whether the student exhibits the problem behavior in multiple settings or whether the behavior is isolated to one location. Do problems occur only in the classroom? Does the student have difficulty in the halls or in special settings like the library and music room, the playground, or the cafeteria? Do the parents report similar problems at home? When problems are pervasive across all settings, the misbehavior may be firmly ingrained in the student's repertoire, or the repertoire may lack the expected behavior. On the other hand, when the problem occurs only in one or two settings, something specific about the setting may lead to problems.
- *When do the problems tend to occur?* Look for any pattern in the timing of the misbehavior. Do problems occur during certain times of the day? Are mornings better than afternoons? Do problems tend to occur more frequently on certain days? If you detect a pattern, it may help with intervention planning.
- *Do specific conditions seem to increase the likelihood that problem behavior will occur on any given day?* In some situations, certain events or conditions that happen before an antecedent increase the likelihood that a problem behavior will occur. When present, these conditions, called *setting events*, increase the likelihood that an identified antecedent will trigger problem behavior (Wahler & Fox, 1981). For example, when a student misses breakfast, he may be agitated and irritable and more likely to throw a tantrum when his teacher asks him to work on his seatwork. Because this condition can change each day, the student may be more likely to respond appropriately to his teacher's redirection on the days when he has breakfast and more likely to throw a tantrum on days when he misses breakfast. An intervention can address a setting event by preventing the setting event from occurring or by incorporating strategies to reduce the impact that specific conditions have on the student's behavior.

From the information that you gathered in these questions, use the checkboxes to indicate possible antecedents and setting events that predict problem behavior. Select antecedents that seem to occur most often and have the greatest likelihood of triggering problem behavior. If needed, ask additional questions to understand the specific features of the situation that may be predicting problem behavior. For example, if the teacher says that the student often tantrums in the mornings, ask more questions about what goes on in the classroom in the morning. What activities take place? What is expected of the student during this time? What happens right before the problem behavior occurs?

Item 9: Identify the function of the behavior, or the consequences that seem to be maintaining or reinforcing problem behavior. Considering function just means you are asking two basic questions: What is the student getting from the behavior? What is the underlying reason for the behavior?

To determine what the student seems to achieve through the behavior, ask the following questions:

- *What typically happens right after the problem behavior occurs?* What do you (the teacher) do? What do other students do? How might these responses reinforce the student's problem behavior?
- *Is the student trying to avoid something?* Are there certain situations or activities that the student is motivated to avoid or escape? Does engaging in the problem behavior get the student out of these situations or activities?
- *Is the student trying to get something?* Are there certain privileges or items that the student is motivated to obtain through problem behavior? Does the student gain access to these privileges or items after demonstrating the problem behavior?
- *Does the student lack certain skills or self-awareness that may be contributing to the problem?* Does the student lack the ability or awareness to exhibit the expected behavior? NOTE: If you suspect that an academic skill deficit may be contributing to the behavior problem, see "Academic Concerns" on pages 128–129.

Once you have asked these questions, guide the teacher toward developing a hypothesis about the function of the behavior. Why is the problem occurring chronically? Why is it so resistant to simpler solutions? You're not diagnosing, you're just developing a guess. See "Developing a Functional Hypothesis" on pages 130–133 for a list of possible functions to help develop your hypothesis.

Considering function just means you are asking two basic questions: What is the student getting from the behavior? What is the underlying reason for the behavior?

---

9. Identify the function of the behavior, or the consequences that seem to be maintaining or reinforcing problem behavior. What typically happens right after the problem behavior occurs? What do you do? What do other students do?

Are there certain situations or activities that the student is motivated to avoid or escape?

Are there certain privileges or items that the student is motivated to obtain through problem behavior?

Does the student lack certain skills or an awareness of their behavior that may be contributing to the problem?

excerpt p. 4 of 9

Hypothesized function(s):

Deficits	Trying to Get Something	Trying to Avoid Something
☐ Lacking awareness	☐ Seeking adult attention	☐ Avoiding overly difficult or overly simple work
☐ Lacking ability:	☐ Seeking peer attention	☐ Avoiding nonpreferred activities and tasks
☐ Physical/Neurological	☐ Seeking access to activities	☐ Avoiding peer interactions
☐ Academic	☐ Seeking power or control	☐ Avoiding adult interactions
☐ Social/Emotional		

continued on page 134

ACADEMIC CONCERNS

Behavior and academic success are intricately interwoven. Often, what appears to be a behavior problem has an academic component. Academic frustration leads to behavior problems, and poor behavioral choices often result in academic problems.

For some students, misbehavior may serve the function of escape from academic tasks that may be too difficult. Students may also misbehave as a way to regain a sense of power and control when they struggle with feeling inadequate or unable to complete academic tasks. Assessing a student's current academic ability and needs can provide important information to help staff determine whether the student may benefit from additional academic support.

If the student is failing to meet academic expectations in one or more areas, examine existing information and identify patterns of academic behavior. Does the student perform poorly in some subject areas but not others? Are some types of tasks more difficult than others (e.g. paper and pencil tasks vs. project-based tasks; group vs. independent work)? Does the student consistently struggle with behavior in tasks or activities that require a particular academic skill (e.g., reading, writing, math)?

In addition, it's important to evaluate whether academic difficulties are a product of a skill deficit (i.e., the student cannot do the work) or a performance deficit (i.e., the student will not do the work). This Can't Do/Won't Do assessment can be extremely useful in guiding intervention efforts (VanDerHeyden & Witt, 2008).

For a student with a performance deficit, behavior intervention strategies that offer incentives for effort (e.g., reinforcement systems, behavior contracts, self-monitoring systems) may be effective in improving academic performance and remedying related behavior problems.

For a student who cannot do the work, refer the student to your school's process for academic evaluation and initiation of academic support services.

Support services and strategies will depend on available resources and procedures in place within your school, but possibilities include:

- Teaching the student to create and use framed outlines and graphic organizers
- Providing study guides
- Preteaching essential vocabulary

- Teaching the student to manage homework and use organizational strategies
- Assigning the student a peer tutor
- Initiating additional support services (e.g., Title 1, Tier 2 reading support, etc.)
- Evaluating for special education eligibility

It is outside the scope of this book to provide a comprehensive overview of the process for assessing for academic deficits and implementing strategies for adapting instruction and remediating academic deficits. If you suspect that a student is experiencing an academic problem, follow your school's protocol for evaluating for and initiating additional academic support services. A list of academic assessment and intervention resources is provided below, including resources for conducting a Can't Do/Won't Do assessment.

Because addressing academic deficits is a complex and time-consuming task, make sure to concurrently move forward with selecting and implementing intervention strategies to address and prevent behavior issues and improve student connectedness at school.

Resources

Archer, A., & Gleason, M. (1992). *Skills for school success.* North Billerica, MA: Curriculum Associates. Designed for students in the elementary and middle grades who struggle with organizational issues, this program systematically teaches students critical organizational and study skills to succeed at school.

Eckert, T. L., Codding, R. M., Truckenmiller, A. J., & Rheinheimer, J. L. (2009). Improving children's fluency in reading, mathematics, spelling, and writing: A review of evidence-based academic interventions. In K. A. Akin-Little, S. N. Little, M. Bray, & T. Kehle (Eds.), *Handbook of behavioral interventions in schools* (pp. 111–124). Washington, DC: American Psychological Association.

Shapiro, E. S. (2011). *Academic skills problems: Direct assessment and intervention* (4th ed.) New York, NY: Guilford Press. A practitioner-friendly text that presents an effective problem-solving approach to evaluating and remediating academic skills problems.

VanDerHeyden, A. M., & Witt, J. C. (2008). Best practices in can't do/won't do assessment. In A. Thomas & J. Grimes (Eds.). *Best practices in school psychology* (5th ed., pp. 131–140). Bethesda, MD: National Association of School Psychologists.

Developing a Functional Hypothesis

Every behavior that occurs repeatedly serves some function for the individual who exhibits the behavior—whether it's gaining attention from peers by misbehaving in class, obtaining access to a reinforcing item by bullying another student, or escaping academic work by wandering around the classroom (O'Neill et al., 1997).

When you are thinking about the function of a misbehavior, remember that you are not developing a diagnosis, merely a guess or hypothesis about why the behavior is occurring. If the function-based intervention is successful in changing the student's behavior, your hypothesis is probably correct. If the behavior does not change, your hypothesis may be incorrect.

Below is a list of possible functions that may be factors in the student's problem behaviors. Consider three broad categories when thinking about function:

- Does the student have deficits, such as lacking the ability or awareness to exhibit the expected behavior?
- Is the student trying to get something?
- Is the student trying to avoid or escape something?

Use this list to help develop a hypothesis about why the behavior is occurring.

Does the student lack the ability or awareness to exhibit the expected behavior?

Lacking awareness. Some students act inappropriately because they don't realize they're behaving badly. For example, imagine a fidgety student who constantly taps his pencil on the desk. The only time this student is not tapping his pencil is when his knee is bobbing up and down, which he does with equal unawareness. Only when he consciously thinks about keeping his hands and feet still is he completely quiet. He isn't irritating his teacher to get attention—in fact, he's completely unaware that his tapping and bobbing is having any effect at all on the teacher.

A student who raises her voice and gets very loud when she feels strongly about something may also have an awareness problem. Her pattern of speech may reflect the interactions that are common in her home, community, or circle of friends, or they may simply be a product of her temperament and physiological makeup. She may not realize that her behavior is perceived as rude or even threatening, and she may be genuinely confused when adults get angry with her or when teachers refer her for insubordination.

Intervention strategies: Interventions may involve accommodation, but should also involve signals or prompts, teaching replacement behavior, self-monitoring, positive reinforcement, and other strategies to help behavior improve over time. Providing a Koosh ball to a fidgety student is an example of an accommodation—giving the student something to do with his hands instead of the distracting behavior. You would concurrently implement some form of self-monitoring, positive reinforcement, or other strategy as a long-term intervention designed to change the behavior.

Lacking ability. Some students act inappropriately because they're incapable of exhibiting the expected behavior or because they don't realize they're behaving badly. Lack of ability should always be considered and ruled out before proceeding with an intervention. Here are a few examples of students who lack the physiological or neurological ability to meet expectations:

- Physical/Neurological: A student with Tourette syndrome cannot control his actions. Whenever the underlying condition is at least partly neurological or physiological, the intervening teacher must work closely with the student's physician to determine which behaviors are reasonable to treat and which behaviors should be tolerated and accommodated.
- Social/Emotional: A student with autism refuses to share toys and playground equipment at recess. The student struggles with seeing another person's perspective and understanding the expectation that he must share with his peers.
- Academic: A student with severe academic deficits does nothing during independent work periods. The student is not trying to avoid the work. She just knows she cannot complete the work and there's no point in trying. See "Academic Concerns" (pp. 128–129) for more discussion.

Consider a student who has been identified as having attention deficit/hyperactivity disorder (ADHD) and cannot stay seated. ADHD is a special case because some combination of modified expectations and accommodations may be the best course. While the student who can't stay seated for long periods of time may have difficulty doing what comes easily to other students, it is not beyond that student's ability to learn how to sit still. It is perfectly reasonable to design a plan to try to help a student with ADHD practice and learn improved behavior. Some children with ADHD will overcome the difficulties associated with this condition, while others will continue to struggle and may benefit from an adjustment of expectations while they are learning new skills such as self-control and impulse control, staying still, and keeping their attention focused on a task. Teachers, while making some reasonable accommodations, can still hold high standards and firm behavior expectations for their students with ADHD (DuPaul & Eckert, 1997).

Intervention strategies: If the behavior is outside the student's ability to control (Tourette syndrome, for example), merely create accommodations. If the behavior is within the student's ability to learn to control (ADHD tendencies, for example), interventions should involve making temporary accommodations while concurrently teaching replacement behaviors. With many students, do not expect immediate or complete behavior change.

Is the student trying to get something?

Seeking adult attention. Some students seek positive attention in inappropriate ways—an example is the student who chronically tattles on others. Another example is the student who constantly seeks reassurance or validation: "Look at my work! Look what I did!" The student's motive is positive, but the method quickly becomes trying for the teacher.

Some students may be trying to get negative attention from the teacher—a scolding, a reprimand, a threat of disciplinary action. These students may have had little success getting positive attention in the past. They may be struggling academically. They may be trying to impress their friends, appease their antagonizers, or take advantage of any opportunity to argue with adults. Whatever the reason, consequences that are negative or aversive for most students may be serving as positive reinforcers for these students.

Intervention strategies: Interventions will involve planned ignoring and increasing the ratio of positive interactions—that is, delivering many more positive interactions than corrective interactions.

Seeking peer attention. The class clown is seeking laughter and social approval. The show-off wants to be seen as talented and popular. Conversely, some students want negative attention. They have found that they get attention from their peers only by annoying them, bullying them, or arguing with them.

Intervention strategies: Interventions will involve trying to increase the amount of attention the student receives from peers in prosocial ways, usually by teaching the student better social skills for interacting with peers and making friends. It may occasionally involve working directly with the peer group to reduce the amount of attention the student receives for acting out.

Seeking access to activities or tangibles. The student may use misbehavior to obtain access to desirable activities, privileges, or items. For example, a student may push and trip kids on the way to line up for lunch in order to secure a place near the front of the line. Or a student might use intimidation and name-calling to get other students to vacate the playground equipment that she wants to use.

Intervention strategies: Interventions will involve limiting access to preferred activities and tangibles to only when the student demonstrates appropriate alternative behaviors to the misbehavior.

Seeking power and control. This is an extreme form of attention-getting behavior in which the student truly seems to want to get adults angry. Instead of being satisfied with any type of attention, the student actively tries to push the teacher's buttons. An emotional reaction from an adult is like fanning the flames of a fire and can be highly reinforcing to students who are deliberately trying to provoke such a response.

Intervention strategies: The intervention will often involve giving the student more control by putting her in charge of some aspects of the classroom environment or of her own situation when she exhibits positive behaviors. At the same time, reduce any control (such as emotional reactions) that the student elicits from adults through misbehavior.

Is the student trying to avoid or escape something?

Avoiding overly difficult or overly simple work. The student may use misbehavior to avoid or escape overly difficult or overly simple work. For example, suppose you set up a round-robin reading activity, with each student reading a paragraph in turn. A student who knows he is a poor reader might misbehave to escape having to read aloud in front of his friends. In other cases, a student might find the assignment extremely dull or simple and misbehave to avoid boredom more than the work itself.

Intervention strategies: Adapt instruction to fit the student's academic abilities. If you know that a certain assignment will be too easy for a student, consider letting that student complete an alternative task instead. For example, if a student hasn't been completing work he finds boring, try to create more interesting assignments while letting him know that occasionally he'll have to do the regular assignment. If the work is too difficult for the student, adapt content to the student's level and provide necessary support.

Avoiding nonpreferred activities and tasks. In this scenario, the student would rather do something other than the assigned task or activity. An example is a very young child who, instead of doing her work, walks around the classroom or does other activities.

Intervention strategies: When a student is seeking different stimuli than the activity provides, the intervention will involve reducing access to outside reinforcers so that the reinforcers inherent in the desired activity are the best and most accessible ones available. It may also involve setting up a procedure for the student to request breaks.

Avoiding peer interactions. Most students go to some lengths to avoid negative, harsh, or embarrassing situations. For example, knowing that the tough kids like to hang out in the restroom, a student might avoid going into the restroom during passing times to escape harassment. At some point during the day, that student will demand to be excused from class or perhaps do something extremely negative to get thrown out of class so she can use the restroom while other students are not present.

Intervention strategies: Try to restructure the student's environment so that exposure to the anxiety-producing stimulus is minimized. Also reduce the ways the student can easily escape unpleasant but necessary situations.

Avoiding adult interactions. Some students avoid interactions with adults they find overly harsh, caustic, or critical. Even if the student isn't truly afraid of a teacher, the prospect of interacting with that teacher may be too much to handle, so the student searches for some escape, such as getting kicked out of class or chronic absenteeism. Because they have had such bad relationships with adults, some students have learned, "If an adult gets close to me, they are likely to abuse or abandon me." So even if the current teacher or teachers are never harsh or abusive, the student still may try offend the adult to drive the adult away—thus avoiding a personal relationship.

Intervention strategies: Gather more information about the dynamic between the student and adult to determine which aspects of the interaction are aversive to the student. Is the teacher overly critical? Do the student and adult engage in frequent power struggles? Does the student feel connected to other adults in the school? Intervention strategies might include encouraging the teacher to increase the ratio of positive interactions with the student, working with the teacher to develop corrections that the student may perceive as less critical, or structuring opportunities at the school for the student to interact with an adult the student likes and feels comfortable around.

BEHAVIOR CHANGES FROM TRAUMA

For some students, changes in behavior and school performance may result from a trauma experience. If you know or suspect that the student has experienced a traumatic event, refer to the trauma-informed intervention recommendations included in Appendix A for a discussion of signs of trauma, the impact of trauma on children, and intervention strategies to consider when working with students who have experienced trauma.

Item 10: Describe student awareness of the problem and motivation to change behavior. Ask whether the teacher (or someone else) has discussed the issue with the student. Does the teacher think the student is aware that the behavior is problematic and unacceptable at school? If yes, how motivated is the student to change the behavior?

Item 11: Has the parent been contacted about this problem? Note how interactions with parents have gone in the past. How has the problem been presented to parents? How have parents reacted to indications that their student needs to change the behavior? What levels of support have parents shown? Include any information that parents may have provided in previous contacts.

Item 12. Is there other relevant information that the teacher would like to share? This is the time to throw any other information on the table for consideration. Does the teacher know anything else that might be useful to consider? Ask if the teacher has heard anything from other adults or students that should be investigated. Find out if the teacher has information about the student's medical history and involvement with outside agencies. At this stage, it is important for all information to be considered and kept in play. As interventions are designed, implemented, redesigned, and reimplemented, any and all information about the student may prove to have value.

> *excerpt p. 4 of 9*
>
> 10. Describe student awareness or the problem and motivation to change behavior.
>   Is the student aware of the problem? Yes / No / Unsure   Notes: _____
>   _____
>   Does the student seem motivated to improve the behavior? Yes / No / Unsure   Notes: _____
>   _____
> 11. Has the parent been contacted about this problem? Yes / No / Unsure   Notes: _____
>   _____
> 12. Is there other relevant information that the teacher would like to share (input from other adults who know the student—e.g., teachers, assistants, specialists, school counselors, information from student records)? _____
>   _____
>   _____

PARENT INVOLVEMENT

Parental contact and involvement are necessary components of intervention planning. All too often, an interventionist brought into planning realizes that the teacher has never interacted with a student's parents. It is essential to try to bring parents in as partners in the earliest stages of the problem-solving process. At this point, a staff member should have already contacted parents and obtained permission for intervention planning. If this has not been done, contact the parents immediately before any further planning or action takes place.

NOTE: If you are conducting this meeting as a background session before using the 25-Minute Planning Process with an intervention team, conclude the meeting with the teacher at this time. Inform the teacher that the team will consider many intervention options at the planning meeting but that the first minutes will be used to review the problem, trends and patterns, and any data that were uncovered in the current meeting. If the intervention planning is conducted one-on-one, continue to the next step of the Teacher Interview.

Step 3: Consider possible solutions and select intervention strategies.

At this point, you will use all of the information gathered so far to consider and select intervention strategies that will form the basis of the student's support plan. Your skill in describing how interventions might actually be implemented and suggesting combinations of interventions that may be particularly powerful for addressing the function of the misbehavior comes into play here. Though you may provide suggestions, the teacher still has a deciding role in what the final intervention plan will include.

Step 3. Consider possible solutions and select intervention strategies.

13. Identify examples of appropriate behavior and/or student strengths to encourage and examples of inappropriate behavior to discourage.

Appropriate Behavior	Inappropriate Behavior

excerpt p. 5 of 9

Item 13. Identify examples of appropriate behavior and/or student strengths to encourage and examples of inappropriate behavior to discourage. Work with the teacher to consider the goal identified in Item 7 and clearly define the positive behaviors that will lead to achieving this goal and the negative behaviors that will detract from it. Identify the line between *appropriate* behaviors that should be encouraged and *inappropriate* behaviors that need to be reduced or eliminated.

Appropriate behaviors include behaviors that are currently in the student's repertoire as well as behaviors that need to be learned. Inappropriate behaviors include a list of specific behaviors that are identified and tied to corrective consequences. For example, if the student is working on managing her own in-class work, appropriate behaviors might include listening to directions, writing down the assignment, getting started right away, and sharpening pencils before class. Inappropriate behaviors might include daydreaming while the teaching is giving directions, not writing down the assignment, and fooling around in the desk rather than getting started on work.

Relative to the goal behavior, you will want only two categories of behavior: *appropriate* and *inappropriate*, with no gray areas in between. For some problems, the line between appropriate and inappropriate behavior is very clear and you will need to spend little time defining it. For example, if a student does not turn in his seatwork, responsible behavior clearly involves handing in the work.

With other problems, the line between desired and undesired behavior is very hard to distinguish, which makes it difficult to teach expectations to the student and difficult for teachers to implement the plan. For such problems, this step of intervention planning is perhaps the most difficult.

Consider a student for whom the focus of the behavior plan is to decrease disrespectful interactions with adults. If you don't define the behaviors that constitute disrespect as well as those considered respectful, the student will move into a hazy, unclear area in which sometimes a behavior is acceptable and sometimes it isn't. Teachers will implement the intervention plan inconsistently if this line is not clearly defined—and inconsistency can sabotage any other progress that is made in the intervention.

Work with the teacher to be very clear about which is which. Explore a variety of scenarios and situations to help clarify. What if you ask the student to do something and he says OK, but his tone of voice is negative or sarcastic? Is that respectful or disrespectful? The teacher should feel prepared to respond to as many of the student's behaviors as possible, quickly identifying them as *appropriate* or *inappropriate*.

See Section 3, Task 5, Step 1 for more guidance in defining limits of behavior.

Item 14. Identify a list of possible strategies to implement to encourage appropriate behavior and discourage inappropriate behavior. In the first part of this item, list all potentially relevant ready-to-use interventions that are already in place in your school (see Section 1, Task 3 for examples of these ready-to-use interventions). Consider the goal you and the teacher outlined in Item 7 and include any and all interventions that might be a good fit in helping the student meet this goal.

---

excerpt p. 5 of 9

14. Identify a list of possible strategies to implement to encourage appropriate behavior and discourage inappropriate behavior.

   a. List ready-to-use interventions that already exist in your building.
   - _____
   - _____
   - _____
   - _____
   - _____

   b. Using the Intervention Decision Guide on the next page, review the list of *presenting behaviors* and check each one that describes the student or context of the problem.

The second part of this item presents the Intervention Decision Guide (full form pages shown on pp. 153–154), which lists possible intervention strategies to consider. Note that your school or district may have its own list of protocols to choose from. The guide suggests one or more intervention strategies for each presenting behavior listed in the first column.

Overview of the Intervention Decision Guide

Assessing Classroom Management Practices and Addressing Academic Needs
The first two interventions listed on the Intervention Decision Guide should be ruled out or tried before considering any other solution. For example, if nine students in a classroom are all having the same problem, start by first looking at the teacher's classroom management approach. If eight out of nine of the students respond well to a change in procedures, designing an individual intervention for the remaining student becomes a more manageable task. Similarly, if a student is failing to meet academic expectations in one or more areas, it is important to examine existing information and identify patterns of academic behavior. Often, what appears to be a behavior problem has an academic component. If you suspect that a student is experiencing an academic problem, concurrently follow your school's protocol for evaluating for and initiating additional academic support services.

Early-Stage Interventions
Consider these strategies next, as they represent some of the most powerful and easy-to-implement interventions. We recommend that all teachers be trained in early-stage intervention strategies (see Section 1, Task 6, Step 1 for guidance). Ideally, some of these strategies should have been attempted with the

Intervention Decision Guide

Presenting behavior	Check if true	Intervention strategy	Date implemented	Effective? (+/−)
More than three students in class misbehave	☐	Assess classroom management practices		
The student has an underlying academic problem	☐	Address academic needs		
The student is not aware of the problem, or no individual supports have been tried yet	☐	Early-stage interventions		
The student doesn't know what is expected or lacks the ability to exhibit the expected behavior	☐	B. Change work requirements D. Change expectations or procedures F. Use precorrections I. Re-teach classroom expectations J. Provide demonstrations and modeling K. Provide positive practice and feedback L. Provide opportunities for verbal practice M. Deliver praise and specific feedback		
Adult attention seems to reinforce misbehavior	☐	G. Increase opportunities to respond M. Deliver praise and specific feedback O. Send positive news home P. Ignore misbehavior W. Increase the frequency of noncontingent positive attention		
Peer attention seems to reinforce misbehavior	☐	A. Change assigned seating Q. Reduce peer attention		
Escape seems to reinforce misbehavior	☐	B. Change work requirements C. Provide breaks D. Change expectations or procedures E. Offer viable choices S. Assign time owed		
Access to tangibles, activities, or privileges seems to reinforce misbehavior	☐	N. Offer rewards V. Revoke a privilege		
Specific consequences for misbehavior are necessary	☐	R. Use gentle verbal reprimands or warnings		
Misbehavior may be positively affected by changes to structural features of the classroom (e.g. classroom layout, schedule)				
The student misbehaves under periods of low supervision or structure				
Previously used consequences for misbehavior don't seem to work, or misbehavior is a firmly established part of the student's behavior				

excerpt pp. 6–7 of 9

Intervention Decision Guide (continued)

Presenting behavior	Check if true	Intervention strategy	Date implemented	Effective? (+/−)
The student acts impulsively or seems to be unaware of engaging in inappropriate behavior	☐	3. Self-Monitoring and Self-Evaluation		
The student has difficulty maintaining emotional control	☐	5. Managing Emotional Escalation		
The student seems anxious, depressed, or withdrawn	☐	6. Supporting Students with Internalizing Challenges		
The student doesn't seem connected to peers or adults at school	☐	W. Increase the frequency of noncontingent positive attention X. Assign a meaningful duty or responsibility at school Y. Encourage and facilitate the student's participation in clubs, after-school activities, and other school events Z. Connect the student with an adult or peer mentor at school		
The student's behavior is so disruptive that the teacher cannot continue	☐	Code Red Situation: Consult school policies for responding to severely disruptive behavior 4. Behavior Emergency Planning U. Assign out-of-class timeout		
The student's behavior is unsafe or dangerous to self or others	☐	Code Red Situation: Consult school policies for responding to unsafe or physically dangerous behavior 4. Behavior Emergency Planning U. Assign out-of-class timeout		

targeted student before the intervention planning meeting was called. However, if early-stage intervention strategies have not yet been implemented, we highly recommended incorporating them into your current planning. If the teacher has already implemented early-stage interventions without seeing any student progress, you can consider trying other strategies, combining strategies, or moving to more specialized and intensive interventions that have not yet been implemented.

Note that procedures for implementing the first three types of intervention strategies listed on the Intervention Decision Guide are described in other Safe & Civil Schools resources, namely *CHAMPS: A Proactive and Positive Approach to Classroom Management* (Sprick, 2009), *Discipline in the Secondary Classroom* (Sprick, 2013), and *Foundations* Module F (Sprick et al., 2014). However, you don't necessarily have to use these resources. Your school or district can use many other available resources on classroom management and academic assistance to help you design these suggested interventions.

Foundational Intervention Strategies
Foundational intervention strategies are designed to be used in accordance with the functional hypothesis you developed to explain why the misbehavior is occurring in the first place. Foundational strategies, listed by letters A–Z, are the basis of your behavior intervention plan and fall under five categories.

- *Antecedent strategies* address events and conditions (e.g., times, places, people, activities) that occur before the student's misbehavior.
- *Teaching strategies* provide the student with positive replacement behaviors for misbehavior.
- *Positive consequence strategies* outline rewards and responses from staff that are intended encourage appropriate behavior and discourage misbehavior.
- *Corrective consequence strategies* are designed to increase the consistency and efficacy of corrective consequences that are implemented when misbehavior occurs.
- *Interactional strategies* are designed to provide students with a high rate of positive interactions and help them feel connected to school.

For minor problems, you might need to include strategies from only one or two categories. For more severe or chronic problems that have not been remedied by initial intervention efforts, you'll likely need to address all categories in your intervention plan. Generally, if you can manipulate something in all five categories, even through relatively minor adjustments, the resulting behavior plan will be much stronger than if you incorporate strategies from only one category. Procedural recommendations for implementing foundational intervention strategies are discussed in Section 3.

Specialized Intervention Strategies
The remaining interventions listed on the Intervention Decision Guide target more severe or ingrained problems. Specialized intervention strategies, listed by numbers 1–6, expand on the foundational intervention strategies presented in this section by packaging together multiple foundational strategies (e.g., behavior contracts that outline both positive and corrective consequences) or

applying foundational strategies to specific types of behavior (i.e., internalizing and mental health issues, unsafe or highly disruptive behavior, and behavior that escalates). Generally, these interventions are designed for students whose behavior problems require a greater level of individualization, resources, or expertise. Intervention specialists such as school psychologists, school counselors, special education teachers, administrators, and anyone involved in an intervention planning team should be well versed in these interventions, but classroom teachers are not likely to be trained in these methods. These interventions will probably be implemented by or with the assistance of an interventionist, not by the classroom teacher alone. Guidelines for using specialized intervention strategies appear in Section 4.

If your district uses other approved interventions, you may wish to bring them to the table for consideration. You will also want to modify the Intervention Decision Guide to reflect your district's list of evidence-based interventions.

With the teacher, review each presenting behavior. Each describes the type of behavior that might be best addressed by the intervention strategies listed in the next column. If a presenting behavior is true for the student, place a check in the second column. Leave the checkbox blank if the statement is false.

Next, review the list of intervention strategies. Procedures and considerations for implementing these intervention strategies appear in Sections 3 and 4. If any of the strategies have already been tried, indicate the approximate date of implementation and degree of effectiveness. If an intervention strategy was successful, or the teacher thinks it might be successful in combination with other strategies, check the second column to include it in your list of intervention strategies to consider.

Marking an intervention strategy as applicable does not mean you will implement it. In some cases, only four strategies may be applicable to the problem, and in other cases you may end up with 15 check marks on the first pass. As a general rule, it is somewhat better to have more applicable strategies because the initial intervention plan will likely include up to three intervention strategies for a combined, multifaceted approach. If the initial intervention strategies fail but nine more are worth trying, you have fallback options. If only three intervention strategies are marked, this puts great pressure on the success of the initial intervention.

Item 15. Select a manageable set of strategies to implement. Consulting your list of potentially relevant ready-to-use interventions and list of checked intervention strategies from the Intervention Decision Guide, select a manageable number of intervention strategies to implement.

The Intervention Plan Summary table (shown on the next page) in Item 15 provides space to detail different components of your intervention plan, organized in approximate order from least to most resource and time intensive. Start by considering foundational and ready-to-use intervention strategies that require few resources before selecting specialized intervention strategies that require more individualization, staffing, materials, and expertise.

Consider each category of foundational strategy (e.g., antecedent, teaching, positive consequence, corrective consequence, and interactional) when designing your intervention plan. While you may not need to include strategies from all categories, making small adjustments to the structure of a classroom, re-teaching expectations, increasing praise,

RECORD KEEPING

Encourage teachers to keep a complete file on any student with whom they attempted an individualized intervention plan—both what worked and what did not. Any subsequent intervention planning will be more efficient because relevant information will already be collected and ready for review. When you design an intervention plan, it is important to capitalize on anything that worked in the past and to avoid interventions that have proven ineffective.

INTERVENTIONS: SUPPORT FOR INDIVIDUAL STUDENTS WITH BEHAVIOR CHALLENGES

excerpt p. 8 of 9

15. Select a manageable set of strategies to implement. Describe how, where, and when strategies will be implemented and the responsibilities of staff members involved.

Intervention Plan Summary

Intervention Strategy Type		Description of Intervention Strategy	Start Date
Ready to Use			
Foundational	Antecedent strategies		
	Teaching strategies		
	Positive consequence strategies		
	Corrective consequence strategies		
	Interactional strategies		
Specialized			

and outlining consistent corrective procedures can go a long way, especially in the early stages of a problem, with a relatively minimal amount of effort and change to the environment. Section 3 provides more detail on these foundational strategies.

If you decide that an existing, ready-to-use intervention is a good fit for the student, list the intervention and describe how often the student will participate, who will be responsible for enrolling and introducing the student to the intervention, and when participation will begin.

Finally, list any specialized intervention strategies to be used and outline details for how these will be implemented. Section 4 offers step-by-step guidance in planning and implementing the specialized strategies.

Considerations in Choosing Intervention Strategies

Selecting appropriate and effective interventions requires a thorough knowledge of the interventions. Interventionists should be familiar with each of the interventions listed on the Intervention Decision Guide as well as any other district-approved interventions, including the ready-to-use interventions in place in your school. This knowledge can be gained by studying this resource and participating in training on all of the interventions. Because the teacher is involved in this planning stage, provide additional explanation about each of the possible interventions as needed. The teacher may also wish to look at the interventions more closely, either by reviewing the Intervention Decision Guide summary or by exploring the corresponding section or chapter in this book.

When selecting interventions to implement, try to balance the following, sometimes competing, considerations:

Make sure the intervention plan is related to the identified goal or desired outcome. When considering an intervention strategy, keep in mind the overall goal of the intervention: What are you trying to achieve through intervention? How will this intervention strategy help achieve this goal? Some interventions may appeal to the teacher, maybe because the teacher is comfortable with the procedures or can implement them with minimal effort, but unless the intervention strategy is likely to produce behavior change, it won't be worthwhile to implement. For example, changing a student's seating arrangement so that she is seated in a separate area of the classroom may help limit the amount of peer attention that she gets from misbehaving. However, if the goal is for the student to learn how to appropriately recruit attention from peers and follow expectations for when interaction with peers is permitted and when it isn't, a singular seat rearrangement isn't likely to teach the student much. Instead, it may be more effective to re-teach expectations, reinforce appropriate peer interactions, and allow the student to choose her seat when she demonstrates that she can follow expectations.

Ensure that the intervention plan incorporates your hypothesis about the function of the misbehavior. Function-based intervention plans are more effective in reducing problem behaviors than plans designed without considering behavior function (Ingram, Lewis-Palmer, & Sugai, 2005). Focus on the variables you identified as being most important according to your hypothesis regarding the function of the misbehavior. For example, if the student's problem is awareness, make sure that your plan incorporates components that teach expectations and increase awareness. After thinking about the possible function of the student's misbehavior, take care to avoid reinforcing the misbehavior—your planned response should not feed into the behavior. For example, if the student's misbehavior serves to gain attention, keep your corrections brief and detached—you don't want to give the misbehaving student any more attention than necessary.

Ensure that the intervention seems manageable for the teacher. Even the most cooperative teachers are likely to be overwhelmed by interventions that are too difficult to manage (Elliott & Dweck, 1988; Perepletchikova & Kazdin, 2005). Classroom teachers cannot implement an intervention that makes it impossible to meet the needs of other students or the normal responsibilities of teaching. Furthermore, the ability of teachers to implement intervention strategies will vary greatly. In some cases, the teacher will perceive an intervention as easy to implement. Consider using cueing to stop a student's whistling during class. This intervention involves a relatively simple set of procedures, but the teacher attention required to consistently use this strategy may not be feasible in certain situations. When relying on cues to interrupt the progression of a tantrum, the teacher might think, "To prevent Eric from a full-blown tantrum, I need to catch his fidgeting symptoms early on. I honestly don't think I could monitor and cue him in time without disrupting my ability to teach." When considering an intervention, think about how intrusive the intervention will be (i.e., how much teacher time and effort will be required). If an intervention seems unwieldy or would put undue stress on the teacher, it would not be wise to use it.

Assess the teacher's willingness and readiness to work on an intervention. Try to assess how frustrated the teacher is with the student and the problem situation. The greater the degree of teacher frustration, the more important it is to look for solutions that do not require too much work from the teacher. Similarly, if the teacher seems resistant to an intervention for any reason, it is probably better to look for other options. Without high levels of classroom support, interventions are not likely to be implemented consistently (Finn & Sladeczek, 2001; Gunter & Denny, 1996). At this stage in the problem-solving process, offer a lot of decision-making power to the teacher. While you will guide the decisions, you are essentially saying to the teacher, "This is your intervention. I will help and guide you, but you will be living with it on a daily basis, so your input is essential."

Determine the amount of support available to the teacher. Given the right resources, interventions that seem unmanageable for the teacher to implement may, in fact, be possible. One way to avoid overburdening a classroom teacher is to have an administrator, special education teacher, school counselor, school psychologist, well-trained teacher assistant, or other interventionist implement highly structured interventions. For example, if the teacher cannot manage cueing Eric's fidgety symptoms but a classroom aide is scheduled in the room for 90 minutes a day, the aide might be assigned to monitor the student and cue him when he first shows escalating behaviors. Of course, this covers only the 90 minutes, but if the intervention shows dramatic progress, the teacher may see that the cueing process is not as difficult to manage as first assumed. Likewise, if teaching a particular skill (e.g., calming down when angry) seems promising but is too time consuming for the teacher to take on, you might ask the school counselor to conduct daily lessons.

Assess the degree of student responsibility and motivation. Select interventions that encourage the student to assume the greatest amount of responsibility for change, but make sure that these interventions provide enough support and structure for success. Interventions that require students to be more independent (e.g., self-monitoring) take less time to set up, implement, and monitor. Further, because students are required to take more responsibility, they are more likely to attribute success to their own abilities rather than feeling that adults made them change (Menzies, Lane, & Lee, 2009). Use more independent interventions for relatively mild behaviors (i.e., ones that do not require a large change in behavior from the student), with more mature students, and for behaviors the student is motivated to change. Other interventions provide high degrees of structure and adult support to ensure student success. They tend to require more effort and support from teachers and other involved adults. More time is needed to set up, implement, and monitor such interventions. However, because of the structure and support provided, the probability of success is higher, especially with less mature or more troubled students. These interventions are appropriate for students who have a long history of problem behavior or who have fairly severe problems that are likely to be resistant to change.

Step 4: Collect data to monitor progress.

Generally, at this point, teachers will be the primary staff responsible for data collection. Try not to overburden them when selecting data collection procedures. Make sure the data collection plan you choose is feasible and acceptable to the teacher. In cases when other staff will be responsible for data collection (e.g., ready-to-use intervention coordinator, facilitator of a specialized intervention), also consider procedures that maximize the ease with which data are collected, summarized, and shared with others.

Step 4. Collect data to monitor progress.

16. Identify data that will be used to track progress toward the goal, including who will collect data and how.

17. Identify follow-up date(s) to check in about progress:

18. Identify at least two ways to determine whether the plan is working at the next follow-up meeting.

19. Describe plans to monitor and evaluate implementation fidelity.

excerpt p. 9 of 9

Item 16. Identify data that will be used to track progress toward the goal, including who will collect data and how. Review the goal that was developed in Item 7 and determine how data will be collected and recorded to track the intervention plan's progress. Identify at least one source of objective data to collect for each goal behavior. You may simply be able to continue or modify monitoring procedures that are already in place, or you may need to develop a new system.

Objective data collection might include any of these methods.

a. *Existing data and work products.* When the goal of an intervention is to increase the quality or quantity of a student's work, the evaluation procedures should consider the student's work products. Data sources may include the percentage of assignments completed, test scores, grades, and number of written words in a journal. In most cases, this method does not require additional work for teachers, only periodic analysis of data already collected. A teacher's grade book may provide a major source of data on any problem that involves work products.

b. *Frequency data.* During observation, a count is taken whenever the student engages in a particular behavior (e.g., the number of times the student gets out of her seat in a day or the number of times the student interacts disrespectfully with the teacher). The teacher might make a simple tally of the number of times the student engages in the behavior. To take frequency data, for example, the teacher might carry a small index card in a pocket. Whenever the student engages in the targeted behavior, the teacher marks a tally on the card. If the student engages in tantrums, the teacher might keep a record on a calendar of the number of tantrums per day.

c. *Duration data.* Evaluation information might also include the amount of time a student engages in a particular behavior, or a duration count. For example, if a student engages in tantrums, the teacher might record the number of tantrums (a frequency count) and use a stopwatch to track the amount of time the student spent tantruming (a duration count). At the end of the day, the teacher has a record of the amount of time the student spent in temper tantrums. For example, Joey had three tantrums today for a total of 58 minutes.

d. *Latency data.* Sometimes it is appropriate to track latency: how much time it takes for a particular behavior to begin after a stimulus occurs. For example, if a student has trouble following the teacher's directions, it may be appropriate to record the length of time between when the instruction was given and when the student begins to comply.

e. *Interval recording.* Interval recording involves recording whether the behavior occurs during a particular time interval. This is typically conducted by an external observer and requires a timing device. Interval recording is an alternative way of measuring the duration of behavior and can be useful when target behaviors are not easily counted (e.g., behavior occurs at high rates or it is difficult to tell exactly when behavior begins or ends).

f. *Rating scales.* Ratings on the quality of student behavior can provide valuable information. Although this method has a subjective aspect, rating scales are usually accompanied by criteria for judging student behavior, which makes the evaluation more specific and clear. For example, for a student who is learning to follow directions, you may rate his behavior on a three-point scale, where 2 = followed all directions pleasantly and cooperatively, 1 = followed some directions pleasantly and cooperatively, and 0 = failed to follow directions and was uncooperative.

g. *Data from self-monitoring or reinforcement systems.* If your intervention plan will include self-monitoring or a reinforcement system, the recording forms used in these strategies offer a built-in source of data that can provide information about the effectiveness of the intervention. For example, initial data may show that the student blurted out answers 10 times during a half-hour discussion and never raised his hand. After the student used self-monitoring forms for 2 weeks, the data show that he raised his hand 50% of the time and blurted out responses 50% of the time. Although this is not perfect, the student is clearly making progress. (More information about how to set up and use data from a self-monitoring intervention or structured reinforcement system can be found in the chapters on these topics in Section 4).

Section 3, Task 8 provides a more detailed description of the options presented above, as well as sample forms to use for collecting data.

Item 17. Identify follow-up date(s) to check in about progress. Follow-up involves regular meetings with the teacher, the student, and the family to review data being collected to determine if the situation is getting better, staying the same, or getting worse. Schedule the first follow-up meeting for about two weeks after implementation is scheduled to begin. While you may schedule only one or two follow-up meetings at this point, inform the teacher that you plan to continue the intervention process until the student is no longer having problems and that the people involved will do everything they can to reduce the possibility that the student will fall through the cracks.

Item 18. Identify at least two ways to determine whether the plan is working at the next follow-up meeting. Ahead of your scheduled follow-up meeting, work with the teacher to determine guidelines for judging the effectiveness of your intervention plan. This item expands on the goal you defined in Item 7 and the data collection procedures you outlined in Item 16. Here, you'll consider how to specifically interpret your data to evaluate the plan's effectiveness. In other words, you'll create decision rules that indicate whether the student has made sufficient progress under the plan.

When developing decision rules, be as specific as possible. Instead of saying, "The plan is working if the frequency of Marco's tantrums has decreased," consider using numbers and timelines to clearly define how much of a decrease will be considered sufficient. For example: "After 2 weeks of implementation, the plan is working if Marco tantrums no more than twice per week and if his tantrums last for less than 5 minutes."

To effectively monitor intervention plans and avoid misperceptions in the data, two independent means of evaluating progress are recommended. These can include any of the objective data sources that you selected in Item 16 as well as other sources, such as:

- *Observations.* You might ask if the teacher would be open to you or another staff member conducting periodic observations of the student. Observations can yield important information that can help evaluate the effectiveness of an intervention. An outside observer might formally collect frequency, duration, or latency data to supplement or validate data already being collected by the teacher, or informally record notes and impressions about what's going on in the classroom, how the student is behaving, and whether the situation has changed since the intervention plan took effect. To determine progress, schedule observations to take place before the intervention plan begins and then periodically after its implementation. To increase the usability of data collected by outside observers, schedule observations for times when the student has the greatest difficulty and conduct follow-up observations during the same time periods and for the same length of time.
- *Subjective perceptions.* A supplemental method of evaluating the effectiveness of an intervention is to gather subjective impressions from the teachers, parents, and students involved. Is the situation better, the same, or worse? This is the easiest and least time-consuming evaluation procedure. Although subjective perceptions alone are not sufficiently reliable, a clear picture of the intervention's effectiveness generally emerges when they are used in conjunction with another evaluation procedure. If you use subjective impressions as a measure of effectiveness, the plan should specify how, when, and from whom opinions about student progress will be solicited. Anecdotal records or interviews can provide subjective evaluations. For example, the interventionist might conference with the teacher and student after 2, 4, and 6 weeks of implementation to determine how the intervention is working.

Item 19. Describe plans to monitor and evaluate implementation fidelity. Ensuring fidelity includes securing adequate resources, staffing, and training to properly implement the plan and monitoring whether core components of the intervention plan are actually being implemented (Gresham et al., 2000). Think about how to establish accountability and make sure that the plan is implemented as designed. Discuss the purpose of monitoring fidelity with the teacher. Provide assurances that fidelity monitoring is designed to assess the plan's effectiveness and appropriateness, and will not be used to evaluate or check up on the teacher. Fidelity monitoring might include having the teacher use a self-assessment checklist when providing lessons, or scheduling an external observation of the teacher's use of praise with the student. In your plans, define what "good" fidelity looks like and outline a schedule for monitoring fidelity. See Section 3, Task 9 for more in-depth recommendations and options for monitoring implementation fidelity.

At this point, you will conclude the interview. Ask if the teacher has any questions or could use additional support or resources. Also plan to prepare and share with relevant team members a written summary of the intervention plan that outlines each person's responsibilities. Conclude the meeting with words of encouragement and thank the teacher for taking the time to participate.

Check in after the first day or two of implementation to discuss progress and anything that was not anticipated. Any glitches in the plan or procedures that need clarification can be taken care of quickly. If necessary, schedule observations or assistance before the first scheduled follow-up meeting.

Step 5: Evaluate whether supports are working.

In all subsequent follow-up meetings, the interventionist and the teacher will evaluate progress and make modifications to the plan as needed. As a general rule, the intervention plan should be implemented for at least 2 weeks before your initial follow-up meeting. If the student is absent during part of that time, continue the plan for a longer period.

Item 20. Provide date and summary of follow-up meetings. Record the date of your follow-up meeting and provide a summary of the data collected to date, any changes made to the plan, and any follow-up actions that are needed moving forward. At these meetings, make a clear determination: Should the intervention be maintained, modified, replaced, or faded? See "Guidelines for Maintaining, Modifying, Replacing, and Fading Plans" for more details.

Step 5. Evaluate whether supports are working.

excerpt p. 9 of 9

20. Provide date and summary of follow-up meetings. Describe any modifications that are made to the intervention plan.

Date _____ Summary:

Date _____ Summary:

Date _____ Summary:

GUIDELINES FOR MAINTAINING, MODIFYING, REPLACING, AND FADING PLANS

If the student is making good progress: Maintain the intervention plan. If the student is steadily progressing toward the goal, the plan should be maintained until the student demonstrates continuous and consistent success in achieving the goal. You want to ensure that the student experiences a period of success long enough to make sure that more natural reinforcers in the setting (e.g., grades, praise, increased attention) are likely to maintain the behavior without additional intervention supports. This period may be a few weeks, or it may be a couple of months or even the rest of the school year.

If progress is slow or comes to a halt: Modify the plan to provide more support. Because intervention planning involves trial and error, it may become apparent that the student needs more assistance. When you make changes to the plan, it is important to note the planned changes and the date they will begin. This will allow you to make an objective decision about the effectiveness of the modified intervention.

If the student makes no progress or the problem gets worse: Assess fidelity or develop a new intervention plan. When a student shows no progress over the course of 2 weeks, the plan may need to be redesigned. However, before abandoning a plan, look carefully at the data and assess fidelity of implementation. If a student has been making good progress but blows it one day, a teacher may feel the student hasn't made any progress at all, when in fact the objective data show the student has been making progress on most days. Similarly, if no progress has been made but you're not sure whether strategies were actually implemented, it's important to assess implementation fidelity and follow-up to ensure that the plan is actually implemented as intended before you design a new plan. Evaluation information and the support of the interventionist can help the teacher and student stay on course.

If the student is consistently achieving the goal and there is a high probability that the student can maintain success: Fade the intervention. Fading is accomplished by gradually providing less structure and support. Some intervention plans are automatically faded as the student becomes successful. For example, cueing may be used less and less as a student demonstrates success on her own. Eventually, the cueing can stop completely. With a student whose language skills are fairly sophisticated, the student can be part of the process of deciding whether the intervention can be faded successfully.

Summary of the Teacher Interview

Although the Teacher Interview can serve as a rudimentary FBA, it is primarily a means of gathering as much information as possible from the most direct source and using it to form an initial intervention plan. The teacher interacts with the student day after day. The teacher is the one who is experiencing the problem and is the one who will carry out the initial intervention. The teacher's information, input, buy-in, and full participation are crucial to the success of any intervention in the classroom (Kratochwill et al., 2002; Roach & Elliott, 2008). The Teacher Interview also serves as a guide to brainstorming everything that is known about the student. At this early point, all information is valuable and needs to be documented in a single place so that it stays in play throughout the intervention process.

INTERVENTIONS: SUPPORT FOR INDIVIDUAL STUDENTS WITH BEHAVIOR CHALLENGES

REPRODUCIBLE 2.2 *Teacher Interview (1 of 9)*

Teacher Interview

Student _____ Age ____ Grade ____ Date _____

Teacher _____ Support Coordinator/Interviewer _____

Other participants _____

Step 1. Define the problem.

1. Describe the problem or reason for referral:

2. How often do the problems occur? How long does the behavior last? How intense is the problem?

3. **Code Red Situations:** Is the student's behavior unsafe or severely disruptive to the classroom? Yes / No
   If yes, consult your school's protocol for handling severely disruptive or dangerous behavior.

4. What are the student's strengths?

5. List interventions tried in the Intervention History table on the next two pages.

6. Prioritize 1–2 major behaviors that are most problematic or urgent:

   ☐ Physical aggression   ☐ Anxiety   ☐ Off task
   ☐ Self-injury   ☐ Disruption   ☐ Depression, withdrawal
   ☐ Peer conflict   ☐ Absenteeism   ☐ Inappropriate language
   ☐ Damage to property   ☐ Bullying others   ☐ Tardiness
   ☐ Noncompliance   ☐ Other: _____   ☐ Other: _____

7. Narrow the scope of the problem and identify a goal for improvement.

REPRODUCIBLE 2.2 *Teacher Interview (2 of 9)*

Teacher Interview

Intervention History

Intervention/Strategy	Were data collected?	How effective was the intervention/strategy at addressing problem behavior?
	☐ Yes / ☐ No Describe:	☐ Not at all / ☐ Somewhat / ☐ Very Notes:
	☐ Yes / ☐ No Describe:	☐ Not at all / ☐ Somewhat / ☐ Very Notes:
	☐ Yes / ☐ No Describe:	☐ Not at all / ☐ Somewhat / ☐ Very Notes:
	☐ Yes / ☐ No Describe:	☐ Not at all / ☐ Somewhat / ☐ Very Notes:
	☐ Yes / ☐ No Describe:	☐ Not at all / ☐ Somewhat / ☐ Very Notes:

REPRODUCIBLE 2.2 *Teacher Interview (3 of 9)*

Teacher Interview

Intervention/Strategy	Were data collected?	How effective was the intervention/strategy at addressing problem behavior?
	☐ Yes / ☐ No Describe:	☐ Not at all / ☐ Somewhat / ☐ Very Notes:
	☐ Yes / ☐ No Describe:	☐ Not at all / ☐ Somewhat / ☐ Very Notes:
	☐ Yes / ☐ No Describe:	☐ Not at all / ☐ Somewhat / ☐ Very Notes:
	☐ Yes / ☐ No Describe:	☐ Not at all / ☐ Somewhat / ☐ Very Notes:
	☐ Yes / ☐ No Describe:	☐ Not at all / ☐ Somewhat / ☐ Very Notes:

REPRODUCIBLE 2.2 *Teacher Interview (4 of 9)*

Teacher Interview

Step 2. Analyze the problem. — 5 minutes

8. Identify relevant triggers (antecedents) and conditions (setting events) that predict when behavior is likely to occur. Are there specific situations that seem to set off the problem behavior?

    Where do the problems tend to occur?

    When do the problems tend to occur?

    Possible Antecedents and Setting Events:

    - ☐ Unstructured time
    - ☐ Whole group instruction
    - ☐ Small group activities
    - ☐ Independent work
    - ☐ Transitions
    - ☐ Change in routine
    - ☐ Specific tasks: _____

    - ☐ Peers present
    - ☐ Peer conflict
    - ☐ After adult correction or reprimands
    - ☐ Corrective consequence or loss of privilege
    - ☐ Other: _____

    - ☐ Hunger
    - ☐ Conflict or stressors at home
    - ☐ Illness, pain, discomfort
    - ☐ Missed medications
    - ☐ Lack of sleep

9. Identify the function of the behavior, or the consequences that seem to be maintaining or reinforcing problem behavior. What typically happens right after the problem behavior occurs? What do you do? What do other students do?

    Are there certain situations or activities that the student is motivated to avoid or escape?

    Are there certain privileges or items that the student is motivated to obtain through problem behavior?

    Does the student lack certain skills or an awareness of their behavior that may be contributing to the problem?

    Hypothesized function(s):

    Deficits
    - ☐ Lacking awareness
    - ☐ Lacking ability:
        - ☐ Physical/Neurological
        - ☐ Academic
        - ☐ Social/Emotional

    Trying to Get Something
    - ☐ Seeking adult attention
    - ☐ Seeking peer attention
    - ☐ Seeking access to activities
    - ☐ Seeking power or control

    Trying to Avoid Something
    - ☐ Avoiding overly difficult or overly simple work
    - ☐ Avoiding nonpreferred activities and tasks
    - ☐ Avoiding peer interactions
    - ☐ Avoiding adult interactions

10. Describe student awareness or the problem and motivation to change behavior.

    Is the student aware of the problem? Yes / No / Unsure   Notes: _____

    Does the student seem motivated to improve the behavior? Yes / No / Unsure   Notes: _____

11. Has the parent been contacted about this problem? Yes / No / Unsure   Notes: _____

12. Is there other relevant information that the teacher would like to share (input from other adults who know the student—e.g., teachers, assistants, specialists, school counselors, information from student records)? _____

REPRODUCIBLE 2.2 *Teacher Interview (5 of 9)*

Teacher Interview

Step 3. Consider possible solutions and select intervention strategies.

13. Identify examples of appropriate behavior and/or student strengths to encourage and examples of inappropriate behavior to discourage.

Appropriate Behavior	Inappropriate Behavior

14. Identify a list of possible strategies to implement to encourage appropriate behavior and discourage inappropriate behavior.

   a. List ready-to-use interventions that already exist in your building.

   - _____
   - _____
   - _____
   - _____
   - _____

   b. Using the Intervention Decision Guide on the next page, review the list of *presenting behaviors* and check each one that describes the student or context of the problem.

REPRODUCIBLE 2.2 *Teacher Interview (6 of 9)*

Teacher Interview

Intervention Decision Guide

Presenting behavior	Check if true	Intervention strategy	Date implemented	Effective? (+/−)
More than three students in class misbehave	☐	Assess classroom management practices		
The student has an underlying academic problem	☐	Address academic needs		
The student is not aware of the problem, or no individual supports have been tried yet	☐	Early-stage interventions		
The student doesn't know what is expected or lacks the ability to exhibit the expected behavior	☐	B. Change work requirements D. Change expectations or procedures F. Use precorrections I. Re-teach classroom expectations J. Provide demonstrations and modeling K. Provide positive practice and feedback L. Provide opportunities for verbal practice M. Deliver praise and specific feedback		
Adult attention seems to reinforce misbehavior	☐	G. Increase opportunities to respond M. Deliver praise and specific feedback O. Send positive news home P. Ignore misbehavior W. Increase the frequency of noncontingent positive attention		
Peer attention seems to reinforce misbehavior	☐	A. Change assigned seating Q. Reduce peer attention		
Escape seems to reinforce misbehavior	☐	B. Change work requirements C. Provide breaks D. Change expectations or procedures E. Offer viable choices S. Assign time owed		
Access to tangibles, activities, or privileges seems to reinforce misbehavior	☐	N. Offer rewards V. Revoke a privilege		
Specific consequences for misbehavior are necessary	☐	R. Use gentle verbal reprimands or warnings S. Assign time owed T. Assign in-class timeout V. Revoke a privilege		
Misbehavior may be positively affected by changes to structural features of the classroom (e.g. classroom layout, schedule)	☐	A. Change assigned seating B. Change work requirements D. Change expectations or procedures		
The student misbehaves under periods of low supervision or structure	☐	D. Change expectations or procedures H. Increase monitoring and supervision		
Previously used consequences for misbehavior don't seem to work, or misbehavior is a firmly established part of the student's behavior	☐	1. Behavioral Contracting 2. Structured Reinforcement		

REPRODUCIBLE 2.2 *Teacher Interview (7 of 9)*

Teacher Interview

Intervention Decision Guide (continued)

Presenting behavior	Check if true	Intervention strategy	Date implemented	Effective? (+/−)
The student acts impulsively or seems to be unaware of engaging in inappropriate behavior	☐	3. Self-Monitoring and Self-Evaluation		
The student has difficulty maintaining emotional control	☐	5. Managing Emotional Escalation		
The student seems anxious, depressed, or withdrawn	☐	6. Supporting Students with Internalizing Challenges		
The student doesn't seem connected to peers or adults at school	☐	W. Increase the frequency of noncontingent positive attention X. Assign a meaningful duty or responsibility at school Y. Encourage and facilitate the student's participation in clubs, after-school activities, and other school events Z. Connect the student with an adult or peer mentor at school		
The student's behavior is so disruptive that the teacher cannot continue	☐	Code Red Situation: Consult school policies for responding to severely disruptive behavior 4. Behavior Emergency Planning U. Assign out-of-class timeout		
The student's behavior is unsafe or dangerous to self or others	☐	Code Red Situation: Consult school policies for responding to unsafe or physically dangerous behavior 4. Behavior Emergency Planning U. Assign out-of-class timeout		

Interventions © 2019 Ancora Publishing

REPRODUCIBLE 2.2 *Teacher Interview (8 of 9)*

Teacher Interview

15. Select a manageable set of strategies to implement. Describe how, where, and when strategies will be implemented and the responsibilities of staff members involved.

Intervention Plan Summary

Intervention Strategy Type		Description of Intervention Strategy	Start Date
Ready to Use			
Foundational	Antecedent strategies		
	Teaching strategies		
	Positive consequence strategies		
	Corrective consequence strategies		
	Interactional strategies		
Specialized			

REPRODUCIBLE 2.2 *Teacher Interview (9 of 9)*

Teacher Interview

Step 4. Collect data to monitor progress.

16. Identify data that will be used to track progress toward the goal, including who will collect data and how.

17. Identify follow-up date(s) to check in about progress:

18. Identify at least two ways to determine whether the plan is working at the next follow-up meeting.

19. Describe plans to monitor and evaluate implementation fidelity.

Step 5. Evaluate whether supports are working.

20. Provide date and summary of follow-up meetings. Describe any modifications that are made to the intervention plan.

Date _____ Summary:

Date _____ Summary:

Date _____ Summary:

The 25-Minute Planning Process

At this stage, the support coordinator works in collaboration with the problem-solving team in place within your school. The 25-Minute Planning Process is designed to guide a problem-solving team through developing a worthwhile plan of action in less than half an hour.

The 25-Minute Planning Process may be appropriate under the following conditions:

- More information is needed about the student and the context of the problem in order to proceed with identifying appropriate supports.
- No appropriate ready-to-use interventions are available in your building, or the problem is complex enough to warrant a more detailed intervention plan that incorporates strategies outside of your menu of ready-to-use interventions.
- Interventions have been in place for 2 weeks or more, but the student has not shown sufficient improvement.

Although collaborative problem-solving is often more effective than individual planning, it does have certain drawbacks when not conducted in a structured fashion. The more people involved in the meeting, the more ideas and perspectives will be gained. The concern, however, is that the meeting will become longer and longer as individuals get stuck at certain points in planning. The 25-Minute Planning Process attempts to correct some of these common pitfalls associated with team-based problem solving:

- *Too much time spent on problem admiring, not problem solving.* Team meetings can easily turn into collective gripe sessions in which the majority of planning time is spent venting and complaining about a student or a student's family. These comments can push the meeting to an unnecessary length. There is a point in any planning meeting when it is necessary to say, "Now we know the problems, so what are we going to do about them?" This is significantly easier to do with a predetermined structure and time limits.
- *A focus on reactive consequences rather than proactive procedures.* The meeting's focus may become a discussion of consequences, cycling through menus of corrections that are probably not powerful enough to create lasting change. Members of planning teams often fall into the pattern of "We can try this, but he doesn't care about that," or "We might try this, but it probably won't work because he gets a lot worse punishment at home." The problem with these conversations is that correction is weak in the spectrum of intervention effectiveness. At best, correction will produce a momentary interruption in negative behavior. But used alone, it will probably not bring relief from ingrained misbehaviors or yield long-term success (Bambara & Kern, 2005; Scheuermann & Hall, 2008). To counter this pitfall, the 25-Minute Planning Process directs intervention meeting time toward creating proactive plans and allots only a small amount of time for corrective consequences.
- *A meeting that goes on and on.* Another risk of collaborative problem-solving is that the meeting will stretch on for hours because of members' excitement and enthusiasm about creating a successful intervention. It is true that an intervention plan will be stronger after 90 minutes of discussion than it will be after 25. However, in the early stages of a problem, long planning meetings that detract from busy

teachers' prep, grading, or personal time can leave teachers feeling resentment toward the student who took away important minutes of the day. Long meetings will probably also leave members feeling like they have *the* plan rather than *a* plan. The sense of finality that may follow a long, open-ended meeting leaves little hope for other solutions to follow. Although a 25-minute plan may be flawed, the probability that members will be willing to try other options is much greater. Therefore, in the early stages of intervention planning, team members should set finite time limits for each stage of the process. At the end of a meeting, it's OK if the perception is this: *We came up with a solution. It's not perfect, but it's worth a try.*

By setting time limits, the 25-Minute Planning Process creates an efficient team-based problem-solving structure to start with. If plans from the 25-minute meeting prove to be ineffective at solving the problem, the team can follow up with a longer and more intensive process, such as the Multidisciplinary Team Planning Process (discussed later in this section). However, if every problem were to be worked on with that level of intensity, there would likely be long lists of problems waiting to be addressed.

The 25-Minute Planning Process may be used:

- *To match the student with an existing ready-to-use intervention or to develop an intervention plan:* If a problem has been referred to your intervention team, you can use this process as the first step in dealing with problems. By identifying situations that predict when the problem behavior will occur and generating an initial hypothesis about why the behavior is occurring, the team can identify an existing ready-to-use intervention that may be a good fit for the student or other intervention strategies to put into place. The teacher or teachers should be invited to take part in the 25-Minute Planning Process to provide information for Steps 1 and 2 of the problem-solving process and offer input into the intervention design.
- *In conjunction with the Teacher Interview:* The Teacher Interview is used for Steps 1 and 2 of the problem-solving model to gather information about the student and the problem, and the 25-Minute Planning Process is used for Steps 3 through 5 to guide team-based intervention design and planning.
- *After the Teacher Interview has been completed:* If an initial intervention has been designed and implemented as a result of the Teacher Interview but the student's behavior hasn't improved, use the 25-Minute Planning Process to make adjustments to the original intervention plan.

Guidelines for Conducting the 25-Minute Planning Process

To ensure that problem-solving meetings are effective and efficient, follow these guidelines.

Establish ground rules for meetings. Set ground rules with the planning team, either in advance of the meeting or immediately before discussion begins. Ground rules establish expectations for the team's behavior during the process. Nothing is more discouraging to a team than meetings that chronically start late, end after the announced time, and turn into gripe sessions rather than productive problem-solving sessions. Ground rules can help ensure that everyone collaborates, listens to each other, accepts and acknowledges different points of view, and stays positive. Ground rules can also give teachers the

---

PLANNING MEETING

You will need to make a decision about which staff members to invite to participate in the problem-solving process. If you know the problem happens only during one class or in a specific school setting, include the teacher of that class or the staff member in charge of supervising the targeted setting in the 25-Minute Planning Process meeting. If you are unsure whether the problem occurs across periods or settings, distribute the Student Status Report (Reproducible 2.1, p. 117) to all of the student's teachers. Use this information to determine whether the focus of the intervention should involve one or more teachers and invite these teachers to participate in the 25-Minute Planning Process meeting.

sense that the group is truly focused on helping them find a way to help the student be more successful.

We suggest you develop ground rules as a team and review them often, especially at the start of the school year. Also post them in the meeting room. Set the expectation that team members will acknowledge behaviors that violate the rules. See Figure 2.2 for a sample set of ground rules. Ground rules should cover the following topics:

- Attendance
- Punctuality
- Listening to each other and avoiding side conversations
- Team members can disagree, but must be respectful
- Confidentiality
- Making the teacher feel welcome and an important contributor to the process
- Active participation by all team members

FIGURE 2.2 *Sample Ground Rules for Meetings*

1. Everyone arrives on time.
2. Five members must be present to hold a meeting.
3. We listen while others talk.
4. What is said at the meeting stays within the team.
5. Everyone participates.
6. We stick to the agenda and the timelines.
7. We make the referring teacher and parent feel welcomed and important.

Determine time limits. Decide in advance whether the planning team will use time limits in the meeting. Although not essential, time limits help keep the meeting productive and a reasonable length. Time limits may feel oppressive at first, so you may wish to set a longer time limit, such as 50 minutes total, for the first one or two times your team implements this process. Then, for the next couple of cases, make it a 35-minute process. Only after becoming fully familiar with how the process works would you adhere to the 25-minute limit. This takes a lot of pressure off participants while they learn the process. Also, any time team members adequately complete a step in less than the allotted time, they can move immediately to the next step. For example, if they are scheduled for a 35-minute process but two of the steps go very smoothly, they may be done in 30 minutes. This would indicate that the team is getting close to achieving the fluency needed to operate within the 25-minute limit. On the next page, see Figure 2.3, Time Breakdown for Planning Meeting, for how to structure each step for meetings of different lengths.

FIGURE 2.3 *Time Breakdown for Planning Meeting*

Steps	Minutes		
Step 1: Define the problem.	5	5	10
Step 2: Analyze the problem.	5	10	10
Step 3: Consider possible solutions and select intervention strategies.	10	15	20
Step 4: Collect data to monitor progress.	5	5	10
Total >	25	35	50

When possible, provide participants the option of following the agenda in the 25-minute period or proceeding without time limits. Without time limits, the meeting will be more casual and responsive to the needs of participants, but it is likely to last much longer. If participants decide to stay within the time limits, the meeting will move very efficiently. However, if the planning format hasn't been jointly agreed on in advance, staff or family members may feel rushed into accepting an intervention plan.

Assign job roles. Clearly defining team roles helps ensure an effective and efficient team planning process. Include a list of assigned jobs in the written record of the referral/planning process and regularly rotate jobs so that each member has an opportunity to become skilled in different roles and does not get burned out on any one role.

- *Team Leader:* Assign one person the role of team leader. The key task for the team leader is to make sure all members are actively involved, on task, and working. The team leader works to keep the agenda moving and participants on track in each step of the process. If conversation begins to stray from the topic at hand or participants begin to cycle on a subject, the team leader should gently prompt the group to return to the designated step. Other responsibilities of this role may include receiving problem-solving referrals, developing the meeting agenda, and maintaining a file of completed forms and meeting notes for every student referred to the team. In some schools, the problem-solving team leader may also oversee the support coordinator program and may take on responsibilities for reviewing red-flag indicators, universal behavior screening results, and teacher referrals and assigning support coordinators to students identified as at risk. See Section 1, Task 4 (p. 45) for additional considerations regarding a support coordinator program.

  Some teams find it helpful to have co-leaders. Splitting the leadership responsibilities between two members prevents one person from being overwhelmed. It also allows one leader to conduct a meeting if the other leader happens to be the support coordinator for the student or cannot attend a meeting.

- *Timekeeper:* If you will keep time limits, designate one person as timekeeper. This person's responsibility is to use a watch, kitchen timer, or computer timer to remind team members how much time is left in a specific part of the meeting (problem analysis, for example). The timekeeper's role is critical in ensuring that the meeting proceeds efficiently from step to step.

- *Recorder:* The recorder takes notes on all parts of the discussion and completes the team's official copy of the problem-solving form. When designating a recorder, consider the person's ability to multitask. The recorder should be able to take notes and participate at the same time, because the team will want to benefit from

every member's expertise. This person should not be the support coordinator or the referring teacher. These individuals need to be free to think, listen, talk, and participate without having to concentrate on taking notes.
- *Mediator:* The mediator should have excellent interpersonal skills and be sensitive to people's feelings and emotions. This job entails ensuring that team members work together, support each other, and stay positive and proactive throughout the process. Emotions may sometimes run high during meetings, and the mediator's role is to watch for body language and facial expressions that indicate a participant feels alienated from or unhappy with the process. The mediator then tries to bring that person back into the process. For example, if a parent suddenly sits back with arms crossed, the mediator might say something like, "I think Mr. Jones has some concerns about the way we're describing Sam's behaviors. Let's see if we can clarify and restate our description."

Make sure that team members are familiar with the entire range of behavior intervention strategies available in the building. These include classroom management and early-stage intervention strategies as well as ready-to-use, foundational, and specialized intervention strategies. If the school uses a specific intervention program or set of strategies, the team can divide up the interventions so that each person is responsible for knowing only a portion of the body of knowledge in depth. However, everyone on the team should be somewhat familiar with the purpose and general implementation procedures for all possible intervention strategies.

Finally, consider incorporating these additional suggestions for ensuring effective and efficient meetings:

- Have comfortable chairs and a large table with plenty of space for writing.
- Ensure privacy and confidentiality—close the door.
- A wall clock will help everyone stick to time limits.
- Use a computer with a monitor that everyone can easily see. As the recorder fills in the problem-solving form, everyone can read it.
- Have the support coordinator sit next to the teacher. This can help convey the idea that the support coordinator is supporting the teacher and they are working together to present the student's case to the team and work toward a solution.
- Establish a schedule of regular meetings for the semester or (preferably) for the entire school year. It is easier to cancel a meeting if there isn't a referred case than to find a convenient time to meet on short notice.

Step-by-Step Directions for Conducting the 25-Minute Planning Process

This section describes how to implement each step of the process shown on the 25-Minute Planning Process worksheet (Reproducible 2.4, pp. 182–190). Each section of the form includes specific questions to help the team gather information for all steps of the problem-solving model. Before conducting the planning meeting, make sure to:

- *Obtain parent permission for problem-solving and invite parents and older students to participate.* Check to make sure someone has discussed the problem with the student and parents. If this has not been done, do so immediately before any other steps take place. Once the parents have been made aware of concerns, a staff member should explain the purpose of the team intervention process and invite them to participate. Be sure to obtain written permission from parents to conduct interventions, regardless of whether they choose to be involved in the planning.

A sample Parent Permission Form (Reproducible 2.3) is shown on page 181. If the parents want to attend the planning meeting, explain the time constraints of the meeting and allow the parents to express their concerns in full in advance of the meeting. Otherwise, the parents may take up a large portion of the 25 minutes, leaving very little time to plan the intervention. If team members try to keep the meeting on schedule by cutting the parents off, the parents may be alienated from the process. The support coordinator can facilitate a pre-meeting discussion with parents to forestall these scenarios. Finally, if the student is older, say in high school, you may also wish to invite the student to attend the meeting. The effectiveness of any intervention is likely to be greatly enhanced if the student's input is taken into account (Arra & Bahr, 2005; Carr, Nicholson, & Higbee, 2000).

- *Have the support coordinator meet with the teacher to go over background information about the student and the problem.* The teacher and support coordinator should meet to compile as much detailed information about the student, the problem, and the goal for the intervention as time permits. This can be accomplished by an informal discussion about the student and the context, or by formally working through the first part of the problem-solving model by completing Step 1 and Step 2 of the Teacher Interview (Reproducible 2.2) or the 25-Minute Planning Process worksheet (Reproducible 2.4). This background meeting may take 30 minutes or more, but it will help the support coordinator and teacher efficiently summarize and relate all relevant background information to other participants during the planning team meeting.

    Depending on the comfort and openness of the teacher at this point, the support coordinator might arrange to observe the student before the planning meeting. This may allow the interventionist to gather additional information or, in the case of a teacher whose relationship with the student has become hostile, identify trends or positive attributes that the teacher has not seen or shared.

At the beginning of the planning meeting, make sure to:

- *Set a positive tone.* Convene the planning meeting by setting a positive and collaborative tone. Welcome each participant and establish an atmosphere of support and advocacy for the student. Convey a sense of optimism that with the expertise at the table, there is an excellent chance of developing an efficient and effective intervention plan that will help the student and the teacher.
- *Hand out copies of the 25-Minute Planning Process worksheet (Reproducible 2.4) to each meeting participant.* Although the recorder will be the person who actively takes notes on the form, all attendees should have a copy so they can follow along as you work through each step. If the support coordinator has already collected background information from the teacher, you may wish to fill out this information on each participant's planning form before beginning the meeting. This will allow each member to reference the student's history as the team comes up with a plan of action.

- *Review ground rules.* Review time limits and other ground rules that will be used. If any participants, such as parents, the student, or new members of the planning team, are unfamiliar with the 25-Minute Planning Process, explain the format and procedure for structured time limits. Say something like: *When the timer goes off for each step, someone will call time and we will immediately move on. This may seem rude or rushed at times, but we are using finite time limits that will help us come up with an initial plan of action that we can implement now, then develop further in the future. We can discuss any points that don't seem finalized at a later time if we feel it is necessary.*

Step 1: Define the problem. *(5 minutes)*

In this step, the teacher and support coordinator describe the presenting problem and other relevant background information for the rest of the planning team. If the Teacher Interview has already been conducted, the teacher and support coordinator can summarize that information. For example:

Support Coordinator: Mr. Winfrey [classroom teacher] and I worked through background information on Charlie's problem at our meeting on Thursday. We'll try to give you a summary of some important things we identified in that meeting, but I would like to invite you to ask questions and help us get a deeper understanding as we move through the information. When we first talked, Mr. Winfrey said that he was worried about Charlie because she has difficulty working independently. As we talk here today, we'll try to get a handle on the problem so we can develop a plan to help Charlie become more independent. In Step 1, we want to discuss the problems, Charlie's strengths, and things that have been tried so far. Mr. Winfrey, why don't you begin by filling us in on what you see in the classroom?

> The steps and items shown here correspond directly to the **25-Minute Planning Process** form (Reproducible 2.4, pp. 182–190).

Item 1: Describe the problem or reason for referral. Ask the teacher or support coordinator to summarize the problem or situation that resulted in the request for help.

Item 2: How often do the problems occur? How long does the behavior last? How intense is the problem? Review information about the frequency, duration, and severity of the problem.

Step 1. Define the problem.   *excerpt p. 1 of 9*

1. Describe the problem or reason for referral:

2. How often do the problems occur? How long does the behavior last? How intense is the problem?

3. **Code Red Situations:** Is the student's behavior unsafe or severely disruptive to the classroom? Yes / No
   If yes, consult your school's protocol for handling severely disruptive or dangerous behavior.

4. What are the student's strengths?

Item 3: Code Red Situations: Is the student's behavior unsafe or severely disruptive to the classroom? Code Red situations involve behaviors that are either so dangerous or so disruptive that classes cannot continue. Under Code Red circumstances, you will skip simple intervention strategies and move directly to the protocol that your district has in place for handling severely disruptive or dangerous behavior. If your district does not have such a policy, or if the policy is vague and does not define specific procedural actions, see Section 1, Task 6: Establish Processes for Responding to Code Red Situations for a description of how to set up schoolwide policies, and Behavior Emergency Planning for guidelines on creating a safety plan for an individual student. Once temporary procedures are put into place for defusing or responding to Code Red situations, you can return to developing a long-term intervention plan that will help the student learn appropriate behavior.

Item 4: What are the student's strengths? Ask the teacher to identify 2–3 positive features or strengths that the student brings to the classroom. Pausing to reflect on student strengths is important—it encourages the teacher and problem-solving team to see that the student brings more to the classroom than the problems that are the focus of the problem-solving discussion. Additionally, if you can plan an intervention that builds on the student's strengths, the problematic misbehavior may just go away because the strength-based behaviors are more likely to take over more of the student's behavioral repertoire (Seligman & Csikszentmihalyi, 2000; Tedeschi & Kilmer, 2005).

Item 5: List interventions tried in the Intervention History table. Review any interventions and strategies that the teacher or other school staff have already tried in responding to the problem. For interventions that have already been tried, indicate the date and effectiveness. Determine the following:

- Does the teacher believe the intervention lasted long enough?
- Were there glimmers of success?
- Should the effort be part of a comprehensive intervention, or abandoned?
- Is any other relevant information available?

Fully document the efforts and outcomes of each intervention and strategy. This list of interventions can be archived, expanded, and used in subsequent problem-solving meetings. Note that if a previous intervention was run for less than 2 weeks or may not have been implemented consistently with fidelity, that intervention may be worth considering in the development of future behavior improvement plans.

Item 6: Prioritize 1–2 major behaviors that are most problematic or urgent. Once the teacher or support coordinator has summarized the full scope of the student's problems, select 1–2 major behaviors or categories to address first with intervention. With multidimensional problems, you will need to limit the scope of what everyone hopes to accomplish. For example, if the student needs to get to school on time, use better hygiene, stay on task, complete academic work, learn new social skills with peers, and learn to work cooperatively in the classroom, having intervention goals to address each of these would be overwhelming. If the intervention plan tries to focus on too many goals, it may be overwhelming to the student, but is even more likely to be overwhelming to the teacher (Forman & Burke, 2008). When you narrow objectives and begin with obtainable goals, students have a greater chance of success.

When you narrow objectives and begin with obtainable goals, students have a greater chance of success.

SECTION 2: EMBEDDING A PROBLEM-SOLVING MODEL INTO EACH TIER OF SUPPORT

To identify priorities for the initial intervention, ask the following questions.

- *Which behavior changes will help the student feel successful in the shortest period of time?* An intervention plan should initially target behaviors that have the highest probability of changing in the least amount of time. Once the student begins to experience success and to understand the value of positive behavior, the team can focus on more long-term problems that require greater commitment, motivation, and effort. For example, if a student has problems with peer interactions, academic difficulties, and a significant weight problem tied to low self-esteem, reducing the student's weight would not be the first target for intervention. Although this might be a worthy long-range goal, success may be difficult to achieve and results won't be seen for a long period of time. The student is likely

---

excerpt p. 1 of 9

5. List interventions tried in the Intervention History table on the next two pages.
6. Prioritize 1–2 major behaviors that are most problematic or urgent:

   ☐ Physical aggression ☐ Anxiety   ☐ Off task
   ☐ Self-injury   ☐ Disruption   ☐ Depression, withdrawal
   ☐ Peer conflict   ☐ Absenteeism   ☐ Inappropriate language
   ☐ Damage to property   ☐ Bullying others ☐ Tardiness
   ☐ Noncompliance   ☐ Other: _____ ☐ Other: _____

7. Narrow the scope of the problem and identify a goal for improvement.

Intervention History

excerpt pp. 2–3 of 9

Intervention/Strategy	Were data collected?	How effective was the intervention/strategy at addressing problem behavior?
	☐ Yes / ☐ No Describe:	☐ Not at all / ☐ Somewhat / ☐ Very Notes:
	☐ Yes / ☐ No Describe:	☐ Not at all / ☐ Somewhat / ☐ Very Notes:
	☐ Yes / ☐ No Describe:	☐ Not at all / ☐ Somewhat / ☐ Very Notes:

☐ Very

☐ Very

to experience success sooner by first working on improving peer interactions and academic skills. Once the student begins to experience the sense of satisfaction that accompanies success, helping the student with other problems becomes progressively easier.

- *Which behavior changes will help the teacher see improvements in the shortest period of time?* The second major consideration in setting intervention priorities is to address problems that interfere with the teacher's ability to instruct or with other students' ability to learn. The more a problem interferes with the smooth operation of a classroom, the sooner the problem needs to be addressed. If a problem disrupts the natural flow of a classroom, the likelihood increases that the problem will escalate to more serious proportions, lead to other problems, or distract other students from learning. For example, a teacher who is frustrated with a particular student's behavior may become less interested in or optimistic about helping that student. As time goes on, the teacher may become less effective in teaching the rest of the class as a result of her stress and frustration with the problem student. To reduce the impact of the problem on teachers and other students, place high priority on addressing behaviors that interfere with the teacher's ability to instruct or other students' ability to learn.

Item 7. Narrow the scope of the problem and identify a goal for improvement. Carefully guide the team toward developing a clear, reasonable, and achievable goal for the student's behavior. When selecting behaviors to target with intervention, make sure to:

- *Select observable behaviors.* State the goal in such a way that it can be measured. "To increase respect in the classroom," for example, is too broad because it does not clarify the specific behaviors that need to change. An alternative statement, such as "respond to teacher instructions in a respectful tone of voice or with no reply," would be more appropriate.
- *Identify a positively stated goal.* Whether the goal is to reduce a negative behavior or increase a positive one, it's important to state the goal in positive terms. Although many intervention plans are designed to help students overcome problems, positively stated goals allow students to take pride in their accomplishments and focuses on building appropriate behaviors. For a student who takes other student's things, for example, "learning to be trustworthy by touching only your own things" can help that student develop a sense of self-worth, while "learning not to steal" may simply reinforce her sense of untrustworthiness.
- *Include numbers and timelines.* Defining timelines and degrees of accomplishment are useful in specifying measurable goals. Collaborate with the teacher to incorporate numbers and timelines into your goals, such as: "By the end of the quarter, Damari will turn in at least 80% of his math assignments."
- *Choose ambitious but obtainable objectives.* Avoid selecting goals that are overly ambitious. Instead, start by setting an initial goal that is closer to the student's baseline level of performance than the ultimate goal for behavior. For example, if a student engages in disruptive behavior several times each hour, it would be

unrealistic to select a goal to eliminate all disruptive behavior within 2 weeks. Instead, the team might define a more obtainable goal such as: "Within 2 weeks, the number of disruptive acts will be reduced by 50%, and within 2 months, the number of disruptive acts will decrease by 80%."

If the team has trouble narrowing the scope of the problem, ask the teacher to think about what behaviors interfere most with teaching effectively. Student success is determined to a large extent by the teacher's perceptions. Therefore, an intervention must focus not only on improving student behavior but also on addressing any misbehaviors that the teacher cannot tolerate. Conduct the process as an advocate for the student, but also make it clear that you are an equal advocate for the teacher—in other words, you want the intervention process to be win-win for both parties. For example:

Support Coordinator: Let's review what we have identified as Charlie's work-related problem behaviors.
Team Member: Charlie wanders around the room playing with things like the pencil sharpener and talking to others when she should be working. She hums and makes noises at her desk. The net result is that she doesn't get her work done.
Support Coordinator: Thank you. Mr. Winfrey, can you identify which behaviors interfere the most with Charlie's success and make it hard for you and the other students to get work done?
Teacher: I guess there are two major problems. She causes problems when she wanders around, and she is very off-task at times. Actually, I guess her biggest problem is wandering around. If she weren't roaming, maybe she'd be more on task, and if she were on task, she'd get her work done.
Team Member: What about the humming and other noises she makes at her desk?
Teacher: They don't seem to bother the other students, and I don't think they would bother me if I knew she was getting her work done.
Team Member: If we made the initial focus of the intervention learning to stay in her assigned place, would that seem like a good starting place?
Teacher: Yes, but what if she does not get her work done?
Support Coordinator: Maybe Charlie's goal could be to learn to manage her work time and space. The outcome would be getting her work done.
Teacher: Sounds good. Mrs. Metzger, what do you think?
Parent: I like that. We have the same problem at home when she does homework. She is all over the place and doesn't get it done.
Support Coordinator: Good. Time to move on. We were a few seconds long in this step, so let's try to make it up in the next step.

INTERVENTIONS: SUPPORT FOR INDIVIDUAL STUDENTS WITH BEHAVIOR CHALLENGES

Step 2: Analyze the problem. *(5 minutes)*

The next questions guide the team in looking for trends in the student's behavior by determining the *when, where, how,* and *why* of the most urgent problem behavior identified in Item 6.

---

excerpt p. 4 of 9

Step 2. Analyze the problem. *5 minutes*

8. Identify relevant triggers (antecedents) and conditions (setting events) that predict when the behavior is likely to occur. Possible Antecedents and Setting Events:

☐ Unstructured time ☐ Peers present ☐ Hunger
☐ Whole group instruction ☐ Peer conflict ☐ Conflict or stressors at home
☐ Small group activities ☐ After adult correction or reprimands ☐ Illness, pain, discomfort
☐ Independent work ☐ Corrective consequence or loss ☐ Missed medications
☐ Transitions   of privilege ☐ Lack of sleep
☐ Change in routine ☐ Other: _____
☐ Specific tasks: _____

Data sources that support this hypothesis: _____

9. Identify the function of the behavior, or the consequences that seem to be maintaining or reinforcing problem behavior. Hypothesized function(s):

Deficits **Trying to Get Something** **Trying to Avoid Something**
☐ Lacking awareness ☐ Seeking adult attention ☐ Avoiding overly difficult or overly simple work
☐ Lacking ability: ☐ Seeking peer attention ☐ Avoiding nonpreferred activities and tasks
  ☐ Physical/Neurological ☐ Seeking access to activities ☐ Avoiding peer interactions
  ☐ Academic ☐ Seeking power or control ☐ Avoiding adult interactions
  ☐ Social/Emotional

Data sources that support this hypothesis: _____

10. Record notes on student awareness and motivation.
    Is the student aware of the problem? Yes / No / Unsure Notes: _____

    Does the student seem motivated to improve the behavior? Yes / No / Unsure Notes: _____

11. Record notes on parent contact.
    Has the parent been contacted about this problem? Yes / No If yes, when did first contact occur? _____
    Who contacted the parent? _____
    How did the parent respond? _____
    Was the parent invited to participate in planning meetings? Yes / No Notes: _____

12. Summarize other relevant information.
    Notes from other staff members _____

    Notes from student records (e.g., medical history, family history, school history, test data) _____

STEP 2 NOTE

In most situations, you should have narrowed the scope of the problem so that this step can be completed with one major category or set of related behaviors in mind. In some instances, you may need to address a set of unrelated problem behaviors at the same time. If this is the case, answer Items 8 and 9 separately for each behavior category.

In this step, other members of the team should be asking probing questions to gain a deeper understanding of the student's problems and abilities and what the teacher is facing on a daily basis. For example:

> Teacher: Charlie has the greatest difficulty during independent work times. I worry about her because she doesn't seem to be able to

	get anything done unless I'm standing over her. She wanders aimlessly about, sharpens her pencil, gets a drink of water, and often bothers the other children.
Team Member:	How do the other students respond to her?
Teacher:	They don't seem to mind her interruptions. Charlie is very likable. She has a good sense of humor.
Team Member:	So one problem is that she wanders and bothers other kids, but one strength is her social skills.
Parent:	Yes, Charlie has a lot of friends.
Teacher:	Everyone likes Charlie, so she can easily pull other students off task. She doesn't harass anyone.
Team Member:	How does she do during instructional periods?
Teacher:	She does better when I'm working directly with her in a small group or even when I'm teaching the entire class, if I remember to call on her often enough.
Team Member:	So being off-task is a problem during independent work, but not when you are around. How is the quality of Charlie's work?
Teacher:	She gets it done if I keep her in from recess to do it. She does good work and seems capable, but she wastes so much time in class that she needs the extra time during recess. I don't mind giving up my break once in a while, but it's getting to be an everyday occurrence.
Parent:	I think that's one of the reasons Charlie doesn't like school. She really enjoys her time with the other kids at recess.
Support Coordinator:	We clearly need to come up with a different solution. Mr. Winfrey, is Charlie disruptive when she's at her desk?
Teacher:	When the whole class is working with me, she does fairly well. But during work times, she hums, sings, and talks to the other kids. I have her desk moved away from the other students, but it hasn't done much good because she just gets up to bother them.
Team Member:	How does she do in other settings? The hall, playground, music class?
Support Coordinator:	In PE and art she does just fine. Once in a while, she's been a little loud in the hallways and cafeteria, but nothing out of line. The problem is really in the classroom. Let's explore how she does with different activities in the classroom.

Item 8: Identify relevant triggers (antecedents) and conditions (setting events) that predict when the behavior is likely to occur. The following questions may help to determine which triggers and conditions are contributing to the problem:

- What situations seem to set off the problem behavior?
- Where do the problems tend to occur?
- When do the problems tend to occur?
- What specific conditions seem to increase the likelihood that problem behavior will occur on any given day?

From the information that you gathered from these questions, place a check mark next to possible antecedents and setting events that predict problem behavior. Select the antecedents that seem to occur most often and have the greatest likelihood of triggering problem behavior.

If you have already gathered information about antecedents and setting events from the Teacher Interview, a formal functional behavior assessment, or via other means, summarize the hypothesis and the sources that support the hypothesis here.

Item 9: Identify the function of the behavior, or the consequences that seem to be maintaining or reinforcing problem behavior. To determine what the student seems to achieve through the behavior, ask the following questions:

- What typically happens right after the problem behavior occurs? What does the teacher do? What do other students do? How might these responses reinforce the student's problem behavior?
- Is the student trying to get something? Are there privileges or items that the student is motivated to obtain through the problem behavior? Does the student get access to these privileges or items after demonstrating the problem behavior?
- Is the student trying to avoid something? Are there situations or activities that the student is motivated to avoid or escape? When the student engages in problem behavior, does that behavior get the student out of these situations or activities?
- Does the student lack certain skills or an awareness of the behavior that may be contributing to the problem? Does the student lack the ability or awareness to exhibit the expected behavior? NOTE: If you suspect that an academic skill deficit may be contributing to the behavior problem, see "Academic Concerns" (pp. 128–129).

Once you ask these questions, generate a hypothesis to guide development of a function-based intervention plan. See "Developing a Functional Hypothesis" (pp. 130–133) for a list of possible functions to help in developing this hypothesis.

Item 10. Record notes on student awareness and motivation. Is the student aware of the problem? Does the student seem motivated to improve the behavior?

Item 11. Record notes on parent contact. Has the family been contacted about this problem? When was the parent first contacted? Who contacted the parent? How did the parent respond? Was the parent invited to participate in planning meetings?

Item 12. Summarize other relevant information. Review notes from other staff members and from the student's records. Consider the following when reviewing the student's records:

- Medical history: diagnosed illnesses or diseases, developmental issues, medications
- Family history: who lives with the student, siblings, education level and employment of parents, involvement of outside agencies
- School history: special education status, school changes and moves, absenteeism, retentions, academic grade averages
- Test data: standardized and state test results, psychological evaluations

---

FUNCTION-BASED INTERVENTION

As described previously, *function-based intervention* simply means that the intervention should be designed to help the student get needs met by exhibiting responsible and appropriate behavior rather than through misbehavior. For example, with a student who seeks attention, an intervention plan should be designed to reduce the amount or intensity of attention the student receives for disruptive behavior while increasing the attention the student receives for productive, appropriate behavior.

Step 3: Consider possible solutions and select intervention strategies. *(10 minutes)*

This section of the process guides the team and teacher in defining appropriate and inappropriate behaviors, identifying possible solutions to the problem, and planning an intervention.

Step 3. Consider possible solutions and select intervention strategies.	*10 minutes*
13. Identify examples of appropriate behavior and/or student strengths to encourage and examples of inappropriate behavior to discourage.	
Appropriate Behavior	**Inappropriate Behavior**

excerpt p. 6 of 9

Item 13. Identify examples of appropriate behavior and student strengths to encourage and examples of inappropriate behavior to discourage. In this item, clearly define the positive behaviors that will lead to achievement of the goal and the negative behaviors that will detract from it. Identify the line between *appropriate* behaviors to encourage and *inappropriate* behaviors to discourage (if needed, see Section 3, Task 5, Step 1 for more guidance on defining limits of behavior). This step can help adults teach students the behaviors they hope to see for achieving the goal while providing clarity for the teacher on precisely when to assign corrective consequences for misbehavior.

Appropriate behaviors include behaviors that are currently in the student's repertoire as well as behaviors that need to be learned. Inappropriate behaviors include a list of specific behaviors that are identified and tied to corrective consequences. For example, if the student is working on improving interactions with adults, appropriate behaviors might include saying hello in the morning, using a respectful tone of voice, nodding when the teacher addresses the student, and answering patiently when the teacher asks a question. Inappropriate behaviors might include giving the teacher a dirty look, answering the teacher in a sarcastic tone, or mimicking the teacher.

Team members should ask probing questions to help the teacher create a clear picture of the boundary between what is acceptable and what is not. What if you ask the student to do something and he says OK, but simply shrugs his shoulders and doesn't do what you asked? How about if he responds in an acceptable manner but then kicks the chair as he walks away? What if he doesn't respond at all but follows the instruction? Explore as many scenarios and situations as possible to ensure that everyone fully understands what is appropriate and what is inappropriate. For example:

Support Coordinator: Our main goal for Charlie is for her to learn to manage her workspace and time during independent work. Now we need to clarify what exactly we expect to see for positive and negative behavior as Charlie works toward that goal. We know that

	we don't want Charlie to disturb the other kids while they are working. What if she has a question about her work?
Teacher:	I let the other kids help each other. I don't mind if Charlie asks a neighbor a question, but I don't want her asking the kids unnecessary questions. That's going to be hard to distinguish, isn't it?
Team Member:	Maybe. We may need to think of a different way for Charlie to get help. I'm going to make a note under intervention strategies to suggest a question card. For now, Charlie may not be able to make the fine distinction between when it's OK to go talk to another student and when it isn't OK.
Support Coordinator:	Let's talk about out-of-seat behavior. What if her pencil lead breaks? Can she get out of her seat to sharpen it?
Teacher:	That would be fine, unless she abuses the privilege.
Team Member:	Maybe we should clarify what that means.
Teacher:	It would be irresponsible if she does it all the time or bothers other people on her way to the sharpener. It would also be irresponsible if she used sharpening her pencil as an excuse to get out of her seat and wander around for a long time. Unfortunately, this is another privilege with a lot of qualifiers.
Team Member:	You may be right. Especially by the time you add in other valid reasons for getting out of her seat, such as getting a drink, turning in her work, and getting materials.
Teacher:	Maybe for Charlie, just being out of her seat is inappropriate, but I hate to be unfair.
Support Coordinator:	Perhaps when we look at ways to encourage appropriate behavior, we can think of ways Charlie might earn back the privilege. What things should she be doing during independent work times? We'll need to create a clear list of what she should be doing during independent work times and what she should not be doing.
Parent:	Charlie's always had a hard time sitting still. I'm not sure she can.
Teacher:	I know Charlie can stay with a task. She does it when I'm with her. But I really don't care whether she is sitting down or not. I just want her to be on task and not bothering others.
Team Member:	When another student had a similar problem, we defined lines by marking his space with masking tape. We told him he could work in that area, at his desk, on the floor, sitting, or standing. It didn't matter as long as he stayed in that space. We called it his office, and he loved it.
Parent:	I could see Charlie loving that, too. Is it possible to do that for her?
Support Coordinator:	I like that idea. I think it could work.
Team Member:	Good. I'll write that down under responsible behaviors. Irresponsible behavior would include leaving the office area without permission and that would be when you launch into ignoring mode.

Item 14. Identify a list of possible strategies to implement to encourage appropriate behavior and discourage inappropriate behavior. In the first part of this item, list all potentially relevant ready-to-use interventions already in place within your school that might be a good fit for the student (see Section 1, Task 3 for examples of ready-to-use interventions).

> 14. Identify a list of possible strategies to implement to encourage appropriate behavior and discourage inappropriate behavior.
>   a. List ready-to-use interventions already existing in your building.
>   - _____
>   - _____
>   - _____
>   - _____
>   - _____
>   b. Using the Intervention Decision Guide on the next page, review the list of *presenting behaviors* and check each one that describes the student or context of the problem.
>   c. Brainstorm and list any other possible interventions strategies not included above.

excerpt p. 6 of 9

In the second part, review each presenting behavior listed on the Intervention Decision Guide. If the statement is true for the student, place a check in the second column. Leave the column blank if the statement is false. Next, review the list of intervention strategies. If any of the strategies have already been tried, indicate the approximate date of implementation and degree of effectiveness. If an intervention strategy was successful, or the teacher thinks it might be successful in combination with other strategies, place a mark in the second column (Check if true) to include the strategy for consideration. All strategies are described in more detail in Sections 3 and 4 of this book.

The purpose of this item is to identify as many applicable intervention strategies as possible. Not all of the strategies listed here will be incorporated into the student's intervention plan. In some cases, only a few intervention strategies may be applicable to the student's goal. In other situations, the team may develop a long list of potential strategies that could address the problem. Either way, in the initial intervention you will implement only a few strategies first. If they don't adequately address the problem, the team can return to the list and select other intervention options to try next. A detailed overview of the Intervention Decision Guide appears on pages 136–139 (see full form pages on pp. 187–188).

Item 15. Select a manageable set of strategies to implement. From your list of possibly relevant ready-to-use interventions and checked intervention strategies from the Intervention Decision Guide, select a manageable number of intervention strategies to implement. When selecting intervention strategies to implement, make sure that the intervention plan:

- Is related to the identified goal
- Takes into account your hypothesis about the function of the misbehavior
- Seems manageable and acceptable to the teacher

Also see "Considerations in Choosing Intervention Strategies" on pages 141–142.

INTERVENTION DECISION GUIDE

Team members should have some familiarity with each of the interventions listed on the Intervention Decision Guide as well as any other district-approved interventions, including the ready-to-use interventions in place within your school. They can achieve this familiarity by studying this resource (Sections 3 and 4) or attending training in the interventions. The team may also divide up the interventions so that each person is responsible for knowing only a portion of the body of knowledge. Team members should also be familiar with the concept of *function*, specifically, that any chronic misbehavior serves some function for the student. As the team explores possible consequences for the student's misbehavior, team members should take into account the hypothesized function and avoid consequences that are likely to reinforce problem behavior.

INTERVENTIONS: SUPPORT FOR INDIVIDUAL STUDENTS WITH BEHAVIOR CHALLENGES

Intervention Decision Guide

Presenting behavior	Check if true	Intervention strategy	Date implemented	Effective? (+/-)
More than three students in class misbehave	☐	Assess classroom management practices		
The student has an underlying academic problem	☐	Address academic needs		
The student is not aware of the problem, or no individual supports have been tried yet	☐	Early-stage interventions		
The student doesn't know what is expected or lacks the ability to exhibit the expected behavior	☐	B. Change work requirements D. Change expectations or procedures F. Use precorrections I. Re-teach classroom expectations J. Provide demonstrations and modeling K. Provide positive practice and feedback L. Provide opportunities for verbal practice M. Deliver praise and specific feedback		
Adult attention seems to reinforce misbehavior	☐	G. Increase opportunities to respond M. Deliver praise and specific feedback O. Send positive news home P. Ignore misbehavior W. Increase the frequency of noncontingent positive attention		
Peer attention seems to reinforce misbehavior	☐	A. Change assigned seating Q. Reduce peer attention		
Escape seems to reinforce misbehavior	☐	B. Change work requirements C. Provide breaks D. Change expectations or procedures E. Offer viable choices S. Assign time owed		
Access to tangibles, activities, or privileges seems to reinforce misbehavior	☐	N. Offer rewards V. Revoke a privilege		
Specific consequences for misbehavior are necessary	☐	R. Use gentle verbal reprimands or warnings S. Assign time owed T. Assign in-class timeout V. Revoke a privilege		
Misbehavior may be positively affected by changes to structural features of the classroom (e.g. classroom layout, schedule)	☐	A. Change assigned seating B. Change work requirements D. Change expectations or procedures		
The student misbehaves under periods of low supervision or structure	☐	D. Change expectations or procedures H. Increase monitoring and supervision		
Previously used consequences for misbehavior don't seem to work, or misbehavior is a firmly established part of the student's behavior	☐	1. Behavioral Contracting 2. Structured Reinforcement		

excerpt pp. 6–7 of 9

			Date implemented	Effective? (+/-)
		f-Evaluation		
		calation		
		th Internalizing		
		of noncontingent		
		X. Assign a meaningful duty or responsibility at school Y. Encourage and facilitate the student's participation in clubs, after-school activities, and other school events Z. Connect the student with an adult or peer mentor at school		
The student's behavior is so disruptive that the teacher cannot continue	☐	Code Red Situation: Consult school policies for responding to severely disruptive behavior 4. Behavior Emergency Planning U. Assign out-of-class timeout		
The student's behavior is unsafe or dangerous to self or others	☐	Code Red Situation: Consult school policies for responding to unsafe or physically dangerous behavior 4. Behavior Emergency Planning U. Assign out-of-class timeout		

Use the Intervention Plan Summary to outline all the components of your intervention plan. This table is organized in approximate order from least to most resource- and time-intensive strategies. Start by considering foundational and ready-to-use intervention strategies that require few resources before selecting specialized intervention strategies that require more individualization, staffing, materials, and expertise.

15. Select a manageable set of strategies to implement. Describe how, where, and when strategies will be implemented and the responsibilities of staff members involved.

excerpt p. 8 of 9

Intervention Plan Summary

Intervention strategy type		Description of intervention strategy	Start date
Ready to Use			
Foundational	Antecedent strategies		
	Teaching strategies		
	Positive consequence strategies		
	Corrective consequence strategies		
	Interactional strategies		
Specialized			

INTERVENTION PLAN SUMMARY

The Intervention Plan Summary sets the stage for a carefully designed, targeted intervention plan. During implementation, staff must follow through with their responsibilities. If any member of the intervention team is unable to continue with their responsibilities for any reason, it is essential that a replacement be found immediately so that support for the student continues throughout the process. The support provided by collaborative planning groups and individuals can ultimately make the difference in whether an intervention plan works or not.

Consider each category of foundational strategy (e.g., antecedent, teaching, positive consequence, corrective consequence, and interactional) when designing your intervention plan. You may not need to include intervention strategies from each category, but it is important to consider how manipulating variables in each category might encourage behavior change.

The teacher knows the student's tendencies and has to live with and carry out the plan, so the final decision about which interventions will be manageable and effective should be the teacher's. The support coordinator and the planning team should help guide the teacher to a reasonable plan and clarify procedures, as needed. For example:

Support Coordinator: Let's look at what we have and then decide on one to three strategies to implement.

Teacher: These are all such great ideas. I'd like to do them all.

Support Coordinator: It would be easy to take on too much. We should start with just a few so we don't overwhelm you or Charlie. Then we can revisit the plan after a few weeks to see if we want to switch to different strategies or add some.

Teacher: OK. A lot of these suggestions seem pretty easy to implement. Mrs. Metzger, I'd like your input, too. I like the idea of marking Charlie's work space with masking tape. What do you think?

Parent: I think Charlie would like that. Ms. Trent, when we are through, could you help me work out something for Charlie's homework?

Support Coordinator: I'd like to do that. Let's finish looking at the list and finalize the school plan. Then you and I can work on a homework plan.

Teacher: Mrs. Metzger, I'm really glad you came in. I think we can help make this a better year for Charlie. Let's see. We've got the masking-tape office. I'd rather not get into a point system.

Team Member: Why don't I circle the things you want to do?

Teacher: Circle self-monitoring. It would be good to get Charlie focused on her own behavior. I'd like to do everything else.

Support Coordinator: Let's eliminate a few more—maybe one or two of the more time-consuming ones? I think the rest are manageable. Most of this will require time up front, but then the strategies will become fairly routine.

Teacher: Let's definitely do a self-monitoring system. I think Charlie would like it. We could set up an assignment sheet for her to monitor her office work. That would keep the focus on work completion.

Team Member: I have several self-monitoring forms that I could leave in your box. They might help you come up with something for Charlie.

Teacher: That would be great. Actually, could I take a look at the intervention chapter that covers self-monitoring? I think it would be helpful. I'd also like to have her help me with something like making a bulletin board. It would give her some extra attention, and we can work on positive interactions. Mrs. Metzger, would you have 5 or 10 minutes to read with Charlie before bedtime?

Parent: Yes. We got out of that habit when she learned to read. She still asks me to read sometimes, though, so I know she would like that.

When completing the Intervention Plan Summary, lay out the final details and outline everyone's role in implementing the plan. This includes identifying ways in which other members of the planning team can assist with implementation, determining whether other people in or outside of school should be involved, and summarizing each person's responsibilities. For example, if a self-monitoring form will be used, can one of the team members provide a sample for the teacher or develop a first draft? Also specify:

- Who will talk to the student and when
- Who will teach and model positive behaviors to the student
- When the plan can reasonably start
- If parents aren't present, how and when the plan will be shared with them
- If a substitute teacher will be asked to implement the plan, how instructions will be communicated
- Which staff members need to be notified of the plan

Participants in planning meetings often get carried away as they develop intervention plans for students. Enthusiasm runs high in the meeting, but a few days later nothing has happened. Implementation is the hardest step, so it is imperative that all people involved are clear about their duties and responsibilities for implementing the plan.

Step 4: Collect data to monitor progress. *(5 minutes)*

The next few items guide the team in identifying methods to use to evaluate the effect of the intervention plan on the student's target behaviors.

Step 4. Collect data to monitor progress.   *5 minutes*

16. Identify data that will be used to track progress toward the goal, including who will collect data and how.

17. Identify follow-up date(s) to check in about progress:

18. Identify at least two ways to determine whether the plan is working at the next follow-up meeting.

19. Describe plans to monitor and evaluate implementation fidelity.

excerpt p. 9 of 9

Item 16. Identify data that will be used to track progress toward the goal, including who will collect data and how. Review the goal that was developed in Item 7 and determine how data will be collected and recorded to track the intervention's progress. Identify at least one source of objective data to collect for each goal behavior. If the goal is not defined in terms of measurable and observable behaviors, go back to Item 7 and redefine the goal. One of the best tests for whether the goal for intervention is reasonable and behaviorally specific enough is whether you can easily measure and evaluate intervention effectiveness. Objective data collection might include rating scales, work products, self-monitoring data, data from a reinforcement system intervention, audio or video records, or frequency, duration, or latency data. Section 3, Task 8 provides a detailed description of data collection options and sample forms to use in collecting data.

Item 17. Identify follow-up date(s) to check in about progress. Schedule the first follow-up meeting for about two weeks after implementation is scheduled to begin.

Item 18. Identify at least two ways to determine whether the plan is working at the next follow-up meeting. Before concluding the planning meeting, work with the team to determine decision rules that indicate whether the student has made sufficient progress under the plan. This item expands on the goal you defined in Item 7 and the data collection procedures you outlined in Item 16. Decision rules should be specific and include numbers and timelines to clearly define how much improvement will be considered sufficient.

Select at least two ways to evaluate progress. These can include any of the objective data sources that you selected in Item 16 as well as observations from an outside observer or subjective perceptions from the teacher or other staff. For example:

- After 2 weeks of implementation, the plan is working if Marco tantrums no more than twice per week and if these tantrums last for less than 5 minutes.
- After 2 weeks of implementation, the plan is working if weekly rating scales competed by the teacher show an improvement.
- If observations by the school psychologist indicate a 50% decrease in off-task behavior, the plan is working.

When choosing a progress monitoring approach, try not to overburden staff. Make sure the plan you have chosen is feasible and acceptable to the teacher or staff responsible for collecting data. Also consider how to streamline procedures so that data can be easily summarized and shared with others. For example:

Support Coordinator: We need to identify a couple of ways to determine whether the plan is working. Let me suggest some ideas. One possibility would be to monitor the time Charlie spends out of her seat. You start a stopwatch when she leaves her seat and then stop it when she returns to her space. The next time she leaves, you start the watch again. At the end of the day, you have the total number of minutes Charlie spent out of her seat. We could create a simple chart to record each day's total time, and then we can easily see if she is getting better or worse, or staying the same. Another option would be to see how you are feeling about things. Is this plan working? Is it feasible to maintain, or is it wearing down your patience? We could just have an informal talk about this once a week. A third possibility would be to have Charlie use a self-monitoring system and periodically check it.

Teacher: I doubt I'd remember to start and stop a watch, so I'd prefer not to do that one. It also would be problematic if she gets up for some legitimate reason and then gets distracted along the way. But I think a self-monitoring system would be good, and I will be monitoring work completion anyway, so that can be a measure. I think I'd also like to debrief with you once a week.

Support Coordinator: Good. That's all we need for now.

Item 19. Describe plans to monitor and evaluate implementation fidelity. If a plan is put into place but isn't working, your problem-solving team will need to verify that strategies were implemented in the way they were designed to be. Therefore, it is important to proactively embed procedures for monitoring fidelity within the intervention plan itself. Select a method for monitoring and evaluating implementation fidelity (e.g., directly observe implementation, evaluate permanent products, have the teacher or interventionist self-monitor) and define what "good" fidelity looks like. Also identify a schedule for monitoring fidelity. Consider ways to encourage good implementation and provide follow-up support as needed. See Section 3, Task 9 for more in-depth recommendations and options for monitoring implementation fidelity.

At this point, you will conclude the planning meeting. Ask if the teacher has any questions or could use additional support or resources from the team. Share a written summary of the plan that outlines each person's responsibilities with all team members and applicable staff (e.g., distribute copies of the Intervention Plan Summary). Conclude the meeting with words of encouragement and thank all participants for their time and input.

The support coordinator should check in with the teacher or other involved staff after the first day or two of implementation. If there are problems or anything that was not anticipated, the support coordinator can help troubleshoot and get the intervention plan on track.

Step 5: Evaluate whether supports are working.

In all subsequent follow-up meetings, the team will evaluate progress and modify the plan as needed. Make sure that interventions are implemented for at least 2 weeks before your initial follow-up meeting.

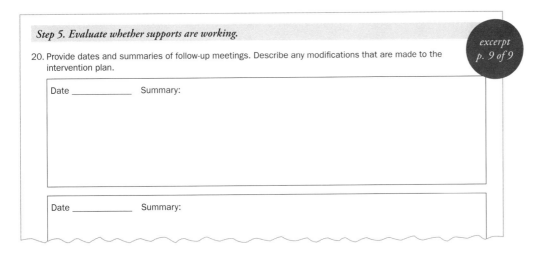

Consider graphing evaluation data prior to the follow-up meeting. Interventions rarely run a smooth and gradual course toward success; therefore, it is important to identify trends that will help determine whether the intervention is having a positive effect on student behavior. Examples of types of behavior you might graph include:

- Number of times each day the student uses profanity
- Number of minutes spent in timeout each day
- Total number of minutes owed for delays in following an instruction

- Number of pluses, which represent specified periods of time on task, earned during the day
- Average ratings of how hard the student worked for 15-minute periods throughout the school day
- Percentage of assignments completed

Item 20. Provide dates and summaries of follow-up meetings. Record the date of your follow-up meeting and provide a summary of the data that have been collected to date, any changes made to the plan, and any follow-up actions needed moving forward.

At these meetings, make a clear determination: Should the intervention be maintained, modified, replaced, or faded? To help make this decision, see "Guidelines for Maintaining, Modifying, Replacing, and Fading Plans" on page 147.

Summary of the 25-Minute Planning Process

The 25-Minute Planning Process provides a structured, step-by-step, timed process for intervention planning teams to use to guide their problem analysis and intervention design. By combining the expertise of a group of professionals, you gain a broader perspective and range of expertise. The timed and structured agenda reduces the chance that meetings will be too long, off-task, or negative in tone. When intervention planning teams function well, they can quickly and efficiently design interventions that have a high probability of helping the student in ways that earlier-stage interventions did not.

REPRODUCIBLE 2.3 *Parent Permission Form*

Parent Permission Form

Dear _____,

We would like to develop a plan to support _____
_____
_____

To assist us in developing the most useful plan possible, we would like your permission to informally assess your child's academic skills and work habits. This process may include any or all of the following:

_____
_____
_____
_____
_____
_____
_____

Please sign the slip below and return it to school by _____. As soon as the assessment has been completed, we will be in touch.

Thank you for your assistance.

Sincerely,

- -

_____ has my permission to informally assess _____'s academic skills and work habits and to develop a plan of assistance.

_____   _____
Parent/Guardian signature   Date

Interventions © 2019 Ancora Publishing   REPRODUCIBLE 2.3

REPRODUCIBLE 2.4 *25-Minute Planning Process (1 of 9)*

25-Minute Planning Process

Student _____ Age _____ Grade _____ Date _____

Teacher _____ Support Coordinator _____

Other participants _____

Step 1. Define the problem.   *5 minutes*

1. Describe the problem or reason for referral:

2. How often do the problems occur? How long does the behavior last? How intense is the problem?

3. **Code Red Situations:** Is the student's behavior unsafe or severely disruptive to the classroom? Yes / No
   If yes, consult your school's protocol for handling severely disruptive or dangerous behavior.

4. What are the student's strengths?

5. List interventions tried in the Intervention History table on the next two pages.

6. Prioritize 1–2 major behaviors that are most problematic or urgent:

   ☐ Physical aggression   ☐ Anxiety   ☐ Off task
   ☐ Self-injury   ☐ Disruption   ☐ Depression, withdrawal
   ☐ Peer conflict   ☐ Absenteeism   ☐ Inappropriate language
   ☐ Damage to property   ☐ Bullying others   ☐ Tardiness
   ☐ Noncompliance   ☐ Other: _____ ☐ Other: _____

7. Narrow the scope of the problem and identify a goal for improvement.

Interventions © 2019 Ancora Publishing   — 1 of 9 —   REPRODUCIBLE 2.4

REPRODUCIBLE 2.4 *25-Minute Planning Process (2 of 9)*

25-Minute Planning Process

Intervention History

Intervention/Strategy	Were data collected?	How effective was the intervention/strategy at addressing problem behavior?
	☐ Yes / ☐ No Describe:	☐ Not at all / ☐ Somewhat / ☐ Very Notes:
	☐ Yes / ☐ No Describe:	☐ Not at all / ☐ Somewhat / ☐ Very Notes:
	☐ Yes / ☐ No Describe:	☐ Not at all / ☐ Somewhat / ☐ Very Notes:
	☐ Yes / ☐ No Describe:	☐ Not at all / ☐ Somewhat / ☐ Very Notes:
	☐ Yes / ☐ No Describe:	☐ Not at all / ☐ Somewhat / ☐ Very Notes:

Interventions © 2019 Ancora Publishing

REPRODUCIBLE 2.4 *25-Minute Planning Process (3 of 9)*

25-Minute Planning Process

Intervention/Strategy	Were data collected?	How effective was the intervention/strategy at addressing problem behavior?
	☐ Yes / ☐ No Describe:	☐ Not at all / ☐ Somewhat / ☐ Very Notes:
	☐ Yes / ☐ No Describe:	☐ Not at all / ☐ Somewhat / ☐ Very Notes:
	☐ Yes / ☐ No Describe:	☐ Not at all / ☐ Somewhat / ☐ Very Notes:
	☐ Yes / ☐ No Describe:	☐ Not at all / ☐ Somewhat / ☐ Very Notes:
	☐ Yes / ☐ No Describe:	☐ Not at all / ☐ Somewhat / ☐ Very Notes:

REPRODUCIBLE 2.4 *25-Minute Planning Process (4 of 9)*

25-Minute Planning Process

Step 2. Analyze the problem. — 5 minutes

8. Identify relevant triggers (antecedents) and conditions (setting events) that predict when the behavior is likely to occur. Possible Antecedents and Setting Events:

   - ☐ Unstructured time
   - ☐ Whole group instruction
   - ☐ Small group activities
   - ☐ Independent work
   - ☐ Transitions
   - ☐ Change in routine
   - ☐ Specific tasks: _____

   - ☐ Peers present
   - ☐ Peer conflict
   - ☐ After adult correction or reprimands
   - ☐ Corrective consequence or loss of privilege
   - ☐ Other: _____

   - ☐ Hunger
   - ☐ Conflict or stressors at home
   - ☐ Illness, pain, discomfort
   - ☐ Missed medications
   - ☐ Lack of sleep

   Data sources that support this hypothesis:

9. Identify the function of the behavior, or the consequences that seem to be maintaining or reinforcing problem behavior. Hypothesized function(s):

   Deficits
   - ☐ Lacking awareness
   - ☐ Lacking ability:
     - ☐ Physical/Neurological
     - ☐ Academic
     - ☐ Social/Emotional

   Trying to Get Something
   - ☐ Seeking adult attention
   - ☐ Seeking peer attention
   - ☐ Seeking access to activities
   - ☐ Seeking power or control

   Trying to Avoid Something
   - ☐ Avoiding overly difficult or overly simple work
   - ☐ Avoiding nonpreferred activities and tasks
   - ☐ Avoiding peer interactions
   - ☐ Avoiding adult interactions

   Data sources that support this hypothesis:

10. Record notes on student awareness and motivation.

    Is the student aware of the problem? Yes / No / Unsure   Notes: _____

    Does the student seem motivated to improve the behavior? Yes / No / Unsure   Notes: _____

11. Record notes on parent contact.

    Has the parent been contacted about this problem? Yes / No   If yes, when did first contact occur? _____

    Who contacted the parent? _____
    How did the parent respond? _____
    Was the parent invited to participate in planning meetings? Yes / No   Notes: _____

12. Summarize other relevant information.

    Notes from other staff members _____

    Notes from student records (e.g., medical history, family history, school history, test data) _____

REPRODUCIBLE 2.4 *25-Minute Planning Process (5 of 9)*

25-Minute Planning Process

Step 3. Consider possible solutions and select intervention strategies.   10 minutes

13. Identify examples of appropriate behavior and/or student strengths to encourage and examples of inappropriate behavior to discourage.

Appropriate Behavior	Inappropriate Behavior

14. Identify a list of possible strategies to implement to encourage appropriate behavior and discourage inappropriate behavior.

   a. List ready-to-use interventions already existing in your building.

   - _____
   - _____
   - _____
   - _____
   - _____

   b. Using the Intervention Decision Guide on the next page, review the list of *presenting behaviors* and check each one that describes the student or context of the problem.

   c. Brainstorm and list any other possible interventions strategies not included above.

Interventions © 2019 Ancora Publishing

REPRODUCIBLE 2.4 *25-Minute Planning Process (6 of 9)*

25-Minute Planning Process

Intervention Decision Guide

Presenting behavior	Check if true	Intervention strategy	Date implemented	Effective? (+/-)
More than three students in class misbehave	☐	Assess classroom management practices		
The student has an underlying academic problem	☐	Address academic needs		
The student is not aware of the problem, or no individual supports have been tried yet	☐	Early-stage interventions		
The student doesn't know what is expected or lacks the ability to exhibit the expected behavior	☐	B. Change work requirements D. Change expectations or procedures F. Use precorrections I. Re-teach classroom expectations J. Provide demonstrations and modeling K. Provide positive practice and feedback L. Provide opportunities for verbal practice M. Deliver praise and specific feedback		
Adult attention seems to reinforce misbehavior	☐	G. Increase opportunities to respond M. Deliver praise and specific feedback O. Send positive news home P. Ignore misbehavior W. Increase the frequency of noncontingent positive attention		
Peer attention seems to reinforce misbehavior	☐	A. Change assigned seating Q. Reduce peer attention		
Escape seems to reinforce misbehavior	☐	B. Change work requirements C. Provide breaks D. Change expectations or procedures E. Offer viable choices S. Assign time owed		
Access to tangibles, activities, or privileges seems to reinforce misbehavior	☐	N. Offer rewards V. Revoke a privilege		
Specific consequences for misbehavior are necessary	☐	R. Use gentle verbal reprimands or warnings S. Assign time owed T. Assign in-class timeout V. Revoke a privilege		
Misbehavior may be positively affected by changes to structural features of the classroom (e.g. classroom layout, schedule)	☐	A. Change assigned seating B. Change work requirements D. Change expectations or procedures		
The student misbehaves under periods of low supervision or structure	☐	D. Change expectations or procedures H. Increase monitoring and supervision		
Previously used consequences for misbehavior don't seem to work, or misbehavior is a firmly established part of the student's behavior	☐	1. Behavioral Contracting 2. Structured Reinforcement		

Interventions © 2019 Ancora Publishing

REPRODUCIBLE 2.4 *25-Minute Planning Process (7 of 9)*

25-Minute Planning Process

Intervention Decision Guide (continued)

Presenting behavior	Check if true	Intervention strategy	Date implemented	Effective? (+/-)
The student acts impulsively or seems to be unaware of engaging in inappropriate behavior	☐	3. Self-Monitoring and Self-Evaluation		
The student has difficulty maintaining emotional control	☐	5. Managing Emotional Escalation		
The student seems anxious, depressed, or withdrawn	☐	6. Supporting Students with Internalizing Challenges		
The student doesn't seem connected to peers or adults at school	☐	W. Increase the frequency of noncontingent positive attention X. Assign a meaningful duty or responsibility at school Y. Encourage and facilitate the student's participation in clubs, after-school activities, and other school events Z. Connect the student with an adult or peer mentor at school		
The student's behavior is so disruptive that the teacher cannot continue	☐	Code Red Situation: Consult school policies for responding to severely disruptive behavior 4. Behavior Emergency Planning U. Assign out-of-class timeout		
The student's behavior is unsafe or dangerous to self or others	☐	Code Red Situation: Consult school policies for responding to unsafe or physically dangerous behavior 4. Behavior Emergency Planning U. Assign out-of-class timeout		

Interventions © 2019 Ancora Publishing

REPRODUCIBLE 2.4 *25-Minute Planning Process (8 of 9)*

25-Minute Planning Process

15. Select a manageable set of strategies to implement. Describe how, where, and when strategies will be implemented and the responsibilities of staff members involved.

Intervention Plan Summary

Intervention strategy type		Description of intervention strategy	Start date
Ready to Use			
Foundational	Antecedent strategies		
	Teaching strategies		
	Positive consequence strategies		
	Corrective consequence strategies		
	Interactional strategies		
Specialized			

REPRODUCIBLE 2.4 *25-Minute Planning Process (9 of 9)*

25-Minute Planning Process

Step 4. Collect data to monitor progress.   5 minutes

16. Identify data that will be used to track progress toward the goal, including who will collect data and how.

17. Identify follow-up date(s) to check in about progress:

18. Identify at least two ways to determine whether the plan is working at the next follow-up meeting.

19. Describe plans to monitor and evaluate implementation fidelity.

Step 5. Evaluate whether supports are working.

20. Provide dates and summaries of follow-up meetings. Describe any modifications that are made to the intervention plan.

Date _____ Summary:

Date _____ Summary:

Date _____ Summary:

The Multidisciplinary Team Planning Process

The Multidisciplinary Team Planning Process is intended to guide a problem-solving team in bringing the most resources to the table when addressing a student's behavior problem. At this point, earlier interventions designed as part of Stage 1 and Stage 2 problem-solving efforts have proven to be ineffective, or more expertise, additional data, and comprehensive intervention supports are required to remedy the problem. The Multidisciplinary Team Planning Process may be appropriate under the following conditions:

- Collaborative problem-solving efforts have taken place, but interventions have not resulted in adequate improvements in student behavior.
- The problem is complex and requires more extensive problem analysis or specialized input into intervention design.

This stage of problem-solving is more comprehensive, detailed, and time consuming than the previous stages. Because the multidisciplinary team is composed of highly trained and experienced staff members such as the school counselor, school psychologist, school social worker, special education teacher, behavior specialist, school nurse, and administrator, the goal is to develop and implement a comprehensive intervention plan that reflects the best of what the school and district have to offer the student and the classroom teacher.

The Multidisciplinary Team Process may be used:

- *After the Teacher Interview, 25-Minute Planning Process, or initial interventions have failed to adequately address the problem.* If an initial intervention has been designed and implemented as a result of earlier problem-solving efforts, but the student's behavior hasn't improved, the Multidisciplinary Team Planning Process can be used to develop a comprehensive intervention plan.
- *When the problem is complex and requires more extensive problem analysis or specialized input into intervention design.* If the problem is specific, chronic, or severe enough to warrant expertise from specialists, such as speech pathologists, behavior specialists, or school social workers, the Multidisciplinary Team Planning Process may be a good option for building an intervention plan. In some cases, the team may opt to use this process instead of the Teacher Interview or 25-Minute Planning Process to describe, analyze, and generate solutions for the problem in more detail, which may involve additional data collection or the expertise of specialized team members. For example, the Multidisciplinary Team Planning Process might be suitable for:
  - A transfer student who has a history of requiring behavior supports or accommodations at his previous school
  - A student whose behavior is so severe or complex that efficient problem-solving processes wouldn't likely allow enough time or resources to adequately analyze the problem, collect data, and design a comprehensive intervention plan
  - A student who has specialized needs, such as speech-language needs, health impairments, or a mental-health diagnosis

- *As a vehicle for completing a functional behavior analysis (FBA) and designing a comprehensive behavior intervention plan.* If some members of the team meet the training qualifications needed to conduct a full functional behavior analysis, the multidisciplinary team could use or modify the Multidisciplinary Team Planning Process form to carefully document completion of the FBA along with reporting all interventions developed and implemented as part of initial support efforts (i.e., completing Steps 1 and 2 of the process). The team may also use results from the FBA to develop a comprehensive behavior intervention plan in Steps 3 and 4 of the process. Note that the Multidisciplinary Team Planning Process is not intended to fulfill all FBA procedural requirements for establishing and documenting potential eligibility for special education.

The problem-solving framework used during the Multidisciplinary Team Planning Process is similar to processes for earlier problem-solving stages of the MTSS continuum. The key substantive difference is that the multidisciplinary team will devote more time and resources to problem-solving, collect more and better quality data, and develop a comprehensive intervention plan for high-risk students. However, for the Multidisciplinary Team Planning Process to be effective, your earlier problem-solving efforts must be effective and successful in addressing the majority of students with behavior difficulties. Otherwise, the number of referrals to the Multidisciplinary Team Planning Process can easily overwhelm the multidisciplinary team and make it very difficult to conduct the in-depth problem-solving and intervention planning this process requires.

Guidelines for Conducting the Multidisciplinary Planning Process

To ensure that problem-solving meetings are effective and efficient, follow these guidelines.

Establish ground rules for meetings. Establishing expectations, or ground rules, for the team's behavior during the planning process helps ensure that everyone collaborates, listens to each other, accepts and acknowledges different points of view, and stays positive. Ground rules should cover the following:

- Attendance
- Punctuality
- Listening to each other and avoiding side conversations
- Team members can disagree, but must be respectful
- Confidentiality
- Making the teacher feel welcome and an important contributor to the process
- Active participation by all team members

See Figure 2.2 on page 159 for a sample set of ground rules.

In addition to this basic set of ground rules, the Multidisciplinary Team Planning Process relies heavily on brainstorming as a critical piece of the process. We suggest you establish ground rules for brainstorming so that all team members are respectful of others and feel they can contribute. The Recorder should include all suggestions in the meeting minutes so that all possibilities will be available for future use even if not used in the initial plan.

Following are some sample ground rules for brainstorming:

- Anything goes and any idea or strategy is acceptable; don't hold back.
- Piggybacking (i.e., going in a different direction with someone else's idea) is encouraged.
- Team members should not comment or ask questions about strategies until after the brainstorming.
- Avoid looking to the referring teacher for approval when offering an idea (looking at the teacher can encourage the teacher to comment on the suggested strategy).
- Each team member should provide at least one strategy.

Define general guidelines for how long each meeting should last. The team should establish broad guidelines for how long each part of the Multidisciplinary Team Planning Process should last, including setting a target date for when the full process will be completed. If you don't clarify, for example, "we hope to be done with this entire multidisciplinary team process within 6 weeks," a case could drag out for 3 months or a whole semester and the teacher will feel like it never ended. In addition, the team should establish suggested time parameters for how long each meeting should last to keep discussions focused and productive.

The Multidisciplinary Team Planning Process is divided into ten sections:

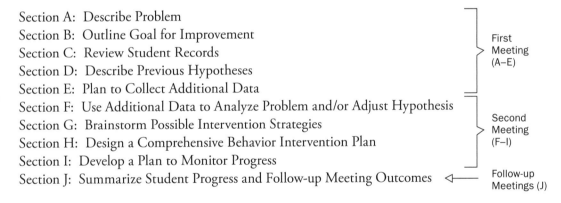

Section A: Describe Problem
Section B: Outline Goal for Improvement
Section C: Review Student Records
Section D: Describe Previous Hypotheses
Section E: Plan to Collect Additional Data
Section F: Use Additional Data to Analyze Problem and/or Adjust Hypothesis
Section G: Brainstorm Possible Intervention Strategies
Section H: Design a Comprehensive Behavior Intervention Plan
Section I: Develop a Plan to Monitor Progress
Section J: Summarize Student Progress and Follow-up Meeting Outcomes

First Meeting (A–E)
Second Meeting (F–I)
Follow-up Meetings (J)

These sections can be completed over the course of at least three meetings:

- First meeting (15–20 minutes): In this meeting, the team will describe the problem, outline the goal for improvement, update the student's intervention history, review student records, describe previous hypotheses, and develop a plan for collecting additional data. Completing Sections A–E will carry the team through Step 1 and part of Step 2 of the problem-solving model. Some of this information can be gathered and compiled ahead of time by the support coordinator or referring teacher to help facilitate this meeting.
- Second meeting (30–45 minutes): The team will meet after additional data have been collected to incorporate new information into the problem analysis step, adjusting hypotheses as needed. Then the team will move on to brainstorm possible intervention strategies to implement, design a comprehensive behavior intervention plan, and outline procedures for monitoring progress under

the plan. Completing Sections F–I finishes Step 2, Step 3, and Step 4 of the problem-solving model.
- Third meeting and beyond (10–15 minutes): Subsequent follow-up meetings are conducted for Step 5 of the problem-solving model—evaluate whether supports are working. In these meetings, the team summarizes student progress and determines whether the intervention should be modified, maintained, or faded, depending on the progress of the student.

If the problem is physically dangerous or otherwise urgent, the timeline and goals of these meetings may, of necessity, change.

Determine team membership and assign job roles. Your school should already have a functioning multidisciplinary team. If it does not, see Section 1, Task 2 (p. 30) for guidelines on establishing one. Such teams usually comprise school-based and itinerant staff members who represent different disciplines in the school and district, such as school counselor, school psychologist, school social worker, school nurse, special education personnel (for example, behavior specialist and speech/language specialist), curriculum specialist (for example, reading teacher and instructional coach), and administrator. Some teams include personnel from outside agencies. In some cases, a master general education teacher may also serve on the team.

As in the other problem-solving processes, the student's classroom teacher should be viewed as an equal partner and active participant in the Multidisciplinary Team Planning Process. With secondary students, or a student who exhibits misbehavior across settings, you may want to invite multiple teachers and staff members who regularly interact with the student. If you are unsure about who to include, distribute the Student Status Report (Reproducible 2.1) to all of the student's teachers and invite those who are most affected by the student's behavior and report having the greatest concerns about the student's performance to participate in the Multidisciplinary Team Planning meeting.

Establishing and nurturing a collaborative relationship with the student's teacher will enable the team to provide crucial support needed for the teacher to faithfully implement the intervention plan that is developed.

Because the student has already gone through several phases of the MTSS problem-solving continuum, one or more of the team members may have already been part of the service delivery for this student—served as the interventionist or worked with an intervention planning team, for example. If this is the case, the multidisciplinary team's work will be enhanced by this existing knowledge of the student's needs and the teacher's efforts to intervene.

As discussed in the 25-Minute Planning Process, clearly defined team roles help ensure that planning meetings are effective and efficient. Review the description of each role on pages 160–161 and identify who will serve as team leader, recorder, and mediator for your multidisciplinary team.

Make sure that team members are familiar with the entire range of behavior intervention strategies available in the building. Strategies include classroom management and early-stage interventions as well as foundational, ready-to-use, and specialized interventions. Not everyone on the multidisciplinary team needs in-depth knowledge of all available intervention strategies, but team members should be familiar with the purpose and general implementation procedures for all possible strategies. If needed, the team can divide up the interventions so that each person is responsible for knowing only a portion of the body of knowledge in depth. The overall goal is to ensure that the team can bring together individual expertise and knowledge to consider the full continuum of available supports during planning discussions.

Step-by-Step Directions for Conducting the Multidisciplinary Team Planning Process

This section describes how to implement each step of the process shown on the Multidisciplinary Team Planning Process worksheet (Reproducible 2.5, pp. 217–230). Before conducting the planning meeting, make sure to:

- *Obtain parent permission for problem-solving and invite parents and older students to participate.* At this point, parents should be well informed about the problem and problem-solving efforts underway at school. Check to make sure that someone has discussed the problem with the parent and invited parents and the student (if appropriate) to participate in the Multidisciplinary Team Planning Process. Also make sure that district or school policies for obtaining parental consent for assessment and intervention have been followed.
- *Review student records.* Before the planning meeting, the support coordinator should gather and review the student's records and fill in relevant information in Section 3 of the Multidisciplinary Team Planning Process. This will save time in the meeting and allow the support coordinator to offer a brief summary of the student's medical, family, school, and assessment history for the team to consider when analyzing the problem and generating possible solutions.
- *Gather documentation from previous problem-solving team meetings.* If the Teacher Interview and 25-Minute Planning Process were conducted at earlier stages of the problem, bring documentation of these meetings to the Multidisciplinary Team Planning meeting. Specifically, copies of the Intervention History, Intervention Decision Guide, and Intervention Plan Summary sections will be very helpful in informing intervention planning.
- *Meet with the student's teachers.* Even if the Teacher Interview was previously completed or the support coordinator has already met with the student's teacher to collect background information, it is still important that the support coordinator meet with all participating teachers before the Multidisciplinary Team Planning meeting. This allows the support coordinator to update the information collected earlier and to continue establishing a collaborative relationship with the teacher. If possible, arrange to conduct this meeting in the teacher's room when students are not there. Meeting in the teacher's room will increase the teacher's comfort level and allow easy access to records and work samples.

    In this meeting, the support coordinator should:

    ○ Gather any relevant data and work samples in preparation for the planning meeting.
    ○ Explain the purpose of the Multidisciplinary Team Planning meeting and familiarize the teacher with the process. Provide the teacher with

a copy of the Multidisciplinary Team Planning Process worksheet that will be used in the meeting.
- Demonstrate good listening skills and show support for the teacher. Given the likelihood that the teacher is frustrated by the student's continued disruptiveness and resistance to change despite previous intervention efforts, the support coordinator must continue efforts to build rapport and trust with the teacher.

At the beginning of the planning meeting, make sure to:

- *Welcome participants and introduce the purpose of the meeting.* The support coordinator or team leader should start the meeting by stating the goal: "Today we are meeting so we can support the student's behavioral needs by evaluating the information and data already collected and by working together to develop a comprehensive intervention plan."
  This introduction should:
  - Provide a brief overview of how the Multidisciplinary Team Planning Process works, including the purpose of each meeting and approximate timelines for completing each part of the process.
  - Review guidelines for ensuring confidentiality. Specify who will have access to the completed Multidisciplinary Team Planning Process worksheet, and review district or school policies around student privacy.
  - Go over team member roles, including who will serve as team leader, recorder, and mediator. Also note the positions that team members hold in the school, district, or community (e.g., social worker, school counselor).
  - Emphasize the importance of ensuring that the outcome of the meeting results from collaboration between the teacher and the multidisciplinary team, wherein everyone works together to create an intervention plan that the teacher selects and develops with guidance and help from the multidisciplinary team.
  - Review established ground rules for the planning meeting (e.g., guidelines for brainstorming, accepting and acknowledging different points of view, staying positive, etc.).

- *Hand out copies of the Multidisciplinary Team Planning Process to each group member.* Providing team members with a copy of the worksheet offers an agenda for the meeting and helps members follow along as you work through each step. To save time, you may transfer relevant information from previously completed Teacher Interview or 25-Minute Planning Process forms to the worksheet, or provide participants with a copy of the previously completed forms. The Intervention History, Intervention Decision Guide, and Intervention Plan Summary will be particularly helpful in the planning meeting, allowing each member to refer to the student's history and previous problem-solving efforts when developing a plan of action.

SECTION 2: EMBEDDING A PROBLEM-SOLVING MODEL INTO EACH TIER OF SUPPORT

Step 1: Define the problem.

SECTION A: DESCRIBE THE PROBLEM

The support coordinator and teacher will be the primary team members leading this section of the meeting. They will work in tandem to introduce the team to the student and the context of the problem, describing the student's problematic behaviors, personal strengths, history of intervention, and outcomes of previous intervention efforts.

> The steps and items shown here correspond to the **Multidisciplinary Team Planning Process form** (Reproducible 2.5, pp. 217–230).

Step 1. Define the problem. *excerpt p. 1 of 14*

SECTION A: DESCRIBE THE PROBLEM

1. Describe the problem or reason for referral:

2. How often do the problems occur? How long does the behavior last? How intense is the problem?

3. **Code Red Situations:** Is the student's behavior unsafe or severely disruptive to the classroom?   Yes / No
   If yes, consult your school's protocol for handling severely disruptive or dangerous behavior.

4. What are the student's strengths?

Item 1. Describe the problem or reason for referral. Provide a summary of the presenting problem, including the reason for the initial referral and what the problematic behavior looks like currently.

Item 2. How often do the problems occur? How long does the behavior last? How intense is the problem? Review information about the frequency, duration, and severity of the problem.

Item 3: Code Red Situations: Is the student's behavior unsafe or severely disruptive to the classroom? Indicate whether the problem is a Code Red situation that involves behaviors that are either so dangerous or so disruptive that classes cannot continue. If Code Red plans have already been put in place, have the teacher describe what was done and the outcomes. If Code Red plans are needed, make note of this, consult the school's protocol for handling severely disruptive or dangerous behaviors, and incorporate these protocols in the student's behavior intervention plan. If your district does not have such a policy, or if the policy is vague and does not define specific procedural actions, see Section 1, Task 6: Establish Processes for Responding to Code Red Situations. Also review Behavior Emergency Planning for guidelines on creating a safety plan for an individual student.

Item 4. What are the student's strengths? Have the teacher describe at least three of the student's strengths for the team. Strengths can be revisited as building blocks for the development of supports for the student. Ask the teacher to describe if and how any previous interventions attempted to capitalize on the strengths, including how effective the interventions were.

Item 5. List interventions tried in Intervention History table. (See the next page.) Review the history of intervention strategies that have already been implemented to address the problem. Ask the teacher to provide a detailed summary of the strengths and weaknesses of previous interventions. This information will be useful in developing future supports.

INTERVENTIONS: SUPPORT FOR INDIVIDUAL STUDENTS WITH BEHAVIOR CHALLENGES

excerpt pp. 2–3 of 14

Intervention History

Intervention/Strategy	Were data collected?	How effective was the intervention/strategy at addressing problem behavior?
	☐ Yes / ☐ No Describe:	☐ Not at all / ☐ Somewhat / ☐ Very Notes:
	☐ Yes / ☐ No Describe:	☐ Not at all / ☐ Somewhat / ☐ Very Notes:
	☐ Yes / ☐ No Describe:	☐ Not at all / ☐ Somewhat / ☐ Very Notes:

Have the teacher describe previously used corrective consequence strategies. The support coordinator can help facilitate this summary by asking questions such as:

- What consequences did you use in the past (e.g., verbal reprimand, time owed, timeout, points lost, referral to the office) and for what misbehavior?
- How did the student respond to the consequences?
- How effective where these consequences? Were any consequences more effective than others?
- How consistently were consequences delivered for each occurrence of the misbehavior?
- Were there times or days of the week when consequences seemed more or less effective?

Also ask the teacher to describe all proactive strategies used as part of previous intervention efforts by asking these questions:

- Which positive strategies were used in the past (e.g., noncontingent positive attention, positive feedback, intermittent celebrations, incentives, and rewards)?
- Which positive strategies were most effective? How did you know?

- Which behaviors earned intermittent celebrations, incentives, or rewards?
- How often did the student earn incentives? Which incentives appeared to be more powerful and effective?
- Which positive strategies and incentives were not effective?
- Did the parents deliver any positive strategies or incentives? If yes, how consistent were the parents? How effective were the home incentives?

In addition, if the student's parents are not attending the meeting, the support coordinator should confirm that the parents have been informed of the student's problems, discuss how the parents responded, and indicate whether or not the parents were involved with any previously attempted interventions.

SECTION B: OUTLINE GOAL FOR IMPROVEMENT

In this section, the team will work together to determine which behaviors to prioritize in the intervention plan and whether to modify the previous goal for improvement.

SECTION B: OUTLINE GOAL FOR IMPROVEMENT *excerpt p. 1 of 14*

6. Prioritize 1–2 major behaviors that are most problematic or urgent:

☐ Physical aggression	☐ Anxiety	☐ Off task
☐ Self-injury	☐ Disruption	☐ Depression, withdrawal
☐ Peer conflict	☐ Absenteeism	☐ Inappropriate language
☐ Damage to property	☐ Bullying others	☐ Tardiness
☐ Noncompliance	☐ Other: _____	☐ Other: _____

7. Determine whether the existing goal should be maintained or if a new goal should be defined. Describe the goal for improvement:

---

6. Prioritize 1–2 major behaviors that are most problematic or urgent. As emphasized in earlier problem-solving processes, identifying intervention priorities is critical. At this point, if misbehavior hasn't been affected by previous intervention efforts, pause to reflect on the most important behavior that your intervention plan needs to address. Consider:

- Which behavior is most problematic, disruptive, or dangerous?
- Which behavior is of most concern to the teacher?
- Which behavior is of most concern to the student's parents?
- Which behaviors have worsened over time?
- What behavior changes are likely to make the greatest difference to the student's success or well-being?
- What behavior changes have the highest probability of success?

7. Determine whether the existing goal should be maintained or if a new goal should be defined. Describe the goal for improvement. Consider the goals that were established previously: Are they still the teacher's main priority? If the team decides to modify a goal, make sure the new goal is *observable, positively stated, specific,* and *obtainable*.

INTERVENTIONS: SUPPORT FOR INDIVIDUAL STUDENTS WITH BEHAVIOR CHALLENGES

SECTION C: REVIEW STUDENT RECORDS

Ideally, the support coordinator should complete this section before the meeting begins. When the team reaches this section, the support coordinator can provide an overview of relevant details from the student's records.

SECTION C: REVIEW STUDENT RECORDS *excerpt p. 4 of 14*

8. Provide details about the student's relevant medical history.

   Any diagnosed illnesses or diseases? Yes / No / Unsure   If yes, describe illness and impact on student: ___

   Mother's age when child was born? ____   Significant birth or developmental history? ____

   History of medications? Yes / No / Unsure   If yes, identify medications, impact on student, and any known side effects: ____

   Wears glasses? Yes / No   Hearing loss? Yes / No   Is the student psychologically/neurologically capable of controlling their behavior? Yes / No / Unsure   If no, describe evidence to support this claim: ____

9. Describe the student's family situation.

   Who does the student live with? ☐ Both parents ☐ Mother only ☐ Father only ☐ Shared custody ☐ Grandparent(s) ☐ Other guardian: ____

   Siblings? Yes / No   Ages and genders: ____

   Education level and job of parents/guardians: ____

   Have one or both parents died? Yes / No   If yes, describe situation: ____

   Any agency involvement (e.g., social worker, Dept. of Human Services, private psychologist?) Yes / No   If yes, please describe: ____

10. Provide details about the student's school history.

    Is or was the student served by special education? Yes / No   If so, which classification, how long, and what level of service? ____

    How many school changes/moves? ____   If yes, where? ____

    History of absenteeism? Yes / No   If yes, describe (e.g., few absences vs. excessive absences [more than 20 per year], which years): ____

    Any retentions? Yes / No   If yes, when? ____

    Summary of the history of report card grades: ____

    Strong and weak subjects from report card grades: ____

    Describe any negative conduct ratings and comments from report cards: ____

11. Describe outcomes from assessments that were administered to the student.

    Summarize results from standardized and state accountability testing within the past 3 years: ____

    Has the school conducted other assessments with the student? Yes / No   If yes, describe the assessments given, when administered, and overall results: ____

    Has the student been evaluated by an outside agency or psychologist? Yes / No   If yes, describe the time frame, purpose, overall results, and outcome of the evaluation: ____

---

8. Provide details about the student's relevant medical history. Record whether records indicate that the student has any diagnosed illnesses or diseases, developmental delays, a history of medication, issues with hearing or eyesight, or other medical issues.

9. Describe the student's family situation. Describe the student's family composition, whether any outside agencies are involved with the student or student's family, and other relevant information about the home situation.

10. **Provide details about the student's school history.** Describe the student's school history. Include a summary of report cards and conduct ratings, indicate whether the student has ever received special education services, and note any history of absenteeism, grade retention, or mobility.

11. **Describe outcomes from assessments that were administered to the student.** Record general results from recent standardized and state test administrations, describe any additional assessments conducted with the student, and indicate whether an outside agency or psychologist has evaluated the student.

Step 2: Analyze the problem.

SECTION D: DESCRIBE PREVIOUS HYPOTHESES

In this section, the team will review previous hypotheses that were made about why the problem is occurring.

Step 2. Analyze the problem.
SECTION D: DESCRIBE PREVIOUS HYPOTHESES

12. What relevant triggers (antecedents) and conditions (setting events) were previously hypothesized to predict when behavior is likely to occur?

    Did interventions confirm that these situations triggered problem behavior? Yes / No / Unsure
    Select level of confidence in hypothesized antecedents: ☐ High ☐ Medium ☐ Low

13. What was the previous functional hypothesis of behavior, or the consequences that seem to be maintaining or reinforcing problem behavior?

    Did interventions confirm that this functional hypothesis explained problem behavior? Yes / No / Unsure
    Select level of confidence in functional hypothesis: ☐ High ☐ Medium ☐ Low

excerpt p. 5 of 14

---

12. **What relevant triggers (antecedents) and conditions (setting events) were previously hypothesized to predict when behavior is likely to occur?** In earlier problem-solving efforts, what antecedents and setting events did the team identify as likely to predict when behavior would occur? Since interventions were put into place, is there any evidence that these situations actually triggered the problem behavior? For example, if the presence of certain peers was hypothesized as an antecedent to aggressive behavior, did moving the student to another seat during independent work time lead to reductions in aggressive incidents? In this item, determine whether the efficacy of previous interventions and ongoing data collection make it clear that these hypothesized factors predict behavior or suggest that another explanation may be more accurate. Indicate the teacher's and team's level of confidence in the original hypothesis.

13. **What was the previous functional hypothesis of behavior, or the consequences that seem to be maintaining or reinforcing problem behavior?** Similarly, determine the accuracy of the original functional hypothesis in explaining the problem behavior. For example, if adult attention was originally identified as the function of misbehavior, did the previous intervention plan that focused on manipulating this variable by having the teacher ignore certain misbehaviors increase the rate of praise for replacement behaviors? Did following a protocol for avoiding power struggles have an effect on the student's behavior? If not, might an alternative function (e.g., peer attention) better explain why the problem behavior is occurring? Indicate the teacher's and team's level of confidence in the original hypothesis.

INTERVENTIONS: SUPPORT FOR INDIVIDUAL STUDENTS WITH BEHAVIOR CHALLENGES

SECTION E: PLAN TO COLLECT ADDITIONAL DATA

The team will outline a plan for collecting additional data in this section.

SECTION E: PLAN TO COLLECT ADDITIONAL DATA

excerpt p. 5 of 14

14. If *medium* or *low* levels of confidence were indicated for any of the previous two items, consider what data sources can provide additional information about why the problem is occurring, and outline a plan for collecting these data.

Additional Data Collection Plan

Data source and purpose	Description	Who, when, where
☐ Direct observation Purpose:		
☐ Staff interview Purpose:		
☐ Student interview Purpose:		
☐ Parent/Guardian interview Purpose:		

---

14. If *medium* or *low* levels of confidence were indicated for any of the previous two items, consider what data sources can provide additional information about why the problem is occurring, and outline a plan for collecting these data. A variety of data collection methods can help the team gather additional evidence about the context of the problem.

   a. *Direct observation:* A crucial aspect of understanding the student's behavior and the context in which it occurs is to conduct a third-party observation of the student in the classroom and other school settings. Identify which behaviors related to the goal should be observed and establish a schedule of observations by determining the crucial settings and times of the day to observe. Do any specific days of the week, times of day, and school settings seem more problematic for the student? The team should consider conducting at least two structured observations of the student in key settings where the behavior has the greatest impact. The team should also identify the type of observational data needed, such as frequency, duration, or latency data. If needed, refer to Section 3, Task 8 for a detailed description of data collection options and sample forms to use in collecting data.

   b. *Staff interview:* Interviewing key people who have worked or are working with the student can be another important source of information. Identify staff members who interact with the student regularly or who knew the student in previous years. Ask questions such as:

- What student strengths have you noticed?
- What problematic behaviors has the student exhibited around you?
- What strategies have you tried when working with the student?
- How has the student responded to these strategies?
- Do you have any suggestions for better supporting the student at school?

c. *Parent/guardian interview:* Insights from a parent or guardian can help the multidisciplinary team understand the student and develop an appropriate plan. Discuss the extent of parent involvement up to this point. If the parent has not been interviewed, assign the team member with the best rapport with the parents to conduct an interview. Questions to ask the parents may include:

- What are some of the strengths that you appreciate in your child?
- What problematic behaviors have you noticed at home or in the community?
- Are you supportive of the identified goal? If not, what would you change?
- What other goals or objectives do you have?
- Can you think of other relevant information or circumstances that may be contributing to your child's behavior problems at school (e.g., history of help your child has received, counseling from resources outside the school, any relevant medical or developmental history, family assets and resources, significant family crises within the past six months)?
- How can school staff better support your child and your family?

d. *Student interview:* Interviewing the student can also yield important insights. Consider asking the following questions:

- What are some of your favorite things about school?
- What things at school are challenging for you (e.g., specific subjects, tasks, teachers, peer activities, etc.)?
- Are you aware of any behaviors that get you into trouble at school?
- Has an adult talked to about these behaviors? When?
- How motivated are you to improve?
- How might your teachers help you to stay out of trouble at school?
- What types of things (e.g., rewards, celebrations, attention) would you like to work toward earning?

e. *Assessments:* Assessments are useful for determining the degree to which a student may be experiencing problems and levels of maladjustment that warrant additional services. Students who exhibit problematic behavior may demonstrate a variety of symptoms that may not be evident unless you specifically look for them, such as struggles with low self-esteem, feelings of helplessness or sadness, social withdrawal and isolation, or excessive worrying and anxiety. Further, administering additional assessments may be worthwhile to gather more information about the severity of externalizing and other more overt behavior problems. To fully assess a problem, you often need to gather information from multiple sources (e.g., teachers, parents, self-report). If the student displays symptoms of any of the following problems, considering initiating additional assessments:

- Internalizing disorders, such as depression and anxiety: signs that the student feels unhappy, sad, or hopeless; lacks energy, enthusiasm, or motivation; is socially withdrawn or isolated; demonstrates excessive worrying or agitation, or frequently reports somatic systems (e.g., headache, sore throats/cough/colds, poor appetite)
- Attention deficit/hyperactivity disorder: inattention, hyperactive or impulsive behaviors, forgetfulness, disorganization
- Oppositional defiant disorder: argumentative and defiant behavior, noncompliance, angry and irritable mood, spiteful or hostile behaviors toward others
- Substance abuse: physical signs or evidence of drug use (e.g., frequent nosebleeds, bloodshot eyes, impaired coordination, smell of smoke or alcohol, skin abrasions or bruises, possession of drug paraphernalia), emotional instability or changes in behavior (e.g., irritability, agitation, or anxiety, declining grades, attendance, or motivation)

ADDITIONAL ASSESSMENTS

If the team opts to administer additional assessments, make sure to follow your district's protocol for obtaining parental consent for assessment. Additional information gathered from observations, interviews, and assessments should be considered confidential, meaning that the information should be shared with only those staff members who have a legitimate reason to know.

At this point, it may also be worthwhile to further examine the student's academic performance and consider whether academic demands may be contributing to the misbehavior. For some students, misbehavior may serve the function of escape from academic tasks that may be too difficult. Assessing the student's current academic ability can provide important information that will allow staff to determine whether the student may benefit from additional academic support. Assessments can also help you determine whether academic difficulties are a product of a skill deficit (i.e., academic expectations are not met because the student cannot do the work) or a performance deficit (i.e. expectations are not met because the student will not do the work). If you suspect that an academic skill deficit may be contributing to the behavior problem, see "Academic Concerns" on pages 128–129.

Further, many students who come to the attention of your problem-solving team will have experienced trauma. When making a plan to collect additional data about the student and the context of the problem, make sure to look for signs of trauma. See Trauma-Informed Intervention (Appendix A) for a list of potential signs of trauma as well as recommendations for intervention strategies to consider when working with students who have experienced trauma.

Use the Additional Data Collection Plan table to describe the methods and purpose for data collection, as well as who will be responsible for collecting data and when and where data collection will occur. The team leader should ask staff members involved in the additional data collection plan to briefly summarize their observations, interviews, and assessment outcomes in a one-page summary, preferably using charts or tables when appropriate, so that the data can be easily shared with the team at the next meeting.

NOTE: In most cases, you will conclude the first meeting at this point. Make sure that all people involved in collecting additional data are aware of their responsibilities and the timeline. It's helpful to make copies of the data collection plan to share with relevant team members. Set a date to meet again to discuss the outcomes of data collection and begin developing a comprehensive behavior intervention plan for the student. Depending on the number of observations, interviews, and assessments that need to be completed, the meeting should be scheduled within 1–2 weeks of the first meeting. If the team decides that no additional data are needed to understand the problem, skip to Section G on page 7 of the worksheet to begin developing a comprehensive behavior intervention plan for the student.

SECTION F: USE ADDITIONAL DATA TO ANALYZE PROBLEM/ADJUST HYPOTHESIS

The second meeting of the Multidisciplinary Team Planning Process will begin with completing Section F, where the team will use additional data to analyze the problem and adjust the hypothesis, if needed. At the beginning of the meeting, the team leader should facilitate any necessary introductions, review team roles and ground rules, and provide an overview of the purpose of the second meeting—which is to review additional data that has been collected and develop a comprehensive intervention plan for the student.

SECTION F: USE ADDITIONAL DATA TO ANALYZE PROBLEM/ADJUST HYPOTHESIS

excerpt p. 6 of 14

15. Summarize general findings from additional data collection:

16. Identify relevant triggers (antecedents) and conditions (setting events) that predict when behavior is likely to occur. Possible Antecedents and Setting Events:
    - ☐ Unstructured time
    - ☐ Whole group instruction
    - ☐ Small group activities
    - ☐ Independent work
    - ☐ Transitions
    - ☐ Change in routine
    - ☐ Specific tasks: _____
    - ☐ Peers present
    - ☐ Peer conflict
    - ☐ After adult correction or reprimands
    - ☐ Corrective consequence or loss of privilege
    - ☐ Other: _____
    - ☐ Hunger
    - ☐ Conflict or stressors at home
    - ☐ Illness, pain, discomfort
    - ☐ Missed medications
    - ☐ Lack of sleep

    Data sources that support this hypothesis:

---

15. Summarize general findings from additional data collection. Once the introductions and overview are completed, the team leader can distribute copies of summaries of the additional observations, interviews, and assessments completed since the previous meeting. Each person responsible for writing a summary should provide the team with a brief 1- or 2-minute review of key findings. This sharing may take anywhere from 5 to 10 minutes, depending on the amount of new data to review. To avoid devoting too much time to sharing the information, the team leader can remind each person to be concise and brief, then give reminders about the time, as needed.

16. Identify relevant triggers (antecedents) and conditions (setting events) that predict when behavior is likely to occur. After all new data have been reviewed, the team leader should direct the team to consider how this additional information informs hypotheses about antecedents and setting events.

To help guide this discussion, ask questions such as:

- Which situations seem to set off the problem behavior?
- Where and when do problems tend to occur?
- What conditions seem to increase the likelihood that problem behavior will occur on any given day?
- What evidence from observations, interviews, assessments, and other data collection efforts supports this hypothesis?

Once the team decides to either keep the original hypotheses or adjust them to align better with the recently collected data, note the data sources that support the current hypotheses (e.g., observational data, information from student records, assessment results, data from interviews with the teacher, other staff, student, or parents).

17. Identify the function of behavior, or the consequences that seem to be maintaining or reinforcing problem behavior. Also consider how additional data support or counter the original hypothesis about the function of misbehavior. Determine what the student seems to achieve through the behavior by asking questions such as:

- Does the student lack certain skills or an awareness of the behavior that may be contributing to the problem?
- Is the student trying to get something?
- Is the student trying to avoid something?
- What evidence from observations, interviews, assessments, and other data collection efforts supports this hypothesis?

---

excerpt p. 7 of 14

17. Identify the function of the behavior, or the consequences that seem to be maintaining or reinforcing problem behavior. Hypothesized function(s):

Deficits
- ☐ Lacking awareness
- ☐ Lacking ability:
  - ☐ Physical/Neurological
  - ☐ Academic
  - ☐ Social/Emotional

Trying to Get Something
- ☐ Seeking adult attention
- ☐ Seeking peer attention
- ☐ Seeking access to activities
- ☐ Seeking power or control

Trying to Avoid Something
- ☐ Avoiding overly difficult or overly simple work
- ☐ Avoiding nonpreferred activities and tasks
- ☐ Avoiding peer interactions
- ☐ Avoiding adult interactions

Data sources that support this hypothesis:

Again, decide whether to keep the original functional hypothesis or develop a new one informed by the data that have been gathered. Note the data sources that offer support for the hypothesized function. If needed, refer to "Developing a Functional Hypothesis" on pages 130–133 for more guidance in considering function.

Step 3: Consider possible solutions and select intervention strategies.

SECTION G: BRAINSTORM POSSIBLE INTERVENTION STRATEGIES

The team will use this section to develop a list of possible strategies to incorporate into the student's behavior intervention plan.

18. Identify examples of appropriate behavior and student strengths to encourage and examples of inappropriate behavior to discourage. Revisit the list of appropriate and inappropriate behaviors that problem-solving teams identified previously. Are these the

> ### Step 3. Consider possible solutions and select intervention strategies.
> #### SECTION G: BRAINSTORM POSSIBLE INTERVENTION STRATEGIES
>
> 18. Identify examples of appropriate behavior and student strengths to encourage and examples of inappropriate behavior to discourage.
>
> | Appropriate Behavior | Inappropriate Behavior |
> |---|---|
> | | |
>
> *excerpt p. 7 of 14*
>
> 19. Identify a list of possible strategies to implement to encourage appropriate behavior or discourage inappropriate behavior.
>
>   a. List ready-to-use interventions already existing in your building.
>
>   - _____
>   - _____
>   - _____
>   - _____
>   - _____
>
>   b. Using the Intervention Decision Guide on the next page, review the list of *presenting behaviors* and check each one that describes the student or context of the problem.
>
>   c. Brainstorm and list any other possible interventions strategies not included above.

same behaviors that the team would like to target with intervention? Do they align with the goal identified in Item 7? If not, adjust accordingly. The team may need to include new appropriate behaviors that have been added to the student's repertoire and additional inappropriate behaviors that have emerged, remove behaviors that were inappropriate but are no longer a concern, and more precisely define behaviors in either category, if needed. Make sure to clearly define the positive behaviors that will lead to achieving the goal and the negative behaviors that will detract from it, identifying the line between *appropriate* behaviors to encourage and *inappropriate* behaviors to discourage. If needed, refer to Section 3, Task 5, Step 1 for more guidance in defining limits of behavior.

19. Identify a list of possible intervention strategies to implement. (See the next page, or pp. 224–225 for full-page thumbnails.) If previous problem-solving efforts used the Teacher Interview and/or 25-Minute Planning Process, you may wish to refer to the documentation for those meetings. As part of both of those processes, a problem-solving team may have already created a list of potential intervention strategies. The team can consider whether to incorporate any of those strategies that haven't yet been tried.

In the first part of this item, list all ready-to-use interventions already in place within your school that might be a good fit for the student. In the second part, review each presenting behavior listed on the Intervention Decision Guide and place a check in the second column if it is true for the student. If any of the interventions have already been tried, indicate the approximate date of implementation and degree of effectiveness. If an intervention strategy was successful, or the team thinks it might be successful in combination with other strategies, place a mark in the second column (Check if true) to include the intervention for consideration.

INTERVENTIONS: SUPPORT FOR INDIVIDUAL STUDENTS WITH BEHAVIOR CHALLENGES

Once the team has a list of all potentially relevant ready-to-use interventions and possible intervention strategies checked on the Intervention Decision Guide, brainstorm any additional intervention strategies not included on these two lists.

Because the intervention plan should include prevention, corrective consequences, and positive reinforcement strategies, the team should consider conducting two separate brainstorming sessions, each lasting 3 to 5 minutes. We recommend that the first brainstorming session focus on options for consequences, followed by a session on possible positive and preventive strategies.

excerpt pp. 8–9 of 14

Intervention Decision Guide

Presenting behavior	Check if true	Intervention strategy	Date implemented	Effective? (+/–)
More than three students in class misbehave	☐	Assess classroom management practices		
The student has an underlying academic problem	☐	Address academic needs		
The student is not aware of the problem, or no individual supports have been tried yet	☐	Early-stage interventions		
The student doesn't know what is expected or lacks the ability to exhibit the expected behavior	☐	B. Change work requirements D. Change expectations or procedures F. Use precorrections I. Re-teach classroom expectations J. Provide demonstrations and modeling K. Provide positive practice and feedback L. Provide opportunities for verbal practice M. Deliver praise and specific feedback		
Adult attention seems to reinforce misbehavior	☐	G. Increase opportunities to respond M. Deliver praise and specific feedback O. Send positive news home P. Ignore misbehavior W. Increase the frequency of noncontingent positive attention		
Peer attention seems to reinforce misbehavior	☐	A. Change assigned seating Q. Reduce peer attention		
Escape seems to reinforce misbehavior	☐	B. Change work requirements C. Provide breaks D. Change expectations or procedures E. Offer viable choices S. Assign time owed		
Access to tangibles, activities, or privileges seems to reinforce misbehavior	☐	N. Offer rewards V. Revoke a privilege		
Specific consequences for misbehavior are necessary	☐	R. Use gentle verbal reprimands or warnings S. Assign time owed T. Assign in-class timeout V. Revoke a privilege		
Misbehavior may be positively affected by changes to structural features of the classroom (e.g. classroom layout, schedule)	☐	A. Change assigned seating B. Change work requirements D. Change expectations or procedures		
The student misbehaves under periods of low supervision or structure	☐	D. Change expectations or procedures H. Increase monitoring and supervision		
Previously used consequences for misbehavior don't seem to work, or misbehavior is a firmly established part of the student's behavior	☐	1. Behavioral Contracting 2. Structured Reinforcement		

(continued)

Intervention strategy	Date implemented	Effective? (+/–)
...and Self-Evaluation		
...ional Escalation		
...dents with Internalizing		
...quency of noncontingent ...n		
...gful duty or ...school		
...acilitate the student's ...lubs, after-school ...her school events ...dent with an adult or ...chool		
Consult school ...ing to severely		
...ncy Planning ...ss timeout		
Consult school ...ing to unsafe or physically dangerous behavior		
4. Behavior Emergency Planning U. Assign out-of-class timeout		

Come up with as many strategies as possible in the time allotted. Be sure to move through each suggestion quickly, not getting stuck on one possibility. Pros and cons of each strategy can be discussed at a later time. The team leader must be assertive at this step to keep the process moving. Consider a broad range of options and be as creative as possible. The more possible intervention strategies that the team can identify, the greater the likelihood the intervention plan will successfully address both the student's and the teacher's needs. The recorder should write down every suggestion so that all possibilities will be available for future use whether they are used in the initial plan or not. Consider incorporating these suggestions to facilitate brainstorming:

- After 30 seconds of silence, read the list aloud to stimulate more ideas.
- Write down a summary statement or phrase for every strategy or idea.
- Record the ideas on chart paper, white board, or computer with LCD projector so everyone can see them.

When brainstorming is completed, the team leader should allow 2 or 3 minutes for any team member to ask questions about specific suggestions. Be sure to encourage the teacher to ask questions, especially about any suggested strategies that are not familiar.

SECTION H: DESIGN A COMPREHENSIVE BEHAVIOR INTERVENTION PLAN

In this section, the multidisciplinary team and teacher will work together to design the intervention plan. While this stage of the problem-solving continuum is specifically designed to bring the highest level of expertise and experience to developing a comprehensive intervention plan, team members need to be careful about advocating for a specific intervention. The degree of teacher buy-in, effort, and fidelity of the intervention plan can be easily compromised if teachers feel that they had little or no input into what was selected (Kratochwill et al., 2002; Roach & Elliott, 2008). To achieve a balance between team recommendations and teacher investment in the plan, the team should provide guidance while actively seeking input and buy-in from the teacher.

To achieve a balance between team recommendations and teacher investment in the plan, the team should provide guidance while actively seeking input and buy-in from the teacher.

When selecting interventions to implement, make sure that the intervention plan:

- Is related to the identified goal
- Takes into account the hypothesis about the function of the misbehavior
- Seems manageable and acceptable to the teacher

Also see "Considerations in Choosing Intervention Strategies" on pages 141–142.

20. Select intervention strategies to implement. Use the Comprehensive Behavior Intervention Plan table provided to outline a detailed plan for implementing intervention strategies to address misbehavior, encourage appropriate behavior, and help meet the student's needs at school. This plan includes a description of each intervention strategy that will be implemented, as well as responsibilities and timelines for the staff members involved. The table is divided into five sections:

- *Antecedent strategies* to address events that occur immediately before the student's inappropriate behavior (antecedents) or to target situations or conditions that increase the likelihood that inappropriate behavior will occur (setting events)

- *Teaching strategies* to help the student learn positive replacement behaviors
- *Positive consequence strategies* that outline rewards and responses from staff intended to encourage appropriate behavior and discourage misbehavior
- *Corrective consequence strategies* that will be used to respond to student misbehavior and ensure that staff corrects misbehavior fluently
- *Interactional strategies* to provide the student with a high rate of noncontingent positive attention and help the student feel connected to school

Refer to Section 3, Tasks 2–6 for more detailed descriptions of these foundational intervention strategies and guidance on selecting appropriate strategies within each category.

SECTION H: DESIGN A COMPREHENSIVE BEHAVIOR INTERVENTION PLAN

20. Select intervention strategies to implement. Describe how, where, and when strategies will be implemented and the responsibilities of staff members involved.

excerpt p. 10 of 14

Comprehensive Behavior Intervention Plan

a. Identify antecedent intervention strategies.

Plan for using antecedent strategies	Staff responsible	Start date

b. Identify teaching intervention strategies.

Plan for teaching appropriate/replacement behaviors	Staff responsible	Start date

SECTION 2: EMBEDDING A PROBLEM-SOLVING MODEL INTO EACH TIER OF SUPPORT

c. Identify positive consequence intervention strategies.

Plan for using positive consequence intervention strategies	Staff responsible	Start date

excerpt pp. 11–12 of 14

List of possible rewards and praise statements:

d. Identify corrective consequence intervention strategies.
   Step 1: Categorize problem behaviors and define limits.
   List categories of problem behaviors to correct.

   Step 2: Select corrective consequence strategies.

Plan for using corrective consequence strategies		

e. Identify strategies to increase noncontingent positive interactions and school connectedness.
   Step 1: Determine baseline ratio of positive to corrective interactions.
   - Do baseline data reflect at least a 3:1 positive to corrective ratio of interactions? Yes / No
   - Identify when and where to direct efforts to improve ratio of interactions:

   Step 2: Select strategies to increase noncontingent positive interactions and school connectedness.

Plan for increasing positive interactions and school connectedness	Staff responsible	Start date

f. Describe other group interactions, academic supports, accommodations, or specialized intervention strategies.

Plan for incorporating other intervention strategies	Staff responsible	Start date

REPRODUCIBLE 2.5

211

In many cases, you may opt to incorporate intervention strategies that are not fully captured in the categories defined above. Note these in the space provided. These may include:

- Existing interventions from your building or district menu of ready-to-use interventions (e.g., check-and-connect, social skills groups, mentorship programs)
- Academic supports (e.g., participation in supplementary reading skill groups, extra time on tests)
- Accommodations for specific disabilities or impairments (e.g., adaptations to the environment and curriculum materials for a student with visual impairment)
- Specialized intervention strategies for addressing certain types of problematic behavior (e.g., mental health issues, dangerous or highly disruptive behavior) or detailed systems for delivering strategies (e.g., self-monitoring and self-evaluation, structured reinforcement). Refer to Section 4 for descriptions and procedures for implementing specialized intervention strategies.

Once the team outlines strategies for each section of the intervention plan, the next step requires nailing down all the details of the intervention. No matter how powerful the intervention strategies, the success of the intervention plan depends on developing and documenting details. Record the logistical details of the plan (i.e., who, what, where, and when) and be sure to identify resources the teacher will need (e.g., modeling, coaching, observations, forms, materials).

Step 4: Collect data to monitor progress.

SECTION I: DEVELOP A PLAN TO MONITOR PROGRESS

In this section, the team will identify methods that can be used to evaluate the effect of the intervention plan on the student's target behaviors.

Step 4. Collect data to monitor progress. *excerpt p. 13 of 14*

SECTION I: DEVELOP A PLAN TO MONITOR PROGRESS

21. Identify data that will be used to track progress toward the goal, including who will collect data and how.

22. Identify follow-up dates to check in about progress.

23. Identify at least two ways to determine whether the plan is working at the next follow-up meeting.

24. Describe plans to monitor and evaluate implementation fidelity.

---

21. Identify data that will be used to track progress toward the goal, including who will collect data and how. Review the goal that the team defined in Item 7. Identify at least one source of objective data to collect for each goal behavior. Objective data collection might include rating scales, work products, self-monitoring data, data from a reinforcement system intervention, audio or video records, and frequency, duration, or latency data. If needed, refer to Section 3, Task 8 for a detailed description of data collection options and sample forms to use in collecting data.

22. **Identify follow-up date(s) to check in about progress.** Schedule the first follow-up meeting for about two weeks after implementation is scheduled to begin.

23. **Identify at least two ways to determine whether the plan is working at the next follow-up meeting.** Define the decision rules that the team will use to determine whether the student has made sufficient progress under the plan. This item expands on the goal defined in Item 7 and the data collection procedures outlined in Item 21. Decision rules should be specific and include numbers and timelines to clearly define how much improvement will be considered sufficient.

Select at least two ways to evaluate progress. These can include any of the objective data sources that you selected in Item 21 as well as observations by an outside observer or subjective perceptions from the teacher or other staff. For example:

- After 2 weeks of implementation, the plan is working if Jasmine accurately completes her self-monitoring forms at least 4 out of 5 days of the week, turns in 80% of her daily assignments, and checks in with her mentor at least once per week.
- The plan is working if Kyle meets his point goal 80% of the time and rating scales competed by the teacher show an improvement in his peer interactions.
- Over the course of 2 weeks, if weekly structured observations by the behavior specialist reflect at least a 50% decrease in inappropriate behavior toward peers at recess and the recess supervisor reports no major infractions, the plan is working.

Item 24. Describe plans to monitor and evaluate implementation fidelity. If you put a plan into place but it isn't working, your problem-solving team will need to verify that the strategies were implemented in the way they were designed to be. Select a method for monitoring and evaluating implementation fidelity (e.g., directly observing implementation, evaluating permanent products, or having the teacher or interventionist self-monitor) and define what "good" fidelity looks like. Also identify a schedule for monitoring fidelity and consider ways to encourage good implementation and provide follow-up support as needed. Refer to Section 3, Task 9 for more in-depth recommendations and options for monitoring implementation fidelity.

NOTE: At this point, you will conclude the second planning meeting. Ask if the teacher, parents, or other team members have any questions or need additional support or resources from the team. Make sure that all people involved in the intervention plan are aware of their responsibilities and know what steps to take next to initiate implementation. Share copies of the Comprehensive Behavior Intervention Plan with all team members and applicable staff. Thank all meeting attendees for their input and participation in the intervention plan design.

The support coordinator should check in with the teacher or other involved staff after the first day or two of implementation. If there are problems or anything not anticipated, the support coordinator can help troubleshoot and get the plan on track.

INTERVENTIONS: SUPPORT FOR INDIVIDUAL STUDENTS WITH BEHAVIOR CHALLENGES

Step 5: Evaluate whether supports are working.

SECTION J: SUMMARIZE STUDENT PROGRESS AND FOLLOW-UP MEETING OUTCOMES

In all subsequent follow-up meetings, the team will evaluate progress and modify the plan, as needed. Make sure that intervention plans are implemented for at least 2 weeks before the initial follow-up meeting.

Follow-Up Meetings

excerpt pp. 13–14 of 14

Step 5. Evaluate whether supports are working.
SECTION J: SUMMARIZE STUDENT PROGRESS AND FOLLOW-UP MEETING OUTCOMES

25. Provide a summary of follow-up meetings. Describe any modifications that are made to the intervention plan.

Follow-up Meeting #1   Date: _____

Team members present: ☐ Support Coordinator   ☐ Gen Ed Teacher   ☐ Special Ed Teacher
☐ Student   ☐ Parent   ☐ Speech-Language Pathologist
☐ Behavior Specialist   ☐ School Psychologist   ☐ Administrator

Other participants _____

Summary of data collected since last meeting:

Summary of teacher's perceptions of how well the plan has addressed the target behavior:

Team recommendations (e.g., continue implementation as is, revise plan, refer to special education, etc.):

Who will share outcomes of meeting with: Classroom teacher? _____ Parent/student? _____

Team members present: ☐ ... Teacher   ☐ Special Ed Teacher
☐ Speech-Language Pathologist
☐ ... Psychologist   ☐ Administrator

... essed the target behavior:

... ise plan, refer to special education, etc.):

Who will share outcomes of meeting with: Classroom teacher? _____ Parent/student? _____

Follow-up Meeting #3   Date: _____

Team members present: ☐ Support Coordinator   ☐ Gen Ed Teacher   ☐ Special Ed Teacher
☐ Student   ☐ Parent   ☐ Speech-Language Pathologist
☐ Behavior Specialist   ☐ School Psychologist   ☐ Administrator

Other participants _____

Summary of data collected since last meeting:

Summary of teacher's perceptions of how well the plan has addressed the target behavior:

Team recommendations (e.g., continue implementation as is, revise plan, refer to special education, etc.):

Who will share outcomes of meeting with: Classroom teacher? _____ Parent/student? _____

25. Provide a summary of follow-up meetings. Describe any modifications made to the intervention plan. At the start of each meeting, record which team members are present. Ask participants to share any data collected since the last meeting, and record a summary of these data. Ask the teacher and intervention coordinator to share informal impressions about how the plan is working to address the targeted behaviors. Based on data and these impressions, the team should determine whether the intervention plan should be maintained, modified, replaced, or faded. The following are possible options the team might consider:

- If the interventions are working, continue implementation. The team needs to encourage the teacher to celebrate the improvements and to provide the student and parents with positive feedback about the interventions.
- Continue the interventions as designed, but adjust implementation to ensure greater fidelity.
- Revise the intervention to address weaknesses or gaps. Implement the modified plan for another 2 weeks and continue to collect data.
- Amend the intervention to address other target behaviors. Implement the revised intervention for 2 weeks and continue to collect data.
- Refer the student to special education or other appropriate school or district services or programs.
- Begin to phase out the intervention plan as a result of its successful effect on the target behavior. Set a gradual phase-out schedule and be sure to celebrate the student's success. Once phase-out is completed, discontinue the intervention plan and connect the student to any universal supports in the school that can meet the student's needs and ensure successful adjustment. Note that this fading is unlikely to occur until an intervention successfully maintains the goal behavior over a period of several months.

Once the team determines how to proceed, outline a plan to share team recommendations with the classroom teacher, parent, and student. Also decide if and when any additional follow-up meetings are needed. Once the referral is closed, the multidisciplinary team should carefully document its recommendations and findings on the Multidisciplinary Team Planning Process and attach copies of relevant forms, collected data, and charts. This documentation should be kept in a confidential location that ensures appropriate access for involved staff members. Follow district policy on whether this documentation should be placed in the student's official school records.

Summary of the Multidisciplinary Team Planning Process

Although the problem-solving process implemented by the multidisciplinary team is very similar to that of both the Teacher Interview and the 25-Minute Planning Process, it differs in scope. The process involves more skilled professionals to create a greater breadth of perspective and includes collection of much more information in the form of observations, interviews, and assessments to ensure that all available information and resources (district and community) are brought to bear in designing a comprehensive intervention. As we have stated many times, MTSS is about matching the intensity of problem-solving and intervention to the needs of the student. This multidisciplinary process is occurring only because less intense processes have failed to yield a successful intervention. At this stage, every effort must be made to find something that will help the student succeed.

Section Summary

This section provided information useful in designing any intervention. By using a consistent five-step problem-solving process, interventionists can objectively define and analyze any problem, consider and select evidence-based intervention strategies, use data to monitor progress, and evaluate the efficacy or lack thereof of the intervention plan. In addition, three tools for applying this process were covered: A Teacher Interview protocol, a 25-Minute Planning Process agenda for use by a team of professionals, and a detailed and extensive Multidisciplinary Team Planning Process. This section can be used to guide the work of an individual interventionist and anyone on a school's problem-solving or multidisciplinary team.

REPRODUCIBLE 2.5 *Multidisciplinary Team Planning Process (1 of 14)*

Multidisciplinary Team Planning Process

Student _____ Age _____ Grade _____ Date _____

Teacher _____ Support Coordinator _____

Meeting 1

Date of meeting: _____

Team members present:
- ☐ Support Coordinator
- ☐ Student
- ☐ Behavior Specialist
- ☐ Gen Ed Teacher
- ☐ Parent
- ☐ School Psychologist
- ☐ Special Ed Teacher
- ☐ Speech-Language Pathologist
- ☐ Administrator

Other participants _____

Step 1. Define the problem.

SECTION A: DESCRIBE THE PROBLEM

1. Describe the problem or reason for referral:

2. How often do the problems occur? How long does the behavior last? How intense is the problem?

3. **Code Red Situations:** Is the student's behavior unsafe or severely disruptive to the classroom? Yes / No
   If yes, consult your school's protocol for handling severely disruptive or dangerous behavior.

4. What are the student's strengths?

5. List interventions tried in the Intervention History table on the next two pages.

SECTION B: OUTLINE GOAL FOR IMPROVEMENT

6. Prioritize 1–2 major behaviors that are most problematic or urgent:

   - ☐ Physical aggression
   - ☐ Self-injury
   - ☐ Peer conflict
   - ☐ Damage to property
   - ☐ Noncompliance
   - ☐ Anxiety
   - ☐ Disruption
   - ☐ Absenteeism
   - ☐ Bullying others
   - ☐ Other: _____
   - ☐ Off task
   - ☐ Depression, withdrawal
   - ☐ Inappropriate language
   - ☐ Tardiness
   - ☐ Other: _____

7. Determine whether the existing goal should be maintained or if a new goal should be defined. Describe the goal for improvement:

Interventions © 2019 Ancora Publishing

Multidisciplinary Team Planning Process

Intervention History

Intervention/Strategy	Were data collected?	How effective was the intervention/strategy at addressing problem behavior?
	☐ Yes / ☐ No Describe:	☐ Not at all / ☐ Somewhat / ☐ Very Notes:
	☐ Yes / ☐ No Describe:	☐ Not at all / ☐ Somewhat / ☐ Very Notes:
	☐ Yes / ☐ No Describe:	☐ Not at all / ☐ Somewhat / ☐ Very Notes:
	☐ Yes / ☐ No Describe:	☐ Not at all / ☐ Somewhat / ☐ Very Notes:
	☐ Yes / ☐ No Describe:	☐ Not at all / ☐ Somewhat / ☐ Very Notes:

REPRODUCIBLE 2.5 *Multidisciplinary Team Planning Process (3 of 14)*

Multidisciplinary Team Planning Process

Intervention/Strategy	Were data collected?	How effective was the intervention/strategy at addressing problem behavior?
	☐ Yes / ☐ No Describe:	☐ Not at all / ☐ Somewhat / ☐ Very Notes:
	☐ Yes / ☐ No Describe:	☐ Not at all / ☐ Somewhat / ☐ Very Notes:
	☐ Yes / ☐ No Describe:	☐ Not at all / ☐ Somewhat / ☐ Very Notes:
	☐ Yes / ☐ No Describe:	☐ Not at all / ☐ Somewhat / ☐ Very Notes:
	☐ Yes / ☐ No Describe:	☐ Not at all / ☐ Somewhat / ☐ Very Notes:

REPRODUCIBLE 2.5 *Multidisciplinary Team Planning Process (4 of 14)*

Multidisciplinary Team Planning Process

SECTION C: REVIEW STUDENT RECORDS

8. Provide details about the student's relevant medical history.

    Any diagnosed illnesses or diseases? Yes / No / Unsure   If yes, describe illness and impact on student: ___
    _____

    Mother's age when child was born? ____   Significant birth or developmental history? _____

    History of medications? Yes / No / Unsure   If yes, identify medications, impact on student, and any known side effects: _____

    Wears glasses? Yes / No   Hearing loss? Yes / No   Is the student psychologically/neurologically capable of controlling their behavior? Yes / No / Unsure   If no, describe evidence to support this claim: _____
    _____

9. Describe the student's family situation.

    Who does the student live with?   ☐ Both parents   ☐ Mother only   ☐ Father only   ☐ Shared custody
    ☐ Grandparent(s)   ☐ Other guardian: _____

    Siblings? Yes / No   Ages and genders: _____

    Education level and job of parents/guardians: _____

    Have one or both parents died? Yes / No   If yes, describe situation: _____
    _____

    Any agency involvement (e.g., social worker, Dept. of Human Services, private psychologist?) Yes / No   If yes, please describe: _____

10. Provide details about the student's school history.

    Is or was the student served by special education? Yes / No   If so, which classification, how long, and what level of service? _____

    How many school changes/moves? ____   If yes, where? _____

    History of absenteeism? Yes / No   If yes, describe (e.g., few absences vs. excessive absences [more than 20 per year], which years): _____

    Any retentions? Yes / No   If yes, when? _____

    Summary of the history of report card grades: _____

    Strong and weak subjects from report card grades: _____
    _____

    Describe any negative conduct ratings and comments from report cards: _____
    _____

11. Describe outcomes from assessments that were administered to the student.

    Summarize results from standardized and state accountability testing within the past 3 years: _____
    _____

    Has the school conducted other assessments with the student? Yes / No   If yes, describe the assessments given, when administered, and overall results: _____
    _____

    Has the student been evaluated by an outside agency or psychologist? Yes / No   If yes, describe the time frame, purpose, overall results, and outcome of the evaluation: _____

REPRODUCIBLE 2.5 *Multidisciplinary Team Planning Process (5 of 14)*

Multidisciplinary Team Planning Process

Step 2. Analyze the problem.

SECTION D: DESCRIBE PREVIOUS HYPOTHESES

12. What relevant triggers (antecedents) and conditions (setting events) were previously hypothesized to predict when behavior is likely to occur?

    Did interventions confirm that these situations triggered problem behavior? Yes / No / Unsure
    Select level of confidence in hypothesized antecedents: ☐ High ☐ Medium ☐ Low

13. What was the previous functional hypothesis of behavior, or the consequences that seem to be maintaining or reinforcing problem behavior?

    Did interventions confirm that this functional hypothesis explained problem behavior? Yes / No / Unsure
    Select level of confidence in functional hypothesis: ☐ High ☐ Medium ☐ Low

SECTION E: PLAN TO COLLECT ADDITIONAL DATA

14. If *medium* or *low* levels of confidence were indicated for any of the previous two items, consider what data sources can provide additional information about why the problem is occurring, and outline a plan for collecting these data.

Additional Data Collection Plan

Data source and purpose	Description	Who, when, where
☐ Direct observation Purpose:		
☐ Staff interview Purpose:		
☐ Student interview Purpose:		
☐ Parent/Guardian interview Purpose:		

Interventions © 2019 Ancora Publishing

REPRODUCIBLE 2.5 *Multidisciplinary Team Planning Process (6 of 14)*

Multidisciplinary Team Planning Process

Data source and purpose	Description	Who, when, where
☐ Assessments Purpose:		
☐ Other Purpose:		

Meeting 2

Date of meeting: _____

Team members present: ☐ Support Coordinator ☐ Gen Ed Teacher ☐ Special Ed Teacher
  ☐ Student ☐ Parent ☐ Speech-Language Pathologist
  ☐ Behavior Specialist ☐ School Psychologist ☐ Administrator

Other participants _____

SECTION F: USE ADDITIONAL DATA TO ANALYZE PROBLEM/ADJUST HYPOTHESIS

15. Summarize general findings from additional data collection:

16. Identify relevant triggers (antecedents) and conditions (setting events) that predict when behavior is likely to occur. Possible Antecedents and Setting Events:

    ☐ Unstructured time
    ☐ Whole group instruction
    ☐ Small group activities
    ☐ Independent work
    ☐ Transitions
    ☐ Change in routine
    ☐ Specific tasks: _____

    ☐ Peers present
    ☐ Peer conflict
    ☐ After adult correction or reprimands
    ☐ Corrective consequence or loss of privilege
    ☐ Other: _____

    ☐ Hunger
    ☐ Conflict or stressors at home
    ☐ Illness, pain, discomfort
    ☐ Missed medications
    ☐ Lack of sleep

    Data sources that support this hypothesis:

Interventions © 2019 Ancora Publishing

REPRODUCIBLE 2.5 *Multidisciplinary Team Planning Process (7 of 14)*

Multidisciplinary Team Planning Process

17. Identify the function of the behavior, or the consequences that seem to be maintaining or reinforcing problem behavior. Hypothesized function(s):

    Deficits
    ☐ Lacking awareness
    ☐ Lacking ability:
      ☐ Physical/Neurological
      ☐ Academic
      ☐ Social/Emotional

    Trying to Get Something
    ☐ Seeking adult attention
    ☐ Seeking peer attention
    ☐ Seeking access to activities
    ☐ Seeking power or control

    Trying to Avoid Something
    ☐ Avoiding overly difficult or overly simple work
    ☐ Avoiding nonpreferred activities and tasks
    ☐ Avoiding peer interactions
    ☐ Avoiding adult interactions

    Data sources that support this hypothesis:

    ### Step 3. Consider possible solutions and select intervention strategies.
    #### SECTION G: BRAINSTORM POSSIBLE INTERVENTION STRATEGIES

18. Identify examples of appropriate behavior and student strengths to encourage and examples of inappropriate behavior to discourage.

Appropriate Behavior	Inappropriate Behavior

19. Identify a list of possible strategies to implement to encourage appropriate behavior or discourage inappropriate behavior.

    a. List ready-to-use interventions already existing in your building.

    - _____
    - _____
    - _____
    - _____
    - _____

    b. Using the Intervention Decision Guide on the next page, review the list of *presenting behaviors* and check each one that describes the student or context of the problem.

    c. Brainstorm and list any other possible interventions strategies not included above.

Interventions © 2019 Ancora Publishing

REPRODUCIBLE 2.5 *Multidisciplinary Team Planning Process (8 of 14)*

Multidisciplinary Team Planning Process

Intervention Decision Guide

Presenting behavior	Check if true	Intervention strategy	Date implemented	Effective? (+/−)
More than three students in class misbehave	☐	Assess classroom management practices		
The student has an underlying academic problem	☐	Address academic needs		
The student is not aware of the problem, or no individual supports have been tried yet	☐	Early-stage interventions		
The student doesn't know what is expected or lacks the ability to exhibit the expected behavior	☐	B. Change work requirements D. Change expectations or procedures F. Use precorrections I. Re-teach classroom expectations J. Provide demonstrations and modeling K. Provide positive practice and feedback L. Provide opportunities for verbal practice M. Deliver praise and specific feedback		
Adult attention seems to reinforce misbehavior	☐	G. Increase opportunities to respond M. Deliver praise and specific feedback O. Send positive news home P. Ignore misbehavior W. Increase the frequency of noncontingent positive attention		
Peer attention seems to reinforce misbehavior	☐	A. Change assigned seating Q. Reduce peer attention		
Escape seems to reinforce misbehavior	☐	B. Change work requirements C. Provide breaks D. Change expectations or procedures E. Offer viable choices S. Assign time owed		
Access to tangibles, activities, or privileges seems to reinforce misbehavior	☐	N. Offer rewards V. Revoke a privilege		
Specific consequences for misbehavior are necessary	☐	R. Use gentle verbal reprimands or warnings S. Assign time owed T. Assign in-class timeout V. Revoke a privilege		
Misbehavior may be positively affected by changes to structural features of the classroom (e.g. classroom layout, schedule)	☐	A. Change assigned seating B. Change work requirements D. Change expectations or procedures		
The student misbehaves under periods of low supervision or structure	☐	D. Change expectations or procedures H. Increase monitoring and supervision		
Previously used consequences for misbehavior don't seem to work, or misbehavior is a firmly established part of the student's behavior	☐	1. Behavioral Contracting 2. Structured Reinforcement		

REPRODUCIBLE 2.5 *Multidisciplinary Team Planning Process (9 of 14)*

Multidisciplinary Team Planning Process

Intervention Decision Guide (continued)

Presenting behavior	Check if true	Intervention strategy	Date implemented	Effective? (+/–)
The student acts impulsively or seems to be unaware of engaging in inappropriate behavior	☐	3. Self-Monitoring and Self-Evaluation		
The student has difficulty maintaining emotional control	☐	5. Managing Emotional Escalation		
The student seems anxious, depressed, or withdrawn	☐	6. Supporting Students with Internalizing Challenges		
The student doesn't seem connected to peers or adults at school	☐	W. Increase the frequency of noncontingent positive attention X. Assign a meaningful duty or responsibility at school Y. Encourage and facilitate the student's participation in clubs, after-school activities, and other school events Z. Connect the student with an adult or peer mentor at school		
The student's behavior is so disruptive that the teacher cannot continue	☐	Code Red Situation: Consult school policies for responding to severely disruptive behavior 4. Behavior Emergency Planning U. Assign out-of-class timeout		
The student's behavior is unsafe or dangerous to self or others	☐	Code Red Situation: Consult school policies for responding to unsafe or physically dangerous behavior 4. Behavior Emergency Planning U. Assign out-of-class timeout		

REPRODUCIBLE 2.5 *Multidisciplinary Team Planning Process (10 of 14)*

Multidisciplinary Team Planning Process

SECTION H: DESIGN A COMPREHENSIVE BEHAVIOR INTERVENTION PLAN

20. Select intervention strategies to implement. Describe how, where, and when strategies will be implemented and the responsibilities of staff members involved.

Comprehensive Behavior Intervention Plan

a. Identify antecedent intervention strategies.

Plan for using antecedent strategies	Staff responsible	Start date

b. Identify teaching intervention strategies.

Plan for teaching appropriate/replacement behaviors	Staff responsible	Start date

REPRODUCIBLE 2.5 *Multidisciplinary Team Planning Process (11 of 14)*

Multidisciplinary Team Planning Process

c. Identify positive consequence intervention strategies.

Plan for using positive consequence intervention strategies	Staff responsible	Start date

List of possible rewards and praise statements:

d. Identify corrective consequence intervention strategies.

Step 1: Categorize problem behaviors and define limits by example or quantity.

List categories of problem behaviors to correct.

Step 2: Select corrective consequence strategies.

Plan for using corrective consequence strategies	Staff responsible	Start date

REPRODUCIBLE 2.5 *Multidisciplinary Team Planning Process (12 of 14)*

Multidisciplinary Team Planning Process

e. Identify strategies to increase noncontingent positive interactions and school connectedness.

Step 1: Determine baseline ratio of positive to corrective interactions.
- Do baseline data reflect at least a 3:1 positive to corrective ratio of interactions? Yes / No
- Identify when and where to direct efforts to improve ratio of interactions:

Step 2: Select strategies to increase noncontingent positive interactions and school connectedness.

Plan for increasing positive interactions and school connectedness	Staff responsible	Start date

f. Describe other group interactions, academic supports, accommodations, or specialized intervention strategies.

Plan for incorporating other intervention strategies	Staff responsible	Start date

REPRODUCIBLE 2.5 *Multidisciplinary Team Planning Process (13 of 14)*

Multidisciplinary Team Planning Process

Step 4. Collect data to monitor progress.
SECTION I: DEVELOP A PLAN TO MONITOR PROGRESS

21. Identify data that will be used to track progress toward the goal, including who will collect data and how.

22. Identify follow-up dates to check in about progress.

23. Identify at least two ways to determine whether the plan is working at the next follow-up meeting.

24. Describe plans to monitor and evaluate implementation fidelity.

Follow-Up Meetings

Step 5. Evaluate whether supports are working.
SECTION J: SUMMARIZE STUDENT PROGRESS AND FOLLOW-UP MEETING OUTCOMES

25. Provide a summary of follow-up meetings. Describe any modifications that are made to the intervention plan.

Follow-up Meeting #1   Date: _____

Team members present: ☐ Support Coordinator ☐ Gen Ed Teacher ☐ Special Ed Teacher
☐ Student ☐ Parent ☐ Speech-Language Pathologist
☐ Behavior Specialist ☐ School Psychologist ☐ Administrator

Other participants _____

Summary of data collected since last meeting:

Summary of teacher's perceptions of how well the plan has addressed the target behavior:

Team recommendations (e.g., continue implementation as is, revise plan, refer to special education, etc.):

Who will share outcomes of meeting with: Classroom teacher? _____ Parent/student? _____

REPRODUCIBLE 2.5 *Multidisciplinary Team Planning Process (14 of 14)*

Multidisciplinary Team Planning Process

Follow-up Meeting #2   Date: _____

Team members present: ☐ Support Coordinator   ☐ Gen Ed Teacher   ☐ Special Ed Teacher
☐ Student   ☐ Parent   ☐ Speech-Language Pathologist
☐ Behavior Specialist   ☐ School Psychologist   ☐ Administrator

Other participants _____

Summary of data collected since last meeting:

Summary of teacher's perceptions of how well the plan has addressed the target behavior:

Team recommendations (e.g., continue implementation as is, revise plan, refer to special education, etc.):

Who will share outcomes of meeting with: Classroom teacher? _____   Parent/student? _____

Follow-up Meeting #3   Date: _____

Team members present: ☐ Support Coordinator   ☐ Gen Ed Teacher   ☐ Special Ed Teacher
☐ Student   ☐ Parent   ☐ Speech-Language Pathologist
☐ Behavior Specialist   ☐ School Psychologist   ☐ Administrator

Other participants _____

Summary of data collected since last meeting:

Summary of teacher's perceptions of how well the plan has addressed the target behavior:

Team recommendations (e.g., continue implementation as is, revise plan, refer to special education, etc.):

Who will share outcomes of meeting with: Classroom teacher? _____   Parent/student? _____

References

Alberto, P. A., & Troutman, A. C. (2012). *Applied behavior analysis for teachers* (9th ed.). Merrill/Prentice Hall: Upper Saddle River, NJ.

Allen, S. J., & Graden, J. I. (2002). Best practices in collaborative problem-solving for intervention design. In A. Thomas & J. Grimes (Eds.), *Best practices in school psychology IV* (pp. 414–435). Bethesda, MD: National Association of School Psychologists.

Archer, A., & Gleason, M. (1992). *Skills for school success.* North Billerica, MA: Curriculum Associates.

Arra, C. T., & Bahr, M. W. (2005). Teachers' and students' preferences for mathematics interventions: Implications for teacher acceptability in consultation. *Journal of Educational and Psychological Consultation, 16*(3), 157–174.

Bambara, L. M., & Kern, L. (Eds.). (2005). *Individualized supports for students with problem behaviors: Designing positive behavior plans.* New York, NY: Guilford Press.

Carr, J. E., Nicolson, A. C., & Higbee, T. S. (2000). Evaluation of a brief multiple-stimulus preference assessment in a naturalistic context. *Journal of Applied Behavior Analysis, 33*(3), 353–357.

DuPaul, G. J., & Eckert, T. L. (1997). School-based interventions for children with attention-deficit/hyperactivity disorder: A meta-analysis. *School Psychology Review, 26,* 5–27.

Eckert, T. L., Codding, R. M., Truckenmiller, A. J., & Rheinheimer, J. L. (2009). Improving children's fluency in reading, mathematics, spelling, and writing: A review of evidence-based academic interventions. In K. A. Akin-Little, S. N. Little, M. Bray, & T. Kehle (Eds.), *Handbook of behavioral interventions in schools* (pp. 111–124). Washington, DC: American Psychological Association.

Elliott, E. S., & Dweck, C. S. (1988). Goals: An approach to motivation and achievement. *Journal of Personality and Social Psychology, 54*(1), 5.

Esler, A. N., Godber, Y., & Christenson, S. L. (2002). Best practices in supporting home-school collaboration. In A. Thomas,& J. Grimes (Eds.), *Best practices in school psychology IV* (pp. 389–412). Bethesda, MD: National Association of School Psychologists.

Finn, C. A., & Sladeczek, I. E. (2001). Assessing the social validity of behavioral interventions: A review of treatment acceptability measures. *School Psychology Quarterly, 16*(2), 176.

Forman, S. G., & Burke, C. R. (2008). Best practices in selecting and implementing evidence-based school interventions. In A. Thomas & J. Grimes (Eds.), *Best practices in school psychology V* (Vol. 3, pp. 799–811). Bethesda, MD: National Association of School Psychologists.

Gresham, E, MacMillan, D. L., Beebe-Frankenberger, M. B., & Bocian, K. M. (2000). Treatment integrity in learning disabilities intervention research: Do we really know how treatments are implemented? *Learning Disabilities Research and Practice, 15,* 198–205.

Gresham, F., Watson, T., & Skinner, C. (2001). Functional behavioral assessment: Principles, procedures, and future directions. *School Psychology Review, 30,* 156–172.

Gunter, P. L., & Denny, R. K. (1996). Research issues and needs regarding teacher use of classroom management strategies. *Behavioral Disorders, 22*(1), 15–20.

Gutkin, T. B., & Curtis, M. J. (1999). School-based consultation: The art and science of indirect service delivery. In C. R. Reynolds & T. B. Gutkin (Eds.), *The handbook of school psychology* (3rd ed., pp. 598–637). New York, NY: Wiley.

Henderson, A. T., & Mapp, K. L. (2002). *A new wave of evidence: The impact of school, family, and community connections on student achievement.* Austin, TX: National Center for Family and Community Connections with Schools.

Ingram, K., Lewis-Palmer, T., & Sugai, G. (2005). Function-based intervention planning: Comparing the effectiveness of FBA function-based and non–function-based intervention plans. *Journal of Positive Behavior Interventions, 7*(4), 224–236.

Kratochwill, T. R., Elliott, S. N., & Callan-Stoiber, K. (2002). Best practices in school-based problem-solving consultation. In A. Thomas & J. Grimes (Eds.), *Best practices in school psychology IV* (pp. 583–608). Bethesda, MD: National Association of School Psychologists.

Lasky, S. (2000). The cultural and emotional politics of teacher–parent interactions. *Teaching and Teacher Education, 16*(8), 843–860.

Menzies, H. M., Lane, K. L., & Lee, J. M. (2009). Self-monitoring strategies for use in the classroom: A promising practice to support productive behavior for students with emotional or behavioral disorders. *Beyond Behavior, 18*(2), 27–35.

O'Neill, R. E., Horner, R. H., Albin, R. W., Sprague, J. R., Storey, K., & Newton, J. S. (1997). *Functional assessment and program development for problem behavior: A practical handbook.* New York, NY: Brooks/Cole.

O'Shea, L., Algozzine, R., Hammittee, D., & O'Shea, D. (2000). *Families and teachers of individuals with disabilities: Collaborative orientations and responsive practices.* Boston, MA: Allyn & Bacon.

Perepletchikova, F., & Kazdin, A. E. (2005). Treatment integrity and therapeutic change: Issues and research recommendations. *Clinical Psychology: Science and Practice, 12*(4), 365–383.

Roach, A. T., & Elliott, S. N. (2008). Best practices in facilitating and evaluating intervention integrity. In A. Thomas & J. Grimes (Eds.), *Best practices in school psychology V* (pp. 195–208). Bethesda, MD: National Association of School Psychologists.

Rosenfield, S. (2008). Best practices in instructional consultation and instructional teams. In A. Thomas & J. Grimes (Eds.), *Best practices in school psychology V* (pp. 1645–1660). Bethesda, MD: NASP. Retrieved from http://www.nasponline.org/assets/documents/Resources%20and%20Publications/Books%20and%20Products/1645_BPV119_103.pdf

Scheuermann, B., & Hall, J. A. (2008). *Positive behavioral supports for the classroom.* Upper Saddle River, NJ: Pearson/Merrill Prentice Hall.

Seligman, M. E., & Csikszentmihalyi, M. (2000). *Positive psychology: An introduction* (Vol. 55, No. 1). Washington, DC: American Psychological Association.

Shapiro, E. S. (2011). *Academic skills problems: Direct assessment and intervention* (4th ed.) New York, NY: Guilford Press.

Tedeschi, R. G., & Kilmer, R. P. (2005). Assessing strengths, resilience, and growth to guide clinical interventions. *Professional Psychology: Research and Practice, 36*(3), 230.

Tilly III, W. D. (2008). The evolution of school psychology to science-based practice: Problem solving and the three-tiered model. In A. Thomas & J. Grimes (Eds.), *Best practices in school psychology IV* (pp. 17–36). Bethesda, MD: National Association of School Psychologists.

Tryon, G. S., & Winograd, G. (2011). Goal consensus and collaboration. *Psychotherapy, 48*(1), 50–57.

VanDerHeyden, A. M., & Witt, J. C. (2008). Best practices in can't do/won't do assessment. In A. Thomas & J. Grimes (Eds.). *Best practices in school psychology V* (pp. 131–140). Bethesda, MD: National Association of School Psychologists.

Wahler, R. G., & Fox, J. J. (1981). Setting events in applied behavior analysis: Toward a conceptual and methodological expansion. *Journal of Applied Behavior Analysis, 14*(3), 327–338.

SECTION THREE

Designing an Effective Behavior Intervention Plan

Simply put, *behavior intervention* can be thought of as a planned response to a behavior or set of behaviors that is interfering with a student's success in school. However, to go a little deeper, Tilly & Flugum's (1995, p. 485) definition aligns well with the processes and goals of intervention as presented in this book, where intervention is defined as "a planned modification of the environment made for the purpose of altering behavior in a pre-specified way."

Three key phrases in this definition call attention to the following features of behavior interventions:

> An intervention is *planned* ahead of time. It provides an important roadmap for addressing misbehavior by clarifying the specific actions that will take place and the responsibilities of those involved in its implementation.

> An intervention seeks to *alter behavior in a pre-specified way.* It is goal directed, with the desired outcomes of the intervention outlined prior to its implementation.

> An intervention is focused on *modifying the environment,* rather than the individual, by determining variables that can be changed to encourage appropriate behavior and discourage misbehavior.

What Are the Components of a Behavior Intervention Plan?

Research indicates that an effective behavior intervention plan does the following:

1 Clearly defines target behaviors and goals in objective, measurable terms (Alberto & Troutman, 2006).

Interventions are designed to change behavior—but you must know what behaviors to target for change and what magnitude of change is desired. By specifying target behaviors—both undesired problematic behaviors and desired replacement behaviors—and outlining a goal for how much these behaviors should decrease or increase, you can create a targeted intervention plan that is more likely to actually produce the behavior change you want to see.

2 Includes a variety of antecedent, teaching, and consequence strategies that address the context and function of problem behavior (O'Neill et al., 1997).

> **EVIDENCE-BASED INTERVENTION STRATEGIES**
>
> All behavior intervention plans should be created from a menu of strategies that have a proven track record of success—that is, evidence in the research literature shows that they have been effective in improving student outcomes. All of the intervention strategies included in this book are based on research and best-practice recommendations.

Function-based intervention plans include strategies that address the primary function, or purpose, of a student's misbehavior. In other words, the plan is designed so that the student can access motivating consequences (e.g., peer attention) by either refraining from misbehavior or replacing the misbehavior with more appropriate replacement behaviors. Research indicates that function-based intervention plans are more effective in reducing problem behaviors than are plans designed without consideration of the function of the behavior (Ingram, Lewis-Palmer, & Sugai, 2005). In addition, while an intervention plan will typically specify consequence strategies (e.g., redirection, de-escalation, clearly outlined consequences, crisis management procedures), the goal of behavior intervention is not just the absence of misbehavior. Positive, proactive intervention plans place an emphasis on strategies that prevent problem behavior (antecedent strategies) and that explicitly teach and reinforce alternative desired behaviors (teaching strategies). Compared with reactive interventions that rely on punitive consequence strategies alone, proactive interventions are more likely to produce lasting behavior change.

3 Includes strategies that increase positive interactions and improve student feelings of connectedness with school (Centers for Disease Control and Prevention, 2009).

Students enter the classroom with a diversity of needs and backgrounds. Some have received a lot of positive attention since infancy, and some have received little attention of any kind from adults. Unfortunately, others may have received primarily negative attention all their lives. However, all children want and need attention of some sort. Recognizing the needs of students as individuals is essential to building authentic relationships with them, tailoring help to meet their needs, and intervening appropriately and effectively with students whose needs may be different from those of their classmates. Designing a behavior intervention plan that seeks to achieve at least a 3:1 ratio of positive to corrective interactions with adults at school has the potential to dramatically improve student-staff relationships and a student's feeling of connectedness to the school—both important predictors of educational and long-term success (see "School Connectedness").

4 Specifies procedures for collecting data and monitoring progress (Maag, 2003).

Data collection generates the information needed to evaluate the goal of the intervention. Without data to evaluate an intervention's effectiveness, teachers and interventionists must rely on subjective impressions, which can be a notoriously cloudy barometer. Emotions, preconceptions, distractions, and being busy with teaching can all diminish the usefulness of subjective impressions. In addition, the data collected will form the basis of all subsequent intervention planning. From this point on, what you do next with any intervention will depend on the data you collect. Should an intervention be maintained? Faded? Replaced with a different intervention? Data give collaborating teachers, administrators, and interventionists a common point of reference for looking at the issue objectively and constructively.

5 Outlines a plan for monitoring implementation fidelity (Gresham, MacMillan, Beebe-Frankenberger, & Bocian, 2000).

Once a plan for intervention is outlined and put into place, it is important to establish accountability and make sure that the plan is implemented as designed. This includes ensuring that adequate resources, staffing, and training are provided, that follow-up occurs, and that someone is monitoring whether core components of the intervention plan are actually being implemented. To monitor fidelity, for example, you might provide a self-assessment checklist for the interventionist to use when providing lessons, schedule an external observation of a teacher's use of praise statements during small group reading instruction, or informally check in with the staff members involved in the plan's implementation during follow-up problem-solving team meetings.

Embedding each of these components into a student's behavior intervention plan will set the student up for the greatest chance of success.

SCHOOL CONNECTEDNESS

The Centers for Disease Control and Prevention (2009) defines *school connectedness* as "the belief by students that adults and peers in the school care about their learning as well as about them as individuals." A growing body of research suggests that school connectedness is a powerful predictor of educational and behavioral outcomes, such as increased school attendance and school completion, higher grades and test scores, and reduced likelihood of engaging in risk-taking behaviors, substance use, and violence (Blum, 2005; Catalano, Haggerty, Oesterle, Fleming, & Hawkins, 2004; Klem & Connell, 2004; Shochet, Dadds, Ham, & Montague, 2006; Thapa, Cogen, Guffey, & Higgins-D'Alessandro, 2013; Whitlock, 2006).

Proactively working to increase a student's sense of connectedness with school can serve as a potential protective factor, help address social needs, promote the development of interpersonal skills, and improve the student's chances for academic and social success.

How to Build a Behavior Intervention Plan

An understanding of environmental variables that contribute to the student's behavior provides the problem-solving team with critical information for developing an effective behavior intervention plan. In other words, a hypothesis about what tends to occur before, during, and after a student misbehaves can lead to a plan that incorporates an array of intervention strategies to prevent, defuse, and respond to problematic behavior at school. Section 2 introduced several problem-solving tools to help teams develop a hypothesis about why a student exhibits a specific behavior. This hypothesis is based on information you gather about relevant triggers (i.e., antecedents) and conditions (i.e., setting events) that predict when the target behavior is likely to occur, and relevant consequences that seem to be maintaining or reinforcing the behavior (i.e., the function of the behavior).

The tasks presented next offer a step-by-step approach to designing a behavior intervention plan that is directly linked to this hypothesis and incorporates each of the five core components presented at the beginning of this section. These tasks can be carried out by problem-solving teams and interventionists to design any behavior intervention plan. After defining target behaviors and goals of the plan (Task 1), you will select intervention strategies from five categories to make up the foundation of your behavior intervention plan:

- *Antecedent strategies* to address events and conditions (e.g., times, places, people, activities) that occur before the student's misbehavior (Task 2)
- *Teaching strategies* that provide the student with positive replacement behaviors for misbehavior (Task 3)
- *Positive consequence strategies* that outline rewards and responses from staff intended to encourage appropriate behavior and discourage misbehavior (Task 4)
- *Corrective consequence strategies* designed to increase the consistency and efficacy of corrective consequences that are implemented when misbehavior occurs (Task 5)
- *Interactional strategies* designed to provide the student with a high rate of noncontingent positive attention and help the student feel connected to school (Task 6)

These *foundational intervention strategies* offer a framework for thinking about intervention and can be used to build any intervention plan. For minor problems, you might need to include strategies from only one or two categories. For more severe or chronic problems that initial intervention efforts have not remedied, your intervention plan will likely need to address all categories. Generally, if you can manipulate something in all five categories, even with relatively minor adjustments, the resulting behavior plan will be much stronger than if you incorporate strategies from only one category.

As you develop a plan, in many cases you may need to incorporate other intervention strategies that are not fully captured in the list of 26 foundational strategies shown in Figure 3.1. In Task 7, you will specify any additional intervention strategies to incorporate into a student's plan. These may include:

- Existing interventions from your building or district menu of ready-to-use interventions (e.g., check-and-connect, social skills groups, mentorship programs)
- Academic supports (e.g., participation in supplementary reading skill groups, extra time on tests)

> **CONTINUUM OF SUPPORT**
>
> As a reminder, your multi-tiered system of support (MTSS) should offer a continuum of problem-solving and intervention supports and use these resources efficiently so that the intensity of support matches the intensity of the problem. Build your intervention plans with this goal in mind.

FIGURE 3.1 *Foundational Intervention Strategies*

Antecedent strategies
- A. Change assigned seating.
- B. Change work requirements.
- C. Provide breaks.
- D. Change expectations or procedures.
- E. Offer viable choices.
- F. Use precorrections.
- G. Increase opportunities to respond.
- H. Increase monitoring and supervision.

Teaching strategies
- I. Re-teach classroom expectations.
- J. Provide demonstrations and modeling.
- K. Provide positive practice and feedback.
- L. Provide opportunities for verbal practice.

Positive consequence strategies
- M. Deliver praise and specific feedback.
- N. Offer rewards.
- O. Send positive news home.

Corrective consequence strategies
- P. Ignore misbehavior.
- Q. Reduce peer attention.
- R. Use gentle verbal reprimands or warnings.
- S. Assign time owed.
- T. Assign in-class timeout.
- U. Assign out-of-class timeout.
- V. Revoke a privilege.

Interactional strategies
- W. Increase the frequency of noncontingent positive attention.
- X. Assign a meaningful duty or responsibility at school.
- Y. Encourage and facilitate the student's participation in clubs, after-school activities, and other school events.
- Z. Connect the student with an adult or peer mentor at school.

- Accommodations for specific disabilities or impairments (e.g., adaptations to the environment and curriculum materials for a student with visual impairment)
- Specialized intervention strategies for addressing certain types of problematic behavior (e.g., mental health issues, dangerous or highly disruptive behavior) or detailed systems for delivering strategies (e.g., self-monitoring and self-evaluation systems, structured reinforcement systems). Figure 3.2 below lists the six specialized intervention strategies discussed in detail in Section 4.

FIGURE 3.2 *Specialized Intervention Strategies*

1. Behavioral Contracting
2. Structured Reinforcement
3. Self-Monitoring and Self-Evaluation
4. Behavior Emergency Planning
5. Managing Emotional Escalation
6. Supporting Students With Internalizing Challenges

When developing any behavior intervention plan, start by considering those intervention strategies that seem to have the highest likelihood of success and fewest barriers to implementation—in other words, strategies that are likely to produce the quickest, easiest solution with the smallest amount of resources. Also consider the following:

- Are resources, staff skills, or processes for implementing the strategy available or already in place in the school? For example, the school already offers a social skills group to teach anger management skills.
- Does the strategy align with the function of the student's misbehavior? For attention-seeking behavior, for example, a positive consequence strategy can provide access to desired attention.
- Is the strategy age appropriate and contextually relevant? For example, consider whether the intervention strategy will be embarrassing to a student in middle school.
- Is the student likely to comply and accept the chosen strategy? For example, the potential to earn certain rewards may motivate the student.

The Behavior Intervention Planning Form (Reproducible 3.1, pp. 240–243) is designed to align with the step-by-step approach below, but you can also use your school or district's forms in conjunction with reading and applying this section.

TASK 1 Clearly define target behaviors and goals in objective, measurable terms.

While it may sound easy, it can sometimes be quite challenging to objectively describe a student's behavior without injecting subjective impressions. For example, "He is so immature" and "She acts like a five-year-old" are both subjective statements. Subjective statements make it virtually impossible to collect valid data. Instead, you must break down subjective impressions of a student's behavior into objective descriptions of what the behavior looks and sounds like. Likewise, specifying measurable goals will allow you to objectively evaluate whether intervention efforts are making a meaningful difference in the student's behavior.

STEP 1 Objectively describe problematic behavior.

The goal here is to describe behavior in such detail that the teacher or any other third-party observer can easily see or hear it. Figure 3.3 compares subjective descriptions that can't be measured (from a data collection perspective) with objective statements that can be measured. At this point, you will prioritize one or two major misbehaviors to target in your intervention plan. Determine the behaviors that are the most problematic or that should be the focus of initial intervention efforts for another reason. If you are dealing with a student who has many problems, where are you going to start? If the student has hygiene problems, peer relation problems, anger management and self-control issues, academic deficits, and difficulty completing assigned tasks, you will not be able to correct all of these problems at once. A broad-based intervention plan that targets too many changes

FIGURE 3.3 *Subjective Versus Objective Descriptions of Behavior*

Subjective descriptions (unmeasurable)	Objective descriptions (measurable)
Bad attitude	• Makes disrespectful comments to the teacher and other students • Says she always messes up when writing and spelling
Unmotivated	• Doesn't complete classwork or homework • Doesn't answer questions in class • Reads a book when assigned to do math problems
Off in his own world	• Stares out the window • Doodles on his paper • Plays quietly with items in his desk
Poor self-image	• Makes negative statements about self, such as "I'm stupid" and "I can't read"
Attention-deficit problems	• Fidgets while sitting in chair (rocks her chair, sits on her feet) • Gets out of her chair and wanders around the room • Makes tapping noises with a pencil on the desk or with her foot on the leg of the desk
Emotional problems	• Responds with angry verbal outbursts when asked to read • Cries when frustrated • Doesn't interact with students when approached

at once is likely to frustrate the student and teacher and yield fewer positive results. When you narrow the scope of the intervention to a focused plan that is truly manageable, you have the greatest probability of success. Likelihood is high that if the student begins to experience success and increased confidence with a targeted intervention, other problem behaviors may naturally improve on their own.

Once you gather information about the full scope of the student's problems, work with the student's teachers to identify one or two major behaviors or categories to address first through intervention. If a teacher wants to change too many behaviors, help narrow the scope of the initial intervention.

To identify priorities for the initial intervention, ask the following questions:

- *How often do the problems occur? How long does the behavior last? How intense is the problem?* Identify the misbehaviors that occur most frequently, last the longest, or are most severe.
- *What behavior changes will help the student feel successful in the shortest period of time?* Select behaviors that have the highest probability of success in the least amount of time.
- *What behavior changes will help the teacher see improvements in the shortest period of time?* Determine not only what the teacher hopes to accomplish but also those misbehaviors the teacher can't live with any longer.

continued on page 244

REPRODUCIBLE 3.1 *Behavior Intervention Planning Form (1 of 4)*

Behavior Intervention Planning Form

☐ **TASK 1: CLEARLY DEFINE TARGET BEHAVIORS AND GOALS IN OBJECTIVE, MEASURABLE TERMS.**

Step 1: Objectively describe problematic behaviors:

Step 2: Objectively describe appropriate/replacement behaviors:

Step 3: Specify measurable goals for both the problematic and the appropriate/replacement behaviors:

☐ **TASK 2: IDENTIFY ANTECEDENT INTERVENTION STRATEGIES.**

Plan for using antecedent strategies	Staff responsible	Start date

☐ **TASK 3: IDENTIFY TEACHING INTERVENTION STRATEGIES.**

Plan for teaching appropriate/replacement behaviors	Staff responsible	Start date

Interventions © 2019 Ancora Publishing

REPRODUCIBLE 3.1 *Behavior Intervention Planning Form (2 of 4)*

Behavior Intervention Planning Form

☐ **TASK 4: IDENTIFY POSITIVE CONSEQUENCE INTERVENTION STRATEGIES.**

Plan for using positive consequence intervention strategies	Staff responsible	Start date

List of possible rewards and/or praise statements:

☐ **TASK 5: IDENTIFY CORRECTIVE CONSEQUENCE INTERVENTION STRATEGIES.**

Step 1: Categorize problem behaviors and define limits by example or quantity.

List categories of problem behaviors to correct.

Step 2: Select corrective consequence strategies.

Plan for using corrective consequence strategies	Staff responsible	Start date

REPRODUCIBLE 3.1 *Behavior Intervention Planning Form (3 of 4)*

Behavior Intervention Planning Form

☐ **TASK 6: IDENTIFY INTERACTIONAL STRATEGIES.**

Step 1: Determine baseline ratio of positive to corrective interactions (optional).
- Do baseline data reflect at least a 3:1 positive to corrective ratio of interactions? Y N
- Identify when and where to direct efforts to improve ratio of interactions:

Step 2: Select strategies to increase noncontingent positive interactions and school connectedness.

Plan for increasing positive interactions and school connectedness	Staff responsible	Start date

☐ **TASK 7: DESCRIBE OTHER GROUP INTERVENTIONS, ACADEMIC SUPPORTS, ACCOMMODATIONS, OR SPECIALIZED INTERVENTION STRATEGIES.**

Plan for incorporating other intervention strategies	Staff responsible	Start date

REPRODUCIBLE 3.1 *Behavior Intervention Planning Form (4 of 4)*

Behavior Intervention Planning Form

☐ **TASK 8: SPECIFY PROCEDURES FOR COLLECTING DATA AND MONITORING PROGRESS.**

Step 1: Select a data collection method.
Identify data that will be used to track progress toward the goal, including who will collect data and how:

Step 2: Determine how to summarize and interpret data.
- Identify follow-up date(s) to check in about progress and describe how data will be summarized for these check-ins:

- Identify at least two ways to determine whether the plan is working at the next follow-up meeting.

☐ **TASK 9: MAKE A PLAN TO MONITOR AND ENSURE IMPLEMENTATION FIDELITY OF THE PLAN.**

Step 1: Identify a method for monitoring and evaluating implementation fidelity.
- Describe how fidelity will be measured, how often monitoring will take place, and who will be responsible for monitoring and follow-ups:

- Using measurable terms, define what "good" fidelity means:

Step 2: Make a plan to encourage good implementation and provide follow-up support as needed.
If fidelity monitoring reveals problems with implementation, what follow-up actions will be taken?

> *Does the student exhibit any Code Red behavior? Is the student's behavior unsafe or severely disruptive to the classroom?* Code Red situations involve behaviors that are either so dangerous or so disruptive that classes cannot continue. Prioritize any Code Red behaviors—move directly to the protocol that your district has in place or develop an individual Behavior Emergency Plan for the student. Once temporary procedures are in place for responding to Code Red situations, you can return to developing a long-term intervention plan that will help the student learn appropriate behavior. See Section 1, Task 6: Establish Processes for Responding to Code Red Situations (p. 54) for a description of how to set up schoolwide policies, and Section 4.4: Behavior Emergency Planning for guidelines on creating a safety plan for an individual student.

CODE RED SITUATIONS

Code Red situations involve behaviors that are either unsafe or so disruptive that classes cannot continue. These behaviors include:

- Overt aggressive behavior toward others (e.g., kicking, hitting, fighting)
- Threats of targeted violence toward others
- Brandishing items that could be used as weapons
- Carrying weapons
- Self-injurious behavior
- Vandalism or property destruction
- Sexual assault
- Clear signs of using controlled substances (drugs and alcohol)
- Running away from school property
- Sustained confrontational or defiant behavior resulting in refusal to follow immediate, reasonable adult directions.

STEP 2   Objectively describe appropriate/replacement behaviors.

Once you have a clear description of what the problem behavior looks and sounds like, you can begin to identify what appropriate behaviors (i.e., replacement behaviors) should look and sound like.

To identify replacement behaviors, consider the *positive opposite* of the problem behavior. In other words, try to name specific, observable behaviors that would not be problematic if the student engaged in them in place of the negative behaviors. Figure 3.4 on the next page shows examples.

Follow these steps to use the Replacement Behavior Worksheet (Reproducible 3.2, p. 246) to identify replacement behaviors:

- List all problem behaviors in the first column of the worksheet.
- For each behavior, develop a hypothesis about the function of the misbehavior (see pp. 130–133 for guidance in developing a functional hypothesis).
- In the Goal column, identify the desired outcome of the intervention.
- In the Brainstorming column, identify several possible replacement behaviors that might address the problem and goal.
- In the remaining columns, evaluate the potential efficacy of the replacement behaviors before you begin implementing the intervention.

A good candidate for a replacement behavior will capitalize on the student's strengths. If a basketball team is having trouble with a particular aspect of the game, the coach may come up with new plays that make better use of things the team is good at—passing, fast breaks, perimeter shooting, and so on. These could be considered replacement behaviors. If the players execute new plays with some success, the new behaviors will automatically tend to replace the behaviors that were failing them before. In the same way, rechanneling a behavior with replacement behaviors can become more powerful as the new behaviors bring success and, through that success, become self-sustaining.

When you are trying to identify a replacement behavior, also give some thought to the function or purpose of the misbehavior. Think of a context in which a student has been disruptive. If the student uses disruptive behavior to get attention, choose

FIGURE 3.4 *Problem Behaviors and Appropriate Replacements*

Problem behaviors	Appropriate/Replacement behaviors
• Hits and kicks other male students when angry. • When angry, pinches female students until they cry. • Often yells and screams when he hits, kicks, and pinches peers. • Sometimes uses profanity when yelling. • When frustrated, sometimes throws objects (e.g., pencils, books) at students and staff	• Stay two to three feet away from other students when angry or frustrated. • Talk with students and teachers in a quiet voice without using profanity. • Tell the teacher when he is starting to feel angry or frustrated. • Go to a designated spot in the classroom for cool down time. • Take 10 deep breaths when feeling angry.

a replacement behavior that teaches the student alternative ways to get attention that are prosocial and within the student's current behavioral skill set. If students try these new strategies and find that their needs are met, they may pursue the strategies with keener interest.

If the problem is lack of awareness, choose a replacement behavior that helps the student develop better self-awareness of the behavior. For example, if Raoul taps his pencil incessantly and seems to be unaware of that behavior, an effective replacement behavior might be to teach him to use a Koosh ball or other stress-relieving device. In this case, the intervention might logically include some form of cueing to support the development of awareness. For example, the teacher might cue Raoul to use the Koosh ball when he begins drumming on his desk. Over time, the student will learn to pick up the Koosh ball and squeeze it instead.

If a student often falls into power struggles with the teacher (i.e., the student argues to engage the teacher emotionally), you might teach the student a phrase to use whenever she wants to argue, such as, "Mrs. Thompson, I think that's unfair. Can I schedule an appointment to speak with you later?" Explain that when she tries to argue during class, the teacher is going to ignore her. Teach, practice, and rehearse variations on the phrase until it rolls off the student's tongue automatically. Essentially, you're teaching the student that she can actually have more power by making an appointment and calmly stating her case. When she tries to argue and make demands, she has less power and makes less of an impact. In other words, the student will learn that she is more likely to get what she wants by exhibiting the replacement behavior.

If the function of a misbehavior is to escape work that the student thinks is too difficult, teach the student how and when to ask for assistance, and arrange to provide needed assistance when the student requests it. A replacement behavior for escapist misbehaviors should also close off less appropriate avenues for escape.

Figure 3.5, shown on p. 247, presents examples of common problem behaviors and acceptable alternatives that might be taught to help students replace the behaviors. To identify a possible replacement behavior, brainstorm a list of reasonable alternatives and then determine which might be most appropriate for the specific situation.

REPLACEMENT BEHAVIORS

You can identify replacement behaviors as part of problem-solving efforts (e.g., Item 13 of the Teacher Interview and 25-Minute Planning Process and Item 18 of the Multidisciplinary Team Planning Process) or by using the Replacement Behavior Worksheet (Reproducible 3.2 on the next page).

REPRODUCIBLE 3.2 *Replacement Behavior Worksheet*

Replacement Behavior Worksheet

Student _____ Grade/Class _____ Date _____

Teacher _____

Define the problem	Consider the function		Identify replacement behaviors	Does the proposed replacement:		Is the proposed replacement:	
Behavior	Lacking awareness or ability, trying to get something, trying to avoid something	Goal	Brainstorm ideas	Meet the needs/ serve the function?	Capitalize on student's strengths?	Concrete, observable, and teachable?	Within the student's repertoire?

FIGURE 3.5 *Examples of Replacement Behaviors*

Problem	Goal	Replacement Behavior
Anger when work is corrected	Calmly accepting feedback	Nodding acceptance; saying "OK, I'll fix it."
Swearing	Appropriate response or exclamation	Silence; "Shoot!" "Shizzle!" "Wow!" etc.
Aggression	Calming down without aggressive acts	Deep breathing; self-imposed timeout
Oversensitivity	Responding maturely to teasing	Ignoring; use of "I" statements
Not completing work	Staying focused and on task	Ignoring distractions; returning to work quickly

When selecting replacement behaviors, also consider the following:

- Is the proposed replacement concrete, observable, and teachable?
- Is the proposed replacement within the student's repertoire—is the student physically and mentally capable of performing the desired behavior?

STEP 3 Specify measurable goals for both the problematic and the appropriate/replacement behaviors.

In addition to objectively defined target behaviors, effective interventions will clearly outline goals for these behaviors. These goals should answer the question: *What are you trying to accomplish through intervention?*

Stating the goal of the intervention in observable and measurable terms establishes criteria that the interventionist and teacher can use to determine the success or failure of the intervention. If the goal can't be counted or measured somehow, it may be too broad or subjective. If this is the case, revisit and revise the definitions you created in the previous two steps.

Goals should:

- *Be positively stated.* Whether the goal is to reduce a negative behavior or increase a positive one, it's important to state the goal in positive terms. For a student who is aggressive when angry, *learning to calm down and manage emotions when angry* can help that student develop an important skill set and sense of self-efficacy. In contrast, *not hitting other students* is a more limited goal that focuses only on problematic target behaviors. Such a goal may be less motivating or feel demeaning to the student.
- *Include numbers and timelines.* Define timelines and degrees of accomplishment when creating measurable goals. By incorporating numbers and timelines into your goals, you'll be able to clearly determine whether the goal was met at the time of evaluation. For example, "By the end of the semester, Chelsea will increase attendance to 95%."
- *Be ambitious but obtainable.* Avoid selecting goals that are overly ambitious. Instead, start by setting an initial goal that is closer to the student's baseline level

Stating the goal of the intervention in observable and measurable terms establishes criteria that the interventionist and teacher can use to determine the success or failure of the intervention.

of performance than to the ultimate goal for behavior. For example, if Jason is completing none of his seatwork during math class, it would be unrealistic to set a goal of completing 100% of assignments by the end of the month. Instead, you might define a more obtainable, tiered goal, such as: "Within 2 weeks, Jason will turn in 80% of his assignments, whether they are finished or not. Within 1 month, at least 50% of the assignments Jason turns in will be fully completed. Within 2 months, Jason will be turning in assignments daily, with 80% of these fully completed."

TASK 1 SUMMARY

In this task, you:

- ☑ Prioritized one or two major misbehaviors to target in your intervention plan.
- ☑ Developed an objective, observable description of the problem behavior.
- ☑ Identified appropriate/replacement behaviors that align with the function of the misbehavior.
- ☑ Specified measurable goals for both the problem behavior and the appropriate/replacement behaviors.

Antecedent strategies are designed to prevent misbehavior before it starts.

Now that you have clear definitions of target behaviors and goals, you can begin to consider different intervention strategies to include in the student's behavior intervention plan.

TASK 2: Identify antecedent intervention strategies.

Antecedent strategies are designed to prevent misbehavior before it starts. With many students, misbehavior will occur at predictable times—for example, during math work groups, in the cafeteria, or when particular peers are present. Pinpoint problematic times by asking these questions:

- *When do the problems tend to occur?* Look for a pattern in the timing of the misbehavior. Do problems occur during certain times of the day? Are mornings worse than afternoons? Do problems tend to occur more frequently at the end of the week?
- *Where do the problems tend to occur?* Determine if the student exhibits the problem behavior in multiple settings or if the behavior is isolated to one location. Do problems occur only outside the classroom? Does the student have difficulty in the halls, on the playground, or in the cafeteria?
- *What other situations seem to trigger problem behavior?* Are assemblies particularly difficult for the student? Does misbehavior occur more often at the beginning of the day when the student takes the bus than when the student is dropped off

SECTION 3: DESIGNING AN EFFECTIVE BEHAVIOR INTERVENTION PLAN

by a parent? Does the student get into fights when particular students are present? When you identify specific triggers, the intervention can focus on increasing supervision when these conditions are present.

NOTE: If you follow the problem-solving model and tools introduced in Section 2, at the point of intervention design you should have already developed a hypothesis about the settings and situations that tend to trigger problem behavior. Use this information to consider which antecedent strategies may be appropriate. If you need additional support in identifying relevant triggers and conditions that predict when behavior is likely to occur, see Item 8 of the Teacher Interview and 25-Minute Planning Process.

Reviewing the information that you have gathered about events (i.e., antecedents) and conditions (i.e., setting events) that predict when and where problematic behavior is likely to occur, consider whether any of the following evidence-based strategies may help to prevent behavior from occurring in the first place.

A. Change assigned seating. The easiest alteration of the physical environment is to change where a student sits in the room. Research has found that when desks are arranged in rows, students stay more on-task, talk out less, and complete more work (e.g., Bennett & Blundell, 1983; Wheldall & Lam, 1987). Other examples of changes to seating arrangements include:

- If a student always talks when seated with certain peers, have her sit in a different area of the room.
- If a student is highly distractible, move him as far away as possible from high-traffic areas.
- If a student is angling for adult attention, move her closer to the teacher so that she gets more attention when on task.
- Likewise, if a student is trying for peer attention, moving him closer to an adult will make his peer interactions easier to monitor.

B. Change the work requirements. A mismatch between task difficulty and a student's instructional level (i.e., presenting a task that is either too hard or too easy) can often result in higher levels of inappropriate behavior (Center, Deitz, & Kaufman, 1982; Umbreit, Lane, & Dejud, 2004). Therefore, it may be necessary to alter or modify the curriculum to fit the student's needs (Davis et al., 2004). Examples of work modifications include:

- If a student frequently fails to complete work, arrange for her to get feedback on the first part of assignments (e.g., her teacher may say, "When I give an assignment, do the first five problems and then raise your hand, and I'll come over to correct those first five and help you.")
- If a student gets frustrated with certain tasks, ask the teacher to provide initial assistance on those tasks or embed scaffolds into the tasks to make them easier.
- If a student acts out during tasks that aren't adequately challenging, consider ways to increase the difficulty of a task.

C. Provide breaks. Intentionally scheduling break opportunities allows students to move around, change activities, or redirect attention without having to misbehave to get relief from challenging or nonpreferred activities. Decreasing the overall task length or offering periodic breaks can be an effective strategy for reducing problem behavior, especially for students who demonstrate escape-maintained misbehavior (Boyd & Anderson, 2013; Moore, Anderson, & Kumar, 2005). Examples include:

- If students are expected to remain seated during a 30-minute work period and several generally fail to comply, ask the teacher to give the whole class a chance to stand up and stretch halfway through.
- If only one student struggles to get through the work time, create a process for that student to ask for breaks (e.g., placing a card on the desk to signal a break request), or have the teacher ask the student to run an errand or pass out some papers.

D. Change expectations or procedures. If you judge that the student's learning (and the teacher's sanity) won't be negatively affected, consider modifying a rule or mode for completing a particular task that a student has trouble following consistently. For students who consistently struggle to comply with classroom expectations, providing an alternative way to complete a task or modifying a rule to be more flexible may help to reduce problem behaviors (Kern, Childs, Dunlap, Clark, & Falk, 1994). Examples include:

- For a student who struggles with tasks that require a lot of written output, provide an alternative mode for work completion, such as using a computer or verbally presenting a response.
- For a young student, create a masking tape box on the floor around her desk and give her permission to stand and work if she wants, as long as she does not leave her "office."
- If you know a student is being perpetually harassed in the hallway after class, ask the teacher to excuse the student 1 or 2 minutes early to get to the next class—enabling him to avoid the harassment and make his time in the next class more productive.

E. Offer viable choices. Sometimes students rebel when they believe they have no influence over their school experience. Offering a viable choice as an element of control over situations that agitate or set off such a student can have a calming effect (Dunlap et al., 2004; Kern, Mantegna, Vorndran, Bailin, & Hilt, 2001). *Viable* means that you present the student with a *real* choice, not a choice between doing exactly what you want and a corrective consequence. Instead of "You can either get your work done or you can stay in from recess," a viable choice means providing a range of options: "You can do this, this, or this, and they would all be perfectly acceptable. Which of them would you prefer?" With that in mind, here are a few examples of viable choices you and the teacher might consider:

- Offer a choice of work locations.
- Allow the student to choose the order in which to complete a series of tasks.
- Set a self-initiated timeout: "You have my permission to go to the designated quiet area whenever you need to take a timeout and regroup." Train the student not

to abuse the privilege, and explain that work must still be completed and turned in. The idea here is that it's better for students to learn to calm themselves down before they get so upset that the teacher needs to intervene anyway: "As long as you continue to get your work done, you can use that area any time you need to.

F. Use precorrections. Precorrections are used to anticipate and prevent an inappropriate social or academic behavior by "correcting" the behavior *before* it occurs (Colvin, Sugai, & Patching, 1993; Ennis, Schwab, & Jolivette, 2012). Essentially, precorrections are verbal or nonverbal reminders about the expected behavior. For example:

- For a student who often runs in the hallway, the teacher says, "Remember, we walk quietly to the lunch room. Show me what walking quietly looks like."
- For a student who struggles with sharing playground equipment, the teacher checks in before recess and says, "I know you'll do a great job taking turns on the swings at recess today."
- For a student who often forgets to turn in assignments on time, the teacher stops at the student's desk before the end of class to ask whether the student wrote down the due date or has any questions about the assignment.
- The teacher tells the class: "When I touch my left ear, it means 'Remember to pay close attention to what I'm about to say.'"

G. Increase opportunities to respond. An opportunity to respond includes any teacher behavior that prompts or solicits a student response (verbal, written, or gesture). Increasing the rate of opportunities to respond is one of the most powerful strategies for increasing the likelihood that students will be engaged with instruction and demonstrate appropriate and on-task behavior (Partin, Robertson, Maggin, Oliver, & Wehby, 2009; Simonsen, Fairbanks, Briesch, Myers, & Sugai, 2008). Further, when you increase active student engagement, students have less time to misbehave. Following are examples of ways teachers can increase opportunities to respond:

- Invite a group of students to read a passage aloud in unison.
- Ask students to write answers to a math problem on individual whiteboards and hold them up.
- Direct students to think about what might happen next in a science demonstration, write down one sentence explaining the reasoning for their guess, and share their guess and reason with a neighboring peer.
- Model different ways to put away materials in the classroom and ask students to give a thumbs-up if the example is the right way and a thumbs-down if the example shows the wrong way.

H. Increase monitoring and supervision. Students commonly misbehave in settings and situations with limited adult supervision. If no adults are watching, it's likely that misbehavior will go unnoticed and continue to be reinforced. Increasing adult supervision can ensure that when misbehavior is observed, it's addressed appropriately. In addition, the simple presence of an adult can prevent misbehavior from occurring in the first place; most students will automatically try to behave better when they know that they are being observed (Colvin, Sugai, Good, & Lee, 1997; Johnson-Gros, Lyons, & Griffin, 2008).

Once you know when and where misbehavior might occur, you can work to increase monitoring in these settings and situations. For example:

- During problematic times, have the supervising adult move unpredictably throughout the classroom or other setting.
- Ask recess supervisors to simply spend more time standing near specific students than they have in the past.
- Increase visual scanning of areas close to individual students. Great teachers do not really have "eyes in the back of their heads" — they just seem to because they always know what is going on in all parts of the classroom.
- Assign additional supervisors to problematic locations. While it may not be feasible to hire more staff members specifically for this purpose, you can be creative in how you position adult staff members throughout the school. For example, you might have teachers stand in their doorway during passing times, assign students jobs that free adults up for supervision (e.g., students help serve food in the cafeteria), or reassign existing supervisors to zones in the cafeteria, on the playground, and in the hallways to ensure that supervisors are spread out and closely monitoring individual students or situations that have been problematic in the past for one or more students.

TASK 2 SUMMARY

In this task, you:

☑ Selected antecedent intervention strategies to implement to prevent misbehavior from occurring in the first place.

TASK 3 Identify teaching intervention strategies.

Adults frequently take appropriate behavior for granted because most students have learned these skills incidentally at home or at an earlier age. Some students, however, have not learned these skills and need to be taught how to replace misbehaviors with appropriate behaviors. For example:

- A student who does not know how to respond to feedback without becoming angry needs to be taught how to accept feedback with grace and dignity.
- A student who has poor listening skills needs to be taught how to keep her attention focused on the speaker, sit reasonably still, and answer questions related to the topic.
- A student who shouts during a disagreement needs to learn to listen actively and talk calmly.
- A student who fights when problems occur needs to learn to think about choices and act responsibly.

The point of teaching replacement behaviors is this: If you can successfully teach and get a student to replace problem behavior with a positive opposite that serves the same function or fulfills the same need, the problem no longer exists. A well-considered replacement behavior will bring the student more success, as it is more desirable and acceptable, and will also gradually squeeze out the problem behavior. Teaching students to replace problem behaviors with their positive opposite will thus resolve many problems naturally.

Teaching the positive opposite means teaching a student how to practice a behavior that is incompatible with the problem behavior. For example:

- For a student who is unable to stay on task, teach specific skills for concentrating, staying focused, and self-monitoring work behaviors. The concept of being able to manage your attention—reminding yourself to get back to work, noticing when you're staring out the window, developing strategies to bring yourself back to what's happening right now—may be entirely foreign to some students, and consciously teaching the skill can make a difference in their behavior.
- For a student who gets upset when you correct his work, teach him a range of acceptable responses, such as telling himself that "mistakes are OK," taking a deep breath and counting to 10, or fixing mistakes and taking a computer break.
- For a student who struggles with accepting a compliment, teach her to say "thanks" or reciprocate with a compliment.

Note that *teaching* is not the same thing as *telling*. Teaching involves repeated instruction across time until mastery is achieved. Instruction may involve modeling, creating frequent practice opportunities, providing positive and corrective feedback, combining simple, previously mastered behaviors into more complex chains of behavior, and providing context instruction (i.e., in this situation do this, but in another situation do that). Teaching also involves encouraging students to use and practice newly learned behaviors on a regular basis. A masterful basketball coach who repeatedly drills players every day on skills and techniques is a good example of someone who is actively teaching rather than telling.

Based on the replacement behaviors and goals you specified in Task 1, consider how to incorporate the following teaching strategies into a student's behavior intervention plan:

I. Re-teach classroom expectations. While most teachers introduce classroom rules at the beginning of the school year, it is important to regularly revisit and review these rules throughout the year in order to remind students about the behavior expectations (Rosenberg, 1986; Simonsen et al., 2008). Spending time re-teaching expectations will save time—potentially a lot of it—later on. Re-teaching expectations may be worthwhile in the following situations:

- Review classroom expectations a few months into the school year, after holiday breaks, or when a new student joins the class.
- If several students are having trouble following classroom rules, re-teach expectations to the whole class.
- If everybody in the class but Zach is doing well, individualize teaching expectations to Zach. Explain to him one-to-one when he can talk, how he can get help, and any other concepts that seem to be unclear or unnecessary to him.

The point of teaching replacement behaviors is this: If you can successfully teach and get a student to replace problem behavior with a positive opposite that serves the same function or fulfills the same need, the problem no longer exists.

J. Provide demonstrations and modeling. Students singled out for intervention are probably quite familiar with injunctions such as *stay on task, work harder,* and *behave yourself,* but they may have no understanding of how to actually put these phrases into practice. When a new behavior is introduced, the student should have an opportunity to see what it looks like in action. Modeling involves demonstrating the specific behaviors or language associated with a new skill (Brophy & Good, 1986; Rosenshine, 1995).

A powerful demonstration model is to give a positive-negative-positive example. To do this, demonstrate the right way, show the wrong way (i.e., the way the student has behaved in the past), and then show the right way again. In effect, you are sandwiching the example of what you don't want to see between two examples of the behavior you'd like to see, helping the student make the connection without unduly stressing the "bad" behavior. For example:

- First, show the student the right way to exhibit the behavior. Model it and break it down: "Watch how I do this. Notice what I'm saying, how I gesture, what my face is doing."
- Then demonstrate a negative behavior you've seen: "This is the wrong way to do it." Explain, "I've seen this behavior from you or other students in the past. Here's why it's not OK, and why it won't work as well for you as what I'm showing you."
- Finally, return to modeling a positive example: "Now watch me do it the right way again."

K. Provide positive practice and feedback. Schedule time for students to rehearse new behaviors. This provides repeated opportunities for staff to offer specific feedback on student performance, which will strengthen existing knowledge, address any problems in the use of the new behaviors, and help students apply skills to new settings and situations (Kluger & DeNisi, 1996; MacKenzie-Keating & McDonald, 1990). For effective structured practice, incorporate these tips:

- Simulate situations that resemble the real settings and events that the student has had difficulty managing in the past.
- Each time the student acts out the replacement behavior, provide positive feedback if it was done well. If you need to provide corrective feedback, try to come up with at least three positive aspects of the rehearsal so that your work together maintains a 3:1 positive-to-corrective ratio. For example: "Good! You talked about needing an appointment. You didn't demand that it be now. And something you did really, really well was use a very calm voice. But you got a little too close—you were a little too much in my face. Sometimes that can make people not want to listen to what you have to say. But you're saying it so well! Stand back a step or two, and let's try it again."
- As you practice, ask the student *what, why, how, when,* and *where* questions about the rationale for the replacement behavior. If the student has trouble answering, provide the information and then repeat the question. For example: "When can you ask for a break? What signal will I give you if a break is OK? Where can you go? What should you be doing?"

L. Provide opportunities for verbal practice. Asking students to verbally rehearse what they will do when faced with challenging situations gives them the opportunity to "think aloud" about their behavior (Gresham, 2002). By verbalizing the behavior or strategy, students demonstrate an understanding of what they should be doing. Verbal practice also allows a student to practice a behavior before trying it, minimizing the risk of failure. If more explanation or practice in the new behavior is needed, verbal practice will help you identify areas that need more work before the student enters the classroom. This is especially important if the new behavior will be difficult for the student. Examples of verbal practice include:

- Having a student practice asking her teacher for a break when she is feeling anxious or overwhelmed.
- Asking a student to describe the detailed steps he will take to complete that evening's homework (e.g., writing down assignment details, gathering materials before leaving school, setting up a work space at home, etc.).
- Having a student verbalize the actions he will take when encountering a bully (e.g., take two deep breaths, say "that was disrespectful," walk away).

Planning Recommendations for Teaching Strategies

When creating a plan that includes teaching strategies, make sure to address and incorporate the following components.

- *Determine who will provide the lessons and where they will occur.* Someone the student feels relatively comfortable with and enjoys working with should conduct these initial practice lessons. If the skill being taught is fairly simple, the classroom teacher may be able to present the replacement behavior and conduct informal lessons with the student individually for a few minutes several times a week. Sometimes the classroom teacher can skillfully and unobtrusively find time to provide 5-minute behavior lessons while other students work independently or in small groups. If other classmates need improvement in the same skills that are being taught to the individual student of concern, consider teaching the lessons to a small group of students or the whole class. For example, if the target student needs to learn how to work independently, the classroom teacher could teach the class strategies such as getting help from other students, circling a problem and moving on until the teacher is free, "guesstimating" answers, and ignoring distractions. In this way, the targeted student can practice the replacement behavior along with peers, who will also benefit.

    However, if the lessons will be fairly involved and require daily practice, the classroom teacher may not be in the best position to provide lessons due to time constraints. A member of the school's problem-solving team, such as the school counselor, principal, school psychologist, or school nurse, might conduct initial sessions. It might be useful to have a paraprofessional, mentor, or parent volunteer teach some of the lessons under the guidance of the interventionist. One arrangement might be to have a paraprofessional conduct the daily lessons, with the interventionist participating and observing once a week. In all cases, as the student becomes more competent, ongoing support for new skills will gradually be transferred to the "real" environment of the classroom and the student's teacher.

- *Determine how much time will be needed and how often lessons will occur.* Because a replacement behavior may not be in the student's current repertoire, providing frequent opportunities for practice is essential. Five minutes of practice each day will usually produce better results than 45 minutes once a week. As a rule of thumb, the greater the change you hope to effect, the more often you should conduct the lessons.

- *Plan to conduct lessons in a manner and place that will not embarrass the student.* At-risk students often respond positively to supportive adult attention in one-to-one lessons, but conditions that cause unintended embarrassment or agitation may lead to resistance. Keep practice sessions with the student private and unobtrusive. The student must feel comfortable enough in sessions to quell any fear of failure. Lessons should provide the student with "safe" practice. With secondary students, these lessons probably need to be conducted away from peers (e.g., in an empty classroom or counselor's office).

- *Plan to gradually increase the difficulty of the lessons.* As the student gains competence, plan to gradually increase the difficulty of the lessons until the student adopts the behavior in everyday situations. In the early stages, lessons should be conducted in an environment that is relatively free of distractions. As the student becomes more successful, conduct the lessons in more complex contexts that assume more of the characteristics of the actual setting in which the student usually has problems. Eventually, the goal is to teach the student to employ the new behavior in the problematic school setting for progressively longer periods of time. Lesson difficulty can be increased by asking the student to deal with more complex situations, by increasing the expected length or duration of the behavior, and by removing adult assistance.

- *Make a conscious effort to recognize student success outside of the practice sessions.* As the student begins to practice new behavior in the real classroom environment, the teacher and other staff should monitor key times when the student is likely to engage in the new behavior. As the student gains competence, all adults should try to catch the student exhibiting the goal behavior outside of structured lesson times. Share behavior goals with adults who regularly interact with the student and encourage them to provide positive feedback on the student's efforts to use new skills in different settings.

TASK 3 SUMMARY

In this task, you:

☑ Selected strategies for teaching and practicing appropriate behavior.

SECTION 3: DESIGNING AN EFFECTIVE BEHAVIOR INTERVENTION PLAN

TASK 4: Identify positive consequence intervention strategies.

Positive consequence strategies are designed to encourage appropriate behavior and discourage misbehavior through the use of reinforcement. Used in response to behavior, these strategies are intended to increase the likelihood that students will choose to engage in positive behaviors in the future. Examples of positive consequence strategies include:

- Praising a student who walks quietly in the hallway.
- Awarding a student extra time on the computer for turning in her homework.
- Recording points on a chart every time a student remembers to raise his hand and allowing him to select a prize when he earns 10 points.
- Sending a positive note home at the end of a week in which the student had no problems at recess.
- Allowing the student to pick her seat in the afternoon if she completed all of her seatwork.

Consider how the following strategies may help to increase the appropriate/replacement behaviors and/or decrease misbehaviors that you specified in Task 1.

M. Deliver praise and specific feedback. When students behave appropriately, teachers should consciously give them attention, praise, and positive feedback (Hattie & Timperley, 2007). For students who have historically gained attention from adults and peers through misbehavior, praise and feedback for positive, appropriate behavior are critical elements in redirecting behavior patterns (Becker, Madsen, Arnold, & Thomas, 1967). Likewise, for a student who is learning a new skill or behavior, feedback that describes what the student was doing responsibly helps the student learn exactly what responsible behavior looks and sounds like (Brookhart, 2017). When delivering praise and feedback, keep these guidelines in mind:

- Be descriptive, concrete, and specific with feedback so that the student knows exactly what to do more or less of next time.
- Avoid the "good job" syndrome and nonspecific rote comments such as "terrific," "super," or "nice job." When this happens, positive comments become background noise. Students may not even notice the attention because no usable information is provided.
- Link positive feedback to a student's goals or general class rules. When specific behavior is linked to goals or to classroom rules, students will begin to understand how their actions are related to more global or sophisticated expectations. Students need to know how their specific actions translate into being "responsible," "on task," "polite," and so on.

Positive consequence strategies are designed to encourage appropriate behavior and discourage misbehavior through the use of reinforcement.

N. Offer rewards. When problems have been resistant to change or when a student needs additional encouragement to demonstrate appropriate behavior, offering rewards for increased positive behavior or decreased rates of inappropriate behavior can provide an extra boost of motivation and help make success a reality for a student (Alberto & Troutman, 2012). Rewards can be a powerful motivating component to any behavior intervention plan. In order to be effective, rewards need to be a) valued by the student, b) delivered consistently and as immediately as possible, and c) paired with social acknowledgment (Cooper, Heron, & Heward, 2007). Rewards can take many forms, including:

- Special privileges (e.g., early dismissal from class, first-in-line privileges)
- Tangible items (e.g., snacks, pencils, stickers)
- Access to preferred activities (e.g., computer time, free choice)
- Points or tokens that can be exchanged for something of value to the student

REWARDS AND REINFORCERS

See Appendix B for a list of ideas for rewards and reinforcers.

NOTE ABOUT REWARDS AND REINFORCERS

While *reward* and *reinforcer* are often used interchangeably, there is an important distinction between the two terms.

A *reinforcer* is defined by its effects on future behavior. A reinforcer is something that, when presented after a behavior, increases the likelihood that behavior will occur again in the future in the given situation. In contrast, a *reward* is not defined by its effects on behavior. Rewards are generally assumed to be positive, but they may not actually increase future behavior (Alberto & Troutman, 2006; Skinner, 1953).

We use the term *reward* throughout this book to refer to tangible items, special privileges, access to preferred activities, and points or tokens that are delivered after desired behavior occurs. Praise and specific feedback are social rewards that occur after desired behavior. When integrating positive consequence strategies into your behavior intervention plan, remember that the tangible and social rewards that you specify are only *hypothesized* reinforcers until they effectively increase the likelihood of future desired behavior. If behavior doesn't improve, you may need to revisit and adjust your list of possible rewards.

O. Send positive news home. Regularly communicating with parents to celebrate a student's progress can be a powerful component in maintaining student motivation to change (Barth, 1979 ; Carlson & Christenson, 2005). Acknowledge a student's positive efforts and success in meeting expectations and making progress toward goals by:

- Writing a note home to inform parents about a student's exceptional effort.
- Calling parents to discuss positive examples of student behavior during the week.
- Sending home a weekly report card that displays the progress a student has made toward behavior goals.

Planning Recommendations for Positive Consequence Strategies

When creating a plan to include positive consequence strategies, consider the following recommendations.

- *Create a list of rewards and possible praise and feedback statements.* Identify some possible rewards that may be motivating to the student and that match the function of the student's misbehavior (e.g., offering priority access to preferred recess equipment for improved behavior may be an appropriate reward for a student who in the past bullied other students to gain access to preferred equipment). To be effective at reinforcing appropriate behavior, rewards must be individualized and valued by the student. A special privilege may be extremely reinforcing to one student and aversive to another. When considering different types of rewards to offer the student, be careful to select only options that the student is likely to value. You might develop a list of possible rewards and ask students to identify those they would feel motivated to work toward. Appendix B provides a list of potential rewards to consider.

    Similarly, create a list of opportunities to provide praise and possible feedback statements to use in these moments. Proactively identifying opportunities and specific statements can help a teacher more fluently deliver high rates of praise and feedback. For example, opportunities to provide praise may include:

    - Noticing when the student is kind or helpful to peers.
    - Looking for times when the student puts in extra effort on academic work.
    - Recognizing when the student is applying new skills or knowledge to a task or activity.

    Possible feedback statements include:

    - "I really appreciated how quiet you were when entering the classroom after recess."
    - "I saw that you turned your homework into the box before class. Great job getting it in on time."
    - When providing feedback to the whole class, make extra efforts to include the student specifically, for example: "Students, I can tell by your comments that you are listening respectfully to your classmates. Duane, your comment about whales eating plankton is very knowledgeable."

- *Plan to deliver feedback in a manner and place that will not embarrass the student.* Be sure to recognize that every student responds differently to praise, and structure your interactions accordingly. Some students will misbehave simply to avoid receiving compliments they find embarrassing or patronizing. Other students may respond well to private comments, but are embarrassed by public comments.

Students may respond better when comments are emotionally neutral as well. "Ellen, you have produced a very creative story" may be more acceptable than, "Oh, Ellen! I loved your story about the sea monster. It was so imaginative! I enjoyed it so much!" If a student seems embarrassed by verbal feedback, consider working out a nonverbal signal in advance. The teacher can look the student in the eye, give a prearranged signal such as a nod of the head, and then resume teaching. If the teacher has discussed the signal with the student, eye contact and a nod of the head will clearly communicate the message: *That was a good example of self-control.* Specific feedback, while important, should always be delivered in a way that is acceptable to the student.

- *Recognize important behavior and avoid praising overly simple behavior.* If a student is working on improving self-control, saying something like "Good sitting" is not meaningful and is in fact potentially demeaning. Appropriate and relevant feedback might be, "You demonstrated self-control by listening patiently while I was giving instructions." Give praise for tasks or behavior that are new or difficult so that feedback is meaningful. Remember that the same behavior may be simple for one student but new and complex for another.
- *Provide honest feedback.* Give honest positive feedback by catching students as they legitimately demonstrate responsible behavior. If Kenny is tapping his pencil, it would not be appropriate to praise him for sitting in his seat. Praise is not appropriate when the student is misbehaving. If inappropriate behavior triggers a positive comment, the interaction is negative because the teacher is responding to misbehavior. In this case, the misbehavior should be ignored or a consequence implemented in accordance with the consequences that were previously set.

NOTE: An exception to this guideline may be made when behavior is so severe that it needs to be gradually shaped. In this case, it might be appropriate to provide positive feedback about an appropriate behavior while the student is engaged in an unrelated misbehavior. For example, you might praise a student with a developmental delay for staying on task and keeping his hands to himself, even though he is making inappropriate noises while he works.

TASK 4 SUMMARY

In this task, you:

☑ Selected positive consequence strategies to use in reinforcing and encouraging the student's demonstration of appropriate behavior at school.

TASK 5 — Identify corrective consequence intervention strategies.

Corrective consequence strategies are designed to increase the consistency and efficacy of the corrective consequences implemented when misbehavior occurs. Though negative consequences in isolation are weak strategies for reducing chronic or severe misbehavior, their use is often necessary. In combination with other proactive strategies, they can be extremely powerful in changing student behavior.

Fluency is key to implementing consequences successfully. A fluent response to an incident of misbehavior is given in a way that continues the flow of the instructional activity as much as possible. This means that what is done to correct a student's misbehavior is of less importance than continuing instruction. For example, if a student makes a disrespectful comment during teacher-directed instruction and the teacher matter-of-factly states, "That was disrespectful. I would like to speak to you after class. Now, class, the next paragraph states . . . ," the flow of the lesson is maintained. On the other hand, if the teacher immediately takes the student into the hall or gets into an argument about assigning detention, the flow of the lesson is lost.

A fluent correction is performed calmly, consistently, briefly, and immediately. It is specific, direct, and, above all, respectful. As straightforward as fluency may sound, it is surprisingly difficult to achieve. You must define the fine line between acceptable and unacceptable behaviors before consequences can be used effectively. This will allow teachers to make the quick judgments necessary to follow through with consequences for infractions without undue strain on the flow of instruction. At the same time, predetermining boundaries will help determine which behaviors to encourage. By carefully delineating what is and what is not acceptable behavior, you are teaching students positive expectations for their behavior and setting appropriate limits. Once limits are clarified, it is easier to calmly and fluently implement a prearranged consequence every time a student crosses the line into unacceptable behavior.

A fluent correction is performed calmly, consistently, briefly, and immediately.

STEP 1 — Categorize problem behaviors and define limits.

Start by identifying and categorizing all problem behaviors that the student exhibits. You may not address all the misbehaviors that you identify, but write down every behavior the student exhibits that could be considered inappropriate or bordering on inappropriate. A complete list will help you define the parameters of selected intervention strategies.

> **NOTE ABOUT CONSEQUENCES AND PUNISHMENT**
>
> Similar to the distinction between *reward* and *reinforcer* discussed on page 258, *consequences* and *punishment* are defined differently based on their effects on future behavior. A *punisher* is something that, when presented after a behavior, decreases the likelihood that behavior will occur again in the future in a given situation. A *consequence* is assumed to be negative, but is only punishing (or corrective) if it effectively decreases the frequency, intensity, or duration of future behavior (Alberto & Troutman, 2006; Skinner, 1953).

To capture as many problem behaviors as possible, ask the following questions:

- Does the student say or do anything that bothers the teacher or other staff?
- Does the student say or do anything that disrupts the class?
- Does the student say or do anything that interferes with the student's or others' learning?
- Does the student comply with instructions?
- Does the student get along with other students?
- Does the student get academic work done? Is it satisfactory?
- Where and when does the student display problem behavior? (E.g., in the classroom, before or after school, on the bus, in common areas such as hallways, cafeteria, playground, etc.)

Next, examine the list to determine how misbehaviors can be categorized. For example, if the list includes pencil tapping, chair screeching, and making animal noises, combine these behaviors into one category: "making noises." If the student tells classmates to pick their own things up, tells the teacher to watch the clock, tells other students to sharpen their pencils, and so on, combine these behaviors into a category such as "bossiness." Continue consolidating similar or redundant items on the list until you have created a comprehensive set of categories. Figure 3.6 shows an example of categorized behaviors.

Once you've categorized the problem behaviors, select one or two general behaviors as priorities for assigning corrective consequences. When identifying priorities, consider:

- *Urgency of the problem.* Deal with the most pervasive or disruptive problems first. Less intrusive problems can be handled once the student is experiencing success. Sometimes less important problems resolve themselves as the student experiences success in other areas.
- *Manageability of change for the student and teacher.* Though many problems may exist, it is important to consider the sophistication and ability of the student and the manageability of corrective consequences for the teacher and other staff. If the student is intellectually limited or a vast change is required, it may be best to select only one problem to address with corrective consequences. If you select too many problems, the teacher and the student are likely to become overwhelmed and discouraged.

Finally, work with one category at a time, beginning with the highest priority, to define limits by identifying examples of acceptable and unacceptable behavior in particular situations, or, in some cases, in terms of quantity (i.e., how much of a behavior is acceptable).

- *Define limits by example.* Because an element of subjectivity is unavoidable in deciding whether a behavior is appropriate or inappropriate, providing examples will help define consistent limits for misbehaviors in the classroom. To define limits by example, start by identifying a few typical situations in which the student has misbehaved. For each situation, list ways the student might handle the situation appropriately and ways the student might handle the situation inappropriately. It's

FIGURE 3.6 *Examples of Categorized Behaviors*

Misbehavior	Category
When Mrs. Parson says, "Good morning," Carly responds: • "Good morning, Mrs. Parson," in a singsong, sarcastic tone. • "Oh, good. Another day with Mrs. Parsley."	disrespect disrespect
When Carly is tardy, she: • Tries not to be counted tardy. • Implies that Mrs. Parson treats her unfairly compared with other students.	negotiating complaining
When Mrs. Parsons calls on Carly during discussions, she says: • "Who cares about [*blank*]? This is stupid." • "No one else is interested." • "Why would I care?" • "If you don't know the answer, you're pretty stupid."	disrespect disrespect disrespect disrespect
When Mrs. Parson gives group directions like "Line up for recess" or "Everyone get cleaned up," Carly mimics Mrs. Parson.	disrespect
When Mrs. Parson gives assignments, Carly says: • "Why should I do it?" • "What a laugh. Here we go with another of Mrs. Parsley's dumb assignments." • "OK, I'll do it," in a sulky, obnoxious tone. • "No one else has to do so much."	negotiating disrespect disrespect complaining
Carly tries to evade assignments by saying: • "I don't see why I have to do it. I already did it once." • "Can't I fix just one problem? I understand it."	complaining complaining
Carly has to have the last word. She says, "You always give us too much work."	disrespect
When asked to clean up after some types of work, Carly has complained that Mrs. Parson never gives enough time.	complaining
When Mrs. Parson tries to talk with Carly, Carly: • Walks away from her. • Glares at her. • Sighs in a disgusted manner.	disrespect disrespect disrespect
Carly sometimes forgets her homework.	homework
Carly sometimes makes inappropriate noises, such as belching.	inappropriate noises
Carly doesn't seem to have many friends.	friends

not necessary to include examples of everything the student might do—focus on those things the student has done or seems likely to do. What's most important is to describe or model examples that fall near the border between appropriate and inappropriate behavior. In baseball, you can explain the strike zone by pointing and explaining: "If the pitch is here, it would be a strike, but if the pitch is here, it would be a ball." By demonstrating similar minimal distinctions with respect to behavior, adults can clarify the difference between acceptable and unacceptable behavior in their own minds. See Figure 3.7 for examples.

- *Define limits in terms of quantity (how much is too much).* While limits for most behaviors can be made plain by generating a sufficient number of examples, behavior that is unacceptable because it is excessive rather than inappropriate may need to have its limits defined in a different way. In this case, provide the student with information about how often a behavior is appropriate. Quantity limits are especially useful for behaviors that teachers do not want to eliminate but hope to reduce. An example is the student who clowns around too much:

> *Tony, we all love your great sense of humor, but you need to learn how to curb it a bit. Your jesting is interfering with what we need to accomplish in class. Therefore, I am going to give you five "laugh" tickets for the day. Use the tickets wisely. Once they are gone, you cannot take class time for jokes and fun comments. If you take time to entertain us after your tickets are gone, you will owe time after the bell.*

To determine quantity-based limits, consider what would be acceptable from any student, what teachers can reasonably manage, and whether the student can reasonably meet expectations.

STEP 2   Select corrective consequence intervention strategies.

Once you list problem behaviors and define their limits, select consequences for each category of behavior. Work collaboratively with the teacher, administrator, and problem-solving team to identify appropriate consequences. If you want to include the student in the process of selecting consequences, first review the list of possible consequences and select some you think would be most reasonable.

Many options for consequences are available, including:

P. Ignore misbehavior. If attention is what the student wants, constant nagging, repeated corrections, and increasingly severe consequences will not improve misbehavior and may in fact be reinforcing to an attention-starved student. In these cases, withholding attention may be the most effective consequence to implement (Alberto & Troutman, 2012; Gable, Hester, Rock, & Hughes, 2009). Categories of misbehavior that can be ignored include behaviors that do not interfere with teaching or other students' learning. However, the use of ignoring is counterintuitive to many adults and therefore difficult to implement. To ignore misbehavior effectively:

- Act as though you did not see or hear the misbehavior. This means staying calm and physically relaxed. A rigid body response or even a glance at the student might be reinforcing.
- Ignore misbehavior consistently. As with all responses to misbehavior, consistency is the key to ignoring effectively. If the plan calls for ignoring Harvey for blurting out responses, then he must be ignored every time he blurts out a response. If the teacher ignores Harvey the first two or three times he blurts out answers and

FIGURE 3.7 *Examples of Defining Limits*

If the problem is inappropriate language, the following kinds of examples might be used to define behavior limits.

Situation: Thomas trips in the classroom.

Acceptable responses:
"Darn!"
"Oops!"

Unacceptable responses:
"D*mn!"
"Sh*t!"

Situation: Thomas misses a ball in four square.

Acceptable responses:
"Darn!"
"Shoot!"
No comment.

Unacceptable responses:
"D*mn!"
"Sh*t!"
"F*ck!"

If the problem is hitting, physical examples might be used to define behavior limits.

Situation: Brenda wants to get someone's attention.

Acceptable touching:
Touching someone like this
(tap the student's shoulder).

Unacceptable hitting:
Touching someone like this
(hit the wall to demonstrate).

If the problem is putting others down, the following kinds of examples might be used to define behavior limits.

Situation: Someone says something that Salim already knows.

Acceptable responses:
Nodding his head.
"I noticed that, too."

Unacceptable responses:
"Isn't that obvious?"
"Bravo, aren't you smart!"

---

then responds with a consequence, the previous ignoring will not be effective and intervention fidelity will be compromised. Harvey will soon learn that persistence pays when he wants to get attention through misbehavior—and you'll be hearing a lot more from Harvey.

- Simultaneously, seek opportunities to give the student attention by interacting positively—saying "hello" to the student, engaging in friendly interactions, and providing positive feedback when possible. When you ignore irresponsible behavior and interact when the student is behaving responsibly, the student will learn that behaving responsibly is the easier way to get attention.

CAUTION: Ignoring is a difficult technique to implement. If a student misbehaves to get teacher attention, behavior is likely to worsen before it gets better. Students who have a long history of getting attention through negative means will try harder to get attention in the way they have been most successful—through misbehavior. Though difficult to deal with, worsening behavior is a sign that ignoring will eventually work.

Give ignoring at least 2 weeks of consistent implementation before making a judgment regarding its effectiveness.

Q. Reduce peer attention. If a student has received a lot of peer attention for misbehavior in the past, it may be necessary to implement strategies that remove this attention (Broussard & Northrup, 1997; Solomon & Wahler, 1973). One way to accomplish this is by teaching other students in the classroom to ignore misbehavior when it occurs. To reduce peer attention:

- Identify specific behaviors to teach the class to ignore, and model and role-play what these behaviors look like and sound like. Explain that when students witness any student engaging in inappropriate behavior, they should either a) turn away and ignore the behavior, or b) ignore the behavior but tell the teacher what happened.
- Simultaneously, teach students to pay increased attention to students who demonstrate appropriate behavior. Model examples linked to classroom or schoolwide expectations to clarify what appropriate behavior looks like and provide some age-appropriate options for what positive attention for these behaviors might look like (e.g., a thumbs-up, a smile, a compliment).

CAUTION: Before implementing this strategy, make sure to consider whether this approach is likely to make the student feel ostracized by peers. Peer intervention should be used only when the majority of students are willing to ignore inappropriate behavior *and* provide increased attention to the student during positive times.

R. Use gentle verbal reprimands or warnings. A gentle verbal reprimand or warning reminds students that they are engaging (or about to engage) in inappropriate behavior. When students do not know that a behavior is unacceptable or are unaware of when they engage in a particular behavior, a gentle verbal reprimand, given in a neutral or supportive tone, provides them with useful information about the nature of their behavior (Jenson & Reavis, 1996; Matheson, Starkweather, & Shriver, 2005). For example: "Malcolm, when I hear that edge in your voice, I know you are starting to get argumentative. Please try that statement again, but in a less argumentative tone."

In addition, when a student's misbehavior starts to slide from appropriate into inappropriate behavior, a verbal warning may be an appropriate consequence prior to a more severe consequence (such as in-class timeout or time owed). For example, as the student's behavior begins to deteriorate, the teacher might say something like: "Ellis, your tone of voice is starting to sound impatient. You need to take a deep breath. Then lower your voice." When providing a gentle verbal reprimand or warning, keep the following in mind:

- Move to the student if possible. Reprimands from across the room tend to be ineffective.
- Calmly state what the student should be doing.
- Offer praise as soon as the student begins to exhibit more acceptable behavior.
- Avoid increasing the emotional intensity of repeated feedback if a reprimand must be repeated. A short, neutral statement is less likely to reinforce the student for the misbehavior than an angry or lengthy attempt to correct the behavior.

RESOURCE: REDUCING PEER ATTENTION

For young students (Pre-K to Grade 2) who need a greater level of support in learning to use prosocial behaviors in the classroom, *FIRST STEP Next* is a comprehensive intervention that combines peer intervention strategies with one-on-one coaching, explicit instruction in behavioral skills, and a home component that links skills introduced at school to the home environment. For more information and to purchase, visit Ancora Publishing at ancorapublishing.com.

S. Assign time owed. When a student wastes class time by engaging in frequent misbehavior, time owed communicates to the student that wasted class time will be repaid during a time that the student values (Sprick, 2009). For example, when a student engages in misbehavior, a teacher may calmly say, "That was an example of [*blank*]. You owe 1 minute of recess." To implement time owed:

- Use only small amounts of time owed for each infraction. A common error is to have the student owe an entire recess or passing period for each infraction. With frequent misbehavior, you soon run out of recesses and passing periods to take away. The teacher and student end up without needed breaks, and any potential impact from the consequence is soon lost. In most cases, owing 15 seconds to 1 minute per infraction is more effective than owing larger amounts of time. These small amounts of time owed also allow the teacher to be consistent with every incidence of misbehavior. If Keone causes 10 disruptions that waste class time, he still owes less than 3 minutes, which is a manageable period of time for the teacher to implement. In comparison, the teacher who implements 5 minutes of time owed for each infraction would face close to an extra hour with the frequently misbehaving student. This teacher will probably end up implementing consequences inconsistently or progressively, both of which can do as much harm as good.
- Decide what the student should be doing during time owed. In some early cases of misbehavior, the time might be used to discuss the problem with the student. If time is owed repeatedly and frequently, the student should sit and do nothing. The more boring you can make time owed, the better, because students will be thinking of the many other things they would rather be doing than sitting silently.

CAUTION: This consequence may be difficult to implement by secondary teachers and elementary teachers who have students for only one period, such as librarians, PE teachers, and music specialists, as there are fewer opportunities during the day to implement time owed. These teachers might consider in-class timeouts as an alternative.

T. Assign in-class timeout. When a student engages in misbehavior frequently, an in-class timeout communicates that taking part in class activities is a privilege. Considerable research suggests that in-class timeout can be a successful consequence strategy for reducing misbehavior (e.g., Brantner & Doherty, 1983; Clark, Rowbury, Baer, & Baer, 1973). When a student engages in unacceptable behavior, the teacher may calmly say something like: "That was an example of [*blank*]. Go to timeout and think about other ways you might have handled that situation. You may return to your seat when the timer rings." Timeout in the room may be as simple as having the student go to a chair at the side of the classroom or to a study carrel. To effectively use timeout:

- Decide in advance whether to specify how long the student will spend in timeout. Some teachers assign specific durations. Others structure timeout as more flexible, according to the student's behavior: "Come back and join the group when you are ready." If the timeout is to be a specific length, keep it short and set a timer so that the student isn't forgotten. Time begins when the student is in the timeout area and sitting quietly. For students in sixth grade and above, 5 minutes is a reasonable period of time. With older students who refuse or delay going to the timeout area, record the amount of time they take to get to timeout and explain that they will owe that time from recess or after school. For younger students, timeout should be shorter and based on the age and sophistication of the student. One-minute timeouts are appropriate for kindergarten and first-grade students, who may need to be escorted to the timeout area.

- During an in-class timeout, the student should sit and do nothing. If academically capable, the student can fill out a Behavior Improvement Form (Reproducible 3.3). If a student misbehaves after returning from timeout, calmly tell the student to return to the timeout area and repeat the process. It is not unusual for a student to be sent to timeout 5, 10, or even 20 times in the first several days of implementing a new timeout procedure. As long as the time period is not unduly harsh and you have established that the student is capable of exhibiting the expected behavior, this high level of implementation is OK. With consistency, persistence, and time, this approach has the potential to resolve many chronic behavior problems.

BEHAVIOR IMPROVEMENT FORM

It may be useful to have students who engage in misbehavior without thinking fill out a Behavior Improvement Form (Reproducible 3.3) so that they can reflect on their actions and think about ways to avoid future problems. The Behavior Improvement Form requires students to think about their actions, begin assuming responsibility, and learn how to take control by identifying more-acceptable ways of handling similar situations. When a student misbehaves, calmly say, "That was an example of [*blank*]. You need to think about what you did and fill out a Behavior Improvement Form."

NOTE: This form requires sophisticated reading and writing skills and is not appropriate for a student who struggles academically.

CAUTION: The proper use of the term *timeout* references the original procedure called "timeout from positive reinforcement," meaning that the purpose of timeout is to remove a student's access to a reinforcing situation or environment (Harris, 1985; Taylor & Miller, 1997). For a student whose misbehavior is maintained by offering escape from difficult or nonpreferred situations, it is very likely that timeout will inadvertently reinforce the misbehavior.

U. Assign out-of-class timeout. When the misbehavior is too disruptive for the student to remain in the classroom, an out-of-class consequence may be necessary. However, this consequence should be reserved only for behavior that is highly disruptive or dangerous—in other words, Code Red situations—such as overt defiance toward adults, loud and sustained noncompliance, screaming, or highly aggressive behavior such as hitting or hair pulling (Busch & Shore, 2000; Rozalski, Yell, & Boreson, 2006). When a behavioral episode is escalating toward a Code Red situation and the misbehavior of one or more students is so severe as to warrant removal from the classroom, staff must know exactly what procedures to follow. These procedures should have been set in advance, possibly on a schoolwide basis (Ryan, Peterson, Tetreault, & Hagen, 2007). See Section 1, Task 6: Establish Processes for Responding to Code Red Situations for a description of how to set up schoolwide policies, and Section 4.4: Behavior Emergency Planning for guidelines on creating a safety plan for an individual student.

If you select out-of-class timeout as a consequence, make sure to address the following questions in advance:

- Which behaviors warrant removal from the classroom?
- Where will the student go for an out-of-class timeout?
- How long will the student spend in the timeout location?
- What will the student do while in timeout?
- Who will supervise the student while in timeout?
- How will the student transition back to the classroom?

REPRODUCIBLE 3.3 *Behavior Improvement Form*

Behavior Improvement Form

Name _____ Grade/Class _____

Teacher _____ Period/Time _____

1. What was your behavior? _____
_____
_____
_____
_____
_____

2. What could you do differently? _____
_____
_____
_____
_____
_____

3. Will you be able to do that? _____
_____
_____
_____
_____
_____

Interventions © 2019 Ancora Publishing

REPRODUCIBLE 3.3

Because dismissing students from their regularly scheduled class has the potential to cause as many problems as it solves (e.g., escalating the behavior), answers to these questions are important. Where should the student be if not in the classroom? Typical out-of-class detention locations include the hallway, the office, another classroom, or a designated timeout room.

CAUTION: The only occasion when you should use an out-of-class consequence is when a behavior simply cannot be tolerated in the classroom because it impedes the learning of other students or threatens the student or others. Be sure your school administrators are in agreement about which behaviors are severe enough to warrant a student's removal from class and where students whose behavior crosses that threshold should be sent.

V. Revoke a privilege. For some students, the reinforcing value of misbehavior may be so powerful and ingrained that other reinforcement and consequence strategies may not effectively motivate them to change their behaviors. In such cases, it may be useful to remove a highly valued privilege as a consequence for misbehavior (Bear, 2008; Walker, 1983). As with all consequences to be implemented, be sure to tell the student in advance which privilege will be removed as a consequence for engaging in misbehavior. Also keep these other considerations in mind:

- The revoked privilege should be mild and fairly immediate. Appropriate examples are loss of computer game time, loss of recess for that day, or loss of choice of seat for the day.
- Avoid removing major privileges or privileges that are scheduled far in the future, such as losing recess every day for the next month or not being able to go on a field trip scheduled for next month. Each classroom can define the range of what are considered privileges.
- In many cases, it may be worthwhile to offer the student a chance to earn back privileges by demonstrating appropriate behavior.

CAUTION: If you choose to revoke recess privileges, avoid restricting the student from recess entirely. Instead, consider removing a few minutes of recess or restricting the student to a tighter structure at recess (e.g., the student has to select between two highly supervised activities).

Guidelines for Selecting Consequences

Keep the following in mind when selecting corrective consequences.

- *Choose consequences that can be implemented consistently.* It is easier to consistently implement a mild consequence than a severe consequence. If the behavior occurs 18 times a day, choose a consequence that can be easily implemented 18 times a day. Well-meaning educators sometimes set tough consequences for mild to moderate misbehavior and then find they aren't willing to go through with the consequences in all cases or with every student because they seem too harsh. If gentle reprimands are chosen as a consequence, make sure that the teacher will use them every time. Getting angry after issuing five gentle reprimands not only fractures the consistency that characterizes fluent correction, but it can potentially teach or reinforce a host of unwelcome behaviors as the student learns that persistence is the trick to getting the teacher riled up. Emotional responses from a teacher simply reinforce a student's feelings of power or control. This point is important enough to reiterate: *Staff response to misbehavior should be something they can do each and every time the student exhibits the problem behavior.*

- *Choose consequences that take into account the function of the misbehavior, and when possible, have a logical association to the misbehavior.* Consider the function of the student's misbehavior when selecting consequences, ensuring that consequences for inappropriate behavior aren't inadvertently reinforcing to the student. For example, timeout in a more enjoyable environment may be reinforcing for students who act out during class activities that they don't like. If you are taking into account the function the misbehavior serves, your planned response should not feed into it. If a student is looking for attention, long lectures, harangues, and even gentle and supportive corrections that go on too long may be reinforcing the misbehavior.

    In addition, when possible, choose consequences that are logically connected to the misbehavior. For example, when DeSean is off-task during morning independent work time, a logical consequence might be time owed during recess. Consequences that prevent students from getting something from misbehavior are more likely to encourage behavior change. Requiring DeSean to make up work at recess will prevent him from escaping work altogether. In addition, students who place a high value on recess may be less likely to act out during morning work time if they know that they'll have to complete the work during recess.

Also review "Consequences That Aren't Recommended" on the next page.

Planning Recommendations for Corrective Consequence Strategies

Finally, make sure to incorporate the following components into your plan for using corrective consequences.

- *Determine who will be responsible for implementing the specified corrective consequences.* Train all relevant staff to recognize and consistently respond to the student's misbehavior. Make sure that staff who regularly interact with the student know how to effectively use preplanned corrections. This may involve teaching and practicing responses with staff, documenting a plan for using corrective responses, informing all staff who work with the student about the details of this plan, and monitoring staff response to ensure that corrective responses are delivered effectively and consistently. Discuss guidelines in "Tips to Assist Staff in Delivering Fluent Corrections" (p. 273) with relevant staff members. Make adjustments if any part of the plan feels unworkable. Staff should feel that they can and will implement the procedures every time a misbehavior occurs.

    Additionally, if the student exhibits severely disruptive or unsafe behavior, make sure that staff know how to follow your school's protocol and individual student safety plan for responding to such behavior.

CONSEQUENCES THAT AREN'T RECOMMENDED

After-school or lunchtime detentions. Generally, after-school or lunchtime detentions are not effective for frequent or chronic misbehavior. The delay between the misbehavior and the consequence simply dilutes the consequence's effectiveness. If Charlie misbehaves early in the day and is informed that he will have detention, the consequence can't be imposed again if the misbehavior occurs a second time. The functional result is that teachers are unable to respond consistently to misbehavior.

Parental contact. Having an open dialogue with parents is a vital part of any intervention plan. However, parental notification should not typically be viewed as an effective consequence for chronic misbehavior, and parents should generally not be put in the position of "enforcing" classroom or school rules at home. However, if the student rarely engages in misbehavior and has firm but supportive parents, parental contact as a consequence may be an option—but be wary. It is not uncommon for the parent of a student with chronic misbehavior problems to fume in exasperation, "What am I supposed to do? My child talks back to the teacher at school, and the teacher expects me to do something about it at home? As if I don't have enough to deal with." The aftermath of this kind of contact—defensiveness, a sense of helplessness, perhaps a highly emotional confrontation with the student—will likely be at best ineffective and at worst abusive.

Differential consequences based on the severity of the problem. Though it may seem logical to establish a set of consequences based on the severity of the misbehavior, such as a set of mild/medium/severe consequences, subjectivity may affect a teacher's ability to be consistent. For example, if Cade has trouble being respectful, he might be reprimanded for a minor comment, given a timeout for a moderate incident, and sent to the office for flagrant disrespect. The problem with this type of system is that it forces the teacher to make continual judgments about the severity of the misbehavior. If the misbehavior occurs frequently, even the most tolerant teacher can be stressed out and nonobjective at making numerous judgments throughout the day while still trying to teach. Even if the teacher effectively implements a system of differentiated consequences, students may believe the system is spurious: "Sometimes the teacher does nothing, and other times she gets all bent out of shape and sends me to the principal." Consequences tend to be more effective when they are clear and consistent: "Each time you are disrespectful, you will go to the timeout area and write down what you did that was disrespectful."

Sequential consequences. In a sequential plan, consequences become progressively more severe each time a student engages in misbehavior. For example, the system might dictate that the student's name be written on the board as a warning for the first infraction. For the second infraction, the student owes time after class. For the third infraction, the student is kept after school and parents are contacted, and for the fourth infraction, the student is sent to the office.

Sequential consequences tend to be effective for students who engage in misbehavior infrequently, and they may work for a teacher who has the misbehaving student for only one period. However, sequential systems are difficult to implement when teachers have the same students throughout the day. If a student engages in frequent mild misbehavior and the teacher is consistent, the student may end up in the office by the middle of each morning for several incidents of mild misbehavior. The teacher will have to make the difficult choice of being consistent or overly harsh every time students engage in a mild misbehavior, such as making annoying noises or talking at inappropriate times. Because they are reluctant to send students to the office for minor misbehavior, many teachers opt for a second mistake—inconsistency. The first time Tim misbehaves, his name goes on the board. Ten minutes later, Tim engages in a minor misbehavior and owes time after class. But a half hour later, he commits another minor misbehavior—a disrespectful comment—and the teacher begins stalling. "Oh, Tim's comments weren't so bad. I don't want to have to call his parents about him being mildly sarcastic." As the student grows a little bolder, another check might go on the board and the teacher has to face a call to the parents. Now things get very tricky for the teacher. If Tim is disrespectful again, according to the system he must be sent to the office, but perhaps it is only 10 a.m. Because sequential consequences tend to become harsher as time goes on, they are difficult to implement with fairness or consistency.

> **TIPS TO ASSIST STAFF IN DELIVERING FLUENT CORRECTIONS**
>
> **Be calm:** Correcting calmly avoids reinforcing the behavior and demonstrates to other students that you are positive and in control.
>
> **Be consistent:** Consistency can't be part-time. Anything other than full-time implementation is inconsistent, and for most students, getting away with something part of the time is tremendously reinforcing.
>
> **Be brief:** Keep corrections short—don't talk too much. The length of the interaction or the intensity risks reinforcing the misbehavior of some students. In addition, being brief helps you get back to a positive footing. It keeps the duration, emphasis, and focus of your time on positive interactions and instruction, not on student misdeeds or negativity. Preplanning and discussing your response with students ahead of time will allow you to be briefer at the time of the infraction.
>
> **Be immediate:** Correct closer to the moment of a misbehavior rather than later. The closer your correction is to the behavior that triggered it, the more likely it is to be effective. If a consequence must be delayed, as with assigning detention, you can still assign it immediately—promptly and briefly describe what the student did, let the student know that you are assigning detention, then continue with instruction.
>
> **Minimize attention:** The student should get very little adult or peer attention when you are implementing a consequence for misbehavior. When staff stay calm when implementing consequences, their behavior is less likely to reinforce the student.
>
> **Be respectful:** When staff implement any consequence, the student must be treated with dignity and respect. Belittlement has no place in any educator's repertoire. The consequence should be implemented as privately as possible; the student should not be "put on display."

- *Plan to meet with the student to discuss corrective consequences.* It's important to meet with the student in advance of implementing consequences. In this meeting, you will inform the student of what to expect when misbehavior occurs—how staff will react, whether consequences will be used, and what behaviors will result in which consequences. This discussion should clearly and directly define behaviors and consequences. "If you do *that*, the consequence will be *this*." In some cases, this discussion might occur before you use any consequences with the student. In other cases, this discussion may help to clarify limits and remind the student that continued misbehavior will result in the specified consequences.

    During this meeting, ensure that the student understands the boundary between appropriate and inappropriate behavior and the response or consequences that will be used for different types of misbehavior. If you are defining *disrespect*, for example, you might tell the student it is acceptable to ask a question in a conversational voice and then model such behavior. Then explain how a snide tone of voice is disrespectful and unacceptable—demonstrate such a tone and then model the positive example again. Whenever you model an unacceptable behavior, be sure to demonstrate the positive replacement both before and after the unacceptable example. This will ensure that the student sees the positive example twice for each negative example. By sandwiching the unacceptable example between positive ones, you communicate high expectations and eliminate any risk that all the student remembers is the negative example.

In addition, use this meeting as an instructional opportunity to discuss ways that the student can behave more responsibly. Ask questions like:

- What should you be doing instead of [*misbehavior*]?
- If [*trigger*] happens, what are some appropriate ways to handle this situation?
- What is your plan so this problem will not happen in the future?

Guide the student from thinking about past incidents to thinking about how to handle future situations more responsibly. If the student does not have strategies for behaving more responsibly, make arrangements to incorporate instruction in appropriate behavior into the student's intervention plan.

- *If the use of corrective consequences is likely to prompt an escalation in behavior, incorporate defusion strategies into the plan.* Some students may respond negatively to reprimands and consequences, perhaps by arguing, challenging the staff member, refusing to follow directions, or escalating into unsafe or severely disruptive behavior. If adults react by becoming agitated or confrontational, they run the risk of reinforcing the behavior or inadvertently escalating the situation. In these cases, plan to use defusion strategies in conjunction with corrective consequences and in response to escalating behavior. With relevant staff members, discuss how to remain calm, respectful, and detached when delivering consequences and when student behavior begins to escalate. See "Strategies for Defusing Escalating Behavior" on the next page for simple strategies to use in defusing escalating behavior, or refer to Section 4.5: Managing Emotional Escalation for detailed guidance in designing a plan to manage the cycle of a student's emotional escalation.
- *Make a conscious effort to recognize appropriate behavior that the student demonstrates.* In addition to reducing the amount of attention the student gets for misbehavior, the success of this strategy depends on increasing attention to responsible behavior. Adults must clearly demonstrate that students have a higher probability of getting adult attention when they behave than when they misbehave. If corrective consequences are used on their own, there is a chance that increased attention will be reinforcing for the student and result in higher rates of misbehavior. Because corrective consequences increase adult attention to students for misbehavior, it is essential that staff employ strategies for correcting fluently—briefly, calmly, and consistently—while simultaneously increasing the attention they pay to students when they are behaving appropriately. Positive consequence strategies (Task 4) and interactional strategies (Task 6) can help staff pay more attention to appropriate behavior.

TASK 5 SUMMARY

In this task, you:
- ☑ Defined limits of behavior to correct.
- ☑ Identified appropriate corrective consequence strategies to use in response to misbehavior.

STRATEGIES FOR DEFUSING ESCALATING BEHAVIOR

The following strategies can help staff members when dealing with students whose behavior escalates when they receive corrective consequences.

Use reminders and cues: If you have already discussed expectations for responding appropriately to corrective consequences, embed a reminder into the correction when you deliver it—for example, "Samir, that was an example of using your art materials inappropriately. Please move to the timeout desk for 3 minutes. I know that you can do this calmly, with your hands to yourself, and practice your deep breathing exercises while you are in timeout."

Minimize body language and signs of anxiety or frustration: When a student's behavior escalates, avoid showing signs of panic or anxiety. If possible, pause and take a few deep breaths before addressing the situation. The less you allow yourself to be drawn in, the more effective you can be in defusing the situation.

Withdraw from the student: When behavior begins to escalate, simply withdraw from the student and direct your attention to the other students. At the same time, keep a close eye on the student. This simple act of withdrawing may stave off further escalation.

Expect compliance: After delivering a direction or consequence, convey an expectation that the student will comply by stating that you will time how long it takes for the student to follow your direction. Overtly use a stopwatch to record the time between your direction and the moment in which the student fully complies with the direction. For example, "Kylie, please return your tablet to the shelf, gather your books, and take a seat over at my desk. I'm going to time how long it takes for you to follow my direction."

Jot it Down: After you deliver a direction that the student refuses to follow, pause, let the student know that you are recording their decision, and write the direction and the student's inappropriate response on paper. This action slows the momentum toward more serious conflict between you and the student—and the student might just comply with your original direction during this interlude.

TASK 6 — Identify interactional strategies.

It is easy to believe that having a classroom full of positive interactions springs from having responsible students who are exceedingly well behaved and responsible. Many skilled educators work from similar assumptions, and yet this belief is exactly backward. In truth, positive interactions are more like the fuel that drives good behavior and personal responsibility.

Unfortunately, some students with chronic behavior problems have learned it is easier and more reliable to get attention by doing things wrong than by following the rules. Positive interactions are even more important with these students who tend to provoke or draw out negative interactions from their teachers and peers—those who exhibit chronic behavior problems, have a poor self-image, or underperform academically. These students have found that responsible behavior goes unnoticed, while behavior that annoys the teacher or disrupts the class results in riveted attention from the entire class, including the teacher, almost every time. Other students may not misbehave to get attention, and they may not seek any attention at all—the passive, quiet kids. In this case, the problem is not one of a negatively skewed ratio of interactions, but one of no interactions at all.

Noncontingent positive interactions, such as greeting a student or asking about interests, occur simply because the student is part of the class community, meaning that the student does not have to *do* anything to get this attention. In contrast, the use of positive consequence strategies, such as positive feedback, praise, and delivery of a reward, are considered *contingent* responses because they follow, and are dependent on, the student's exhibiting appropriate behavior.

Used in conjunction with contingent positive consequences for appropriate behavior (e.g., specific feedback, praise, or rewards), noncontingent positive attention can be powerful in increasing student motivation to change. In increasing positive interactions with students, you are teaching them that not only is it easier to engage in appropriate behavior, it's simply more enjoyable. In time, the rewards of good behavior and interacting positively become intertwined, and a new habit is born.

NOTE: While these strategies, like the others in this book, are structured within a one-to-one framework, improving your ratio of positive to corrective interactions is equally effective and important with a whole class. A teacher's ratio of interactions should be predominantly positive with students of all grade levels and abilities.

Further, because lack of school connectedness is a factor that has been correlated with dropping out of high school and other negative behavioral outcomes, such as drug and alcohol abuse (e.g., Catalano, Haggerty, Oesterie, Fleming, & Hawkins, 2004; Klem & Connell, 2004; Shochet et al., 2006), it is important that each student feels linked to school. Many students establish this link through involvement with sports or arts activities. Another way for a student to build this connection is to establish a friendship with an adult involved in the school community. Schools are full of students who desperately need an adult in their lives to talk to and get support from, someone who will ask on a weekly basis: *How is your week going? Do you have any questions? Can I help you in any way?* The effect of such interactions may not always be immediate or measurable, but our experience has taught us that the long-term payoff is profound.

> *Noncontingent positive interactions occur simply because the student is part of the class community, meaning that the student does not have to do anything to get this attention.*

Before proceeding, review "Defining Positive and Corrective Interactions" on the next page.

STEP 1 Determine baseline ratio of positive to corrective interactions (optional).

Assessing the typical rate of positive and corrective interactions that the student experiences at school will provide a baseline level of understanding about teacher-student interactions. It will also help determine whether to initiate efforts to increase positive interactions. By gathering objective information through observation or self-monitoring, you can capture valid, subtle patterns of behavior that often go unnoticed by teachers who are busy teaching. The purpose of this assessment is to determine whether a teacher is interacting with a student at least three times more often when the student is behaving responsibly than when misbehaving—to determine if the teacher is maintaining at least a 3:1 ratio of positive to corrective interactions.

First, identify when to gather data. If you know that certain activities or situations are difficult for the student, gather data on interactions during these times of the day. For secondary students, you may want to compare ratios of interactions across different periods with different teachers. Ideally, you'll want to assess the ratio of interactions across as much of the student's day as possible to get an accurate sense of the baseline amount and quality of interactions the student experiences on a regular basis.

Second, determine whether to collect data through third-party observation or via self-monitoring forms completed by the teacher. In both approaches, you can use either the Ratio of Interactions Monitoring Form (Reproducible 3.4, p. 279) or the Ratio of Interactions Detailed Observation Form (Reproducible 3.5, p. 280).

Ratio of Interactions Monitoring Form: Outside observers and teachers who wish to self-monitor their own interactions can use the Ratio of Interactions Monitoring Form (Reproducible 3.4). Whenever the teacher interacts with the student, mark a tally in the corresponding box (Positive Interactions or Corrective Interactions). As discussed at the beginning of this section, use the definitions to ensure that you accurately categorize positive and corrective interactions:

- *Interaction:* Any attention that the teacher directs to an individual student.
- *Positive interaction:* An interaction that occurs directly after a student engages in appropriate behavior.
- *Corrective interaction:* An interaction that occurs directly after a student engages in inappropriate behavior.

After tallying is complete, calculate the ratio of positive to corrective interactions.

For a more detailed record, you can create a coding system to include more information about each interaction (e.g., type of instructional activity [I = Independent Work, G = Group Work], specific type of attention, severity of the misbehavior, etc.). If other variables were used to code interactions, calculate separate ratios for each category to determine whether specific situations, activities, or behaviors are associated with different ratios of interactions.

continued on page 281

DEFINING POSITIVE AND CORRECTIVE INTERACTIONS

Although *positive* and *corrective interactions* may seem relatively straightforward, there are important distinctions you should be aware of before proceeding with the intervention process. Following are a few definitions to clarify the differences.

Interactions. Classroom interactions occur any time an adult pays attention to a student. The interaction can be verbal (making a comment or discussing something with the student) or nonverbal (smiling, frowning, moving closer, tensing up, or nodding to a student), as subtle as a shrug or as intense as physical restraint. An interaction occurs whenever an adult expresses approval or disapproval, or simply recognizes a student. For the purposes of intervention, consider any attention directed to an individual student an interaction.

Whether an interaction is considered positive or corrective is determined by *what the student is doing* in the moments immediately before and during the interaction. To determine whether an interaction that just occurred is positive or corrective, ask yourself what the student was doing immediately prior to it. For example, if the teacher says to a student during an independent work time, "How are things going, DJ? Do you have any questions?" she has clearly initiated an interaction.

Was the interaction positive or corrective? Without more contextual information, you have no way of knowing. It depends entirely on what DJ was doing when the teacher initiated the interaction. If he was following directions, it was a positive interaction. If he was off task and the teacher was asking the question as a gentle way to reengage him, it was a corrective interaction.

Classify interactions based on the student's behavior at that moment, not the teacher's assumed intent. The difference is in the timing (what was DJ doing?), not the tone (how did I sound?).

Positive interactions. As it turns out, DJ was busy checking answers on his assignment. When the teacher asked DJ how things were going, the interaction was positive—she paid attention when he was appropriately engaged in the task. Although the teacher may have made no attempt to reinforce DJ and did not specifically praise him, you would count the interaction as positive.

Corrective interactions. Again, a corrective interaction has nothing to do with the tone or substance of what the teacher says. It has everything to do with the inappropriate, irresponsible, or incorrect behavior exhibited by the student just before the teacher initiates an interaction.

Suppose you now realize—(oops!)—that DJ was actually checking over his assignment *after* you explicitly told your class to put away their schoolwork and line up by the door. No matter how kindly and gently you said, "How are things going, DJ? Do you need any help?" you must now classify the interaction—the exact *same* interaction—as corrective. The context has changed, so the classification of the behavior has also changed.

Although the interactions that follow may be quite pleasant and supportive, each represents a corrective interaction:

- A student is off task, and the teacher says, "Kris, you need to get back to work or you won't have time to finish."
- A student in a cooperative learning group is getting angry, and the teacher reminds the student, "Jorge, try to state your opinion in a less emotional way."
- A student ignores a teacher's direction to put away her art project. The teacher says, "Shawna, I am looking at my watch. If it takes you longer than 1 minute to get the project put away, you will owe me that much time after school."
- A student is off task, and the teacher redirects her by saying, "Amy, just a few minutes ago you were working very hard. Let's get back to it."
- A student is disruptive, and the teacher says, "Kareem, we have discussed this before. You need to go to the timeout area and think about how to work quietly without disturbing others at your table."

The goal is not to eliminate corrective interactions. Gentle corrections are as much a part of instruction as negative interactions are a fact of life. However, if a teacher interacts more frequently with students when they misbehave, there is a risk that this attention itself will reinforce the student's misbehavior. Improving a teacher's ratio of interactions so that the positive ones significantly outnumber the corrective ones will ensure that students learn that it is easier (and more gratifying) to access adult attention by behaving responsibly than by misbehaving.

NOTE: We recommend striving for at least a 3:1 ratio of positive to corrective interactions, both with individual students and your class as a whole. Although this number may seem high or difficult to achieve, many other behavior specialists recommend up to a 9:1 ratio of interactions with individual students.

REPRODUCIBLE 3.4 *Ratio of Interactions Form*

Ratio of Interactions Monitoring Form

Name _____ Grade/Class _____

Teacher _____ Date _____

Coding system used (e.g., to indicate specific activities or transitions):

Directions: Tally *every* interaction you have with the student.

Positive Interactions	Corrective Interactions
(Praise or noncontingent attention while student is behaving appropriately)	(All attention while student is misbehaving)

Calculate ratio: _____ : _____ (positive interactions to corrective interactions)

Analysis and plan of action:

Interventions © 2019 Ancora Publishing

REPRODUCIBLE 3.5 *Ratio of Interactions Detailed Observation Form*

Ratio of Interactions Detailed Observation Form

Student Duane Williams   Grade/Class 2

Teacher Mrs. Saltzman   Date 11/2

Observer Mr. Umaki   Subject math

Activities Teacher demo, discussion, guided practice

Time	Description of student behavior	Description of teacher interaction
10:30	(When I arrived, Duane immediately came over. I told him I could not talk with him as I had work to do, but that I'd stop by to see him when I left. Duane returned to his seat.)	(None.)
10:32	Listening and participating in lesson.	(None.)
10:35	Blurts out answer.	"Yes, Duane. That's correct and that was a hard problem."
10:36	Begins to fidget and tap pencil like a drum.	"Duane, you need to listen, not play the drums."
10:37	He stops tapping and appears to listen.	(None.)
10:39	Gets out of seat and goes and draws on board.	"Duane, get back to your seat."
10:39	Starts back to seat, but stops and talks to James.	Stares at Duane and motions him back to his seat.
10:40	Gets back to his seat and begins to work on the problems assigned.	
10:43	Continuing to work	Circulating, looks at Duane's work and says, "Nice job on these problems, Duane."
10:47	Gets out of his seat while the teacher is presenting and goes to the pencil sharpener, but taps kids on the way.	"Duane, that is not fair to the other students. Keep your hands to yourself."
10:50	Duane is still at the pencil sharpener.	"That is enough, Duane. Get back to your seat."
10:51	Duane takes his seat and appears to participate in lesson.	(None.)
10:58	As the lesson concludes, Duane takes the completed (?) paper to hand in, but on the way pokes students, drums on desks, and talks to other students.	(None.)
11:00	Still bouncing around the room	(None.)

Interventions © 2019 Ancora Publishing

REPRODUCIBLE 3.5

Ratio of Interactions Detailed Observation Form: As an alternative to the tallying method used with the Ratio of Interactions Monitoring Form, you can use the Ratio of Interactions Detailed Observation Form to keep a scripted log of interactions. This will provide an anecdotal record of positive and corrective interactions between the teacher and student.

While the scripted log may be more time consuming to implement and analyze, it can yield detailed information about the nature of interactions with students that will be relevant to intervention planning. On the form, use Column 1 to note the time an interaction takes place. In Column 2, record what the student is doing immediately before the interaction or during the time of the interaction. In Column 3, record exactly what the teacher does or says during the interaction.

This anecdotal record may be kept by an outside observer or by a teacher who is self-monitoring through use of an audio or video recording.

NOTE: You may use both of these tools—the Ratio of Interactions Monitoring Form and the Ratio of Interactions Detailed Observation Form—to collect data on the ratio of interactions between the teacher and a group of students or a whole classroom. This may be particularly useful in situations where an outside observer is available to collect data, when interactions between the teacher and individual student of concern are few, or when you suspect that the teacher's interactions with students may be contributing to a classroom environment that is more directed toward correcting the inappropriate behaviors of all students.

See the sample filled-out version of the Ratio of Interactions Detailed Observation Form for examples of teacher-student interactions.

When you have a teacher use either of these forms to self-monitor, consider the following options:

- *Live recording:* The teacher keeps the form on a clipboard and marks a tally or records notes whenever an interaction with the target student occurs.
- *Audio recording:* The teacher simply records a class session and later transcribes and analyzes exchanges with students. Audio recording is easy to set up but somewhat limited because only verbal interactions are recorded. What the student was doing at the time of an interaction often has to be reconstructed from memory, and such reflection is invariably less accurate than data recorded in the moment by a third-party observer. Even so, audio recording is an easy way to monitor and improve classroom interactions.
- *Videotaping:* To conduct videotaped monitoring, set up a stationary camcorder, record a class session, and transcribe and analyze teacher-student interactions at a later point. Videotaping often captures interactions that go unnoticed by busy classroom teachers. After the initial novelty wears off and students are accustomed to having a camera in the classroom, behavior tends to be natural. Because teachers can see as well as hear their interactions, the accuracy of their observations will be pretty good, almost on par with a direct observation. Teachers will also be able to observe their body language, facial expressions, and the activity students are engaged in at the time of an interaction.

PARENT PERMISSION

Make sure to consult your school or district policies for obtaining permission to video or audiotape students.

Once the interactions have been recorded, review the interactions to determine the ratio of positive to corrective interactions. Also consider:

- Are there certain activities where positive interactions are more or less frequent?
- Does the teacher tend to provide more positive or corrective attention to certain students?
- Which appropriate behaviors are noticed and which go unnoticed?

Asking these types of questions can help you identify when, where, and how to direct efforts to increase positive interactions.

If overall interactions do not reflect at least a 3:1 positive to corrective ratio, use one or more of the strategies presented in the next step to decrease attention to inappropriate behavior and increase attention to appropriate behavior.

If the baseline ratio of interactions meets this 3:1 threshold, provide positive feedback to the student's teacher and encourage staff to continue interacting with the student in positive ways.

STEP 2 Select strategies to increase noncontingent positive interactions and school connectedness.

Once you've determined the baseline ratio of interactions, consider how to incorporate the following approaches into a plan for increasing positive interactions.

W. Increase the frequency of noncontingent positive attention. Noncontingent positive interactions are nonevaluative and simply tell students that they are important. They may include the teacher greeting students in the morning, asking about their weekend, or chatting about a shared interest. All students need and deserve noncontingent positive interactions. Though it may feel awkward at first to increase friendly interactions, students respond to them. Eventually, these interactions become second nature.

Students in classrooms with teachers who were assigned to provide a ratio of 5:1 positive to corrective interactions displayed significantly fewer disruptive behavior problems and higher academic engaged time compared with students in control classrooms (Cook et al., 2017).

The impact of positive interactions can be increased by soliciting the help of other adults. PE and music teachers, the librarian, playground supervisors, cafeteria and custodial staff, bus drivers, office staff, and instructional assistants can all provide students with additional positive adult interactions. As the student experiences the support and recognition of adults throughout the school, the need for attention in the classroom will be reduced. The student will also feel a greater sense of connection and self-worth in the school community, which will often improve motivation. Inform staff members who have contact with the student about the student's goals and encourage them to watch for opportunities to provide the student with additional positive interactions. Help from staff may be solicited individually, via a letter, or in a staff meeting. When the school is large, it is sometimes useful to show a picture of the student. Ask staff members to greet the student, make eye contact, nod to the student in recognition, and acknowledge the student in other specific ways. See "Common Concerns About Increasing Positive Interactions" on pages 284–285 for tips on dealing with staff concerns.

X. Assign a meaningful duty or responsibility at school. Providing a student with a specific and meaningful job within the school can be a great way to meet a student's basic needs, whether it is a need for attention, for purpose and belonging, or simply to get to school on time. Giving a job or responsibility can be particularly helpful for a student who seeks power and control. If a student craves attention, a job that furnishes a lot of attention can help—trash can duty, for instance, or helping the teacher pass out papers the students will need when they come back from recess. A student who likes technology could be asked to clean keyboards or computer enclosures, or reboot and maintain systems in the computer lab. Two minutes of positive time with an adult through these kinds of tasks may be enough to substantially reduce the times the student attracts attention in negative ways.

See *Meaningful Work* (Wise, Marcum, Haykin, Sprick and Sprick, 2011) for ideas for student jobs and more details about how to implement this strategy. Learn more: ancorapublishing.com/product/meaningful-work/

Y. Encourage and facilitate the student's participation in clubs, after-school activities, and other school events. Participation in after-school programs and activities has the potential to effect a range of positive learning and behavioral outcomes. Research confirms the positive benefits associated with extracurricular involvement, including improvements in academic achievement, social/emotional skills, and health and wellness (Little, Wimer, & Weiss, 2008). For students who already demonstrate chronic misbehavior, attendance in after-school programs can help reduce their likelihood of engaging in risky behavior during the hours after school (between 3 p.m.–6 p.m.), where there are ample opportunities for juvenile crime, sexual activity, and drug and alcohol use (Goldschmidt, Huang, & Chinen, 2007; Philliber, Kaye, Herrling, & West, 2002).

To encourage student participation in extracurricular activities:

- Meet with the student to discuss individual interests and identify existing activities or clubs that align with those interests.
- Ask staff members who manage clubs to personally invite the student to join.
- Work with the student to identify a peer who might accompany the student or consider ways that you can support the student's attendance at the first several club meetings.

Z. Connect the student with an adult or peer mentor at school. While many students will establish their link with school through involvement with sports or arts activities, another way for a student to build this connection is to establish a friendship with an adult who is involved in the school community. As noted earlier, many students are missing the presence of an adult in their lives who they can talk to, someone who checks with them regularly to see how things are going and whether they need support in any way. Mentoring programs recognize that misbehavior is often a function of a need for attention and that many students need more attention than they typically receive from adults in the school. Establishing a cadre of mentors who are willing and able to provide individual attention for students whose problem behavior appears to be maintained by adult attention may be a simple but powerful way to address student needs from a functional perspective (DuBois, Holloway, Valentine, & Harris, 2002; Pryce, Kelly, & Keller, 2007; Sipe, 2002).

COMMON CONCERNS ABOUT INCREASING POSITIVE INTERACTIONS

Teachers who have experienced a student's chronic misbehavior may be reluctant or skeptical about focusing on increasing positive interactions. Below are responses to some common concerns expressed by these teachers.

Is it appropriate to give even more time and attention to students who misbehave?

Students who misbehave can usurp unfair amounts of teacher time. When a student is constantly demanding your attention through misbehavior, it may be difficult to imagine giving that student *more* of your time. The trick is to give that extra time and attention when the student is *not* acting up. Increasing positive interactions does not mean that you give a misbehaving student more attention. It means you will work to reduce the amount of attention the student gets for misbehavior as you increase the amount of attention for behaving responsibly and respectfully. Instead of saying, "Quit making those noises, Magali. You are disturbing those around you," take advantage of opportunities to say hello to the student, ask how she's doing, and compliment her at appropriate times. What you're aiming for is a shift in focus. This can be difficult when the student is acclimatized to a deeply entrenched pattern of interacting with teachers only when she is misbehaving. By focusing on the student's positive qualities and responsible behavior, you are helping her do the same.

Do problem students deserve extra positive attention?

It isn't a question of what students "deserve." You should have already set consequences for unacceptable behavior, which you apply calmly and consistently. "Less positive attention" shouldn't be one of them! All students flourish in the rays of extra positive attention. But some students do not know how to invite a positive interaction—how to look at someone, nod, smile, and in other ways initiate the positive interactions they want. These students may rarely or never experience the normal positive interactions others enjoy—simple pleasantries and quiet exchanges that let them know they are valued. These students do not deserve any less than others to hear you say, "Hi, Ericka. How are you today?" or "Ericka, I appreciated your use of class time today." Whether these students show it or not, the lack of positive interactions with others leaves a void that they struggle to fill. If they have not learned appropriate ways of doing this, you will be dealing with their inappropriate attempts for some time to come. With a student who does not know how to gain attention appropriately or interact positively, you need to take the lead.

Isn't selectively granting extra attention unfair to the other students?

Treating students *fairly* does not necessarily mean treating students *equally*. Some students have a greater need for adult attention and may misbehave in order to get that need met. Those students who are striving to do their best and behave appropriately are telling you through positive behavior that their needs for attention and recognition are being met. Any time a student's behavior begins to deteriorate, this intervention can be a promising experiment to determine if the deterioration is a function of the student's need for more attention and recognition.

Won't the student think that the positive attention is phony?

Making a conscious effort to change your ratio of interactions with a student may initially feel phony. However, practicing over time will lessen any awkwardness. At the start, the student may not know how to respond. However, positive interactions eventually become the new norm, and the student is likely to invite positive interactions: "Hi, Mr. Chang. How did your softball game last night go?" There's little likelihood of overdoing it, but if the possibility concerns you, think of the number of positive interactions you typically have with your favorite students—those who are socially and academically successful. If you can match that with a student who has difficulties, the frequency and tone of your interactions will not seem phony—because they won't be.

What can I do when I just don't like the student?

Because teaching involves people and people have feelings, it is possible to have a student in your class who is difficult for you to like. However, liking or disliking a student should have nothing to do with the quality of professional effort given to the student. Physicians cannot give patients they do not like a substandard quality of care, and retail store owners don't reserve courtesy and service just for patrons they like. Teaching is no different. All students, like all patients, should be guaranteed the best possible care. The venerable educator Siegfried Engelmann was once asked, "What do you do when you just don't like a student?" He replied, "You can't dislike kids on company time." In teaching, as in any profession, professionalism means keeping personal feelings separate from work; ratios of positive to corrective interactions should have nothing to do with your personal feelings about a student.

Doesn't changing ratios of interactions give misbehaving students their own way?

Some students are desperate for adult attention. If you are not providing more positive attention, these student will demand attention the only way they know how—through misbehavior. Though making an effort to improve your ratio of interactions with these students might feel like caving in or giving the students their own way, the opposite is true. You are changing your behavior on your terms, initiating positive interactions when you "catch" a student being friendly, responsible, considerate, or engaged in any behavior you would like to see more of, rather than on the student's terms—initiating interactions only when the student acts out.

Planning Recommendations for Interactional Strategies

When creating a plan, make sure to incorporate the following components.

- *Develop a list of possible phrases staff can use when providing noncontingent positive attention.* A list of possible noncontingent positive interactions prompts adults to try interacting positively with a student who has behavior problems. Work with teachers and other staff members who regularly interact with the student to develop a list of phrases or actions that they feel comfortable using regularly with the student.

    Here are some examples:

    - Say hello when the student enters the classroom.
    - Walk with the student in the hall when escorting the class to the cafeteria.
    - Greet the student returning from lunch or recess.
    - Wish the student a happy vacation.
    - Say things like "I look forward to seeing you tomorrow" at the end of the day.
    - Chat about a shared interest.

- *Plan to reframe corrective interactions to minimize attention.* Meet with teachers and other staff members who regularly interact with the student and explain how they can minimize attention when interacting with the student to redirect behavior, deliver a prompt or warning, or implement a corrective consequence.

    Tips for minimizing attention include:

    - Be calm: Correcting calmly avoids reinforcing the behavior and demonstrates to other students that you are a positive and in-control teacher.
    - Be brief: Keep corrections short and don't talk too much. Brief corrections keep the duration, emphasis, and focus of your time on positive interactions and instruction, not on student misdeeds or negativity.
    - Preplan and discuss corrective responses with students ahead of time: Telling the student how you will respond to misbehavior ahead of time will enable you to be briefer at the time of the infraction.

    When corrective interactions are conducted in a calm, brief, and planned manner, attention given to the student is minimized and the teacher's behavior is less likely to reinforce the student.

- *Plan to have an adult meet informally with the student to discuss progress.* In addition to increasing positive interactions throughout the school day, an adult should occasionally meet with the student in a one-to-one conference or informal conversation to offer feedback about the student's progress at school. This effort takes time, but offers a productive opportunity to positively interact with the student. Further, this one-on-one time may be especially meaningful to a student who is motivated by attention from adults.

- *Plan to reassess ratios of interactions.* After working with the student's teachers to increase positive interactions, make sure to follow up and reassess ratios of interactions after a few weeks. If ratios haven't improved, it will be important to continue to work with staff to identify ways to provide high rates of positive attention and minimize attention for misbehavior.

> ### TASK 6 SUMMARY
>
> In this task, you:
> - ☑ Determined the baseline ratio of positive to corrective interactions.
> - ☑ Developed a plan for increasing the ratio of positive to corrective interactions the student experiences at school.
> - ☑ Considered possible strategies to improve the student's feelings of connectedness to school.

Describe other group interventions, academic supports, accommodations, or specialized intervention strategies to include in the student's plan.

In many cases, you may need to incorporate into a student's plan intervention strategies that are not fully captured in the list of 26 foundational strategies presented in Tasks 2–6. These may include:

- Existing interventions from your building or district menu of ready-to-use interventions (e.g., check-and-connect, social skills groups, mentorship programs). See Section 1, Task 5: Develop a Menu of Ready-to-Use Interventions on page 49 for more detailed description and guidance in establishing these types of interventions in your building.
- Academic supports (e.g., participation in supplementary reading skill groups, extra time on tests)
- Accommodations for specific disabilities or impairments (e.g., adaptations to the environment and curriculum materials for a student with visual impairment)
- Specialized intervention strategies for addressing certain types of problematic behavior (e.g., mental health issues, dangerous or highly disruptive behavior) or detailed systems for delivering strategies (e.g., self-monitoring and self-evaluation systems, structured reinforcement systems). See "Specialized Interventions" on the next page for a summary of the specialized intervention strategies covered in Section 4 of this book.

SPECIALIZED INTERVENTIONS

Section 4 presents procedures for designing and implementing *specialized intervention strategies.* These specialized interventions expand on the foundational intervention strategies presented in this section by packaging together multiple foundational strategies (e.g., behavior contracts that outline both positive and corrective consequence strategies) or by applying foundational strategies to specific types of behavior (i.e., internalizing and mental health issues, unsafe or highly disruptive behavior, and behavior that escalates).

Specialized intervention strategies will be applicable only to certain types of situations and intervention goals. Review the following summaries of the specialized intervention chapters included in Section 4 to determine whether any may be relevant to the context and goals of your intervention plan.

Behavioral Contracting: Behavioral Contracting is a collaborative method of defining behavior expectations, setting goals, specifying rewards, and clarifying consequences in writing. Developed through negotiation with the student, behavioral contracting can increase the student's motivation and investment in changing behavior.

Structured Reinforcement: A Structured Reinforcement system offers external rewards for behavior improvements to motivate students to break deeply ingrained cycles of inappropriate behavior. When problems have been resistant to change or when a student needs additional encouragement to demonstrate desired behavior, a structured system for rewarding increased positive behavior or decreased rates of inappropriate behavior can provide an extra boost of motivation and help make success a reality for the student.

Self-Monitoring and Self-Evaluation: Self-Monitoring and Self-Evaluation helps students become more aware, responsible, and in control of their own behavior. In *self-monitoring,* the student observes and records the occurrence or nonoccurrence of certain behaviors. *Self-evaluation* is a modified form of self-monitoring in which the student evaluates and records the quality of some aspect of behavior. Both strategies are designed to help students better understand their own behavior and use this information to change behavior over time.

Behavior Emergency Planning: A Behavior Emergency Plan skips over preventive strategies and moves directly to specifying the protocol for responding immediately to behaviors that have escalated to a Code Red situation. Code Red situations involve behaviors that are either so dangerous or so disruptive that classes cannot continue. These behaviors include overt aggressive behavior toward others (e.g., kicking, hitting, fighting), threats of targeted violence toward others, carrying weapons, self-injurious behavior and suicidality, vandalism or property destruction, sexual assault, drug or alcohol use or signs of inebriation at school, elopement behaviors (i.e., running away from school property), and refusal to follow immediate, reasonable adult direction (i.e., defiance or insubordination). Behavior Emergency Planning is appropriate when the student has exhibited one or more Code Red behaviors in the past or misbehavior has escalated to the point where the possibility of a Code Red situation is likely.

Managing Emotional Escalation: Managing Emotional Escalation is designed to help defuse and resolve any behaviors that are the result of emotional escalation. This strategy can help prevent and control escalated behaviors, such as tantrums, volatile or explosive behavior, and sustained disruptions, and is applicable when misbehavior tends to escalate as the student becomes more agitated or when the teacher and student frequently engage in power struggles. It can also be used as a long-term intervention for students whose chronic disruptive or dangerous behavior warrants a Behavior Emergency Plan.

Supporting Students With Internalizing Challenges: Designed to assist students with symptoms associated with depression and anxiety, Supporting Students With Internalizing Challenges provides an overview of the nature of internalizing problems and includes detailed descriptions of strategies, considerations for using them effectively, and troubleshooting when students need more assistance.

In the space provided on the Behavior Intervention Planning Form, record relevant details of any other intervention strategies. Include a short description of the strategy, how often the student will participate, who will be responsible for initiating supports or implementing the intervention, and when participation will begin.

TASK 7 SUMMARY

In this task, you:

☑ Considered and noted other intervention strategies currently in place or planned (e.g., existing group interventions, academic supports, accommodations, or specialized interventions).

TASK 8 Specify procedures for collecting data and monitoring progress.

Now that you've clearly identified target behaviors related to the student's goal and selected intervention strategies, you'll need to consider what kind of data will be useful to evaluate the progress and effectiveness of your chosen strategies. This data collection plan is a critical component of the intervention plan you are about to implement—it will help you evaluate progress, determine the effectiveness of your chosen strategies, and guide decisions around all future intervention efforts.

This data collection plan is a critical component of the intervention plan—it will help you evaluate progress, determine the effectiveness of your chosen strategies, and guide decisions around all future intervention efforts.

NOTE: Collecting data requires that you define the problem in an objective manner, which allows you to measure in a way that will enable you to assess progress. As you think about data collection methods to use, review your original definitions of target behaviors and goals and make sure you have defined them in an observable way. Imagine that you are concerned about a student's progress relative to the rest of the class. Are you thinking about the student's work completion—a measurable behavior—or are you worried about the student's flagging motivation? A student's lack of motivation is not measurable, but a student's work completion is. Before considering data collection methods, make sure you have objectively defined the target behaviors and goals of your intervention plan.

STEP 1 Select a data collection method.

Data on student behavior can be collected in many ways. The list below includes the most common types of data collection methods and tools. Read through these to find a method that fits the nature of the problem and aligns with the teacher's or interventionist's style and preferences. The amount of data collected will correspond with the complexity and seriousness of the problem. In many situations, you may need to select more time-intensive data collection methods (e.g., using external observers to collect data vs. using data collected by the classroom teacher) or include multiple sources of data for each target behavior (e.g., collecting a frequency count and completing a daily rating scale on disruptive behavior). Common data collection methods include:

a. Existing data. Obviously, the easiest sources of data to gather will be those you already have, such as grade books, attendance records, tardiness records, and other class records. If your concern is work completion, the teacher probably already has a good source for data in her grade book—for example, the number of assignments completed versus the number given. From these data, you might calculate the percentage of work completed on a weekly basis. Attendance and tardiness are other problem behaviors that may already have existing records.

b. Basic frequency count. The most common type of behavior data collected is a frequency count—simply the number of occurrences of a positive or negative behavior. The simplest way to keep a frequency count for an individual student is with a tally of hash marks, which can be kept on a card in the teacher's pocket or on a sheet of paper on a clipboard. Alternatively, the teacher might use a golf counter or transfer paper clips from one pocket to the other each time the student exhibits the target behavior. Some interventionists recommend always counting the positive behaviors you want to increase rather than any negative behaviors you are trying to decrease. This is a nice idea, but it's not always easy to do. You could, for example, count the frequency with which Artem raises his hand instead of counting how frequently he blurts out answers, but opportunities for hand-raising vary from day to day. This means the count may actually show a positive increase in hand-raising, masking the negative reality that Artem is also blurting out more often. In this example, you may want to count both behaviors, which gives you the ability to compute and display a percentage (appropriately raising hand vs. blurting out).

In some cases, it is not feasible to count a positive behavior. If classroom disruptions are of concern, for example, it would be very difficult to count the absence of those disruptions or the times when a student is not being disruptive! The simplest solution would probably be just to count the number of disruptions the student causes, as shown in the Happy Cat/Sad Dog form (Reproducible 3.6). This form is a basic frequency count for monitoring the behavior of younger students. Note that the top half shows happy cats, while the bottom half shows happy dogs, giving both cat fanciers and dog lovers among your primary-age students equal opportunity to indicate positive behavior with the animal pal of their choice.

c. Public frequency counts. As a way to record data overtly, consider using a *countoon*, a public frequency count that can be used to record positive behavior, negative behavior, or both. This method of recording data is most appropriate with younger students. The countoon will be publicly posted, so you need to make sure that it is OK with the student or students involved, and you may want to consider counting only positive behaviors. Data reporting should never be embarrassing to a child. A natural use would be in resource rooms or special education classrooms in which most, if not all, students have a behavioral or academic goal that is being recorded and charted. In this way, the countoon doesn't stand out as odd or appear to single out one particular student. The countoon in Reproducible 3.7 is for a student who is frequently off task. Once you've seen a countoon in action, you can be creative and devise ones of your own.

SECTION 3: DESIGNING AN EFFECTIVE BEHAVIOR INTERVENTION PLAN

REPRODUCIBLE 3.6 *Happy Cat/Sad Dog form*

Happy Cat/Sad Dog

Name _____   Behavior _____

Directions: Each time you remember, color the smiling cat. When you forget, color the sad dog.

Interventions © 2019 Ancora Publishing

REPRODUCIBLE 3.6

REPRODUCIBLE 3.7 *Countoon Behavior Counting form*

Countoon Behavior Counting

Name _____   Grade/Class _____
Teacher _____   Date _____

Optional: Draw an example and nonexample of the desired behavior to the right of each grid.

Positive Behavior

Negative Behavior

Interventions © 2019 Ancora Publishing

REPRODUCIBLE 3.7

291

d. Advanced frequency count. You can get even more sophisticated with frequency counts, as long as the extra effort doesn't overtax your resources. For example, if a student continually argues with the teacher and teaching assistant, you could divide the tally into two columns, one representing the teacher and the other the aide. To refine the data further, use one-letter codes to indicate more specific information about the arguing, such as *A* for a.m. and *P* for p.m. Without taking any more time than a simple frequency count, this advanced count can yield more granular data. Figure 3.8 is an example of a frequency count that uses anecdotal notes and does not require a dedicated form. Frequency Count Chart (Reproducible 3.8) can be used to tally targeted behaviors that occur each day across different activities. This detailed information has tremendous potential for aiding the design of a very targeted intervention plan.

FIGURE 3.8 *Example of Advanced Frequency Count*

Notes on Alexa's Arguing — 11/4
Frequency

With Teacher	With Assistant
AA PPPP	AAAA PPPPPP PPPP

NOTES:

9:05 Mr. Yarborough (assistant) told Alexa that she needed to clean up the Science Center when she finished. Alexa argued that it was a mess before she got there. They went back and forth several times until Alexa was almost shouting. I went over to find out what was going on, and Alexa told me to stay out of it and then started to argue with me.

9:50 When I was collecting the science papers, Alexa told me that I did not give her enough time to finish. I reminded her that she should take the work home as homework just like anyone else, but she kept demanding that I explain why I never give enough time to finish assignments.

1:00 I told the students that they needed to hand in their long-term project proposals. Alexa asked why I didn't remind them yesterday. I told her that I had reminded them yesterday, but she kept insisting that I hadn't. After a few back-and-forth exchanges, several other students told her I was right. That silenced her.

3:15 This afternoon was typical. Alexa didn't think that she should have to do the art project, she didn't want Mr. Y to correct her work, she didn't know that we had given out book order forms, and on and on.

REPRODUCIBLE 3.8 *Frequency Count Chart*

Frequency Count Chart

Name _____ Grade/Class _____ Teacher _____

Behavior _____

Directions: Put a tally mark in the corresponding box each time the student engages in the targeted behavior.

ACTIVITY	Week:					Week:					Week:					Week:				
	M	U	W	T	F	M	U	W	T	F	M	U	W	T	F	M	U	W	T	F
TRANSITION	M	U	W	T	F	M	U	W	T	F	M	U	W	T	F	M	U	W	T	F

Interventions © 2019 Ancora Publishing

e. *Classwide frequency counts.* Frequency counts can also be used to track the frequency of rule violations and other misbehaviors with the entire class. If the teacher is already using a record-keeping form to track the misbehaviors of all students in the class, it should be easy to convert the information into useful data on a particular student. For example, a teacher who is tracking the disruptions and off-task behavior of the entire class can easily track those two behaviors for a particular student and add a tally of true versus untrue statements. The Daily Misbehavior Recording Sheet (Reproducible 3.9) is useful for teachers who have the same group of students for the entire day, such as elementary or special education teachers. The Weekly Misbehavior Recording Sheet (Reproducible 3.10, p. 296), intended for a full week of data collection, is designed for secondary teachers who have students for only one class period.

f. *Duration recording.* When a behavior does not occur regularly but tends to last a long time when it does occur, you may want to record the duration of the behavior instead of or in addition to counting the frequency of the behavior. Jot down the time of day each occurrence begins and ends, or use a stopwatch or wristwatch to record duration. If you are using a stopwatch, don't reset it after each instance. Simply stop the time and restart it if the behavior begins again. At the end of the day, you will have recorded the cumulative amount of time the student engaged in the behavior. If you also monitored the frequency of behavior, you can divide this accumulated time by the number of behavioral episodes that occurred to get the average duration of the behavior.

g. *Latency data.* Sometimes it is helpful to record how much time it takes for a particular behavior to begin. For example, if a student has trouble following the teacher's directions, it may be appropriate to record the length of time between when the instruction was given and when the student begins to comply.

h. *Interval recording.* Interval recording involves marking whether the behavior occurs during a particular time interval. This is typically completed by an external observer and requires a timing device. Interval recording is an alternative way to measure the duration of behavior and can be useful when target behaviors are not easily counted (e.g., behavior occurs at high rates, or it is difficult to tell exactly when behavior begins or ends [Alberto & Troutman, 2006]). As shown on the Peer Comparison Interval Recording Form (Reproducible 3.11, p. 297), a 15-minute observation is broken into 90 ten-second intervals during which occurrences of target behaviors are recorded. This observation captures the proportion of 10-second intervals in which the student engages in a given behavior and compares the student's behavior with that of other students in the classroom. For example, in recording off-task behavior, if the student is engaged for the entire 10-second interval, the observer records a + (plus sign) in the box. If the student is off task at any point during the interval (e.g., talks to peers, leaves seat), a – (minus sign) is recorded. Rotating through different comparison peers at each interval, the observer uses the same recording process for the comparison peer, noting whether the peer was on task or off task during the interval. At the end of the 15-minute observation, the proportion of intervals that the student was on task is calculated and compared with the proportion of intervals that the peers were on task.

continued on page 298

REPRODUCIBLE 3.9 *Daily Misbehavior Recording Sheet*

Daily Misbehavior Recording Sheet

Date _____   Reminders _____

Name	1st Hour	2nd Hour	3rd Hour	4th Hour	5th Hour	Total

Interventions © 2019 Ancora Publishing

REPRODUCIBLE 3.10 *Weekly Misbehavior Recording Sheet*

Weekly Misbehavior Recording Sheet

Date _____   Reminders _____

Name	Mon.	Tues.	Wed.	Thur.	Fri.	Total

Interventions © 2019 Ancora Publishing

REPRODUCIBLE 3.11 *Peer Comparison Interval Recording Form (15-Minute Observation)*

Peer Comparison Interval Recording Form

Student _____ Date _____

Teacher _____ Observer _____

Definition of target behavior _____

Directions: For each interval, observe both the focus student and a randomly selected peer. Rotate through peers at each interval.

- ☐ Partial interval recording: If the student exhibits the target behavior *at any point* during the 10-second interval, record a plus (+). If the student does not exhibit the target behavior at all during the interval, record a minus (−).

- ☐ Whole interval recording: If the student exhibits the target behavior for the *entire* 10-second interval, record a plus (+). If the student does not exhibit the target behavior for the *entire* interval, record a minus (−).

At the end of the 15-minute observation, calculate the percentage of intervals that the focus student engaged in target behavior and compare to the average percentage for peers.

[Grid: Student/Peer rows for intervals 1 min., 2 min., 3 min.]

[Grid: Student/Peer rows for intervals 4 min., 5 min., 6 min.]

[Grid: Student/Peer rows for intervals 7 min., 8 min., 9 min.]

[Grid: Student/Peer rows for intervals 10 min., 11 min., 12 min.]

[Grid: Student/Peer rows for intervals 13 min., 14 min., 15 min.]

Percentage of Intervals with Target Behavior: Add the number of pluses for each student, divide by 90 (total number of recorded intervals in 15 minutes), and multiply by 100.

Focus student _____ / 90 x 100 = _____ %   Peers _____ / 90 x 100 = _____ %

Interventions © 2019 Ancora Publishing

Recording behavior in 10-second intervals will be feasible only when an external observer conducts the observation. However, the length of intervals can be adjusted to allow a teacher or student who is self-monitoring to record whether behavior occurred during set intervals. The Interval Recording Form (Reproducible 3.12) allows you to specify the length of the interval, which can be anywhere from 10 seconds to a full class period. This form can be used for partial interval recording (where target behavior is recorded if it occurs *at any point* during the interval) or whole interval recording (where target behavior is recorded if it occurs for the *entire* duration of the interval).

i. *Rating scale.* Rating scales are another measure that can add to your understanding of the problem. Rating scales may be completed by a teacher and/or the student to record the quality or intensity of a student's behavior on a simple scale. Though more subjective than the other methods, a rating scale can be made more objective by consistent application of judgments over time and across activities. The sample Reproducible 3.13 on page 300 shows a rating scale in which a student receives a point for each of three behaviors that is exhibited appropriately during an activity. Another example of a rating scale involves ranking a particular behavior on a scale of 1 to 5. If the ratings have a specific descriptor, this type of form is called an *anchored rating scale*. A partially anchored scale may have descriptors for only the first and last numeral ratings, but a fully anchored scale may be more objective. Though any rating scale is admittedly more subjective than data collected by other methods, this body of information can provide another useful window into a student's behavior over time. Reproducible 3.14 on page 301 shows an anchored scale to assess a student's class participation.

When selecting a data collection method, make sure your plan includes details about:

- When data collection will take place (e.g., during math periods, from 10 a.m.–11 a.m. on Mondays and Wednesdays, every time a direction to line up at recess is given, at the end of the week when the teacher records assignments in the gradebook)
- Who will be responsible for collecting the data

Finally, make sure the data collection method you have chosen is feasible and acceptable to the teacher. In cases when other staff will be responsible for data collection (e.g., intervention coordinator, facilitator of a specialized intervention), also consider procedures that will maximize the ease in which data are collected, summarized, and shared with others.

STEP 2 Determine how to summarize and interpret data.

When outlining plans for summarizing and interpreting data, make sure to:

- *Identify a follow-up date to check in about progress.* Follow-up involves regular meetings to review collected data to determine if the situation is getting better, staying the same, or getting worse. Schedule the first follow-up meeting for about two weeks after implementation is scheduled to begin.

continued on page 302

DATA COLLECTION FORMS

Blank templates of the data collection forms discussed in this section are available for download. See page 564 for directions.

REPRODUCIBLE 3.12 *Interval Recording Form*

Interval Recording Form

Student _____ Interval Length _____ Date _____

Teacher _____ Observer _____

Definition of target behavior _____

Directions: For each interval, record whether the student exhibited the target behavior.

☐ Partial interval recording: If the student exhibits the target behavior *at any point* during the interval, record a plus (+). If the student does not exhibit the target behavior at all during the interval, record a minus (–).

☐ Whole interval recording: If the student exhibits the target behavior for the *entire* interval, record a plus (+). If the student does not exhibit the target behavior for the *entire* interval, record a minus (–).

At the end of the recording period, calculate the percentage of intervals during which the student engaged in the target behavior.

Intervals: 1 2 3 4 5 6 7 8 9 10 11 12 13 14 15 16 17 18

Intervals: 19 20 21 22 23 24 25 26 27 28 29 30 31 32 33 34 35 36

Intervals: 37 38 39 40 41 42 43 44 45 46 47 48 49 50 51 52 53 54

Intervals: 55 56 57 58 59 60 61 62 63 64 65 66 67 68 69 70 71 72

Intervals: 73 74 75 76 77 78 79 80 81 82 83 84 85 86 87 88 89 90

Percentage of Intervals with Target Behavior:
Add the number of pluses, divide by the total number of recorded intervals, and multiply by 100. _____%

Interventions © 2019 Ancora Publishing

REPRODUCIBLE 3.12

REPRODUCIBLE 3.13 *Rating Scale*

Rating Scale

Student __Alita__   Grade/Class __3__
Teacher __Mr. Johns__   Period/Time __6__

SUBJECT

	Behavior	Reading	Math	Computer	L.Arts	Soc. St	
MONDAY	uses appropriate language	①　0	①　0	1　0	1　0	1　0	1　0
	cooperates with others	①　0	1　⓪	1　0	1　0	1　0	1　0
	problem-solves positively	①　0	1　⓪	1　0	1　0	1　0	1　0

	Behavior						
TUESDAY		1　0	1　0	1　0	1　0	1　0	1　0
		1　0	1　0	1　0	1　0	1　0	1　0
		1　0	1　0	1　0	1　0	1　0	1　0

	Behavior						
WEDNESDAY		1　0	1　0	1　0	1　0	1　0	1　0
		1　0	1　0	1　0	1　0	1　0	1　0
		1　0	1　0	1　0	1　0	1　0	1　0

	Behavior						
THURSDAY		1　0	1　0	1　0	1　0	1　0	1　0
		1　0	1　0	1　0	1　0	1　0	1　0
		1　0	1　0	1　0	1　0	1　0	1　0

	Behavior						
FRIDAY		1　0	1　0	1　0	1　0	1　0	1　0
		1　0	1　0	1　0	1　0	1　0	1　0
		1　0	1　0	1　0	1　0	1　0	1　0

Interventions © 2019 Ancora Publishing

REPRODUCIBLE 3.14 *Participation Evaluation Record*

Participation Evaluation Record

Student _____ Grade/Class _____

Teacher _____ Period/Time _____

Directions: For each subject, circle the number that best describes your level of participation.

RATING SCALE:
0 = Did not participate verbally and did not take notes
1 = Participated verbally at least once but did not take notes
2 = Took notes but did not participate verbally
3 = Participated verbally at least once and took notes

Subject	Monday	Tuesday	Wednesday	Thursday	Friday
	0 1 2 3	0 1 2 3	0 1 2 3	0 1 2 3	0 1 2 3
	0 1 2 3	0 1 2 3	0 1 2 3	0 1 2 3	0 1 2 3
	0 1 2 3	0 1 2 3	0 1 2 3	0 1 2 3	0 1 2 3
	0 1 2 3	0 1 2 3	0 1 2 3	0 1 2 3	0 1 2 3
	0 1 2 3	0 1 2 3	0 1 2 3	0 1 2 3	0 1 2 3
	0 1 2 3	0 1 2 3	0 1 2 3	0 1 2 3	0 1 2 3

Subject	Monday	Tuesday	Wednesday	Thursday	Friday
	0 1 2 3	0 1 2 3	0 1 2 3	0 1 2 3	0 1 2 3
	0 1 2 3	0 1 2 3	0 1 2 3	0 1 2 3	0 1 2 3
	0 1 2 3	0 1 2 3	0 1 2 3	0 1 2 3	0 1 2 3
	0 1 2 3	0 1 2 3	0 1 2 3	0 1 2 3	0 1 2 3
	0 1 2 3	0 1 2 3	0 1 2 3	0 1 2 3	0 1 2 3
	0 1 2 3	0 1 2 3	0 1 2 3	0 1 2 3	0 1 2 3

Subject	Monday	Tuesday	Wednesday	Thursday	Friday
	0 1 2 3	0 1 2 3	0 1 2 3	0 1 2 3	0 1 2 3
	0 1 2 3	0 1 2 3	0 1 2 3	0 1 2 3	0 1 2 3
	0 1 2 3	0 1 2 3	0 1 2 3	0 1 2 3	0 1 2 3
	0 1 2 3	0 1 2 3	0 1 2 3	0 1 2 3	0 1 2 3
	0 1 2 3	0 1 2 3	0 1 2 3	0 1 2 3	0 1 2 3
	0 1 2 3	0 1 2 3	0 1 2 3	0 1 2 3	0 1 2 3

Interventions © 2019 Ancora Publishing

- *Decide where to keep the data for safekeeping.* Consider what safeguards to put into place to make sure that data aren't lost. If the teacher jots notes on slips of paper instead of using a form, make sure that information is transferred to a master recording sheet on a daily basis. Slips of paper are easily lost, and you don't want to negate several days of work by being careless with data. Data can also be recorded electronically, via a spreadsheet on a tablet or computer, to help ensure that records aren't lost.
- *Decide how to best summarize data to share with others.* How you summarize and share data will dictate the quality of interpretation and affect everyone's understanding of the data's meaning. Give some careful thought to how you will display data at follow-up meetings. Think about whether a table, bar graph, pie chart, or scatterplot will make trends and patterns most apparent. Display changes across time so you can illustrate the progress the student is making. You may want to employ statistical techniques such as drawing the line of best fit, either by hand or automatically using a spreadsheet application such as Excel.
- *Set decision rules ahead of time to help with data interpretation.* Establishing decision rules before you implement the intervention plan will help the teacher or problem-solving team better understand what collected data mean and how to proceed after assessing progress. Ahead of your scheduled follow-up meeting, work with the teacher or problem-solving team to determine guidelines for judging the effectiveness of your intervention plan. Decision rules should be as specific as possible and aligned with the goals of the intervention plan that you defined in Task 1. For example, if the goal is to reduce blurt-outs by 30% by the end of 2 weeks, decision rules might include:

  - If the student reduces blurt-outs by 30%, the plan will stay in place for another 2 weeks.
  - If the student demonstrates at least a 50% reduction after 2 weeks, the goal will be increased moving forward.
  - If the student reduces blurt-outs by less than 10%, the problem-solving team will meet to discuss how to modify positive and corrective consequences and incorporate precorrections to encourage a greater reduction in behavior.

TASK 8 SUMMARY

In this task, you:

- ☑ Selected a data collection method.
- ☑ Determined when data collection will take place and who will be responsible.
- ☑ Identified a follow-up date to check in about progress.
- ☑ Decided where to keep collected data for future reference and retrieval.
- ☑ Considered ways to best summarize data to share with others.
- ☑ Set decision rules to help with data interpretation.

TASK 9: Make a plan to monitor and ensure implementation fidelity of the plan.

In order to establish accountability and make sure that the plan is implemented as designed, it is critical to proactively embed procedures for monitoring fidelity within the intervention plan itself. If a plan is put into place but isn't working, your problem-solving team will need to verify that strategies were implemented in the way they were designed to be. To return to a medical metaphor, you cannot know whether antibiotics will work if you do not take the medication. This creates a tricky political balance. You do not want staff to feel like you are checking up on them, but you owe it to the student to ensure that if an intervention is unsuccessful, some thought is given to whether it was the intervention itself or its quality of implementation.

Numerous factors can impact implementation fidelity, including intervention complexity, implementation time required, materials required, number of personnel involved, perceived and actual effectiveness of the plan, and motivation of the teachers or interventionists responsible for implementing the plan (Gresham, 2000). In general, as the intervention plan increases in terms of complexity, time requirements, materials needed, and number of people involved, the level of implementation fidelity decreases. In addition, fidelity can suffer if staff responsible for implementing the plan don't fully buy into it or express doubts about its effectiveness or appropriateness. Therefore, when creating a behavior intervention plan, it's important to consider the factors that might impact fidelity, reflect on whether plans can be simplified and still meet the needs of the student, and proactively address any potential barriers to implementation.

Consider the factors that might impact fidelity, reflect on whether plans can be simplified and still meet the needs of the student, and proactively address any potential barriers to implementation.

STEP 1   Identify a method for monitoring and evaluating implementation fidelity.

There are a number of ways to assess implementation fidelity, including:

- *Direct observation:* A third party observes the teacher or interventionist during implementation and records whether critical components of the intervention are implemented as intended. Ideally, the observer is also trained in the intervention procedures and is in a position to provide corrective feedback (e.g., acts as a consultant or coach).
- *Permanent products:* Student self-monitoring sheets, reward charts, and student work samples can tell a story about how, when, and if intervention strategies were implemented. If these types of products are produced on a regular basis, consider reviewing them as a way to assess implementation fidelity.
- *Teacher or interventionist self-monitoring:* The person responsible for implementing the intervention uses a checklist to record whether essential components have been implemented as planned. However, keep in mind that self-monitoring checklists don't always align with assessments completed by a third-party observer. Research has shown that teachers tend to self-report that they are implementing the intervention as designed, but direct observation finds lower levels of fidelity (Wickstrom, Jones, LaFleur, & Witt, 1998).

When deciding how to monitor implementation fidelity, you will also need to:

- *Using measurable terms, define what "good" fidelity means.* The research literature defines five major dimensions of implementation fidelity to consider (e.g., Durlak & DuPre, 2008; Dusenbury, Brannigan, Falco, & Hansen, 2003):

    ○ *Adherence:* How well do we stick to the plan? What proportion of components of the plan are delivered as prescribed?
    ○ *Exposure:* How often and how long does the student participate in the intervention?
    ○ *Quality of delivery:* How well is the intervention delivered? How prepared, enthusiastic, communicative, etc., is the interventionist?
    ○ *Student engagement:* How engaged and involved are students in the intervention?
    ○ *Program differentiation:* How distinguishable are the critical components of the intervention from other interventions offered in your building?

    Considering the details of the plan, goals for student behavior, and method you've selected for assessing fidelity, reflect on which of the above dimensions are most important to a plan's implementation and most likely to have an impact on student outcomes. Then, define what "good" fidelity means by specifying measurable criteria as a threshold.

    For example, let's say an interventionist self-monitors fidelity by checking off essential components of each social and emotional learning lesson that she conducts with the student. She also gathers reward charts from the student's classroom teacher at the end of the week. In this case, the team decides to define good fidelity as: a) an average of 90% of lesson components checked off and b) 90% of reward charts completed.

    In another example, an external observer monitors fidelity by observing the student during his math period and collecting data on the frequency of cues and precorrections that the teacher uses, the ratio of positive to corrective interactions the student experiences, and the time the student spends on task and engaged in instruction. The team decides to define good fidelity as: a) clear and appropriate use of cues and precorrections as needed (yes/no), b) at least a 3:1 ratio of positive to corrective interactions, and c) at least 85% of time on task.

- *Identify a schedule for monitoring fidelity.* How often will fidelity data be gathered and when will the data be evaluated? As mentioned before, the more complex and resource intensive an intervention plan is, the more likely fidelity will be affected. At the minimum, fidelity data should be compiled and examined after 2 weeks of first implementing a plan to promptly address any problems. If implementation levels are high, you can monitor fidelity monthly moving forward.

    However, we recommend monitoring fidelity on a weekly basis until implementation levels are consistently meeting the threshold for good fidelity in the following cases:

    ○ Teachers or other staff members are initially learning how to implement an intervention strategy.

- Progress-monitoring data indicates little or no progress, or the student's behavior is deteriorating.
- Previous fidelity checks revealed implementation levels below your defined threshold.

- *Identify who will assume primary responsibility for monitoring fidelity.* This person will be tasked with conducting fidelity checks, collecting and summarizing fidelity data, scheduling check-ins and meetings, and providing follow-up support if implementation levels are low. This person will also work in conjunction with the teacher or problem-solving team to evaluate student progress and guide decisions about maintaining, modifying, and fading interventions.

STEP 2 Make a plan to encourage good implementation and provide follow-up support as needed.

Some ways to support implementation fidelity include:

- *Explicitly outline all roles and responsibilities for implementing the plan.* Provide all participants with a written summary of the behavior intervention plan, with a list of their responsibilities highlighted. When summarizing plans, watch for inconsistencies, omissions, and potential glitches or places where the participants might need additional assistance. Also make sure to identify:

    - Who will meet with the student to discuss the plan.
    - Who will be responsible for implementing each strategy included in the plan.
    - Who will be responsible for data collection, and how data will be collected and summarized.
    - Who will need training.

- *Ensure that the plan is fully understood by all staff involved in its implementation.* When an intervention is fairly complex or involves new skills, rehearse the plan with teachers or staff responsible for implementing strategies. Exploring questions about what might happen is also useful. (*What might happen if . . .? What might you do when . . .?*) A dry run may help participants clarify parts of the plan and work out any glitches. Offer to model the new procedures, giving the teacher or interventionist a chance to learn by watching.
- *Provide training to teachers and other adults who will be implementing the plan.* All adults who will be involved in the plan's implementation should receive training on procedures. Plan to explain the goals of the plan, which behaviors to encourage and praise, how to respond to misbehavior, procedures for using strategies effectively, and how to collect data. See "Tips for Implementing a Behavior Intervention Plan" on pp. 307–310 for procedures to review with staff. Implementation Guidelines: Behavior Intervention Plan (Reproducible 3.15, pp. 311–314), available for download, also covers this information.

- *Clearly specify and provide materials.* If materials are needed, your written summary should specify them. Additionally, it is worthwhile to help overburdened teachers by providing or developing any materials needed to implement the plan.
- *Ensure that the plan is understood by the student.* When explaining a plan to the student, have the student paraphrase the information. If the student doesn't have the language skills to paraphrase, ask questions to make sure the student understands the plan, and have the student practice or role-play relevant parts of the plan.
- *Use fidelity checklists included in intervention materials.* Many intervention programs and curricula include fidelity checklists to support implementation. Fidelity checklists are provided for the specialized intervention strategies in Section 4. In addition, a general fidelity checklist—Fidelity Checklist: Behavior Intervention Planning (Reproducible 3.16, p. 315)—aligns with the essential components of behavior intervention planning presented in this section.

If fidelity monitoring indicates problems with a plan's implementation, it is important to address these issues in a timely manner. What follow-up actions will be taken to increase fidelity? These actions may include:

- *Provide additional training or coaching to the teacher or interventionist.* Poor fidelity may result from interventionists who are not adequately trained in delivering intervention procedures or who are unable to troubleshoot implementation problems when they arise. In these cases, additional training and coaching may be necessary to increase fidelity.
- *Increase the frequency of check-ins and collaborative meetings.* Scheduling regular check-ins and meetings can help reduce feelings of isolation that a teacher or interventionist may have when implementing the plan. It also communicates the availability of ongoing support, increases accountability, and offers a regular opportunity to address implementation questions and concerns.
- *Reassess the contextual fit of intervention strategies.* If the intervention design process was not collaborative, failed to consider contextual aspects of the problem or the classroom, or doesn't have adequate buy-in from staff or the student, reassess the intervention plan and adjust to better fit the needs and limitations of staff and the student.

TASK 9 SUMMARY

In this task, you:
- ☑ Identified a method for monitoring and evaluating implementation fidelity.
- ☑ Defined what "good" fidelity means in measurable terms.
- ☑ Specified a schedule for monitoring fidelity.
- ☑ Identified who will be responsible for monitoring fidelity and providing follow-up support.

By embedding procedures for monitoring fidelity into your intervention plan, you will increase accountability, improve quality of implementation, and increase the likelihood that the plan will actually be effective in changing behavior.

> ### Tips for Implementing a Behavior Intervention Plan
>
> **Before implementing the plan, meet with the student to discuss and finalize the plan.** In the initial meeting with the student, it is important to establish a sense of trust. The student should understand that intervention strategies are being initiated to assist in their efforts to be more successful. Use professional judgment to determine who will be present when the plan is discussed with the student. Some students are more responsive to a discussion when only one adult is present. In other cases, it will be important to include parents, an administrator, or an interventionist who will be working with the student. Schedule the discussion at a time when the student and adult can be relatively relaxed. Prior to the discussion, the student's teacher should let the student know in private that the meeting is coming up and the goal of the meeting. By prearranging the meeting with the student, the teacher can communicate that the discussion is important—it is not a punishment for past behavior, but an opportunity to set up a plan for the future.
>
> During this meeting:
>
> - Explain that you would like to assist the student in being more successful at school.
> - Describe the plan objectives and goals.
> - Model, practice, and role-play appropriate, replacement behavior. Make sure the student understands the line between appropriate and inappropriate behavior.
> - Communicate an age-appropriate rationale for the replacement behavior. Emphasis should be placed on *why* the replacement behaviors are necessary and how they can help. Why is this important? Why will the replacement behavior you're suggesting work out better for the student and the teacher than the old behavior? The older the student, the more important your *why* rationale becomes. High school students require a more carefully explained rationale than primary students, who are on the whole more willing to practice just for the sake of practice.
> - If rewards are part of the student's plan, discuss options and identify a list of rewards that the student is motivated to work for. Clearly explain what the student must do to earn rewards, when and where rewards can be earned, and how rewards will be delivered once they are earned.
> - Specify whether any corrective consequences will be used in response to misbehaviors. Be transparent with the student about which misbehaviors will lead to consequences, how consequences will be delivered, and how the student should respectfully comply with assigned consequences.
> - Encourage student buy-in with the intervention plan. As much as possible, engage the student in helping to plan the system, and encourage and discuss any suggestions, questions, and concerns.

- Make sure the student understands the goals of the plan, the desired outcome, and the benefits. The more engaged the student is in the discussion, the greater the likelihood that the student will take ownership of the plan.

Meet and debrief with the student regularly.

Meet with the student during the first week of the plan to make any necessary modifications. If the plan is working, celebrate the student's success and continue using the system without any changes for another week or so. Once the plan seems to be working well, check in with the student on a weekly basis. Review any collected data with the student, highlight successes, and discuss any behaviors that can be improved.

If the plan is not working after the first week, identify whether there are any minor adjustments you can make to improve the chance of student success. Consider:

- *Does the student understand the plan and its goals?* To check for understanding, ask the student to explain the goals of the plan, tell you what must be done to earn a reward, or describe behaviors that will result in corrective consequences.
- *Is the system designed so the student has little chance of success?* Check whether the behavior expectations require too much change at once and adjust the plan accordingly.
- *Does the student care about the rewards that have been identified?* If not, brainstorm with the student to identify alternatives that may be more motivating.
- *Is the student getting too much attention from the teacher or peers for exhibiting the problem behaviors?* If so, identify ways to minimize adult attention for misbehavior and increase the ratio of positive to corrective interactions with the student.

Keep in contact with the parents or guardians.

Maintain ongoing communication with parents to celebrate progress, keep parents informed of any major incidents, and discuss concerns and questions. This may be accomplished via regularly scheduled progress reports (e.g., a weekly note sent home with the student, phone conference, or e-mail communication).

Use data to make periodic revisions and adjustments to the plan as necessary.

Gradual improvements over a long period of time are more likely to occur than immediate and dramatic improvements. Wait at least 2 weeks before evaluating the success of the student's behavior intervention plan. After these 2 weeks, review data on student behavior that have been gathered.

If the interventions are working, continue their implementation. Continue to celebrate improvements and to provide the student and parents with positive feedback about progress.

If the student's behavior did not gradually improve over the first 2 weeks, consider the following options.

- Schedule an observation to make sure that the teacher has effectively improved the ratio of positive to corrective interactions. If the teacher is having difficulty interacting positively with the student, additional practice with positive interactions or self-monitoring can help the teacher learn to interact in a positive manner more effectively.
- Ensure that intervention fidelity is maintained. Have the teacher or an external observer assess fidelity by using or adapting Fidelity Checklist: Behavior Intervention Planning (Reproducible 3.16), or the fidelity checklists associated with the specialized interventions in Section 4.
- Provide additional training or coaching support to staff responsible for the plan's implementation.
- Modify aspects of the plan to increase its effectiveness. Are rewards motivating to the student? Are consequences inadvertently reinforcing misbehavior? Should antecedent strategies be used at different times of the day or in different settings? If needed, adjust your plan to better fit the needs of the student and align with the context of the problem.
- Incorporate additional foundational strategies, existing interventions from your building or district menu of ready-to-use interventions, specialized strategies presented in Section 4, or academic supports and accommodations that might help to encourage improvement in the student's behavior.
- Review information about the context of the problem and determine if additional data should be collected to more accurately identify contributing factors and uncover the function of problematic behavior.

Once the student demonstrates consistent success, consider fading procedures.
Supports may be faded once a student is consistently meeting the goals. The rate at which you fade the intervention should be determined by the rate at which the student is successful. The more quickly the student displays the new behavior, the sooner and more rapidly you can fade the intervention. Typically, fading is unlikely to occur until an intervention has successfully maintained the goal behavior over a period of a couple of months. Based on data and impressions of the student's support team, determine whether the intervention plan should be maintained, modified, replaced, or faded.

If the intervention plan will be faded as a result of its successful effect on the target behavior, make sure to gradually introduce fading procedures. Set a gradual phaseout schedule and be sure to continue to celebrate the student's success. Once the phaseout is complete, discontinue the intervention plan and connect the student to any universal supports in the school that meet the student's needs and can help ensure a successful adjustment.

Some students will readily agree to discontinuing their participation in supports, while others will be more reluctant. If a student isn't yet ready to give up the structure of the intervention, or if there are concerns about whether the student will be able to maintain gains after discontinuing the system, consider the following options:

- Continue to implement the plan for the rest of the school year. As long as the plan is relatively easy to implement and not too resource intensive, continue it as needed. The team can reevaluate the situation at the beginning of the next school year.

- Transition the student to self-manage all aspects of supports, introducing a self-monitoring plan for the student to monitor and record data.
- Amend strategies to address other target behaviors that were lower on your list of initial priorities. Implement the revised interventions for 2 weeks and continue to collect data.
- Continue to implement antecedent strategies, but fade the frequency of teaching and practice sessions (e.g., from once weekly to every 2 weeks).
- Transition from using specified rewards and consequences to relying on praise for appropriate behavior and gentle reprimands when necessary.

If the student's behavior deteriorates after you introduce fading procedures, revert back to the previously implemented plan or adjust the fading procedures to be more gradual. Once the student is able to maintain behavior gains, you can consider reintroducing fading procedures.

Once the intervention has been faded, provide continued follow-up, support, and encouragement.

Once an intervention plan has been faded, continue monthly check-ins with the student and parents for the remainder of the school year. Check-ins can be accomplished through an occasional phone call or informal discussion. As interventions are gradually removed and behavior shows generalization to real-life settings, continue to provide encouragement to students about their increasing ability to manage their own behavior. Students will need continued support in recognizing the sense of power they have gained as they manage situations on their own. If students lapse into old habits of misbehavior, create a modified plan to help them get back on track. Avoid making a student feel guilty about sliding backward, or the intervention will begin to take on negative or punitive connotations. As long as a student needs support, provide it. When the student again becomes more successful, gradually fade procedures and continue support with encouragement and positive feedback.

Section Summary

When a student's behavior or motivation problems have risen to the attention of the problem-solving team or an individual interventionist, the next step is designing and implementing an intervention that has a high likelihood of helping the student. This section provided suggestions for building evidence-based interventions that will define target behaviors and goals in objective, measurable terms; collect data; monitor progress; determine effectiveness; and monitor implementation fidelity. Twenty-six foundational interventions were provided as a menu for designing the actual intervention — that is, choosing the strategies the behavior intervention plan will include. Each of these foundational intervention strategies fits within one of the five categories that should be included in a comprehensive behavior intervention plan: antecedent, teaching, positive consequence, corrective consequence, and interactional. Put in a colloquial manner, this section puts the interventional meat on the skeletal structure of the problem-solving process described in Section 2.

REPRODUCIBLE 3.15 *Implementation Guidelines: Behavior Intervention Plan (1 of 4)*

Implementation Guidelines: Behavior Intervention Plan

What Is a Behavior Intervention Plan?

Simply put, *behavior intervention* can be thought of as a planned response to a behavior or set of behaviors that is interfering with a student's success in school. A *behavior intervention plan* is the roadmap that outlines this planned response, clarifying specific actions that will take place to address misbehavior and responsibilities of the people involved in these actions. In describing how an educational setting will be changed to increase student success, a behavior intervention plan focuses on modifying variables in the student's environment.

Behavior intervention plans include a variety of strategies designed to encourage appropriate behavior and discourage misbehavior:

- *Antecedent strategies* are designed to structure and organize the environment to set the student up for the best chance for success and to prevent misbehavior from occurring in the first place.
- *Teaching strategies* are designed to model, teach, and provide positive practice in appropriate, replacement behaviors for misbehavior.
- *Positive consequence strategies* are designed to acknowledge and encourage the student's efforts and appropriate behaviors.
- *Corrective consequence strategies* help ensure that misbehavior is addressed consistently and fluently.
- *Interactional strategies* increase positive interactions at school to help foster positive student-staff relationships and increase a student's feelings of connectedness with school.

In addition, a behavior intervention plan will include clear, objective descriptions of target behaviors, goals for improvement, a process for collecting data on behaviors and evaluating the plan's effectiveness, and procedures for monitoring fidelity and ensuring that the plan is implemented as it was designed.

Tips for Implementing a Behavior Intervention Plan

1. **Meet with the student to discuss and finalize the plan.**

    In the initial meeting with the student, it is important to establish a sense of trust. The student should understand that intervention strategies are being initiated to help their efforts to be more successful. Use professional judgment to determine who will be present when the plan is discussed with the student. Some students are more responsive to a discussion when only one adult is present. In other cases, it will be important to include parents, an administrator, or an interventionist who will be working with the student. Schedule the discussion at a time when the student and adults can be relatively relaxed. Before the discussion, the student's teacher should let the student know in private that the meeting is coming up and the goal of the meeting. By prearranging the meeting with the student, the teacher can communicate that the discussion is important—it is not a punishment for past behavior, but an opportunity to set up a plan for the future.

    During this meeting with the student, you will:

    - Explain that you would like to help the student be more successful at school.
    - Describe the plan objectives and goals.
    - Model, practice, and role-play appropriate, replacement behavior. Make sure the student understands the line between appropriate and inappropriate behavior.
    - Communicate an age-appropriate rationale for the replacement behavior. Emphasize why the replacement behaviors are necessary and how they can help: *Why is this important? Why will the replacement behavior you're suggesting work out better for the student and the teacher than the old behavior?* The older the student, the more

REPRODUCIBLE 3.15 *Implementation Guidelines: Behavior Intervention Plan (2 of 4)*

Implementation Guidelines: Behavior Intervention Plan

important your *why* rationale becomes. High school students require a more carefully explained rationale than primary students, who are on the whole more willing to practice just for the sake of practice.

- If rewards are part of the student's plan, discuss options and identify a list of rewards that the student is motivated to work for. Clearly explain what the student must do to earn rewards, when and where rewards can be earned, and how they will be delivered once they are earned.
- Specify any corrective consequences that will be used in response to misbehaviors. Be transparent with the student about the misbehaviors that will lead to consequences, how consequences will be delivered, and how the student should respectfully comply with assigned consequences.
- Encourage student buy-in to the intervention plan. As much as possible, engage the student in helping to plan the system and in voicing any suggestions, questions, or concerns.
- Make sure the student understands the goals of the plan, the desired outcome, and the benefits. The more engaged the student is in the discussion, the greater the likelihood that the student will take ownership of the plan.

2. **Implement antecedent strategies consistently.**

To create a predictable environment that encourages appropriate behavior instead of misbehavior, use antecedent strategies consistently in accordance with the details of the student's behavior intervention plan.

Specific recommendations for staff who use antecedent strategies include:

- If the intervention plan incorporates student choice as an antecedent strategy, remember to offer real, viable choices ("You can do this, this, or this, and they would all be perfectly acceptable. Which would you prefer?")
- If precorrections will be used to anticipate misbehavior, try to be as consistent as possible in delivering them before challenging situations, and focus on reviewing expectations and appropriate behaviors when the student engages in an upcoming task or situation.
- If increased monitoring and supervision are part of the student's intervention plan, make sure that when adults observe misbehavior, they know how to respond appropriately.

3. **Regularly review the student's goals and the rationale for replacement behavior.**

When teaching new behaviors or re-teaching expectations, review the student's goals at the beginning of each session and link these goals to the focus of the session. Also, periodically review the rationale for the replacement behavior that you are teaching: *What will this get for the student? Why will this behavior help?* The older the student, the more critical it is that you back up the proposed replacement behaviors with well-considered reasoning that will be meaningful to the student.

During teaching and practice sessions, also incorporate these recommendations:

- When modeling appropriate behavior, use a positive-negative-positive example framework—that is, demonstrate the right way, show the wrong way (the way the student has behaved in the past), and then show the right way again. Always sandwich a demonstration of the wrong way between two examples of the right way.
- Provide ample opportunities for positive practice. Simulate situations that resemble the real settings and events that the student has had difficulty managing in the past. As you practice, ask the student *what, why, how, when,* and *where* questions directed at the rationale for the replacement behavior. If the student has trouble answering, provide the information and then repeat the question.
- Each time the student acts out the replacement behavior, provide positive feedback if it was done well. If you need to point out a negative, try to come up with at least three positive aspects of the rehearsal so that your work together remains at a 3:1 positive-to-corrective ratio.

REPRODUCIBLE 3.15 *Implementation Guidelines: Behavior Intervention Plan (3 of 4)*

Implementation Guidelines: Behavior Intervention Plan

4. **Be consistent, immediate, and descriptive when delivering praise, feedback, and rewards.**

   When working with the student on a daily basis, remember to consistently provide praise, specific feedback, and rewards based on the details of the intervention plan.

   Maximize the effectiveness of positive consequence strategies by incorporating the following tips:
   - Be descriptive, concrete, and specific with feedback so that the student knows exactly what to do more of or less of next time.
   - Remember to focus on appropriate behavior. Avoid comments that remind the student of any negative behavior. Rather than saying, "Nice job, José. You didn't get in trouble at recess today," focus on the goal behavior: "Thanks, José—you followed the playground rules and lined up with the class on time. You've earned 2 extra minutes of computer time this afternoon."
   - Deliver praise and rewards as immediately as possible. The longer the student has to wait, the less effective the positive consequence will be. This is particularly true for younger students.
   - Be enthusiastic. Pair feedback and rewards with congratulatory comments and excitement. This will help strengthen the value of your acknowledgments.

5. **Correct misbehavior fluently. Tips for fluent corrections include:**
   - *Be calm:* Correcting calmly avoids reinforcing the behavior and demonstrates to other students that you are positive and in control.
   - *Be consistent:* Consistency can't be part-time. Anything other than full-time implementation is inconsistent, and for most students, getting away with something part of the time is tremendously reinforcing.
   - *Be brief:* Keep corrections short—don't talk too much. The length or the intensity of the interaction risks reinforcing the misbehavior of some students. In addition, being brief helps you get back on a positive footing; it keeps the duration, emphasis, and focus of your time on positive interactions and instruction, not on student misdeeds or negativity. Preplanning and prediscussing your response with students will allow you to be briefer at the time of the infraction.
   - *Be immediate:* Correct closer to the moment of a misbehavior rather than later. The closer your correction is to the behavior that triggered it, the more likely it is to be effective. If a consequence must be delayed, as with assigning detention, you can still be immediate in assigning it—promptly and briefly describe what the student did, assign detention to the student, and then continue with instruction.
   - *Minimize attention:* The student should get very little adult or peer attention when you are implementing a consequence for misbehavior. When a teacher stays calm when implementing a consequence, the teacher's behavior is less likely to reinforce the student.
   - *Be respectful:* When any consequence is implemented, the student must be treated with dignity and respect. Belittlement has no place in a teacher's repertoire. The consequence should be implemented as privately as possible; the student should not be put on display.

   When delivering a consequence, also keep the following in mind:
   - Move to the student if possible. Reprimands from across the room tend to be ineffective.
   - Calmly state what the student should be doing.
   - Offer praise as soon as the student begins to exhibit more acceptable behavior.
   - Avoid increasing the emotional intensity of repeated feedback if you must repeat a reprimand. The student is less likely to be reinforced for the misbehavior by a short, neutral statement than by an angry or lengthy attempt to correct the behavior.
   - If time owed or timeouts are used as a consequence for misbehavior, remember to use only small amounts of time for each infraction. For students in sixth grade and above, 5 minutes is a reasonable period of time. For

REPRODUCIBLE 3.15 *Implementation Guidelines: Behavior Intervention Plan (4 of 4)*

Implementation Guidelines: Behavior Intervention Plan

younger students, timeout should be shorter and based on the age and sophistication of the student. In addition, be clear about what the student should be doing during time owed or timeouts. The more boring you can make time owed or timeout, the better, because the student will be thinking of the many other things they would rather be doing than sitting silently.

6. **As frequently as possible, provide noncontingent, positive attention to the student.**

   Noncontingent positive interactions occur simply because the student is part of the class community, meaning that the student does not have to do anything to get this attention. Noncontingent positive interactions are nonevaluative and simply tell students that they are important. They may include greeting students in the morning, asking about their weekend, or chatting about shared interests. Find opportunities throughout the day to interact positively with the student in ways that go beyond providing feedback. If you've made a list of possible phrases to use when providing noncontingent positive attention and contingent praise, consult this list regularly and add to it as needed. On a daily basis, strive for at least a 3:1 positive to corrective ratio of interactions.

7. **Meet and debrief with the student regularly.**

   Meet with the student during the first week of the plan to make any necessary modifications. If the plan is working, celebrate the student's success and continue using the system without any changes for another week or so. Once the plan seems to be working well, check in with the student on a weekly basis. Review any collected data with the student, highlight successes, and discuss any behaviors that can be improved.

   If the plan is not working after the first week, identify any minor adjustments you might make to improve the chance of student success. Consider:

   - *Does the student understand the plan and its goals?* To check for understanding, ask the student to explain the goals of the plan, tell you what must be done to earn a reward, or describe behaviors that will result in corrective consequences.
   - *Is the system designed so the student has little chance of success?* Check whether the behavioral expectations require too much change at once and adjust the plan accordingly.
   - *Does the student care about the rewards that have been identified?* If not, brainstorm with the student to find other alternatives that they might be more motivated to earn.
   - *Is the student getting too much attention from the teacher and/or peers for exhibiting the problem behaviors?* If so, try to minimize the amount of attention given to misbehavior and increase the number of positive interactions you have with the student.

   If the system is still not working after minor adjustments, collaborate with your problem-solving team to discuss next steps.

8. **Keep in contact with the parents or guardians.**

   Maintain ongoing communication with parents to celebrate progress, keep parents informed of any major incidents, and discuss concerns and questions. This may be accomplished via regularly scheduled progress reports (e.g., a weekly note sent home with the student, phone conference, or e-mail communication).

9. **Use data to make periodic revisions and adjustments to the plan as necessary.**

   Monitor student progress and collaborate with your problem-solving team to make adjustments to the plan as needed.

REPRODUCIBLE 3.16 *Fidelity Checklist: Behavior Intervention Planning*

Fidelity Checklist
Behavior Intervention Planning

Essential Planning Steps

- [ ] Objectively describe problematic behaviors.
- [ ] Objectively describe appropriate/replacement behaviors.
- [ ] Specify measurable goals for both problematic and appropriate/replacement behaviors.
- [ ] Identify antecedent strategies.
- [ ] Identify teaching strategies.
- [ ] Identify positive consequence strategies.
- [ ] Identify corrective consequence strategies.
- [ ] Select interactional strategies to increase positive interactions and student connectedness to school.
- [ ] Describe other group interventions, academic supports, accommodations, and specialized intervention strategies to include in the student's plan.
- [ ] Select a data collection method.
- [ ] Determine how to summarize and interpret data.
- [ ] Identify a method for assessing implementation fidelity.
- [ ] Make a plan to encourage good implementation and provide follow-up support as needed.
- [ ] Outline roles and responsibilities for implementing the plan.
- [ ] Provide training to teachers and other adults who will be implementing the plan.

Essential Implementation Components

- [ ] Meet with the student to discuss and finalize the plan.
- [ ] Implement antecedent strategies consistently.
- [ ] Regularly review the student's goals and the rationale for replacement behavior.
- [ ] Be consistent, immediate, and descriptive when delivering praise, feedback, and rewards.
- [ ] Correct misbehavior fluently.
- [ ] As frequently as possible, provide noncontingent attention to the student.
- [ ] Meet and debrief with the student regularly.
- [ ] Keep in contact with the parents or guardians.
- [ ] Use data to make periodic revisions and adjustments to the plan as necessary.

Interventions © 2019 Ancora Publishing

References

Alberto, P. A., & Troutman, A. C. (2012). *Applied behavior analysis for teachers* (9th ed.). Upper Saddle River, NJ: Merrill/Prentice Hall.

Barth, R. (1979). Home-based reinforcement of school behavior: A review and analysis. *Review of Educational Research, 49*(3), 436–458.

Bear, G. G. (2008). Classroom discipline. In A. Thomas & J. Grimes (Eds.), *Best practices in school psychology V* (pp. 1403–1420). Bethesda, MD: National Association of School Psychologists.

Becker, W. C., Madsen, C. H., Arnold, C. R., & Thomas, D. R. (1967). The contingent use of teacher attention and praise in reducing classroom behavior problems. *Journal of Special Education, 1,* 287–307.

Bennett, S. N., & Blundell, D. (1983). Quantity and quality of work in rows and classroom groups. *Educational Psychology, 3,* 93–105.

Blum, R. (2005). *School connectedness: Improving students' lives.* Baltimore, MD: Johns Hopkins Bloomberg School of Public Health.

Boyd, R. J., & Anderson, C. M. (2013). Breaks are better: A tier II social behavior intervention. *Journal of Behavioral Education, 22*(4), 348–365.

Brantner, J. P., & Doherty, M. A. (1983). A review of timeout: A conceptual and methodological analysis. In S. Axelrod (ed.), *Effects of punishment on human behavior* (pp. 87–132). Cambridge, MA: Academic Press.

Brookhart, S. M. (2017). *How to give effective feedback to your students* (2nd ed.). Alexandria, VA: ASCD.

Brophy, J., & Good, T. L. (1986). Teacher behavior and student achievement. In M. C. Wittrock (Ed.), *Handbook of research on teaching* (3rd ed., pp. 328–375). New York, NY: MacMillan Publishing.

Broussard, C., & Northup, J. (1997). The use of functional analysis to develop peer interventions for disruptive classroom behavior. *School Psychology Quarterly, 12*(1), 65–76.

Busch, A., & Shore, M. (2000). Seclusion and restraint: A review of recent literature. *Harvard Review of Psychiatry, 8,* 261–270.

Carlson, C., & Christenson, S. (Eds.). (2005). Evidence-based parent and family interventions in school psychology [Special issue]. *School Psychology Quarterly, 20*(4).

Catalano, R. F., Haggerty, K. P., Oesterie, S., Fleming, C. B., & Hawkins, J. D. (2004). The importance of bonding to schools for healthy development: Findings from the social development research group. *The Journal of School Health, 74*(7), 252–262.

Center, D. B., Deitz, S. M., & Kaufman, M. E. (1982). Student ability, task difficulty, and inappropriate classroom behavior: A study of children with behavior disorders. *Behavior Modification, 6,* 355–374.

Centers for Disease Control and Prevention. (2009). *School connectedness: Strategies for increasing protective factors among youth.* Atlanta, GA: U.S. Department of Health and Human Services.

Clark, H. B., Rowbury, T., Baer, A. M., & Baer, D. M. (1973). Timeout as a punishing stimulus in continuous and intermittent schedules. *Journal of Applied Behavior Analysis, 6*(3), 443–455.

Colvin, G., Sugai, G., Good, R.H., III, & Lee, Y. Y. (1997). Using active supervision and precorrection to improve transition behaviors in an elementary school. *School Psychology Quarterly, 12*(4), 344–361.

Colvin, G., Sugai, G., & Patching, W. (1993). Pre-correction: An instructional strategy for managing predictable behavior problems. *Intervention, 28,* 143–150.

Cook, C., Grady, E., Long, A., Henshaw, T., Codding, R., Fiat, A., & Larson, M. (2017) Evaluating the impact of increasing general education teachers' ratio of positive to negative interactions on students' classroom behavior. *Journal of Positive Behavior Interventions, 19*(2), 67–77.

Cooper, J. O., Heron, T. E., & Heward, W. L. (2007). *Applied behavior analysis* (2nd ed.). Upper Saddle River, NJ: Pearson/Merrill Prentice Hall.

Davis, C. A., Lane, K. L., Sutherland, K., Gunter, P. L., Denny, R. K., Pickens, P., & Wehby, J. (2004). Differentiating curriculum and instruction on behalf of students with emotional and behavioral disorders within general education settings. In L. M. Bullock, R. A. Gable, & K. J. Melloy (Eds.), *Effective disciplinary practices: Strategies and positive learning environments for students with challenging behaviors*. Arlington, VA: Council for Children with Behavior Disorders.

DuBois, D., Holloway, B., Valentine, J., & Harris, C. (2002). Effectiveness of mentoring programs for youth: A meta-analytic review [Special issue]. *American Journal of Community Psychology, 30*(2), 157–197.

Dunlap, G., dePerczel, M., Clarke, S., Wilson, D., Wright, S., White, R., & Gomez, A. (1994). Choice making to promote adaptive behavior for students with emotional and behavioral challenges. *Journal of Applied Behavior Analysis, 27,* 505–518.

Durlak, J. A., & DuPre, E. P. (2008). Implementation matters: A review of research on the influence of implementation on program outcomes and the factors affecting implementation. *American Journal of Community Psychology, 41*(3–4), 327.

Dusenbury, L., Brannigan, R., Falco, M., & Hansen, W. B. (2003). A review of research on fidelity of implementation: Implications for drug abuse prevention in school settings. *Health Education Research, 18*(2), 237–256.

Ennis, R. P., Schwab, J. R., & Jolivette, K. (2012). Using precorrection as a secondary-tier intervention for reducing problem behaviors in instructional and noninstructional settings. *Beyond Behavior, 22*(1), 40–47.

Gable, R., Hester, P., Rock, M., & Hughes, K. (2009). Back to basics: Rules, praise, ignoring, and reprimands revisited. *Intervention in School and Clinic, 44*(4), 195–205.

Goldschmidt, P., Huang, D., & Chinen, M. (2007). *The long-term effects of after-school programming on educational adjustment and juvenile crime: A study of the LA's BEST after-school program.* Retrieved from http://lasbest.org/wp-content/uploads/2018/05/CRESST-2007-LASBEST_DOJ_Final-Report.pdf

Gresham, F. M. (2002). Best practices in social skills training. In A. Thomas & J. Grimes (Eds.), *Best practices in school psychology IV* (pp. 1029–1040). Washington DC: National Association of School Psychologists.

Gresham, F., MacMillan, D. L., Beebe-Frankenberger, M. B., & Bocian, K. M. (2000). Treatment integrity in learning disabilities intervention research: Do we really know how treatments are implemented? *Learning Disabilities Research and Practice, 15,* 198–205.

Harris, K. R. (1985). Definitional, parametric, and procedural considerations in timeout interventions and research. *Exceptional Children 51*(4), 279–288.

Hattie, J., & Timperley, H. (2007). The power of feedback. *Review of Educational Research, 77*(1), 81–112.

Ingram, K., Lewis-Palmer, T., & Sugai, G. (2005). Function-based intervention planning: Comparing the effectiveness of FBA function-based and non–function-based intervention plans. *Journal of Positive Behavior Interventions, 7*(4), 224–236.

Jenson, W. R., & Reavis, H. K. (1996). Reprimands and precision requests. In H. Reavis, M. Sweeten, W. Jenson, D. Morgan, D. Andrews, & S. Fister (Eds.), *Best practices: Behavioral and educational strategies for teachers* (pp. 49–55). Longmont, CO: Sopris West.

Johnson-Gros, K. N., Lyons, E. A., & Griffin, J. R. (2008). Active supervision: An intervention to reduce high school tardiness. *Education and Treatment of Children, 31*(1), 39–53.

Kern, L., Childs, K., Dunlap, G., Clarke, S., & Falk, G. (1994). Using an assessment-based curricular intervention to improve the classroom behavior of a student with emotional and behavioral challenges. *Journal of Applied Behavior Analysis, 27,* 7–19.

Kern, L., Mantegna, M. E., Vorndran, C. M., Bailin, D., & Hilt, A. (2001). Choice of task sequence to reduce problem behaviors. *Journal of Positive Behavior Interventions, 3*(1), 3–10.

Klem, A., & Connell, J. (2004). Relationships matter: Linking teacher support to student engagement and achievement *Journal of School Health*, *74*(7), 262–273.

Kluger, A. N., & DeNisi, A. (1996). The effects of feedback interventions on performance: A historical review, a meta-analysis, and a preliminary feedback intervention theory. *Psychological Bulletin*, *119*(2), 254.

Little, P., Wimer, C., & Weiss, H. B. (2008). After-school programs in the 21st century: Their potential and what it takes to achieve it. *Issues and Opportunities in Out-of-School Time Evaluation*, *10*(1–12).

Maag, J. W. (2003). Targeting behaviors and methods for recording their occurrences. In M. J. Breen & C. R. Fiedler (Eds.), *Behavioral approach to assessment of youth with emotional/behavioral disorders: A handbook for school-based practitioners* (2nd ed., pp. 297–333). Austin, TX: PRO-ED.

MacKenzie-Keating, S. E., & McDonald, L. (1990). Overcorrection: Reviewed, revisited, and revised. *The Behavior Analyst*, *13*(1), 39–48.

Matheson, A., Starkweather, A., & Shriver, M. D. (2005). Training teachers to give effective commands: effects on student compliance and academic behaviors. *School Psychology Review, 34,* 202–219.

Moore, D. W., Anderson, A., & Kumar, K. (2005). Instructional adaptation in the management of escape-maintained behavior in a classroom. *Journal of Positive Behavior Interventions*, *7*(4), 216–223.

O'Neill, R. E., Horner, R. H., Albin, R. W., Sprague, J. R., Storey, K., & Newton, J. S. (1997). *Functional assessment and program development for problem behavior: A practical handbook* (2nd ed.). Pacific Grove, CA: Brooks/Cole.

Partin, T. C. M., Robertson, R. E., Maggin, D. M., Oliver, R. M., & Wehby, J. H. (2009). Using teacher praise and opportunities to respond to promote appropriate student behavior. *Preventing School Failure: Alternative Education for Children and Youth*, *54*(3), 172–178.

Philliber, S., Kaye, J. W., Herrling, S., & West, E. (2002). Preventing pregnancy and improving health care access among teenagers: An evaluation of the Children's Aid Society-Carrera program. *Perspectives on Sexual and Reproductive Health*, *1*(5), 244–251.

Pryce, J., Kelly, M., & Keller, T. (2007). What makes mentoring effective? How research can guide you in selecting a program. *Focal Point*, *21*(2), 19–21.

Rosenberg, M. S. (1986). Maximizing the effectiveness of structured classroom management programs: Implementing rule-review procedures with disruptive and distractible students. *Behavior Disorders*, *11*(4), 239–248.

Rosenshine, B. (1995). Advances in research on instruction. *The Journal of Educational Research*, *88*(5), 262–268.

Rozalski, M. E., Yell, M. L., & Boreson, L. A. (2006). Using seclusion, timeout, and physical restraint: An analysis of state policy, research, and the law. *Journal of Special Education Leadership*, *19*(2), 13–29.

Ryan, J. B., Peterson, R., Tetreault, G., & Hagen, E. V. (2007). Reducing seclusion, timeout, and restraint procedures with at-risk youth. *Journal of At-Risk Issues*, *13*(1), 7–12.

Shochet, I. M., Dadds, M. R., Ham, D., & Montague, R. (2006). School connectedness is an underemphasized parameter in adolescent mental health: Results of a community prediction study. *Journal of Clinical Child & Adolescent Psychology*, *35*(2), 170–179.

Simonsen, B., Fairbanks, S., Briesch, A., Myers, D., & Sugai, G. (2008). Evidence-based practices in classroom management: Considerations for research to practice, *Education and Treatment of Children, 31,* 351–380.

Sipe, C. L. (2002). Mentoring programs for adolescents: A research summary. *Journal of Adolescent Health*, *31*(6), 251–260.

Skinner, B. F. (1953). *Science and human behavior.* New York, NY: Macmillan.

Solomon, R. W., & Wahler, R. G. (1973). Peer reinforcement control of classroom problem behavior. *Journal of Applied Behavior Analysis*, *6*(1), 49–56.

Sprick, R. (2009) *CHAMPS: A proactive and positive approach to classroom management* (2nd ed.). Eugene, OR: Ancora Publishing.

Taylor, J., & Miller, M. (1997). When timeout works some of the time: The importance of treatment integrity and functional assessment. *School Psychology Quarterly, 12*(1), 4.

Thapa, A., Cohen, J., Guffey, S., & Higgins-D'Alessandro, A. (2013). A review of school climate research. *Review of Educational Research, 83*(3), 357–385.

Tilly, W. D., III, & Flugum, K. R. (1995). Ensuring quality interventions. In A. Thomas & J. Grimes (Eds.), *Best practices in school psychology III* (pp. 485–500). Washington, DC: National Association of School Psychologists.

Umbreit, J., Lane, K. L., & Dejud, C. (2004). Improving classroom behavior by modifying task difficulty: Effects of increasing the difficulty of too-easy tasks. *Journal of Positive Behavior Interventions, 6*(1), 13–20.

Walker, H. (1983). Application of response cost in school settings: Outcomes, issues, and recommendations. *Exceptional Education Quarterly, 3*(4), 4–55.

Wheldall, K., & Lam, Y. Y. (1987). Rows versus tables II: The effects of two classroom seating arrangements on classroom disruption rate, on-task behavior, and teacher behavior in three special school classes. *Educational Psychology, 7,* 303–312.

Whitlock, J. L. (2006). Youth perceptions of life at school: Contextual correlates of school connectedness in adolescence. *Applied Developmental Science, 10*(1), 13–29.

Wickstrom, K. F., Jones, K. M., LaFleur, L. H., & Witt, J. C. (1998). An analysis of treatment integrity in school-based behavioral consultation. *School Psychology Quarterly, 13*(2), 141.

Wise, B. J., Marcum, K., Haykin, M., Sprick, R. S., & Sprick, M. (2011). *Meaningful work: Changing student behavior with school jobs.* Eugene, OR: Ancora Publishing.

NOTES

SECTION FOUR

Specialized Intervention Strategies

This section covers procedures for planning and implementing six *specialized intervention strategies*. These intervention strategies are a powerful group of tools that may be more time intensive to plan and more time consuming to implement. The following specialized intervention strategies are covered:

Strategy 1: Behavioral Contracting (p. 322): A collaborative method of defining behavior expectations, setting goals, specifying rewards, and clarifying consequences in writing

Strategy 2: Structured Reinforcement (p. 344): A system to motivate students to break deeply ingrained cycles of inappropriate behavior by offering external rewards for behavior improvements

Strategy 3: Self-Monitoring and Self-Evaluation (p. 373): A strategy to help students become more aware, responsible, and in control of their own behavior

Strategy 4: Behavior Emergency Planning (p. 406): A plan that skips over preventive strategies and moves directly to specifying the protocol for responding immediately to behaviors that have escalated into a Code Red situation

Strategy 5: Managing Emotional Escalation (p. 433): A strategy designed to help defuse and resolve any behaviors that are the result of emotional escalation

Strategy 6: Supporting Students with Internalizing Challenges (p. 469): A strategy to assist students with symptoms associated with depression and anxiety

Section 4.1

SPECIALIZED INTERVENTION STRATEGY ONE

Behavioral Contracting

The student needs help in managing specific behaviors and setting goals

Purpose

Behavioral Contracting is a collaborative method of defining behavior expectations, setting goals, specifying rewards for improvements, and clarifying consequences in writing.

Behavioral Contracting can be used to help students:

- Increase engagement in particular skills or behavior, such as amount of work completed, time on task, and positive interactions with peers.
- Reduce or eliminate the frequency of negative behavior, such as using profanity, fighting, and interacting disrespectfully with adults.

Rationale

A behavior contract is a written and signed agreement between a student and a teacher or other school staff member (e.g., school counselor, administrator) that outlines the specific student behaviors to be increased and misbehaviors to be decreased (Kidd & Saudargas, 1988). Having the student and an adult sign the contract formalizes the agreement and helps make the student more accountable for actions at school. Developed through negotiation with the student, behavior contracts provide structure and can be used across settings to encourage progress toward both academic and behavioral goals (Houmanfar, Maglieri, Roman, & Ward, 2008). Behavioral contracting has a long history of use in changing behavior (e.g., Bailey, Wolf, & Phillips, 1970), and a large body of research provides evidence of its beneficial effects for students regardless of grade level, gender, or disability status (Bowman-Perrott, Burke, de Marin, Zhang, & Davis, 2015).

Behavior contracts package together several effective behavior management components, including explicitly defining expectations, clarifying the difference between appropriate and inappropriate behavior, and offering feedback and rewards when the student meets expectations (Miltenberger, 2008). Rewards might include stickers, privileges, special activities, and other reinforcers that the student is motivated to obtain. Rewards are contingent on the student's meeting the behavior goals specified in the contract—which is why behavioral contracting is also sometimes referred to as *contingency contracting* (Cantrell, Cantrell, Huddleston, & Woolridge, 1969).

Behavior contracts are cost effective and flexible, and teachers, school psychologists, and other educators can easily use them (Downing, 1990). You can create a behavior contract at any time during the school year and adjust it over time—as long as the process remains collaborative and the student and adult both agree to the modified terms.

Essential Planning Steps

The Student Behavior Contract (Reproducible 4.1a) shown on the next page is an example of a behavior contract that you can use to draft details of your plan. You can use other contract forms or draft your own, but the steps below follow the format in this example.

STEP 1 Identify target behaviors and describe the general goals of the contract.

Using examples of the problematic behavior, identify 1–2 major misbehaviors to decrease and target in the contract. Objectively define these behaviors in observable, measurable terms. If you are working with a student who exhibits many behavior problems, prioritize the behaviors that are most problematic by asking the following questions:

- *How often do the problems occur? How long does the behavior last? How intense is the problem?* Identify the misbehaviors that occur most frequently, last the longest, or are most severe.
- *Which changes in behavior will help the student feel successful in the shortest period of time?* Select behaviors that the student is most likely to improve in the least amount of time.
- *Which changes in behavior will help the teacher see improvement in the shortest period of time?* Determine not only what the teacher hopes to accomplish, but also which misbehaviors the teacher can't live with any longer.

Be cautious about targeting too many behaviors in your original contract. Aiming for many changes at once is likely to frustrate or overwhelm the student and the teacher. Narrowing the scope of the contract to a few manageable behavior changes will result in the greatest likelihood of success.

NOTE: If the student exhibits any unaddressed Code Red behaviors, which are behaviors that are either so dangerous or so disruptive that classes cannot continue, move directly to the protocol that your district has in place or develop an individual Behavior Emergency Plan for the student. See Section 1, Task 6: Establish Processes for Responding to Code Red Situations (p. 54) for a description of how to set up schoolwide policies and Behavior Emergency Planning (Section 4.4) for guidelines on creating a safety plan for an individual student. Once temporary procedures are in place for responding to these situations, you can return to developing a long-term intervention plan, which may include behavioral contracting, to support the student.

Once you've identified the problematic behaviors to address, also identify 1–2 appropriate/replacement behaviors that you'd like to increase. These could include appropriate behaviors already in the student's repertoire or newly introduced replacement behaviors that act as positive opposites to misbehavior (i.e., behaviors that are maintained by the same function as the misbehavior, but are more socially appropriate). For example, for a student who tends to blurt out obscenities when frustrated, an appropriate replacement behavior might be raising his hand and asking for help from the teacher.

> **BEFORE IMPLEMENTING THIS STRATEGY**
>
> Before implementing Behavioral Contracting, discuss the problem and general goals for improvement with the teacher and student. Gather any relevant background information that may help in designing and implementing the intervention. Contact the student's parents or guardian to discuss the problem, and keep them informed of all aspects of the intervention plan.

REPRODUCIBLE 4.1a *Student Behavior Contract*

Student Behavior Contract

1. I, _Arletta_, agree to work on the following goals:

    Use respectful words toward my teachers
    Raise my hand when I want to contribute to the class discussion

2. To meet these goals, I will achieve the following:

    Each day, I will earn a point if I make no more than two disrespectful or disruptive comments in science and English periods

3. When these goals are met, I will earn the following rewards:

    Once I have earned 5 points, I can exchange these points for a no-homework pass in English class or an extra hour of Internet time at home.

4. Bonus opportunity: _I will earn 3 bonus points at the end of the week if I had no more than three total incidents in English class for the week._

5. Penalty clause: _____

6. The terms of this contract will be applied in the following settings/situations: _Second and third periods, English and math_

7. Dates effective: This contract will begin on _November 2nd_ and remain active until _November 13th_.

_____   _____
Student signature   Adult signature

                                 _____
                                 Adult signature

Interventions © 2019 Ancora Publishing   REPRODUCIBLE 4.1a

Finally, make sure you have a clear idea about what the contract is designed to achieve—that is, what will be different about the student's behavior after the contract is in place? Which behaviors do you want to see more often? Which behaviors do you want to observe less frequently? In addition to frequency, can you identify desired changes in the quality, intensity, or duration of certain behaviors? When and where should these changes take place? In Step 3, you will translate these general goals into objective, measurable goals. These measurable goals will act as criteria for determining whether the student has met the terms of the agreement.

Try to frame these overall goals in positive terms, even if the contract will be primarily designed to reduce a misbehavior. When you explain the purpose of a behavioral contract to a student who acts aggressively when frustrated, "learning to calm down and ask for help" can help the student develop an important skill set. Contrast this goal with "not throwing a tantrum," which focuses only on misbehavior and may be less motivating or feel demeaning to the student.

Write these overall goals in Item 1 on the Student Behavior Contract.

1. I, *Arletta*, agree to work on the following goals:
   use respectful words toward my teachers
   Raise my hand when I want to contribute to the class discussion

STEP 2 Choose a method to monitor target behaviors.

Once you identify target behaviors, select a method for monitoring these behaviors. Behavior can be monitored in a number of different ways.

a. *Existing data*: Grade books, attendance records, tardiness records, and other class records offer a source of routinely collected data. If data are already being collected on the behaviors included in the contract, you might consider just using those data to monitor the student's fulfillment of contract goals.

b. *Frequency counts of appropriate and inappropriate behavior*: For discrete behaviors, such as swearing, throwing items, delivering compliments, or turning work in on time, teachers can simply record the number of occurrences of a positive or negative behavior. In such cases, you might use the monitoring system shown in Positive/Negative Behavior Scaling Form (Reproducible 4.1b), where a student earns points or rewards based on the ratio of appropriate to inappropriate behaviors. For example, Kendra, who has problems with negative self-talk, might earn credit to the school store for every period that her positive comments about herself or others exceed negative self-talk statements.

c. *Interval recording of appropriate and inappropriate behavior*: Interval recording involves marking whether the behavior occurs during a particular time interval, which might be as short as 10 seconds or as long a full class period. Depending on the baseline frequency of behavior, select time intervals that allow the student to see a high rate of success. Start with intervals that guarantee success at least 50% of the time with no changes to current behavior. As the student shows progress, gradually adjust the time intervals. Interval Recording Form (Reproducible 4.1c) is a sample form for interval recording.

continued on page 328

STEP 1 NOTE

If you use the problem-solving model and tools that were introduced and applied at different stages of a problem in Section 2, when you design the intervention you should have already defined target behaviors, identified replacement behaviors, and set goals for improvement. Use this information to complete Step 1. If you need additional support, see Section 3, Task 1 (p. 238).

REPRODUCIBLE 4.1b *Positive/Negative Behavior Scaling Form*

Positive/Negative Behavior Scaling Form

Name _____   Grade/Class _____

Teacher _____   Date _____

Goal _____

Time	Positive	1	2	3	4	5	6	7	8	9	10
_____	Negative	1	2	3	4	5	6	7	8	9	10

Time	Positive	1	2	3	4	5	6	7	8	9	10
_____	Negative	1	2	3	4	5	6	7	8	9	10

Time	Positive	1	2	3	4	5	6	7	8	9	10
_____	Negative	1	2	3	4	5	6	7	8	9	10

Time	Positive	1	2	3	4	5	6	7	8	9	10
_____	Negative	1	2	3	4	5	6	7	8	9	10

Time	Positive	1	2	3	4	5	6	7	8	9	10
_____	Negative	1	2	3	4	5	6	7	8	9	10

Interventions © 2019 Ancora Publishing

REPRODUCIBLE 4.1c *Interval Recording Form*

Interval Recording Form

Student _____ Interval Length _____ Date _____

Teacher _____ Observer _____

Definition of target behavior _____

Directions: For each interval, record whether the student exhibited the target behavior.

☐ Partial interval recording: If the student exhibits the target behavior *at any point* during the interval, record a plus (+). If the student does not exhibit the target behavior at all during the interval, record a minus (–).

☐ Whole interval recording: If the student exhibits the target behavior for the *entire* interval, record a plus (+). If the student does not exhibit the target behavior for the *entire* interval, record a minus (–).

At the end of the recording period, calculate the percentage of intervals during which the student engaged in the target behavior.

Intervals: 1 2 3 4 5 6 7 8 9 10 11 12 13 14 15 16 17 18

Intervals: 19 20 21 22 23 24 25 26 27 28 29 30 31 32 33 34 35 36

Intervals: 37 38 39 40 41 42 43 44 45 46 47 48 49 50 51 52 53 54

Intervals: 55 56 57 58 59 60 61 62 63 64 65 66 67 68 69 70 71 72

Intervals: 73 74 75 76 77 78 79 80 81 82 83 84 85 86 87 88 89 90

Percentage of Intervals with Target Behavior:
Add the number of pluses, divide by the total number of recorded intervals, and multiply by 100. _____ %

Interventions © 2019 Ancora Publishing

REPRODUCIBLE 4.1c

d. *Counting work or task completion:* If the goal of the contract is to increase work or task completion, you might opt to monitor the number of assignments, problems, or tasks completed in a specified period of time. For example, a teacher could award points for each assignment completed, for a certain number of problems completed, or for each time the student remembers to record details and due dates of daily homework assignments in a planner.
e. *Behavior rating scales:* If the frequency of a behavior is difficult to count, or if you'd like to monitor certain qualities or multiple dimensions of behavior, a rating scale may be a good choice. With a rating scale, the teacher awards a variable number of points based on the degree to which the student exhibits a particular behavior. For example, as shown in the sample Behavior Rating Form (Reproducible 4.1d), a student might receive points based on how well he is able to follow directions, where 0 = Not at all, 1 = Needed reminders, and 2 = Followed directions independently. (You can download a blank version of the Behavior Rating Form so that you can define what 0, 1, and 2 look like for a specific target behavior. See p. 564 for download directions.)
f. *Duration recording:* For behaviors that last a long time (e.g., tantruming) or when the goal of the contract is to increase the duration of behavior (e.g., on-task behavior), consider keeping track of the amount of time a student engages in those behaviors. While more labor intensive than other methods, duration recording can be useful when target behaviors occur too frequently to warrant a frequency count. In addition, with some behaviors you may see gradual improvements in duration before you see changes in frequency (e.g., out-of-seat behavior). To monitor duration, the teacher or other staff member simply starts a stopwatch any time the student engages in the target behavior, stops the watch when the behavior ceases, and restarts it when the behavior begins again. If the stopwatch is not reset, the amount of time the student engages in the target behavior will be recorded cumulatively throughout the day. You can then deliver points or rewards when the total time is above or below a predetermined amount.

> *Objective, measurable goals serve as criteria for determining whether the student has held up their side of the contract agreement.*

When considering options for monitoring target behaviors, make sure that the system you choose is feasible to implement and acceptable to the teacher or other staff member who will be in charge of monitoring. See Section 3, Task 8 (p. 289) for more monitoring options, additional considerations in selecting data collection methods, and examples of reproducible data collection forms.

STEP 3 Outline a plan for implementation and data collection.

When creating a plan, make sure to incorporate the following components.

State the criteria for meeting each goal in observable and measurable terms. Based on the overall goals specified in Step 1 and the method for monitoring target behaviors selected in Step 2, establish objective, measurable goals to serve as criteria for determining whether the student has held up their side of the agreement. For example:

> *Goal:* Learn to calm down and ask for help.
> *Method of monitoring target behavior:* Frequency counts of throwing materials, yelling, and asking for help; grade book for assignment completion

REPRODUCIBLE 4.1d *Sample Behavior Rating Form*

Behavior Rating Form

Name Jaydon

Goal Follow directions

POINTS:

0 = Not at all
1 = Needed reminders
2 = Followed directions independently

Week of: 4/12

Day	AM	PM	Total
Monday	⓪ 1 2	0 ① 2	1
Tuesday	0 ① 2	0 ① 2	2
Wednesday	0 1 ②	0 ① 2	3
Thursday	0 1 ②	0 1 ②	4
Friday	0 1 ②	0 ① 2	3

Week of:

Day	AM	PM	Total
Monday	0 1 2	0 1 2	
Tuesday	0 1 2	0 1 2	
Wednesday	0 1 2	0 1 2	
Thursday	0 1 2	0 1 2	
Friday	0 1 2	0 1 2	

Week of:

Day	AM	PM	Total
Monday	0 1 2	0 1 2	
Tuesday	0 1 2	0 1 2	
Wednesday	0 1 2	0 1 2	
Thursday	0 1 2	0 1 2	
Friday	0 1 2	0 1 2	

Interventions © 2019 Ancora Publishing

Criteria: Each day during math class, Aaron will meet his goal by turning in his completed math worksheet without throwing materials or yelling, and by asking for help when needed.

Goal: Arrive on time and prepared for class to begin.
Method of monitoring target behavior: Frequency counts of tardies
Criteria: Claudia will meet her goal by having no more than one tardy per week.

When developing criteria for goals, remember to:

- *Include numbers and timelines.* Incorporating numbers and timelines into your goals allows you to clearly evaluate whether the student met the goal. It will also specify how often the student can earn rewards. Students should earn rewards quickly in the initial phases of the intervention so that they view behavior goals and the criteria for earning rewards as achievable. Begin by choosing goals with shorter timelines (no more than one week) to give the student the opportunity to earn rewards quickly.
- *Select goals that are ambitious but obtainable.* If the ultimate goal for behavior is far from the student's current level of performance, set intermediate goals and renegotiate contract terms at a later point. For example, if Leon refuses to remain in his seat for any part of the morning reading period, it is unrealistic to expect him to be in his seat 100% of the time on the first day the contract goes into place. Instead, you might define a more obtainable, tiered goal such as, "On Week 1, Leon will meet his goal each day by being in his seat 50% of the time. On Week 2, Leon will meet his goal by being in his seat 60% of the time, etc."
- *Use cumulative criteria when possible and appropriate.* Try to avoid arbitrary time limits (e.g., earn 20 points by the end of the week). If a student earns 20 points by Thursday afternoon, she may realize she can resort to inappropriate behaviors on Friday and still earn the reward. Consecutive criteria (e.g., demonstrate 5 consecutive days of good behavior) can also be problematic. If the student is successful for 3 days in a row, but struggles on the fourth day, she may give up trying if the consecutive count starts over. Instead, use cumulative criteria. For example, offer a reward for 5 days of good behavior or when the student accumulates 20 points, instead of for 5 consecutive days of good behavior or 20 points by the end of the week. This may not always be feasible given the goals of the contract or the limits of monitoring procedures, but you should proactively consider whether time limits or consecutive criteria might interfere with the success of the individual student. If problems seem likely, consider alternative goal criteria.

Once you develop criteria for each goal included in the student's behavior contract, record these details in Item 2 on the Student Behavior Contract (Reproducible 4.1a).

2. To meet these goals, I will achieve the following:

    Each day, I will earn a point if I make no more than two disrespectful or disruptive comments in science and English periods

Create a menu of possible rewards. Generate a list of reward suggestions to share with the student. Rewards should be inexpensive, feasible to deliver, and tailored to the interests of the student. Remember that privileges and responsibilities are often as powerful as material things. When you meet with the student to negotiate the terms of the contract, the student will select rewards from this menu. Try to include a few reward options that align with the function of the student's misbehavior. For example, a student who bullies other students at recess in order to play on preferred playground equipment could work to earn special access to that equipment. A list of reward ideas appears in Appendix B.

At this point, record the list of possible rewards separately from the draft contract. You can fill in Item 3 on Student Behavior Contract when you meet with the student to discuss the contract.

> 3. When these goals are met, I will earn the following rewards:
>
> Once I have earned 5 points, I can exchange these points for a no-homework pass in English class or an extra hour of Internet time at home.

Consider including a bonus opportunity to provide extra motivation to change behavior. A bonus opportunity outlines additional rewards the student can earn for exceptional effort or quick improvements in behavior. Examples include:

- Aaron can earn one week of no homework if he completes and scores above 90% on all math worksheets in the unit.
- Claudia can earn a pizza party at the end of the quarter if she has no more than three tardies during the quarter.

If you choose to include a bonus opportunity, describe the reward that is available to earn and specify the criteria for earning it in Item 4 on Student Behavior Contract.

> 4. Bonus opportunity: I will earn 3 bonus points at the end of the week if I had no more than three total incidents in English class for the week.

Consider including a penalty clause that specifies consequences for not meeting the contract's behavior expectations. In some cases, it may be advantageous to include a penalty clause in the contract, especially in cases where rewards may not be adequately motivating to the student. For example, if Lashinda's peers provide highly reinforcing attention and encouragement for misbehaving, the rewards offered to motivate her to change behavior may not compare with the social rewards she is already accessing by misbehaving. In these cases, a penalty clause can be a useful addition to the student's contract. For example, for a student who avoids participating in seatwork by socializing with peers, a consequence might include staying in for recess to complete work. If you intend to include a penalty clause, make sure to consider the function of the student's problem behavior to ensure that consequences aren't inadvertently reinforcing to the student.

If you do include a penalty clause, explicitly outline the behaviors that will warrant penalty consequences and describe the consequences that will be assigned in Item 5 on Student Behavior Contract (Reproducible 4.1a).

> 5. Penalty clause: _____
> _____
> _____

Clarify when and where contract terms will be applied. You may opt to apply the terms of the behavior contract for the whole school day, part of the day, or during certain situations and activities. This decision will largely depend on the frequency and severity of the problem and the method chosen to monitor student behavior.

If misbehavior occurs frequently across multiple settings, don't expect change to occur all at once. Instead, start by using the contract in one setting, for part of the day, or during specific activities that are challenging for the student. As the student achieves success, you can gradually expand the contract's use to longer periods of time or across settings. If the contract will be applied across multiple settings or situations, your monitoring and data collection plan must extend to these as well. For example, if the contract's goal is to reduce name-calling across all settings, adults need to monitor and collect data on this behavior in all settings. If this isn't feasible, either start by limiting the contract's application to certain time periods or adjust data collection plans so that staff can feasibly monitor student behavior across all targeted settings and situations. For example, you might adjust the goal so that the student initially works on reducing name-calling at recess.

Use Item 6 of the Student Behavior Contract to document the settings and situations that the terms of the contact will apply to.

> 6. The terms of this contract will be applied in the following settings/situations: _Second and third periods, English and math_

After the contract expires, you can meet with the student and discuss continuing the contract, renegotiating its terms, or discontinuing its use.

Specify the contract's timeline. Specifying the dates that the contract will remain in effect is also important. You can choose to structure this timeline around the academic calendar (e.g., at the end of the quarter or semester) or with consideration of the student's goals (e.g., for weekly goals, an ending date in 8 weeks may be appropriate). After the contract expires, you can meet with the student and discuss continuing the contract, renegotiating its terms, or discontinuing its use.

NOTE: This timeline should only be viewed as an estimate. It is designed to help communicate the scope and purpose of the contract to the student. A staff member should check in with the student about progress at least once per week and make adjustments to the plan as often as needed.

Once you identify the timeline, use Item 7 of the contract to document the dates the contract will remain in effect and a date on which to review terms.

> 7. Dates effective: This contract will begin on _November 2nd_ and remain active until _November 13th_.

Contact the student's parents/guardians to discuss the contract. Introduce the behavioral contracting plan, share the goals of the contract, and invite the parent to be an active partner in its implementation. You might ask the parent about any rewards or privileges at home that the student might earn in addition to, but not in place of, the rewards or privileges that can be earned at school. In this case, make a plan for communicating with parents about the points the student has earned at school and ensure that they are willing to follow through if they volunteer to offer home-based rewards.

Make a plan for data collection and monitoring. Identify ways to determine whether the intervention is helping the student reach the goals. If you monitoring system uses forms, these offer a built-in record of student progress. Keep dated records so that you can analyze progress and adjust the system periodically.

Consider supplemental intervention strategies to incorporate into the plan. Identify other strategies that might support or increase the effectiveness of the behavior contract in changing behavior. For example:

- *Antecedent strategies:* Consider whether to modify structural elements to maximize the effectiveness of your contract. Think about whether changing seating arrangements, schedules, work requirements, expectations, or procedures can increase the likelihood that the student will meet the goal.
- *Teaching strategies:* If the contract requires the student to learn and practice a new behavior, schedule short, regular lessons with the interventionist, a teacher, a trained paraprofessional, or a volunteer.
- *Positive consequence strategies:* In addition to incorporating rewards into the contract, think about ways to ensure that the student receives high rates of praise and specific feedback for appropriate behavior, making efforts, and meeting goals. For example, share the goals of the contract with other staff members who regularly interact with the student, or send positive news home when the student makes a concentrated effort.
- *Corrective consequence strategies:* If negative attention has sustained the misbehavior, consider ways to minimize adult or peer attention for misbehavior. Further, if the student's goal involves eliminating or reducing an inappropriate behavior, make sure that your intervention plan is comprehensive enough to ensure that adult response to misbehavior is consistent and fluent. This may require defining the limits of behavior in more detail, preplanning a range of corrective responses, explicitly teaching limits and discussing corrective consequences with the student, and working closely with staff members to ensure that corrections are delivered fluently and effectively.
- *Interactional strategies:* Consider ways to increase the frequency of noncontingent positive attention, and, if needed, encourage student engagement in the school community through participating in school clubs or activities, assuming a meaningful role in the school, or connecting with an adult or peer mentor.

- *Specialized strategies:* Once a student is successful in meeting goals, it could be worthwhile to transition to Self-Monitoring and Self-Evaluation (Section 4.3). Also, the reward component of Behavioral Contracting can be implemented through Structured Reinforcement (Section 4.2).

Outline roles and responsibilities for implementing the plan. At this point, you should have a draft of the behavior contract to present to the student for negotiation. The contract should clearly state its goals for changing student behaviors and the amount of behavior change required for the student to receive rewards. You should also specify any bonus or penalty clauses that will be included and have a list of possible rewards to discuss with the student. Also make sure to identify:

- Who will meet with the student to introduce the contract and negotiate its terms and rewards.
- Who will be responsible for administering the contract's rewards and penalties.
- Who will be responsible for data collection, and how data will be collected and summarized.
- Who will need training.

Provide training to teachers and other adults who will be implementing the plan. Anyone involved in monitoring student behavior, delivering rewards, or assigning penalties as part of the contract's implementation should receive training on procedures. Plan to explain when and how to monitor student behavior, how to respond to misbehavior, and how to deliver rewards when the student earns them. Use the Implementation Guidelines: Behavioral Contracting (Reproducible 4.1e, pp. 339–341) to review procedures with staff. Also make sure to distribute a copy of the contract and relevant forms for monitoring progress.

Case Example: Arletta

Arletta, a seventh-grade student at a large middle school, is frequently disruptive and disrespectful to adults during class time. She makes disparaging comments when the teacher presents lessons, seemingly with the purpose of embarrassing or frustrating the teacher. If the teacher tries to speak to her, even with a greeting in the hall, Arletta is likely to shrug and walk away, or verbally lash out with an angry comment. The concern is initially brought to the problem-solving team by Arletta's English teacher, who has started to keep a frequency count of Arletta's disrespectful and disruptive comments. During third-period English class, Arletta makes between 3–8 comments each day. In discussing Arletta with the seventh-grade team, the problem-solving team learns that Arletta is academically successful in all of her classes, but exhibits these disruptive and disrespectful behaviors in five of her six classes. Her science teacher reports that she does not exhibit these behaviors, but is relatively quiet in class. When the school counselor asks Arletta about science class, she says she likes the class and feels that Mr. Thompson, the science teacher, respects her.

The team decides to try a behavior contract for 2 weeks. The contract focuses on second-period science class and third-period English class. Negotiation of the initial contract is guided by the school counselor and includes Arletta and her mother; Mr. Thompson, the science teacher; and Ms. Aziz, the English teacher. Together, they identify two goals for Arletta:

1. Use respectful words toward my teachers.
2. Raise my hand when I want to contribute to the class discussion.

The team also defines the types of comments considered disrespectful or disruptive. For each disrespectful or disruptive comment, the teacher plans to quietly say, "Arletta," and make a hash mark on a frequency count card. Comments made in class that are respectful and nondisruptive will receive a positive acknowledgment in the form of a head nod or verbal specific praise from the teacher.

Aletta can earn a point each day for no more than two incidents of disrespectful or disruptive comments across both second and third periods. She can also earn three bonus points at the end of the week if she has no more than three total incidents in English class for the week. At the end of each week, Arletta will meet with the school counselor to review frequency count data from her science and English classes. Arletta selects a range of school and home-based rewards that she can exchange accrued points for, including extra time to use the Internet at home and a no-homework pass in English class. At this point, the team decides not to include a penalty clause in the contract. If the 2-week contract is successful during second and third period, the team plans to negotiate a new contract that will include other class periods.

Essential Implementation Procedures

The teacher or interventionist responsible for implementing the plan should make sure to:
1. **Meet with the student to discuss and finalize the plan.** During this meeting:

- Explain that you would like to help the student be more successful at school.
- Present the goals of the contract, explain why a contract is necessary, and describe how it can help the student reach their goals. Let the student know that while you are open to negotiating the details of the contract, its implementation is not negotiable.
- Discuss contract terms, including reward options and criteria for earning rewards. Negotiate the contract with the student, ask for input, and work together to come up with an acceptable version of the contract. Using the menu you created in Step 3 as a starting point, develop a list of rewards that the student is motivated to work for.
- Describe how the monitoring system will work and clarify how and when rewards will be delivered.
- If a bonus clause is part of the contract, discuss how the bonus can be earned. If a penalty clause is included, explain what the consequences are and when they will be assigned.

Items 1–9 are also shown on **Implementation Guidelines** (Form 4.1e, pp. 339–341). Share with teachers and other adults who are responsible for implementing the plan.

BEFORE MEETING WITH THE STUDENT

Once a draft of the contract has been created, determine who will meet with the student to discuss the problem behavior, the goals, and the reinforcement system. This meeting may include the interventionist, the teacher, adults who will be working with the student, and the student's parents. However, it is important to convene a group that will not overwhelm the student.

- Discuss the contract's timeline. Set a date to review and possibly renegotiate the contract.
- Make sure the student understands the goals of the system, the desired outcome, and the benefits. The more engaged the student is in the discussion, the greater the likelihood that the student will take ownership of the plan.
- Before concluding the meeting, have everyone involved (student, teacher, parent, counselor, etc.) sign the contract. Provide a copy of the finalized contract for the student and the student's family.

2. Practice and role-play appropriate responses with the student. Conduct any needed instruction and practice in behaviors or skills that the student needs in order to comply with the terms of the contract. For example, if the goal is to "interact respectfully with peers," the student may need additional instruction on the difference between respectful and disrespectful comments. Generate a list of examples and non-examples, present hypothetical situations, and discuss appropriate and inappropriate ways to act in different situations the student is likely to encounter.

3. Follow through with the contract terms during specified times and settings. Make sure to consistently monitor student behavior, deliver rewards, and follow through with bonus and penalty clauses in accordance with the details of the contract. Staff and parents who sign the contract must understand the importance of upholding their end of the deal. Deliver rewards as immediately as possible. Students may lose motivation when they have to wait too long for an earned reward to be given.

4. Acknowledge and encourage the student's efforts. Provide ample praise when the student follows expectations and demonstrates appropriate behavior. Be enthusiastic about progress and encouraging about the student's ability to fulfill the terms of the contract.

5. Respond calmly and consistently to misbehavior. If you need to deliver a correction or implement a penalty clause, minimize attention by remaining calm and using brief, neutral statements. The student is less likely to be reinforced for the misbehavior when corrections are calm, brief, and consistent.

6. Meet and debrief with the student regularly. After the first week of using the contract, meet with the student to discuss the experience so far, review goals, highlight successes, and address any problems. Continue to meet with the student on a weekly basis until the end of the contract's timeline.

If the system is not working after the first week, identify any minor adjustments you might make to improve the chance of student success. Consider:

- *Does the student understand the terms of the contract?* To check for understanding, ask the student to list the goals of the contract or explain what must be done to earn a reward.
- *Does the student care about the rewards that have been identified?* If not, brainstorm with the student to find other alternatives that might be more motivating. If the student is interested only in big rewards, consider a reinforcement ladder, which allows the student to earn smaller rewards on the way to an ultimate goal (see Figure 4.1a).
- *Is the system designed so the student has little chance of success?* Check whether the contract's goals require too much change at once and adjust the system accordingly.

FIGURE 4.1a *Reinforcement Ladder*

Reward	Points
Pizza with the principal	100
Read to the kindergarten students	90
15 minutes game time with friend	80
15 minutes computer time	70
Choose a class job	60
Certificate from the principal	50
Pick a prize	40
Run off papers	30
Certificate from teacher	20
Game with teacher	10

- *Is the student getting too much attention from the teacher or peers for exhibiting the problem behaviors?* If so, identify ways to minimize adult attention for misbehavior and increase the ratio of positive to corrective interactions with the student. (See strategies for increasing contingent and noncontingent positive interactions in Task 4 and Task 6 of Section 3.)

7. Use data to make periodic revisions and adjustments to the plan as necessary. Use monitoring data and information from the weekly debriefing meeting to make adjustments to the contract as needed. If the student's behavior isn't improving, ask the following questions:

- *Are all essential components of the plan being implemented as intended?* Ensure that intervention fidelity is maintained by having the teacher or external observer complete the Fidelity Checklist: Behavioral Contracting (Reproducible 4.1f, p. 342).
- *Which aspects of the plan can be modified to increase its effectiveness?* Are the rewards no longer motivating to the student? Do rewards take too long to earn, so the student is not able to experience regular success? If so, adjust the system.
- *What supplemental strategies can be introduced to support the effectiveness of the plan?* Incorporating other intervention strategies, such as explicitly teaching replacement behaviors, increasing ratios of positive to corrective interactions, or introducing self-monitoring procedures might help encourage improvement in the student's behavior.
- *Is the plan meeting the student's needs?* Review information about the context of the problem and determine whether to collect additional data to more accurately identify contributing factors and uncover the function of the problematic behavior.

Continue to use the contract, regularly reviewing progress, until the student is consistently meeting high standards for the selected behaviors.

8. At the end of the contract's timeline, meet with the student to discuss whether to renew the contract, renegotiate its terms, or discontinue it. During this meeting, review the contract goals and discuss the student's progress toward meeting these goals. Share a summary of monitoring data gathered during the contract's use, highlighting successes and providing specific feedback on the improvements you've observed. Then, present one or more of the following options to discuss with the student:

- *Renew the contract with the same terms.* If the student has just recently started to meet the contract's goals, if success has been inconsistent, or if there are concerns about whether the student will be able to maintain gains, it may be a good idea to extend the contract's timeline, offering the student more time to keep working on meeting the original terms.
- *Renew the contact, but renegotiate new terms.* If the original goals specified in the contract were intermediate goals (i.e., set somewhere between the student's baseline level of performance and the ultimate goal for behavior), or if the student engages in other problematic behaviors not targeted in the original contract, you might renegotiate the terms to target new goals, increase expectations for appropriate behavior, or make the criteria for earning rewards more challenging.
- *Renew the contract, but transition to self-monitoring.* If the student isn't yet ready to give up the structure of the contract but is consistently meeting goals, consider transitioning the student to self-manage all aspects of the contract, including recording data on behaviors and evaluating whether goals are met. (See Section 4.3: Self-Monitoring and Self-Evaluation.)
- *Renew the contract, but fade the use of rewards.* If the student has been consistently successful in meeting the contract's goals with the use of rewards, you might gradually fade rewards over time and transition the student to working for more natural reinforcers found in the classroom (e.g., praise and encouragement). If the student's behavior deteriorates after you introduce fading procedures, offer the option of reverting back to the previously implemented plan, or adjust fading procedures to be more gradual.
- *Discontinue the contract.* If the student has made sufficient improvements in behavior and readily agrees to discontinuing the system, you may opt to end the contract. Make sure to continue to acknowledge appropriate behavior and monitor whether the student is maintaining behavioral gains.

9. Provide continued follow-up, support, and encouragement. Whether you decide to renew, renegotiate, or discontinue behavioral contracting, remember to continue to praise appropriate behavior, acknowledge the student's efforts and improvements, and offer ongoing encouragement and support to help the student experience success at school.

Strategy Summary

Behavioral Contracting is a simple, effective goal-setting and planning tool for improving student behavior. As a collaborative agreement between the teacher and the student, behavior contracts encourage student buy-in with the process of changing behavior, provide structure for clarifying and monitoring specific behaviors, and offer a framework for rewarding progress and celebrating student successes.

REPRODUCIBLE 4.1e *Implementation Guidelines: Behavioral Contracting (1 of 3)*

Implementation Guidelines
Behavioral Contracting

Overview

Behavioral Contracting is a collaborative method of defining behavior expectations, setting goals, specifying rewards for improvements, and clarifying consequences in writing. Developed through negotiation with the student, behavior contracts provide structure and can be used across settings to encourage progress toward both academic and behavioral goals.

Behavioral Contracting can be used to help students:

- Increase engagement in particular skills or behavior, such as amount of work completed, time on task, and positive interactions with peers.
- Reduce or eliminate the frequency of negative behavior, such as using profanity, fighting, and interacting disrespectfully with adults.

A behavior contract is a written and signed agreement between a student and a teacher or other school staff member (e.g., school counselor, administrator) that outlines the specific student behaviors to be increased and misbehaviors to be decreased. Having the student and an adult sign the contract formalizes the agreement and helps to make the student more accountable for actions at school.

Implementation Steps

1. **Meet with the student to discuss and finalize the plan.**

    During this meeting:

    - Explain that you would like to assist the student in being more successful at school.
    - Present the goals of the contract, explain why a contract is necessary, and describe how it can help the student reach their goals. Let the student know that while you are open to negotiating the details of the contract, its implementation is not negotiable.
    - Discuss contract terms, including reward options and criteria for earning rewards. Negotiate the contract with the student, ask for input, and work together to come up with an acceptable version of the contract. Create a list of rewards that the student is motivated to work for.
    - Describe how the monitoring system will work and clarify how and when rewards will be delivered.
    - If a bonus clause is part of the contract, discuss how the student can earn the bonus. If a penalty clause is included, explain what the consequences are and when they will be assigned.
    - Discuss the contract's timeline. Set a date to review and possibly renegotiate the contract.
    - Make sure the student understands the goals of the contract, the desired outcome, and the benefits. The more engaged the student is in the discussion, the greater the likelihood that they will take ownership of the plan.
    - Before concluding the meeting, have everyone involved (student, teacher, parent, counselor, etc.) sign the contract. Provide a copy of the finalized contract for the student and the student's family.

REPRODUCIBLE 4.1e *Implementation Guidelines: Behavioral Contracting (2 of 3)*

Implementation Guidelines: Behavioral Contracting

2. **Practice and role-play appropriate responses with the student.**

    Conduct any needed instruction and practice in behaviors or skills that the student needs to comply with the terms of the contract. For example, if the goal is to "interact respectfully with peers," the student may need additional instruction on the difference between respectful and disrespectful comments. Generate a list of examples and non-examples, present hypothetical situations, and discuss appropriate and inappropriate ways to act in different situations that the student is likely to encounter.

3. **Follow through with the contract terms during specified times and settings.**

    Make sure to consistently monitor student behavior, deliver rewards, and follow through with bonus and penalty clauses in accordance with the details of the contract. Staff and parents who sign the contract must understand the importance of upholding their end of the deal. Deliver rewards as immediately as possible. Students may lose motivation if they have to wait too long to receive an earned reward.

4. **Acknowledge and encourage the student's efforts.**

    Provide ample praise when the student follows expectations and demonstrates appropriate behavior. Be enthusiastic about progress and encouraging about the student's ability to fulfill the contract's terms.

5. **Respond calmly and consistently to misbehavior.**

    If you need to deliver a correction or implement a penalty clause, minimize attention by remaining calm and using brief, neutral statements. The student is less likely to be reinforced for the misbehavior when corrections are calm, brief, and consistent.

6. **Meet and debrief with the student regularly.**

    After the first week of using the contract, meet with the student to discuss the experience so far, review goals, highlight successes, and address any problems. Continue to meet with the student on a weekly basis until the end of the contract's timeline.

    If the system is not working after the first week, identify any minor adjustments you might make to improve the chance of student success. Consider:

    - *Does the student understand the terms of the contract?* To check for understanding, ask the student to list the goals of the contract or explain what must be done to earn a reward.
    - *Does the student care about the rewards that have been identified?* If not, brainstorm with the student to find other alternatives that may be more motivating.
    - *Is the system designed so the student has little chance of success?* Check whether the contract's goals require too much change at once and adjust the system accordingly.
    - *Is the student getting too much attention from the teacher or peers for exhibiting the problem behaviors?* If so, identify ways to minimize adult attention for misbehavior and increase the ratio of positive to corrective interactions with the student.

    If the contract is still not working after minor adjustments, collaborate with your problem-solving team to discuss next steps.

REPRODUCIBLE 4.1e *Implementation Guidelines: Behavioral Contracting (3 of 3)*

Implementation Guidelines: Behavioral Contracting

7. **Use data to make periodic revisions and adjustments to the plan as necessary.**

   Use monitoring data, information from the weekly debriefing meetings, and input from your problem-solving team to make adjustments to the contract as needed.

8. **At the end of the contract's timeline, meet with the student to discuss whether to renew the contract, renegotiate terms, or discontinue the contract.**

   During this meeting, review the contract goals and discuss the student's progress in meeting these goals. Share a summary of monitoring data gathered during the contract's use, highlighting successes and providing specific feedback on the improvements you've observed. Then, present one or more of the following options to discuss with the student:

   - *Renew the contract with the same terms.* If the student has just recently started to meet the contract's goals, if success has been inconsistent, or if there are concerns about whether the student will be able to maintain gains, it may be a good idea to extend the contract's timeline, offering the student more time to keep working on meeting the original terms.
   - *Renew the contact, but renegotiate the terms.* If the original goals specified in the contract were intermediate goals (i.e., set somewhere between the student's baseline level of performance and the ultimate goal for behavior), or if the student engages in other problematic behaviors not targeted in the original contract, you might renegotiate the terms to target new goals, increase expectations for appropriate behavior, or make the criteria for earning rewards more challenging.
   - *Renew the contract, but transition to self-monitoring.* If the student is consistently meeting goals but isn't yet ready to give up the structure of the contract, consider transitioning the student to self-manage all aspects of the contract, including recording behavior data and evaluating whether goals are met.
   - *Renew the contract, but fade the use of rewards.* If the student has been consistently successful in meeting the contract's goals with the use of rewards, you might gradually fade rewards over time and transition the student to working for more natural reinforcers found in the classroom (e.g., praise and encouragement). If the student's behavior deteriorates after you introduce fading procedures, offer the option of reverting back to the previously implemented plan, or adjust the fading procedures to be more gradual.
   - *Discontinue the contract.* If the student has made sufficient improvements in behavior and readily agrees to discontinuing the system, you may opt to end the contract. Make sure to continue to acknowledge appropriate behavior and monitor the student's ability to maintain behavior improvements.

9. **Provide continued follow-up, support, and encouragement.**

   Whether you decide to renew, renegotiate, or discontinue behavioral contracting, remember to continue to praise appropriate behavior, acknowledge the student's efforts and improvements, and offer ongoing encouragement and support to help the student experience success at school.

REPRODUCIBLE 4.1f *Fidelity Checklist: Behavioral Contracting*

Fidelity Checklist
Behavioral Contracting

Essential Planning Steps

- ☐ Identify target behaviors and describe general goals of the contract.
- ☐ Choose a method for monitoring target behaviors.
- ☐ State the criteria for meeting each goal in observable and measurable terms.
- ☐ Create a menu of possible rewards.
- ☐ Clarify when and where contract terms will be applied.
- ☐ Specify the contract's timeline.
- ☐ Contact the student's parents/guardians to discuss the contract.
- ☐ Make a plan for data collection and monitoring.
- ☐ Outline roles and responsibilities for implementing the plan.
- ☐ Provide training to teachers and other adults who will be implementing the plan.

Essential Implementation Components

- ☐ Meet with the student to discuss and finalize the plan.
- ☐ Practice and role-play appropriate responses with the student.
- ☐ Follow through with the contract terms during specified times and settings.
- ☐ Acknowledge and encourage the student's efforts.
- ☐ Respond calmly and consistently to misbehavior.
- ☐ Meet and debrief with the student regularly.
- ☐ Use data to make periodic revisions and adjustments to the plan as necessary.
- ☐ At the end of the contract's timeline, meet with the student to discuss whether to renew the contract, renegotiate terms, or discontinue the contract.
- ☐ Provide continued follow-up, support, and encouragement.

References

Bailey, J. S., Wolf, M. M., & Phillips, E. L. (1970). Home based reinforcement and the modification of pre-delinquents' classroom behavior. *Journal of Applied Behavior Analysis, 3,* 223–233.

Bowman-Perrott, L., Burke, M. D., de Marin, S., Zhang, N., & Davis, H. (2015). A meta-analysis of single-case research on behavior contracts: Effects on behavioral and academic outcomes among children and youth. *Behavior Modification, 39*(2), 247–269.

Cantrell, R. P., Cantrell, M. L., Huddleston, C. M., & Wooldridge, R. L. (1969). Contingency contracting with school problems. *Journal of Applied Behavior Analysis, 2,* 215–220.

Downing, J. A. (2002). Individualized behavior contracts. *Intervention in School and Clinic, 37*(3), 168–172.

Houmanfar, R., Maglieri, K. A., Roman, H. R., & Ward, T. A. (2008). Behavioral contracting. In W. T. O'Donohue & J. E. Fisher (Eds.), *Cognitive behavioural therapy: Applying empirically supported techniques in your practice* (pp. 53–59). Hoboken, NJ: John Wiley.

Kidd, T. A., & Saudargas, R. A. (1988). Positive and negative consequences in contingency contracts: Their relative effectiveness on arithmetic performance. *Education and Treatment of Children, 11,* 118–126

Miltenberger, R. G. (2008). Behavioral contracts. In R. G. Miltenberger, *Behavior modification: Principles and procedures* (pp. 521–536). Belmont, CA: Wadsworth Publishing.

SECTION 4.2

SPECIALIZED INTERVENTION STRATEGY TWO

Structured Reinforcement

The student has deeply ingrained cycles of inappropriate behavior

Purpose

A structured reinforcement system motivates students to break deeply ingrained cycles of inappropriate behavior by offering external reinforcements or rewards for behavior improvements. Once the student begins to experience success, external reinforcements can be faded and eventually removed.

Structured reinforcement systems can be used to help students:

- Increase engagement in particular skills or behavior, such as amount of work completed, time on task, and positive interactions with peers.
- Reduce or eliminate the frequency of negative behavior, such as using profanity, fighting, and interacting disrespectfully with adults.

This strategy may be applicable when a student:

- Demonstrates patterns of deeply ingrained behavior problems that have been resistant to simpler solutions.
- Requires additional encouragement to demonstrate desired behavior.

Rationale

Many students find natural success and encouragement in the classroom. They take pride in their accomplishments and feel a sense of satisfaction at completing a task. These students share these positive interactions at home: "Hey, Mom! Mrs. Dubach said she'd like to borrow my book. She hasn't read it yet." Feedback is taken seriously: "Mrs. Dubach said that we need to be more careful when we multiply with decimals." These students are fueled by a sense of well-being. Their motivation to cooperate and do their best is deeply ingrained. Other students may require more motivation in order to meet expectations and succeed in school (Stipek, 1993; Brophy, 2004). This may be the case when:

- *The student doesn't yet value school success.* Motivation to change may initially require an external reward to link school success with something worthwhile and important to the student. Some students do not initially value praise and positive attention or value learning for itself. They need an external reward to boost their interest until these values become important (Ryan & Deci, 2000).
- *Inappropriate behavior has provided a way for the student to meet needs in the past.* For example, if an attention-seeking student is often rewarded by peer laughter when he misbehaves in class, he will likely need different and powerful motivators to encourage him to access attention in more appropriate ways. The motivation to change may initially require an external, tangible reward (O'Neill, Albin, Storey, Horner, & Sprague, 2015).

- *Learning and using new behavior requires a lot of effort.* Because change is difficult, the motivation to change must outweigh the difficulty. Sometimes students need an external motivator to overcome the challenges of ending habitual behavior problems. In the early phases of learning something new or difficult, some students (particularly those who have experienced past failure) are not likely to be motivated simply by the value of learning, knowledge, or improving themselves. These students often need the boost of external reinforcement to get started (Jovanovic & Matejevik, 2014).

When problems have been resistant to change or when a student needs additional encouragement to demonstrate desired behavior, a structured system for rewarding increased positive behavior or decreased inappropriate behavior, and novel applications of positive reinforcement, such as the use of spinners and mystery motivators (Jenson, Rhode, & Reavis, 2009), can provide an extra boost of motivation and help make success a reality.

Common Concerns about Using Reinforcement

Despite its benefits for students, a structured reinforcement system raises several common and legitimate concerns from educators that need to be addressed.

Shouldn't students behave appropriately without rewards? Students should behave appropriately, and they should be motivated to be successful. However, some students need to be taught to value appropriate behavior. When less structured early-stage interventions have not been effective, staff are left with two options: (a) let the student continue to engage in inappropriate behavior, or (b) provide a highly structured reinforcement system to motivate the student to change the pattern of behavior as quickly as possible. The longer misbehavior goes unchanged, the more deeply ingrained it becomes and the more likely it is to worsen.

It may be helpful to think of rewards as extrinsic motivators. Extrinsic motivation occurs when someone engages in a behavior because of the pleasant consequences that are not directly related to the essential nature of the behavior—they engage in behavior to gain a particular prize, grade, praise, and so on. These motivators differ from intrinsic motivators, which are pleasant consequences related to the essential nature of the behavior—someone engages in a behavior to learn new things, relax, have fun, and so on.

Some people believe that the only valid kind of motivation is intrinsic—students should want to learn simply for the value of knowledge—and teachers should not give students praise or rewards. Other people believe that motivators such as praise and good grades are acceptable, but other extrinsic reinforcement, in the form of tangible rewards, should not be used. The simple truth is that the line between intrinsic and extrinsic motivation is not as distinct as it may seem, and tangible and intangible reinforcers are not terribly different—they all are intended to engage students in school. Teachers often must use a combination of techniques to motivate their students to learn and grow. For the student who has experienced little academic success or who has had behavior problems, you may initially need to use tangible reinforcers to spark the student's motivation. In most cases, you will need to enhance both intrinsic (e.g., making a science lesson more engaging) and extrinsic (e.g., writing an encouraging note on returned homework) motivation.

Because change is difficult, the motivation to change must outweigh the difficulty.

Won't students stop working as soon as the rewards are removed? If you overuse structured reinforcement systems, students may learn to work only for tangible rewards and fail to learn the value of working hard, getting along with others, being cooperative, taking pride in a job well done, and other intrinsic rewards in school and life. However, with carefully planned steps you can fade a structured reinforcement system that assists in the initial process of making a behavior change. If a system is removed suddenly, the student may stop working. A carefully designed system is a long, involved process that gradually teaches the student to value success.

Why should students who misbehave get extra rewards or privileges? Students probably shouldn't get extra rewards and privileges as a result of misbehavior. In an ideal world, everything would be equal and fair. However, students do not enter school as equals. Therefore, *equal* treatment cannot mean the *same* treatment when working with students of different backgrounds and abilities. Some students bring background knowledge and values that support cooperation, responsibility, and hard work. These students have already learned to value the attitudes and behaviors that bring success. Reinforcement for these students is inherent in the natural school environment and in their homes without external rewards. Students with behavior problems have more to learn. They may be discouraged by or suspicious of efforts to help them change. These students may need additional incentives to learn how to behave responsibly.

Shouldn't we avoid reinforcing students and focus more on encouraging them and facilitating learning? In education, we often get wrapped up in words. The distinction between *reinforcement* and *encouragement* is largely semantic. If a student is working hard and the teacher stops to engage in a friendly interaction, one person might say, "The teacher is facilitating learning by encouraging the student's interest." Another person might say, "The teacher's attention is reinforcing the on-task behavior." In both cases, the teacher does the same thing; only the words describing the situation are different. Regardless of semantics, reinforcement procedures can be either implemented carefully to support and encourage students or implemented poorly so students do not learn to value effort and accomplishment.

Won't other students object? Students expect the school system to treat them fairly and equitably. Therefore, special rewards for some students can cause problems with other students. It might appear that students who misbehave are rewarded, and those who behave are punished because they are denied access to the reinforcement. You can deal with this in several different ways, depending on the situation:

- Design the reinforcement system in such a way that it is not obvious to other students.
- Discuss the reinforcement system with other students prior to implementing the system and solicit their assistance in the spirit of cooperation and support.
- Let the entire class earn a special reward or privilege occasionally as a way of celebrating the target individual's success.

Will students become the kind of people who always ask, "What will you give me if I do that?" If reinforcement systems are not handled carefully, this potential drawback may become a reality. All adults involved in this intervention must carefully focus on the accomplishments that lead to the reward versus the reward itself. If adults systematically focus interactions on student accomplishments, eventually students develop a sense of satisfaction that takes the place of the actual reward. For example:

Ms. Mayberry:	Scott, here is the mechanical pencil you earned. Tell me what you did to earn it.
Scott:	I read at home for 10 days.
Ms. Mayberry:	You must be exceptionally proud of yourself. You are getting to be a stronger reader because of this kind of practice. When you go home today, be sure to tell your folks how you earned that pencil.

If possible, students should be encouraged to make improvements through positive interactions and strategies that honor hard work, cooperation, kindness, and responsibility. However, there are times when some students won't understand or be motivated by less structured interventions. A high-powered reinforcement system may be necessary to get these students moving in the right direction.

CAUTION: Structured reinforcement systems can help students make difficult behavior changes. However, if the reinforcement system is not carefully planned and gradually removed, the above concerns with this approach may become realities. Be prepared for a long, involved process if you want the system to have a long-term impact on the student's ability to take responsibility.

Essential Planning Steps

STEP 1 Define the problem, describe its context, and identify replacement behaviors.

Review the problem and overall goals for the student. Defining the nature and scope of the problem provides critical information for developing a successful intervention. Be sure you have a clear idea of the specific goals the intervention will be designed to achieve—that is, what will be different about the student's behavior after the intervention?

Once you determine the overall goals, identify exactly what the student must do or not do to demonstrate improvement. Is the objective to increase a positive behavior or decrease a negative behavior? Is the purpose to do more of something or less of something? If work completion is a problem, the goal will be to increase work completion. In the case of swearing or throwing tantrums, the goal will be to reduce the negative behavior. In some instances, the objective will be to decrease a negative behavior and increase a positive one. For example, if a student has poor peer interactions, the goal will be to decrease negative interactions while increasing positive interactions.

BEFORE IMPLEMENTING THIS STRATEGY

Before this intervention can be successfully implemented, be sure that you have discussed the problem and general goals for improvement with the teacher and student. Gather any relevant background information that may help in designing and implementing the intervention. Contact the student's parents or guardian to discuss the problem, and keep them informed of all aspects of the intervention plan.

In addition to determining what the student must do, you should identify when and where the student will be expected to make changes. If major changes are required, the student will need to make improvements in small increments. Change should not be expected all at once in all settings. Prioritize the settings and periods of the day that are most problematic and urgent to address.

NOTE: If you use the problem-solving model and tools that were introduced and applied at different stages of a problem in Section 2, at the point of intervention design you should have already defined target behaviors, identified replacement behaviors, and set goals for improvement. Use this information to complete Step 1. If you need additional support, see Section 3, Task 1 (p. 238).

STEP 2 Choose a method for monitoring student behaviors and counting points.

Once you identify specific behaviors, select a method for monitoring behavior and providing the student with rewards for successfully meeting objectives. Behavior can be monitored in a number of different ways.

a. *Count a positive, appropriate behavior.* If the goal of the intervention is to increase the frequency of a specific discrete behavior, counting the number of times a student engages in a positive behavior may be an effective monitoring system. For example, if a shy student doesn't interact with peers, you might design a system to count the number of times she interacts with classmates. If a student blurts out inappropriate answers, you might count the number of times he raises his hand, waits to be called on, and makes reasonable contributions to a discussion.

The monitoring system might be as simple as the Behavior Counting Grid (Reproducible 4.2a). Each time the student demonstrates the desired behavior, circle a number. You might also use a tally system (Figure 4.2a) or a simple graph (Reproducible 4.2b, p. 350) to count and record positive behaviors. In all of these systems, the student would earn a point for each positive behavior demonstrated.

FIGURE 4.2a *Positive Comments Tally*

Number of Positive Comments
ℎℎℎ̶ II

b. *Count both an appropriate behavior and an inappropriate behavior.* If the goal of the intervention is to encourage an appropriate behavior and reduce a related inappropriate one, counting both types of behavior may be necessary. Monitoring

REPRODUCIBLE 4.2a *Behavior Counting Grid*

Behavior Counting Grid

Name _____   Class/Period _____
Teacher _____

Behavior _____   Date _____

1	2	3	4	5	6	7	8	9	10
11	12	13	14	15	16	17	18	19	20

Behavior _____   Date _____

1	2	3	4	5	6	7	8	9	10
11	12	13	14	15	16	17	18	19	20

Behavior _____   Date _____

1	2	3	4	5	6	7	8	9	10
11	12	13	14	15	16	17	18	19	20

Behavior _____   Date _____

1	2	3	4	5	6	7	8	9	10
11	12	13	14	15	16	17	18	19	20

Interventions © 2019 Ancora Publishing

REPRODUCIBLE 4.2b *Behavior Counting Graph*

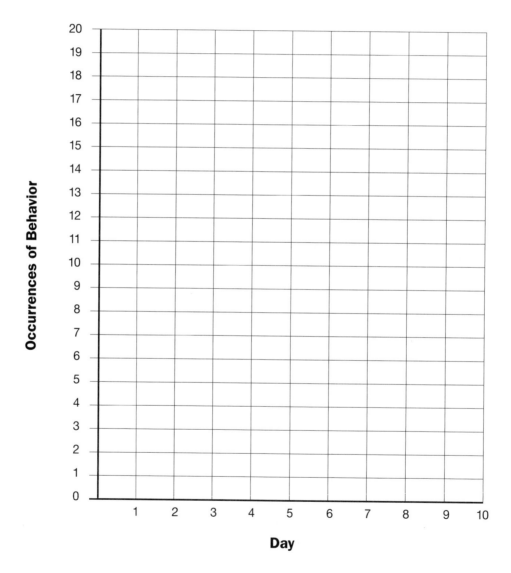

only appropriate behavior may present a false picture, as the tally will not reflect inappropriate behaviors that are still occurring and problematic. For example, a student who has difficulty interacting in a friendly manner with adults might also have a corresponding problem of aggressive, adversarial interactions with adults. If the intervention monitors only friendly interactions, the student may appear to be more successful than he is: "Nathan engaged in five positive interactions" presents a very different picture from "Nathan engaged in five positive interactions and fifteen adversarial interactions."

In such a case, you might choose the monitoring system shown on the Positive/Negative Behavior Scaling Form (Reproducible 4.2c), where a student earns points based on the ratio of appropriate to inappropriate behaviors. For example, a student who makes negative comments to peers might earn a point for every hour that her positive comments exceed her negative comments to classmates.

c. *Record appropriate or inappropriate behavior that occurs within specific time intervals.* Many interventions are designed to help a student eliminate annoying, disruptive, or immature behaviors. Although the goal of the intervention should always be stated positively, success may actually be determined by the absence or reduction of an inappropriate behavior within a specified time interval. For example, if a student throws tantrums, the goal may be to demonstrate self-control. In this case, the monitoring system would track the number of tantrums that occur within a specified time interval and award points for reductions in the number of outbursts.

The sample Positive/Negative Behavior Tracking Form—30-Min Intervals (Reproducible 4.2d) shows a system for monitoring a student's goal behavior in half-hour intervals. This monitoring schedule would be appropriate for use with a student who tends to engage in inappropriate behavior four to six times per day. The short monitoring intervals allow the student to experience success despite the high rate of inappropriate behavior. For example, the teacher records a plus (+) for every interval in which the student treats others with dignity and respect, and a minus (-) for any interval in which the student makes negative comments toward peers. The student then earns a point for every interval with a plus (+) recorded.

Positive/Negative Behavior Tracking Form—90-Min Intervals (Reproducible 4.2e) shows the same type of system designed for use with a student who engages in problematic behavior less frequently. For example, a student who tantrums once or twice per day might earn a point for each interval in which he exhibits the goal behavior—demonstrating self-control.

Finally, another simple system to consider involves recording every incidence of the misbehavior during a specified interval of time and determining whether the total number of occurrences is less than (for inappropriate behavior) or greater than (for appropriate behavior) a defined goal. For example, you might count each disrespectful comment a student makes during a specified time interval. The student's goal is to make no more than a prespecified number of disrespectful comments during each interval. A point will be awarded for each interval in which the student keeps negative comments below the predetermined number.

continued on page 355

REPRODUCIBLE 4.2c *Positive/Negative Behavior Scaling Form*

Positive/Negative Behavior Scaling Form

Name _____ Grade/Class _____

Teacher _____ Date _____

Goal _____

Time	Positive	1	2	3	4	5	6	7	8	9	10
_____	Negative	1	2	3	4	5	6	7	8	9	10

Time	Positive	1	2	3	4	5	6	7	8	9	10
_____	Negative	1	2	3	4	5	6	7	8	9	10

Time	Positive	1	2	3	4	5	6	7	8	9	10
_____	Negative	1	2	3	4	5	6	7	8	9	10

Time	Positive	1	2	3	4	5	6	7	8	9	10
_____	Negative	1	2	3	4	5	6	7	8	9	10

Time	Positive	1	2	3	4	5	6	7	8	9	10
_____	Negative	1	2	3	4	5	6	7	8	9	10

Interventions © 2019 Ancora Publishing

REPRODUCIBLE 4.2e *Positive/Negative Behavior Tracking Form (30-minute intervals)*

Positive/Negative Behavior Tracking Form (30-minute intervals)

Name **Zach Turnball** Grade/Class **6**
Teacher **Ms. Howard** Week of **3/15**
Goal **Treat others with dignity and respect**

Time	Rating (+/−)				
	Monday	Tuesday	Wednesday	Thursday	Friday
8:00 – 8:30	N/A				
8:30 – 9:00	+				
9:00 – 9:30	+				
9:30 – 10:00	−				
10:00 – 10:30	+				
10:30 – 11:00	+				
11:00 – 11:30	−				
11:30 – 12:00	−				
12:00 – 12:30	+				
12:30 – 1:00	+				
1:00 – 1:30	+				
1:30 – 2:00	−				
2:00 – 2:30	+				
2:30 – 3:00	N/A				
Points earned	8				

Interventions © 2019 Ancora Publishing

REPRODUCIBLE 4.2d

REPRODUCIBLE 4.2e *Positive/Negative Behavior Tracking Form (90-minute intervals)*

> A version with blank intervals is available to download (see Reproducible 4.2e Alt).

Positive/Negative Behavior Tracking Form (90-minute intervals)

Name: __Shelly Burnquist__ Grade/Class: __6__
Teacher: __Ms. Howard__ Week of: __3/15__
Goal: __Demonstrate self-control__

Time	Rating (+/−) Monday	Tuesday	Wednesday	Thursday	Friday
8:00 – 9:30	+				
9:30 – 11:00	−				
11:00 – 12:30	+				
12:30 – 2:00	+				
2:00 – 3:30	−				
Points earned	3				

Time	Rating (+/−) Monday	Tuesday	Wednesday	Thursday	Friday
8:00 – 9:30					
9:30 – 11:00					
11:00 – 12:30					
12:30 – 2:00					
2:00 – 3:30					
Points earned					

Time	Rating (+/−) Monday	Tuesday	Wednesday	Thursday	Friday
8:00 – 9:30					
9:30 – 11:00					
11:00 – 12:30					
12:30 – 2:00					
2:00 – 3:30					
Points earned					

Interventions © 2019 Ancora Publishing

Positive/Negative Behavior Limit Form—30-Min Intervals (Reproducible 4.2f) shows an example of what this system would look like.

Versions of the Positive/Negative Behavior Tracking and Limit forms with customizable time intervals are provided for download (see p. 564 for directions). Select time intervals that allow the student to see a high rate of success. A rule of thumb is to establish intervals that guarantee success at least 50% of the time without making any changes to current behavior. The student who experiences success in the early stages of the intervention will be motivated to make improvements. As the student shows progress, you can gradually adjust the time intervals.

d. *Count completed work.* If the goal of the intervention is to increase work completion, consider monitoring the number of assignments or problems completed in a specified period of time. With this monitoring system, award the student points for each assignment completed, each half assignment completed, or for a certain number of problems completed, depending on the severity of the problem. Create a system where the chances of success are high. If the student rarely completes an assignment, avoid setting goals that are too stringent. As the student achieves goals, the student will begin to learn that success feels good.

Make sure to also clarify expectations in terms of correctness and neatness. Because some students may focus solely on work completion and neglect quality, the system should specify that points will be earned not only for quantity of work completed, but also for the quality of the work. The criteria for quantity and quality should be based on what the student can reasonably do. Use a copy of acceptable work previously completed by the student as a model for neatness. Set the criterion for correctness at 80%, 90%, or even 100% with opportunities to correct errors. The criterion for success can gradually be increased as the student gains competency. The fact that work will not earn any points until it meets quality expectations reduces the chance that the student will rush simply to get the work done.

e. *Rate a behavior on a predetermined scale.* If the target behavior is difficult to count, or if the student is just learning to exhibit a replacement behavior and can demonstrate only certain elements of that behavior, consider using a rating scale. Rating scales are useful when behavior needs to improve in quality or across a number of dimensions.

With a rating scale, award a variable number of points based on the degree to which the student exhibits a particular behavior. For example, as shown in the sample Behavior Rating Form (Reproducible 4.2g), Nila might receive points based on how well she is able to follow directions, where 0 = Not at all, 1 = Needed reminders, and 2 = Followed directions independently.

You can download a version of the Behavior Rating Form (Reproducible 4.2g Alt) with blank anchors so that you can define what 0, 1, and 2 look like for a specific target behavior.

f. *Record the length of time a student engages in a particular behavior.* If the student's goal includes reducing not only the frequency of a behavior but also the duration, you may need to keep track of the amount of time the student engages in that behavior. For example, if a student engages in lengthy and frequent crying bouts, the goal might be to become more self-sufficient, to learn self-control, or to act more grown up. Monitoring only the number of times the student cries may not

continued on page 358

REPRODUCIBLE 4.2f *Positive/Negative Behavior Limit Form (30-minute intervals)*

> A version with blank intervals is available to download (see Reproducible 4.2f Alt).

Positive/Negative Behavior Limit Form (30-minute intervals)

Name: **Alexa Bropohy** Grade/Class: **6**
Teacher: **Ms. Howard** Week of: **3/15**
Goal: **Talk respectfully to others (less than four disrespectful comments in any half hour demonstrates improvement for this week).**

Time	Number of Behaviors								
8:00 – 8:30	①	②	③	④	⑤	6	7	8	9	10
8:30 – 9:00	①	②	③	④	5	6	7	8	9	10
9:00 – 9:30	①	②	③	④	⑤	⑥	⑦	8	9	10
9:30 – 10:00	①	②	3	4	5	6	7	8	9	10
10:00 – 10:30	①	②	3	4	5	6	7	8	9	10
10:30 – 11:00	①	②	③	④	5	6	7	8	9	10
11:00 – 11:30	①	②	3	4	5	6	7	8	9	10
11:30 – 12:00	①	②	③	④	⑤	⑥	⑦	⑧	⑨	10
12:00 – 12:30	①	②	3	4	5	6	7	8	9	10
12:30 – 1:00	①	②	③	④	⑤	6	7	8	9	10
1:00 – 1:30	①	②	③	④	⑤	⑥	⑦	8	9	10
1:30 – 2:00	①	②	③	④	5	6	7	8	9	10
2:00 – 2:30	①	②	③	④	⑤	6	7	8	9	10
2:30 – 3:00	①	②	③	4	5	6	7	8	9	10

Interventions © 2019 Ancora Publishing

REPRODUCIBLE 4.2g *Positive/Negative Behavior Limit Form (30-minute intervals)*

Behavior Rating Form

Name Nila Purdy
Goal Follow directions right away

POINTS:
- 0 = Not at all
- 1 = Needed reminders
- 2 = Followed directions independently

Week of: 5/12

Day	AM			PM			Total
Monday	0	1	②	⓪	1	2	2
Tuesday	0	1	②	0	①	2	3
Wednesday	0	1	2	0	1	2	
Thursday	0	1	2	0	1	2	
Friday	0	1	2	0	1	2	

Week of:

Day	AM			PM			Total
Monday	0	1	2	0	1	2	
Tuesday	0	1	2	0	1	2	
Wednesday	0	1	2	0	1	2	
Thursday	0	1	2	0	1	2	
Friday	0	1	2	0	1	2	

Week of:

Day	AM			PM			Total
Monday	0	1	2	0	1	2	
Tuesday	0	1	2	0	1	2	
Wednesday	0	1	2	0	1	2	
Thursday	0	1	2	0	1	2	
Friday	0	1	2	0	1	2	

Interventions © 2019 Ancora Publishing

REPRODUCIBLE 4.1d

be sufficient to determine whether the student is meeting the goal. Six short incidents will appear far worse than a two-hour-long sobbing bout if only frequency is recorded. Duration recording may be more appropriate in this situation.

To monitor duration, simply start a stopwatch any time the student engages in the inappropriate behavior, stop the watch when the behavior ceases, and restart it if the inappropriate behavior begins again. If the stopwatch is not reset, the total amount of time the student engages in the inappropriate behavior will be recorded cumulatively throughout the day. Award points when the total duration of the inappropriate behavior remains below a predetermined amount.

When considering options for monitoring target behaviors and counting points, make sure that the system you choose is feasible to implement, acceptable to the teacher or other staff member who will be in charge of monitoring, and age appropriate and interesting to the student. See Section 3, Task 8 (p. 289) for more monitoring options, additional considerations in selecting data collection methods, and examples of reproducible forms.

STEP 3 Outline a plan for implementation and data collection.

When creating a plan for using a structured reinforcement system, make sure to incorporate the following components.

Specify when and where the reinforcement system will be used. Determine what settings, activities, or time intervals to monitor and when points will be awarded. You may decide to use the system for the whole school day, part of the day, or during certain situations and activities. This decision will largely depend on the frequency and severity of the problem and the method you have chosen to monitor student behavior. Plan to start using the reinforcement system in a setting or during an activity that is challenging for the student, but where the student has the highest likelihood of experiencing success. Don't expect change to occur all at once across all settings. For example, if a student has a difficult time with on-task behavior, the first 5 minutes of an activity may be best to target as your initial focus. As the student achieves success, you can gradually expand objectives for longer periods of time and across settings so that the new skills generalize.

Create a menu of possible rewards. When you meet with the student to discuss the structured reinforcement system, the student will select rewards from this menu. Consider rewards that are tailored to the interests of the student. Remember that privileges and responsibilities are often as powerful as material items. The list of possible rewards is endless. (A list of reward ideas appears in Appendix B.) Some ideas include:

- Providing a homework pass (i.e., a chance to skip one assignment)
- Calling the student's grandmother with a good report
- Initiating an activity at home, such as playing a game with Mom
- Spending extra time on the computer
- Granting 5 minutes to play outside
- Getting to be a messenger
- Making cookies after school in the home economics room
- Operating equipment
- Taking care of a class pet

When you create a menu of possible rewards:

- *Provide suggestions and then brainstorm other ideas with the student.* Encourage as many ideas as possible when brainstorming. When the list is completed, help the student select rewards that are feasible.
- *Try to include a few reward options that align with the function of the student's misbehavior.* For example, a student who fails to complete seat work because she is frequently out of seat and socializing with peers could work to earn her choice of seat once she earns enough points from completing her assignments.
- *Consider incorporating mystery rewards.* Adding an unknown component to the reinforcement system can increase student interest in and excitement about the system. For example, write the name of each reward from your menu on a piece of paper, put these papers in an envelope, and have the student draw a paper once they have earned enough points for a reward. Alternatively, create or adapt a game-type spinner, divided into five or more sections of various sizes, with the name of a different reward on each section. When the student reaches a point goal, they can spin the spinner to determine their reward.

Determine how many points will be required for the student to earn each reward. When setting goals for the amount or quality of the goal behavior that the student must demonstrate to earn a reward, consider the monitoring system, the amount of time and effort required of the student, the sophistication of the student, and the value of the reward in terms of cost and adult time required. As you work out the details of the plan, consider these guidelines:

The student should view the behavior goals and the criteria for earning rewards as achievable

- *Rewards should be quickly earned in the initial phases of the intervention.* The student should view the behavior goals and the criteria for earning rewards as achievable. When presented with the system, the student should be thinking, "I can do that." A common error is to design a reinforcement system that requires the student to make large and fairly immediate changes in behavior. If the system is too difficult, the student may not try or may not be able to sustain the effort.
- *Reinforcement menus are useful so that the student has a variety of rewards from which to choose.* However, if the student is likely to select rewards that will take too long to earn, structure an initial menu of only easy-to-earn rewards. As the student gains sophistication, more difficult-to-earn rewards can be added to the menu.
- *If the student shows no interest in small rewards but needs fairly immediate gratification, structure a reinforcement ladder.* This type of reinforcement system allows the student to earn smaller rewards on the way to the ultimate goal. As each reward is earned, the student does not "spend" the required points. Instead, points accumulate as the student proceeds up the ladder. Figure 4.2b on the next page shows a reinforcement ladder.
- *Avoid putting time limits on what the student must do to earn rewards.* Systems that involve a certain number of points by the end of the day or by the end of the week have some inherent weaknesses. First, they tend to be too inflexible. If a student must complete five homework assignments in a week to earn a reward but she completes only four assignments, she may feel discouraged by having to

FIGURE 4.2b *Reinforcement Ladder*

Reward	Points
Pizza with the principal	100
Read to the kindergarten students	90
15 minutes game time with friend	80
15 minutes computer time	70
Choose a class job	60
Certificate from the principal	50
Pick a prize	40
Run off papers	30
Certificate from teacher	20
Game with teacher	10

begin over again the next week. Always give credit for success the student has achieved, irrespective of the student's pace. Time limits also create problems if the student begins the day or week unsuccessfully. The student may realize early in the week that success is not possible no matter how well she does the rest of the week. Reinforcement systems must have forgiveness built in. A bad day or a bad hour should not overshadow positive efforts, negate previous efforts, or eliminate reinforcement for future efforts. Therefore, instead of setting up a system as "Earn 5 points by Friday," set it up as, "As soon as you earn 5 points, you can spend them on a reward."

Contact the student's parents/guardians to discuss the reinforcement system. Introduce the plan, share the goals of the reinforcement system, and invite the parent to be an active partner in its implementation. The easiest and safest way to do this is to have the student earn rewards or privileges at home in addition to, but not in place of, the rewards or privileges earned at school. Develop a menu of home-based rewards in addition to a menu of school-based rewards and make a plan for communicating with parents about the points the student has earned at school. Make sure that parents are willing to follow through if they volunteer to offer home-based rewards. In spite of assurances, there is a risk that if the student misbehaves at home, the parents will not provide the reward for school-based points, which would defeat any positive gains from the system. At a minimum, therefore, ensure that school-based points lead to school-based rewards. That way, if the parents wish to assist, home-based rewards are simply a nice supplement to the program.

Make a plan for data collection and monitoring. Identify ways to determine whether the intervention is helping the student reach the goals. The forms that your reinforcement system requires offer a built-in record of student progress. Keep dated records so that you can analyze progress and adjust the system periodically.

Consider supplemental intervention strategies to incorporate into the plan. Identify other strategies that might support or increase the effectiveness of the structured reinforcement system in changing behavior. For example:

- *Antecedent strategies:* Consider whether modifying structural elements, such as changing seating arrangements or schedules, delivering precorrections to remind

- *Teaching strategies:* If the reinforcement system involves demonstrating new behaviors or generalizing behaviors to a new setting, schedule short, regular lessons with the interventionist or teacher to provide opportunities for the student to practice, refine, and receive feedback on these behaviors.
- *Positive consequence strategies:* In addition to the contingent rewards that will be delivered when the student makes progress, ensure that the student receives high rates of praise and specific feedback for demonstrating appropriate behavior, making efforts, and meeting goals. For example, share behavior goals and successes with the student's family and other staff members who regularly interact with the student and ask them to provide as much encouragement, feedback, and praise as possible.
- *Corrective consequence strategies:* If the student's goal involves eliminating or reducing an inappropriate behavior, staff should be prepared to respond fluently and consistently to misbehavior. You may need to define the limits of appropriate and inappropriate behavior in more detail, preplan a range of corrective responses, explicitly teach limits and discuss corrective consequences with the student, and work closely with staff members to ensure that they deliver corrections fluently and effectively.
- *Interactional strategies.* Consider ways to increase the frequency of noncontingent positive attention across different settings and situations at school. If needed, encourage the student to engage in the school community through participating in school clubs or activities, assuming a meaningful role in the school, or connecting with an adult or peer mentor.
- *Specialized strategies:* To help clarify goals and procure a more formal commitment from the student to work on changing behavior, the structured reinforcement system may be implemented in conjunction with a behavior contract (see Section 4.1: Behavioral Contracting). Once the student is successful in meeting goals, it may be useful to have the student begin self-monitoring and progressively take on more responsibility for tracking their own behavior and evaluating progress (see Section 4.3: Self-Monitoring and Self-Evaluation).

Outline roles and responsibilities for implementing the plan. At this point, the intervention plan should include objectives for improved behavior, a monitoring system, a menu of possible rewards, proposed point values for earning rewards, and specification of consequences if needed. Summarize the plan and then try to anticipate any possible glitches by asking *what-if* questions. The more time you spend mentally rehearsing how the system will work, the greater the likelihood that you will find and remedy glitches before they sabotage an otherwise strong intervention. Also make sure to identify:

- Who will meet with the student to discuss the plan and negotiate rewards.
- Who will be responsible for keeping track of points and delivering rewards.
- Who will work with the student to teach and practice new behaviors, if needed.
- Who will be responsible for data collection, and how data will be collected and summarized.
- Who will need training.

Provide training to teachers and other adults who will be implementing the plan. All adults who will be involved in awarding points and implementing the reinforcement system should receive training on procedures. Plan to explain when, why, and how to award points, how to respond to misbehavior, and how to collect data. Use Implementation Guidelines: Structured Reinforcement (Reproducible 4.2h, pp. 367–370) to review procedures with staff. Also make sure to distribute relevant forms for recording points and monitoring progress.

Case Example: Tracy

Tracy is a second-grade student who always moves extremely slowly. When the teacher, Mr. Dryer, says, "Put your things away and line up," all of the students follow instructions and are in line before Tracy even starts to put her things away. Because Mr. Dryer cannot leave Tracy or the class unsupervised, everyone must wait for her. Even with constant reminders and peer pressure, Tracy continually keeps everyone waiting. This happens several times a day. When at recess, Tracy walks slowly around the playground or just stands in one place. Watching Tracy is like watching a very old person, not a seven-year-old child.

Tracy's mother is under doctor's care and is heavily medicated for psychiatric problems. Her father is a long-haul trucker who is rarely at home. When meeting with Tracy's mother, the school counselor, Ms. Thompson, sees an older version of Tracy. Tracy's mother operates as if she is moving underwater—everything is slow and laborious, including speech. Although communication is difficult, Tracy's mother does say that she hopes that school will help Tracy learn to do things "more like other little girls." She adds, "I am just too tired to help." Working with Tracy's mother, Ms. Thompson arranges for Tracy to be examined by a physician. The physician concludes that Tracy is in perfect health and that her slow behavior is not a medical problem.

Based on the above information, the problem-solving team determines that teaching Tracy to move more efficiently should be the goal of the intervention plan. In analyzing the nature of the problem, the team hypothesizes that Tracy's slow-moving behavior is learned, and may be motivated by the attention Tracy receives from the adults and peers in school as they try to make her move faster.

The team plans to have Tracy meet with Ms. Thompson daily for 10-minute lessons to learn and practice moving efficiently. Once Tracy demonstrates that she can move efficiently 80% of the time during the practice sessions, Tracy will begin working on moving efficiently during four specific transitions that occur each day in the classroom. After each transition, Mr. Dryer will rate the efficiency of Tracy's movement on a 0–3 scale, where:

3 = Efficient—Moves independently, quickly, and purposefully during the transition

2 = Better—Moves quickly, but needs one reminder to stay focused on the transition

1 = OK—Moves slowly, but stays focused on the transition
0 = Not OK—Needs more than one reminder about staying focused on accomplishing the transition

These ratings will be translated into points, with each point equating to 30 seconds, that Tracy can save up and use to purchase 5 minutes of computer game time or time with Mr. Dryer during lunch. Tracy has the opportunity to earn a total of 12 points each day. Mr. Dryer will record the points that Tracy earns each day.

Every 2 weeks, the team will evaluate Tracy's progress. Once Tracy is earning 80% of possible points on 4 out of 5 days each week, a self-evaluation process will be introduced, in which Tracy will rate her own behavior during each transition. Ms. Thompson will continue daily lessons with Tracy, but will begin expanding the context of moving efficiently. For example, Ms. Thompson will provide guidance on interacting with peers on the playground and playing a game during recess. Mr. Dryer and Ms. Thompson will meet monthly to subjectively assess whether Tracy's "efficient behavior" is generalizing to other contexts. If it is not, they will expand the structured reinforcement system to apply beyond the four daily transitions initially targeted in the plan.

Essential Implementation Procedures

The teacher or interventionist responsible for implementing the plan should make sure to:

1. **Meet with the student to discuss and finalize the plan.** During this meeting:

- Explain that you would like to help the student be more successful at school.
- Present the goals of the system and how they will help the student be more successful at school.
- Discuss possible rewards and create a list of rewards that the student is motivated to work for.
- Explain how the structured reinforcement system works, clearly outlining what the student must do to earn points, when and where points can be earned, and the process for exchanging points for rewards.
- Specify behaviors that will not earn points and any corrective consequences that will be used in response to certain misbehaviors.
- Encourage student buy-in to the rewards and the system itself. As much as possible, engage the student in helping to plan the system and encourage the student to voice any suggestions, questions, or concerns.
- Make sure the student understands the goals of the system, the desired outcome, and the benefits. The more engaged the student is in the discussion, the greater the likelihood that the student will take ownership of the plan.

2. **Practice and role-play appropriate responses with the student.** Once you identify the expectations or plan objectives, model the expected behaviors and have the student role-play or verbally rehearse them. Practice recording and summarizing behavior on the monitoring forms so the student will be prepared for what this looks like.

> Items 1–9 are also shown on **Implementation Guidelines** (Form 4.2h, pp. 367–370). Share with teachers and other adults who are responsible for implementing the plan.

> **BEFORE MEETING WITH THE STUDENT**
>
> Once the system has been carefully outlined, determine who will meet with the student to discuss behavior goals and plans for using the reinforcement system. This meeting may include the interventionist, the teacher, other staff members, and the student's parents.

3. Implement the reinforcement system during specified times and settings. When working with the student on a daily basis, make sure to consistently implement the system and award points based on the details of the intervention plan. Maximize the effectiveness of the system by incorporating the following tips:

- Deliver points and rewards as immediately as possible. The longer the student has wait, the less effective the reward will be as positive reinforcement. This is particularly true for younger students (Cooper, Heron, & Heward, 2007).
- Be enthusiastic. Pairing congratulatory comments and excitement with point delivery will strengthen the value of the reward (Alberto & Troutman, 2012). It will also help you set the stage for the later transition from external rewards to more natural reinforcers, such as praise and acknowledgment.

4. Acknowledge the student whenever they earn a point. Whenever the student earns a point, offer specific praise or nonverbal positive feedback (e.g., a thumbs-up or nod). Feedback should focus on appropriate behavior. Avoid comments that remind the student of any negative behavior. Rather than saying, "Nice job, Tracy. You didn't keep the class waiting before lunch," focus on the goal behavior: "Tracy, nice job. You put your things away fairly quickly and lined up with the class. You've earned another point."

5. Respond calmly and consistently to misbehavior. If you need to deliver a correction, minimize attention by remaining calm and using brief, neutral statements. The student is less likely to be reinforced for the misbehavior when corrections are calm, brief, and consistent.

6. Meet and debrief with the student regularly. Meet with the student during the first week of the plan to see how things are going and to determine whether the plan needs revision. If the system is working, celebrate the student's success and continue using the system without any changes for another week or so. Once the intervention seems to be working well, check in with the student on a weekly basis. Review any collected data with the student, highlight successes, and discuss any behaviors that can be improved.

If the system is not working after the first week, identify any minor adjustments you might make to improve the chance of student success. Consider:

- *Does the student understand the system?* To check for understanding, ask the student to explain the system or show you what must be done to earn a point or reward.
- *Does the student care about the rewards that have been identified?* If not, brainstorm with the student to find alternatives that they might be more motivated to earn. If the student is interested only in big rewards, consider a reinforcement ladder (Figure 4.2b).
- *Is the system designed so the student has little chance of success?* Check whether the behavior expectations require too much change at once and adjust the system accordingly.
- *Is the student getting too much attention from the teacher or peers for exhibiting the problem behaviors?* If so, identify ways to minimize adult attention for misbehavior and increase the ratio of positive to corrective interactions with the student. (See strategies for increasing contingent and noncontingent positive interactions in Task 4 and Task 6 of Section 3.)

7. Use data to make periodic revisions and adjustments to the plan as necessary. As you monitor the student's progress, make adjustments to the plan as needed. If the student's behavior isn't improving, ask the following questions:

- *Are all essential components of the plan being implemented as intended?* Ensure that intervention fidelity is maintained by having the teacher or external observer complete the Fidelity Checklist: Structured Reinforcement (Reproducible 4.2i, p. 371).
- *Which aspects of the plan can you modify to increase its effectiveness?* Are rewards no longer motivating to the student? Do rewards take too long to earn, so the student is not able to experience regular success? If so, adjust the system.
- *What supplemental strategies can you introduce to support the effectiveness of the plan?* Incorporating other intervention strategies, such as using precorrections to remind the student of behavior expectations, reducing peer attention for misbehavior, and providing more opportunities for practice and feedback on new behaviors might help to encourage improvement in the student's behavior.
- *Is the student getting their needs met through the plan?* Consider whether your plan adequately addresses the student's needs and hypothesized function of misbehavior by reviewing information and collecting more data about the problem's context.

8. Once the student demonstrates consistent success, implement fading procedures. After a reinforcement system is successful, you should gradually modify it so the student becomes motivated by reinforcers that are part of the teacher's daily routine and inherent in the classroom atmosphere—praise, positive interactions, notes on papers, grades, satisfaction, and others. After at least 2 weeks of success, introduce one or more of these fading procedures.

- *Require more points to earn the same rewards.* Once the student is consistently successful in earning rewards, increase the price of rewards. For example, rewards that used to cost 4 points might now cost 6 points.
- *Increase the time monitored before the student earns points.* If the student is earning points for demonstrating self-control during half-hour intervals, you might increase the intervals to 45 minutes.
- *Move to intermittent reinforcement:* Provide a reward only on some occasions when the student meets the performance criteria. For example, Luis is initially rewarded each day he meets his point goal. After a few weeks of daily success, the system is modified so that a reward is given only on some randomly selected days when Luis meets the point goal. He does not know in advance which days are reward days and which are not.
- *Redefine expectations.* For a student who aimlessly wanders around the classroom, the initial expectation might be to stay in a specific work area. When the student has successfully met this expectation for a couple of weeks, you might expand the expectation to be staying in her seat for a specific length of time.
- *Move to more natural reinforcers.* Natural reinforcers are activities or things in the school setting that students find rewarding. Over time, move the student from tangible rewards to internal ones, such as taking pride in success and recognition.

For example, once a student demonstrates she can be on time to class, she might earn the responsibility of being a hall monitor during transitions.

The most important concept in fading the system is the word *gradual*. One of the most frequent errors in using a reinforcement system is to change it abruptly as soon as the student is successful. In most cases, students quickly revert back to problem behaviors. The student must have a couple of weeks of success before you make any change to the system. The student should feel in control of the system before modifications are made.

Each time the system becomes more sophisticated, make sure to inform the student in advance of the change and increase the amount of praise and attention the student receives. Emphasize the student's success and sense of accomplishment. This will help the student accept the changes and take pride in the fact that the system is growing more demanding.

Once the student has experienced 2 or more weeks of success, introduce another very gradual change. Continue adjusting the system until the student is engaging in positive behavior with minimal rewards. Eventually, give the student the option of discontinuing the system.

Some students will readily agree to discontinuing the system, while others will be more reluctant. When a student isn't yet ready to give up the structure, or if there are concerns about whether the student will be able to maintain gains after the system is discontinued, consider the following options:

- Continue to implement the system, but keep introducing fading procedures.
- Transition the student to self-manage all aspects of the system and to work for very minimal rewards (see Section 4.3: Self-Monitoring and Self-Evaluation).
- Continue to implement the system for the rest of the school year. As long as the intervention is easy to implement and not too expensive, continue it as needed. The team can reevaluate the situation at the beginning of the next school year.

If the student's behavior deteriorates after you introduce fading procedures, the change may be too big or too abrupt. Offer the option of reverting back to the previously implemented plan, or adjust fading procedures to be more gradual.

9. Once the intervention has been faded, provide continued follow-up, support, and encouragement. Changing behavior is a difficult process. Once the student has begun achieving the goals, it is easy to take appropriate behavior for granted. Remember that the student will need continued positive feedback throughout the fading process.

Strategy Summary

Setting up structured reinforcement systems may be time consuming, but if simpler solutions have been ineffective, active reinforcement has a high likelihood of jump-starting improvement. Initially, a reinforcement system works by motivating the student to earn rewards, but the sense of satisfaction the student derives from achievement may in time generate more intrinsic motivation to behave appropriately. Over time, success tends to foster more success.

REPRODUCIBLE 4.2h *Implementation Guidelines: Structured Reinforcement (1 of 4)*

Implementation Guidelines
Structured Reinforcement

Overview

A structured reinforcement system motivates students to break deeply ingrained cycles of inappropriate behavior by offering them external reinforcements or rewards. Once the student begins to experience success, external reinforcements can be faded and eventually removed.

Many students find natural success and encouragement in the classroom. They take pride in their accomplishments and feel a sense of satisfaction at completing a task. Other students may require more motivation to meet expectations and succeed in school (Stipek, 1993; Brophy, 2004). For the student who has experienced little academic success or who has had behavior problems, you may initially need to use tangible rewards to spark the student's motivation to change.

When problems have been resistant to change or when a student needs additional encouragement to demonstrate desired behavior, a structured system for rewarding increased positive behavior or decreased rates of inappropriate behavior can provide an extra boost of motivation and help make success a reality for the student.

Plan Summary

A reinforcement system will be used at these times in these settings: _____

to monitor the following behaviors: _____

_____

Points will be awarded when these conditions are met: _____

_____

Menu of rewards and their cost (in points): _____

_____

_____

_____

_____

The person responsible for tracking points and delivering rewards is: _____

Once the student is successful, the system will be faded by: _____

_____

Other notes: _____

_____

REPRODUCIBLE 4.2h *Implementation Guidelines: Structured Reinforcement (2 of 4)*

Implementation Guidelines: Structured Reinforcement

Implementation Steps

1. **Meet with the student to discuss and finalize the plan.**

   In this meeting:

   - Explain that you would like to assist the student in being more successful at school.
   - Present the goals of the reinforcement system and explain how they will help the student be more successful at school.
   - Discuss possible rewards and create a list of rewards that the student is motivated to work for.
   - Explain how the structured reinforcement system works, clearly outlining what the student must do to earn points, when and where points can be earned, and the process for exchanging points for rewards.
   - Specify behaviors that will not earn points and any corrective consequences that will be used in response to certain misbehaviors.
   - Encourage student buy-in to the rewards and the system itself. As much as possible, engage the student in helping to plan the system and encourage any suggestions, questions, or concerns.
   - Make sure the student understands the goals of the system, the desired outcome, and the benefits. The more engaged the student is in the discussion, the greater the likelihood that the student will take ownership of the plan.

2. **Practice and role-play appropriate responses.**

   Once you identify the expectations or plan objectives, model the expected behaviors and have the student role-play or verbally rehearse them. Practice recording and summarizing behavior on the monitoring forms so the student will be prepared for what this looks like.

3. **Implement the reinforcement system during specified times and settings.**

   When working with the student on a daily basis, make sure to consistently implement the system and award points based on the details of the intervention plan. Maximize the effectiveness of the system by incorporating the following tips:

   - Deliver points and rewards as immediately as possible. The longer the student has to wait, the less effective the reward will be as positive reinforcement. This is particularly true for younger students (Cooper, Heron, & Heward, 2007).
   - Be enthusiastic. Pairing congratulatory comments and excitement with point delivery will strengthen the value of the reward (Alberto & Troutman, 2012). It will also help set the stage for later transitioning from external rewards to more natural reinforcers, such as praise and acknowledgment.

4. **Acknowledge the student whenever they earn a point.**

   Whenever a student earns a point, offer specific praise or nonverbal positive feedback (e.g., a thumbs-up or nod). Feedback should focus on appropriate behavior. Avoid comments that remind the student about negative behavior. Rather than saying, "Nice job, Tracy. You didn't keep the class waiting for lunch," focus on the goal behavior: "Tracy, nice job. You put your things away fairly quickly and lined up with the class. You've earned another point."

REPRODUCIBLE 4.2h *Implementation Guidelines: Structured Reinforcement (3 of 4)*

Implementation Guidelines: Structured Reinforcement

5. **Respond calmly and consistently to misbehavior.**

   If you need to deliver a correction, minimize attention by remaining calm and using brief, neutral statements. The student is less likely to be reinforced for misbehavior when corrections are calm, brief, and consistent.

6. **Meet and debrief with the student regularly.**

   Meet with the student during the first week of the plan to see how things are going and to determine whether the plan needs revision. If the system is working, celebrate the student's success and continue using the system without any changes for another week or so. Once the intervention seems to be working well, check in with the student on a weekly basis. Review any collected data with the student, highlight successes, and discuss any behaviors that can be improved.

   If the system is not working after the first week, identify any minor adjustments you might make to improve the chance of student success. Consider:

   - *Does the student understand the system?* To check for understanding, ask the student to explain the system or show you what must be done to earn a point or reward.
   - *Does the student care about the rewards you identified?* If not, brainstorm with the student to find alternatives that might be more motivating.
   - *Is the system designed so the student has little chance of success?* Check whether the behavior expectations require too much change at once and adjust the system accordingly.
   - *Is the student getting too much attention from the teacher or peers for exhibiting the problem behaviors?* If so, identify ways to minimize adult attention for misbehavior and increase the ratio of positive to corrective interactions with the student.

   If the system is still not working after minor adjustments, collaborate with your problem-solving team to discuss next steps.

7. **Use data to make periodic revisions and adjustments to the plan as necessary.**

   Monitor student progress and collaborate with your problem-solving team to make adjustments to the plan as needed.

8. **Once the student demonstrates consistent success, implement fading procedures.**

   After at least 2 weeks of success, introduce one or more of these fading procedures:

   - *Require more points to earn the same rewards.* Once the student is consistently successful in earning rewards, increase the price of rewards. For example, rewards that used to cost 4 points might now cost 6 points.
   - *Increase the time monitored before the student earns points.* If the student is earning points for demonstrating self-control during half-hour intervals, you might increase the intervals to 45 minutes.
   - *Move to intermittent reinforcement.* Provide a reward only on some occasions when performance criteria are met. For example, a student might initially be rewarded each day he meets the point goal. After a few weeks of daily success, you might change the system so that the student receives a reward only on randomly selected days on which the point goal is met. The student does not know in advance which days are reward days.

REPRODUCIBLE 4.2h *Implementation Guidelines: Structured Reinforcement (4 of 4)*

Implementation Guidelines: Structured Reinforcement

- *Redefine expectations.* For the student who aimlessly wanders around the classroom, the first expectation might be to stay in a specific work area. When the student has successfully met this expectation for a couple of weeks, you might expand the expectation to staying in her seat for a specific amount of time.
- *Move to more natural reinforcers.* Natural reinforcers are activities or things in the school setting that students find rewarding. Over time, move the student from tangible rewards to internal ones, such as taking pride in success and recognition. For example, once a student demonstrates that she can be on time to class, she might earn the responsibility of being a hall monitor during transitions.

The most important concept in fading the system is the word *gradual*. Each time the system becomes more sophisticated, make sure to inform the student in advance about the change and increase the amount of praise and attention the student receives. Emphasize the student's success and sense of accomplishment. This will help the student accept the changes and take pride in the fact that the system is asking more from them.

Once the student has experienced 2 or more weeks of success, introduce another very gradual change. Continue adjusting the system until the student is engaging in positive behavior with minimal rewards. Eventually, give the student the option of discontinuing the system.

If the student's behavior deteriorates after you introduce fading procedures, offer the option of reverting back to the previously implemented plan, or adjust fading procedures to be more gradual.

9. **Once the intervention has been faded, provide continued follow-up, support, and encouragement.**

   Changing behavior is a difficult process. Once the student has started to achieve the goals, it is easy to take appropriate behavior for granted. Remember that the student will need continued positive feedback throughout the fading process.

REPRODUCIBLE 4.2i *Fidelity Checklist: Structured Reinforcement*

Fidelity Checklist
Structured Reinforcement

Essential Planning Steps

- ☐ Identify the target behavior or trait to monitor.
- ☐ Choose a method for monitoring target behaviors and counting points.
- ☐ Specify when and where the reinforcement system will be used.
- ☐ Create a menu of possible rewards.
- ☐ Determine how many points the student must accumulate to earn each reward.
- ☐ Contact the student's parents/guardians to discuss the reinforcement system.
- ☐ Make a plan for data collection and monitoring.
- ☐ Outline roles and responsibilities for implementing the plan.
- ☐ Provide training to teachers and other adults who will be implementing the plan.

Essential Implementation Components

- ☐ Meet with the student to discuss and finalize the plan.
- ☐ Practice and role-play appropriate responses with the student.
- ☐ Implement the reinforcement system during specified times and settings.
- ☐ Acknowledge the student whenever they earn a point.
- ☐ Respond calmly and consistently to misbehavior.
- ☐ Meet and debrief with the student regularly.
- ☐ Use data to make periodic revisions and adjustments to the plan as necessary.
- ☐ Once the student demonstrates consistent success, implement fading procedures.
- ☐ Once the intervention has been faded, provide continued follow-up, support, and encouragement.

Interventions © 2019 Ancora Publishing

References

Alberto, P. A., & Troutman, A. C. (2012). *Applied behavior analysis for teachers* (9th ed.). Upper Saddle River, NJ: Merrill/Prentice Hall.

Brophy, J. (2004). *Motivating students to learn* (2nd ed.). Mahwah, NJ: Lawrence Erlbaum.

Cooper, J. O., Heron, T. E., & Heward, W. L. (2007). *Applied behavior analysis* (2nd ed.). Upper Saddle River, NJ: Prentice Hall.

Jenson, W. R., Rhode, G., & Reavis, H. K. (2009). *The Tough Kid Book* (2nd ed.) Eugene, OR: Ancora Publishing.

Jovanovic, D., & Matejevic, M. (2014). Relationship between rewards and intrinsic motivation for learning–Researches Review. *Procedia-Social and Behavioral Sciences, 149*, 456–460.

O'Neill, R. E., Albin, R. W., Storey, K., Horner, R. H., & Sprague, J. R. (2015). *Functional assessment and program development for problem behavior: A practical handbook* (3rd ed.). Stamford, CT: Cengage Learning.

Ryan, R. M., & Deci, E. L. (2000). Self-determination theory and the facilitation of intrinsic motivation, social development, and well-being. *American Psychologist, 55*, 68–78.

Stipek, D. J. (1993). *Motivation to learn: From theory to practice.* Needham Heights, MA: Allyn and Bacon.

SPECIALIZED INTERVENTION STRATEGY THREE

Section 4.3

Self-Monitoring and Self-Evaluation

The student would benefit from developing better awareness and control over their behavior

Purpose

The purpose of Self-Monitoring and Self-Evaluation is to increase students' awareness of a particular behavior so they can learn to take responsibility for their own behavior and control what they do.

In *self-monitoring,* the student observes and records the occurrence or nonoccurrence of certain behaviors. *Self-evaluation* is a modified form of self-monitoring in which the student evaluates and records the quality of some aspect of behavior (Menzies, Lane, & Lee; 2009). Both strategies are designed to help students better understand their own behavior and use this information to change behavior over time.

Self-Monitoring and Self-Evaluation can be used to help students:

- Monitor and increase positive, appropriate behaviors, such as work completion or time on task
- Track and reduce problematic behavior, such as complaining or blurting out

This strategy may be appropriate for students who:

- Seem to be unaware of when they engage in inappropriate behavior
- Act impulsively and have difficulty taking ownership of their behavior
- Are learning to be more independent

Self-Monitoring and Self-Evaluation helps students become more aware, responsible, and in control of their own behavior.

Rationale

Self-Monitoring and Self-Evaluation can be an extremely empowering process for students. By putting students in touch with their actions, this intervention strategy teaches them that they can manage how they act and what they do, encouraging growth, maturation, and the development of self-regulation skills in the process (Graham, Harris, & Reid; 1992). Self-Monitoring and Self-Evaluation is especially effective for students who seem to be motivated but are unaware of their inappropriate behavior (Walker, 1995). To monitor their actions accurately, students must learn to pay close attention to what they are or are not doing. As students count and chart their improvements, the motivation to change becomes intrinsic. Reinforcement is often as simple as the sense of accomplishment students feel as they recognize self-improvement (Carr & Punzo, 1993).

Research indicates that self-monitoring can be successfully used with students of various ages to increase attention to tasks, decrease inappropriate classroom behavior, and build social skills (Bruhn, McDaniel, & Kreigh, 2015; Mooney, Ryan, Uhing, Reid, & Epstein, 2005). In addition, students who develop self-management skills can apply these skills to a variety of behaviors that will help them throughout their school careers and after they graduate (Lan, 2005; Zimmerman, 2002).

Self-Monitoring and Self-Evaluation is a relatively simple and efficient strategy to implement. Once a system is designed, the student is primarily responsible for tracking and monitoring behavior. Because Self-Monitoring and Self-Evaluation teaches students to manage their own behavior, as opposed to having an adult do so, this intervention can free up a substantial amount of teacher time that was previously spent redirecting and correcting (Vanderbilt, 2005). Additionally, by collecting data on their own behavior, students create a record that can be used for regular debriefing and evaluating intervention effectiveness (Rafferty, 2010).

> **BEFORE IMPLEMENTING THIS STRATEGY**
>
> Before this intervention can be successfully implemented, be sure that you have discussed the problem and general goal for improvement with the teacher and student. Gather any relevant background information that may help in designing and implementing the intervention. Defining the nature and scope of the problem provides critical information for developing a successful intervention. In addition, contact the student's parents or guardian to discuss the problem and keep them informed of all aspects of the intervention plan.

Essential Planning Steps

STEP 1 Define the problem, describe its context, and identify replacement behaviors.

Begin planning by identifying the specific behavior or academic task to target in your self-monitoring plan. Target behaviors can be positive, appropriate behaviors (e.g., raise hand before calling out, stay in seat during reading, complete 80% of math worksheet during class period) or problematic behaviors (e.g., yelling at recess, running in the halls, off-task talking in social studies class).

When you select a target behavior for a student to self-monitor, make sure that it meets the following conditions (Rafferty, 2010):

- *The student understands and is able to perform the behavior.* If the behavior is not yet within the student's repertoire, you'll need to first develop a plan to explicitly teach the student how to perform the behavior before introducing a self-monitoring system.
- *The student can control the behavior.* If a student exhibits out-of-control behavior, such as tantrums, self-injury, or highly aggressive behavior, implement alternative specialized intervention strategies, such as Managing Emotional Escalation or Behavior Emergency Planning, to get the behavior under control before attempting a self-management intervention.
- *The behavior occurs frequently.* The behavior should occur frequently enough that the student has ample opportunities to monitor and record it and can demonstrate meaningful changes in the behavior over relatively short periods of time.
- *The behavior can be easily observed and recorded.* For a self-monitoring intervention to be effective, target behaviors must be objectively defined and observable.

Once you identify a target behavior, one of the most important parts of intervention planning is to clearly define the behavior so that it can be taught to the student.

First, create a student-friendly definition of the behavior to be monitored. For example, if Jackson is to tally his on-task and off-task behavior, you might tailor his chart to define *on-task* as "eyes on work, attempting to complete the assignment" and *off-task* as "out of seat, talking to peers." The language you use will vary depending on whether the intervention is intended for an elementary or high school student, but try to define the target behavior in as much detail as possible. If the goal for the student is to increase on-task behavior, ask yourself questions like: What does on-task behavior look like? Does it mean being in the seat, facing forward, with all chair legs on the floor? Must the student complete 80% of math questions with the correct answers, or is simply writing down a response to 80% of the problems sufficient? All of these behaviors can fall under the umbrella of *on-task*, but each behavior is uniquely different. Make sure to clearly define the expectations for behavior in detail so that the self-monitoring process is as unambiguous as possible for the student.

Next, draw the line between acceptable and unacceptable behavior. With a behavior problem such as work completion, this step is easy. The work is either done on time or it is not. However, with most behavior, the borderline between acceptable and unacceptable is fuzzy and requires definition. With a behavior such as talking respectfully to adults, for example, what distinguishes respectful from disrespectful talk? Is it the words? The tone of voice? Does body language play a part? Is it all of these? By discussing limits before asking a student to self-monitor, you let the student know in advance what is acceptable and what is unacceptable. This greatly reduces the natural human urge to test the limits. For more in-depth information in clarifying limits of behavior, see Section 3, Task 5 (p. 261).

Finally, brainstorm several examples of possible student behavior and discuss whether each is acceptable or unacceptable. When the line between acceptable and unacceptable behavior is difficult to distinguish, it is important to define it through examples prior to teaching the student to self-monitor. For example, for a student who is learning to speak respectfully to adults, Figure 4.3a on the next page shows a list of examples generated from the types of misbehavior the student exhibited in the past.

NOTE: If you use the problem-solving model and tools that were introduced and applied at different stages of a problem in Section 2, at the point of intervention design you should have already defined target behaviors, identified replacement behaviors, and set goals for improvement. Use this information to complete Step 1. If you need additional support, see Section 3, Task 1 (p. 238).

STEP 2 Choose a recording system for self-monitoring behavior.

After you identify and define behaviors to monitor, choose a recording system. You can use numerous formats for recording, such as:

  a. *Frequency count of target behavior.* The student records each occurrence of target behaviors. This may be as simple as using a tally chart as shown in Figure 4.3b on the next page, or the student can record behavior on a designated form.

FIGURE 4.3a *Behavior Examples*

Situation: The teacher asks Joan to sit down.

Responsible behavior	Irresponsible behavior
Joan nods and sits down.	Joan sits down but calls the teacher a name or says, "Why should I?"
Joan says, "OK," and sits down.	Joan sits down, but in a sarcastic tone says, "OK, whatever you say."
Joan does not respond to the teacher but immediately goes to her seat.	Joan does not sit down or respond.
Joan asks in a respectful tone, "I need to sharpen my pencil. Is that OK?"	Joan goes to sit down in exaggerated slow motion.

Situation: The teacher says, "Good morning" as Joan enters the classroom.

Responsible behavior	Irresponsible behavior
Joan replies in a polite tone, "Good morning."	Joan responds in a sarcastic tone, "Good morning, teacher."
Joan says, "It hasn't been a good morning. My mom was all over my case this morning."	Joan says, "It might be good for you, but what do you know?"
Joan smiles and nods.	Joan looks disgusted and sighs.

FIGURE 4.3b *Behavior Tally*

On Task	Off Task
‖‖‖‖	‖

For example, as shown in Self-Monitoring Form: Following Directions (Reproducible 4.3a), the student marks a plus (+) for each direction followed without complaining and a minus (-) for each direction that led to complaining.

To record counts for other target behaviors, you can use the customizable Behavior Counting Grid (Reproducible 4.3b) or the Behavior Counting Graph (Reproducible 4.3c, p. 378).

For younger students (grades K–2), the Happy Cat/Sad Dog—Happy Dog/Sad Cat Form (Reproducible 4.3d, p. 379) offers a simplified version of a tally count. Here, the student tracks a behavior by coloring in a drawing. Note that the top half of the reproducible shows happy cats while the bottom half shows happy dogs, giving both cat fanciers and dog lovers equal opportunity to indicate positive behavior with the animal pal of their choice.

b. *Self-rating of behavior or effort.* The student rates behavior or effort after specified activities or periods of the day. For example, the system shown in Self-Evaluation Form: Class Participation (Reproducible 4.3e, p. 380) is designed for a student who has difficulty participating in class.

continued on page 381

REPRODUCIBLE 4.3a *Self-Monitoring: Following Directions*

Self-Monitoring: Following Directions

Student _____ Week of _____

Directions: Mark a "+" for each direction followed without complaining.
Mark a "−" for each direction that led to complaining.

Date/Period	+/− Count

REPRODUCIBLE 4.3b *Behavior Counting Grid*

Behavior Counting Grid

Name _____

Behavior _____ Date/Period _____

1	2	3	4	5	6	7	8	9	10
11	12	13	14	15	16	17	18	19	20

Behavior _____ Date/Period _____

1	2	3	4	5	6	7	8	9	10

REPRODUCIBLE 4.3c *Behavior Counting Graph*

Behavior Counting Graph

Name _____ Grade/Class _____

Teacher _____ Start date _____

Behavior to be counted _____

Occurrences of Behavior (y-axis: 0–20)

Day (x-axis: 1–10)

Interventions © 2019 Ancora Publishing

REPRODUCIBLE 4.3c

REPRODUCIBLE 4.3d   *Happy Cat/Sad Dog and Happy Dog/Sad Cat*

Happy Cat/Sad Dog

Name _____   Behavior _____

Directions: Each time you remember, color the smiling cat. When you forget, color the sad dog.

Interventions © 2019 Ancora Publishing

REPRODUCIBLE 4.3d

- -

Happy Dog/Sad Cat

Name _____   Behavior _____

Directions: Each time you remember, color the smiling dog. When you forget, color the sad cat.

Interventions © 2019 Ancora Publishing

REPRODUCIBLE 4.3d

REPRODUCIBLE 4.3e *Self-Evaluation: Class Participation*

Self-Evaluation: Class Participation

Student _____   Date _____

Period/Class		Level of Participation
	☐ I gave it my best effort.	I raised my hand, and I asked relevant questions. I volunteered information. I listened to others and thought about what they said.
	☐ I did just enough to get by.	I sat quietly and didn't interfere with others.
	☐ I didn't try.	I didn't listen. I made noises that interfered with what other people were saying. I did things that got other people to look at me.
	☐ I gave it my best effort.	I raised my hand, and I asked relevant questions. I volunteered information. I listened to others and thought about what they said.
	☐ I did just enough to get by.	I sat quietly and didn't interfere with others.
	☐ I didn't try.	I didn't listen. I made noises that interfered with what other people were saying. I did things that got other people to look at me.
	☐ I gave it my best effort.	I raised my hand, and I asked relevant questions. I volunteered information. I listened to others and thought about what they said.
	☐ I did just enough to get by.	I sat quietly and didn't interfere with others.
	☐ I didn't try.	I didn't listen. I made noises that interfered with what other people were saying. I did things that got other people to look at me.
	☐ I gave it my best effort.	I raised my hand, and I asked relevant questions. I volunteered information. I listened to others and thought about what they said.
	☐ I did just enough to get by.	I sat quietly and didn't interfere with others.
	☐ I didn't try.	I didn't listen. I made noises that interfered with what other people were saying. I did things that got other people to look at me.
	☐ I gave it my best effort.	I raised my hand, and I asked relevant questions. I volunteered information. I listened to others and thought about what they said.
	☐ I did just enough to get by.	I sat quietly and didn't interfere with others.
	☐ I didn't try.	I didn't listen. I made noises that interfered with what other people were saying. I did things that got other people to look at me.
	☐ I gave it my best effort.	I raised my hand, and I asked relevant questions. I volunteered information. I listened to others and thought about what they said.
	☐ I did just enough to get by.	I sat quietly and didn't interfere with others.
	☐ I didn't try.	I didn't listen. I made noises that interfered with what other people were saying. I did things that got other people to look at me.

Interventions © 2019 Ancora Publishing

REPRODUCIBLE 4.3e

Reproducibles 4.3f through 4.3i are rating forms for self-evaluating different traits, including neatness, complaining behavior, and on-task behavior.

Finally, you can customize open-ended rating forms, such as Reproducibles 4.3j through 4.3m (pp. 384–386), for other target behaviors.

c. *Completion checklist.* The student uses a checklist of tasks that must be completed. For example, a student who needs to improve hygiene might use the Self-Monitoring Form: Personal Hygiene (Reproducible 4.3n, p. 387) to check off things as she does them in the morning.

A student who has difficulty with independent classwork might use Self-Monitoring Form: Work Completion (Reproducible 4.3o, p. 388), which includes writing down assignments, starting an assignment, finishing it, and handing it in. A student who is working on improving homework completion could use Self-Monitoring Form: Homework Completion (Reproducible 4.3p, p. 389).

A blank Self-Monitoring Checklist (Reproducible 4.3q, p. 390) can be customized with tasks for the student to check off as they are completed.

When considering options for the recording system, ensure that the system you choose is aligned with the student's problem and goal, easy for the student to understand and manage, and as unobtrusive as possible. You can select one of the recording systems and associated monitoring forms provided, or design your own to match the student's needs.

Make sure the self-monitoring system doesn't embarrass the student. Self-monitoring can be beneficial to any student, but its power can be diluted if the student is embarrassed (Carr & Punzo, 1993). Especially for older students, the system should involve recording behavior privately, possibly inside a notebook or folder. Younger students tend to be less concerned about embarrassment and often like having a "special system."

You might consider having the student use a handheld computer or mobile device to record behavior. Students are often more motivated to self-record using technology rather than "old-fashioned" pen and paper. In addition, recording data digitally enables you to easily create digital graphs, print data summaries, and e-mail charts to students or their parents.

Choose a recording system that is aligned with the student's problem and goal, easy for the student to understand and manage, and as unobtrusive as possible.

STEP 3   Outline a plan for implementation and data collection.

When creating a plan, make sure to incorporate the following components.

Determine when the student will record behaviors. Using information about the context of the problem, determine the most appropriate times and situations for the student to use the self-monitoring system. Behavior may be monitored:

- *Once a day at a specified time.* If a student has difficulty paying attention during the afternoon, for example, she might monitor her behavior only in the afternoon.
- *Only during certain activities.* If a student has difficulty keeping his hands and feet to himself when students line up or sit together on the floor, he might monitor his behavior only during those specific activities.
- *Whenever the behavior occurs.* If a student is monitoring a behavior such as hand-raising and waiting to be called on, talking respectfully to the teacher, or engaging in positive self-talk, it may be best to have her record the behavior as it occurs. If recording is done at intervals, the student may have difficulty judging whether her behavior during that time was appropriate or inappropriate.

continued on page 391

REPRODUCIBLE 4.3f *Neatness Evaluation Form*

Neatness Evaluation Form

Name _____ Assignment _____ Date _____

Directions: Circle the number that best describes the level of neatness of this assignment. If the assignment is rated 0 or 1, it will have to be cleaned up or redone. If the teacher agrees with your rating, there may be an occasional reward.

4	The paper is whole and flat with no extra marks. The writing sits appropriately on the line. There are spaces between the words. The capitals are big and the small letters are small. The writing is all printing or cursive. The writing is straight or at a uniform slant.
3	The paper is whole and flat with no extra marks. The writing sits appropriately on the line. There are spaces between the words. The capitals are big and the small letters small. The writing is all printing or all cursive.
2	The paper is whole and flat with no extra marks. The writing sits appropriately on the line. There are spaces between the words.
1	The paper is whole and flat, but has extra marks or smudges.
0	The paper is torn or crumpled.

Interventions © 2019 Ancora Publishing

REPRODUCIBLE 4.3g *Self-Evaluation: Complaining Behavior*

Self-Evaluation: Complaining Behavior

Name _____ Date _____

Directions: Circle the number that best describes your level of participation.

When	Went to the health room	Complained about how I felt	Acted sick or tired	Was OK	Was enthusiastic
First Hour	0	1	2	3	4
Second Hour	0	1	2	3	4
Third Hour	0	1	2	3	4
Fourth Hour	0	1	2	3	4
Fifth Hour	0	1	2	3	4
Sixth Hour	0	1	2	3	4
Seventh Hour	0	1	2	3	4

Total points for the day ☐

Interventions © 2019 Ancora Publishing

REPRODUCIBLE 4.3h *Self-Monitoring: On-Task Behavior*

Self-Monitoring: On-Task Behavior

Student _____ Week of _____

Date _____

	Did I stay focused on my task?		
very off task	off task	mostly on task	on task; very focused
1	2	3	4

Date _____

	Did I stay focused on my task?		
very off task	off task	mostly on task	on task; very focused
1	2	3	4

REPRODUCIBLE 4.3i *Self-Monitoring: On-Task Behavior*

Self-Monitoring: On-Task Behavior

Student _____ Week of _____

Date _____

Did I stay focused on my task?

no — 1   2   3   4 — yes

Date _____

Did I stay focused on my task?

no — 1   2   3   4 — yes

INTERVENTIONS: SUPPORT FOR INDIVIDUAL STUDENTS WITH BEHAVIOR CHALLENGES

REPRODUCIBLE 4.3j *Self-Monitoring Form*

Self-Monitoring Form

Student _____   Week of _____

Date _____

I am working on _____

1   2   3   4

Date _____

I am working on _____

1   2   3   4

REPRODUCIBLE 4.3k *Self-Monitoring Form*

Self-Monitoring Form

Student _____   Week of _____

Date _____

I am working on _____

1   2   3   4

Date _____

I am working on _____

1   2   3   4

REPRODUCIBLE 4.3l *Self-Monitoring Form*

Self-Monitoring Form

Name _____ Date _____

Directions: Put a "+" under each header, where earned. Calculate bonus points with tally marks in the column.

Work =			
Behavior =			
Bonus =			
Time	**Work**	**Behavior**	**Bonus**
9:00			
9:30			
10:00			
10:30			
11:00			
11:30			
12:00			
12:30			
1:00			
1:30			
2:00			
2:30			
3:00			
3:30			
Percentage of + marks:		Total:	

Interventions © 2019 Ancora Publishing

REPRODUCIBLE 4.3m *Self-Monitoring: Behavior*

Self-Monitoring: Behavior

Name _____ Date _____

Directions: Put a ✓ under each header, as appropriate.

Target Behavior			
Time	Sad	OK	Happy
8:00 to 8:15			
8:15 to 8:30			
8:30 to 8:45			
8:45 to 9:00			
9:00 to 9:15			
9:15 to 9:30			
9:30 to 9:45			
9:45 to 10:00			
10:00 to 10:15			
10:15 to 10:30			
10:30 to 10:45			
10:45 to 11:00			
11:00 to 11:15			
11:15 to 11:30			
11:30 to 11:45			
11:45 to 12:00			
12:00 to 12:15			
12:15 to 12:30			
12:30 to 12:45			
12:45 to 1:00			
1:00 to 1:15			
1:15 to 1:30			
1:30 to 1:45			
1:45 to 2:00			
2:00 to 2:15			
2:15 to 2:30			
2:30 to 2:45			
2:45 to 3:00			
3:00 to 3:15			
3:15 to 3:30			

Interventions © 2019 Ancora Publishing

REPRODUCIBLE 4.3n *Self-Monitoring: Personal Hygiene*

Self-Monitoring: Personal Hygiene

Student _____

Week of _____

Personal Hygiene	M	T	W	Th	F
1. Get up at 6:30.					
2. Shower and wash hair.					
3. Put on deodorant.					
4. Comb or brush hair.					
5. Brush teeth					

Week of _____

	M	T	W	Th	F
1. Get up at 6:30.					
2. Shower and wash hair.					
3. Put on deodorant.					
4. Comb or brush hair.					
5. Brush teeth					

Week of _____

	M	T	W	Th	F
1. Get up at 6:30.					
2. Shower and wash hair.					
3. Put on deodorant.					
4. Comb or brush hair.					
5. Brush teeth					

Week of _____

	M	T	W	Th	F
1. Get up at 6:30.					
2. Shower and wash hair.					
3. Put on deodorant.					
4. Comb or brush hair.					
5. Brush teeth					

Week of _____

	M	T	W	Th	F
1. Get up at 6:30.					
2. Shower and wash hair.					
3. Put on deodorant.					
4. Comb or brush hair.					
5. Brush teeth					

Interventions © 2019 Ancora Publishing

REPRODUCIBLE 4.3o *Self-Monitoring: Work Completion*

Self-Monitoring: Work Completion

Student _____   Week of _____

		M	T	W	Th	F
Period: _____ Subject: _____	I wrote down the assignment.					
	I started the assignment.					
	I finished the assignment.					
	I handed in the assignment.					
Period: _____ Subject: _____	I wrote down the assignment.					
	I started the assignment.					
	I finished the assignment.					
	I handed in the assignment.					
Period: _____ Subject: _____	I wrote down the assignment.					
	I started the assignment.					
	I finished the assignment.					
	I handed in the assignment.					
Period: _____ Subject: _____	I wrote down the assignment.					
	I started the assignment.					
	I finished the assignment.					
	I handed in the assignment.					
Period: _____ Subject: _____	I wrote down the assignment.					
	I started the assignment.					
	I finished the assignment.					
	I handed in the assignment.					

I will put an "X" in any box where nothing was assigned or due during that period. When a box is successfully completed, I will initial that box.

I will meet with _____ to discuss my progress.

When/Where _____

When I can get _____ of the boxes filled in (including Xs), I will earn _____

I also recognize that when I can get _____ to _____ boxes filled in, my grades will begin to go up and I will feel very responsible.

Interventions © 2019 Ancora Publishing

REPRODUCIBLE 4.3p *Self-Monitoring: Homework Completion*

Self-Monitoring: Homework Completion

Student _____ Week of _____

Due	Assignment	Materials	Done

Before leaving school each day, I will study from _____ to _____ and from _____ to _____ if needed.

	M	U	W	H	F
I have logged long-term assignments not yet finished on tomorrow's assignment sheet.					
I have organized my assignments in my notebook.					
I have packed all my books, materials, and notebook in my backpack.					
I have put my backpack by the door.					

Interventions © 2019 Ancora Publishing

REPRODUCIBLE 4.3p

REPRODUCIBLE 4.3q *Self-Monitoring Checklist*

Self-Monitoring Checklist

Student _____   Behavior _____

		M	T	W	Th	F
Week of _____	1.					
	2.					
	3.					
	4.					
	5.					
Week of _____	1.					
	2.					
	3.					
	4.					
	5.					
Week of _____	1.					
	2.					
	3.					
	4.					
	5.					
Week of _____	1.					
	2.					
	3.					
	4.					
	5.					
Week of _____	1.					
	2.					
	3.					
	4.					
	5.					

Interventions © 2019 Ancora Publishing

- *At specified intervals.* A student who has difficulty with work completion might record the number of problems completed in a 15-minute period.
- *At random intervals.* If a student has difficulty with on-task behavior, having the student monitor behavior at random intervals may be effective. These intervals may be as frequent as every 2 minutes or as infrequent as two per hour, depending on the needs of the student and the objectives of the intervention.

If major changes in behavior are required, the student will need to make improvements in small increments. Start by prioritizing the settings and periods of the day that are most problematic and urgent to address. You might have the student begin self-monitoring during a fairly short period (e.g., 15–30 minutes) and gradually increase the monitoring period as the student becomes more comfortable and accurate with using the system.

Select a cue to prompt the student to record. If the student is counting specific behaviors, the behavior itself acts as a cue:

- *When you hear yourself say something positive, make a tally.*
- *When you raise your hand and wait quietly for the teacher to call on you, make a tally.*
- *When you complete an assignment, check it off.*

Other cases may require an independent cueing mechanism. A student who is monitoring behavior at specified or random intervals will need a cue when it is time to record. You can set up an independent cueing system in a variety of ways, such as:

- *Setting a timer for intervals.* The timer goes off and signals the student to record behavior at that point in time.
- *Using an audio recording of beeps or voice cues spaced at intervals.* The student hears a beep or cue, and records behavior.
- *Using technology.* Computer or tablet applications can be set to emit a sound at regular intervals (e.g., every 15 minutes) or intermittently (e.g., four times an hour at random intervals). Devices such as the MotivAider, a simple electronic device worn on or near the body, can be set to vibrate on a fixed or variable schedule. A search of the Internet for timers, cueing devices, and reminder devices will yield a variety of other possibilities.

With any of these cueing systems, students must be on board with the system so that they don't feel embarrassed or offended. Plan to discuss the different options for cueing systems and allow the student to choose one that is acceptable.

Set a measurable goal to share with the student. Identify a goal aligned with the target behaviors and measurable with the recording system you selected. For example:

- If the student is recording the frequency of different types of interactions with peers, a daily goal might be delivering more compliments than put-downs.
- If the student is using a rating scale of 0–2 points to evaluate effort during study hall, a weekly goal might be 7 or more cumulative points.
- If the student is using a checklist to record completion of each step of a project, a goal might be to complete 100% of the steps by the project's due date.

You may also elect to specify a goal for accurate monitoring (e.g., at least 90% accuracy during teacher accuracy checks) or for regular use of the self-monitoring system (e.g., use self-monitoring forms without being prompted during each study hall period).

Select a goal that is ambitious but obtainable given the student's current level of behavior. If needed, collect baseline data to help determine an appropriate goal.

Plan to conduct occasional accuracy checks. In the early phases of the plan, plan to have an adult monitor the student's progress by doing intermittent checks at least once a week. For example, if a student is learning to stay on task, the teacher might monitor the student's behavior at unpredictable intervals, such as at the first, third, fourth, and eighth intervals, and record whether the student was on task or not. Later, the teacher can check with the student to see whether their recordings match. Adult monitoring during the initial phases of self-monitoring will increase the effectiveness of the intervention (Menzies et al., 2009).

For systems that involve self-rating of behavior or effort, accuracy checks are even more important to make sure that the student is truthfully assessing behavior. Accurate self-assessment is a prerequisite to being able to self-manage a behavior change. For example, if Destinee is rating her level of cooperation every hour, the teacher should also occasionally use the same rating scale to assess Destinee's cooperativeness. Then, the student and teacher can compare ratings and discuss discrepancies. Without these checks, the student has little incentive to rate herself accurately. As the student demonstrates reliable self-monitoring, adult monitoring can be gradually reduced.

Consider whether to incorporate rewards for using the system or for showing progress. If the student needs extra motivation to use the self-monitoring system, consider including a reward component. For example:

- Deliver a small tangible or activity reward when the student meets the weekly goal.
- Have the student use a computer to graph the self-monitoring results after consistently using the system for 5 days.
- Give the student an extra privilege in class (front of the line, homework pass, etc.) when he achieves 90% during accuracy checks.
- Schedule a special time with a parent to discuss improvements.

Contact the student's parents to discuss the plan. Introduce the goals and purpose of the self-monitoring plan, explain how the system works and which behaviors will be monitored, and invite the parent to be an active partner in its implementation.

Make a plan for data collection and monitoring. The records kept by students and adults provide important information about how the self-monitoring system is working. As data are collected, make a plan to graph and discuss student progress. Depending on the behavior, evaluation might also include subjective impressions from the teacher and student, grades, attendance records, office referrals, and so on.

Consider supplemental intervention strategies to incorporate into the plan. Identify other strategies that might support or increase the effectiveness of the self-monitoring system. For example:

- *Antecedent strategies:* Increasing monitoring and supervision or using additional cues and precorrections to remind the student of behavior expectations and when to use self-monitoring procedures might increase the likelihood that the student will learn to successfully self-monitor.

- *Teaching strategies:* Consider practicing and refining behavioral skills and self-monitoring practices with short, regular sessions with an adult. Opportunities for verbal practice and role-playing responses in hypothetical situations may be particularly helpful for students who are learning to self-monitor and manage their own behavior.
- *Positive consequence strategies:* Provide praise, feedback, or rewards when the student effectively uses the self-monitoring system, demonstrates progress, and makes strong efforts to change behavior. Also, to cultivate family collaboration and support, share behavior goals and successes with the student's family and ask them to provide encouragement and praise at home.
- *Corrective consequence strategies:* If the student needs to eliminate or reduce an inappropriate behavior in addition to learning more responsible behaviors, staff should be prepared to respond to misbehavior. Any corrective response should be delivered calmly and consistently, and the limits of behaviors to correct should be clearly defined so that the student knows the line between inappropriate and appropriate behaviors.
- *Interactional strategies.* Increasing a teacher's ratio of positive to corrective interactions is a powerful component of all behavior intervention plans. Also consider how to encourage the student's engagement in the school community (e.g., participating in school clubs or activities, assuming a meaningful role in the school, or connecting with an adult or peer mentor).
- *Specialized strategies:* To formalize the student's agreement to assume more responsibility for changing behavior, you might implement self-monitoring procedures in conjunction with Behavioral Contracting. Self-monitoring may be included as part of a plan for Managing Emotional Escalation or Supporting Students with Internalizing Challenges, or implemented once the student is successful in meeting goals within a Structured Reinforcement system.

Outline roles and responsibilities for implementing the plan. Be sure everyone involved in the plan has a clear understanding of the procedures. Ask *what-if* questions, and discuss contingencies in advance. Address the following details:

- Who will meet with the student to discuss the plan.
- Who will be responsible for conducting periodic accuracy checks.
- Who will work with the student to teach and practice behavior or self-management skills.
- Who will be responsible for data collection, and how will the data be collected and summarized.
- Who will need training.

Provide training to teachers and others who will be implementing the plan. All adults involved in implementing and supporting the self-monitoring system should receive training on procedures, how the system works, what behaviors will be monitored, how to respond to misbehavior, and how to conduct accuracy checks. Use Implementation Guidelines: Self-Monitoring and Self-Evaluation (Reproducible 4.3r, pp. 400–403) to review procedures with staff. Also distribute relevant forms for recording behavior and monitoring progress.

Case Example: Bobby

Bobby is a seventh-grade student in Mrs. Werner's language arts/social studies block. During class, Bobby participates. His class assignments are above average, and he is always pleasant to have in class. Despite Bobby's strong abilities, Mrs. Werner is concerned because he is failing in English and barely passing in social studies. Bobby's problem is homework. Mrs. Werner has discussed the problem with Bobby, but the discussions have not done much good. Mrs. Werner decides to ask the school's problem-solving team for assistance.

The counselor, Mr. Pope, is assigned as Bobby's support coordinator. Mr. Pope reviews Bobby's elementary school records and finds that homework has been a problem since the third grade. Teacher comments describe an academically capable student who is charming but chronically disorganized. Daily report cards were tried in sixth grade, with only partial success. Bobby still missed assignments frequently after the report card program was instituted. Mr. Pope checks with Bobby's other teachers and finds that Bobby is doing fine in PE and photography, but is getting D's or failing grades in all academic subjects. All of his teachers indicate that the problem is homework. Mr. Pope finds that Bobby reads with good fluency and understanding, his writing abilities are average, and he is physically and mentally able to do his homework.

Bobby was two when his parents divorced. They have joint custody, and Bobby switches between homes every Wednesday. Both parents are professionals with demanding careers.

In talking with Bobby's parents, Mr. Pope finds that each parent blames the other for Bobby's problems. His father says that his ex-wife is disorganized and coddles the boy. His mother says that his father is too critical and demanding. Both parents have high aspirations for their son, but beyond that they do not seem to agree. Both parents are amenable to working with Bobby but indicate that they do not want to talk with each other.

Bobby's teachers and Mr. Pope, the support coordinator, decide that Bobby needs to learn to take responsibility for his homework. They plan to have him self-monitor his homework and learn to get work done despite his inconsistent home situation. The problem-solving team creates a self-monitoring plan for Bobby to record all homework as it is assigned and check off homework as he finishes it. Bobby's goals are to:

1. Write down assignments.
2. Self-check to make sure he has all needed materials before leaving school.
3. Stick to a prearranged homework schedule.
4. Stay with the schedule until homework is done.
5. Put completed homework in his notebook.
6. Get his notebook to school in the morning.

To help meet these goals, Bobby will use a daily checklist. See the sample Self-Monitoring Form: Homework Completion (Reproducible 4.3p). During each class period, Bobby will record his assignments and note when they are due. At the end of the day, Bobby will write down when he will study that evening and check off all the materials he needs as he puts them in his notebook or backpack. At home, as he is doing his homework, Bobby will check off each completed assignment. When he is finished with his homework, he will pack everything up and put his backpack by the door.

Self-Monitoring: Homework Completion

Student: Bobby Ross   Week of: 10/15 – 10/19

Due	Assignment	Materials	Done
10/16	math, page 16	math book and folder	X
10/16	The Pearl, pages 42–60	The Pearl	
10/19	Field trip permission slip	Notebook	X

Before leaving school each day, I will study from **2:30** to **3:30** and from **5:00** to **6:00** if needed.

	M	U	W	H	F
I have logged long-term assignments not yet finished on tomorrow's assignment sheet.					
I have organized my assignments in my notebook.	X				
I have packed all my books, materials, and notebook in my backpack.	X				
I have put my backpack by the door.					

Bobby's self-monitoring system will be in effect from the moment he leaves his house in the morning until he packs up his materials in the evening. The team thinks that Bobby will initially need frequent adult guidance as he learns to monitor his homework. For the first week, Bobby will check in at the counseling office at the end of each day. Mr. Pope and Bobby will go over the assignment sheet and make sure Bobby has all needed materials before he gets on the bus. If time permits, they will discuss when Bobby plans to study at home and verbally rehearse how he will use his assignment sheet. In addition, Bobby will stop in to see Mr. Pope at the beginning of the school day for a quick review and discussion of how things went the previous evening. In the following weeks, as Bobby is more successful, these meetings will be faded to three times a week, then two times per week, and eventually once per week.

The problem-solving team agrees to determine the effectiveness of the self-monitoring system by 1) having Bobby summarize his daily checklists by graphing the percentage of homework he completes each week, 2) having Mr. Pope check with Bobby's teachers once a week to determine whether he is keeping up with his homework assignments, and 3) reviewing Bobby's quarterly grades in all academic subjects.

> Items 1–9 are also shown on **Implementation Guidelines** (Form 4.3r, pp. 400–403). Share with teachers and other adults who are responsible for implementing the plan.

Essential Implementation Procedures

The teacher or interventionist responsible for implementing the plan should make sure to:

1. Meet with the student to discuss and finalize the plan. During this meeting, you will:

- Explain that you would like to assist the student in being more successful and more aware of their own behavior at school. Introduce the self-monitoring system, discussing the purpose and the benefits of self-monitoring.
- Describe the behaviors the student will monitor. Provide a student-friendly definition and several examples for each behavior.
- Explain how the self-monitoring system works, including how and when to record behavior, where the student's record will be kept, and when data will be reviewed.
- Describe the cue that should prompt the student to record behavior. For example: "When you say something positive to someone else, circle the next number on your chart" or "When you hear the timer go off, mark a plus if you are on task and doing what you're supposed to be doing and a minus if you are not."
- Share a goal for using the self-monitoring system. This could be a goal for improvement (e.g., if a student rates daily effort in math class on a scale of 0–2 points, strive for at least 7 cumulative points at the end of the week), a goal for accurate monitoring (e.g., at least 90% accuracy during teacher accuracy checks), or a goal for regular use of the self-monitoring system (e.g., use self-monitoring forms without being prompted during each study hall period).
- Inform the student of any rewards that can be earned by using the system and making progress.
- Encourage student buy-in to the system itself. As much as possible, engage the student in helping to plan the system and voicing any suggestions, questions, or concerns.
- Let the student know that you will occasionally monitor using the same system to check for accuracy.

BEFORE MEETING WITH THE STUDENT

Use professional judgment to determine who will be present when the plan is discussed with the student. Some students will be responsive only if the teacher is present. In other cases, it will be important to include a parent, an interventionist, other teachers, or a paraprofessional or volunteer who will be working with the student.

2. Practice using the self-monitoring system and role-play different scenarios. Have the student verbally rehearse and demonstrate the steps of the self-monitoring procedures. Make sure the student can demonstrate the procedures and explain the goal of self-monitoring. If appropriate for the student's academic level, provide a written list of the self-monitoring steps. Such a list can serve as a guide for reviewing the process at periodic intervals during the first several days of the plan.

Also role-play examples of different behaviors. Ask the student to identify whether the example is appropriate or inappropriate behavior and to show how the behavior should be recorded on the self-monitoring form. Provide supportive and corrective feedback about the student's responses. Continue this process using a wide variety of different examples. If the student needs practice beyond the initial meeting, schedule additional practice times.

3. Implement self-monitoring procedures during specified times and settings. Make sure that the student consistently self-monitors in accordance with the details of the intervention plan. Check in with the student often to monitor use of the forms, answer any questions, and provide encouragement and praise for the student's efforts. If rewards are part of the plan, deliver them as immediately as possible.

4. Acknowledge and encourage the student's efforts. Learning new behaviors and discarding old behaviors can be very difficult for some students. Though a particular change may seem simple to an adult, to a child it can be as difficult as learning a new language or musical instrument. The student may need a lot of practice, opportunities to make errors and adjustments, and a lot of encouragement along the way.

5. Respond calmly and consistently to misbehavior. Minimize attention to misbehavior by remaining calm and using brief, neutral statements. Calm, brief, and consistent corrections are less likely to reinforce misbehavior or interrupt the flow of instruction.

6. Conduct accuracy checks and compare results with the student's record. Using the same form that the student is using to record behavior, monitor the student's behavior and record your observations. Depending on the self-monitoring system, you might opt to observe and record behavior during random intervals, for a portion of a targeted period, or for the entire time that the student is self-monitoring. Afterwards, compare your results with the student's. If you both recorded the same behavior in the same way, provide the student with praise and encouragement. Even if the behavior itself has not yet improved, the student is taking the first step toward being responsible—learning how to self-assess behaviors. If the monitoring records do not match, find a time to discuss the reason for the discrepancy. Is the student recording every event? Is the line between appropriate and inappropriate behavior unclear?

7. Meet and debrief with the student regularly. Meet with the student during the first week of the plan to see how things are going and to determine whether the plan needs revision. If the system is working, celebrate the student's success and continue using the system without any changes for another week or so. Once the intervention seems to be working well, check in with the student on a weekly basis. Review any collected data with the student, highlight successes, and discuss any behaviors that can be improved.

If the system is not working after the first week, identify any minor adjustments you might make to improve the chance of student success. Consider:

- *Does the student understand the system?* To check for understanding, ask the student to model the target behavior and explain how to record behavior.

- *Is the target behavior clearly defined?* Determine whether additional clarification or more behavior examples are needed to help the student accurately monitor behavior.
- *Is the student motivated to use the system?* If not, reiterate the goals and benefits of using the system and brainstorm possible rewards to offer for improvements in behavior, recording accuracy, or regular use of the monitoring forms.
- *Is the student getting too much attention from the teacher or peers for exhibiting the problem behaviors?* If so, try to minimize the amount of attention given to misbehavior and increase the number of positive interactions you have with the student. (See strategies for increasing contingent and noncontingent positive interactions in Tasks 4 and 6 of Section 3).

8. Use data to make periodic revisions and adjustments to the plan as necessary. As you monitor the student's progress, make adjustments to the plan as needed. If the student's behavior isn't improving, ask the following questions:

- *Are all essential components of the plan being implemented as intended?* Ensure intervention fidelity by having the teacher or external observer complete Fidelity Checklist: Self-Monitoring and Self-Evaluation (Reproducible 4.3s, p. 404).
- *Which aspects of the plan can you modify to increase its effectiveness?* Consider modifying when and where the student uses the system, how behavior is recorded, and whether to incorporate a reward component. If the plan requires an unrealistic amount of teacher time and energy, modify the plan to reduce teacher monitoring or include another adult.
- *What supplemental strategies can be introduced to support the effectiveness of the plan?* Incorporating other intervention strategies, such as explicitly teaching and modeling target behaviors, delivering precorrections and reminders to record behavior, or providing more specific feedback on behavior might help to encourage improvement.
- *Is the plan meeting the needs of the student?* Review information about the context of the problem and determine whether to collect additional data to more accurately identify contributing factors and the function of problematic behavior.

9. Once the student demonstrates consistent success, implement fading procedures or provide continued follow-up, support, and encouragement. As the student assumes ownership of a new behavior or breaks an old habit, consider whether to fade or discontinue the monitoring system.

A general rule of thumb: Fade the system when the student demonstrates consistent success, but continue to provide any support necessary to maintain the student's behavior improvements. For some students, temporary practice of self-monitoring may be sufficient to impact self-awareness and behavior in the long term. These students will maintain improvements as the system is gradually faded and eventually removed. Other students may require continued support and may need the structure of a sustained self-monitoring system across the school year in order to be successful.

Fading options include:

- *Increasing time intervals between monitoring.* Reduce the number of times or the frequency with which the student self-monitors. For example, if the student has been monitoring on-task behavior all day, fade the system by limiting the monitoring to only certain parts of the day.
- *Modifying goals.* After the student is able to consistently demonstrate and track behaviors originally targeted in the intervention plan, consider increasing the goal for behavior or including new behaviors to monitor. For example, once a student demonstrates success with monitoring on-time completion of assignments, you can transition the student to evaluating neatness, monitoring word count, or rating overall effort on each assignment.
- *Adjusting rewards.* If your plan includes a reward component, consider adjusting the criteria for earning rewards or fading the use of rewards altogether. For example, instead of delivering rewards daily, you might provide a reward for every 2 days the student meets the goal. Or transition from tangible rewards to more natural reinforcers, such as recognition or praise for meeting goals.
- *Decreasing adult guidance and facilitation of the monitoring system.* One very natural way to fade the system is to eliminate the formal self-monitoring form but continue verbal debriefing with the student once or twice a week. This debriefing offers the student a chance to reflect on recent behavior and you a chance to provide feedback to the student.

Each time you adjust the system, make sure to inform the student in advance and increase the amount of praise and attention the student receives during the transition to new procedures.

If the student maintains improvements, continue to adjust procedures as needed to keep the student engaged, or offer the student the option of discontinuing self-monitoring. If the student's behavior deteriorates, offer the option of reverting back to the previous plan, or adjust fading procedures to be more gradual.

Finally, regardless of whether you decide to maintain, fade, or suspend formal self-monitoring procedures, continue to praise appropriate behavior and acknowledge the student's maturity and self-discipline. Though it is easy to take appropriate behavior for granted, remember that the student has made a major change in behavior and will need ongoing encouragement and support to keep being successful at school.

Strategy Summary

Self-Monitoring and Self-Evaluation is a positive, efficient approach to teaching students to be responsible and in charge of their actions. Practice in self-management helps students effectively change behavior today and establish skills that will help them succeed in future schooling and employment.

REPRODUCIBLE 4.3r *Implementation Guidelines: Self-Monitoring and Self-Evaluation (1 of 4)*

Implementation Guidelines
Self-Monitoring and Self-Evaluation

Overview

Self-Monitoring and Self-Evaluation helps students become more aware, responsible, and in control of their own behavior. In self-monitoring, students observe and record the occurrence or nonoccurrence of certain behaviors. Self-evaluation is a modified form of self-monitoring in which students evaluate and record the quality of some aspect of their behavior (Menzies, Lane, & Lee, 2009). Both strategies are designed to help students better understand their own behavior and use this information to change their behavior over time.

Self-Monitoring and Self-Evaluation can be an extremely empowering process for students. By putting students in touch with their actions, this intervention strategy teaches them that they can manage how they act and what they do, encouraging growth, maturation, and the development self-regulation skills in the process (Graham, Harris, & Reid; 1992). Self-Monitoring and Self-Evaluation is especially effective for students who seem to be motivated but are unaware of their inappropriate behavior (Walker, 1995). To monitor their actions accurately, students must learn to pay close attention to what they are or are not doing. As they count and chart their improvements, the motivation to change becomes intrinsic. Reinforcement is often as simple as the sense of accomplishment students feel as they recognize self-improvement (Carr & Punzo, 1993).

Self-Monitoring and Self-Evaluation is a relatively simple and efficient strategy to implement. Once a system is designed, the student is primarily responsible for tracking and monitoring behavior. As the interventionist, you will facilitate the student's use of self-monitoring forms by offering feedback and encouragement, occasionally conducting accuracy checks, and reviewing progress with the student.

Plan Summary

A self-monitoring system will be used at these times in these settings: _____

to monitor the following behaviors: _____

_____

The goal will be: _____

_____

When the student meets this goal, I will: _____

_____

During the first 2 weeks of the plan, I will conduct accuracy checks: _____

_____

After 2 weeks, I will conduct accuracy checks: _____

Once the student is successful, the system will be adjusted or faded by: _____

_____

Other notes: _____

REPRODUCIBLE 4.3r *Implementation Guidelines: Self-Monitoring and Self-Evaluation (2 of 4)*

Implementation Guidelines: Self-Monitoring and Self-Evaluation

Implementation Steps

1. **Meet with the student to discuss and finalize the plan.**

   In this meeting:

   - Explain that you would like to assist the student in being more successful and more aware of their own behavior at school. Introduce the self-monitoring system to the student, discussing the purpose and the benefits of self-monitoring.
   - Describe which behaviors the student will monitor. Provide a student-friendly definition and several examples for each behavior.
   - Explain how the self-monitoring system works, including how and when to record behavior, where the student's record will be kept, and when data will be reviewed.
   - Describe the cue that should prompt the student to record behavior. For example, "When you say something positive to someone else, circle the next number on your chart," or "When you hear the timer go off, mark a plus if you are on-task and doing what you're supposed to be doing, and a minus if you are not."
   - Share a goal for using the self-monitoring system. This could be a goal for improvement (e.g., if a student is rating daily effort in math class on a scale of 0–2 points, have the student strive for at least 7 cumulative points at the end of the week), a goal for accurate monitoring (e.g., at least 90% accuracy during teacher accuracy checks), or a goal for regular use of the self-monitoring system (e.g., use self-monitoring forms without being prompted during each study hall period).
   - Inform the student of any rewards that can be earned by using the system and making progress.
   - Encourage student buy-in to the system itself. As much as possible, engage the student in helping to plan the system, and solicit suggestions, questions, and concerns.
   - Explain that you will occasionally use the same system to monitor the student's behavior to check for accuracy.

2. **Practice using the self-monitoring system and role-play different scenarios.**

   Have the student verbally rehearse and demonstrate the steps of the of the self-monitoring procedures. Make sure the student can demonstrate the process and explain the goal of self-monitoring. If appropriate for the student's academic level, provide a written list of the self-monitoring steps. A short list of the process can serve as a guide for reviewing the process at periodic intervals during the first several days of the plan.

   Also role-play examples of different behaviors. Ask the student to identify whether each example behavior is appropriate or inappropriate and how it should be recorded on the self-monitoring form. Provide supportive and corrective feedback about the student's responses. Continue this process using a wide variety of different examples. If the student needs practice beyond the initial meeting, schedule additional practice times.

3. **Implement self-monitoring procedures during specified times and settings.**

   Make sure that the student consistently self-monitors in accordance with the details of the intervention plan. Check in with the student often to monitor use of the forms, answer any questions, and provide encouragement and praise for the student's efforts. If rewards are part of the plan, deliver them as immediately as possible.

REPRODUCIBLE 4.3r *Implementation Guidelines: Self-Monitoring and Self-Evaluation (3 of 4)*

Implementation Guidelines: Self-Monitoring and Self-Evaluation

4. **Acknowledge and encourage the student's efforts.**

    Learning new behaviors and discarding old behaviors is very difficult for some students. Though a particular change may seem simple to an adult, to a child it can be as difficult as learning a new language or musical instrument. The student may need a lot of practice, opportunities to make errors and adjustments, and a lot of encouragement along the way.

5. **Respond calmly and consistently to misbehavior.**

    Minimize attention to misbehavior by remaining calm and using brief, neutral statements. Calm, brief, and consistent corrections are less likely to reinforce misbehavior or interrupt the flow of instruction.

6. **Conduct accuracy checks and compare results with the student's record.**

    Using the same form that the student is using to record behavior, monitor the student's behavior and record your observations. Depending on the self-monitoring system, you might opt to observe and record behavior during random intervals, for a portion of a targeted period, or for the entirety of the time that the student is self-monitoring. Afterwards, compare results. If both you and the student record the same behavior in the same way, provide the student with praise and encouragement. Even if the behavior itself has not yet improved, the student is taking the first step in being responsible—by learning how to self-assess behaviors. If the student and adult records do not match, find a time to discuss the reason for the discrepancy. Is the student recording every event? Is the line between appropriate and inappropriate behavior unclear?

7. **Meet and debrief with the student regularly.**

    Meet with the student during the first week of the plan to see how things are going and to determine whether the plan needs revision. If the system is working, celebrate the student's success and continue using the system without any changes for another week or so. Once the intervention seems to be working well, check in with the student weekly. Review any collected data with the student, highlight successes, and discuss any behaviors that can be improved.

    If the system is not working after the first week, identify whether there are any minor adjustments you can make to improve the chance of student success. Consider:

    - *Does the student understand the system?* To check for understanding, ask the student to model the target behavior and explain how to record behavior.
    - *Is the target behavior clearly defined?* Determine whether additional clarification or more behavior examples are needed to help the student accurately monitor behavior.
    - *Is the student motivated to use the system?* If not, reiterate the goals and benefits of using the system and brainstorm possible rewards to offer for improvements in behavior, accurate recording, or regular use of the monitoring forms.
    - *Is the student getting too much attention from the teacher or peers for exhibiting the problem behaviors?* If so, try to minimize the amount of attention given to misbehavior and increase the number of positive interactions you have with the student.

    If the system is still not working after minor adjustments, collaborate with your problem-solving team to discuss next steps.

REPRODUCIBLE 4.3r Implementation Guidelines: Self-Monitoring and Self-Evaluation (4 of 4)

Implementation Guidelines: Self-Monitoring and Self-Evaluation

8. **Use data to make periodic revisions and adjustments to the plan as necessary.**

    Monitor student progress and collaborate with your problem-solving team to make adjustments to the plan as needed.

9. **Once the student demonstrates consistent success, implement fading procedures or provide continued follow-up, support, and encouragement.**

    As the student assumes ownership of a new behavior or breaks an old habit, consider whether to fade or discontinue using the monitoring system. Fading options include:

    - *Increasing time intervals between monitoring.* Reduce the amount of time or frequency in which the student self-monitors. For example, if the student has been keeping track of on-task behavior and the monitoring was initially taking place all day, you could fade the system by limiting checks to only certain parts of the day.
    - *Modifying goals.* After the student is able to consistently demonstrate and track behaviors originally targeted in the intervention plan, consider increasing the goal for behavior or including new behaviors to monitor. For example, if the student has demonstrated success at monitoring on-time completion of assignments, you might transition the self-monitoring to evaluating neatness, monitoring word count, or rating overall effort on each assignment.
    - *Adjusting rewards.* If your plan includes a reward component, consider adjusting the criteria for earning rewards or fading the use of rewards altogether. For example, instead of delivering rewards daily, you might provide a reward for every 2 days the student meets the goal, or transition from tangible rewards to more natural reinforcers, such as recognition or praise for meeting goals.
    - *Decreasing adult guidance and facilitation of the monitoring system.* One very natural way to fade the system is to eliminate the formal self-monitoring form but continue verbal debriefing with the student once or twice a week. This debriefing offers the student a chance to reflect on recent behavior and you a chance to provide feedback to the student.

    A general rule of thumb: Fade the system when the student demonstrates consistent success, but continue to provide the student with any support necessary to maintain behavior improvements. For some students, temporary practice of self-monitoring may be sufficient to impact self-awareness and behavior in the long term. These students will maintain improvements as the system is gradually faded and eventually removed. Other students may require continued support and may need the structure of a sustained self-monitoring system across the school year in order to be successful.

    Each time you adjust the system, make sure to inform the student in advance and increase the amount of praise and attention the student receives during the transition to new procedures. If the student maintains improvements, continue to adjust procedures as needed to keep the student engaged, or offer the option of discontinuing self-monitoring. If the student's behavior deteriorates, offer the option of reverting back to the previous plan, or adjust fading procedures to be more gradual.

    Finally, regardless of whether you decide to maintain, fade, or suspend formal self-monitoring procedures, continue to praise appropriate behavior and acknowledge the student's maturity and self-discipline. While it is easy to take appropriate behavior for granted, it's important to remember that the student has made a major change in behavior and will need ongoing encouragement and support to continue being successful at school.

REPRODUCIBLE 4.3s *Fidelity Checklist: Self-Monitoring and Self-Evaluation*

Fidelity Checklist
Self-Monitoring and Self-Evaluation

Essential Planning Steps

- ☐ Identify the target behavior or trait to monitor.
- ☐ Choose a recording system for self-monitoring behavior.
- ☐ Determine when the student will record behaviors.
- ☐ Select a cue to prompt the student to record.
- ☐ Set a measurable goal to share with the student.
- ☐ Plan to conduct occasional accuracy checks.
- ☐ Consider whether to incorporate rewards for using the system or showing progress.
- ☐ Contact the student's parents/guardians to discuss the plan.
- ☐ Make a plan for data collection and monitoring.
- ☐ Outline roles and responsibilities for implementing the plan.
- ☐ Provide training to teachers and other adults who will be implementing the plan.

Essential Implementation Components

- ☐ Meet with the student to discuss and finalize the plan.
- ☐ Practice using the self-monitoring system and role-play different scenarios.
- ☐ Implement self-monitoring procedures during specified times and settings.
- ☐ Acknowledge and encourage the student's efforts.
- ☐ Respond calmly and consistently to misbehavior.
- ☐ Conduct accuracy checks and compare results with the student's record.
- ☐ Meet and debrief with the student regularly.
- ☐ Use data to make periodic revisions and adjustments to the plan as necessary.
- ☐ Once the student demonstrates consistent success, implement fading procedures or provide continued follow-up, support, and encouragement.

Interventions © 2019 Ancora Publishing

References

Bruhn, A., McDaniel, S., & Kreigh, C. (2015). Self-monitoring interventions for students with behavior problems: A systematic review of current research. *Behavioral Disorders, 40*(2), 102–121.

Carr, S. C, & Punzo, R. P. (1993). The effects of self-monitoring of academic accuracy and productivity on the performance of students with behavior disorders. *Behavioral Disorders, 18*(4), 241–150

Graham, S., Harris, K. R., & Reid, R. (1992). Developing self-regulated learners. *Focus on Exceptional Children, 24,* 1–16.

Lan, W. (2005). Self-monitoring and its relationship with educational level and task importance. *Educational Psychology, 25,* 109–127.

Menzies, H. M., Lane, K. L., & Lee, J. M. (2009). Self-monitoring strategies for use in the classroom: A promising practice to support productive behavior for students with emotional or behavioral disorders. *Beyond Behavior, 18*(2), 27–35.

Mooney, P., Ryan, J. B., Uhing, B. M., Reid, R., & Epstein, M. H. (2005). A review of self-management interventions targeting academic outcomes for students with emotional and behavioral disorders. *Journal of Behavioral Education, 14,* 203–221.

Rafferty, L. A. (2010). Step-by-step: Teaching students to self-monitor. *Teaching Exceptional Children, 43*(2), 50–58.

Vanderbilt, A. A. (2005). Designed for teachers: How to implement self-monitoring in the classroom. *Beyond Behavior, 15*(1), 21–24.

Walker, H. M. (1995). *Antisocial behavior in school: Strategies and best practices.* Pacific Grove, CA: Brooks/Cole Publishing.

Zimmerman, B. J. (2002). Becoming a self-regulated learner: An overview. *Theory into Practice, 41*(2), 64–70.

Section 4.4

SPECIALIZED INTERVENTION STRATEGY FOUR

Behavior Emergency Planning

The student exhibits Code Red behaviors—behaviors that are physically dangerous, pose a threat to safety of self or others, or are so severe that the teacher cannot continue to teach.

Purpose

Behavior Emergency Planning can be used to defuse and resolve behaviors that have escalated to a Code Red situation.

Code Red situations involve behaviors that are either unsafe or so disruptive that classes cannot continue. These include behaviors such as:

- Overt aggressive behavior toward others (e.g., kicking, hitting, fighting)
- Threats of targeted violence toward others
- Brandishing items that could be used as weapons
- Carrying weapons
- Self-injurious behavior
- Vandalism or property destruction
- Sexual assault
- Clear signs of using controlled substances (drugs and alcohol)
- Running away from school property
- Sustained confrontational or defiant behavior resulting in refusal to follow immediate, reasonable adult directions

A Behavior Emergency Plan specifies the procedures staff will use in responding immediately to each relevant Code Red situation. Behavior Emergency Planning skips over preventive strategies and moves directly to specifying the protocol for responding to a behavior emergency. After defining emergency response procedures, you can return to planning for other positive, proactive intervention strategies designed to teach the student appropriate behavior and prevent behavior emergencies from occurring in the first place.

Behavior Emergency Planning is appropriate when:

- The student has exhibited one or more Code Red behaviors in the past.
- Misbehavior has escalated, or the possibility of a Code Red situation is likely.

All Behavior Emergency Plans must follow the protocol that your district has in place for handling severely disruptive or dangerous behavior. If your district does not have such a policy, or if the policy is vague and does not define specific procedural actions, see Section 1, Task 6 (p. 54) for a description of how to set up protocols for responding to these types of behaviors.

Rationale

One of the most stressful aspects of working with a severely disruptive student is not knowing how to respond. Often, staff members may have good intentions, but lack the knowledge and skills to manage a student crisis effectively (Long & Brendtro, 1996). Unfortunately, few teachers typically receive training in crisis intervention techniques (Taylor, Hawkins, & Brady, 1991).

When a student engages in highly disruptive or dangerous behavior, the classroom teacher needs to be prepared to respond both immediately and calmly. If the teacher responds to disruptive behavior with anger, the student may actually be reinforced. "Wow, I can make the teacher lose it!" Such students are in control because they can make the teacher go out of control. Similarly, if a teacher responds to disruptive behavior by panicking or appearing unsure about what to do, the student may be reinforced. Again, the student is in control of the situation. In either case, the student may find that disruptive behavior is a powerful way to control both the teacher and what happens in the classroom.

When a behavior episode escalates toward a Code Red situation and student misbehavior is so severe as to warrant removal or require safety procedures, intervention must be decisive and intensive (Rock, 2000). Staff must know exactly what procedures to follow. Just as a fire drill offers practice in procedures to follow in the case of a fire, a Behavior Emergency Plan provides adults with the opportunity to think through and plan a protocol for responding to dangerous or severely disruptive student misbehavior.

Essential Planning Steps

STEP 1   Define the problem and describe its context.

Begin by identifying every type of misbehavior the student has engaged in, regardless of how trivial. Include any behavior the student exhibits that could be considered inappropriate or bordering on inappropriate. While your intervention may not address all the misbehaviors that you list, considering the full range of the student's misbehavior will help to define the parameters of behavior emergency procedures.

Next, use your list to categorize each misbehavior as either minor, severely disruptive, or physically dangerous.

Minor misbehaviors include any behaviors that the teacher can reasonably manage within the classroom. Only misbehaviors that substantially interfere with the teacher's ability to continue instruction or that present a threat to the safety of the student or others will be included in the Behavior Emergency Plan. Other minor misbehaviors can be addressed in supplemental intervention planning efforts.

Severely disruptive behaviors make continuing normal class routines impossible and may include any of the following:

- Severe disruption to the classroom (e.g., screaming, tantruming)
- Vandalism or property destruction
- Sustained confrontational or defiant behavior resulting in refusal to follow immediate, reasonable adult directions (see the box on the next page)

BEFORE IMPLEMENTING THIS STRATEGY

It is critical that any individual plan for responding to Code Red behaviors aligns with the policies and procedures in place within your school or district related to severely disruptive or dangerous behavior. Before you create an individualized plan:

- Review all relevant policies in place within your district, such as the policy on restraint and exclusion, weapons policy, and requirements for contacting the school resource officer.
- Refer to the protocol that your district has in place for handling severely disruptive or dangerous behavior. If your district has not yet defined a protocol, see Section 1, Task 6 on page 54.
- Ensure that an administrator will be involved in all decision-making about behavior emergency planning.

> **REFUSAL TO FOLLOW REASONABLE, IMMEDIATE ADULT DIRECTION**
>
> Noncompliance with adult directions should be considered a Code Red situation only when the student engages in overt and immediate refusal to comply with a reasonable adult direction. Staff might have difficulty defining where to draw the line between typical defiance and extreme insubordination—sometimes it's a judgment call. Because these concepts are so broad and open to interpretation, it's best to avoid labeling behavior as *defiant* or *insubordinate*. As an alternative, *refusal to follow reasonable, immediate adult direction* offers an observable definition of the misbehavior, where:
>
> - *Reasonable* means that the direction is clear and observable. Clear directions are "Sit down at your desk" and "Raise your hand if you want to say something." Unclear and unobservable directions include "Change your attitude" and "Shape up."
> - *Immediate* means that the direction needs to be carried out in the next minute or so. If a teacher instructs a student to bring her homework the next day and she doesn't, that incident should not be viewed as refusal to follow a reasonable direction. However, failing to comply with an immediate direction such as "Get off that desk right now" can be viewed as refusal to follow a direction.

TRAUMATIC EVENTS

Severely disruptive or unsafe behavior at school may sometimes occur as a result of stressful and traumatic experiences at home. If you know or suspect that the student has experienced a traumatic event, refer to Trauma-Informed Intervention recommendations included in Appendix A for a discussion of signs of trauma, the impact of trauma on children, and intervention strategies to consider when working with students who have experienced trauma.

Physically dangerous behaviors pose a threat to the student's own safety or the safety of others. These behaviors include:

- Overt aggressive behavior toward others (e.g., kicking, hitting, fighting)
- Threats of targeted violence toward others
- Brandishing items that could be used as weapons
- Carrying weapons
- Self-injurious behavior
- Sexual assault
- Clear signs of using controlled substances (drugs and alcohol)
- Running away from school property

Make sure to clearly define the limits of severely disruptive and physically dangerous behavior. Staff must be able to quickly identify when a situation warrants initiation of behavior emergency procedures. See Section 3, Task 5 (p. 261) for more guidance in defining limits of misbehavior.

Any behavior you categorize as severely disruptive or physically dangerous is considered a Code Red situation and should be addressed in the student's Behavior Emergency Plan. Be sure your school administrators are in agreement about the behaviors that are at a level of severity to warrant removing the student from class or initiating safety procedures.

STEP 2 Consider strategies for responding to behavior.

For all of the Code Red situations that you identified, select a type of emergency response strategy to incorporate into the student's intervention plan.

a. *For severely disruptive misbehavior that is not physically dangerous, arrange out-of-class consequences.* When a student engages in severe misbehavior that is not physically dangerous, an out-of-class consequence is often necessary. The student must not be allowed to detract unduly from the activities and education of other students. On the other hand, removal of the disruptive student from the classroom should be considered a serious decision and is not without risks and logistical hassles (see "Advantages and Disadvantages of Various Out-of-Class Consequences" on the next page for more in-depth discussion of these issues). Before considering this consequence, make sure your administrator verifies the severity of the misbehavior and supports the use of an out-of-class consequence. Remember that getting the student out of the classroom is a temporary measure that will not solve the problem in and of itself. If an out-of-class consequence is required, carefully follow the remaining steps in this intervention to ensure that improvement occurs.

b. *For physically dangerous behavior, arrange safety procedures.* When a student escalates to physically violent or dangerous acts, staff members must act swiftly to ensure the safety of everyone involved. In all cases, you have three priorities:

1. Reduce the likelihood of anyone getting hurt.
2. Respond in such a way that the student is not reinforced for out-of-control behavior.
3. See that everyone involved, including anyone who provoked or participated in the event, is treated with dignity and respect.

SPECIAL ED STUDENT

If the instigator is an identified special education student, it is vital that you work directly with the building special education personnel and school district when arranging consequences in order to avoid possible violation of federal law. For example, suspension of a special education student may constitute a change of placement and cannot be instituted without due process.

Whenever possible, the preferred method for dealing with out-of-control behavior is to remove everyone else from the threat of violence. In a classroom situation, this would mean a room clear. On a playground, move students in the vicinity away from the student who is out of control. Although physical restraint is the less preferable of the two options, it may be necessary in certain special cases. See "Safety Procedures: Room Clears Versus Physical Restraint" on page 411 for more detailed discussion of these options.

STEP 3 Outline a plan for implementation and data collection.

When creating a plan, make sure to incorporate the following components.

Contact the parents or guardian. Parents must be involved whenever an incident of seriously disruptive or dangerous behavior occurs. Initially, make contact to let the student's parents know there has been a problem. Eventually, a conference should be held to begin the process of collaborative problem-solving. Parents can provide valuable input as staff members determine how to help the student. Depending on the severity of the situation, you may also bring in representatives from other social agencies to help develop a comprehensive plan.

continued on page 412

ADVANTAGES AND DISADVANTAGES OF VARIOUS OUT-OF-CLASS CONSEQUENCES

Consider the pros and cons of these different methods for removing a disruptive student from the classroom.

Send the student to the hallway. Moving a disruptive student into the hallway is a very weak option because the student is unsupervised. Who is responsible for the student out in the hall? What are the liability issues if the student runs away, is injured, or hurts another student? Hallways are also not boring enough. If other students are in the hallway, the misbehaving student is on display. The student might be teased or ostracized, or might pose as a negative hero—"Look how BAD I am. I got sent to the hallway." Finally, if the teacher places a student who has engaged in severe misbehavior in the hallway, the teacher will need to transition the student back into the classroom. If the misbehavior is upsetting, the teacher may find it very difficult to ask the student calmly to clarify what they did and to identify how to behave differently in the future.

Send the student home. At first glance, sending a student home may seem like a logical consequence and the best possible option when the student engages in severe misbehavior. In an ideal situation, a parent is contacted and immediately comes to the school to pick up the student. The student is then taken directly home and not allowed to watch TV, listen to music, read, draw, or play. The child is bored. Later that evening, the parents and child have a serious conversation about the importance of school. The parents let the child know the consequences for this and future problems, and the child learns that the parents are deeply disappointed. Unfortunately, when a child has serious behavior problems, this scenario may be far from reality. It may not be possible to reach a parent immediately. Some parents will not or cannot supervise a student who has been sent home, and often students who are sent home are allowed to do something they would much rather do than schoolwork, like playing a video game or watching TV. Some parents sympathize with the child and talk about "those blankety-blank teachers and that principal—she doesn't know what she's doing." Other children may be physically abused as a punishment for their misbehavior.

Send the student to the office. The office meets the criterion of adequate supervision, but it is hardly a dull place. The office may be the most stimulating environment in the whole school. The student may thoroughly enjoy watching the secretary work, listening to the intercom, greeting the copy machine technician, and so on. These kinds of issues can sometimes be circumvented if you can create a relatively quiet space. For example, it may be possible to position a study carrel in the quietest corner of the office so that the student is visually shielded from high-traffic areas.

Send the student to another classroom. Another classroom may serve as an out-of-class placement. This choice is an option if the alternative classroom is populated with very mature students who are not easily distracted and who will ignore the student. If you select this option, make arrangements in advance with the teacher in the other classroom. The cooperating classroom teacher should tell students that they may have another student join their class once in a while. If this occurs, their job will be simply to provide a quiet space. They will be expected to ignore the student and continue working. The teacher should explain that sometimes people need a place to get away and think. They will be helping others by providing that space.

On engaging in severe misbehavior, the student will be escorted to the alternative classroom and will take a preassigned seat in an unobtrusive location. The other classroom teacher should continue teaching without interruption. This option is not intended to embarrass the student who has engaged in a severe misbehavior, so avoid sending an older student to a classroom of very young children.

Use a timeout room or in-school suspension. Timeout rooms can work very well if a school has the space and personnel to supervise the room. A timeout room is generally supervised by a trained assistant who does not interact with students until they are ready to be transitioned back into the classroom.

NOTE: Though out-of-class placements have inherent problems, they may be necessary. Be aware that out-of-class placements are only temporary responses to misbehavior. It is highly unlikely that the consequence alone will change the behavior, and when they are used too often, consequences may actually reinforce the behavior.

SAFETY PROCEDURES: ROOM CLEARS VERSUS PHYSICAL RESTRAINT

From a practical standpoint, usually only two immediate options are available when a physically threatening incident occurs: (1) get everyone out of the student's way and out of the classroom, referred to as a *room clear*, or (2) have one or more adults physically restrain the student. A room clear is preferable to physical restraint for a number of reasons:

- A room clear is the most direct way to ensure everyone's safety. When students clear the room, they are removed from immediate threats of escalation and physical injury.
- Physical restraint is more likely to result in injury to the student or to the adult attempting to restrain the student.
- Physical restraint may stoke the emotional intensity of the situation. For some students, the sheer intensity of resisting the restraint or fighting an authority figure may be reinforcing for out-of-control behavior.
- Physical restraint is sometimes not an option. It requires an adult who is larger and stronger than the student. Should the student resist strenuously and prolong the struggle, more adults may have to be summoned. Through it all, the risk of injury to others continues.
- A room clear removes the audience and the potential reinforcer of peer attention. If "performing" for other students is reinforcing to the out-of-control student, the attention is removed.
- When physical restraint is used, the entire class witnesses the altercation. The scene can be upsetting and distressing to students, or it can cause outrage and mutinous feelings among classmates sympathetic to the out-of-control student.
- Room clears may help students learn to manage their own behavior. When physical restraint is used to control their behavior, students may mistakenly learn to depend on an adult, an "outside force," to bring their behavior under control. In the long term, such students may come to believe that they are unable to change or control their own behavior. They may grow up afraid of what they might do, or they may continue to depend on others to stop them when they get out of control or "go off."

Use physical intervention only when necessary. Although a room clear is preferable to restraint, it is not always the appropriate response. If a student is about to stab someone with scissors, there may not be time for a room clear. If a student is engaged in self-injurious behavior such as head banging, some form of restraint or physical intervention may be necessary. Sometimes a room clear can be paired with appropriate physical intervention. For example, if two students are involved in a violent fight, the teacher may need to get the other students out of the room, call for help, and, when help arrives, separate and restrain the two students until they calm down enough to be released. If you are considering physical intervention as part of a student's safety plan, carefully review your school or district policies and comply with established protocols. See "Guidelines for Using Physical Restraint" on page 58 in Section 1 for guidance in developing school or districtwide procedures for using physical restraint with students.

When working with parents, staff need to use their professional judgment to determine how involved parents will be in any plan to assist the student at school. You can avoid adversarial stances by letting parents know that staff members are committed to helping the student learn more successful behavior. Parents should not be asked to take full responsibility for problems that occur at school. Parents of students with severe misbehavior problems often do not know what to do at home, much less how to get the student to behave while at school. Instead, staff members should work proactively with parents to develop ways to encourage and support appropriate behavior both at school and at home, while teaching the student to avoid inappropriate behavior.

Establish an out-of-the-room location where the student can be sent if severely disruptive behavior occurs. When selecting a location for an out-of-class consequence, carefully weigh the following three criteria (Ryan, Sanders, Katsiyannis, & Yell, 2007):

- The location should be supervised. Unsupervised locations increase the risk that students will leave the building, destroy property, or hurt themselves.
- The location should be dull. A busy environment may be more interesting to students than the classroom.
- The location should allow a carefully orchestrated transition back into the classroom. Before students return to class, someone will need to help them identify what behavior was inappropriate and what they might do differently in the future.

Good options include sending a student to another classroom or using a timeout room. A timeout room is generally supervised by a trained assistant who does not interact with students until they are ready to be transitioned back into the classroom. Check to ensure that school administrators are in agreement about where students should be sent.

Specify the length of time the student will spend outside the classroom. The length of time the student will spend in an alternative setting should be predetermined. For example, the student may owe a certain number of minutes starting from when they become calm. Or if the infraction occurs in the early morning, the student may need to wait in the out-of-class placement until the end of morning recess. If the severe misbehavior occurs after morning recess, the student may need to eat lunch in the out-of-class placement and remain there until lunch recess is over.

Establish a plan for receiving adult assistance immediately. If a student will be assigned an out-of-class consequence, identify a list of staff members who can go quickly to the classroom and escort the student to the appropriate location.

Plans for providing an immediate response should specify who will respond, a chain of command in case the first person is unavailable, and a communication process to ensure that everyone involved is kept informed. These procedures should be carefully designed and occasionally rehearsed so that the process works smoothly and addresses high-probability contingencies (such as the principal being out of the building). For example, the first person on the list might be the principal. If the principal is out of the building, the next person might be the counselor. If the counselor is unavailable, it might be the teacher in the room next door, whose own room will be covered briefly by a member of the office staff.

Likewise, the classroom teacher will need immediate assistance if a student begins engaging in physically dangerous behavior. Establish procedures for summoning a trained staff person to the classroom immediately. The procedure should include a prearranged signal that indicates a crisis is occurring. Some schools use their intercom system. Others use a specially designed red crisis card that the teacher can give to a student messenger. The messenger takes the crisis card to the office, where an immediate preplanned response is initiated.

Create a backup plan in case the student refuses to comply with an out-of-class consequence. All staff members should be trained to get the student's attention calmly and say that they will go together to the out-of-class placement. If the student fails to comply, the staff member should quietly ask if the student will need assistance. If the student still refuses to comply, the staff member may attempt a gentle physical prompt, such as taking the student by the arm, if school and board policy permit. If the student does not respond appropriately, only three options remain:

- The student can be physically removed if the staff member is large enough and the student is small enough.
- Another adult can be called for assistance to remove the student physically.
- The other students can be removed from the room.

If any of these options are considered, staff should consider the practical and ethical issues that accompany each one, and carefully study their school and board policies to develop contingency plans (Scheuermann, Peterson, Ryan, & Billingsley, 2016).

If room clears are part of the student's safety plan, identify where other students will go and what they will do. Routine provisions should be made to minimize disruption. Students should be taken into the hallway until assistance can be summoned. As soon as another adult arrives, the class should be taken to a predetermined location. Relevant instructional tasks should be prepared in advance. For example, students might be taken to the school stage, where paper and pencils have been stored. If a room clear is necessary, the supervising adult might conduct a spelling bee or have students do a writing assignment, solve math problems, or write a class story.

If you are considering rooms clears or physical intervention as part of the student's safety plan, carefully consider the practical, ethical, and school policy-related issues that accompany these options.

Develop procedures for transitioning the student back into the classroom. The student should be directed to wait quietly while in the out-of-class placement. Determine who will discuss the severe misbehavior with the student and escort the student back to class. At the designated time, the student should discuss with an adult what happened and how to avoid future outbursts. If writing skills are sufficient, the student should write down what happened and what to do differently in the future. If not, the adult should record what happened and what the student could do differently in the future.

It may also be worthwhile to have the student fill out a Behavior Improvement Form (see Reproducible 4.4a on the next page). If time permits, the adult might role-play the problem situation with the student and have the student act out appropriate responses. Upon reentering the classroom, the student should give the teacher the written notes or the Behavior Improvement Form. The teacher should quietly acknowledge the student's return and act as though they were starting a new day.

Identify strategies to focus on appropriate student behaviors and strengths. Because a highly disruptive student usurps so much time and energy when misbehaving, it can be difficult for the teacher to pay attention when the student is being responsible. However, when appropriate behavior is not regularly acknowledged, the student may learn that the only way to access teacher attention is by acting out. To avoid escalation or increases in misbehavior, help the teacher identify ways to direct attention to the

REPRODUCIBLE 4.4a *Behavior Improvement Form*

Behavior Improvement Form

Name _____   Grade/Class _____

Teacher _____   Period/Time _____

1. What was your behavior? _____
_____
_____
_____
_____
_____
_____

2. What could you do differently? _____
_____
_____
_____
_____
_____
_____

3. Will you be able to do that? _____
_____
_____
_____
_____
_____
_____

Interventions © 2019 Ancora Publishing

student's positive behavior and efforts. Working with the teacher, generate a list of student strengths and responsible behaviors. Brainstorm a list of options to focus attention on appropriate behavior and then check those that the teacher believes will be manageable. This is the beginning of a process to set up a long-range positive intervention plan.

Make a plan for data collection and monitoring. From their onset, situations involving severe or dangerous misbehavior should always be recorded. Plan to document the following information:

- Date and time of day the incident occurred
- Location of the incident
- Adults who were supervising at the time of the incident
- Events that occurred prior to the incident
- A detailed description of the student's behavior during the incident, including the duration of the episode and specific details about the behavior
- Actions taken by staff
- Consequences implemented (if any)
- Actions taken to minimize future occurrences

After a Code Red situation occurs, plan to have the classroom teacher or supervising adult provide an account of the incident as soon as possible. This process can provide staff members with an opportunity to talk through incidents that are likely to be disturbing. Debriefing can also help administrators gather and record anecdotal information about each behavior emergency. The Extreme Behavior Log (Reproducible 4.4b on the next page) can be used to create a detailed anecdotal record of all incidents that involve severely disruptive, physically dangerous, or threatening events. When several disruptions from a student are recorded in the log over a period of time, you can summarize the information to help determine the severity of the problem and whether the procedures being used are helping the student improve. Use the Severe Behavior Summary Chart (Reproducible 4.4c, p. 417) to graph incidents at each level of intensity you identify. Use a separate graph for each level of intensity (1, 2, or 3) and record frequency, duration, or both per week.

Finally, check to make sure your plan for documentation addresses any relevant district or building requirements for reporting particular types of behavior to your school resource officer, local police authorities, or other agencies.

Consider supplemental intervention strategies to incorporate into the plan. A Behavior Emergency Plan is primarily focused on defining a set of procedures for staff to follow when an individual student exhibits Code Red behavior. This plan is only the first step in designing supports for the student. Consequences for out-of-control behavior tend to have little effect on preventing future incidents. It is far more important to teach students to control their own behavior. Therefore, this intervention must be accompanied by more intensive planning in other positive, proactive intervention strategies designed to teach students appropriate classroom behavior. Consult the foundational intervention strategies presented in Section 3 and other specialized intervention procedures, such as Behavioral Contracting or Structured Reinforcement, to design a comprehensive behavior support plan to accompany this Behavior Emergency Plan. Interventions for serious behaviors are likely to require multiple components and a long-term approach, with adjustments to accommodate new environments, such as classroom changes across academic years (Kern, Benson, & Clemens, 2009).

REPRODUCIBLE 4.4b *Extreme Behavior Log*

Extreme Behavior Log

Student _____ Grade/Class _____ Teacher _____

Directions: Record Code Red behavior (all incidents of physically dangerous or highly disruptive behavior).

INTENSITY KEY: 1 = Refuses to comply or participate
2 = Verbally abusive or shouting
3 = Physically violent

Date	Start Time	Stop Time	Total Duration	Intensity	Anecdotal Notes

Interventions © 2019 Ancora Publishing

REPRODUCIBLE 4.4b

REPRODUCIBLE 4.4c *Severe Behavior Summary Chart*

Severe Behavior Summary Chart

Name _____ Grade/Class _____

Teacher _____ Date _____

Level of intensity (circle one):   1   2   3

KEY: X = Number of incidents

Frequency (y-axis: 0–30)

Week (x-axis: 1–18)

KEY: ● = Total minutes
        ○ = Average minutes per incident

Duration (minutes) (y-axis: 0–120)

Week (x-axis: 1–18)

Interventions © 2019 Ancora Publishing

REPRODUCIBLE 4.4c

Outline roles and responsibilities for implementing the plan. At this point, the Behavior Emergency Plan should provide clear answers to these questions:

- Which behaviors warrant removal from the classroom?
- Where will the student go for an out-of-class timeout?
- How long will the student spend in the timeout location?
- What will the student do while in timeout?
- Who will supervise the student while in timeout?
- How will the student transition back to the classroom?
- Are there any behaviors that warrant the use of safety procedures? If so, what procedures will be used?

As planning is completed, carefully explore what will be done in unforeseen circumstances by asking *what-if* questions. For example, if the student is to go to another classroom but that teacher is absent, what will happen? Who will transition the student back to class if the responsible staff member is out of the building? A careful discussion of the plan can increase its probability of success.

Finalize your plan by also making sure to identify:

- Who will meet with the student to discuss the plan.
- Who will contact the parents to discuss the plan.
- Who will be responsible for following up with comprehensive intervention planning.
- Who will be responsible for debriefing with staff members after a Code Red situation occurs, and who will collect and monitor data on these behavior emergencies.
- Who will need training.

Provide training to teachers and other adults who will be implementing the plan. Staff who may be responsible for responding to behavior emergencies need to be fully trained. Staff should learn which behaviors qualify as Code Red situations, how to follow emergency procedures, and what documentation and follow-up is required after each behavior emergency. Adults who will supervise an out-of-control student should be trained to stand at the door and determine the actions to take if the situation escalates. If physical restraint is recommended under specified conditions, adults should be trained in how to restrain a student safely.

Use Implementation Guidelines: Behavioral Contracting (Reproducible 4.4d; pp. 426–430) to review procedures with staff. Also make sure to distribute relevant forms for documenting incidents and monitoring progress (e.g., referral forms, Behavior Improvement Forms, Extreme Behavior Log).

> **TRAINING IN PHYSICAL RESTRAINT**
>
> Training in uses and methods of physical restraint requires demonstrations, practice, and rehearsal. It is beyond the scope of this book to provide detailed guidelines. Local law enforcement, mental health organizations, state agencies, and schools with successful violence prevention programs in place may be good resources for strategies and recommendations.

 Case Example: Cynthia

Several days after the start of school in the fall, Cynthia is registered at Adams School by her grandmother. Like many new students in this highly transient neighborhood, Cynthia arrives without any records from her previous school. Cynthia's grandmother promises to try to have those records sent.

Cynthia is placed in Mr. Carmody's fifth-grade classroom. During the first 2 days, Cynthia does very little in class. She seems sullen and quiet. She refuses to participate in any activities, spending most of her time with her head down on her desk. On the third day, Mr. Carmody notices a change. Cynthia seems agitated from the moment she steps into the classroom. By the middle of the morning, Cynthia is wandering around the room, poking and taunting the other students. When Mr. Carmody tells Cynthia to take her seat and begin working, Cynthia responds loudly and angrily, "I don't have to do nothing you tell me to do!" Though Mr. Carmody tries speaking quietly to Cynthia, she becomes more and more agitated, yelling profanities. As Mr. Carmody tries to calm her down, Cynthia picks up a book and throws it. "Leave me alone! You leave me alone!" As Cynthia rages through the classroom, she overturns furniture and pushes nearby students.

Mr. Carmody acts as quickly as possible, implementing previously developed building procedures for dealing with violent behavior. First, he instructs his class to leave the room and immediately report to Mrs. Zugliani's room across the hall. Mrs. Zugliani and Mr. Carmody were paired as Crisis Partners at the beginning of the school year, agreeing to supervise one another's students in the event of a crisis.

Mr. Carmody then calls the office and informs office staff that a crisis is occurring. He asks for assistance, but also indicates that the police are not needed. Mr. Carmody then goes into the hallway and stands where he can observe Cynthia in case she hurts herself.

Meanwhile, because the principal is out of the building, the office secretary contacts Ms. Alton, the counselor. Ms. Alton goes immediately to assist Mr. Carmody, who is watching Cynthia from the hallway to make sure that her out-of-control behavior does not escalate to the point of endangering her own safety. After turning over several desks, Cynthia eventually runs out of steam and sinks to the floor, holding her arms over her head. When Cynthia has been quiet for several minutes, Ms. Alton escorts Cynthia to her office. Twenty minutes have passed.

When it's over, Mr. Carmody feels drained but relieved that he knew how to handle the situation. The entire incident just seemed to explode—he didn't have time to think.

Mr. Carmody takes a few minutes to collect his thoughts and tidy up his classroom. Then he goes to Mrs. Zugliani's room to get his students. The two classes are working on a choral reading of a poem. When they finish, Mr. Carmody thanks both classes for their cooperation. He explains that Cynthia is having a very difficult day and that everyone needs to continue working as a community, welcoming Cynthia into the circle. Cynthia will probably feel very uncomfortable about what happened, so it will be important for everyone to help her feel like a regular fifth grader. Mr. Carmody tells the class that everyone has special goals to work on. He himself is working on being more patient, and Cynthia will be working on handling her angry feelings more constructively.

The secretary is able to contact the principal, Mr. Feinberg, at the district office. He returns to the building immediately. As soon as he returns, he contacts Cynthia's grandmother, who comes to pick her up. Before Cynthia and her grandmother leave the school, the principal sets up a conference with them for the next day to determine a plan for helping Cynthia learn to control herself.

After school, the principal, the counselor, and the classroom teacher meet to establish a plan to present to Cynthia and her grandmother. They identify consequences for Cynthia's outburst, which include spending one hour after school the next day to clean and organize the classroom and writing an apology to Mr. Carmody.

In addition, they establish modifications to the room clear procedure in case Cynthia has similar problems in the future. Mr. Carmody identifies three responsible students whom he will train to get help in the event that he is unable to use the intercom. Two adults are also selected to contact for assistance in the event the principal is out of the building. The chain of command is as follows:

1. Mr. Feinberg—the principal
2. Ms. Alton—the counselor
3. Mr. Black—the special education teacher next door

Together, Mr. Feinberg, Mr. Carmody, and Ms. Alton also clarify exactly how future out-of-control behavior will be handled:

- Students will be moved into the hallway (room clear).
- Mr. Carmody will call the office or instruct one of his trained student helpers to go immediately to the office for assistance.
- If the principal is available, he will immediately drop whatever he is doing and take Mr. Carmody's class to a prearranged location—the cafeteria or stage—where he will conduct prearranged lessons. (If the principal is not available, the office staff will contact the counselor. If both the principal and counselor are out of the building, the office staff will contact Mr. Black, the teacher next door.)
- After the room is clear, Mr. Carmody will remain in the doorway of the classroom to supervise Cynthia and make sure that she does not hurt herself.
- Once Cynthia calms down, Mr. Carmody will quietly inform Cynthia about things that need to be straightened up before the other students can return. When the room is restored to normal, Mr. Carmody will also show Cynthia any broken items that he will store for later replacement.

As Mr. Carmody, Mr. Feinberg, and Ms. Alton map out their plan for Cynthia, they find that one of their most difficult decisions is what to do with Cynthia after an incident. Should there be consequences? Should she be suspended? Mr. Carmody wants Cynthia removed from the classroom and suspended from school for at least a week. Ms. Alton thinks that Cynthia should stay in the room—having to restore the room and face the other students when they return will be consequence enough. Ms. Alton fears that Cynthia might enjoy getting sent home. A middle-ground position is finally determined. Cynthia will be escorted to the office when she is calm enough to follow an adult without a physical confrontation. She will spend the remainder of that day in a timeout room off the front office. The next day she will return to the classroom.

The three also agree that Ms. Alton will spend time with Cynthia investigating her academic abilities and conducting some preliminary lessons on self-control.

Cynthia will spend 30 minutes per day with the counselor for at least a week. At the end of the week, the counselor will assess Cynthia's progress and continue meeting with her on a regular basis.

Temporary restraint is discussed in case Cynthia tries to attack someone before or during the time students are clearing the room. Because Mr. Carmody has training and experience in safe restraint, he will restrain Cynthia only to prevent immediate injury to another student. Once the students are out of danger, Cynthia will be released and Mr. Carmody will go to his position in the hallway. These guidelines ensure that Mr. Carmody is never put in the position of restraining Cynthia without witnesses and that restraint will be used only as a last resort to prevent injury.

Mr. Feinberg also asks Mr. Carmody to begin keeping records. Ms. Alton, Mr. Carmody, and Mr. Feinberg agree to meet whenever a room clear is required. Records will be kept on the duration and frequency of incidents, the events leading to each incident, and the outcome. They decide that it is premature to begin special education referral or to involve the police or other agencies until Cynthia's records arrive.

As Mr. Carmody, Ms. Alton, and Mr. Feinberg finalize the plan, they decide that both Cynthia and her grandmother should be invited to make suggestions about the proposed plan. They agree to begin the conference with Cynthia and her grandmother by outlining two major goals. The first goal is to keep everyone safe, and the second is to help Cynthia learn how to deal with her anger.

Essential Implementation Procedures

The following should be done by the teacher or interventionist responsible for implementing the plan.

1. Meet with the student to discuss and finalize the plan. During this meeting, cover these items:

- Explain that you would like to help the student be more successful at school, learn how to manage their own feelings and actions, and keep everyone safe at school.
- Discuss the problem with the student. Calmly explain why specific behaviors are disruptive or dangerous and provide an age-appropriate rationale for why these behaviors aren't tolerated at school. Make it clear that everyone would like to help the student be successful in the classroom.
- Clearly define the severely disruptive or physically dangerous behavior that will require emergency procedures. Make sure that the student fully understands what behaviors you are referring to. Offer recent incidents involving the student as examples, as needed.
- Review expectations for behavior at school. List examples of different types of appropriate and inappropriate behavior, including examples from the student's own repertoire. Ask the student to explain whether each example meets expectations or violates expectations.

> Items 1–8 are also shown on **Implementation Guidelines** (Form 4.4d, pp. 426–430). Share with teachers and other adults responsible for implementing the plan.

BEFORE MEETING WITH THE STUDENT

Once you outline emergency procedures, determine who will discuss the plan with the student and when the discussion will take place. In most cases, the parents should be invited. The classroom teacher and at least one other staff member should be present. Schedule the conference at a neutral time, not immediately following a disruptive incident, so everyone can discuss problems and plans calmly.

- Explain the procedures that you or other adults will use the next time the student engages in highly disruptive or dangerous behavior. Clearly specify what the student should do to comply with emergency procedures.

    ○ If out-of-class consequences will be used, describe the location, the amount of time the student will spend out of the classroom, and what the student should do during this time.
    ○ If restraint will be used, specify when it will be used and explain that it will stop once it is no longer needed to protect the student or others.

- Inform the student of any consequences that will be delivered. Explain that you will contact the student's parents if behavior escalates to the point of being severely disruptive or dangerous.
- Before concluding this initial meeting, make sure the student is aware of the seriousness of the situation, the behaviors that will require emergency procedures, and what these procedures will look like. Check for understanding of expectations and procedures by asking gentle questions, such as "What will happen if . . . ."

2. Practice and role-play emergency procedures with the student. Have the student practice complying with emergency procedures. Model expected behaviors, such as quietly walking to the timeout room and taking a seat, and have the student role-play or verbally rehearse what to do in different scenarios.

3. Implement behavior emergency procedures when necessary. Whenever behavior escalates to a Code Red situation, follow these steps:

Step 1: Deliver or restate a direction, making sure it is clear, observable, and immediate (e.g., say "Sit down at your desk" instead of "Shape up"). If the student refuses a second time, use the Jot It Down strategy—literally write the direction and the student's inappropriate response on paper. This action slows the momentum toward more serious conflict between you and the student, and the student might sit down while you write. If the student fails to comply or behavior escalates further, move to the next step.

Step 2: If the student fails to comply with the repeated direction, immediately implement emergency procedures.

- First, signal for immediate assistance from another staff member in your identified chain-of-command list.
- If the behavior poses a threat to the safety of the student or others, implement safety procedures (i.e., room clears or physical intervention). Remember the three priorities of safety procedures:

    ○ Reduce the likelihood of anyone getting hurt.
    ○ Respond in such a way that the student is not reinforced for out-of-control behavior.
    ○ See that everyone involved, including anyone who provoked or participated in the event, is treated with dignity and respect.

- If the behavior is severely disruptive but not dangerous, assign an out-of-class consequence. Get the student's attention calmly and say that you (or another adult) will go together to the out-of-class placement. If the student refuses, quietly ask if the student will need assistance. If the student still fails to comply, you may attempt a gentle physical prompt, such as taking the student by the arm, if school and board policy permit. If the student still does not respond appropriately, use the safety procedures outlined in your backup plan (i.e., room clears or physical intervention).
- Make sure to acknowledge the student whenever the student complies with directions, out-of-class consequences, or safety procedures.

Step 3: After the incident, have an adult escort the student back to the classroom. If the student discussed the incident with an administrator or completed a Behavior Improvement Form, collect these notes and quietly acknowledge the student's return. Welcome the student back to class and act as though you are starting a new day.

4. After each behavior emergency, complete all necessary documentation. Adhere to your school's notification or referral procedures, as well as any additional data collection or reporting procedures specified as part of the student's Behavior Emergency Plan, to document all relevant information about the incident.

5. Meet and debrief with the student after each behavior emergency. At a designated time, discuss the incident with the student. Work with the student to complete a Behavior Improvement Form if the student hasn't already done so. If time permits, role-play the problem situation and have the student act out alternative, more appropriate responses. Also, until a more comprehensive plan is developed, check in frequently with the student to see how things are going. Students who have problems with severe misbehavior need continual assurance that, even when they display disruptive behavior, adults will be consistent and supportive.

6. Keep in contact with the parents or guardians. Inform parents about any Code Red incidents and maintain ongoing communication via regularly scheduled progress reports (e.g., a weekly note sent home with the student, phone conference, or e-mail communication).

7. Focus on appropriate student behaviors and strengths as much as possible. When students have severe behavior problems, it is often difficult to give them attention or recognition for appropriate behavior. Unfortunately, such students learn again and again that adult attention is guaranteed during misbehavior and highly unlikely during appropriate behavior. Work to increase the positive attention, praise, and positive feedback you offer the student, while minimizing attention for misbehavior as much as possible.

8. Use data to make periodic revisions and adjustments to the plan as necessary. Referrals and entries in the Extreme Behavior Log provide both a permanent record and a regular opportunity for the teacher to debrief about the student's progress and problems.

Remember that reactive consequences for out-of-control behavior tend to have little effect on preventing future incidents. Rather than evaluating the effectiveness of your Behavior Emergency Plan by looking only for improvements in behavior, consider other outcomes to examine, such as:

- Is behavior getting worse or occurring more frequently?
- Is the safety of the student and others still compromised?
- Are out-of-class consequences resulting in more problems?

If you answer yes to any of the above questions, ask these questions:

- *Are all essential components of the plan being implemented as intended?* Ensure that intervention fidelity is maintained by having the teacher or external observer complete the Fidelity Checklist: Behavior Emergency Planning (Reproducible 4.4e, p. 431).
- *Does the student understand the system?* To check for understanding, ask the student to identify behaviors that will result in out-of-class consequences or safety procedures and the actions adults will take in response.
- *Which aspects of the plan can you modify to increase its effectiveness?* Is the out-of-class consequence too reinforcing to the student? Is the student adequately supervised in this setting? Are procedures to help the student transition back to class supportive enough? Adjust the plan accordingly.
- *Is the student getting too much attention from the teacher or peers for exhibiting the problem behaviors?* If adult attention is an issue, discuss with the teacher ways to minimize the amount of attention given to misbehavior when implementing emergency procedures. If peer attention is reinforcing the student's misbehavior, the other students may need to be taught to ignore inappropriate behavior.
- *What supplemental strategies can you introduce to support the effectiveness of the plan?* As you begin to develop a more comprehensive support plan, consider strategies that may help to increase the effectiveness of your emergency procedures, such as introducing self-monitoring procedures or incorporating a reinforcement system for calming down and complying with adult directions.

Again, because a Behavior Emergency Plan only outlines a set of reactive procedures to address Code Red behavior, the plan is just the first step in designing supports for the student. To encourage lasting behavior improvement, this intervention must be followed by more intensive planning in other positive, proactive intervention strategies designed to teach the student appropriate classroom behavior.

> **PROVIDE ONGOING SUPPORT FOR THE TEACHER**
>
> Once the Behavior Emergency Plan is in place, be sure to follow up with support for the classroom teacher. The classroom teacher dealing with a student who exhibits severely disruptive behavior needs to know that other staff members will provide ongoing support and assistance. This support and assistance may include:
>
> - Asking other teachers and staff members to agree to step in or provide backup support if needed. This can help reassure the teacher that the situation will never be entirely out of control.
> - Setting up a series of observations and conferences with the classroom teacher to take a more in-depth look at the severity of the misbehavior.
> - Checking in while debriefing after a Code Red situation to see how the teacher is feeling, what additional support might be helpful, and whether emergency protocols are working.
> - Inviting the teacher to take part in problem-solving team meetings and efforts to develop more comprehensive supports for the student.
>
> Working on a daily basis with a severely disruptive student can be extremely stressful. The more others can assist and offer support, the less pressure the teacher will experience while trying to help the student and teach a classroom of students at the same time.

Strategy Summary

When a plan for responding to a behavior emergency is *not* defined and in place, staff members may be unsure about which behaviors are considered emergencies and how they are supposed to respond. A Behavior Emergency Plan should be used only when behavior simply cannot be tolerated in the classroom because it impedes the learning of other students or threatens the student or others. This intervention provides temporary relief for a difficult situation while a more proactive plan is developed. As soon as possible, conduct a series of observations and use all the information gathered to develop a more comprehensive, long-term plan.

REPRODUCIBLE 4.4d *Implementation Guidelines: Behavior Emergency Planning (1 of 5)*

Implementation Guidelines
Behavior Emergency Planning

Overview

A Behavior Emergency Plan can be used to defuse and resolve behaviors that have escalated to a Code Red situation. Code Red situations involve behaviors that are either so dangerous or so disruptive that classes cannot continue. These include:

- *Severely disruptive behaviors* that make continuing normal class routines impossible, such as:
    - Severe disruption to the classroom (e.g., screaming, tantruming)
    - Vandalism or property destruction
    - Sustained confrontational or defiant behavior that results in refusal to follow immediate, reasonable adult directions

- *Physically dangerous behaviors* that pose a threat to the student's own safety or the safety of others, such as:
    - Overt aggressive behavior toward others (e.g., kicking, hitting, fighting)
    - Threats of targeted violence toward others
    - Brandishing items that could be used as weapons
    - Carrying weapons
    - Self-injurious behavior
    - Sexual assault
    - Clear signs of using controlled substances (drugs and alcohol)
    - Running away from school property

One of the most stressful aspects of working with a severely disruptive student is not knowing how to respond. When a student engages in highly disruptive or dangerous behavior, adults need to be prepared to respond both immediately and calmly. When a behavior episode escalates toward a Code Red situation and student misbehavior is so severe as to warrant removal or require safety procedures, intervention must be decisive and intensive. Staff must know exactly what procedures to follow. Just as a fire drill offers practice in procedures to follow in the case of a fire, a Behavior Emergency Plan provides adults with the opportunity to think through and plan a protocol for responding to dangerous or severely disruptive student misbehavior.

Note that Behavior Emergency Planning skips over preventive strategies and moves directly to specifying the protocol for responding to a behavior emergency. Once you define emergency response procedures, you will need to implement other positive, proactive intervention strategies to teach appropriate behavior and help the student get their needs met.

REPRODUCIBLE 4.4d *Implementation Guidelines: Behavior Emergency Planning (2 of 5)*

Implementation Guidelines: Behavior Emergency Planning

Plan Summary

The following *severely disruptive behaviors* will be considered behavior emergencies: _____
_____

Describe the out-of-class consequences that will be used to respond to severely disruptive behaviors: _____
_____

The following *physically dangerous behaviors* will be considered behavior emergencies: _____
_____

Describe the safety procedures that will be used to respond to dangerous behaviors: _____
_____

When a behavior emergency occurs, the teacher will use this signal to request immediate assistance from other staff:
_____

List staff members to contact for immediate assistance, in order of contact:

1) _____

2) _____

3) _____

4) _____

Describe documentation requirements and data collection procedures: _____
_____

Other notes: _____
_____
_____

REPRODUCIBLE 4.4d *Implementation Guidelines: Behavior Emergency Planning (3 of 5)*

Implementation Guidelines: Behavior Emergency Planning

Implementation Steps

1. **Meet with the student to discuss and finalize the plan.**

   During this meeting:

   - Explain that you would like to help the student be more successful at school and learn how to manage feelings and actions, as well as keep everyone safe at school.
   - Discuss the problem with the student. Calmly explain why specific behaviors are disruptive or dangerous, and provide an age-appropriate rationale for why these behaviors aren't tolerated at school. Make it clear that everyone would like to help the student be successful in the classroom.
   - Clearly define the severely disruptive or physically dangerous behavior that will require emergency procedures. Make sure that the student fully understands what behaviors you are referring to. Offer examples of the student's recent incidents, as needed.
   - Review expectations for behavior at school. List examples of different types of appropriate and inappropriate behavior, including examples from the student's own repertoire, and ask the student to explain whether each example meets expectations or violates expectations.
   - Explain the procedures that you or other adults will use the next time the student engages in highly disruptive or dangerous behavior. Clearly specify what the student should do to comply with emergency procedures.

     ○ If out-of-class consequences will be used, describe the location, amount of time the student will spend out of the classroom, and what the student should do during this time.
     ○ If restraint will be used, specify when it will be used and explain that it will stop once it is no longer necessary to protect the student or others.

   - Inform the student of any consequences that will be delivered. Explain that you will contact the student's parents if behavior escalates to the point of being severely disruptive or dangerous.
   - Before concluding this initial meeting, ensure that the student is aware of the seriousness of the situation, the behaviors that will require emergency procedures, and what those procedures will look like. Check the student's understanding of expectations and procedures by asking gentle questions, such as "What will happen if . . . ."

2. **Practice and role-play emergency procedures.**

   Have the student practice complying with emergency procedures. Model expected behaviors, such as quietly walking to the timeout room and taking a seat, and have the student role-play or verbally rehearse what to do in different scenarios.

3. **Implement behavior emergency procedures when necessary.**

   Whenever behavior escalates to a Code Red situation, staff should follow these steps:

   Step 1: Deliver or restate a direction, making sure it is clear, observable, and immediate. (e.g., say "Sit down at your desk" instead of "Shape up"). If the student refuses a second time, use the Jot it Down strategy—literally write the direction and the student's inappropriate response on paper. This action slows the momentum toward more serious conflict between you and the student, and the student might sit down while you write. If the student fails to comply or behavior escalates further, move to the next step.

REPRODUCIBLE 4.4d *Implementation Guidelines: Behavior Emergency Planning (4 of 5)*

Implementation Guidelines: Behavior Emergency Planning

Step 2: If the student fails to comply with the repeated direction, immediately implement emergency procedures.

- First, signal for immediate assistance from another staff member in your identified chain-of-command list.
- If the behavior poses a threat to the safety of the student or others, implement safety procedures (i.e., room clears or physical intervention). Remember the three priorities of safety procedures:
  - Reduce the likelihood of anyone getting hurt.
  - Respond in such a way that the student is not reinforced for out-of-control behavior.
  - See that everyone involved, including anyone who provoked or participated in the event, is treated with dignity and respect.
- If the behavior is severely disruptive but not dangerous, assign an out-of-class consequence. Get the student's attention calmly and say that you (or another adult) will go together to the out-of-class placement. If the student refuses, quietly ask if the student will need assistance. If the student still fails to comply, you can attempt a gentle physical prompt, such as taking the student by the arm, if school and board policy permit. If the student still does not respond appropriately, use the safety procedures outlined in your backup plan (i.e., room clears or physical intervention)
- Make sure to acknowledge when the student complies with directions, out-of-class consequences, or safety procedures.

Step 3: After the incident, have an adult escort the student back to the classroom. If the student has discussed the incident with an administrator or completed a Behavior Improvement Form, collect these notes from the student and quietly acknowledge the student's return. Welcome the student back to class and act as though you are starting a new day.

4. **After each behavior emergency, complete all necessary documentation.**

    Adhere to your school's notification or referral procedures, as well as any additional data collection or reporting procedures specified as part of the student's Behavior Emergency Plan, to document all relevant information about the incident.

5. **Meet and debrief with the student after each behavior emergency.**

    At a designated time, discuss the incident with the student. If the student hasn't yet completed a Behavior Improvement Form, complete one with the student. If time permits, role-play the problem situation and have the student act out alternative, more appropriate responses. Also, until you develop a more comprehensive plan to support the student, check in frequently with the student to see how things are going. Students who have problems with severe misbehavior need continual assurance that, even when they display disruptive behavior, adults will be consistent and supportive.

REPRODUCIBLE 4.4d *Implementation Guidelines: Behavior Emergency Planning (5 of 5)*

Implementation Guidelines: Behavior Emergency Planning

6. **Keep in contact with the parents or guardians.**

    Inform parents about any Code Red incidents and maintain ongoing communication via regularly scheduled progress reports (e.g., a weekly note sent home with the student, phone conference, or e-mail communication).

7. **Focus on appropriate student behaviors and strengths as much as possible.**

    It is often difficult to give a student who has severe behavior problems attention or recognition for appropriate behavior. Unfortunately, the student learns again and again that adult attention is guaranteed during misbehavior and highly unlikely during appropriate behavior. Work to increase the rate of positive attention, praise, and positive feedback you offer the student, while minimizing attention for misbehavior as much as possible.

8. **Use data to make periodic revisions and adjustments to the plan as necessary.**

    Monitor student progress and collaborate with your problem-solving team to make adjustments to the plan as needed. If you notice escalation in student behavior or an increase in the frequency of Code Red situations, contact your administrator or problem-solving team immediately to discuss next steps.

REPRODUCIBLE 4.4e *Fidelity Checklist: Behavior Emergency Planning*

Fidelity Checklist
Behavior Emergency Planning

Essential Planning Steps

- ☐ Identify all Code Red behaviors and categorize each as either severely disruptive or physically dangerous.
- ☐ Contact the parents or guardian.
- ☐ Establish an out-of-the-room location where the student can be sent if severely disruptive behavior occurs.
- ☐ Specify the length of time the student will spend outside of the classroom.
- ☐ Establish a plan for getting adult assistance immediately.
- ☐ Create a backup plan in case the student refuses to comply with an out-of-class consequence.
- ☐ If room clears are part of the student's safety plan, identify where other students will go and what they will do.
- ☐ Develop procedures for transitioning the student back into the classroom.
- ☐ Identify strategies to focus on appropriate student behaviors and strengths.
- ☐ Make a plan for data collection and monitoring.
- ☐ Outline roles and responsibilities for implementing the plan.
- ☐ Provide training to teachers and other adults who will be implementing the plan.

Essential Implementation Components

- ☐ Meet with the student to discuss and finalize the plan.
- ☐ Practice and role-play emergency procedures with the student.
- ☐ Implement behavior emergency procedures when necessary.
- ☐ After each behavior emergency, complete all necessary documentation.
- ☐ Meet and debrief with the student after each behavior emergency.
- ☐ Keep in contact with the parents or guardians.
- ☐ Focus on appropriate student behaviors and strengths as much as possible.
- ☐ Use data to make periodic revisions and adjustments to the plan as necessary.
- ☐ Provide ongoing support for the teacher.

References

Kern, L., Benson, J. L., & Clemens, N. H. (2009). Strategies for working with severe challenging and violent behavior. In G. G. Peacock, R. A. Ervin, E. J. Daly, & K. W. Merrell (Eds.), *Practical handbook of school psychology: Effective practices for the 21st century* (pp. 459–474). New York, NY: Guilford Press.

Long, N. J., & Brendtro, L. K. (1996). A double struggle incident. *Reclaiming Children and Youth: Journal of Emotional and Behavioral Problems, 5*(1), 56–60.

Rock, M. L. (2000). Effective crisis management planning: Creating a collaborative framework. *Education and Treatment of Children, 23*(3), 248–264.

Ryan, J. B., Sanders, S., Katsiyannis, A., & Yell, M. L. (2007). Using time-out effectively in the classroom. *Teaching Exceptional Children, 39*(4), 60–67.

Scheuermann, B., Peterson, R., Ryan, J. B., & Billingsley, G. (2016). Professional practice and ethical issues related to physical restraint and seclusion in schools. *Journal of Disability Policy Studies, 27*(2), 86–95.

Taylor, R. D., Hawkins, J., & Brady, M. P. (1991). Extent, type, preferences and consequences of crisis intervention training for teachers. *Educational Psychology, 11*(2), 143–150.

SPECIALIZED INTERVENTION STRATEGY FIVE

Managing Emotional Escalation

The student is impulsive and has difficulty with emotional control

Purpose

Managing Emotional Escalation is designed to help defuse and resolve any behaviors that result in emotional escalation. Use Managing Emotional Escalation to help prevent and control:

- Tantrums
- Out-of-control behavior
- Buildup of angry behavior
- Volatile or explosive behavior
- Verbal or physical outbursts
- Sustained disruptions
- Physically dangerous or severely disruptive behavior (e.g., Code Red situations)

This strategy may be applicable when:

- The student struggles with controlling anger or frustration.
- Misbehavior tends to escalate as the student becomes more agitated.
- The teacher and student engage in power struggles.
- The student has exhibited one or more Code Red behaviors in the past, or a Code Red situation is likely to occur.

Problem behaviors that escalate to serious acting-out behavior are typically emotionally based and fueled by students' reactive responses to successive events—often negative interactions with others. These cases usually involve a cycle of behavior that follows a recognizable sequence of stages or phases, in which each successive behavior becomes more serious than the previous one (Colvin & Scott, 2014). Learning to understand and manage this cycle of emotional escalation can be a powerful way for a teacher or interventionist to intervene and defuse a potentially volatile confrontation. Coupled with self-monitoring strategies, Managing Emotional Escalation can also be used to eventually teach students to manage their own behavior and learn to stay in control without outside assistance.

NOTE: If the student engages in dangerous behavior, such as aggression toward others, behavior that affects the safety of others, or self-injurious behavior (i.e., Code Red behavior), collaborate with an administrator and other specialists (e.g., school counselor, school psychologist, behavior specialist) to develop a Behavior Emergency Plan (Section 4.4) to accompany this intervention.

Rationale

The cycle of emotional escalation typically progresses through seven distinct phases:

1. Calm
2. Triggers
3. Agitation
4. Acceleration
5. Peak
6. De-escalation
7. Recovery

Though behaviors in each phase may manifest differently from student to student, the signature of each remains readily identifiable. That is, at each phase each student exhibits predictable behavior that can readily be recognized (see "Characteristics of Emotional Escalation" on the next page). Once you correlate a student's behavior with a specific phase, you can use corresponding strategies to arrest the behavior before further escalation occurs (Colvin & Scott, 2014). Knowledge of the seven phases of emotional escalation will allow you to help the student settle down in the short term and to develop a problem-solving plan in the long term.

Several key assumptions underlie this intervention's approach to managing emotionally escalated behavior:

- Escalating behavior is expressed in many ways, but the cycle of emotional escalation and acting out is almost always accompanied by distinctive and readily identifiable behavior patterns that you can learn to recognize and pinpoint.
- Escalating behavior may occur with students of all ages and abilities.
- Escalating behavior is rarely an isolated event. It tends to happen repeatedly over time as part of an established behavior chain or pattern.

WHEN TO USE MANAGING EMOTIONAL ESCALATION

Managing Emotional Escalation is designed as a long-term intervention for students whose seriously disruptive or dangerous behavior warrants a Code Red intervention (see Section 4.4: Behavior Emergency Planning). The approaches in this intervention presume that you have already witnessed a student's behavior build to a serious level, or that you have seen lower-level behavior on more than one occasion and you anticipate that the student's impulsiveness may eventually lead to seriously disruptive or unsafe behavior. If you have reason to believe an outburst was a one-time event (perhaps caused by a current crisis, such as parents getting a divorce or going through a relocation), the structured analyses and detailed breakdown of behavioral phases in this intervention may not be necessary. In such cases, timely support and close supervision may be what is needed. If, on the other hand, you suspect the student's escalating behavior may be part of a recurring pattern, the strategies in this chapter can help you effectively manage the cycle.

- To be successful in the long term, analysis and intervention must address the entire chain—all phases of the cycle of emotional escalation in every setting—both prior to and following an incident.
- The most effective intervention is to intervene early in the chain of the escalated cycle.

Characteristics of Emotional Escalation

The seven phases of escalation are depicted in Figure 4.5a below. Note that the graph rises as the interaction escalates and falls away as the student's behavior de-escalates. Following are descriptions of each phase in the cycle of emotional escalation.

Phase 1: Calm—*Overall behavior is cooperative and acceptable.*

The student is to some degree able to exhibit behaviors essential to being successful in class: staying on task, following rules and expectations, responding to praise, initiating appropriate behavior, and responding to goals and successful outcomes.

Phase 2: Triggers—*Events or circumstances prompt emotional reactions.*

Triggers are events that set off emotionally escalating behavior, propelling the student toward a tipping point. The student may be engaged appropriately as in the first phase,

FIGURE 4.5a *Seven-Phase Model of Emotional Escalation*

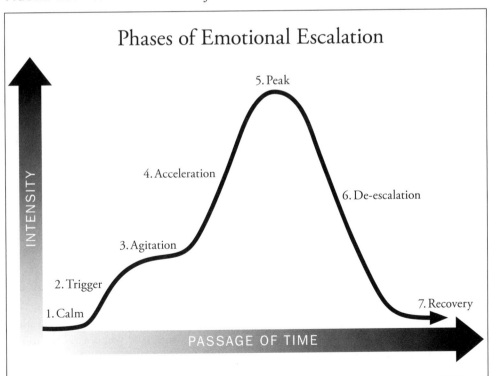

and a trigger comes into play that sets the stage for problem behavior. Other names for triggers include antecedents, setting events, aversive stimuli, and negative circumstances. Triggers are classified either as school based—arising from situations at school—or non-school based, a catchall for all outside influences the student brings to class.

School-based triggers can include:

- *Conflicts.* Conflicts tend to arise at school when students who have limited impulse control are denied something they want or when something negative is inflicted on them.
- *Changes in routine.* Students who are easily driven to escalating behavior will often react negatively to sudden changes in routine, especially if the current activity is something they enjoy or isn't quite finished.
- *Peer provocations.* Unfortunately, classmates sometimes see easily triggered students as fair game and enjoy getting a rise out of these students. In these situations, antagonizing by peers can predictably cause students to escalate and get into trouble.
- *Pressure.* Students are expected to comply with a wide variety of directions and complete a number of complex tasks during the course of a school day. Students who exhibit escalating emotional behavior may not have the necessary skills to meet these expectations. Consequently, they may feel they are under constant pressure and react inappropriately.
- *Ineffective problem solving.* Students who escalate generally have limited strategies for identifying the source of their problems, generating adaptive options, evaluating their choices, negotiating with others, or putting a plan into action.
- *Handling challenging work.* When these students face new or challenging work, they often show avoidance behavior that can readily escalate to help them avoid facing difficulties and their perception of probable failure.
- *Facing correction.* Easily triggered students often have problems receiving feedback on errors and accepting assistance with the task.

Non-school-based triggers may include:

- *High-needs homes.* Students who escalate often come from homes where many critical needs are not met. For example, at an early age the students may experience poverty or inadequate shelter, food, support, and nurturing.
- *Health problems.* Students from low-income homes may not have health insurance or receive regular medical care. Students may be hungry or malnourished and may also be getting inadequate sleep, making it very difficult to behave or participate appropriately. Deficits in any of these areas, which are outside the school's control, adversely affect not only a student's health and well-being, but also the student's behavior during school time.
- *Substance abuse.* Students who use drugs and alcohol often exhibit serious and unpredictable escalating behavior at school.
- *Gangs and deviant peer groups.* Membership in gangs and deviant peer groups may set the stage for serious problems at school, especially when it comes to the authority of school personnel and relationships with other peers. Problem behavior,

in this case escalated behavior, may be perceived as a badge of honor by members of the deviant peer group.
- *Multiple diagnoses.* In some cases, students may have received various medical or psychological diagnoses, and their respective treatments may interact negatively with each other.

Phase 3: Agitation—*Overall behavior is unfocused and distracted.*

Agitation is a general behavioral term that covers a range of emotional states, such as being angry, upset, depressed, on edge, withdrawn, worried, disturbed, frustrated, or anxious. Students often display high outward levels of agitation as a function of their inability to control or manage emotional triggers. Agitation is often readily observed either by *increases* in certain behaviors or *decreases* in behaviors.

Increases in behavior might include:

- *Darting eyes.* Students look here and look there with a certain level of intensity but with little focus or apparent purpose to their eye movements.
- *Busy hands.* Students who are agitated often display a noticeable increase in hand movements that resemble those of a student with hyperactivity, except that the student does not exhibit these behaviors during the Calm phase. This behavior is particularly prevalent among students with severe disabilities, especially in areas of language and communication deficits.
- *Moving in and out of groups.* These students often want to join a group, but when they do, they quickly want to join another group or do something else.
- *Off-task and on-task cycle.* Similarly, students in the agitation phase may start a task or activity, stop, and then start up again. They may appear to be preoccupied and may give little, if any, fixed or sustained attention to academic tasks or classroom activities.

Decreases in behavior might include:

- *Staring into space.* Students may stare into space and appear to be daydreaming or fixated on something, but their minds are somewhere else.
- *Veiled eyes.* Students will often avoid eye contact by looking away, looking down, using a hat to cover their eyes, or pulling a jacket up and sinking as low into it as possible.
- *Nonconversational language.* Agitated students respond in monosyllabic and noncommittal ways, making it difficult to build a conversation. Their body language and words communicate "I don't want to talk to you."
- *Contained hands.* Where some students signal agitation with busy hands, other agitated students may hide their hands by sitting on them, folding their arms, or putting their hands behind their back.
- *Withdrawal.* These students may withdraw from groups, shut down, show a clear preference for independent activities, or move to isolated areas. The implicit message is, "Leave me alone."

Phase 4: Acceleration—*Behavior engages others.*

In this phase, the subtext to the student's behavior is "I want to engage you." The student's words, deeds, and body language all convey this message. The student may bait, try to pull the teacher in, or exhibit behavior that is highly likely to obtain a response from staff.

Typical engaging behaviors include:

- *Questioning and arguing.* Some students need help or ask questions and then proceed to argue about the response they receive or continue to question details of the task at hand.
- *Noncompliance and defiance.* Students may accelerate the situation by refusing to cooperate with instructions, classroom rules, or teacher expectations, setting up confrontations or further negative interactions.
- *Off-task behavior.* These students may stop working or deliberately stray off task, expecting that the teacher will respond.
- *Provoking others.* Some students intentionally irritate or antagonize the teacher or another student, hoping to provoke a reaction. The stronger the reaction, the more positively reinforcing it may be to these students, thus setting the stage for further negative interactions.
- *Partial compliance.* This behavior is a form of limit testing. It could be compliance accompanied by additional inappropriate behavior. Students complete tasks or follow stated directions, but also exhibit one or more additional social behaviors they know are unacceptable. Partial compliance is often described as passive-aggressive behavior.
- *Criterion defiance.* Another form of testing the limits occurs when students perform at standards clearly below the expected level, and the teacher knows, based on their previous work, that they are capable of better performance.
- *Rule violation.* Still another way students who have difficulty maintaining emotional control may test the limits is to break a rule deliberately—knowing that staff will have to respond with correction procedures that often involve established consequences. After provoking the desired response from staff, students are likely to instigate further negative interactions.
- *Whining and crying.* By engaging in these behaviors, students hope to obtain immediate teacher attention or support. In some cases, students may seek to irritate or frustrate the teacher and provoke a confrontation.
- *Avoidance and escape.* Students who aim at engaging staff may seek to avoid certain tasks or responsibilities, knowing that this behavior will usually secure a response from the teacher. Avoidance is often characterized with "You can't make me" comments and behaviors.
- *Threats and intimidation.* By threatening staff members, students may hope to intimidate, but they may also have a secondary objective. If a targeted staff member responds in kind—that is, in any way that suggests a challenge—it is highly likely that the student will swiftly escalate into a serious confrontation involving potentially unsafe or violent behavior.
- *Verbal abuse.* Similarly, students who use offensive or abusive language toward staff may expect and want staff to address the behavior immediately—teachers

typically react strongly to offensive language. This reaction sets the stage for the accelerating student to respond with more serious behavior.
- *Destruction of property.* Some students may deliberately damage or deface property, expecting that staff will take immediate action and counting on further negative interactions as a result.

Phase 5: Peak—*Behavior is out of control.*

In this phase, a student's behavior is so unsafe or disruptive that class cannot continue or can continue only with great difficulty. Peak behaviors are the most serious in the whole chain of emotional escalation.

Dangerous or disruptive behaviors can include:

- *Serious destruction of property.* Students who have reached the peak phase of the cycle of emotional escalation can cause substantial and costly damage to property.
- *Physical attacks.* Students may target others with the intent to cause physical harm (e.g. punching, kicking, throwing objects, hair pulling). Even more serious behaviors include attacks with objects or weapons.
- *Self-abuse.* Peak behaviors may include self-directed harmful behaviors such as face slapping, hitting, pinching, hair pulling, head banging, and scratching.
- *Severe tantrums.* These students may exhibit tantrum behaviors such as screaming, yelling, throwing objects, pushing desks over, and flailing on the floor.
- *Running away.* Students who are out of control will often exhibit a fight-or-flight response. They either continue to escalate the situation or elect to escape it by running away. Their departure may be accompanied by explosive behavior—yelling, cursing, banging doors, or kicking walls and furniture.

NOTE: If a student exhibits peak behaviors that are unsafe or severely disruptive, consult your school's protocol for addressing Code Red situations (or see Section 1, Task 6, p. 54) and refer to Section 4.4: Behavior Emergency Planning for guidance in developing an individual plan for immediately responding to these behavior.

Phase 6: De-escalation—*Overall behavior shows confusion and lack of focus.*

This phase might be thought of as a *reintegration process*. The student begins to disengage, with a corresponding reduction in the intensity of behavior. However, the student remains generally uncooperative or unresponsive to adult social influence. In effect, the student is moving from out-of-control behavior to a phase of uncertainty and confusion. Think about times you have been very angry. Once you start to calm down, you do not immediately revert to a calm state. There is a transition period between an emotional peak and complete calm, during which you are poised between the two states.

Behaviors common at this phase include:

- *Confusion.* Students who are coming down from an episode of out-of-control behavior often appear confused. They may display seemingly random behaviors or a lack of focus.

- *Reconciliation.* Some students make peace overtures, attempt to make up, or try testing the water to see where they stand with the teacher.
- *Withdrawal.* De-escalating students may drop their heads down and may even appear to be asleep. This can be a way to withdraw from the situation or a response to genuine fatigue. Students may also simply need time to pull themselves together after a prolonged behavior episode.
- *Denial.* These students may deny their recent behavior, especially the most serious behaviors. They may genuinely not remember what sent them into this state or how they ended up on the floor or in the principal's office. They may see the whole episode as one big blur.
- *Blaming others.* This is another form of denial, which is frequently accompanied by animated body language and an attempt to convey compelling conviction that the incident was caused by someone else. They blame someone else for starting it all in the first place.
- *Avoidance of discussion.* In this phase, students may avoid discussion, debriefing, or invitations to problem-solve. Consistent with reluctance to participate in class discussions or activities, students may obviously avoid talking about the episode, the behavior, or events leading up to the incident. In this case, postpone debriefing to the Recovery phase because the student needs more time to recover.
- *Responsiveness to directions—specifically involving manipulative or mechanical tasks.* For students who have just had an out-of-control behavior episode, this is not the time for direct discussions. It is an excellent time to give them concrete directions—especially regarding an activity to do. Many adult supervisors have found that students will cooperate, almost willingly, with concrete directions at this stage. Students often appear distracted in the de-escalation phase, and a clear, concrete direction can provide a needed focus. If possible, direct students to engage in tasks that are physically manipulative or fairly mechanical—something that they can do easily to help them focus on something unrelated to the incident and help with the process of regrouping.

Phase 7: Recovery—*Behavior shows an eagerness for busy work and reluctance to interact.*

In the final phase, students slowly return to their original state, becoming progressively less agitated and more able to resume normal classroom activities.

This phase is evident by specific behavioral characteristics such as:

- *Eagerness for independent work or activity.* Students in the Recovery phase become engaged in or actively seek some kind of relatively independent busy work.
- *Subdued behavior in group work or class discussion.* Activities that involve interactions with other students or staff may be very difficult for these students at this time.
- *Defensiveness.* Students may display guarded behavior that is cautious and almost measured.

Essential Planning Steps

STEP 1 Define the problem and describe its context.

First, specify the appropriate behaviors the student exhibits when calm. In other words, describe what behavior looks like when the student hasn't escalated. These behaviors are categorized as Phase 1: Calm. When in this phase, the student is able to exhibit behaviors essential to succeeding in class: staying on task, following rules and expectations, responding to praise, initiating appropriate behavior, and responding to goals and success.

Next, identify contexts that trigger escalation. Context can be any task, situation, setting, antecedent, or trigger that precedes the problem behavior. Look for a causal link among contexts, triggers, and the problem behavior. What specific events or circumstances seem to set off problem behavior? Triggers are classified as either school based—arising from situations at school—or non-school based, which encompasses all outside influences the student brings to class. Because non-school-based triggers occur outside the school, the student comes to school already upset. Easily triggered students may come to school with additional challenges that teachers may be unaware of. These triggers are often called *setting events*. The student is already aroused, then when another event at school serves as a trigger, the student quickly escalates.

Note that school-based and non-school-based triggers often act in combination to amplify escalating behavior. Students who are triggered in a mix of ways are often best supported by wraparound services that involve a combination of medical, psychological, behavioral, and academic interventions. The key with wraparound services is that you must use a team approach, with all participants on the same page and informed about what each one is doing to best serve the student.

> **BEFORE IMPLEMENTING THIS STRATEGY**
>
> Be sure that you have discussed the problem and general goals for improvement with the teacher and student. Gather any relevant background information that may help in designing and implementing the intervention. Contact the student's parents or guardian to discuss the problem, and keep them informed of all aspects of the intervention plan.

NOTE: If you use the problem-solving model and tools that were introduced and applied at different stages of a problem in Section 2, at the point of intervention design you should have already developed a hypothesis about the settings and situations that tend to trigger problem behavior. Use this information to complete Step 1. If you need additional support in identifying conditions that predict when behavior is likely to occur, see "Characteristics of Emotional Escalation" earlier in this section for examples of triggers, or review guidance provided in Item 8 on the Teacher Interview or 25-Minute Planning Process presented in Section 2.

Finally, identify the student's specific behaviors for each of the remaining phases in the cycle of emotional escalation. Refer to "Characteristics of Emotional Escalation" for a general description of phases and examples of specific behaviors typical of each phase. Compare these descriptions and examples with the typical behaviors that your student of concern exhibits during emotional escalation. This will allow you to identify the behaviors the student exhibits at each point and help you select strategies to appropriately respond and defuse the situation before it escalates any further.

You can use the first column of the Plan Summary table shown on the next page in Implementation Guidelines: Managing Emotional Escalation (Reproducible 4.5a, pp. 461–466) to list triggers and document typical student behaviors within each phase.

REPRODUCIBLE 4.5a *Implementation Guidelines: Managing Emotional Escalation (Plan Summary, 2 of 6)*

Implementation Guidelines: Managing Emotional Escalation

Plan Summary

Phase 1: Calm	Student behaviors:	Prevention Strategies:
Phase 2: Triggers	Student behaviors:	Strategies to Address Triggers:
Phase 3: Agitation	Student behaviors:	Anxiety-Reducing Strategies:
Phase 4: Acceleration	Student behaviors:	Defusion Procedures:
Phase 5: Peak	Student behaviors:	Behavior Emergency Procedures:
Phase 6: De-escalation	Student behaviors:	Debriefing Procedures:
Phase 7: Recovery	Student behaviors:	Reintegration Strategies:

Once you identify a pattern of behavior escalation, you are in a much stronger position to intervene early and interrupt the cycle before it spirals into a seriously disruptive and unsafe situation. Next, you will select strategies for managing behavior in each phase.

STEP 2 Consider strategies and procedures for managing behavior at each phase of the cycle.

The seven-phase conceptual model of emotional escalation allows you to develop a list of preferred strategies that correspond to each phase. This list will help you map and defuse the cycle of problem behavior and should include:

- Prevention strategies for Phase 1 (Calm) and Phase 2 (Triggers)
- Anxiety-reducing strategies for Phase 3 (Agitation)
- Defusion procedures for Phase 4 (Acceleration)
- Emergency procedures for Phase 5 (Peak)
- Debriefing procedures for Phase 6 (De-escalation)
- Reintegration strategies for Phase 7 (Recovery)

Prevention Strategies—Phases 1 (Calm) and 2 (Triggers)

Prevention strategies are designed to keep students calm. They can address anticipated triggers before escalation begins to snowball. An effective classroom management approach and engaging instruction will often prevent the conditions that lead to escalation—students who are on task, challenged, and successfully engaged in activities are not likely to embark on the cycle of emotional escalation. In addition, knowledge of a student's individual triggers will allow adults to proactively anticipate and manage the conditions that seem to set off the problem behavior.

Be prepared to use the following strategies as needed to prevent the cycle of escalation from occurring in the first place.

- a. *Modify the context.* Modifications are intended to increase the chance that expected behavior will occur while decreasing the likelihood that problem behavior will occur. Examples of modifying the context include assigning the student to sit in the part of the room farthest from classmates who may tease the student or modifying assigned work to reduce frustration and increase task success.
- b. *Re-teach expectations.* If the trigger is unavoidable and all students are expected to deal with it, review expectations for desired behavior in any situations that are challenging for the student. Clearly specify relevant classroom rules and be sure that the student understands them. See Section 3, Task 3 for more guidance in developing a plan to teach expectations.
- c. *Increase active supervision.* During situations or settings that have been problematic for the student, ask the teacher or supervising adult to move throughout the room or setting and keep an eye on the student's behavior. The presence of an adult can be effective in preventing misbehavior from occurring in the first place. Increasing supervision can also ensure that if misbehavior or emotional escalation begins, it can be addressed in a timely manner.

PLAN SUMMARY TABLE

The Plan Summary table is part of Implementation Guidelines: Managing Emotional Escalation (Reproducible 4.5a, pp. 461–466), and provides a framework for documenting strategies for each phase. In the first column, describe the types of behaviors or events you see at each phase. In the second column, note strategies that may be useful to implement. Select an array of strategies for addressing and managing escalating behavior at each phase of the cycle.

d. *Provide positive feedback when the student exhibits the expected behavior.* Encourage staff to focus more attention on responsible, appropriate behaviors than on misbehavior and to provide praise and specific feedback when the student meets expectations. For example, if the student correctly follows transition steps (which normally have been difficult), the teacher might acknowledge the student's success and grant extra time on the computer or some preferred activity. Positive feedback can offer the attention a student craves and provide information that describes what the student was doing right, which helps the student learn responsible behavior.

e. *Provide cues and precorrections.* Use cues and precorrections during any contexts that are predictable problems. This will give the student advance notice of expectations and prompt any necessary behavior adjustments. For example, if the student has trouble with writing, you might say, "In a few minutes we will be switching to writing. I know you can do a good job."

Anxiety-Reducing Strategies — Phase 3 (Agitation)

Once an easily escalated student is exposed to a trigger, it is often only a matter of time until the student's behavior escalates. Some students simply do not have the necessary skills to manage their triggers, resolve conflicts, or solve problems. In this phase, you can use supportive, anxiety-reducing strategies to help the student settle down and regain control instead of embarking on a cycle of escalated behavior. These supportive strategies are essentially accommodations that involve slight departures from normal procedures. Talk with the teacher to determine which of the following accommodations best align with the student's personality and needs and which are most feasible to offer on a regular basis:

f. *Offer support and empathy.* Perhaps the most powerful supportive strategy at a teacher's disposal is *empathy*. Teachers and other staff offer empathy by conveying to the student that they understand or recognize the student's agitation.

g. *Provide assurances and accommodations.* Agitated students often feel insecure about their abilities. By offering assurances and accommodations — such as having the teacher stand near the student, offering after-class assistance, or allowing the student more time — the teacher can help the student regain control.

h. *Help the student focus.* Agitated students often have difficulty focusing on their work, staying on task, and concentrating. Consider strategies that assist a student in getting started or resuming work. For example, the teacher might assist the student in getting out needed materials for the next task or offer assistance with the first step in the assigned task. In this way, the teacher can help shift the student's attention away from triggers to the specific tasks of the lesson.

i. *Provide space.* Some agitated students may want to be left alone. Providing the student with some level of space or isolation from the rest of the class will often meet this need, allowing the student time to settle down and regain focus.

j. *Arrange specific types of activities.* An agitated student is often distracted and will find it difficult to concentrate. Consider whether planning any of the following types of activities might help the student settle down.

- *Preferred activities:* One way to help a student refocus is to permit the student to engage in a preferred activity for a short amount of time. This strategy allows students to disengage from what is bothering them and become reconnected with the classroom activity without a sense of pressure. Be sure to set some guidelines for when this strategy is used. Otherwise, the student may not leave the preferred activity, or other students may want to participate.
- *Independent activities*: In addition to serving instructional purposes, independent work offers a simple opportunity to help an agitated student become settled and focused. Independent work can also allow the student to be left alone, giving them time to cool off before any other interactions further escalate the situation.
- *Movement activities:* Movement is a tool you can use to help a student who is agitated. Students who are agitated generally tend to move anyway, so when you direct them to do something that involves movement, such as distributing class materials, this activity helps them become more focused and calm.
- *Passive activities:* Following high-stimulus events such as recess, gym class, or assemblies, the whole class may be overly excited, leaving some students in a state of agitation. After these transitions, consider using passive strategies for the whole class, such as watching a video, quiet reading, or reading out loud to the class. These activities require some attention from students but not much effort in terms of response, which can be useful in calming down both excited and agitated students.

Defusion Procedures—Phase 4 (Acceleration)

Effective defusion approaches are critically important at the Acceleration phase in the cycle of acting-out behavior. Once students reach this phase, their behavior can be characterized as *engaging*—in a sense, the student is inviting others to engage in interactions that will lead to escalation. This student may challenge the teacher, argue, and try to draw others in to get them to respond. If an adult takes the bait and reacts by becoming agitated or confrontational, they run a risk of reinforcing the behavior or inadvertently escalating the situation.

Because the risk for escalation is greatest at this phase, adults interacting with these students should be familiar with *all three* of the following recommendations for when the student's behavior reaches this stage of the cycle.

k. *Identify and avoid escalating prompts.* The kinds of adult responses that are likely to worsen the situation are called *escalating prompt*s. These include:

- Demonstrating agitated behavior, such as shouting or rapid speech.
- Responding very quickly, with reactive, sarcastic, or flippant remarks.
- Cornering or encroaching on the student's space (e.g., leaning forward, exaggerating gestures, pointing directly into the student's face).
- Touching, poking, or grabbing the student.

- Arguing with the student and engaging in power struggles (e.g., "In my classroom you will . . .").
- Using statements that belittle, ridicule, or insult the student (e.g., "This is a high school, not a preschool"). Moreover, if such comments are made within earshot of the rest of the class, other students may become involved and worsen the situation.
- Using body language, such as rigid posture or clenched hands, that communicates anger, frustration, or the sense of losing control of the situation.
- Implementing inconsistent consequences out of anger or frustration.

Talk with the teacher to determine whether any past responses to the student's behavior might be considered an escalating prompt. The teacher may frequently use some of these responses with other students in different situations, but they may serve as escalating prompts with this particular student. Then identify alternative responses that the teacher can use to help defuse the situation.

l. *Approach the student in a nonthreatening manner.* Because the probability is high that the student's behavior will escalate in this phase, staff should approach the student in a manner that is controlled, measured, and nonthreatening, as follows:

- *Move slowly and deliberately toward the problem situation.* Avoid showing signs of panic or anxiety. If possible, engage in some normal, on-task interactions with other students on the way to the target situation.
- *Speak privately.* When possible, take the student aside or ask the student to come to your desk. Talk quietly so as not to be overheard by other students.
- *Speak calmly and respectfully.* Use the student's name and speak in a neutral and businesslike voice. Avoid harsh, angry tones. Be as matter-of-fact as possible. Do not threaten or cajole.
- *Minimize body language.* Be as undemonstrative as possible. Avoid pointing or staring at the student. Use a calm demeanor.
- *Keep a reasonable distance.* Though proximity is generally important, do not get too close or invade the student's space. Don't crowd or get in the student's face. Remember that a squared-off stance, directly facing the student, immediately signals that you are approaching the student in a confrontational manner. Try to speak to the student at an angle.
- *Match the student's eye level, if possible.* Some students react negatively to anyone towering over them. If the student is sitting, sit or squat beside them. If the student is standing, stand as well, perhaps taking a step back to show respect for the student's space. By meeting students at their level, you are showing respect and you are less likely to risk escalation.
- *Be brief.* Keep the interaction brief and simple. Lengthy pronouncements or explanations may prompt negative reactions from some students.
- *Stay with the agenda.* Remain focused on your primary concern. Do not get sidetracked. Deal with lesser problems later. For example, if a student needs to return to her desk, the teacher should calmly and persistently stay with that direction and not be drawn into other topics.

- *Withdraw if the situation begins to escalate toward Phase 5 Peak behavior.* Immediately terminate the discussion—simply withdraw from the student and direct your attention to the other students. At the same time, keep a close eye on the troubled student. Understand that the student will not process things at this stage, so it is better to withdraw before the student reaches the Peak stage. This simple act of withdrawing may stave off further escalation. However, if the student escalates further, entering Phase 5 Peak behaviors, follow your school's emergency procedures for severely disruptive or physically dangerous behavior.

Review guidelines for approaching the student in a nonconfrontational manner with relevant staff members. Remind staff to use common sense and approach the problem in a calm, unhurried, respectful, and preplanned manner to help defuse the situation.

m. *Use nonconfrontational limit-setting procedures.* At the Acceleration phase, staff should be prepared with strategies that are effective in arresting escalating behavior quickly and reliably to facilitate resumption of class activity as seamlessly as possible. The key lies in the delivery of directions. Adults need to communicate clearly and unambiguously that the problem behavior must cease, otherwise consequences will be used—without being construed as confrontational or threatening. This limit-setting protocol is described on page 457. Present this limit-setting protocol to relevant staff members, reviewing each step and the appropriate follow-up responses.

Behavior Emergency Procedures—Phase 5 (Peak)

Behavior in the Peak phase of escalation can cause severe disruption and pose serious safety concerns for the involved student, other students, and intervening adults. The primary objective at this phase is to ensure the safety of all students and staff. The secondary goal is to allow the classroom and school activities to continue and to minimize damage to school property.

If behavior in the Peak phase of escalation is severely disruptive or physically dangerous, it is considered a Code Red situation, and you will need to put behavior emergency procedures in place.

Code Red situations involve behaviors that are either so dangerous or so disruptive that classes cannot continue. These include behaviors such as:

- Overt aggressive behavior toward others (e.g., kicking, hitting, fighting)
- Threats of targeted violence toward others
- Brandishing items that could be used as weapons
- Carrying weapons
- Self-injurious behavior
- Vandalism or property destruction
- Sexual assault
- Clear signs of using controlled substances (drugs and alcohol)
- Running away from school property
- Sustained confrontational or defiant behavior resulting in refusal to follow immediate, reasonable adult directions

The primary objective at the Peak phase is to ensure the safety of all students and staff.

A Behavior Emergency Plan specifies the procedures that will be used in responding immediately to each relevant Code Red situation. If the student has exhibited one or more Code Red behaviors in the past, or misbehavior has escalated or the possibility of a Code Red situation is likely, refer to Behavior Emergency Planning (Section 4.4) to outline emergency procedures. The Behavior Emergency Plan will serve as your protocol for responding to Phase 5 Peak behaviors.

If the student's peak behaviors do not meet the requirements for a Code Red situation (i.e., misbehavior is not severely disruptive or physically dangerous), specify how adults will respond and which consequences will be used when the student reaches this stage of the escalation cycle. Consequences might include sending the student to timeout, making an office referral, removing a privilege, or assigning a prearranged out-of-class consequence. See Section 3, Task 5 for more guidance on selecting appropriate corrective consequences.

ESCALATING MISBEHAVIOR

If a student's escalating misbehavior is maintained by adult attention or escape/avoidance of an activity or situation, consider whether debriefing might inadvertently provide too much adult attention or extend the student's escape from the activity or situation. If so, think of ways to minimize attention (e.g., limit the length of the debriefing session) or prevent escape (e.g., debrief at a different time).

Debriefing Procedures—Phase 6 (De-escalation)

Debriefing is designed to help the student process the serious incident that just occurred, reduce the likelihood that similar incidents will occur in the future, and orient the student toward resuming the current classroom activity.

In general, it is best for the teacher to conduct the debriefing session, especially if the incident occurred in the classroom. However, if the teacher is unavailable or if problems are reoccurring, the counselor or administrator may be a better choice to conduct the debriefing, particularly if they have more time to spend with the student or if the student is more open to discussing the incident with someone other than the teacher.

The debriefing process should occur after the student has been calm for at least 20 minutes and can follow simple directions (e.g., "Let's take a seat and talk about this"). Debriefing should last no longer than 5–10 minutes. Debriefing should not be used as a corrective consequence to reprimand or lecture the student. Rather, the focus should be on prompting appropriate behavior in the future. Adults should be encouraging and optimistic about the student's ability to transition back to class successfully and behave appropriately in the future.

A common debriefing process consists of asking the student the following three questions (also see the Behavior Improvement Form, Reproducible 4.5b).

1. *What did you do?* Have the student label and describe all behaviors that occurred during the cycle of escalation, especially Acceleration and Peak behaviors (refused to follow directions, threw a chair, yelled at the teacher, threatened other students, etc.).
2. *Why did you do it?* Encourage the student to think about why they behaved in that way and identify the reasons or purposes behind it.
3. *What else could you have done?* Prompt the student to think of other behaviors that might meet their needs but would be more acceptable in a classroom. In this way you are recognizing that the student has a need, but also are trying to identify an acceptable way of meeting the need.

REPRODUCIBLE 4.5b *Behavior Improvement Form*

Behavior Improvement Form

Name _____ Grade/Class _____

Teacher _____ Period/Time _____

1. What was your behavior? _____

_____

_____

_____

_____

_____

_____

2. What could you do differently? _____

_____

_____

_____

_____

_____

_____

3. Will you be able to do that? _____

_____

_____

_____

_____

_____

_____

Interventions © 2019 Ancora Publishing

Reintegration Strategies — Phase 7 (Recovery)

Following a serious incident, it is important to have strategies planned for transitioning the student back to the classroom or typical routine. Just because the student has regained composure does not mean that this cooperation will continue upon the student's return to normal classroom activities. Without a carefully planned reintegration strategy, returning to the setting where the problems began (where initial triggers may still be present) can trigger the student to embark on the cycle of escalating behavior again. Consider how to incorporate the following strategies to help ease this transition.

   n. *Provide a reentry task.* Choose a task that is simple for the student to complete successfully and does not require immediate engagement with others. This will allow the student to regain composure and begin acting productively. The teacher should reinforce the student once the student starts the reentry task.
   o. *Provide a strong focus on normal routines.* Once the student has successfully reentered the classroom or other setting, the supervising adult should continue to conduct activities as normal and avoid revisiting the incident or negotiating any consequences that have been assigned.
   p. *Focus on the appropriate behavior the student demonstrates.* It is important for teachers to communicate support and the expectation that the student can succeed upon returning to the classroom. Help the teacher identify ways to direct attention to the student's positive behavior by developing a list of the student's strengths and responsible behaviors, possible praise statements to use, and examples of non-verbal feedback to acknowledge appropriate behavior.

RESOURCES FOR MANAGING BEHAVIOR AT EACH PHASE OF CYCLE

Additional information on the procedures for managing behavior at each phase of the cycle can be found in the following resources developed by Geoff Colvin:

- Colvin, G., & Scott, T. M. (2014). *Managing the cycle of acting-out behavior in the classroom* (2nd ed.). Thousand Oaks, CA: Corwin Press.
- Colvin, G. (2010). *Defusing disruptive behavior in the classroom.* Thousand Oaks, CA: Corwin Press.
- Colvin, G. (2005). *Managing non-compliance: Effective strategies for K-12 teachers* [Video]. Eugene, OR: Iris Media.
- Colvin, G. (2005). *Defusing anger and aggression: Safe strategies for secondary school educators* [Video]. Eugene, OR: Iris Media.

STEP 3 Outline a plan for implementation and data collection.

When creating a plan, make sure to incorporate these components.

For each set of strategies, specify when and where they will be used, and who will be primarily responsible for implementing them. Sometimes a student may exhibit serious problem behavior in several school settings, not just in the classroom. If escalating behavior extends to recess, the hallways, or the cafeteria, simply designing a classroom plan and hoping it will transfer to the other settings is not likely to work. In these cases, the student's behavior plan should encompass all settings where problems occur and involve active participation by all supervisory staff in each of the target settings.

For example, you may decide to put prevention strategies in place across all settings, have the recess and lunch supervisors use anxiety-reducing strategies before and during situations that are challenging for the student, teach the classroom teacher how to use defusion and reintegration procedures, and discuss the debriefing procedure with the school counselor.

Make a plan for data collection and monitoring. Identify ways to determine whether the plan is helping the student reach their goals. Behavior Improvement Forms and documentation of when behavior emergency procedures are initiated can provide a built-in form of data collection. You can use the Extreme Behavior Log (Reproducible 4.5c) to create a detailed anecdotal record of any incidents that involve severely disruptive, physically dangerous, or threatening events. Also consider asking staff to note when different strategies were implemented, at which phase of the emotional escalation cycle they were used, and whether they helped the student calm down or had no effect. Keep dated records so that you can analyze progress and periodically adjust the plan. Develop a communication system so that all staff involved with the student are apprised of the student's progress. For example, the student's homeroom teacher should be informed of the student's performance in targeted settings outside the classroom.

Consider supplemental intervention strategies to incorporate into the plan as needed. The procedures to manage escalating behavior usually involve two steps: first, an immediate response designed to defuse the situation, and second, a systematic plan to solve the problem and prevent it from occurring again. After you identify a set of strategies to use in immediately responding to behavior at different phases of the emotional escalation cycle, consider other preventive and teaching strategies to incorporate into the plan, such as:

- *Antecedent strategies*: Consider whether increasing supervision and monitoring during certain activities or altering schedules, expectations, or the physical arrangement of the room might have a positive impact on preventing or defusing escalating behaviors.
- *Teaching strategies:* Introducing relaxation and emotional management skills via short, regular lessons with the interventionist or teacher can provide opportunities for the student to practice, refine, and receive feedback on these behaviors.
- *Positive consequence strategies:* To help prevent and defuse escalating behavior, focus attention on the positive behaviors that the student demonstrates, providing high rates of praise and specific feedback for appropriate behavior, following directions, and applying self-management skills.

REPRODUCIBLE 4.5c *Extreme Behavior Log*

Extreme Behavior Log

Student _____ Grade/Class _____ Teacher _____

Directions: Record Code Red behavior (all incidents of physically dangerous or highly disruptive behavior).

INTENSITY KEY: 1 = Refuses to comply or participate
2 = Verbally abusive or shouting
3 = Physically violent

Date	Start Time	Stop Time	Total Duration	Intensity	Anecdotal Notes

Interventions © 2019 Ancora Publishing

- *Corrective consequence strategies:* Make sure that the limits between appropriate and inappropriate behavior are described in detail. Also discuss with the student any corrective consequences that will be used and ensure that staff members are prepared to use defusion strategies and deliver corrections fluently and effectively.
- *Interactional strategies.* Identify ways to increase the frequency of noncontingent positive attention that the student receives from adults across all settings and situations at school. If needed, encourage the student to engage in the school community through participating in school clubs or activities, assuming a meaningful role in the school, or connecting with an adult or peer mentor.
- *Specialized strategies:* To help clarify goals, establish a more formal commitment from the student to work on changing behavior, and incorporate rewards into the plan for helping the student manage emotional responses, consider implementing this strategy in conjunction with Behavioral Contracting (Section 4.1) or Structured Reinforcement (Section 4.2). It can also be beneficial to introduce self-monitoring procedures for the student to develop better awareness of their emotional responses and how they manage these responses (see Section 4.3: Self-Monitoring and Self-Evaluation). Finally, if the student's behavior in the Peak phase of escalation is severely disruptive or physically dangerous, it is considered a Code Red situation, and you will need to put behavior emergency procedures in place (see Behavior Emergency Planning [Section 4.4]).

Outline roles and responsibilities for implementing the plan. At this point, the intervention plan should specify the typical behaviors the student exhibits at each phase of the escalation cycle, the strategies for prevention, anxiety reduction, and defusion that staff will employ during the first four phases of the escalation cycle, any behavior emergency procedures or consequences that will used at the Peak phase, and debriefing and reintegration techniques that will be used in the last phases.

Summarize the plan in writing and rehearse its implementation by considering different possible scenarios and asking *what-if* questions. For example, what if the student arrives at school when nearing the Peak phase?

Finalize your plan by making sure to determine:

- Who will meet with the student to discuss the plan.
- Who will contact the parents to discuss the plan.
- Who will be responsible for coordinating any additional behavior emergency planning logistics.
- Who will be responsible for data collection, and how data will be collected and summarized.
- Who will need training.

Provide training to teachers and other adults who will be implementing the plan. Familiarize all staff members who will interact with the student in targeted settings about the procedures and strategies to use when the student demonstrates escalating behavior. With all involved staff members, discuss how to remain calm, respectful, and detached when student behavior begins to escalate. Plan to describe why and when to use prevention and anxiety-reducing strategies, and how to avoid escalating prompts, approach the student in a nonthreatening manner, and use confrontational limit-setting procedures.

You should also cover when and how to implement behavior emergency procedures, and what steps to take in debriefing and reintegrating the student back to a normal routine. Also explain data collection procedures and distribute relevant forms for recording and monitoring progress. Use Implementation Guidelines: Managing Emotional Escalation shown at the end of this section (Reproducible 4.5a, pp. 461–466) to review procedures with staff.

Case Example: Michael

Michael, a sixth-grade student, often fails to complete in-class assignments, refuses to follow adult directions, and sometimes exhibits aggressive behavior toward his teachers. This behavior seems to be triggered by directions and corrections from teachers. For example, during math class Michael will slouch in his chair and do nothing. When the teacher, Ms. Hoang, reminds Michael to get to work, his behavior in the next several minutes escalates in the following way:

Michael: Work on what?
Teacher: The math you did not finish earlier in the period.
Michael: I DID finish it! (*Michael leans back and glares at the teacher.*) When did we have to do 10?
Teacher: I announced that at the beginning of class yesterday. Michael, look at the board and see under assignments: 1 through 10.
Michael: I don't remember that.
Teacher: Michael, this has gone far enough. You need to finish the rest of your assignment. So please get on with it.
Michael: Well, that's the first time I've seen it.
Teacher: OK. Here's your choice. Do the math now, or you will have to do it in detention.
Michael: No way. I'm done! F*** you!
Teacher: Michael, that's verbal abuse. I'm going to give you an office referral.
(*Michael throws his book across the room.*)
Teacher: All right, it's to the office. (*Teacher nudges Michael on the elbow. Michael swings his arm in the teacher's direction and makes solid contact with her arm. The teacher then follows the emergency procedures and calls for help. Michael is escorted to the office.*)

Although this is the first incident with actual physical contact, Michael has had similar interactions (engaged in verbal exchanges, knocked things over, or threw items) on at least four other occasions with two other teachers, Mr. Fischer and Mrs. Jefferson.

The problem-solving team develops a functional hypothesis about Michael's behavior, hypothesizing that Michael has skill deficits in managing frustration and anger and may be motivated by the attention he gets from the power struggles with Ms. Hoang and the other two teachers. Working with the three teachers with whom Michael has demonstrated escalating behavior, the problem-solving team uses the seven-phase model of escalating behavior to identify descriptors for Michael's triggers, behaviors that indicate agitation, behaviors that indicate acceleration, and behaviors he exhibits at the peak level of escalation.

Using this information, the team makes a plan for the school counselor to meet with Michael to help him develop a better awareness of his role in this escalation cycle and learn to maintain emotional control.

The counselor and Michael will discuss:

- Triggers that tend to make him upset
- Strategies to employ to stay calm
- Types of precorrections and reminders that the teachers may use regarding upcoming trigger events
- Types of behaviors that indicate he is becoming agitated
- Strategies to use in returning to calm when he is agitated
- Types of behaviors that indicate he is accelerating toward being out of control
- Strategies to request a self-imposed, in-class timeout when he isn't able to calm down
- Consequences that will result when he escalates to peak behaviors (being sent to the office)
- Expectations for returning to the class activities after an escalation incident

On a daily basis, both Michael and the classroom teacher will rate Michael's behavior on a 0–3 scale, where:

3 = Remained calm the entire class
2 = Needed a reminder to use strategies to calm down or use appropriate language
1 = Needed to use in-class timeout
0 = Needed to go to the office after exhibiting peak behaviors

The initial goal of the plan is for Michael to demonstrate no incidents of peak behavior, and corresponding class removal, for a full week. Once he achieves this goal, the next goal will be no more than one self-imposed timeout per week. Finally, after meeting this goal, Michael will work toward behavior ratings of all 2s and 3s for the week (i.e., zero self-imposed timeouts or peak incidents).

If the first goal is not met by the end of 2 weeks, the team agrees to introduce a structured reinforcement system, where Michael can earn rewards for accumulating points on his self-monitoring and teacher monitoring forms.

INTERVENTIONS: SUPPORT FOR INDIVIDUAL STUDENTS WITH BEHAVIOR CHALLENGES

Items 1–12 are also shown on **Implementation Guidelines** (Form 4.5a, pp. 461–466). Share with teachers and other adults responsible for implementing the plan.

BEFORE MEETING WITH THE STUDENT

Once you outline procedures, determine who will discuss the plan with the student, who should be present, and when and where the meeting will take place. Make sure the location is private. In most cases, the parents should be invited. The classroom teacher and at least one other staff member should be present. Schedule the conference at a neutral time, not immediately following a disruptive incident. All parties need to be able to discuss problems and plans calmly.

Essential Implementation Procedures

The teacher or interventionist responsible for implementing the plan should make sure to:

1. Meet with the student to discuss and finalize the plan. During this meeting:

- Explain that you want the student to be successful in school and to learn how to control the behavior that gets them into trouble.
- Explain that you would like to help the student learn how to calm down when feeling frustrated, angry, overwhelmed, upset, or emotional.
- Discuss the problem with the student. Calmly explain why specific behaviors are disruptive or inappropriate and prevent the student from being successful in school. Provide an age-appropriate rationale for why learning how to control emotions is part of growing up. Emphasize that the student can be successful and that everyone wants to help.
- Considering the student's age and maturity level, explain how emotional escalation happens, what sets escalation off in the first place, what the signs of agitation are, and how it's possible to calm down even after these signs appear. Ask if the student can name things that set them off.
- Explain some of the strategies that you or other adults will use and that other students use when they notice signs of agitation. For example, "If I see that you are getting frustrated, I might come over to you and ask if you'd like to work on your seatwork with me at the back table." Ask the student what helps to calm them down. Specify how the student should respond.
- Clarify strategies for how the student should behave when feeling frustrated, angry, or overwhelmed. For example, "When you feel angry with a classmate, I want you to use your words and keep your hands to yourself. You can ask me to help. You can ask me to take a break on the carpet."
- Explain that you or another adult will suggest some strategies that the student can use when feeling angry or emotional.
- Tell the student that you will check in regularly to discuss how things are going.
- Encourage the student to try hard and cooperate, and communicate that the student can succeed with everyone's help.

    2. Practice and role-play appropriate responses. Model expected behaviors, including any relaxation strategies and self-management techniques that the student will be expected to use. Have the student role-play or verbally rehearse what to do when feeling angry, when an adult gives directions, and when behavior emergency procedures are initiated.

    3. Consistently implement prevention strategies. Incorporate all of the planned prevention strategies in their corresponding settings to help prevent the cycle of escalation from occurring in the first place and to productively engage the student in class activities.

    4. Use anxiety-reducing strategies when a known trigger occurs or at the first signs of agitation in the student. Because anxiety-reducing accommodations are supportive in nature, they must be implemented *before* behavior begins to seriously escalate to be effective. Otherwise, the problem behavior may be reinforced.

    5. Use defusion strategies as soon as behavior begins to accelerate and before it reaches its peak. At the Acceleration phase, the student's behavior has the effect of engaging you. The less staff members allow themselves to be drawn in, the more effective they can be in defusing the situation. If behaviors are not managed successfully during this phase, the student is highly likely to escalate further and exhibit severe problem behaviors. Avoid escalating prompts (i.e., adult responses that are likely to worsen the situation) and interact with calmness, respect, and detachment when addressing students in this acceleration phase.

Approach the student in a nonthreatening manner by following these guidelines:

- Move slowly and deliberately toward the problem situation. Avoid showing signs of panic or anxiety. If possible, engage in some normal, on-task interactions with other students on the way to the target situation.
- Speak privately. When possible, take the student aside or ask the student to come to your desk. Talk quietly so as not to be overheard by other students.
- Speak calmly and respectfully. Use the student's name and speak in a neutral and businesslike voice. Avoid harsh, angry tones. Be as matter-of-fact as possible. Do not threaten, plead, or cajole.
- Minimize body language. Be as undemonstrative as possible. Avoid pointing or staring at the student.
- Keep a reasonable distance. Though proximity is generally important, do not get too close or invade the student's space. Don't crowd or get in the student's face. Remember that a squared-off stance, directly facing the student, immediately signals that you are approaching the student in a confrontational manner. Try to speak to the student more at an angle.
- Match the student's eye-level position, if possible. Some students react negatively to anyone towering over them. Sit or squat beside a student who is sitting. If the student is standing, stand as well, perhaps taking a step back to show respect for the student's space. By meeting students at their level, you are showing respect and are less likely to risk escalation.
- Be brief. Keep the interaction brief and simple. Lengthy pronouncements or repeated explanations may prompt negative reactions from some students.
- Stay with the agenda. Stay focused on your primary concern. Do not get sidetracked. Deal with other problems later.
- Avoid power struggles. Do not be drawn into "I won't" or "you will" engagement.
- If the situation begins to escalate toward Phase 5 Peak behavior, immediately terminate any discussion. Simply withdraw from the student. Use an exit strategy, such as saying, "Just a minute," then withdraw and direct your attention to the other students. At the same time, keep a close eye on the student. This simple act of withdrawing may stave off further escalation.

If the student refuses to follow your directions, use a nonconfrontational limit-setting procedure to encourage compliance without engaging in a power struggle. Follow these steps:

Step 1: Restate the expected behavior or direction, making sure it is clear, observable, and immediate (e.g., say "It is time to sit down at your desk"). If the student cooperates, acknowledge the choice briefly and prompt and cue the current class activity. If the student does not cooperate with the direction, go to Step 2.

Step 2: Present the original direction and a negative consequence as a decision for the student to make. For example, "Michael, you are asked to sit down in your seat or you'll have to miss some recess. You decide."

Step 3: Follow up based on the student's response:

- *If the student decides to follow the direction*, acknowledge the choice *briefly* and continue with the lesson or activity. It is important to acknowledge the student's choice briefly and move to the other students. The student may still be somewhat agitated and a lengthy positive statement may escalate the student.
- *If the student does not follow the direction*—that is, he maintains the current problem behavior—deliver the negative consequence. For example, "Michael, you have decided to miss some recess, so that's what we'll do. The longer you are out of your seat, the more recess you will miss."
- *If the student continues to disrupt the classroom,* document the incident with an office referral.
- *If the student escalates to Phase 5 Peak behaviors,* follow the student's behavior emergency plan protocol or deliver the prearranged consequence.

6. Employ debriefing procedures once the student has fully calmed down. Debrief with the student after any incident that escalates to the Peak phase. The debriefing process should occur after the student has been calm for at least 20 minutes and can follow simple directions (e.g., "Let's take a seat and talk about this"). Debriefing should last no longer than 5–10 minutes. Before attempting to debrief, be certain that the student has had enough time to calm down to avoid the risk of triggering more peak behavior. Refer to your list of the student's common de-escalating behaviors to determine whether the student has moved into this phase (this could be as soon as 10 minutes after an incident or as long as 90 minutes).

Follow these debriefing recommendations:

- To gauge whether the student is calm and ready to discuss the incident, try a small direction, such as "Would you sit over here, please?" or "Pass me that book, please." If the student cooperates with that direction, continue the debriefing steps. If the student does not follow the direction, withdraw and allow the student more time to de-escalate.
- Choose a private setting to discuss the incident.
- Complete the Behavior Improvement Form at this time with the student. If time permits, role-play the problem situation with the student and have the student act out alternative, more appropriate responses.
- Avoid reprimanding or lecturing the student. Instead, the focus should be on prompting appropriate behavior for the future and encouraging the student to successfully transition back to the current classroom activity. Ask the student to describe what is expected in the next setting and discuss whether the student is willing to cooperate with these expectations.
- If the student's behavior begins to escalate during debriefing, withdraw from the discussion and use anxiety-reducing and defusion strategies as needed. Resume the debriefing procedures once the student regains a level of calmness.

7. Help the student reintegrate back to the classroom. Once the student has reentered the classroom or current setting, continue to conduct activities as normal. Look for opportunities to acknowledge the student for appropriate behavior, such as starting the reentry task or resuming normal class activities. Be prepared to provide some prompts to help the student get started and reinforce cooperation.

8. Remember to maintain calmness, respect, and detachment across all phases. When you interact with the student, it is crucial to display calmness, respect, and detachment to greatly lessen the chance of further escalation.

- Achieve calmness by pausing slightly and addressing the student in a calm and measured, yet serious tone.
- Convey respect by focusing on the student's behavior instead of on the student, beginning statements with the student's name, and speaking privately to the student as much as possible.
- Detachment communicates that the student is ultimately responsible for their own behavior. Convey detachment by concisely communicating expectations, concealing emotional responses, and refraining from coaxing or pleading with the student to behave appropriately—in other words, give the student the choice of how the interaction will proceed.

9. Acknowledge cooperation whenever the student disengages from an escalating situation. Strongly acknowledge the student for choosing the expected behavior (e.g., "Thank you, James, for taking your seat and getting on with your work"). At a later time or follow-up meeting, offer more specific praise. Also consider mentioning the positive behavior to other staff members or the student's parents when appropriate.

10. Meet and debrief with the student regularly. Check in with the student on a weekly basis to see how things are going, provide additional praise for cooperation, review behavior expectations, and solve problems that may be arising.

11. Keep in contact with the parents or guardians. Immediately inform parents about any Phase 5 Peak behavior incidents. Also maintain ongoing communication to discuss progress and highlight successes via regularly scheduled progress reports (e.g., a weekly note sent home with the student, phone conference, or e-mail communication).

12. Use data to make periodic revisions and adjustments to the plan as necessary. As you monitor the student's progress, make adjustments to the plan as needed. If the student's behavior is not improving, ask the following questions:

- *Are all essential components of the plan being implemented as intended?* Ensure that intervention fidelity is maintained by having the teacher or external observer complete Fidelity Checklist: Managing the Cycle of Emotional Escalation (Reproducible 4.5d, p. 467).
- *Which aspects of the plan can be modified to increase its effectiveness?* Consider modifying when, where, and how strategies are used throughout phases of escalation.
- *What supplemental strategies can be introduced to support the effectiveness of the plan?* Incorporating other intervention strategies, such as explicitly teaching replacement behaviors, increasing monitoring and supervision, or introducing self-monitoring procedures or relaxation techniques, might help to encourage improvement in the student's behavior.

- *Are the student's needs being met through the plan?* Review information about the context of the problem and determine whether to collect additional data to more accurately understand triggers, identify behaviors at each phase of the escalation cycle, and determine the function that is maintaining problem behavior.

Strategy Summary

Serious emotionally escalated behavior can be described by a conceptual model comprised of seven phases—each characterized by specific, identifiable behaviors. Classifying behavior in this way can help educators understand the behavioral processes and emotional subtexts that enable teachers to determine the kinds of teacher-student interactions that are likely to maintain acceptable behavior, defuse problem behavior, and prevent escalated behavior. By focusing on the student behaviors early in the chain, you are in a position to redirect the student toward appropriate behavior and preempt escalation. Phases 1 through 4 emphasize effective teaching and proactive management practices. In Phase 5, the emphasis is on safety, crisis management, and follow-up. Phases 6 and 7 are designed to enable the student to recover from an incident and resume the classroom activity. Knowing which problematic student behaviors to expect at each stage of a potentially explosive situation and being prepared with an array of strategies for each phase in the cycle can help staff respond immediately, safely, and effectively.

Implementation Guidelines
Managing Emotional Escalation

Overview

Managing Emotional Escalation is designed to help prevent, defuse, and resolve any behaviors that are the result of emotional reactions that may lead to escalation. Problem behaviors that escalate into serious acting-out behavior are often emotionally based and fueled by students' reactive responses to conflict situations—generally negative interactions with another person. These cases usually involve a cycle of behavior that follows a recognizable sequence of stages or phases, in which each behavior becomes more serious than the last. Understanding and effectively managing this cycle of emotional escalation can be a powerful way for a teacher or specialist to intervene and defuse a potentially volatile situation.

The cycle of emotional escalation generally progresses through seven distinct phases (Colvin & Scott, 2014):

- Phase 1: Calm—Overall behavior is cooperative and acceptable.
- Phase 2: Triggers—Events or circumstances prompt emotional reactions.
- Phase 3: Agitation—Overall behavior is unfocused and distracted.
- Phase 4: Acceleration—Behavior engages others.
- Phase 5: Peak—Behavior is out of control.
- Phase 6: De-escalation—Overall behavior shows confusion and lack of focus, perhaps appearing to vacillate between anger and calming down.
- Phase 7: Recovery—Behavior shows an eagerness for busy work and reluctance to interact.

As shown in the figure below, the graph rises as the interaction escalates and falls away as the student's behavior de-escalates.

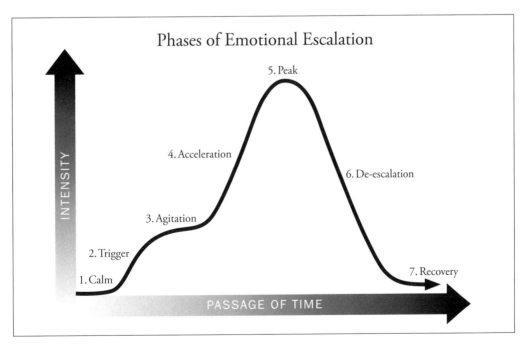

REPRODUCIBLE 4.5a *Implementation Guidelines: Managing Emotional Escalation (2 of 6)*

Implementation Guidelines: Managing Emotional Escalation

Plan Summary

Phase 1: Calm	Student behaviors:	Prevention Strategies:
Phase 2: Triggers	Student behaviors:	Strategies to Address Triggers:
Phase 3: Agitation	Student behaviors:	Anxiety-Reducing Strategies:
Phase 4: Acceleration	Student behaviors:	Defusion Procedures:
Phase 5: Peak	Student behaviors:	Behavior Emergency Procedures:
Phase 6: De-escalation	Student behaviors:	Debriefing Procedures:
Phase 7: Recovery	Student behaviors:	Reintegration Strategies:

Interventions © 2019 Ancora Publishing

REPRODUCIBLE 4.5a *Implementation Guidelines: Managing Emotional Escalation (3 of 6)*

Implementation Guidelines: Managing Emotional Escalation

Implementation Steps

1. **Meet with the student to discuss and finalize the plan.**

    During this meeting with the student, you will:

    - Explain that you want the student to be successful in school and learn to control behavior that gets them into trouble.
    - Explain that you would like to help the student learn how to calm down when feeling frustrated, angry, overwhelmed, or emotional.
    - Discuss the problem with the student. Calmly explain why specific behaviors are disruptive or inappropriate and prevent the student from being successful in school. Provide an age-appropriate rationale for why learning how to control emotions is part of growing up. Emphasize that the student can be successful and that everyone wants to help.
    - Considering the student's age and maturity level, explain how emotional escalation happens, what sets escalation off in the first place, what the signs of agitation are, and how people can calm down even after these signs appear.
    - Explain some of the strategies that you or other adults will use when they notice signs of agitation. For example, "If I see that you are getting frustrated, I might come over to you and ask if you'd like to work on your seatwork with me at the back table." Also discuss strategies other students use to calm down. Ask the student what strategies might help them calm down. Specify how the student should respond.
    - Clarify strategies for how the student should behave when feeling frustrated, angry, or overwhelmed. For example, "When you feel angry at a classmate, I want you to use your words and keep your hands to yourself. You can ask me to help. You can ask me if you can take a break on the carpet."
    - Tell the student that you or another adult will suggest some strategies that the student can use when feeling angry or emotional.
    - Tell the student that you will check in regularly to discuss how things are going.
    - Encourage the student to try hard and cooperate, and communicate that the student can succeed with help.

2. **Practice and role-play appropriate responses.**

    Model expected behaviors, including any relaxation strategies and self-management techniques that the student will be expected to use. Have the student role-play or verbally rehearse what to do when feeling angry, when adult directions are given, and when behavior emergency procedures are initiated.

3. **Consistently implement prevention strategies.**

    Incorporate all of the planned prevention strategies in their corresponding settings to help prevent the cycle of escalation from occurring in the first place and to become productively engaged with the class activities.

4. **Use anxiety-reducing strategies when a known trigger occurs or at the first signs of agitation in the student.**

    Because anxiety-reducing accommodations are supportive in nature, to be effective they must be implemented *before* behavior begins to seriously escalate. Otherwise, the problem behavior may be reinforced.

REPRODUCIBLE 4.5a *Implementation Guidelines: Managing Emotional Escalation (4 of 6)*

Implementation Guidelines: Managing Emotional Escalation

5. **Use defusion strategies as soon as behavior begins to accelerate and before escalating behavior reaches its peak.**

   At this phase, the student's behavior has the effect of engaging you. The less you allow yourself to be drawn in, the more effective you can be in defusing the situation. If behaviors are not managed successfully during this phase, the student is highly likely to escalate further and exhibit severe problem behaviors. Avoid escalating prompts (i.e., adult responses that are likely to worsen the situation), and interact with calmness, respect, and detachment when addressing students in the Acceleration phase.

   Approach the student in a nonthreatening manner by following these guidelines:

   - Move slowly and deliberately toward the problem situation. Avoid showing signs of panic or anxiety. If possible, engage in some normal, on-task interactions with other students on the way to the target situation.
   - Speak privately. When possible, take the student aside or ask the student to come to your desk. Talk quietly so as not to be overheard by other students.
   - Speak calmly and respectfully. Use the student's name and speak in a neutral and businesslike voice. Avoid harsh, angry tones. Be as matter-of-fact as possible. Do not threaten, plead, or cajole.
   - Minimize body language. Be as undemonstrative as possible. Avoid pointing or staring at the student.
   - Keep a reasonable distance. Though proximity is generally important, do not get too close or invade the student's space. Don't crowd or get in the student's face. Remember that a squared-off stance, directly facing the student, immediately signals that you are approaching in a confrontational manner. Try to speak to the student at an angle.
   - Match the student's eye-level position, if possible. Some students react negatively to anyone towering over them. If the student is sitting, sit or squat beside them. If the student is standing, stand as well, perhaps taking a step back to show respect for the student's space. By meeting students at their level, you are showing respect and you are less likely to risk escalation.
   - Be brief. Keep the interaction brief and simple. Lengthy pronouncements or repeated explanations may prompt negative reactions from some students.
   - Stay with the agenda. Stay focused on your primary concern. Do not get sidetracked. Deal with other problems later.
   - Avoid power struggles. Do not be drawn into "I won't" or "you will" types of engagement.
   - If the situation begins to escalate toward Phase 5 Peak behavior, immediately terminate any discussion. Simply withdraw from the student. Use an exit strategy such as saying, "Just a minute," then withdraw and direct your attention to the other students. At the same time, keep a close eye on the escalating student. This simple act of withdrawing may stave off further escalation.

   If the student refuses to follow your directions, use a nonconfrontational limit-setting procedure to encourage compliance without engaging in a power struggle. Follow these steps:

   Step 1: Restate the expected behavior or direction, making sure it is clear, observable, and immediate. (e.g., say "It is time to sit down at your desk"). If the student cooperates, acknowledge the choice briefly, and prompt and cue the current class activity. If the student does not cooperate with the direction, go to Step 2.

   Step 2: Present the original direction and a negative consequence as a decision for the student to make. For example, "Michael, you are asked to sit down in your seat or you'll have to miss some recess. You decide."

REPRODUCIBLE 4.5a *Implementation Guidelines: Managing Emotional Escalation (5 of 6)*

Implementation Guidelines: Managing Emotional Escalation

Step 3: Follow up based on the student's response:

- **If the student decides to follow the direction:** Acknowledge the choice *briefly* and continue with the lesson or activity. It is important to acknowledge the student's choice briefly and move to the other students. The student may still be somewhat agitated, and a lengthy positive statement may escalate the student.
- **If the student does not follow the direction—that is, maintains the current problem behavior:** Deliver the negative consequence. For example, "Michael, you have decided to miss some recess, so that's what we'll do. The longer you are out of your seat, the more recess you will miss."
- **If the student continues to disrupt the classroom:** Document the incident with an incident referral.
- **If the student escalates to Phase 5 Peak behaviors:** Follow the student's beahvior emergency plan protocol or delivery the prearranged consequence.

6. **Employ debriefing procedures once the student has fully calmed down.**

   Debrief with the student after any incident that escalates to the Peak phase. The debriefing process should occur after the student has been calm for at least 20 minutes and can follow simple directions (e.g., "Let's take a seat and talk about this"). Debriefing should last no longer than 5–10 minutes. Before attempting to debrief, be certain that the student has had enough time to calm down to prevent the risk of triggering more peak behavior. Refer to your list of the student's common de-escalating behaviors to determine whether the student has moved into this phase (this could be as soon as 10 minutes after an incident or as long as 90 minutes).

   Follow these debriefing recommendations:

   - To gauge whether the student is calm and ready to discuss the incident, try a small direction such as "Would you sit over here, please?" or "Pass me that book, please." If the student cooperates with these directions, continue the debriefing steps. If the student does not follow the specific directions, withdraw and allow the student more time to de-escalate.
   - Choose a private setting to discuss the incident.
   - Complete the Behavior Improvement Form with the student at this time. If time permits, role-play the problem situation with the student and have the student act out alternative, more appropriate responses.
   - Avoid reprimanding or lecturing the student. Instead, the focus should be on prompting appropriate behavior for the future and encouraging the student to successfully transition back to the current classroom activity. Ask the student to describe what is expected in the next setting and whether they are willing to cooperate with these expectations.
   - If the student's behavior begins to escalate during debriefing, withdraw from the discussion and use anxiety-reducing and defusion strategies as needed. Resume the debriefing procedures once the student regains a level of calmness.

7. **Help the student reintegrate back to the classroom.**

   Once the student has reentered the classroom or current setting, continue to conduct activities as normal. Look for opportunities to acknowledge the student for appropriate behavior, such as starting the reentry task or resuming normal class activities. Be prepared to provide some prompts to help the student get started, and reinforce cooperation.

REPRODUCIBLE 4.5a *Implementation Guidelines: Managing Emotional Escalation (6 of 6)*

Implementation Guidelines: Managing Emotional Escalation

8. **Remember to maintain calmness, respect, and detachment across all phases.**

    It is crucial to display calmness, respect, and detachment when you interact with the student to greatly lessen the chance of further escalation.

    - Achieve calmness by pausing slightly and addressing the student in a calm, measured, yet serious tone.
    - Convey respect by focusing on the student's behavior instead of on the student. Begin statements with the student's name and speak privately to the student as much as possible.
    - Detachment communicates that the student is ultimately responsible for their behavior. Convey detachment by concisely communicating expectations, concealing emotional responses, and refraining from coaxing or pleading with the student to behave appropriately—in other words, give the choice of how the interaction will proceed to the student.

9. **Acknowledge cooperation whenever the student disengages from an escalating situation.**

    Strongly acknowledge the student for choosing the expected behavior (e.g., "Thank you, James, for taking your seat and getting on with your work"). At a later time or in a follow-up meeting, offer more specific praise. Also consider mentioning the positive behavior to other staff members or the student's parents when appropriate.

10. **Meet and debrief with the student regularly.**

    Check in with the student on a weekly basis to see how things are going, to provide additional praise for cooperation, to review behavior expectations, and to solve problems that may be arising.

11. **Keep in contact with the parents or guardians.**

    Inform parents at the earliest opportunity about the student's progress. Highlight successes and be sure to mention any Phase 5 Peak behavior incidents. Also maintain ongoing communication via regularly scheduled progress reports (e.g., a weekly note sent home with the student, phone conference, or e-mail communication).

12. **Use data to make periodic revisions and adjustments to the plan as necessary.**

    Monitor student progress and collaborate with your problem-solving team to make adjustments to the plan as needed. If you notice escalation in student behavior or an increase in the frequency of Code Red situations, contact your administrator or problem-solving team immediately to discuss next steps.

REPRODUCIBLE 4.5d *Fidelity Checklist*

Fidelity Checklist
Managing the Cycle of Emotional Escalation

Essential Planning Steps

- ☐ Identify the student's specific behaviors for each of the phases in the cycle of emotional escalation.
- ☐ Select an array of strategies for addressing and managing escalating behavior at each phase of the cycle.
- ☐ For each set of strategies, specify when and where they will be used, and who will be primarily responsible for implementing them.
- ☐ Make a plan for data collection and monitoring.
- ☐ Outline roles and responsibilities for implementing the plan.
- ☐ Provide training to teachers and other adults who will be implementing the plan.

Essential Implementation Components

- ☐ Meet with the student to discuss and finalize the plan.
- ☐ Practice and role-play appropriate responses.
- ☐ Consistently implement prevention strategies.
- ☐ Use anxiety-reducing strategies when a known trigger occurs or at the first signs of agitation in the student.
- ☐ Use defusion strategies as soon as behavior begins to accelerate and before escalating behavior reaches its peak.
- ☐ If the student escalates to Phase 5 Peak behaviors, follow the student's behavior emergency plan protocol or deliver the prearranged consequence.
- ☐ Employ debriefing strategies once the student has fully calmed down.
- ☐ Help the student reintegrate back to the classroom.
- ☐ Across all phases, maintain calmness, respect, and detachment.
- ☐ Acknowledge cooperation whenever the student disengages from an escalating situation.
- ☐ Meet and debrief with the student regularly.
- ☐ Keep in contact with the parents or guardians.
- ☐ Use data to make periodic revisions and adjustments to the plan as necessary.

References

Colvin, G. (2005a). *Defusing anger and aggression: Safe strategies for secondary school educators* [Video]. Eugene, OR: Iris Media.

Colvin, G. (2005b). *Managing non-compliance: Effective strategies for K-12 teachers* [Video]. Eugene, OR: Iris Media.

Colvin, G. (2010). *Defusing disruptive behavior in the classroom.* Thousand Oaks, CA: Corwin Press.

Colvin, G., & Scott, T. M. (2014). *Managing the cycle of acting-out behavior in the classroom* (2nd ed.). Thousand Oaks, CA: Corwin Press.

SPECIALIZED INTERVENTION STRATEGY SIX

Supporting Students With Internalizing Challenges

The student seems worried, depressed, and socially withdrawn, and/or experiences multiple physical complaints

By Barbara A. Gueldner and
Kenneth W. Merrell

Purpose

This chapter may assist students who have symptoms associated with depression and anxiety. The strategies in this chapter will be of use to school-based interventionists, who may also share the strategies with general education teachers to enhance the interventions and provide additional support to students.

Following are some general guidelines for symptom presentation in students.

Behaviors, Thoughts, and Emotions Associated With Anxiety

- Excessive worry about situations such as school performance, talking to teachers and/or peers, separating from a caregiver, contracting germs or diseases, school bathrooms, or natural disasters
- Misinterpreting common unpleasant or difficult situations so that they seem especially threatening or catastrophic
- Acute fear of particular things or situations: animals, public speaking, vomiting, etc.
- Acute experience of panic symptoms such as racing heart, tingling, numbness, feeling terrified, chest pains, sweating, problem breathing, or feeling like you are losing control
- Avoiding or withdrawing from situations that provoke feelings of discomfort or fear
- Perfectionistic thoughts and behaviors
- Excessive reassurance seeking

Behaviors, Thoughts, and Emotions Associated With Depression

- Feeling sad
- Not being interested in or not finding enjoyment in everyday or enjoyable activities
- Weight gain or loss
- Feeling worthless or guilty
- Hopelessness about the future, helplessness
- Being preoccupied with death

Common Symptom Overlap

- Irritability and anger that appears excessive or prolonged
- Sleep disruption (difficulties falling asleep, sleeping too much or too little)
- Preoccupation with thoughts
- Problems concentrating or making decisions
- Physical restlessness or slowing down
- Physical aches, pains, or other complaints
- Fatigue

 Case Example: Maria

Maria is typically talkative at home, but when she gets to school (the event that triggers her anxiety), she is very quiet. Her body feels tense, she finds it hard to breathe, and she feels like she has a rock in her stomach (the physical experience of anxiety). However much she tries, she cannot get the thought out of her mind that if she talks, she will embarrass herself because people will think her voice sounds strange (thoughts associated with anxiety). As a result, she rarely talks above a whisper (behavior associated with anxiety). Her teacher is interested in using strategies to help Maria learn about this process as a way to support her.

By using a multi-tiered approach to address internalizing problems, you will be able to strategically implement strategies that match each student's needs. A sobering reality is that all students will eventually encounter life stressors that will test their coping resources, whether or not they are considered at-risk or in immediate need. When your approach to student wellness includes providing education and practice with new skills, students whose symptoms have not yet been identified but who are struggling will learn useful strategies and may seek out more help.

Rationale

In and of themselves, anxiety and sadness are not necessarily problematic and in fact are normal emotions. These emotions can be part of typical developmental phases (e.g., separation anxiety, fear of the dark, disappointment, grief) and can also serve to give people information about times when they need to exercise caution, reflect, or problem-solve. However, for some students, persistent and moderate to severe internalizing experiences can be not only concerning, but also very uncomfortable on a day-to-day basis. Internalized thoughts, feelings, and behaviors can be difficult to understand and detect, particularly in children. Worrying, sadness, catastrophic thinking, physical sensations, and, most extremely, thoughts of self-harm or death are not easily seen by an observer, hence the term *internal*-izing. To further confuse matters, sometimes internalizing and externalizing symptoms (e.g., hyperactivity, impulsivity, aggression) occur at the same time, which understandably makes it challenging to consider that a student may be feeling anxious or depressed when their behavior is difficult to manage (Eisenberg et al., 2001). Finally, keep in mind that individuals belonging to different national, ethnic, or regional groups may be less accurate in recognizing emotions across groups, and individuals belonging to a majority group have a more difficult time recognizing emotions in individuals who belong to a minority group (Elfenbein & Ambady, 2002). Thus, internalizing problems can often be misunderstood and underidentified in children and adolescents.

School staff are in an excellent position to support students' mental health at school (Hogan, 2003). School-based interventionists (e.g., counselors, psychologists, and social workers) are trained to identify signs of internalizing challenges and implement strategies known to effectively manage the symptoms of internalizing problems, either through direct contact with students, support for general education teachers in using strategies in the classroom, or coordination of services with community mental health providers. Without proper attention and intervention, potential outcomes of internalizing problems are highly concerning, even devastating, and can affect the lives of students and their loved ones for years to come.

This chapter provides an overview of the nature of internalizing problems and offers strategies for intervention. It includes the steps to take as part of an implementation process, detailed descriptions of strategies, considerations for using them effectively, and troubleshooting when students need more assistance. This information should enhance the school interventionist's knowledge base and skill set, thereby increasing students' access to the assistance that they so very much need.

Common Questions About Internalizing Problems

What do I need to know about internalizing problems?

As listed in the beginning of the chapter, internalizing problems generally are discussed in terms of symptoms associated with anxiety and depression. Diagnosable anxiety, or a set of symptoms that meet criteria established by the *Diagnostic and Statistical Manual of Mental Disorders* (5th ed.; *DSM-5*; American Psychiatric Association, 2013), tends to occur more frequently than depression in preadolescent children (Cartwright-Hatton, McNicol, & Doubleday, 2006), more in females, and affects an estimated 15%–20% of children and adolescents (Beesdo, Knappe, & Pine, 2009). Left untreated, anxiety can be associated with academic and social problems, along with future mental health difficulties (Swan, Cummings, Caporino, & Kendall, 2014).

Although a diagnosable depressive disorder occurs relatively infrequently in childhood, at about 1% of the population, the incidence increases during adolescence, ranging from 5% in early adolescence to about 20% at the end. Depression affects females more than males at a 2:1 ratio (see Thapar, Collishaw, Pine, & Thapar, 2012). Keep in mind that at least one of the two hallmarks of depression—experiencing a sad mood and losing interest or pleasure in everyday activities—must be present to meet the clinical definition of depression. With children—especially younger children—irritable mood is often how depression is expressed. Although the majority of individuals who experience depression improve within a year, the risk of reoccurrence is substantial. And as with anxiety, they are at risk for experiencing a host of other mental health problems, health and social problems, substance abuse, and suicide.

Internalizing problems can also include experiences associated with social withdrawal and somatic complaints, such as stomachaches, headaches, or other physical discomfort that may not otherwise be explained by another medical problem (Merrell, 2008). Symptoms associated with obsessive-compulsive and related disorders (e.g., trichotillomania), trauma, and stress-related disorders can also include internalizing symptoms. Furthermore, internalizing characteristics can occur with other problems that are not classified as primarily internalizing (e.g., eating disorders, bipolar disorders, psychotic disorders, and neurodevelopmental disorders; Whitcomb, 2017, p. 535).

Depression and anxiety often occur together. Out of the children and adolescents diagnosed with a depressive disorder, 30%–75% are also experiencing anxiety (Angold & Costello, 1993; Birmaher et al., 1996, as cited in Bress, Meyer, & Hajcak, 2015). *It is important to note that not all students who experience symptoms of anxiety or depression will meet the criteria for a disorder per se*—behaviors associated with anxiety and depression may be transient, not severe enough to warrant diagnosis, or not particularly impairing or stressful to a student. Although diagnosis can be helpful in some situations, your primary role is to pay attention to the signs and consider how to provide prevention and early intervention services. For students who show signs, assessment will help you understand the scope of the problem and guide specific intervention strategies. From a prevention standpoint, many of the strategies listed in this chapter can assist your students in building their skills to develop general resilience.

We provide information on the symptoms of internalizing problems and occurrence rates to increase awareness of the problem and guide interventions that can help students with these problems. Some assessment and intervention selection tasks are best left to trained mental health professionals, especially when acute, chronic, and serious concerns may require more experience with understanding the nature of psychopathology. The planning team as a group must focus on increased staff awareness, early identification, and intervention planning and implementation. Engaging in these tasks should increase the likelihood that students can build healthy lives.

What causes internalizing problems?

Through the course of your work and study, you have probably heard terms such as *biopsychosocial model, epigenetics,* and *neuroplasticity.* These areas of study are contributing evidence that physical and mental health develops from multiple pathways that constantly interact with one another. We no longer assume that an individual will develop a certain disease due to solely genetic factors or environmental influences—it's not that straightforward. Instead, we must consider *influences* such as biological factors, genes that may be expressed in different ways depending on a variety of circumstances, and students' vast and unique environments, while appreciating that new neural pathways can be forged over time (Garland & Howard, 2009). We know that our brains are able to be flexible (i.e., neuroplasticity), receiving and adapting to influences that can positively alter negative trajectories (Charney & Manji, 2004).

Let's consider some specifics as they pertain to depression and anxiety. Biology (e.g., genetics, psychobiology, temperament), current mental health status, and environmental factors (e.g., stressors, parenting strategies) are believed to contribute to internalizing problems. Interactions among these areas can be highly complex and should not be oversimplified (e.g., the misconception that a student is anxious solely because his parent seems anxious).

In terms of biological influences, parents can pass on anxiety and depression to their biological offspring due to the influence of genes (Beesdo et al., 2009;

CONCERNS ABOUT THE STUDENT

If you are concerned that a student is seriously depressed or anxious, wants to harm themselves, wants to harm others, or is in imminent danger of being harmed, see "Helping Students Who Need More" on page 511. A student experiencing severe and acute or chronic mental health problems may need more comprehensive services than are offered in the typical school setting. Make sure you understand your school's policies and required practices prior to making any referrals.

Levinson, 2006). While no specific gene is identified with developing depression or anxiety, it is more likely that inheriting a certain set of genes makes a person more vulnerable to developing a problem. Second, structures, systems, and neurotransmitters in the brain are associated with anxiety and depressive responses (e.g., the limbic system), suggesting highly complex processes. The hypothalamic pituitary corticoadrenal axis and the sympathetic and parasympathetic nervous systems play a role in how our bodies respond to stress and how we may or may not develop physical and mental health problems (for further information, see Smith and Vale, 2006). The neurotransmitters serotonin, norepinephrine, and dopamine have also been found to play roles (Moret & Briley, 2011). Third, temperamental traits, such as behavioral inhibition or the tendency to experience fear and withdraw when in a new situation, have been associated with developing anxiety and depressive disorders (Biederman et al., 2001).

A variety of environmental (or psychosocial) contributors are also in play and, just like biological factors, do not solely predict who will develop depression and anxiety. Stressful family and social relationships, parental anxiety or depression, adult modeling of maladaptive coping skills, maltreatment, abuse, poverty, acute or chronic illness, gender, bullying, and chronic stress can all be considered risk factors. Events that have the potential to lead to trauma symptoms, such as war, natural disasters, motor vehicle accidents, violence, and others, are gaining more visibility as necessary considerations (see Appendix A). Your school may have recently adopted trauma-informed practices to sensitively consider students' situations and needs.

By now you can see how many ingredients go into the recipe for internalizing problems and how the final product can be different, and yet similar, across variations. The linkages that have been studied and validated to date exceed the scope of this chapter. However, it should be clear that the development of internalizing problems is complex and nonlinear. Simply having a set of genes, a particular temperament, or exposure to stressors or maladaptive modeling does not automatically lead to depression and anxiety. How students perceive, interpret, and cope with events in their lives and the world around them, as well as their personal strengths and resources, also influence their mental health. In other words, the way people think about and respond to the everyday challenges of life influences whether their challenges and vulnerabilities can contribute to the development of depression or anxiety. And perhaps more importantly, our ability to cultivate a warm and supportive environment that can model, respond to, and teach helpful strategies is essential to students' emotional development and health (Denham, Bassett, and Zinsser, 2012).

Fortunately, you aren't expected to perfectly understand the exact causes and mechanisms in order to help students. Instead, you are tasked with maintaining a current understanding of the issues your students face, along with respectful, sensitive, and evidence-based approaches to prevention and early intervention efforts. The goal is to give students practical, useful, and effective skills to offset the negative effects they experience when biological factors cannot be altered and life stressors are unavoidable.

How do internalizing problems affect students in their daily lives?
Students can be anywhere from mildly to significantly affected in their daily functioning when they feel depressed or anxious. There is convincing evidence that students' mental health is directly related to school performance (Masten et

al., 2005). This relationship is bidirectional, meaning that internalizing problems can lead to diminished achievement, and problems in school can be stressful, leading to internalizing problems. Consider some common situations:

- Quinton is frequently restless, daydreams, and asks for reassurance from the teacher every day that he is doing things "right." These problems interfere with his focus in class and take time away from completing his work. It takes him twice as long as classmates to finish an assignment.
- Renae is too depressed to get out of bed in the morning. Her school attendance suffers and she falls behind, leading to more stress and discouragement.
- Nini was bullied last spring. She is fearful to return to school in the fall and develops stomachaches and headaches. She's late to school most days, missing the first hour of instruction.
- Michael earns top grades in all classes. He sleeps about 6 hours per night in order to complete all homework and study thoroughly for tests. He increasingly uses social media to connect with friends, to the exclusion of in-person time. Despite more time on schoolwork, his stress increases and he feels lonely.
- Rafael believes that the teacher thinks he's "not good enough" for an Advanced Placement course, so he doesn't ask for help when he has questions. He receives lower grades that do not reflect his actual knowledge.
- Mallorie has a learning delay and struggles to keep up with writing assignments. She worries about what other students think of her. She's distracted by these thoughts and falls further behind.

Unfortunately, when anxiety and depression go untreated, symptoms may persist and even worsen over time. For some students, these difficulties become so serious and unrelenting that going to school and doing regular activities seem like too much effort. Schoolwork is not completed, and grades drop. This can lead to a vicious cycle in which growing failure in school eventually becomes evidence of perceived internal failures and shortcomings, leading students to a deeper belief in their inability to function in school or with peers. These students may come to believe that they really are worthless or incapable of performing any better. Beliefs such as these may eventually become self-fulfilling prophecies, as the students alienate peers with their dark moods, irritability, and negativity. Alcohol and other substance abuse has also been linked to untreated internalizing problems, including suicidal thoughts and behaviors. Ultimately, school attendance, employment, relationships, and enjoyment of life may be significantly affected if internalizing problems are not addressed.

What can be done to prevent or intervene with internalizing problems?
Schools are in a unique position to bolster students' resilience—their ability to bounce back during difficult times. Because teachers are already trained in effective instructional practices, many teachers are using their expertise to teach strategies that focus on social and emotional education. Evidence is increasing that *resiliency skills* can be learned through explicit instruction and practice (Durlak, Weissberg, Dymnicki, Taylor, & Schellinger, 2011). Students

can learn skills to cope with environmental stressors and biological predispositions. One approach is through a framework such as social and emotional learning (SEL), whereby educators use programs and strategies to teach skills known to help with building resilience and intervening early. You can teach skills to all students as a classwide instructional activity, in small groups, or one-to-one when indicated. The remainder of this chapter will review effective strategies for addressing internalizing problems.

Essential Planning Steps

This section describes the steps you will take to implement an overall approach to interventions for internalizing problems. Use Essential Planning Steps Documentation (Reproducible 4.6a) to guide you through the process.

Step 1: Assess the situation and define goals for improvement.

As a guiding principle, you will measure and monitor internalizing problems by assessing thoughts, feelings (emotions, physiological experiences), and behaviors. For example, you will want to understand the extent to which students are aware of and experience maladaptive thoughts (e.g., "I know I'm going to fail the test," "I'll never feel better and there's nothing I can do about it"), emotions (e.g., anxiety, sadness, hopelessness, helplessness), associated physical sensations (e.g., hyperventilating, lethargy), and behaviors (e.g., avoiding essential tasks, seeking reassurance excessively). It is also important to measure a student's *relationship*—adaptive or maladaptive—to these experiences. For example, a student may experience rapid heartbeat before a test, but feel relatively comfortable in managing the situation and using self-talk to regulate (e.g., "That's my heart telling me I am challenged right now and need to pay attention. I've taken a test before. I know I can do this"). As you develop an assessment plan, keeping these domains in mind will help organize your approach.

   Item a: Gather and summarize assessment data. By now you are likely thinking of students who fit the description of experiencing internalizing problems. You may also be wondering: Because internalizing problems are often hard to detect, what students am I missing and how do we prevent students from experiencing these problems in the first place? Following are descriptions of three options for assessment: 1) universal screening, 2) individual assessment, and 3) socioecological assessment. These three pathways are discussed in order to advocate for *all students* and highlight the need for system reform in the area of internalizing problems—that is, identify students in need as well as move toward a more preventive approach to mental health within a multi-tiered system (Dowdy et al., 2015). This list is not exhaustive.

- *Universal screening:* Universal screening for internalizing problems is, put simply, complex. When it comes to detecting the extent to which students are experiencing mental health problems in general, challenges abound with defining indicators that adequately detect such problems and finding and using methods that are reliable, valid, and feasible (see Miller et al., 2015). Universal screening for

> Steps 1–3 are also shown on Essential Planning Steps Documentation (Form 4.6a, pp. 476–478) that can be used to guide development of an intervention plan.

REPRODUCIBLE 4.6a *Essential Planning Steps Documentation (1 of 3)*

Essential Planning Steps Documentation

Step 1. Assess the situation and define goals for improvement.

a. Gather and summarize assessment data.
   List assessment tools and dates:

   General results of assessments, including skill areas to target in intervention:

b. Identify problem areas, assets, and resources:

c. Define goals:

Step 2. Review potential intervention strategies and programs.

List strategies to consider including in the plan.

Step 3. Outline a plan for implementation, data collection, and training.

a. Use decision-making guidelines (Reproducible 4.6p) to select strategies and determine how, when, and where to implement the strategies. For each strategy, identify who will be responsible for implementation, start date, description of format or setting (e.g., small group, counselor's office), and schedule for delivery (e.g., weekly).

Strategy	Staff responsible	Start date	Format/Setting	Schedule

REPRODUCIBLE 4.6a *Essential Planning Steps Documentation (2 of 3)*

Essential Planning Steps Documentation

Strategy	Staff responsible	Start date	Format/Setting	Schedule

b. Make a plan for data collection and monitoring, including how often monitoring will occur, which behaviors or symptoms will be tracked, and how data will be gathered and summarized. Also specify a date to review data and evaluate the plan's effectiveness.

Monitoring plan	Review date

c. Outline training plans and consultation support.

d. Outline plans to collaborate with community providers.

e. List ideas for next steps for your student.

REPRODUCIBLE 4.6a *Essential Planning Steps Documentation (3 of 3)*

Essential Planning Steps Documentation

List of Interventions for Internalizing Problems

Strategy	Who Can Implement			Setting		
	Interventionist	General Ed Teacher	Community Provider	Classroom	Small Group	Individual
A. Nurture the teacher-student relationship						
Warm, trusting, little conflict	✓	✓	✓	✓	✓	✓
B. Emotion education						
Normalize emotions	✓	✓	✓	✓	✓	✓
Use literature as a tool	✓	✓	✓	✓	✓	✓
Identify comfortable and uncomfortable emotions	✓	✓*	✓	✓	✓	✓
Identify physiological experiences associated with emotions	✓	✓*	✓	✓	✓	✓
Ask the student to finish incomplete sentences	✓	✓*	✓		✓	✓
Use a self-rating inventory for communicating emotions	✓	✓*	✓		✓	✓
C. Emotion coaching						
Awareness of emotions, opportunity to connect, use empathy, label emotions, set limits, and problem-solve	✓	✓*	✓	✓	✓	✓
D. Relaxation training						
Diaphragmatic breathing	✓	✓	✓	✓	✓	✓
Progressive muscle relaxation	✓	✓	✓	✓	✓	✓
E. Behavior change						
Schedule enjoyable activities	✓	✓*	✓	✓	✓	✓
Use operant conditioning techniques	✓	✓*	✓	✓	✓	✓
F. Cognitive change						
Develop an awareness of emotional variability:						
Feelings thermometer	✓	✓*	✓	✓	✓	✓
Emotional pie	✓	✓*	✓	✓	✓	✓
Detect automatic thoughts and identify beliefs:						
Thought chart	✓	✓*	✓		✓	✓
Cognitive replay	✓	✓*	✓		✓	✓
Hypothesizing	✓	✓*	✓		✓	✓
Evaluate automatic thoughts and beliefs:						
Identifying cognitive distortions or thinking errors	✓	✓*	✓		✓	✓
Reframing	✓	✓*	✓		✓	✓
Evaluating positives and negatives	✓	✓*	✓		✓	✓
G. Problem-solving	✓	✓*	✓		✓	✓
H. Social skills training	✓		✓		✓	✓
I. Exposure and response prevention	✓		✓		✓	✓
J. Mindfulness-based practices						
Mindfulness meditation, body scan, breath awareness, yoga, mindfulness-based programs	✓	✓*	✓	✓	✓	✓
K. School-based programs						
Programs to address internalizing symptoms and promote resilience	✓	✓*	✓	✓	✓	✓
Schoolwide positive behavior interventions and supports	✓	✓		✓	✓	✓
Parent training	✓*		✓		✓	✓
L. Referral to and coordination with community healthcare	✓*		✓*			✓

* = Consultation support indicated

Interventions © 2019 Ancora Publishing

internalizing problems specifically can be a new and daunting process for many, if not most, school districts. Schools using a framework such as schoolwide PBIS may provide some guidance as to ways in which identification, measuring outcomes, and linking assessment to intervention can be accomplished with internalizing programs (McIntosh, Ty, & Miller, 2014; Weist et al., 2018)). Potential screening measures may includes the Behavioral and Emotional Screening System (BESS; Kamphaus & Reynolds, 2015), Strengths and Difficulties Questionnaire (SDQ; Goodman, 1997), and Social, Academic, and Emotional Behavior Risk Screener (SAERBS; Kilgus & von der Embse, 2014). For a review, see Allen, Kilgus, Burns, & Hodgson, 2018.

To begin, have your planning team discuss the role screening may play in your school, either at the schoolwide or classroom level. Consult the literature and seek consultation support. Use screening measures that have been tested for use in identifying students with internalizing problems, and understand their psychometric properties (e.g., under which conditions does it identify students who need assistance and those who do not). Anticipate the challenges involved not only in collecting and analyzing data, but also in linking students to appropriate multitiered interventions based on assessment results. In short, the goal for universal screening is to identify students who may benefit from additional assessment. To meet this goal, your team will need to put a procedure in place to conduct such assessments and plan interventions in a timely manner.

- *Individual assessment:* Individualized assessments will help your team identify the problem of concern and describe it in enough detail to understand the exact nature and scope of the problem. As mentioned previously, internalizing problems are often experienced privately and can be confusing to interpret by simply observing behavior. For example, if a student is experiencing repetitive and hopeless thoughts, as well as stomachaches or fatigue, you may notice only that the student goes to the school nurse frequently or seems lethargic. But that does not tell you *the reason for their discomfort*, and you cannot see their thoughts! Furthermore, irritability, refusal or noncompliance, inattention, social communication problems, and verbal or physically aggressive or reclusive behaviors may (or may not) be indicative of internalizing problems (Wehry, Beesdo-Baum, Hennelly, Connolly, & Strawn, 2015). And, as mentioned previously, internalizing problems can occur as a result of a variety of factors, including highly stressful, even traumatic events.

  As a result, a thorough assessment requires that you gather data using a variety of methods (observations, interviews, behavior rating scales), from a variety of sources (student, teacher, parent, community), and in multiple settings (different classes or times of day, at home, in school; Whitcomb & Merrell, 2013). Casting both a wide and a narrow net may help to define the scope and nature of behaviors and experiences that may be contributing to a student's problem. Gathering data that represents a student's strengths, assets, and resources is also important. School personnel who are trained in social, emotional, and behavior-based assessment and data collection are the best resource for gathering and reviewing this data and leading the development of an intervention plan. Use the Social and Emotional Assessment Worksheet (Reproducible 4.6b shown on the next page) to organize, summarize, and analyze assessment data and link them to an appropriate intervention.

continued on page 482

REPRODUCIBLE 4.6b *Social and Emotional Assessment Worksheet (1 of 2)*

Social and Emotional Assessment Worksheet

Student _____ Grade/Class _____

Teacher/Counselor _____ Date _____

1. STUDENT INFORMATION

List major concerns and reason for assessment.

2. SUMMARY OF ASSESSMENT INFORMATION

Write down the most important test scores, observations, and information from interviews or other assessment sources.

3. PROBLEM ANALYSIS

A. List major problems, concerns, diagnostic indicators, and so forth that are indicated and supported by the assessment information.

Adapted from *Helping Students Overcome Depression and Anxiety: A Practical Guide to Internalizing Problems* (2nd ed., pp. 227–228), by K. W. Merrell, 2008, Guilford Press. Copyright 2008 by Guilford Press. Reprinted with permission of Guilford Press.

REPRODUCIBLE 4.6b *Social and Emotional Assessment Worksheet (2 of 2)*

Social and Emotional Assessment Worksheet

Problem analysis (continued)

B. List any hypotheses you have developed regarding the possible origins and functions of any problems listed in Part A.

C. How might these hypotheses be tested?

4. PROBLEM SOLUTION AND EVALUATION

List potential interventions that appear to be appropriate for the identified problems. Include tools or methods that may be useful for monitoring intervention progress and evaluating the intervention outcome.

- *Socioecological assessment:* Understanding the nature of a student's presenting problems also includes examining the student's broader ecological environment (Herman, Merrell, Reinke, and Tucker, 2004). Specifically, try to identify ways in which the school and other socioecological factors may be promoting or worsening students' mental health, and how these factors might be addressed to produce change. To this end, you might inquire into school climate, teacher-student and peer relationships, learning problems, and community, cultural, family, and medical factors. Likewise, when linking assessment to intervention planning, take into consideration student, family, and school preferences, resources, and level of engagement.

Compared with the technological improvements seen in recent decades in the identification of students with externalizing and academic problems, measuring internalizing problems in an objective manner remains a challenge. Few tools are available to measure internalizing problems on a large scale, let alone monitor progress with precision and efficiency (Kilgus, Reinke, & Jimerson, 2015). And, as Dowdy and colleagues note: "Although school-based mental health services should always consider and respond to the needs of students who are suffering and experiencing significant psychological disorders, only focusing on psychopathology falls short of the more universal, aspirational goal of moving all students along a developmental trajectory toward complete, positive mental health" (2005, p. 182).

Indeed, assessment also includes consideration of environmental contributors to problems, as well as an individual's and community's strengths and resources. A more expansive discussion of assessment can be found in *Behavioral, Social, and Emotional Assessment in Children and Adolescents* (5th ed., Whitcomb, 2017). To this end, general guidance for assessment appear in the box "Guidelines for Assessment," and potentially appropriate measures are listed at the end of this chapter.

Item b: Identify problem areas, assets, and resources. After gathering and analyzing relevant data, prioritize one or two problem areas and define them. Two examples follow, one with a group and the other with an individual.

GUIDELINES FOR ASSESSMENT

Assessment of internalizing problems involves a number of considerations:

- A professional trained in assessment methods should lead development of the assessment and intervention plan.
- Assessment methods will often include an initial screening. From there, interviews, observations, and behavior rating scales can be helpful.
- A multimethod, multisource approach is recommended and should include the perspective of the student, a parent, and a teacher.
- Select assessment tools based on their psychometric properties.
- Obtain consent from a student's parent or guardian to conduct assessment, as appropriate.
- Understand your district policies and procedures in regard to assessment, immediate actions to take in response to acute concerns (e.g., suicidal ideation), and the scope of interventions in schools.

Case Examples: Identifying Problem Areas, Assets, and Resources

Example 1: Universal or Indicated Problem Identification

Problem Area: Your data from a universal screening using self-reports and teacher reports from the Behavioral and Emotional Screening System (BESS) with all fifth-grade students indicate that several students have elevated scores on the Internalizing Risk Index, as reported either by the student or teacher, or by both. A review of the test items that are part of the Internalizing Risk Index suggests students experience a range of thoughts, behaviors, and emotions associated with internalizing problems.

Assets and Resources: Data suggest that students attend a school committed to developing resilience and reducing risk. A school mental health professional is available to provide training to teachers on internalizing problems. Parents are engaged as part of the screening process.

Example 2: Targeted Problem Identification

Problem Area: From the results of the initial screening, your team selects five students to assess individually. In one hypothetical case, the individual assessment includes data from a classroom observation and from the student, the primary teacher, and parent (interviews and a broadband measurement [BASC-3]). Results suggest that the student, Taya, may struggle with behaviors associated with anxiety. A narrow-band measure (Multidisciplinary Anxiety Scale for Children, 2nd ed. [MASC-2]) is administered to refine the description of the problem. All data suggest that her primary areas of difficulty are: a) student report of anxious emotions and thoughts regarding communicating with adults, b) low rate of response to teacher prompts for verbal communication (e.g., *Tell me about your paper. How was your weekend? Do you have any questions about the homework?*), and c) low rate of initiating appropriate communication with a teacher (e.g., asking for information about the content of a paper, giving a brief summary of weekend activities, or clarifying a homework assignment). Observational data are collected to establish a base rate for these behaviors, compared with three classmates believed to have average rates of participation.

Assets and Resources: The classroom teacher is engaged. The school psychologist has experience addressing targeted behaviors. The student is hesitant, but willing to engage in the intervention. The parent and teacher will briefly check in every other day to exchange information.

At this point, keep the scope of your initial intervention plan narrow so that the focus is on one or two areas of improvement and so that staff can feasibly deliver high-quality support strategies. Progress-monitoring data will help you keep an eye on any other problem areas that have been (or have yet to be) identified so you can modify goals over time.

Item c: **Define goals.** Next, define your goals to match the prioritized areas of need, including both problematic and helpful behaviors. These goals establish criteria that the interventionist or teacher can use to determine the success or failure of the intervention plan. If the goal is difficult to measure, revise the definitions of target behaviors so that they are more observable and objective.

Case Examples: Defining Goals

Example 1: Universal or Indicated Problem Identification (general internalizing thoughts, emotions, and behaviors for several students)

Goal 1: Students will demonstrate a reduction in symptoms as measured by the BESS Internalizing Risk Index at follow-up testing and after participating in a small group intervention in conjunction with a teacher-led, classroom-based social and emotional learning (SEL) program that focuses on strategies for regulating emotions.

Goal 2: Students who do not experience a reduction in symptoms per the BESS measure at follow-up testing will be referred for further assessment.

Goal 3: Students who experience a reduction in symptoms per the BESS measure will be monitored over time and will continue to participate in a SEL program at the classroom level.

Example 2: Targeted Problem Identification (difficulties in verbal responding and initiating for an individual student)

Goal 1: Taya will increase the frequency of her responses to teacher-initiated communication as measured by observational data and teacher interview.

Goal 2: Taya will increase the frequency at which she initiates communication with a teacher as measured by observational data and teacher interview.

Goal 3: Taya will experience increased feelings of self-efficacy in verbal communication and reduced overall anxiety symptoms, per the MASC-2 and student interview at the follow-up assessment.

Step 2. Review potential intervention strategies and programs.

The most effective strategies for alleviating symptoms of anxiety and depression are based on cognitive behavioral therapy (Tolin, 2010) and recognize that children learn about their emotional worlds through observation, direct instruction, coaching and support from adults, and practice. *Cognitive* means that as humans, people have thoughts and feelings at play in their daily lives. A depressed or anxious student might have unwanted or intrusive thoughts such as:

- I'm stupid.
- They think I'm incompetent.
- I feel dizzy and scared.
- I think I'm going crazy.
- I'll never feel better and there's nothing I can do to help my situation.

Techniques can be used to help a student notice, label, tolerate, and sometimes challenge maladaptive perceptions. *Behavioral* means that behaviors associated with internalizing problems can also be worked with to lead to positive outcomes. Engaging in fun activities and relaxation training are examples.

As mentioned previously, interventions need to expand beyond a sole focus on the student to produce change. To that end, school systems and staff, along with parents, can be excellent conduits to supporting a student in learning adaptive skills. Many strategies can be used with all students and accomplished within the context of a typical school day. Such strategies can be considered foundational to healthy emotional development and are also helpful in the early stages of intervening with internalizing problems. Simply providing information can help students better understand and talk through why they are having certain thoughts and feelings. Other strategies are more targeted. They are best used in small groups or with individual students. Keep in mind that some students will need more intensive school- or community-based services. More information on this topic appears in "Helping Students Who Need More" on page 511.

As a general principle, the higher the level of student need, the more individualized and intensive the intervention should be. For example, as a plan to boost general resilience, the interventionist might recommend or lead strategies for an entire class (e.g., using children's literature or historical figures to discuss emotions, teaching and practicing a relaxation strategy, looking for cognitive errors), or implement an evidence-based program to be coordinated with a schoolwide approach to social and emotional learning. The interventionist may also identify students who are struggling with a particular issue and form a small group to model and practice skills. In some circumstances, individual students will benefit from interventions tailored specifically to their needs, either at school or with a community provider. A good guideline is to start with foundational skills first (teacher-student relationship, emotion education, relaxation training). All students can generally benefit from learning these strategies, and the students who need more intensive assistance typically need these skills as well. To choose the most effective interventions, review the intervention strategies that follow and determine whether they address the symptoms you have targeted for intervention.

The next section reviews intervention strategies and programs in a tiered manner. Table 4.6a on the next page (also repeated on p. 3 of Essential Planning Steps Documentation) lists each intervention and provides guidance regarding the appropriate school- or community-based professional to implement the intervention and whether the intervention is best suited for a large group, small group, or individual setting. An asterisk appears next to interventions that would benefit from additional support from or consultation with an interventionist. However, teachers will most likely appreciate support with all interventions.

Following the table, additional details are provided on each intervention. The first ones reviewed are known to boost resilience and prevent internalizing problems. These strategies (e.g., relationship building, emotion education, emotion coaching, relaxation training) are used in the beginning phase of intervening with internalizing problems. Next come more targeted strategies (e.g., specific behavior and cognitive strategies, problem-solving, social skills, and exposure and response prevention) that are typically used to intervene with internalizing problems in particular. Finally, there is a brief discussion of ways in which you might use programs to meet students' needs.

As you review the following strategies, consider the data you gathered in the initial assessment and note any interventions you think could be effective. Use the space provided in Step 2 on Essential Planning Steps Documentation for this purpose.

TABLE 4.6a *List of Interventions for Internalizing Problems*

Strategy	Who Can Implement			Setting		
	Interventionist	General Education Teacher	Community Provider	Classroom	Small Group	Individual
A. Nurture the teacher-student relationship						
Warm, trusting, little conflict	✓	✓	✓	✓	✓	✓
B. Emotion education						
Normalize emotions	✓	✓	✓	✓	✓	✓
Use literature as a tool	✓	✓	✓	✓	✓	✓
Identify comfortable and uncomfortable emotions	✓	✓*	✓	✓	✓	✓
Identify physiological experiences associated with emotions	✓	✓*	✓	✓	✓	✓
Ask the student to finish incomplete sentences	✓	✓*	✓		✓	✓
Use a self-rating inventory for communicating emotions	✓	✓*	✓		✓	✓
C. Emotion coaching						
Awareness of emotions, opportunity to connect, use empathy, label emotions, set limits, and problem-solve	✓	✓*	✓	✓	✓	✓
D. Relaxation training						
Diaphragmatic breathing	✓	✓	✓	✓	✓	✓
Progressive muscle relaxation	✓	✓	✓	✓	✓	✓
E. Behavior change						
Schedule enjoyable activities	✓	✓*	✓	✓	✓	✓
Use operant conditioning techniques	✓	✓*	✓	✓	✓	✓
F. Cognitive change						
Develop an awareness of emotional variability:						
Feelings thermometer	✓	✓*	✓	✓	✓	✓
Emotional pie	✓	✓*	✓	✓	✓	✓
Detect automatic thoughts and identify beliefs:						
Thought chart	✓	✓*	✓		✓	✓
Cognitive replay	✓	✓*	✓		✓	✓
Hypothesizing	✓	✓*	✓		✓	✓
Evaluate automatic thoughts and beliefs:						
Identifying cognitive distortions or thinking errors	✓	✓*	✓		✓	✓
Reframing	✓	✓*	✓		✓	✓
Evaluating positives and negatives	✓	✓*	✓		✓	✓
G. Problem-solving	✓	✓*	✓		✓	✓
H. Social skills training	✓		✓		✓	✓
I. Exposure and response prevention	✓		✓		✓	✓
J. Mindfulness-based practices						
Mindfulness meditation, body scan, breath awareness, yoga, mindfulness-based programs	✓	✓*	✓	✓	✓	✓
K. School-based programs						
Programs to address internalizing symptoms and promote resilience	✓	✓*	✓	✓	✓	✓
Schoolwide positive behavior interventions and supports	✓	✓		✓	✓	✓
Parent training	✓*		✓		✓	✓
L. Referral to and coordination with community healthcare	✓*		✓*			✓

* = Consultation support indicated

A. Nurture the teacher-student relationship. Relationships play a key role in fostering resilience for everyone (Dryden, Johnson, Howard, & McGuire, 1998). For students, the student-teacher relationship is very important in fostering happiness and success in school (Baker, Grant, & Morlock, 2008). For students with internalizing problems, teacher-student relationships that are warm and trusting, with little conflict, seem to help students perform better (Baker et al., 2008). When the relationship is conflicted, the student has some risk of poor work habits and difficulties adjusting to the classroom. One study found that when middle school students feel supported, instances of depression decrease and self-esteem increases (Reddy, Rhodes, & Mulhall, 2003).

Remember, students with internalizing problems can experience problems in their relationships. For example, students who experience social anxiety often avoid situations where they think they might become embarrassed. As a result, they often miss out on typical social experiences such as lunch in the cafeteria, recess, and extracurricular activities. Sometimes, behaviors such as avoiding eye contact, speaking in a soft voice, or not talking very much appear odd to peers. Subsequently, anxiety symptoms contribute to fewer positive social interactions and less continued practice over time. Also remember variations across cultural norms for social behavior. Some cultural groups value introversion, avoidance of eye contact with authority figures, and a more independent approach to work. It is imperative to evaluate observed behaviors within a multifaceted framework in order to properly understand the issues at hand and support students.

It should be no surprise that when considering the teacher-student relationship as an intervention, staff should consider their relationships with *all* students. Students with internalizing problems can benefit from a relationship with a teacher that is warm and trusting, with little conflict. Everyday qualities that teachers bring to their relationships with students can be a means to resilience (Dryden et al., 1998). In particular, these qualities can positively affect students who experience internalizing problems (Baker et al., 2008). Use Effective Relationships (Reproducible 4.6c on the next page) to reflect and strategize for action.

B. Emotion education. Emotion education essentially involves teaching students about emotions—that's it. Five strategies for emotion education are:

- *Normalize emotions:* It is important to teach students that emotions are part of a normal human being's experience. Doing so is validating and leads to teachable moments. Students should also know that they can talk to someone when they feel their emotions are overwhelming or too much. This excerpt adapted from *Merrell's Strong Kids* curriculum (Carrizales-Engelmann, Feuerborn, Gueldner, & Tran, 2016a, p. 51) illustrates how you might introduce emotions as normal and serving an important function:

> *Just like stop signs and traffic lights, emotions act like signals. When you feel sad, irritated, worried, angry, or even happy or joyful, these emotions are telling you to pay attention to your situation. Emotions can help you figure out if you need to do something or take action. Emotions are sometimes called feelings. Everyone has them! We can also experience more than one emotion at the same time and many different emotions in just one day. Sometimes emotions feel small, and sometimes really big. It can be helpful to talk to an adult about these feelings, especially if you are feeling big emotions for a long time or if they really bother you.*

Items A–L on this and the following pages correspond to the strategies listed in Table 4.6a and page 3 of Reproducible 4.6a.

I especially appreciate the quote by author Toni Morrison, "When a kid walks in the room, your child or anyone else's child, does your face light up? That's what they're looking for." (See the video at youtu.be/9Jw0Fu8nhOc)

—B.G.

REPRODUCIBLE 4.6c *Effective Relationships*

Effective Relationships

Use this worksheet as you reflect on your students in general as well as on students who may be experiencing internalizing problems.

1. Consider the symptoms of internalizing problems and the challenges in detecting them. List new insights now that you have this information. **Example:** *I wonder whether the fact that Ari doesn't communicate very much has something to do with experiencing uncomfortable emotions.*

2. How do I or can I convey a sense of warmth to students who may be experiencing internalizing problems? **Examples:** Smile and greet students as they enter the classroom; ask students about their family; give full attention to a student (it could be 15 seconds); when a student returns to school after an illness, ask, *How are you? I missed having you in class, and we are glad to have you back.*

3. How do I or can I nurture and convey trust in my relationships with students? **Examples:** Talk to students in a quiet voice and in a way that respects their privacy, compliment a student on telling the truth when a mistake was made, apologize to a student when you make a mistake.

4. How do your students know they can count on you to be available to them, to provide support as needed, and to listen with full attention and empathy? **Examples:** Initiate a conversation with a student who may be hesitant to share: *I'd like to know what you were feeling. Tell me more about that.* Validate a student's emotions: *That sounds like it was really disappointing to you. And then you were really angry.* Take a guess: *I wonder if you felt embarrassed. What do you think?*

5. List some strategies that you can apply to managing conflict with a student who is experiencing internalizing symptoms. **Example:** *I asked you to do X, but you want to do Y. Let's figure out where we can meet in the middle.* **Or:** *I know you are having a hard time focusing on your work, but it's really important to finish this project. Let's figure out what we both can do to help.* **Or:** *I know you are really angry right now. It's important that everyone uses appropriate language. How else can you tell me what you are feeling so I can hear it?*

6. Observation and collaboration are means to professional development and personal growth. What strategies do you observe colleagues using to build warmth, trust, and communication, and to diffuse conflict? Which ones would you like to try or adapt to your own style?

7. Action Plan: I'd like to try _____ over the next week or so with _____.

Interventions © 2019 Ancora Publishing

REPRODUCIBLE 4.6c

- *Use literature as a tool:* You can use children's books and other literature to build emotion vocabulary (Doyle & Bramwell, 2006). Just as reading stimulates general vocabulary learning, you can use this same principle to highlight emotion words that can help students understand their emotional worlds. In fact, this strategy incorporates skills that teachers are already using with their students: reading aloud (for younger students) or monitoring reading assignments (with older students), asking questions to check for understanding, highlighting new vocabulary words, and facilitating discussion to promote deeper learning. Remember, students at risk of or who have developed internalizing problems need emotion vocabulary as a foundation for improvement. Using Literature for Emotion Education (Reproducible 4.6d on the next page) outlines a step-by-step approach to this intervention.

  Consider two ways of using this strategy: 1) Choose books that specifically talk about emotions relevant to internalizing problems (e.g., embarrassment, fear, anticipatory anxiety, sadness, grief, loneliness, avoidance), and 2) Infuse a discussion about emotion vocabulary into books (e.g., fiction or nonfiction) students are already reading, either as a class assignment or a personal choice. Nicholson and Pearson (2003) offer some tips. Choose books that:

  ○ Feature characters your students can relate to
  ○ Are relevant to students in terms of developmental level and cultural considerations
  ○ Depict emotions you wish to highlight
  ○ Include problem-solving and coping skills

- *Identify comfortable and uncomfortable emotions:* Emotions can be experienced as comfortable, uncomfortable, or both. Students may have different emotional responses to the same situation (e.g., some find a roller coaster really uncomfortable, but others enjoy it). To help students reflect on how they experience emotions, give them a list or flash cards with emotion words. The Feelings Identification form (Reproducible 4.6e, p. 491) provides a variety of common feelings that students may experience. Ask students to discuss each emotion and when they feel comfortable and uncomfortable with it. Emphasize that there is no correct way to experience the emotion—people can have different perspectives based on their temperament, past experiences, mood, and other factors unique to each individual.
- *Identify physiological experiences associated with emotions:* In addition to identifying emotional experiences as comfortable or uncomfortable, provide information on different physical sensations an individual might experience simultaneously with an emotion. Examples include: stomach discomfort, sweating, flushing, tingling, feeling lightheaded, heart beating faster, feeling lethargic or restless, breathing more rapidly, and so on.
- *Ask the student to finish incomplete sentences:* The goal of an incomplete sentence activity is to increase student awareness of the link between emotions and the situations associated with them. Provide a sentence stem such as "I was really angry when . . ." and ask a student to complete the sentence. Modeling examples can help students who have difficulty with this task. You can use the About My Feelings worksheet (Reproducible 4.6f, p. 492) for this activity.

continued on page 493

REPRODUCIBLE 4.6d *Using Literature for Emotion Education*

Using Literature for Emotion Education

Use these guidelines to choose literature and apply its concepts to internalizing problems.

1. Identify emotions you wish to highlight. Examples include: sadness, depression, loneliness, grief, fear, worry, embarrassment, apprehension, uncertainty, uneasiness, distress.

2. Identify books you can use.
   - For books that specifically address depression and anxiety, talk to your school or community librarian. Internet searches may also be helpful.
   - Is there content from history, language arts, or other classroom books that you can use?
   - Review the guidelines on page 473 for choosing relevant material.

3. Search for content relevant to internalizing-type emotions.

   As your students read aloud and process content, be alert to emotions experienced by the characters that may or may not be expressed overtly in text.

4. Define the emotion words in your own words or use a dictionary definition.

5. Discuss how the emotion words are used in the story.

6. Ask students to relate the emotion words to their own experiences.

7. Ask students to describe how they knew they felt that way (e.g., What did your body feel like? What was the expression on your face? What did you do?).

8. Discuss strategies (helpful and unhelpful) that the story characters use to solve a problem or cope with the situation.

9. Use the emotion words throughout the day in various situations in and out of the classroom. Use your own experiences, as appropriate, to model.

10. If any students disclose information that seems concerning (e.g., persistent and considerable feelings of anxiety or depression, suicidal thoughts, self-harming behaviors), follow up with the student to obtain additional information. Consult with a colleague to support you and determine the next course of action.

NOTE: Some strategies adapted from Doyle and Bramwell (2006) and Nicholson and Pearson (2003).

REPRODUCIBLE 4.6e *Feelings Identification*

Feelings Identification

This activity will help you learn to identify comfortable and uncomfortable feelings.

Comfortable feelings make people feel good. They let people have fun and enjoy life. Uncomfortable feelings make people feel bad. They can also help people grow and change for the better. Uncomfortable feelings can help people notice and appreciate their comfortable feelings.

Directions: For one of the lists on this worksheet, put a plus sign (+) next to any words that you think describe comfortable feelings, and put a minus sign (–) next to any words that you think describe uncomfortable feelings.

Feelings List 1

____ happy	____ lonely	____ scared	____ bored
____ angry	____ sad	____ upset	____ surprised
____ strong	____ proud	____ stupid	____ glad
____ shy	____ worried	____ tired	____ love

Feelings List 2

____ lonely	____ sorry	____ guilty	____ worried
____ happy	____ miserable	____ excited	____ proud
____ confused	____ strong	____ scared	____ loyal
____ crabby	____ surprised	____ upset	____ bored
____ serene	____ inspired	____ warm	____ angry
____ anxious	____ frustrated	____ thrilled	____ furious
____ compassionate	____ ignored	____ embarrassed	____ love

Adapted from *Helping Students Overcome Depression and Anxiety: A Practical Guide to Internalizing Problems* (2nd ed., p. 245), by K. W. Merrell, 2008, Guilford Press. Copyright 2008 by Guilford Press. Reprinted with permission of Guilford Press.

Interventions © 2019 Ancora Publishing

REPRODUCIBLE 4.6e

REPRODUCIBLE 4.6f *About My Feelings*

About My Feelings

Student _____ Grade/Class _____

Teacher/Counselor _____ Date _____

Directions: Complete these sentences in your own words, using real examples about how you feel.

I feel afraid when _____
_____

I am really good at _____
_____

I get excited when _____
_____

Most of the time, I feel _____
_____

I feel upset when _____
_____

I am sad when _____
_____

I am calm when _____
_____

I was really mad when _____
_____

I am thankful for _____
_____

I am lonely when _____
_____

Adapted from *Helping Students Overcome Depression and Anxiety: A Practical Guide to Internalizing Problems* (2nd ed., p. 246), by K. W. Merrell, 2008, Guilford Press. Copyright 2008 by Guilford Press. Reprinted with permission of Guilford Press.

Interventions © 2019 Ancora Publishing

- *Use a self-rating inventory for communicating emotions:* Once students learn how to identify their feelings, self-evaluating how well they communicate these feelings can be beneficial, particularly for older children and adolescents. Use this activity to assess areas for growth and goal setting. Ask students to rate how well they can express common emotions on a scale of *very easy* to *very hard*. Use the Expressing Feelings Inventory (Reproducible 4.6g on the next page) and ask students to rate how easy it is to express the listed feelings to other people. This worksheet can help older students monitor their progress with communicating their feelings.

C. Emotion coaching. As discussed earlier, the teacher-student relationship is important for all students, including those with internalizing problems, and adults play a key role in learning about and regulating emotions. *Emotion coaching* blends both of these areas by helping students learn about and regulate their emotions in the context of a relationship characterized by empathy and attunement. Through emotion coaching, a student experiences a connection with an adult who imagines or relates to the student's emotions, sets limits on behavior, and problem-solves with the student (Gus, Rose, & Gilbert, 2015).

So how does emotion coaching work? To begin, adults influence the emotional development of children through their attitudes about emotional experiences (e.g., accepting, dismissing, or disapproving of emotions, or believing that emotions should be expressed without concern for solving the problem at hand; Gottman, Katz, & Hooven, 1996). Adults also shape emotional development through expressing and managing emotions, how they react when children experience emotions, and adopting a view that coaching during emotions is beneficial (Eisenberg, Cumberland & Spinard, 1998). Seeing children's emotionality as an *opportunity* to connect and coach is different than seeing it as inconvenient and something to shut down quickly. Emotion coaching allows room for empathy, and empathetic responses build connection and relationships. Hence, in emotion coaching, you nurture the relationship and teach students about their emotional worlds in addition to teaching ways to manage emotions *and* behavior.

For this strategy, you'll use five principles, as outlined in Gottman et al., 1996:

- Be aware of your emotions and your students' emotions.
- When you sense any emotion, even a "small" one or those that might be considered positive (e.g., excited, happy), view this as an opportunity to connect and coach.
- Use empathy to identify, understand, and validate emotions.
- Verbally label emotions.
- Set limits on unhelpful behaviors and support problem-solving.

Building Relationships and Emotion Education Through Emotion Coaching (Reproducible 4.6h, p. 495) provides additional information to guide you through using this strategy.

For many adults, this strategy is a paradigm shift in thinking about and responding to children's emotions and behaviors. Often, this is because emotions occur in the context of misbehavior, and most adults were not exposed to being coached in this way. Many adults introduced to emotion coaching have found it to be a refreshing and effective strategy to use with students.

Students develop coping skills by learning about their emotional worlds.

continued on page 496

REPRODUCIBLE 4.6g *Expressing Feelings Inventory*

Expressing Feelings Inventory

Student _____ Grade/Class _____

Teacher/Counselor _____ Date _____

This exercise can help you see how much progress you have made and set goals for changes you might want to make in the future.

Directions: For each of the feeling words listed on the rating form below, think about how easy or hard it is for you to express those feelings to other people. Show whether it is very easy, somewhat easy, somewhat hard, or very hard for you to express those feelings by putting a checkmark in the appropriate box.

When I feel . . .	How easy is it to express this feeling to other people?			
	very easy	somewhat easy	somewhat hard	very hard
angry				
love				
sad				
worried				
joyful				
excited				
surprised				
fearful				
embarrassed				
jealous				
bored				
confident				
lonely				

I think that I am (circle one):

very emotional | somewhat emotional | somewhat unemotional | very unemotional

Adapted from *Helping Students Overcome Depression and Anxiety: A Practical Guide to Internalizing Problems* (2nd ed., p. 251), by K. W. Merrell, 2008, Guilford Press. Copyright 2008 by Guilford Press. Reprinted with permission of Guilford Press.

Interventions © 2019 Ancora Publishing   REPRODUCIBLE 4.6g

REPRODUCIBLE 4.6h *Building Relationships and Emotion Education Through Emotion Coaching*

Building Relationships and Emotion Education Through Emotion Coaching

Use this worksheet as you reflect on your own and your students' experiences of anxiety and depression.

1. **Emotional awareness.** Reflect on your beliefs about sadness and worry for yourself and your students. How do these beliefs help or hinder the teacher-student relationship? Example: *Believing that there's no reason for a student to worry about getting one problem wrong may lead students to feel dismissed.*

2. **Emotions as opportunities.** How can you tell students are experiencing sadness and worry? What do their faces look lke? How about tone of voice or other physical signs? How can you remind yourself to see these signs as an opportunity to connect and coach, rather than fix or stop them?

3. **Empathy and validation.** Show empathy by giving eye contact and full attention to the speaker, nodding, and reflecting back what you hear the speaker saying without criticism. Don't try to fix the problem (*Why don't you try . . .*) or talk the student out of the emotion (*There's no reason to feel . . . Just forget about that . . . At least it wasn't . . . Just think about how great you did with . . .*). You can validate an emotion by guessing it (*You sound really disappointed and sad. Am I getting that right?*) and accepting it, even if it doesn't make sense to you. How might you apply these strategies to a student who is currently experiencing anxiety or sadness?

4. **Label emotions.** Sometimes you can offer a guess as to the emotion a student is feeling (*I wonder if you are feeling embarrassed?*). You can also use pictures of faces experiencing different emotions to help students identify their emotions. As students get older, they can identify nuances of anxiety and depression (e.g., apprehensive, embarrassed, disappointed, dejected, woeful, etc.). List ways you can use these strategies now.

5. **Set limits on inappropriate behaviors, and problem-solve.** Sometimes behaviors give better clues about how a student is feeling. You may also need to put limits on behaviors such as screaming, avoidance, refusal, and verbal aggression. Problem-solving when a student is calm will be more productive than when the student is very upset. Brainstorming solutions with the student can help with problem-solving. List how you might follow Steps 1–4 for a particular student, then apply Step 5.

Based on the five components of emotion coaching identified by Gottman, Katz, & Hooven (1996).

> **WHAT DOES THE RESEARCH SAY ABOUT EMOTION COACHING?**
>
> Most research to date has investigated emotion coaching done by parents (Katz, Maliken, and Stettler, 2012). Early research studied how parents think about their own emotions and those of their children. They found a range regarding the extent to which parents accepted emotions and considered them a typical part of being human, or dismiss emotions as something to be ignored and changed quickly (Gottman et al., 1996). Children whose parents used an emotion coaching style had better emotional development. More recently, there has been increasing interest in teachers using this strategy and with success (Gus et al., 2015; Rose, Gilbert, & McGuire-Snieckus, 2015). Preliminary evidence is encouraging for the use of emotion coaching with youth who experience anxiety (Hurrell, Houwing, & Hudson, 2017), depression (Hunter et al., 2011; Kehoe, Havinghurst, & Harley, 2014), and other problems.

D. Relaxation training. Relaxation skills can help students manage stress in general, but also can be part of a plan to address internalizing symptoms, anxiety in particular. In brief, a relaxation exercise is used to engage the parasympathetic nervous system (the system that calms the body when it is stressed). When students practice this strategy regularly, they will be able to engage this system more readily. Following are two exercises you might use with students. Use your own words to convey the instructions given below.

- *Diaphragmatic breathing:* Also called *belly breathing*, diaphragmatic breathing works by engaging the parasympathetic nervous system to calm down the sympathetic nervous system (i.e., the fight-or-flight system) that is triggered during stress. Ask your students to sit comfortably with their eyes open or closed, feet on the floor, with one hand placed on their abdomen above the belly button. NOTE: Younger children enjoy putting a stuffed animal on their abdomen and watching the animal "move." Before guiding students in this exercise, tell them what they will do and what to expect. You will ask students to take five slow breaths, inhaling through the nose and exhaling through the mouth. They will count slowly to five on each inhale and again to five on each exhale. You can count aloud for students the first couple of times. Students will pay attention to the rise and fall of their abdomens as they breathe in (abdomen moves outward) and breathe out (abdomen moves inward). Some students like to imagine that they are filling up a balloon in their bellies when they inhale and deflating it when they exhale.
- *Progressive muscle relaxation:* This exercise involves tightening and relaxing muscle groups while breathing to a regular count. You will first ask students to sit comfortably and close their eyes. Students will draw in a deep, full breath and inhale, counting to five. You can count aloud for students the first couple of times. Tell students to let the breath out slowly, count to five, and feel their bodies relax as they breathe. Tell students to take four more breaths in the same way. Then, you will ask students to tighten muscle groups as they breathe in for five breaths, then relax the muscles as they breathe out for five breaths. The muscle groups are: toes and feet, legs, stomach, fingers and hands, arms, shoulders (raise shoulders up to

ears), and face (scrunch up the face). When you have finished with the muscle groups, ask students to take two full breaths, then open their eyes.

E. Behavior change. Behavior-based strategies focus on changing behaviors associated with depression and anxiety. Examples include increasing the amount of time spent in purposeful, meaningful activities and having adults pay attention to and reinforce such behaviors. Students who feel depressed and anxious often do not engage in typical childhood activities that can decrease stress (physical activity or peer interactions) and so miss out on fun and enjoyable activities that under other circumstances would boost their mood. For example, these students might avoid social events with peers because of feeling fatigued or worrying what others think about them. To interrupt this negative spiral, introduce positive activities that lead to improved mood, and reward behaviors. These activities are incompatible with depression and anxiety (e.g., smiling, making eye contact, and interacting with peers).

- *Schedule enjoyable activities.* Encourage students to purposefully increase the amount of time they spend in enjoyable activities. Adults will need to help structure these activities, especially in the beginning, because students experiencing internalizing symptoms may not have the energy or the organizational skills to do so. Activities should be simple in the beginning. Providing reinforcers such as praise and encouragement may be necessary to increase the likelihood that the students continue to participate in changing their behavior. The Weekly Planning of Positive Activities form (Reproducible 4.6i on the next page) can help in scheduling daily activities.
- *Use operant conditioning techniques.* Operant conditioning techniques usually involve reinforcing desired behaviors, such as eye contact, to increase the likelihood that prosocial and nondepressed or nonanxious behaviors will continue. Reinforcers can be social (praise) or tangible (obtaining something that is desired or getting out of something) and should be given immediately after you observe the desired behavior. The key is to determine what the student finds reinforcing, because what is reinforcing to one person is not always reinforcing to another.

Doing something enjoyable and being acknowledged for hard work help us feel better.

Case Example: Carlos

Ms. Jackson has been very concerned about Carlos's behavior since the beginning of second grade. Carlos barely talks during large group, does not smile much, and seems tired. He seems to keep to himself on the playground. Ms. Jackson decides to try some operant conditioning techniques. First she identifies the behaviors she will reinforce: Carlos smiling even a little, talking during small and large group, and raising his hand at any time. She explains to Carlos that she will encourage him to do these things and that he will become more comfortable doing them over time. She tells him that when she notices him practicing these behaviors, she will give a quick wink and smile to let him know she noticed without drawing the attention of others in the class. They decide if this doesn't work, they will find something else that will work better.

REPRODUCIBLE 4.6i *Weekly Planning of Positive Activities*

Weekly Planning of Positive Activities

Student _____ Grade/Class _____ Teacher/Counselor _____

Fill in date	Goals for positive activities	People who will be involved	Materials or resources needed
Monday _____			
Tuesday _____			
Wednesday _____			
Thursday _____			
Friday _____			
Saturday _____			
Sunday _____			

Adapted from *Helping Students Overcome Depression and Anxiety: A Practical Guide to Internalizing Problems* (2nd ed., p. 243), by K. W. Merrell, 2008, Guilford Press. Copyright 2008 by Guilford Press. Reprinted with permission of Guilford Press.

Interventions © 2019 Ancora Publishing

F. Cognitive change. As compared with behavior strategies that focus on observable behaviors, cognitive strategies focus on what we cannot see: thoughts and beliefs. To use these strategies, the student must be able to engage in cognitive thinking and reasoning. For this reason, these strategies are best used with typically developed preteens through adolescents and possibly with younger students, depending on how well they grasp the concept (Merrell, 2008). Young children or children with cognitive challenges may gain more benefit from emotional education and behavior change strategies. Cognitive strategies involve three major steps, usually performed in sequence: 1) Develop an awareness of emotional variability. 2) Detect automatic thoughts and identify beliefs. 3) Evaluate automatic thoughts and beliefs.

1. Develop an awareness of emotional variability. First, students learn that thoughts, feelings, and behaviors are connected to one another and that emotions vary in the degree to which they are experienced. These two tools can be used to teach this idea: the Feelings Thermometer (Reproducible 4.6j) and the Emotional Pie (Reproducible 4.6k).

- *Feelings Thermometer.* Students look at a picture of a thermometer, or a volume slider like those found on many electronic devices, and discuss how emotions can be experienced in terms of degrees of intensity or volume (e.g., soft, medium, loud). Students may give examples of situations that provoke particular feelings, such as anger, sadness, irritability, or excitement, and then discuss to what degree they experience the emotion given the situation. Students can use the Feelings Thermometer (Reproducible 4.6j on the next page) to identify the level of intensity of particular emotions they have experienced. This worksheet provides a graphic measurement to help students understand that feelings can be experienced in varying degrees. This exercise can also help promote discussion in a group setting.
- *Emotional Pie.* Ask students to draw a circle and divide the circle into sections, with each slice representing the size of an emotion they experienced as compared with other emotions they felt at that time. The Emotional Pie worksheet (Reproducible 4.6k on p. 501) can facilitate this activity, which helps students understand that they can experience several feelings at once and in varying amounts. Use this worksheet with individual students or in a group setting.

The way in which we think about a situation affects the way in which we are able to manage it.

2. Detect automatic thoughts and identify beliefs. When students are depressed or anxious, they often have thoughts that occur automatically, and they may not evaluate whether or not these thoughts are realistic. In actuality, their thoughts may be distorted or unrealistic. For example, a student who is depressed may automatically think, "I can never do anything right," when presented with a math assignment. Attached to these thoughts are beliefs that can also be automatic and distorted. A student who thinks "I can never do anything right" may also believe that she cannot complete the assignment because "I'm stupid and everyone else is so much smarter." Identifying these automatic thoughts and beliefs is important so that they may then be challenged. You can use three techniques to teach this idea: thought charts, cognitive replay, and hypothesizing/guessing.

- *Thought Chart:* Ask students to keep track of their thoughts during a situation that triggers feelings and thoughts. For example, if a student is chosen last for a basketball team during PE class, he might *feel* hurt because he *believes* he is bad at everything he does. The interventionist can help the student in this process by

continued on page 502

REPRODUCIBLE 4.6j *Feelings Thermometer*

Feelings Thermometer

When _____
       [this happens]

I feel _____
        [this emotion]

Directions: Color in the thermometer below to show how strong your emotion is during this particular situation.

Low emotion   Some emotion   Strong emotion

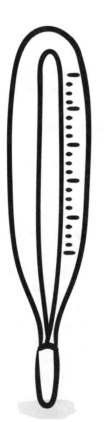

Show how strong that feeling was.

Adapted from Merrell's *Strong Kids—Grades 6–8: A Social and Emotional Learning Curriculum* (2nd ed., p. 73), by D. Carrizales-Engelmann, L. L. Feuerborn, B. A. Gueldner, and O. K. Tran, 2016, Paul H. Brookes Publishing Co., Inc., Baltimore, MD. Copyright 2016 by Paul H. Brookes Publishing Co., Inc. Adapted with permission of the publisher.

Interventions © 2019 Ancora Publishing

REPRODUCIBLE 4.6j

SPECIALIZED INTERVENTION STRATEGIES—SECTION 4.6: STUDENTS WITH INTERNALIZING CHALLENGES

REPRODUCIBLE 4.6k *Emotional Pie*

Emotional Pie

This activity will help you describe how your feelings were divided up during a particular time frame, like a day or a week. Like a pie cut into different-sized slices, our feelings can take up different amounts of room in our life. Sometimes one feeling is bigger than another.

Directions: For the time period that you picked, divide the circle on this sheet into different-sized slices to show how much room different feelings took up in your life during that time. Pick at least two feelings, and label the slices of the pie using the first letter of each feeling. Here are some examples.

N = normal mood, okay   H = happy   S = sad
T = tense   A = angry or mad   W = worried

Write down the names and letters of the feelings you are including in your chart.

____ = _____   ____ = _____   ____ = _____

____ = _____   ____ = _____   ____ = _____

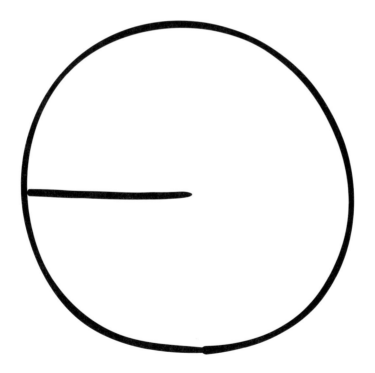

Adapted from *Helping Students Overcome Depression and Anxiety: A Practical Guide to Internalizing Problems* (2nd ed., p. 230), by K. W. Merrell, 2008, Guilford Press. Copyright 2008 by Guilford Press. Reprinted with permission of Guilford Press.

Interventions © 2019 Ancora Publishing

REPRODUCIBLE 4.6k

discussing the student's thoughts when in a particular situation or experiencing a particular emotion. The Thought Chart (Reproducible 4.6l) represents one way to set up this activity. Use the chart to practice identifying automatic thoughts, feelings associated with the thoughts, and the situations that usually provoke these thoughts and feelings. Each student will complete their own thought chart, but the worksheet can also be used to generate a class discussion.

- *Cognitive replay:* Instead of asking a student to chart thoughts independently, guide her through a problem situation that happened recently, asking her to consider feelings, thoughts, and beliefs she associated with the situation.
- *Hypothesizing:* The interventionist offers a hypothesis or guess about the feelings, thoughts, and beliefs the student may have had in a particular situation. This strategy is particularly useful when students are having a difficult time identifying these issues. For example:

> Nikolas: I went to the skate park last night to hang out, but when I got there, no one said hello.
>
> Interventionist: So, what were you feeling? Was it comfortable, uncomfortable, or both? What thoughts were going through your head? What did you believe about yourself?

3. Evaluate automatic thoughts and beliefs. Once a student has identified automatic thoughts and beliefs, evaluate them with the student to determine whether they are realistic and useful, or unrealistic and maladaptive. Students often enjoy this part of using cognitive strategies because for many the idea that something could be faulty in their thinking is a new concept. The goal in this step is not to eliminate uncomfortable thoughts altogether. Remember, emotions are there to tell people something about a situation so they can take appropriate action. Also, life throws unpleasant and unexpected curveballs. Some students, however, need to learn the difference between pervasive unproductive and damaging thoughts and natural negative thoughts that may occasionally occur when something bad happens. When students can recognize automatic thoughts and beliefs and begin to evaluate them, they can cope better with life stressors and bounce back more quickly. Three strategies can assist in this process: identifying cognitive distortions or thinking errors, reframing, and evaluating positives and negatives.

- *Identifying cognitive distortions or thinking errors:* Cognitive distortions or thinking errors can perpetuate depression because of the way in which situations are viewed. For example, if a student tends to view *all* problems as big problems, feelings of being chronically overwhelmed and helpless tend to emerge. Challenging common thinking errors can alleviate these symptoms. In *Merrell's Strong Kids* and *Merrell's Strong Teens* curricula (Carrizales-Engelmann et al., 2016a–c), these eight thinking errors are the focus of lessons on identifying cognitive distortions: Binocular Vision, Black-and-White Thinking, Dark Glasses, Fortune Telling, Making It Personal, the Blame Game, All Alone, and Broad Brush. The Common Thinking Errors worksheet (Reproducible 4.6m) on pages 504–505 provides graphic representations of each error. Use this worksheet to facilitate a discussion about situations that might lead students to think in unhelpful ways that contribute to anxious and depressed emotions and behaviors. A student and

continued on page 506

REPRODUCIBLE 4.6l *Thought Chart*

Thought Chart

Student _____ Grade/Class _____

Teacher/Counselor _____ Date _____

This exercise will help you identify some of your automatic thoughts—thoughts that seem to happen without warning and without you realizing how they got there. When these thoughts are negative, they can lead to feeling depressed.

Directions: Think of some situations from the past few days when you felt bad. Identify the situation and the specific feeling you had. Then identify any automatic thoughts that seemed to go along with the feeling.

The Situation	My Feelings	My Automatic Thoughts

Adapted from *Helping Students Overcome Depression and Anxiety: A Practical Guide to Internalizing Problems* (2nd ed., p. 231), by K. W. Merrell, 2008, Guilford Press. Copyright 2008 by Guilford Press. Reprinted with permission of Guilford Press.

Interventions © 2019 Ancora Publishing

REPRODUCIBLE 4.6m *Common Thinking Errors (1 of 2)*

Common Thinking Errors

Making It Personal

Blaming yourself for things that are not your fault or thinking things are about you when they are not

Example: Your friend is irritable today. You think it's because she's upset with you, even though you can't think of any reason why she might be.

Blame Game

Blaming others for things that are your responsibility

Example: You didn't follow the rules, so your parents took your music away as punishment. You think it's your parents' fault because they don't like you.

All Alone

Thinking you have problems that no one else understands

Example: Your parents can't afford to buy you the pair of shoes you want. You think no one else has money problems in their family.

Broad Brush

Judging something based on one experience with it

Example: You met one person from another country, and you thought that person was rude. Now you think all the people from that country are rude.

Adapted from *Merrell's Strong Kids—Grades 6–8: A Social and Emotional Learning Curriculum* (2nd ed., pp. 133–134), by D. Carrizales-Engelmann, L. L. Feuerborn, B. A. Gueldner, and O. K. Tran, 2016, Paul H. Brookes Publishing Co., Inc., Baltimore, MD. Copyright 2016 by Paul H. Brookes Publishing Co., Inc. Adapted with permission of the publisher.

REPRODUCIBLE 4.6m *Common Thinking Errors (2 of 2)*

Common Thinking Errors

Binocular Vision

Looking at things in a way that makes them seem bigger or smaller than they really are

Example: You have a small pimple on your face. You feel like that's all people see when they look at you.

Black-and-White Thinking

Looking at things in only extreme or opposite ways (e.g., thinking of things as being good or bad, never or always, all or none, friend or enemy)

Example: You had one fight with your good friend. Now you think, "We always fight. She hates me."

Dark Glasses

Thinking about only the negative parts of things

Example: You met with your teacher. Your teacher said many good things about you. He also said your writing needs improvement. Now you think all his comments were bad.

Fortune Telling

Making predictions about what will happen in the future without enough evidence

Example: You don't talk to the new student in class because you think she will not like you.

practitioner can generate problem situations together, identify the student's feelings and thoughts, and determine whether a thinking error is present.
- *Reframing:* In this intervention strategy, students are asked to reflect on alternative ways they might look at their thoughts. Doing so can help them consider other ways of thinking about their situation and their automatic thoughts, rather than believing what may be a cognitive error. Sometimes students need help finding other ways to think about a situation. Two questions guide this reframing strategy:

    1) What thoughts do you have about this situations?
    2) What are some other ways you could think about them? List them.

    Sometimes students have an easier time practicing this strategy by thinking about someone else's problem first, instead of reframing their own. If this is the case, use a real or hypothetical situation to lead the student through the steps above. You can follow up with a problem-solving strategy (discussed later in the chapter) to practice thinking through a variety of actions the student can take to address the problem. For example: Soraya thinks she'll fail seventh grade if she gets a couple of failing grades in science. Soraya's teacher prompts her to write out her thoughts about this situation.

    1. I failed a quiz and a homework assignment. I'm probably going to fail seventh grade.
    2. I'll have to retake seventh-grade science next year and will be humiliated.

    Then Soraya's teacher asks her to consider a couple of other ways to think about the situation.

    1. I guess I'm not sure how the final grades are actually calculated.
    2. I know of a few people who failed a couple of quizzes and still went to eighth grade.

- *Evaluating positives and negatives.* Some students become stuck thinking about the negative aspects of a situation and need reminders to consider the positive. Older children and adolescents may find it helpful to conduct a cost-benefit analysis to evaluate thoughts and beliefs, especially students who have a tendency to look at only the uncomfortable aspects of a situation. Guide students in the initial phase of using this strategy and include the uncomfortable parts, too. After all, few situations are 100% comfortable and pleasant. Consider using Evaluating Positives and Negatives (Reproducible 4.6n) for this activity. This exercise reminds students to consider positive aspects of a situation, especially when they are stuck on thinking about the negative. This technique works particularly well with students who are feeling sad and hopeless.

G. Problem-solving. For students who are experiencing internalizing problems, having a step-by-step plan to solve daily problems can be beneficial. Often, symptoms of anxiety and depression interfere with thinking clearly (remember the thinking errors

REPRODUCIBLE 4.6n *Evaluating Positives and Negatives*

Evaluating Positives and Negatives

Student _____   Grade/Class _____

Teacher/Counselor _____   Date _____

Situation	Pros List the positive things about this situation.	Cons List the negative things about this situation.

Adapted from *Helping Students Overcome Depression and Anxiety: A Practical Guide to Internalizing Problems* (2nd ed., p. 234), by K. W. Merrell, 2008, Guilford Press. Copyright 2008 by Guilford Press. Reprinted with permission of Guilford Press.

Interventions © 2019 Ancora Publishing   REPRODUCIBLE 4.6n discussed earlier?) and taking action. Problem-Solving Steps (Reproducible 4.6o) guides students through a simple problem-solving strategy. Make a plan to check in with the student to review how the plan worked out and discuss any challenges and successes.

H. Social skills training. Social skills training is also commonly used as part of a comprehensive plan to treat internalizing problems. Many students who experience internalizing problems exhibit social skills problems, often due to inhibition, low energy, and lack of practice. For example, a student feels too anxious to initiate a conversation because of fear of rejection, or a student is so sad that he fails to pick up on social cues that would normally tell him to smile, make eye contact, and show interest in the conversation. These symptoms often interfere with opportunities to practice social skills and thus the students often have skill delays.

I. Exposure and response prevention. Exposure and response prevention (ERP) is a technique commonly used for anxiety symptoms when students avoid certain situations because doing so diminishes their anxiety. For example, consider the student who avoids school for fear of saying or doing something that might be embarrassing. Continual avoidance actually perpetuates the problem because the student does not learn how to manage uncomfortable emotions and sensations. This tendency to avoid aspects of normal activities can diminish the overall quality of life over time. Through ERP, students learn how to gradually participate in the very activities that cause discomfort (e.g., speaking to an adult, participating in PE classes, using a public restroom). As they participate, students learn that they can tolerate and, over time, diminish the discomfort that accompanies these situations. In sum, students should engage in typical daily activities so they can practice everyday skills. Doing so keeps them growing in a developmentally healthy manner and is likely to prevent future problems.

NOTE: If you think your student may benefit from social skills training or ERP, it is best to collaborate with a mental health professional at your school. These strategies often require additional assessment and planning to maximize their effectiveness. One valuable resource is the book *Helping Students Overcome Depression and Anxiety* (Merrell, 2008).

J. Mindfulness-based practices. Mindfulness-based practices (MBPs) are increasingly being applied to youth populations and in schools (Meiklejohn et al., 2012). MBPs include strategies such as mindfulness, meditation, body scan, breathing, yoga, and mindfulness-specific programs (e.g., MindUP, Learning to Breathe). As compared with traditional cognitive behavioral therapy (CBT) approaches, in which thoughts are challenged in order to find evidence of their validity and change their content, MBPs encourage students to simply become aware of their thoughts and feelings, adopt a nonjudgmental perspective on these thoughts, and accept them (Semple & Lee, 2007). In the past decade, MBPs have been used to complement existing CBT approaches (e.g., mindfulness-based cognitive therapy) or as stand-alone interventions with youth and in schools. The first approach is applied in the second edition of *Merrell's Strong Kids* curriculum. This program is grounded in cognitive behavioral theory and strategies, but offers a brief MBP as a starting exercise for each lesson (see p. 512 for more about this program). Both approaches have evidence of effectiveness for improving awareness and regulation among youth (e.g., Broderick & Metz, 2009), although CBT has established a longer track record of effectiveness with youth and in schools. Preliminary evidence shows

REPRODUCIBLE 4.6o *Problem-Solving Steps*

Problem-Solving Steps

Problem-Solving Step With Example Problem	Student Reflection
1. Identify the problem. I forgot I had a test today and didn't study.	
2. List some possible solutions. <ul><li>Don't go to school today.</li><li>Go to school, but go to the nurse during the test and say I have a headache.</li><li>Tell myself, *Most people get anxious about tests at some point. I'm going to try my best on the test.* I can also talk to the teacher and see if there is an option to take the test tomorrow. For now, I need to do my breathing strategy!</li></ul>	
3. Evaluate the solutions. <ul><li>If I don't go to school, I'll miss everything that day and get behind in other subjects.</li><li>If I go to the nurse, I'll still have to make up the test.</li><li>Breathing will help calm my body so I can think more clearly. Trying the test and talking to the teacher would probably be OK.</li></ul>	
4. Try a solution. How did it go? I tried the third solution. I still felt a little nervous, but I think I did all right on the test.	

Interventions © 2019 Ancora Publishing

promise for the MBP approach in addressing internalizing problems (e.g., Beauchemin, Hutchins, & Patterson, 2008; Edwards, Adams, Waldo, Hadfield, & Biegel, 2014), building resilience and cognitive skills, and in schools (Zenner, Hernleben-Kurz, & Walach, 2014). If you are considering MBP as part of intervention strategies for students with internalizing problems, consult with evidence-based sources and your colleagues to pursue the best course of action.

K. School-based programs that target internalizing problems, safe school climate and prosocial behavior, and parent support. When you consider such programs, it is wise to review them for appropriateness for your population, whether they have been evaluated for effectiveness, and the extent to which additional support and training may be helpful or needed to implement the program in the way it was intended. The studies cited in this section provide additional information on specific programs.

- *Programs to address internalizing symptoms and promote resilience.* There may be instances when your school team considers programs that specifically target internalizing problems. This approach offers some advantages. The programs were developed to target the very symptoms you wish to address, they use evidence-based strategies, and they were often designed with classrooms in mind. Research suggests that students can benefit from school-based programs. Such programs can reduce not only overall internalizing symptoms, but also the risk that depression and anxiety even develop (Calear & Christensen, 2010; Corrieri et al., 2013; Neil & Christensen, 2009). See the box "Merrell's Strong Kids Programs" on page 512 for an example of curricula designed to address internalizing problems with students in pre-K to grade 12.
- *Schoolwide positive behavior interventions and supports:* Also keep broader ecological variables in mind, namely ways in which your school can support students through positive school climate and programming. Recently, there has been a call for efforts to address internalizing problems in collaboration with schoolwide positive behavior interventions and supports (PBIS). Improving environmental factors by ensuring the environment is more predictable and safe through expectations and consequences, teaching helpful coping behaviors, and so on can decrease students' stress responses and make learning more accessible and comfortable, especially for those who experience internalizing challenges (McIntosh et al., 2014; Weist et al., 2018). Emerging research supports the use of programming commonly associated with social and emotional learning (SEL) in conjunction with PBIS as a potential avenue for integrating existing frameworks to produce positive benefit for students (Cook et al., 2015; McIntosh et al., 2014). As you consider specific programs to use with identified students, consider how they fit into the broader context of schoolwide programming.
- *Parent training:* Finally, parent training and support is a vital part of a comprehensive approach to intervening with internalizing problems (Herman et al., 2004). At minimum, schools should include parents in the assessment phase of intervention planning. Some programs also include parent training as a part of the interventions, and stand-alone interventions can include parents so students can practice their skills at home.

L. Referral to and coordination with community healthcare. Sometimes students experiencing internalizing and associated problems will benefit from additional resources outside of the school setting. A medical evaluation, specialized therapy services, and collaboration with agencies that provide other support services (e.g., tutoring, job coaching, nutrition) may be required to best meet a student's needs. Including these options as part of your intervention inventory recognizes the complex needs of students and helps your team organize training for staff (e.g., understanding signs of internalizing problems, following school policies and procedures regarding services beyond those that are school based, etc.).

HELPING STUDENTS WHO NEED MORE

Sometimes students need more help than is available in a school setting. Students who experience problems that significantly interfere with their ability to function at school, at home, or in the community often need comprehensive services that include community resources for individual and family intervention. Some of your students are also involved in the legal system, which requires further coordination. School personnel often have many responsibilities that do not allow them to provide the additional mental health services students may need, or such services are outside their scope of training and practice. Some schools have developed school-based health clinics as a way of accommodating many of these needs. Other schools have infused family-oriented services on site to provide evidence-based support to students and their caregivers (e.g., the Family Check-Up). Other times, community providers may see students. Make sure you understand your school's policies and requirements prior to making any referrals. Collaborating with these providers can be beneficial to ensure continuity in identifying the problem and delivering interventions.

Immediate response—that is, contacting your school mental health professional as well as community health providers (e.g., emergency department, community therapist), parents, and sometimes law enforcement officials—is required when there is concern that a student wants to self-harm or harm others, is in imminent danger of being harmed, or appears seriously ill. Schools usually have a designated professional (such as an administrator, school psychologist, or counselor) responsible for evaluating and responding to these concerns. Parents should be notified and invited to participate in the assessment and problem-solving process. They should also receive support to follow through with any plan of action. School teams should also plan to provide the student with follow-up support at school after such events, which are often highly stressful and disruptive.

Educators are highly encouraged to consult with colleagues when they are concerned about a student's well-being. As previously mentioned, students who are experiencing depression or anxiety symptoms often go unnoticed due to the very nature of these problems. Symptoms can be challenging to detect, often confusing, and sometimes irritating in their presentation. However, bear in mind that for some students, their verbal or physical aggression, lethargy, refusal, irritability, poor concentration, lack of follow-through, and obsessive thoughts or compulsive behavior may all be signals that they are experiencing internalizing problems. Early intervention is essential. By enacting a team approach to detection and intervention, you can effectively support *many* students who may not otherwise seek or access assistance.

MERRELL'S STRONG KIDS PROGRAMS: SOCIAL AND EMOTIONAL LEARNING CURRICULA

Merrell's Strong Kids programs are designed to teach social and emotional skills, promote resilience, and increase children's and adolescent's coping skills. The curricula also focus on cognitive-behavioral strategies known to be effective in preventing and intervening with internalizing problems. Now in the second edition, the series includes four levels: *Strong Start Pre-K* and *Strong Start* for kindergarten through second grade (Whitcomb & Damico, 2016a–b), *Strong Kids: Grades 3–5*, *Strong Kids: Grades 6–8*, and *Strong Teens: Grades 9–12* (Carrizales-Engelmann et al., 2016a–c). Content includes emotion education, including learning about the interaction among thoughts, feelings, and behaviors; understanding other people's emotions; finding ways to manage anger; learning cognitive strategies such as identifying and challenging thinking errors; dealing with interpersonal conflict; reducing stress; using behavioral strategies to promote a healthy lifestyle; and setting and attaining goals.

Lessons are scripted and intended to be easy to use in the timeframe of one 45- to 60-minute class period over the course of 12 weeks (one lesson per week). Lessons can be divided as necessary to accommodate shorter time periods and attention spans. They are structured to promote instructional excellence: direct teaching of content, opportunities to practice embedded throughout, highlighting examples with sociocultural relevance, checking for students' understanding, flexibility to adapt to student needs, and suggestions about ways to embed the information throughout the course of the school day. The lessons were developed to complement academic skills such as critical thinking, analytical skills, and literacy. Many schools have integrated the lessons into the course of a typical language arts, health, or social studies class. General and special education teachers, school counselors, school psychologists, and other mental health professionals have successfully served as group leaders. The curricula have been used successfully with high- and typical-functioning youth, as well as youth showing early signs of difficulty and those who have already developed significant behavioral and emotional disorders. Table 4.6b lists the lessons in *Merrell's Strong Kids: Grades 3–5* along with a brief description of each lesson.

Several strategies can help you implement the Strong Kids curricula successfully:

- Keep the pace brisk.
- Provide immediate feedback and opportunities to respond and practice.
- Use examples relevant to your students.
- Maintain a high positive to corrective ratio of reinforcement.
- Maintain high student expectations.
- Encourage student participation.
- Consider small groups for activities.
- Use the program as part of a larger schoolwide effort to support social and emotional learning, as well as schoolwide PBIS.
- Integrate the information and skills throughout the day.
- Modify the scripts to shorten them or increase their relevance to the group.

TABLE 4.6b *Merrell's Strong Kids: Grades 3–5 Lessons*

Lesson number and name	Skills addressed
1. About *Strong Kids:* Emotional Strength Training	Introduction to the program and new terms such as *emotions* and *resilience*
2. Understanding Your Feelings, Part 1	Identifying a range of emotions
3. Understanding Your Feelings, Part 2	Discriminating between uncomfortable and comfortable emotions, learning that they vary in intensity
4. Understanding Other People's Feelings	Taking the perspective of others and showing empathy
5. Dealing with Anger	Using strategies to identify sources of and manage anger
6. Clear Thinking, Part 1	Identifying cognitive errors we all make
7. Clear Thinking, Part 2	Reframing strategies to address cognitive errors
8. Solving People Problems	Conflict resolution strategies to boost interpersonal relationships
9. Letting Go of Stress	Identifying sources of stress and using relaxation strategies
10. Positive Living	Incorporating positive habits into daily activities
11. Creating Strong & Smart Goals	Setting SMART goals
12. Finishing Up!	Review and integration of the lesson content

NOTE: For more information about and resources for *Merrell's Strong Kids* programs, visit the website at strongkidsresources.com. Or visit brookespublishing.com for purchase information.

Step 3: Outline a plan for implementation, data collection, and training.

Now that you have reviewed possible intervention strategies, you likely have a better idea of how to help a student or group as well as a list of interventions that could prove effective. Follow these guidelines to create an implementation plan.

Item a: Use decision-making guidelines to select strategies and determine how, when, and where to implement the strategies. The Decision-Making Rules Worksheet (Reproducible 4.6p on the next page) lists decision-making guidelines to help you refine your choices and outline a plan.

These guidelines will help you determine whether the strategy is appropriate for addressing the student's goals and guide you in making decisions about implementation.

- *Choose a format and setting for delivery:* Part of selecting interventions is determining whether you will teach the strategies individually, in a small group, in a large group, or classwide. Most strategies for internalizing problems such as depression

REPRODUCIBLE 4.6p *Decision-Making Rules Worksheet*

Decision-Making Rules Worksheet

Intervention strategy _____

For each intervention strategy you are considering, review the following decision-making rules.

Rules for Decision Making	Notes
Using the data from the assessment worksheet and the information you have about the intervention strategy, how will this intervention target specific goals?	
Is this intervention strategy best used in a group, with an individual, or in a community setting?	
Is this intervention strategy best implemented by an interventionist? Is additional training or support needed? If so, outline a plan.	
Can this intervention strategy be implemented by the general education teacher? If so, is consultation between the interventionist and teacher indicated? If so, outline a plan.	
Is the student working with a community mental health provider or agency? If so, outline a plan for collaboration and how intervention strategies will be used across settings.	

Interventions © 2019 Ancora Publishing

and anxiety can be used in a variety of settings. However, each student's problems are specific to their own unique situation, so you should consider the situation when choosing the setting and format for the intervention. Students dealing with issues that are best addressed in private (serious family stressors, abuse, and specific fears or phobias) will likely benefit from working individually with a school-based mental health professional or being referred to a community agency. On the other hand, students who experience common problems such as chronic worrying or sadness often greatly benefit from participating in a small group where they can share their experiences and be heard and understood by others who have had similar problems. The small group format also allows the intervention to be efficiently delivered. With few exceptions, the interventions listed above are also suited for use with a class. Table 4.6a (p. 486) provides general guidelines on group and individual use for each intervention. Interventionists should still use their professional judgment for each particular situation.

- *Determine whether the intervention can be implemented by a general education teacher or mental health specialist, and if consultation with an interventionist or community mental health provider or agency is required (note any plans for community involvement in Item d):* School-based interventionists can implement most of the interventions in this chapter. Many can also be implemented by general education teachers with the right training and support. It should be encouraging to know that general education teachers and school-based mental health specialists have effectively implemented some of the strategies as part of *Merrell's Strong Kids* curriculum and others. However, teachers will need instruction in areas in which they may not have had training and do not feel particularly comfortable. Interventionists are highly encouraged to consider the feasibility of having a general education teacher deliver chosen interventions and to engage in supportive consultation during implementation. Teachers will likely appreciate feedback on their technique in delivering an intervention and will inevitably have questions and concerns about the issues students bring up during implementation. When in doubt whether you or other educational professionals have the expertise to deliver an intervention, use your professional judgment. Consulting with a colleague can also be helpful.

See the box on the next page for more information on selecting strategies. At this point, also consider whether the student needs more intensive assistance and resources. See "Helping Students Who Need More" on page 511 for guidance.

Item b: Make a plan for data collection and monitoring. Evaluating whether an intervention is successful in improving a student's internalizing problems is essential. Recall that in Step 1 you identified problem areas through assessment and set goals. Use this information to guide your decisions about the problem areas and skills you wish to measure over time.

In terms of progress monitoring, measuring internalizing symptoms at relatively close intervals during the intervention poses some challenges. (Academic progress monitoring, for example, is typically conducted at least once a week.) No standardized measures that have adequate psychometric properties are available for gauging depression and anxiety at brief and regular time intervals. Nonetheless, it is vital to measure how a student is progressing during intervention. A few options include using selected items from

ADDITIONAL CONSIDERATIONS WHEN SELECTING STRATEGIES

Also consider the following when determining the strategies you would like to implement and with whom. Doing so will increase your ability to use a best-practices approach with students.

Cultural Considerations: As with all other school-based prevention and intervention strategies, you must consider cultural factors when problem-solving, considering solutions, and evaluating outcomes (for additional discussion, see Miranda, 2014). These factors can include, but are not limited to, nation of origin, regional norms, religious beliefs and practices, socioeconomic status, stage of acculturation, language, intellectual or physical differences, sexual orientation, gender identification, and educational level and experiences. As educational and mental health professionals, you and your team must first consider your own cultural background and how it has shaped your identities. You must also appreciate historical and current circumstances, viewpoints, policies, and practices that have and continue to marginalize students so that you can respond to students' needs in an ethical and supportive manner. Understanding ways in which internalizing problems are viewed and expressed across individuals is paramount to building relationships and being a supportive voice. Also consider the strengths that cultural influences bring to your life. What assets can you highlight for students to promote their well-being? We highly encourage you to discuss these issues in all assessment and intervention processes for your students. Finally, recognize that the students and families you work with have a range of beliefs about mental health in general, challenges in accessibility, and varying viewpoints on what is considered an acceptable intervention. Some example include:

- The belief that talking about emotions and personal issues is not appropriate
- General distrust of educational and other systems
- The belief that seeing a mental health provider means you are really unwell and that doing so will result in considerable stigma
- Lack of access to healthcare due to provider shortages or cost
- General wariness of taking psychotropic medication for fear of addiction
- Prior negative experiences with mental health systems
- Greater interest in alternative and complementary approaches to health care
- A healthy dose of skepticism due to imperfections in the science and practice of psychology and medicine.

School professionals are urged to approach these issues with respect toward all people and regard for a variety of beliefs and opinions, and to provide education and support as indicated.

Accommodations: Some students receive accommodations via an individualized education plan (IEP) or a 504 Plan. For students who experience anxiety, accommodations may include using the office restroom due to fear of using a community restroom, testing in a private room due to anxiety about testing in the classroom, and giving a speech to the teacher without an audience due to anxiety about speaking in public. Although accommodation strategies are often carefully constructed and well intentioned, research shows that they can actually interfere with an intervention plan and perpetuate the anxiety (Thompson-Hollands, Kerns, Pincus, & Comer, 2014). Escaping discomfort in the short term is highly reinforcing (i.e., if you find a successful way to avoid anxiety, you are bound to repeat the avoidance behavior). Some intervention plans, either set by a school interventionist or a community provider, specify that the student learns and practices coping skills while gradually engaging in the anxiety-provoking situation (e.g., an Exposure and Response Prevention approach), and that any accommodations are faded. Such an approach has considerable evidence for effectiveness. The targeted outcome is for the student to reengage in normal daily living activities (e.g., use the public restroom, take a test in the classroom, give a class presentation). Thus, when considering any accommodations proposed by school personnel, parents, a community provider, or the student, be sure to look at how the accommodation may unintentionally interfere with interventions known to be helpful and how the accommodation will be tapered over time (Swan, Kagan, Frank, Crawford, & Kendall, 2016).

behavior rating scales that represent the identified problem areas, using a weekly mood and behavior rating scale, gathering observation data, or using an application (app) that targets areas and skills of interest. The Weekly Journal Entry With Mood Rating template (Reproducible 4.6q on the next page) is an example of a tool you can use to monitor a student's feelings associated with depression and anxiety and assess progress over time.

As an alternative, you might develop a rating scale and ask the student questions like the following from the Sample Feelings Scale (Figure 4.6a): *On a scale of 0 to 10, where 0 means feeling none of these feelings and 10 means feeling a lot of these feelings, how have you felt in the past day/couple days/week?*

Sad
Irritable or grumpy
Tired or fatigued
*Like life is not worth living
Guilty about things that have happened
Like you want to cry

Worried
Restless or jumpy
Having a hard time concentrating
Problems sleeping
Problems eating
Hopeless about the future

*NOTE: If a student indicates an affirmative answer to "Like life is not worth living," seek consultation immediately for assistance.

FIGURE 4.6a *Sample Feelings Scale*

Behavior rating scales can be used to measure outcomes at the completion of the intervention. Consult the user's manual to determine the intervals at which reliability and validity have been established to guide scheduling a pre- and posttest.

Record the details of your data collection and monitoring plan in the space provided under Step 3 in Essential Planning Steps Documentation (Reproducible 4.6a). Note how often monitoring will occur, list the problem areas that will be tracked, and describe how data will be gathered and summarized. Also indicate a follow-up date for reviewing data and evaluating the effectiveness of the plan.

REPRODUCIBLE 4.6q *Weekly Journal With Mood Rating*

Weekly Journal With Mood Rating

Student _____ Grade/Class _____

Teacher/Counselor _____ Date _____

Describe some of your thoughts over the past week about yourself, your world, and the future.

_____

_____

_____

Describe how you often felt this past week. (Happy, upset, angry, bored, depressed, excited, or something else?)

_____

_____

Describe some of the activities you did this past week. What thoughts and feelings did you have during these activities?

_____

_____

_____

_____

Write down anything else you think was important about this past week.

_____

_____

_____

Rate your usual mood for the past week (circle one):

1	2	3	4	5
Very sad or depressed	Somewhat sad or depressed	Okay, about average (normal mood)	Pretty good, happy	Great! Terrific! Very happy

Adapted from *Helping Students Overcome Depression and Anxiety: A Practical Guide to Internalizing Problems* (2nd ed., p. 242), by K. W. Merrell, 2008, Guilford Press. Copyright 2008 by Guilford Press. Reprinted with permission of Guilford Press.

Interventions © 2019 Ancora Publishing

REPRODUCIBLE 4.6q

Case Example: Developing a Data Collection and Monitoring Plan

Let's return to Example 2 from Step 1 (*Targeted Problem Identification—difficulties in verbal responding and initiating for an individual student*) to illustrate a data collection and monitoring plan. In our example, the assessment measures used included BASC-3 (broadband), MASC-2 (narrowband), observations, and interviews. The team established three goals, all with corresponding measures.

Progress-monitoring plan organized by goals

Goal 1: Taya will increase the frequency of her responses to teacher-initiated communication as measured by observational data and teacher interview.

Four-part plan:

a) School psychologist will take observation data 3 times per week during a class period in which the teacher is known to engage students in group participation.
b) Teacher will also keep a daily tally of instances when she asks Taya a question, recording whether she responds or does not respond. Data will be plotted and graphed accordingly.
c) On a weekly basis, the teacher and school psychologist will discuss general impressions of the intervention and the student's responses.
d) Parent will be contacted to obtain and receive updates and impressions.

Goal 2: Taya will increase the frequency with which she initiates communication with a teacher as measured by observational data and teacher interview.

Four-part plan:

a) School psychologist will gather observation during the same time of day as Goal 1 data collection.
b) Teacher will also keep a daily tally of instances when Taya initiates verbal communication with the teacher. Data will be plotted and graphed.
c) Teacher will provide general impressions during weekly check-in.
d) Parent will be contacted to obtain and receive updates and impressions.

Goal 3: Taya will experience increased feelings of self-efficacy in verbal communication and reduced overall anxiety symptoms, per the *MASC-2* and student interview at follow-up.

Three-part plan:

a) Taya will receive a weekly journal entry form (see Reproducible 4.6q) to self-assess once per week
b) Taya will be interviewed after 4 weeks to determine her perceptions of her progress, define challenges, and refine the intervention as necessary.
c) Parent and teacher will also be interviewed to assess the same areas. The interventionist will consult the *MASC-2* manual to determine the appropriate time for Taya to be reassessed with this measure to evaluate post-intervention status.

Item c: Outline training plans and consultation support. Provide training to teachers and other adults who will be implementing the plan. Training, in conjunction with keen attention to quality implementation of interventions, has been found to result in better student outcomes (Reyes, Brackett, Rivers, Elbertson, & Salovey, 2012). Therefore, anyone who will be responsible for implementing and evaluating strategies should receive training on the intervention, assessment, and overall implementation procedures. You can deliver training in a variety of forms, such as reading, webinars, discussion with colleagues, consultation, and coaching. The type and amount of training will depend on the complexity of the intervention and skill of the interventionist. Use Implementation Guidelines: Supporting Students with Internalizing Challenges (Reproducible 4.6r, pp. 529–534) to review procedures with staff. Also make sure to distribute relevant forms for teaching skills, discussing strategies, and monitoring progress.

Item d: Outline plans to collaborate with community providers. Note any plans to make referrals or collaborate with community providers in the space provided on Essential Planning Steps Documentation (Reproducible 4.6a).

Item e: List ideas for next steps for your student. Lastly, use the data and information you entered into the Essential Planning Steps Documentation worksheet, plus your observations, consultation with colleagues, and reflection, to generate ideas for any next steps that may be helpful to the student. You might decide to refer a student to the school counselor, have another adult check in with the student weekly, or plan to do a refresher on a particular strategy in a month or so. Consider areas where your student will benefit from continued support and learning.

Essential Implementation Procedures

> Items 1–8 are also shown on **Implementation Guidelines** (Form 4.6r, pp. 529–534) that can be shared with teachers and other adults responsible for implementing the plan.

The teacher or interventionist responsible for implementing the plan should make sure to:

1. Meet with the student to discuss and finalize the plan. During this meeting:

- Explain the goal of the intervention plan (e.g., that you would like to assist the student in being more successful at school and in managing worries, stress, sadness, etc.). Discuss the student's perceptions of these goals, along with the student's strengths and resources.
- Communicate an age-appropriate rationale for the goals and skills that you will be working on together. Why are these skills important? How will these goals help the student now and in the future?
- Describe the setting, format, and schedule for planned teaching, coaching, and practice sessions. Let the student know what to expect from these sessions.
- Encourage student participation in and ownership of the intervention plan. As much as possible, engage the student in helping to plan the system and encourage any suggestions, questions, or concerns. Be sure to ask what might make the student uncomfortable and normalize these concerns, as addressing anxiety symptoms in particular can lead to anticipatory anxiety.
- Finalize the plan with the student after taking their input into account. Make sure the student understands the goals of the plan, the desired outcome, and the benefits.

2. Implement teaching, coaching, and practice sessions with the student as planned. Establish a consistent schedule with the student to teach or practice new skills. Follow the details outlined in the intervention plan and ensure that all skills or exercises included in the plan are introduced during sessions. Maximize the effectiveness of sessions through the following recommendations:

- At the beginning of each session, review the student's goals and link these goals to the focus of the session. Also, periodically review the rationale for learning and practicing the new skills (e.g., the student will be able to manage instances of anxious or depressed thoughts, feeling, or behaviors more effectively). For all ages, illustrate the importance and personal relevance of new skills by offering reasoning that will be meaningful to the student. For example: "Improving our skill at identifying triggers that make us feel worried can help us catch ourselves more quickly. We can then use a strategy, if needed, and decrease the likelihood that we will avoid something that might feel uncomfortable but is not harmful or dangerous—for example, taking a test, talking to an adult, or asking a friend to hang out."
- Provide ample opportunities to discuss and simulate situations that resemble the real settings and events that the student has had difficulty managing in the past. Role-play can be an effective strategy to anticipate and practice identified situations that contribute to internalizing signals. For example, Jae identifies feeling sad after looking at another student's social media account. He feels as if he's inferior in some way to this classmate and subsequently avoids talking to him. Using this example, the interventionist initiates a practice activity to explore Jae's thoughts, feelings, and behaviors associated with this experience. They then role-play an interaction between Jae and his classmate while practicing the use of new skills.
- Provide feedback on the student's progress. Feedback can include observations regarding the student's effort ("I can tell you are working hard to pay attention and think during our time together"), possible emotions during practice activities ("Sometimes I wonder if this feels really uncomfortable for you when we are practicing"), and demonstration of skills in intervention meetings as well as settings and situations outside of meetings ("I noticed during lunch you paused before talking to your friend, even though I wondered if she was really bothering you"). Focus on praising effort *and* approximations of the skills that you observe, rather than waiting until the student demonstrates the skill in its desired and final form. Feedback should be descriptive and specific so that the student hears exactly what was done well and what can be modified in the response or strategy the next time.

BEFORE MEETING WITH THE STUDENT

Once the plan has been carefully outlined, determine who will meet with the student to discuss the purpose and goals of each intervention strategy. This meeting may include the interventionist, the teacher, adults who will be working with the student, and the student's parents. Convene a group that will will be supportive and empathic, but not overwhelm the student.

3. Provide ample opportunities for practice and review of skills. There is no question that the more students practice, the more likely it is that they will be able to use the skills across multiple situations and settings. Therefore, finding daily, practical opportunities for practice is essential. Look for ways to infuse strategies into the very fabric of the student's school day—for example, making use of brief, opportune moments during academic instruction, discussions pertaining to social issues within a group, or one-to-one conversations. Review each intervention strategy and consider how you can use nuggets from each during everyday conversations and activities. Furthermore, students often benefit from booster sessions to keep their skills fresh. You can choose a few of the interventions to review with students and see how they are applying these skills 1, 3, or 6 months down the road. Just as everyone needs to exercise regularly to keep their bodies healthy, so too is it beneficial to refresh emotional skills.

4. As frequently as possible, provide noncontingent positive attention to the student. Noncontingent positive interactions are nonevaluative and simply communicate to students that they are recognized, cared for, and part of the school community. In fact, these interactions are known to boost the relationship between teachers and students (Doll et al., 2014), something that is essential for students' success and happiness at school (Rees, Goswami, & Pope, 2013). Noncontingent positive interactions may include greeting the student in the morning, asking about the weekend, or chatting about a known interest. Find opportunities throughout the day to interact positively with the student in ways that go beyond providing feedback. On a daily basis, strive for at least a 3:1 positive to corrective ratio of interactions (Cook et al., 2017). All staff can receive a refresher on the importance of noncontingent attention and examples of how it can be given.

5. Meet and debrief regularly with the student and adults who are directly involved in the implementation plan. A goal of these meetings is to review data and obtain anecdotal information and observations that can help you determine the extent to which the intervention is working, along with any modifications you may need to make. Also highlight successes with the student and address any challenges and concerns.

As you find areas to modify, consider making minor adjustments to improve the chance of student success. Ask questions such as:

- *Is the intervention being implemented as intended?* If you are the interventionist, are you monitoring implementation steps? If others are involved in implementing the intervention, are there gaps in implementation? If so, outline ways to resolve these issues.
- *Does the interventionist need additional training, support, or coaching to effectively deliver the intervention?* Consultation support and training can be especially helpful during inevitably challenging phases of intervention delivery.
- *Do aspects of the intervention that are personally challenging for the interventionist need attention?* Sometimes a student's challenge areas trigger emotional responses in the interventionist during the course of implementation. This is to be expected and a part of the work. Personal reflection and consultation can support the interventionist in working through this particular challenge.
- *Does the student understand the goals and rationale of the strategy?* Review the goals and rationale with the student. Also obtain the student's perspective on ways in which the skills could be helpful in different scenarios.
- *Is the plan designed so the student has little chance of success?* Check whether plan goals and behavior expectations require too much change at once or involve skills that the student needs additional scaffolding to learn, and adjust the plan accordingly.
- *Is the student obtaining reinforcement for escaping uncomfortable situations or tasks?* With internalizing problems, you must balance the need to respond warmly and compassionately to a student's discomfort and facilitating skill development through sometimes uncomfortable exercises. It is important to identify a student's emotions, support problem-solving, and set limits with unhelpful behaviors. At the same time, you must continually evaluate whether attempts to support a

student are interfering with the practice of skills that may make the student feel uncomfortable, especially in the beginning (e.g., providing too much reassurance or other accommodations).

6. Use data to make periodic revisions and adjustments to the plan. As you monitor the student's progress, make adjustments to the plan as needed. The following questions can help guide intervention implementation:

- *Are all essential components of the plan being implemented as intended?* As discussed earlier, fidelity is essential to understanding the extent to which we can claim that the intervention is what led to outcomes, positive or negative. The interventionist or an independent observer can observe the intervention in action and complete Fidelity Checklist: Supporting Students with Internalizing Challenges (Reproducible 4.6s, p. 535).
- *Which aspects of the plan can be modified to increase its effectiveness?* Adaptations to an intervention can be helpful, as long as you maintain the essential ingredients (Durlak and DuPre, 2008). Appropriate adaptations may include finding more opportunities to practice across time and settings, providing more relevant examples, and implementing adaptations relevant to cultural norms.
- *What supplemental strategies can be introduced to support the effectiveness of the plan?* Consider incorporating additional strategies from your original list from Reproducible 4.6a. Also consider strategies that support and encourage the student to participate in intervention activities (e.g., praise for effort, celebration of successes, goal setting, tangible reinforcement for meeting goals).
- *Is the intervention effectively decreasing problem areas and increasing skills?* Review data collected to date and determine: a) the extent to which the student is meeting goals, and b) whether you need additional data to understand the outcomes. It will also be helpful to return to the data collected before intervention and determine whether it might be helpful to address other areas. Analyzing and collecting new data can also extend to contextual contributors to the problem (e.g., family stressors, learning problems).

7. Once the student demonstrates consistent success, implement fading procedures. In addition to progress monitoring during the intervention, you can measure outcomes, in general, by using the same measurement methods to compare pre- and postintervention problem areas. In the case of behavior rating scales, consult the user's manual for testing interval guidelines.

Once data indicate that the student has successfully learned and applied new skills, has met the goals of the intervention plan, or has displayed a consistent change in target symptoms or behavior, it is appropriate to introduce fading procedures. These might include reducing the frequency of teaching, practice, and coaching sessions; conducting shorter check-ins with the student; or transitioning the student from receiving regular feedback from an adult to self-monitoring.

When fading supports, make sure that adjustments are gradual. Give the student advance notice of any changes and present adjustments as a response to the student's success in meeting goals. Continue to provide ongoing acknowledgment of the student's improvements and offer encouragement and support as needed.

Often, a student's behavior can regress after you fade supports. Anticipate this and assure the student that it is a normal occurrence. Also consider whether the thoughts, feelings, and behaviors associated with the identified internalizing problem are actually problematic. Remember, *everyone* experiences feeling anxious and sad at times! If your data indicate that these experiences are interfering with something important (e.g., completing schoolwork, participating socially) or are particularly stressful for the student, mobilize a plan that can support the student. Options include: revisiting the original plan and discussing with the student where to boost learning and practice, initiating additional strategies to support skill development and maintenance (review the list of interventions in Table 4.6a on p. 486), and elicit input and support from the student's parents.

8. Provide continued follow-up, support, and encouragement. The goal is for students to make improvements—experience a reduction in internalizing symptoms, effectively use coping and life skills, and participate in life in a meaningful and effective manner. Periodic check-ins can help achieve this goal, along with fostering a warm, caring, and supportive teacher-student relationship and celebrating successes.

NOTE: For more information and strategies on internalizing problems, see *Helping Students Overcome Depression and Anxiety: A Practical Guide to Internalizing Problems* (2nd ed), by Kenneth W. Merrell (Guilford Press, guilford.com).

PERSONAL EMOTIONAL COMPETENCE

Educators may find it helpful to learn more about the skills we have presented and even try them in their own lives. Doing so may increase confidence in your own skill at implementing them with students, build your own emotional competence, and have a direct impact on your students' well-being (Jennings & Greenberg, 2009). If you have not received training specific to mental health topics in your education to date, you may experience some trepidation with these strategies. A recent study highlighted the paucity of training that educators receive in learning about their own emotional worlds (Schonert-Reichl, Kitil, & Hanson-Peterson, 2017). To increase your knowledge and comfort level to best support students, you may find it beneficial to consult with colleagues, obtain additional training, reflect on practices, and focus on your own social and emotional health. Interestingly, some research has found that teachers who have not had mental health training per se can still be very effective in teaching social and emotional concepts to students (e.g., Sklad, Diekstra, Ritter, Ben, & Gravesteijn, 2012). Above all, paying attention to your own social and emotional experiences helps manage the considerable levels of stress you deal with as an educator and a human being (Roeser et al., 2013)—inarguably a great reason to attend to your own emotional competence.

> **EVALUATING IMPLEMENTATION AND DETERMINING NEEDS**
>
> This chapter reviewed several interventions known to be effective, but you will not fully understand how effective or ineffective they were unless you reflect on the extent and quality with which they were implemented (see Durlak [2015] for additional information). Essential Planning Steps Documentation (Reproducible 4.6a) gives you a means to track your steps through the intervention process. In addition, consider the following questions to supplement this process:
>
> - To what extent were you able to follow the steps of implementation?
> - What sort of additional issues did you consider when choosing an intervention (e.g., age of participants, cultural factors, comfort level with the material)?
> - What adaptations did you make?
> - How well do you think you were able to deliver the intervention? The Fidelity Checklist (Reproducible 4.6s, p. 535) can help here.
> - How did the student respond to the intervention?
> - What sources of support did you have in using the interventions (e.g., consultation, training)?
> - What additional sources of support would be helpful in the future?

Strategy Summary

The emotional well-being of students is a powerful contributor to their academic progress and overall healthy development across their lifespan. Without sufficient skills, students will struggle to cope with the stressors that will inevitably occur in their lives. The danger is that many will needlessly struggle, stumble, and find themselves in an undesirable situation: feeling overwhelmingly anxious or depressed, having difficulties with attending school, avoiding enjoyable activities, and feeling hopeless that their situation will change. Caring for students demands comprehensive attention not only to their health and educational needs, but also to their social and emotional development.

Schools of the 21st century have an important opportunity and challenge to support the relationship between social and emotional health and overall school success by serving as places where students can receive systematic instruction to promote their general development. As educators, you are the best-trained professionals in the area of instruction and can effectively use the strategies presented in this chapter. Consultation with colleagues and school-based mental health interventionists can support your efforts to find efficient and creative ways to implement these techniques in ways that are interesting, relevant, and beneficial to students. Many of the strategies can be easily integrated into the course of the school day, whether the focus is on relationship building, emotion coaching and identification, or teaching one lesson per week from a social and emotional learning (SEL) program. As students learn these skills over the course of their educational career, their emotional resiliency should grow along with their academic skills and carry them through challenging times.

Assessment Resources

Behavior Rating Scales

Achenbach Child Behavior Checklist. Achenbach, T. M., & Rescorla, L. A. (2001). Burlington, VT: University of Vermont, Research Center for Children, Youth, and Families.

The Achenbach Child Behavior Checklist is a series of questionnaires used to evaluate children's behavioral and emotional functioning. The school-age version (CBCL/6-18) is for children ages 6–18 and is available in self-report, teacher-report, and parent-report versions. The internalizing dimension assesses the frequency of anxiety, depression, social withdrawal, and somatic complaints. The externalizing dimension assesses the frequency of rule-breaking behaviors (e.g., stealing, lying, truancy, drug use, etc.) and aggression (e.g., arguing, defiance, teasing, fighting, etc.). Social, thought, and attention problems are also assessed.

Behavior Assessment System for Children (BASC-3, 3rd ed.). Reynolds, C. R., & Kamphaus, R. W. (2015). Bloomington, MN: Pearson.

The Behavior Assessment System for Children measures a wide array of behaviors that represent both behavior problems and strengths, including internalizing and externalizing problems, issues in school, and adaptive skills. Teacher, parent, and student self-report forms are available for youth ages 2–21, as well as the Student Observation System, Structured Developmental History, and Parenting Relationship Questionnaire.

Behavior Assessment System for Children (BASC-3, 3rd ed.): *Behavioral and Emotional Screening System* (BESS). Kamphaus, R. W., & Reynolds, C. R. (2007). Bloomington, MN: Pearson.

Part of the BASC-3 system, the BESS can be used to screen for behavioral and emotional problems and strengths. Teacher, parent, and student forms for youth age 3 to grade 12. Scores are reported as a Behavioral and Emotional Risk Index and Internalizing, Self-Regulation, and Personal Adjustment Risk Indexes.

Children's Depression Inventory-2 (CDI-2). Kovacs, M. (2011). North Tonawanda, NY: Multi-Health Systems.

The Children's Depression Inventory-2 is a brief, 28-item assessment for cognitive, affective, and behavioral signs of depression in children and adolescents ages 7–17. Scores are reported as a total score, two scale scores (Emotional Problems, Functional Problems), and four subscale forms (Negative Mood/Physical Symptoms, Negative Self-Esteem, Interpersonal Problems, and Ineffectiveness). Self-report, teacher-report, and parent-report forms, as well as short and long forms, are available.

Multidimensional Anxiety Scale for Children (MASC-2, 2nd ed.). March, J. S. North Tonawanda, NY: Multi-Health Systems.

The MASC-2 is a narrowband tool that measures characteristics associated with anxiety disorders in students ages 8–19. This 50-item measure can be used to identify youth, monitor symptoms, and develop treatment plans. Parent and self-report forms are available.

Revised Children's Manifest Anxiety Scale-2 (RCMAS-2). Reynolds, C. R., & Richmond, B. O. (2008). Torrance, CA: WPS.

The RCMAS-2 is a narrowband self-report measure for students ages 6–19. It assesses symptoms associated with anxiety on the following scales: physiological anxiety, worry, social anxiety, defensiveness, and an inconsistent responding index. It is available in long and short form.

Reynolds Adolescent Depression Scale-2 (RADS-2, 2nd ed.). Reynolds, W. M. (2002). Lutz, FL: Psychological Assessment Resources.

The RADS-2 is a narrowband self-report measure for students ages 11–20 to assess symptoms associated with depression along four dimensions: dysphoric mood, anhedonia/negative affect, negative self-evaluation, and somatic complaints. This 30-item measure can be used with groups or individual students.

Social-Emotional Assets and Resilience Scales (SEARS). Merrell, K. W. (2011). Lutz, FL: Psychological Assessment Resources.

SEARS is a strengths-based measurement that assesses social and emotional competence, coping skills, problem-solving ability, emotional knowledge, resilience, responsibility, self-regulation, self-esteem, and empathy in students grades K–12. Parent, teacher, and student self-reports are available in long and short forms.

Social Skills Improvement System (SSIS) Rating Scales. Gresham, F., & Elliott, S. N. (2008). San Antonio, TX: Pearson Education.

The Social Skills Improvement System Rating Scales is used for students in grades K–12 and enables teacher, parent, and self-assessment of a child's social skills (communication, cooperation, empathy, assertion, self-control, engagement, and responsibility), problem behaviors that interfere with the development of positive social skills (externalizing problems, internalizing problems, hyperactivity/inattention, autism spectrum, and bullying), and academic competence (reading achievement, math achievement, and motivation).

Suicidal Ideation Questionnaire (SIQ). Reynolds, W. M. (1987). Lutz, FL: Psychological Assessment Resources.

The Suicidal Ideation Questionnaire was developed for use with students in grades 10–12. The SIQ-JR is available for students in grades 7–9. Thirty items are included in the SIQ and 15 are in the SIQ-JR, all focusing on suicidal ideation. Specific items are indicated for review that should raise concern about suicide risk and prompt immediate attention.

Systematic Screening for Behavior Disorders (SSBD). Walker, H., Severson, H., & Feil, E. (2014). Eugene, OR: Ancora Publishing.

The SSBD is a universal screening system that can be used as a multiple-gating assessment procedure with students in grades K–12. Teachers complete this assessment to screen for internalizing and externalizing problems.

Observations

Observation of student behavior can be helpful when the behaviors associated with internalizing problems are observable, defined, and related to the identified internalizing problem. Examples include school absences or tardies, visits to the office or nurse, eye contact, verbal communication with peers and adults, crying, avoiding a situation that same-age peers would not typically avoid (e.g., turning in homework, playing on the playground, using the restroom during school hours). Consulting assessment resources, such as Whitcomb (2017), can assist your team in choosing an appropriate method for observation.

Interviews

Clinical interviewing is an essential component in assessing internalizing problems. This technique can help you gather information that may not be easily obtained via observations and behavioral rating scales (Whitcomb, 2017). Interviews should include the student, teacher, and a parent, with questions focused on identifying thoughts, emotions, behaviors, and physiological sensations associated with anxiety and depression, and on understanding potential functions for behaviors (e.g., the student obtains escape from discomfort by avoiding a stimulus that regularly produces anxious thoughts and feelings). Teachers and parents can also provide information about their observations that can help you generate hypotheses for the problem and establish goals. Teams are strongly encouraged to delegate this portion of assessment to a school-based mental health provider trained in interviewing techniques.

REPRODUCIBLE 4.6r *Implementation Guidelines: Supporting Students With Internalizing Challenges (1 of 6)*

Implementation Guidelines
Supporting Students With Internalizing Challenges

Overview

School-based interventionists and teachers with consultation support can use strategies presented in Supporting Students with Internalizing Challenges to assist students with internalizing symptoms—including behaviors, thoughts, and emotions associated with anxiety and depression.

What do internalizing problems look like?

Symptoms of internalizing problems generally are discussed in terms of symptoms associated with anxiety and depression.

Behaviors, Thoughts, and Emotions Associated With Anxiety:

- Excessive worry about situations such as school performance, talking to teachers or peers, separating from a caregiver, contracting germs or diseases, school bathrooms, natural disasters
- Misinterpreting common unpleasant or difficult situations so that they seem especially threatening or catastrophic
- Acute fear of particular things or situations such as animals, public speaking, vomiting, etc.
- Acute experience of panic symptoms such as racing heart, tingling, numbness, feeling terrified, chest pains, sweating, breathing problems, and feeling like you are losing control
- Avoiding or withdrawing from situations that provoke feelings of discomfort or fear
- Perfectionistic thoughts and behaviors
- Excessive reassurance seeking

Behaviors, Thoughts, and Emotions Associated With Depression:

- Feeling sad
- Not being interested or finding enjoyment in everyday or enjoyable activities
- Weight gain or loss
- Feeling worthless or guilty
- Hopelessness about the future, helplessness
- Preoccupation with death

Common Symptom Overlap:

- Irritability and anger that appears excessive or prolonged
- Sleep disruption (difficulties falling asleep, sleeping too much, too little)
- Preoccupation with thoughts
- Problems concentrating or making decisions
- Physical restlessness or slowing down
- Physical aches, pains, or other complaints
- Fatigue

REPRODUCIBLE 4.6r *Implementation Guidelines: Supporting Students With Internalizing Challenges (2 of 6)*

Implementation Guidelines: Supporting Students With Internalizing Challenges

How common are internalizing problems?

Diagnosable anxiety affects an estimated 15%–20% of children and adolescents (Beesdo, Knappe, & Pine, 2009). Although a diagnosable depressive disorder occurs relatively infrequently in childhood, at about 1% of the population, the incidence increases during adolescence, ranging from 5% in early adolescence to about 20% at the end (Thapar, Collishaw, Pine, & Thapar, 2012). In addition, depression and anxiety often co-occur. Of the children and adolescents diagnosed with a depressive disorder, 30%–75% are also experiencing anxiety (Bress, Meyer, & Hajcak, 2015).

How do internalizing problems affect students in their daily lives?

Children can be anywhere from mildly to significantly affected in their daily functioning when they are depressed or anxious. Internalizing problems can lead to diminished achievement, and problems in school can be stressful, leading to more internalizing problems. Consider some common situations:

- Omari is frequently restless, daydreams, and asks for reassurance from the teacher every day if he is doing things "right." These problems interfere with his focus in class and take time away from completing his work. It takes him twice as long to finish an assignment.
- Udom is too depressed to get out of bed in the morning. School attendance suffers and he falls behind, leading to more stress and discouragement.
- Melinee was bullied last spring. She is fearful to return to school in the fall and develops stomachaches and headaches. She's late to school most days, missing first-hour instruction.
- Jack believes that the teacher thinks he's "not good enough" for an Advanced Placement course, and therefore he doesn't ask for the teacher's help when he has questions. He receives lower grades that do not reflect his actual knowledge.
- Shoni has a learning delay and struggles to keep up with writing assignments. She worries about what other students think of her. She's distracted by these thoughts and falls further behind.

Unfortunately, when anxiety and depression go untreated, symptoms may persist and even worsen over time. For some children, these difficulties become so serious and unrelenting that going to school and doing regular activities seems like too much effort. Schoolwork is not completed, and grades drop. This can lead to a vicious cycle in which growing failure in school eventually becomes evidence of perceived internal failures and shortcomings, leading these students to a deeper belief in their inability to function in school or with peers. They may come to believe that they really are worthless or incapable of performing any better. Beliefs such as these may eventually become self-fulfilling prophecies as these students alienate peers with their dark moods, irritability, and negativity. Alcohol and other substance abuse has also been linked to untreated internalizing problems as well as to suicidal thoughts and behaviors. Ultimately, school attendance, employment, relationships, and enjoyment of life may be significantly affected if internalizing problems are not addressed.

What can be done to prevent or intervene with internalizing problems?

Schools are in a unique position to bolster students' resilience—their ability to bounce back during difficult times. Because teachers are already trained in effective instructional practices, they can use this expertise to teach strategies that focus on social and emotional education. Resiliency skills can be learned through explicit instruction and practice, including the use of packaged, specially designed curricula or strategies commonly referred to as social and emotional learning (SEL). SEL skills can be taught to all students as a classwide instructional activity, in small groups, or in a one-to-one setting.

REPRODUCIBLE 4.6r *Implementation Guidelines: Supporting Students With Internalizing Challenges (3 of 6)*

Implementation Guidelines: Supporting Students With Internalizing Challenges

Plan Summary

Goals of intervention plan: _____

_____

_____

Directions: For each strategy, specify who will be responsible for implementation, select a start date, and describe the format or setting (e.g., small group, counselor's office) and schedule for delivery (e.g., weekly).

Strategy	Staff responsible	Start date	Format/Setting	Schedule

Describe the plan for data collection and monitoring, including how often monitoring will occur, which behaviors or symptoms will be tracked, and how data will be gathered and summarized:

_____

_____

_____

Date to review data and evaluate the plan's effectiveness: _____

Interventions © 2019 Ancora Publishing

REPRODUCIBLE 4.6r *Implementation Guidelines: Supporting Students With Internalizing Challenges (4 of 6)*

Implementation Guidelines: Supporting Students With Internalizing Challenges

Implementation Steps

1. **Meet with the student to discuss and finalize the plan.**

   During this meeting with the student, you will:

   - Explain the goal of the intervention plan (e.g., that you would like to assist the student in being more successful at school and in managing worries, stress, sadness, etc.). Discuss the student's perceptions of these goals, along with the student's strengths and resources.
   - Communicate an age-appropriate rationale for the goals and skills that you will be working on together. Why are these skills important? How will these goals help the student now and in the future?
   - Describe the setting, format, and schedule for planned teaching, coaching, and practice sessions. Let the student know what to expect from these sessions.
   - Encourage student participation in and ownership of the intervention plan. As much as possible, engage the student in helping to plan the system and solicit the student's suggestions, questions, and concerns. Be sure to ask what might make the student uncomfortable and normalize these concerns, because addressing anxiety symptoms in particular can lead to anticipatory anxiety.
   - Finalize the plan with the student after taking their input into account. Make sure the student understands the goals of the plan, the desired outcome, and the benefits.

2. **Implement teaching, coaching, and practice sessions with the student as planned.**

   Establish a consistent schedule with the student to teach or practice new skills. Follow the details outlined in the intervention plan and ensure that all skills or exercises included in the plan are introduced during the sessions. Maximize the effectiveness of the sessions with the following recommendations:

   - At the beginning of each session, review the student's goals and link these goals to the focus of the session. Also, periodically review the rationale for why learning and practicing new skills is relevant to the student (e.g., the student will be able to manage instances of anxious or depressed thoughts, feelings, and behaviors more effectively). For all ages, illustrate the importance and personal relevance of new skills by offering reasoning that will be meaningful to the student. For example: *Improving our skill in identifying triggers to feeling worried can help us catch ourselves more quickly, use a strategy if needed, and decrease the likelihood that we will avoid something that might feel uncomfortable but is not harmful or dangerous, like taking a test, talking to an adult, or asking a friend to hang out.*
   - Provide ample opportunities to discuss and simulate situations that resemble the real settings and events that the student has had difficulty managing in the past. Role-play can be an effective strategy for anticipating and practicing identified situations that contribute to internalizing signals. For example, Raoul mentions feeling sad after looking at another student's social media account. He feels as if he's inferior in some way compared with this classmate and subsequently avoids talking to the student. Using this example, the interventionist initiates a practice activity to explore thoughts, feelings, and behaviors associated with this experience. They then role-play an interaction between Raoul and the other student, in which Raoul practices using new skills.
   - Provide feedback on the student's progress. Feedback can include observations regarding the student's effort (*I can tell you are working hard to pay attention and think during our time together*), the student's possible emotions during practice activities (*Sometimes I wonder if this feels really uncomfortable for you when we are practicing.*), and demonstration of skills in intervention meetings as well as settings and situations outside of meetings (*I noticed during lunch you paused before talking to your friend, even though I wondered if she was really bothering you.*). Focus on praising effort and approximations of the skills that are observed, rather than waiting until the student demonstrates the skill in its desired and final form. Feedback should be descriptive and specific, so that the student hears exactly what was done well and what can be modified in their response or strategy the next time.

REPRODUCIBLE 4.6r *Implementation Guidelines: Supporting Students With Internalizing Challenges (5 of 6)*

Implementation Guidelines: Supporting Students With Internalizing Challenges

3. Provide ample opportunities for practice and review of skills.

There is no question that the more students practice, the more likely it is that they will be able to use the skills across multiple situations and settings. It is important to find daily, practical opportunities for practice. Look for ways to infuse strategies into the very fabric of the school day, such as making use of brief, opportune moments during academic instruction, encouraging discussion about social issues in a group, or engaging in one-to-one conversations. Review each intervention strategy and consider how you can use nuggets from each during everyday conversations and activities. Furthermore, students often benefit from booster sessions to keep their skills fresh. You can choose a few of the interventions to review with students and see how they are applying these skills 1, 3, or 6 months down the road. Just as we need to exercise regularly to keep our bodies healthy, so too is it beneficial to refresh our emotional skills.

4. As frequently as possible, provide noncontingent positive attention to the student.

Noncontingent positive interactions are nonevaluative and simply communicate to students that they are recognized, cared for, and part of the school community. In fact, these interactions are known to boost the relationship between teachers and students (Doll, Brehm, & Zucker, 2014), which is essential for students' success and happiness at school (Rees, Goswami, & Pope, 2013). These interactions may include greeting the student in the morning, asking about the weekend, or chatting about a known interest. Find opportunities throughout the day to interact positively with the student in a way that goes beyond providing feedback. Each day, strive for at least a 3:1 positive to corrective ratio of interactions (Cook et al., 2017). Consider giving all staff a refresher on the importance of noncontingent attention and examples of how to give it.

5. Meet and debrief with the student regularly.

A goal of these meetings is to review data and obtain anecdotal information and observations that can help you determine the extent to which the intervention is working, along with any modifications that may need to be made. Also highlight successes with the student and address any challenges and concerns.

If you encounter any problems with the plan, consider making minor adjustments to improve the chance of student success. Ask questions such as:

- *Does the student understand the goals and rationale of the strategy?* Review the goals and rationale with the student. Also ask for the student's perspective on ways in which the skills could be helpful in different scenarios.
- *Is the plan designed so the student has little chance of success?* Check whether plan goals and behavior expectations require too much change at once or involve skills that require additional scaffolding for learning, and adjust the plan accordingly.
- *Is the student obtaining reinforcement for escaping uncomfortable situations or tasks?* With internalizing problems, you must balance the need to respond warmly and compassionately to a student's discomfort against providing support for skill building—a sometimes uncomfortable task. It is important to identify a student's emotions as well as support the student with problem solving and limit setting with unhelpful behaviors. At the same time, you must continually evaluate whether attempts to support a student (e.g., providing reassurance or other accommodations) are interfering with the practice of skills that may feel uncomfortable, especially in the beginning.
- *Could I or other staff benefit from additional training, support, or coaching to effectively deliver the intervention?* Consultation and training can be especially helpful during inevitably challenging phases of intervention delivery.
- *Are aspects of the intervention personally challenging for me?* Sometimes students' challenge areas trigger emotional responses in the interventionist during the course of implementation. This is to be expected as part of the work. Personal reflection and consultation can help you work through this particular challenge.

REPRODUCIBLE 4.6r *Implementation Guidelines: Supporting Students With Internalizing Challenges (6 of 6)*

Implementation Guidelines: Supporting Students With Internalizing Challenges

6. Use data to make periodic revisions and adjustments to the plan as necessary.

Monitor student progress and collaborate with your problem-solving team to make adjustments to the plan as needed.

7. Once the student demonstrates consistent success, implement fading procedures.

In addition to progress monitoring during the intervention, you can measure outcomes, in general, by repeating the same measurement methods to compare pre- and postintervention problem areas. In the case of behavior rating scales, consult the user's manual for testing interval guidelines.

Once data indicate that the student has been successful in learning and applying new skills or has met the goals of the intervention plan, or there has been a consistent change in target symptoms or behavior, introduce fading procedures, such as reducing the frequency of teaching, practice, and coaching sessions; conducting shorter check-ins with the student; or transitioning the student from receiving regular feedback from an adult to self-monitoring their own behavior.

When fading supports, make sure that adjustments are gradual. Give the student advance notice of any changes and present adjustments as a response to the student's success in meeting goals. Continue to provide ongoing acknowledgment of the student's improvements and offer encouragement and support as needed.

Often, a student's behavior can regress after you fade supports, and thoughts, feelings, and behaviors will occur. It is important to anticipate this possibility and assure the student that it is normal. Also consider whether the thoughts, feelings, and behaviors associated with the identified internalizing problem are actually problematic. Remember, we all feel anxious and sad at times! If your data indicate that these experiences are interfering with something important (e.g., completing schoolwork, participating socially) or are particularly stressful for the student, mobilize a plan to support the student. Options include revisiting the original plan and discussing with the student where to boost learning and practice, initiating additional strategies to support skill development and maintenance, and elicit input and support from the student's parents.

8. Provide continued follow-up, support, and encouragement.

Our goal is for students to make improvements—experience a reduction in internalizing symptoms, effectively use coping and life skills, and participate in life in a meaningful and effective way. Remember that period check-ins can help achieve this goal, In addition, they help develop a warm, caring, and supportive student-teacher relationship and provide an opportunity to celebrate successes.

REPRODUCIBLE 4.6s *Fidelity Checklist: Supporting Students With Internalizing Challenges*

Fidelity Checklist
Supporting Students With Internalizing Challenges

Essential Planning Steps

- ☐ Gather and summarize assessment data.
- ☐ Identify problem areas, assets, and resources.
- ☐ Define goals.
- ☐ Review potential intervention strategies and programs.
- ☐ Use decision-making guidelines to select strategies and determine how, when, and where strategies will be implemented.
- ☐ Make a plan for data collection and monitoring.
- ☐ Outline roles and responsibilities for implementing the plan.
- ☐ Provide training to teachers and other adults who will be implementing the plan.

Essential Implementation Components

- ☐ Meet with the student to discuss and finalize the plan.
- ☐ Implement teaching, coaching, and practice sessions as planned.
- ☐ Provide ample opportunities for practice and review of skills.
- ☐ As frequently as possible, provide noncontingent positive attention to the student.
- ☐ Meet and debrief regularly with the student and adults who are directly involved in the implementation plan.
- ☐ Use data to make periodic revisions and adjustments to the plan as necessary.
- ☐ Once the student demonstrates consistent success, implement fading procedures.
- ☐ Provide continued follow-up, support, and encouragement.

Interventions © 2019 Ancora Publishing

References

American Psychiatric Association. (2013). *Diagnostic and statistical manual of mental disorders* (5th ed.). Washington, DC: Author.

Allen, A., Kilgus, S., Burns, M., & Hodgson, C. (2018). Surveillance of internalizing behaviors: A reliability and validity generalization study of universal screening evidence. *School Mental Health,* 10/8/2018.

Angold, A., & Costello, E. J. (1993). Depressive comorbidity in children and adolescents. *American Journal of Psychiatry, 150*(12), 1779–1791. https://doi.org/10.1176/ajp.150.12.1779

Baker, J. A., Grant, S., & Morlock, L. (2008). The teacher-student relationship as a developmental context for children with internalizing or externalizing behavior problems. *School Psychology Quarterly, 23*(1), 3. https://doi.org/10.1037/1045-3830.23.1.3

Beauchemin, J., Hutchins, T. L., & Patterson, F. (2008). Mindfulness meditation may lessen anxiety, promote social skills, and improve academic performance among adolescents with learning disabilities. *Complementary Health Practice Review, 13*(1), 34–45. https://doi.org/10.1177/1533210107311624

Beesdo, K., Knappe, S., & Pine, D. S. (2009). Anxiety and anxiety disorders in children and adolescents: Developmental issues and implications for DSM-V. *The Psychiatric Clinics of North America, 32*(3), 483–524.https://doi.org/10.1016/j.psc.2009.06.002

Biederman J., Hirshfeld-Becker D. R., Rosenbaum J. F., Herot C., Friedman D., Snidman N., et al. (2001). Further evidence of association between behavioral inhibition and social anxiety in children. The *American Journal of Psychiatry, 158,* 1673–1679. https://doi.org/10.1176/appi.ajp.158.10.1673

Birmaher, B., Ryan, N. D., Williamson, D. E., Brent, D. A., Kaufman, J., & Dahl, R. E. (1996). Childhood and adolescent depression: A review of the past 10 years. *Journal of the American Academy of Child and Adolescent Psychiatry , 35,* 1427–1439. https://doi.org/10.1097/00004583-199611000-00011

Bress, J. N., Meyer, A., & Hajcak, G. (2015). Differentiating anxiety and depression in children and adolescents: Evidence from event-related brain potentials. *Journal of Clinical Child & Adolescent Psychology, 44*(2), 238–249. https://doi.org/10.1080/15374416.2013.814544

Broderick, P. C., & Metz, S. (2009). Learning to BREATHE: A pilot trial of a mindfulness curriculum for adolescents. *Advances in School Mental Health Promotion, 2*(1), 35–46. https://doi.org/10.1080/1754730X.2009.9715696

Calear, A. L., & Christensen, H. (2010). Systematic review of school-based prevention and early intervention programs for depression. *Journal of adolescence, 33*(3), 429–438. https://doi.org/10.1016/j.adolescence.2009.07.004

Carrizales-Engelmann, D., Feuerborn, L., Gueldner, B. A., & Tran, O. (2016a). *Merrell's strong kids: Grades 3-5: A social and emotional learning curriculum* (2nd ed.). Baltimore, MD: Paul H. Brookes Publishing.

Carrizales-Engelmann, D., Feuerborn, L., Gueldner, B. A., & Tran, O. (2016b). *Merrell's strong kids: Grades 6-8: A social and emotional learning curriculum* (2nd ed.). Baltimore, MD: Paul H. Brookes Publishing.

Carrizales-Engelmann, D., Feuerborn, L., Gueldner, B. A., & Tran, O. (2016c). *Merrell's strong teens: Grades 9-12: A social and emotional learning curriculum for students* (2nd ed.). Baltimore, MD: Paul H. Brookes Publishing.

Cartwright-Hatton, S., McNicol, K., & Doubleday, E. (2006). Anxiety in a neglected population: Prevalence of anxiety disorders in pre-adolescent children. *Clinical Psychology Review, 26*(7), 817–833. https://doi.org/10.1016/j.cpr.2005.12.002

Charney, D. S. & Manji, H. K. (2004). Life stress, genes, and depression: Multiple pathways lead to increased risk and new opportunities for intervention. *Science's STKE, 225*(5). https://doi.org/10.1126/stke.2252004re5

Cook, C. R., Frye, M. F., Slemrod, T., Lyon, A. R., Renshaw, T. L., & Zhang, Y. (2015). An integrated approach to universal prevention: Independent and combined effects of PBIS and SEL on youths' mental health. *School Psychology Quarterly, 30*(2), 166–183. https://doi.org/10.1037/spq0000102

Cook, C., Grady, E., Long, A., Henshaw, T., Codding, R., Fiat, A. & Larson, M. (2017). Evaluating the impact of increasing general education teachers' ratio of positive to negative interactions on students' classroom behavior. *Journal of Positive Behavior Interventions, 19*(2), 67–77.

Corrieri, S., Heider, D., Conrad, I., Blume, A., König, H. H., & Riedel-Heller, S. G. (2013). School-based prevention programs for depression and anxiety in adolescence: A systematic review. *Health Promotion International, 29*(3), 427–441. https://doi.org/10.1093/heapro/dat001

Denham, S. A., Bassett, H. H., & Zinsser, K. (2012). Early childhood teachers as socializers of young children's emotional competence. *Journal of Early Childhood Education, 40*, 137–143. https://doi.org/10.1007/s10643-012-0504-2

Doll, B., Brehm, K., & Zucker, S. (2014). *Resilient classrooms: Creating healthy environments for learning* (2nd ed.). New York, NY: Guilford Press.

Dowdy, E., Furlong, M., Raines, T. C., Bovery, B., Kauffman, B., Kamphaus, R. W., . . . & Murdock, J. (2015). Enhancing school-based mental health services with a preventive and promotive approach to universal screening for complete mental health. *Journal of Educational and Psychological Consultation, 25*(2–3), 178–197. https://doi.org/10.1080/10474412.2014.929951

Doyle, B. G., & Bramwell, W. (2006). Promoting emergent literacy and social–emotional learning through dialogic reading. *The Reading Teacher, 59*(6), 554–564. https://doi.org/10.1598/rt.59.6.5

Dryden, J., Johnson, B., Howard, S., & McGuire, A. (1998). *Resiliency: A comparison of construct definitions arising from conversations with 9 year old–12 year old children and their teachers.* Retrieved from http://files.eric.ed.gov/fulltext/ED419214.pdf

Durlak, J. A. (2015). What everyone should know about implementation. In J. A. Durlak, C. E. Domitrovich, R. P. Weissberg, & T. P. Gullota (Eds.), *Handbook of social and emotional learning* (pp. 395–405). New York, NY: Guilford Press.

Durlak, J. A., & DuPre, E. P. (2008). Implementation matters: A review of research on the influence of implementation on program outcomes and the factors affecting implementation. *American Journal of Community Psychology, 41*, 237–350. https://doi.org/10.1007/s10464-008-9165-0

Durlak, J. A., Weissberg, R. P., Dymnicki, A. B., Taylor, R. D., & Schellinger, K. B. (2011). The impact of enhancing students' social and emotional learning: A meta-analysis of school-based universal interventions. *Child Development, 82*, 405–432. https://doi.org/10.1111/j.1467-8624.2010.01564.x

Edwards, M., Adams, E. M., Waldo, M., Hadfield, O. D., & Biegel, G. M. (2014). Effects of a mindfulness group on Latino adolescent students: Examining levels of perceived stress, mindfulness, self-compassion, and psychological symptoms. *Journal for Specialists in Group Work, 39*(2), 145–163. https://doi.org/10.1080/01933922.2014.891683

Eisenberg, N., Cumberland, A., & Spinrad, T. L. (1998). Parental socialization of emotion. *Psychological Inquiry, 9*(4), 241–273. https://doi.org/10.1207/s15327965pli0904_1

Eisenberg, N., Cumberland, A., Spinrad, T. L., Fabes, R. A., Shepard, S. A., Reiser, M., . . . & Guthrie, I. K. (2001). The relations of regulation and emotionality to children's externalizing and internalizing problem behavior. *Child Development, 72*(4), 1112–1134. https://doi.org/10.1111/1467-8624.00337

Elfenbein, H. A., & Ambady, N. (2002). On the universality and cultural specificity of emotion recognition: A meta-analysis. *Psychological Bulletin, 128*(2), 203–235. https://doi.org/10.1037//0033-2909.128.2.203

Garland, E. L., & Howard, M. O. (2009). Neuroplasticity, psychosocial genomics, and the biopsychosocial paradigm in the 21st century. *Health & Social Work, 34*(3), 191–199. https://doi.org/10.1093/hsw/34.3.191

Glaser, S. E., & Shaw, S. R. (2014). Best practices in collaborating with medical personnel. In P. L. Harrison & A. Thomas (Eds.), *Best practices in school psychology: Systems-level services* (pp. 375–388). Bethesda, MD: National Association of School Psychologists.

Goodman, R. (1997). The Strengths and Difficulties Questionnaire: A research note. *Journal of Child Psychology and Psychiatry, 38*, 581–586. https://doi.org/10.1111/j.1469-7610.1997.tb015 45.x.

Gottman, J. M., Katz, L. F., & Hooven, C. (1996). Parental meta-emotion philosophy and the emotional life of families: Theoretical models and preliminary data. *Journal of Family Psychology, 10*(3), 243–268. https://doi.org/10.1037/0893-3200.10.3.243

Gus, L., Rose, J., & Gilbert, L. (2015). Emotion coaching: A universal strategy for supporting and promoting sustainable emotional and behavioural well-being. *Educational & Child Psychology, 32*(1), 31–41. Retrieved from https://www1.bps.org.uk/publications/member-network-publications/member-publications/educational-child-psychology

Herman, K. C., Merrell, K. W., Reinke, W. M., & Tucker, C. M. (2004). The role of school psychology in preventing depression. *Psychology in the Schools, 41*(7), 763–775. https://doi.org/10.1002/pits.20016

Hogan, M. F. (2003). New freedom commission report: The president's new freedom commission: Recommendations to transform mental health care in America. *Psychiatric Services, 54*(11), 1467–1474. https://doi.org/10.1176/appi.ps.54.11.1467

Hunter, E. C., Katz, L. F., Shortt, J. W., Davis, B., Leve, C., Allen, N. B., & Sheeber, L. B. (2011). How do I feel about feelings? Emotion socialization in families of depressed and healthy adolescents. *Journal of Youth and Adolescence, 40*(4), 428–441. https://doi.org/10.1007/s10964-010-9545-2

Hurrell, K. E., Houwing, F. L., & Hudson, J. L. (2017). Parental meta-emotion philosophy and emotion coaching in families of children and adolescents with an anxiety disorder. *Journal of Abnormal Child Psychology, 45*(3), 569–582. Retrieved from https://link.springer.com/article/10.1007/s10802-016-0180-6

Jennings, P. A., & Greenberg, M. T. (2009). The prosocial classroom: Teacher social and emotional competence in relation to student and classroom outcomes. *Review of Educational Research, 79*(1), 491–525. https://doi.org/10.3102/0034654308325693

Kamphaus, R. W., & Reynolds C. R. (2007). Behavior Assessment System for Children (BASC-2; 2nd ed.): Behavioral and Emotional Screening System (BESS). Bloomington, MN: Pearson.

Kamphaus, R. W., & Reynolds, C. R. (2015). BASC-3 behavioral and emotional screening system. Minneapolis, MN: Pearson.

Katz, L. F., Maliken, A. C., & Stettler, N. M. (2012). Parental meta-emotion philosophy: A review of research and theoretical framework. *Child Development Perspectives, 6*(4), 417–422. https://doi.org/10.1111/j.1750-8606.2012.00244.x

Kehoe, C. E., Havighurst, S. S., & Harley, A. E. (2014). Tuning in to teens: Improving parent emotion socialization to reduce youth internalizing difficulties. *Social Development, 23*(2), 413–431. https://doi.org/10.1111/sode.12060

Kilgus, S. P., Reinke, W. M., & Jimerson, S. R. (2015). Understanding mental health intervention and assessment within a multi-tiered framework: Contemporary science, practice, and policy. *School Psychology Quarterly, 30*(2), 159–165.

Kilgus, S. P., & von der Embse, N. P. (2014). *Unpublished technical manual of the Social, Academic, and Emotional Behavior Risk Screener.*

Levinson, D. F. (2006). The genetics of depression: A review. *Biological Psychiatry, 60*(2), 84–92. https://doi.org/10.1016/j.biopsych.2005.08.024

Masten, A. S., Roisman, G. I., Long, J. D., Burt, K. B., Obradovic, J., Riley, J. R., ... & Tellegen, A. (2005). Developmental cascades: Linking academic achievement and externalizing and internalizing symptoms over 20 years. *Developmental Psychology, 41*(5), 733–746. https://doi.org/10.1037/0012-1649.41.5.733

McIntosh, K., Ty, S. V., & Miller, L. D. (2014). Effects of school-wide positive behavior support on internalizing problems: Current evidence and future directions. *Journal of Positive Behavior Interventions, 16,* 209–218.

Meiklejohn, J., Phillips, C., Freedman, M. L., Griffin, M. L., Biegel, G., Roach, A., ... & Isberg, R. (2012). Integrating mindfulness training into K–12 education: Fostering the resilience of teachers and students. *Mindfulness, 3*(4), 291–307. https://doi.org/10.1007/s12671-012-0094-5

Merrell, K. W. (2007). *Behavioral, social, and emotional assessment of children and adolescents.* Mahwah, NJ: Erlbaum/Routledge.

Merrell, K. W. (2008). *Helping students overcome depression and anxiety: A practical guide to internalizing problems* (2nd ed.). New York, NY: Guilford Press.

Miller, F. G., Cohen, D., Chafouleas, S. M., Riley-Tillman, T. C., Welsh, M. E., & Fabiano, G. A. (2015). A comparison of measures to screen for social, emotional, and behavioral risk. *School Psychology Quarterly, 30*(2), 184–196. https://doi.org/10.1037/spq0000085

Miranda, A. H. (2014). Best practices in increasing cross-cultural competency. In P. L. Harrison & A. Thomas (Eds.) *Best practices in school psychology: Foundations* (pp. 9–20). Washington DC: National Association of School Psychologists.

Moret, C., & Briley, M. (2011). The importance of norepinephrine in depression. *Neuropsychiatric Disease and Treatment, 7*(1), 9–13. https://doi.org/10.2147/NDT.S19619

Neil, A. L., & Christensen, H. (2009). Efficacy and effectiveness of school-based prevention and early intervention programs for anxiety. *Clinical Psychology Review, 29*(3), 208–215. https://doi.org/10.1016/j.cpr.2009.01.002

Nicholson, J. I., & Pearson, Q. M. (2003). Helping children cope with fears: Using children's literature in classroom guidance. *Professional School Counseling, 7*(1), 15–19.

Reddy, R., Rhodes, J. E., & Mulhall, P. (2003). The influence of teacher support on student adjustment in the middle school years: A latent growth curve study. *Development and Psychopathology, 15*(1), 119–138. https://doi.org/10.1017/S0954579403000075

Rees, G., Goswami, H., & Pople, L. (2013). *The good childhood report 2013.* London, UK: The Children's Society.

Reyes, M. R., Brackett, M. A., Rivers, S. E., Elbertson, N. A., & Salovey, P. (2012). The interaction effects of program training, dosage, and implementation quality on targeted student outcomes for the RULER approach to social and emotional learning. *School Psychology Review, 41*(1), 82–99.

Roeser, R. W., Schonert-Reichl, K. A., Jha, A., Cullen, M., Wallace, L., Wilensky, R., . . . & Harrison, J. (2013). Mindfulness training and reductions in teacher stress and burnout: Results from two randomized, waitlist-control field trials. *Journal of Educational Psychology, 105*(3), 787–804. https://doi.org/10.1037/a0032093

Rose, J., Gilbert, L., & McGuire-Snieckus, R. (2015). Emotion coaching-a strategy for promoting behavioural self-regulation in children/young people in schools: A pilot study. *European Journal of Social & Behavioural Sciences, 13,* 1766–1790. https://doi.org/10.15405/ejsbs.159

Schonert-Reichl, K. A., Kitil, M. J., & Hanson-Peterson, J. (2017). *To reach the students, teach the teachers: A national scan of teacher preparation and social and emotional learning.* Report prepared for the Collaborative for Academic, Social, and Emotional Learning (CASEL). Vancouver, BC: University of British Columbia.

Semple, R. J., & Lee, J. (2007). *Mindfulness-based cognitive therapy for anxious children: A manual for treating childhood anxiety.* Oakland, CA: New Harbinger Publications.

Sklad, M., Diekstra, R., Ritter, M. D., Ben, J., & Gravesteijn, C. (2012). Effectiveness of school-based universal social, emotional, and behavioral programs: Do they enhance students' development in the area of skill, behavior, and adjustment? *Psychology in the Schools, 49*(9), 892–909. https://doi.org/10.1002/pits.21641

Smith, S. M., & Vale, W. W. (2006). The role of the hypothalamic-pituitary-adrenal axis in neuroendocrine responses to stress. *Dialogues in Clinical Neuroscience, 8*(4), 383–395. Retrieved from https://www.ncbi.nlm.nih.gov/pmc/articles/PMC3181830/

Swan, A. J., Cummings, C. M., Caporino, N. E., & Kendall, P. C. (2014). Evidence-based interventions approaches for students with anxiety and related disorders. In H. M. Walker and F. M. Greshem (Eds.). *Handbook of evidence-based practices for emotional and behavioral disorders: Applications in schools* (pp. 324–343). New York, NY: Guilford Press.

Swan, A. J., Kagan, E. R., Frank, H. E., Crawford, E., & Kendall, P. C. (2016). Collateral support: involving parents and schools in treatment for youth anxiety. *Evidence-Based Practice in Child and Adolescent Mental Health, 1*(1), 3–15. https://doi.org/10.1080/23794925.2016.1158625

Thapar, A., Collishaw, S., Pine, D. S., & Thapar, A. K. (2012). Depression in adolescence. *The Lancet, 379*(9820), 1056-1067. https://doi.org/10.1016/S0140-6736(11)60871-4

Thompson-Hollands, J., Kerns, C.E., Pincus, D.B., Comer, J.S. (2014). Parental accommodation of child anxiety and related symptoms: range, impact, and correlates. *Journal of Anxiety Disorders, 28*(8), 765–773. https://doi.org/10.1016/j.janxdis.2014.09.007

Tolin, D. F. (2010). Is cognitive–behavioral therapy more effective than other therapies?: A meta-analytic review. *Clinical Psychology Review, 30*(6), 710–720. https://doi.org/10.1016/j.cpr.2010.05.003

Wehry, A. M., Beesdo-Baum, K., Hennelly, M. M., Connolly, S. D., & Strawn, J. R. (2015). Assessment and treatment of anxiety disorders in children and adolescents. *Current Psychiatry Reports, 17*(7), 52.

Weist, M., Eber, L., Horner, R., Splett, J., Putnam, R., Barrett, S, . . . Hoover, S. (2018). Improving multitiered systems of support for students with "internalizing" emotional/behavioral problems. *Journal of Positive Behavior Interventions, 20*(3), 172–184.

Whitcomb, S. A. (2017). *Behavioral, social, and emotional assessment of children and adolescents* (5th ed.) Abingdon, UK: Routledge.

Whitcomb, S. A., & Damico, D. M. P. (2016a). *Merrell's Strong Start—Pre-K: A social and emotional learning curriculum.* Baltimore, MD: Paul H. Brookes Publishing.

Whitcomb, S. A., & Damico, D. M. P. (2016b). *Merrell's Strong Start—Kindergarten-Grade 2: A social and emotional learning curriculum.* Baltimore, MD: Paul H. Brookes Publishing.

Whitcomb, S. A., & Merrell, K. W. (2013). *Behavioral, social, and emotional assessment of children and adolescents* (4th ed.). Abingdon, UK: Routledge.

Zenner, C., Herrnleben-Kurz, S., & Walach, H. (2014). Mindfulness-based interventions in schools—a systematic review and meta-analysis. *Frontiers in Psychology, 5,* 1–20. https://doi.org/10.3389/fpsyg.2014.00603

APPENDIX A

Trauma-Sensitive Practices

All schools include children who have experienced trauma. Trauma occurs everywhere and affects children from all socioeconomic, racial, ethnic, and cultural backgrounds. Many of the students who come to the attention of your problem-solving team will have experienced trauma, and it is important to provide stability, create a safe space, and connect caring adults to these children as part of your intervention efforts. By being aware of and sensitive to a student's trauma experiences, educators can help break the cycle of trauma, prevent re-traumatization, and best engage a child in learning and the school community.

What is trauma?

A wide variety of experiences can lead to childhood trauma. Traumatic events include those in which the child experiences, witnesses, or is confronted with actual or threatened death, serious injury, or sexual violence (American Psychiatric Association, 2013). Trauma is often associated with violence, but not always. Traumatic events can also include other adverse childhood experiences (ACEs), such as psychological abuse or neglect, witnessing domestic violence, or living with household members who are mentally ill, suicidal, substance abusers, or were ever incarcerated (Felitti et al., 1998).

Who experiences trauma?

Research on the prevalence of childhood trauma indicates that between half and two-thirds of all school-aged children experience trauma (Felitti et al., 1998). Recent estimates from the National Survey of Children's Health (NSCH) confirm these findings: Nationally, 45% of U.S. children have experienced at least one ACE and 10% have experienced three or more ACEs, placing them in a category of especially high risk (Sacks & Murphy, 2018).

What is the impact of trauma?

Simply put, trauma is toxic to the brain and body (Souers & Hall, 2016). While traumatic events are external, they can quickly become incorporated into the mind (Terr, 1990) and the body (Van der Kolk, 2003). Childhood trauma is considered a response to a negative external event or series of events that renders a child temporarily helpless and surpasses the child's ordinary coping and defensive operations (Terr, 1991). When experiencing a traumatic event, the child's body will respond with a fight, flight, or freeze response, activating the stress response system. Under conditions of repeated trauma, rather than serving a protective function, this stress response can become overreactive and dangerous to the brain (McInerney & McKlindon, 2014).

By living in what trauma experts call a constant state of emergency, these children may experience:

- Difficulties with paying attention and processing new information (Streeck-Fischer & Van der Kolk, 2000)
- Challenges in responding to social cues, participating in social situations, and forming and maintaining normal relationships (Van der Kolk, 2003)
- Reduced ability to regulate, identify, and express emotions (Lubit, Rovine, Defrancisci, & Eth, 2003)

In sum, experiences of trauma have a negative impact on a student's readiness to learn. The more adverse childhood experiences that a child is exposed to, the greater the risk for developing difficulties in attendance, behavior, coursework, and health later on (Blodgett & Lanigan, 2018; Chartier, Walker, & Naimark, 2010).

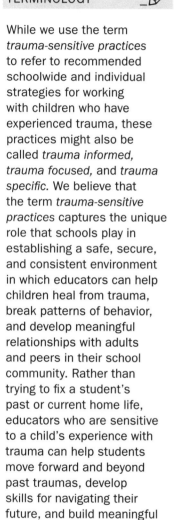

TERMINOLOGY

While we use the term *trauma-sensitive practices* to refer to recommended schoolwide and individual strategies for working with children who have experienced trauma, these practices might also be called *trauma informed, trauma focused,* and *trauma specific.* We believe that the term *trauma-sensitive practices* captures the unique role that schools play in establishing a safe, secure, and consistent environment in which educators can help children heal from trauma, break patterns of behavior, and develop meaningful relationships with adults and peers in their school community. Rather than trying to fix a student's past or current home life, educators who are sensitive to a child's experience with trauma can help students move forward and beyond past traumas, develop skills for navigating their future, and build meaningful relationships with adults as part of this process. —R. S.

How do we work with students who have experienced trauma?

Fortunately, research has shown that the effects of early trauma can be reversed and that schools are in an important position to help facilitate recovery through the use of trauma-sensitive practices (Blaustein, 2013). Integrating research on children's social and neurological development, the importance of a positive school climate, and best practices in behavior support, trauma-sensitive practices have the potential to increase positive outcomes for all students — not just students who have experienced trauma.

The Substance Abuse and Mental Health Services Administration's concept of a trauma-sensitive approach is structured around a set of four assumptions.

A program, organization, or system that is trauma informed:

1. *Realizes* the widespread impact of trauma and understands potential paths for recovery;
2. *Recognizes* the signs and symptoms of trauma in clients, families, staff, and others involved with the system;
3. *Responds* by fully integrating knowledge about trauma into policies, procedures, and practices; and
4. Seeks to actively resist *re-traumatization.* (SAMSHA, 2014, p. 9)

Trauma-sensitive practices fit well within a multi-tiered system of support (MTSS) framework and are consistent with the principles of positive behavior interventions and supports (PBIS). A trauma-sensitive school will anticipate when and where challenging behaviors occur, teach children the skills to manage stress and develop self-awareness, build supports to avoid re-traumatization, and encourage healthy, positive relationships between staff and students.

Review the following recommendations and consider how to embed trauma-sensitive practices into your building's schoolwide policies and practices for working with individual students.

Schoolwide Practices

Maintain a physically and emotionally safe school environment. A safe and welcoming school environment fosters better connections among students, staff members, and families, which will help students experience a sense of belonging and security (Hamre & Pianta, 2006). This includes having safe and secure school grounds and buildings, clear behavior expectations and procedures across all settings, and a welcoming environment for family members to partner in their children's education.

Ensure that each classroom reflects school values and conveys high positive expectations for the success of all students. Children who have experienced trauma often worry about what's going to happen next. Each teacher in your building can teach high expectations and maintain predictable structure by developing a proactive, positive, and instructional classroom management plan. Consistent expectations and routines, such as morning rituals, regularly scheduled activities, and assigned seats, can help these students know what to expect when they are at school and feel safe and secure.

Build strong relationships with students. Positive relationships with teachers provide children with the opportunity to acquire the security needed to form relationships with others. Teachers can't rescue children from past trauma, but they can help them move beyond these events by being a reliable source of support. This includes regularly greeting students when they arrive at school, engaging in meaningful conversations, asking about interests and goals for future, and helping students manage stress, effectively problem-solve, and resolve conflict with others.

Adopt trauma-sensitive discipline policies. Because zero-tolerance policies can be ineffective and counterproductive in changing student behavior (American Psychological Association Zero Tolerance Task Force, 2008), a trauma-sensitive approach involves discipline policies that hold students responsible for their actions through fair and consistent responses to misbehavior delivered by supportive and caring adults (National Association of School Psychologists, 2015). Schools should reflect on whether any of the disciplinary practices commonly used within the building have the potential for contributing to re-traumatization and whether they might be replaced by other methods that promote skillbuilding. For example, timeout and seclusion procedures may trigger fear and remind a child of past experiences with isolation or abandonment. Instead of assigning timeouts, a teacher could prompt students to take a "time-in," during which they remain at their seat, put their head down on the desk, and pay attention to their feelings and thoughts for the next 5 minutes. After a time-in, the teacher checks in to see how the student is

Teachers can't rescue children from past trauma, but they can help them move beyond these events by being a reliable source of support.

feeling, talks through any problem-solving that needs to occur, and praises the student for being able to calm down and manage their feelings.

Incorporate restorative approaches to discipline when possible. Rather than focusing on punishment for wrongdoing, a trauma-sensitive response to misbehavior may seek to use restorative approaches to discipline to strengthen relationships and repair harm that has been done (Craig, 2016). This can be accomplished by helping students learn how to recognize and take responsibility for hurting someone's feelings, actively listen to what others have to say, effectively apologize, and discuss actions they can take in the future to avoid harming others. Students can role-play active listening skills, read scripted conversations that illustrate successful conflict resolution, practice perspective taking by discussing alternative explanations of events in a nonjudgmental manner, or work with peers on projects that require negotiation.

Teach staff to recognize the symptoms of children who have experienced trauma. Trauma can present itself in many ways. Some children may appear unmotivated, avoid new experiences, give up once tasks become challenging, avoid making choices or decisions, fight for control, or withdraw from interacting with others. The National Child Traumatic Stress Network Schools Committee (2008) recommends that teachers be sensitive to the following signs of potential trauma:

- Fear and anxiety
- Changes in behavior (e.g., decreased ability to concentrate; increased or decreased activity levels; regressive behaviors; withdrawal from family, peers, and extracurricular activities; anger and irritability; and changes in school performance or attendance)
- Increased complaints about headaches, stomachaches, and other somatic symptoms
- Over- or underreacting to loud noises, physical contact, lighting, or sudden movements
- Difficulty with authority, redirection, or criticism

Also, staff should be able to recognize what flight, fight, or freeze might look like in the classroom (Souers & Hall, 2016):

- *Flight* behaviors include withdrawing or disengaging from class activities, fleeing the classroom, skipping class, and hiding or wandering.
- *Fight* behaviors include aggression, acting hyperactive, arguing or yelling, and refusing to following directions.
- *Freeze* behaviors include refusing to answer or respond to others, refusing to get needs met, and feeling unable to move or act.

Assess for trauma. Obtain a trauma history for new students and watch for signs of exposure to trauma among current students. Few schools have protocols in place to obtain trauma histories from transfer students, who may transfer schools because of events related to trauma, such as a change in living situation or disciplinary action (Taylor & Siegfied, 2005). Similarly, children who are involved in the dependency or delinquency system have a high likelihood of being affected by trauma (Marsh, Dierkhising, Decker, & Rosiak, 2015). For students new to your school, create a standardized protocol to assess past trauma, including procedures for collecting student records and conducting additional assessments for high-risk students. For current students, make sure staff are trained to recognize symptoms of trauma and know how to follow up or initiate additional support for students who show these signs. Though research has not yet clarified best practices for school-based universal screening in identifying trauma-exposed youth, ongoing attention and research may eventually shed light on useful tools and practices for universal screening in this area (Eklund & Rossen, 2016).

Provide instruction in social and emotional skills. Through explicit instruction and practice, students can learn skills to cope with stress and the impact of biological predispositions and trauma-related effects. Adopting a social and emotional learning (SEL) curriculum or teaching skills to all students as a classwide instructional activity or in small groups can help students learn how their brains work, how to identify feelings, and how to effectively problem-solve and resolve conflict (Chafouleas, Johnson, Overstreet, & Santos, 2016; Durlak, Weissberg, Dymnicki, Taylor, & Schellinger, 2011). For example, teaching students how to use relaxation techniques such as deep breathing, movement, or visualizing a peaceful, safe place can provide them with useful strategies to use when they feel frustrated, scared, uncomfortable, or angry.

Conduct trauma-sensitive functional behavior assessments (FBA). A good, comprehensive FBA should take into account the kinds of information that will make assessment and intervention trauma sensitive—including consideration of trauma-related physiological responses as possible motivators of behavior, adverse experiences that occurred in the child's past or present environments that may increase the likelihood of problem behavior, and antecedents in the school environment that seem to trigger a student's fight, flight, or freeze responses.

Collaborate with community agencies. The majority of students who have experienced trauma don't receive mental health services, and among those that do, schools are often the initial point of entry to these services (Kutash, Duchnowski, & Lynn, 2006; Ko et al., 2008) Consult with experts and build partnerships with mental health organizations to facilitate provision of services for students with trauma histories.

Provide professional development for staff. Ensure that all staff receive ongoing training that focuses on building awareness around the signs of trauma and its impact on children, using effective discipline and support strategies with students experiencing stress and trauma, and implementing strategies to prevent burnout and compassion fatigue. A set of training resources is provided at the end of this appendix.

Guidelines for Working With Individual Students

Avoid judging misbehavior. Challenging behavior at school may sometimes spring from stressful and traumatic experiences at home. For students with a trauma history, you might think of their misbehavior as a direct or indirect result of an injury, often inflicted by a caretaker through physical, emotional, or social maltreatment (Craig, 2015). When children's needs for connection, love, and trust are met, they are able to form relationships and connect with others, adjust to their environment, and regulate emotions. Without nurturing relationships, many children may adopt survival strategies to cope with this disconnection, leading to challenging behavior in the classroom. When faced with misbehavior from a student with a trauma history, try to remain objective. Rather than labeling the student as *bad, noncompliant*, or *out of control*, work to understand the feelings behind behaviors and the needs that the child is trying to meet. While you are not the cause of the problem, you do offer the best hope of positively reaching the student and helping them move beyond their trauma history.

Demonstrate unconditional positive care. One of the major goals of trauma-sensitive intervention is to reestablish adults as safe, caring, and reliable resources that children can turn to for support (Souers & Hall, 2016). Healing happens through building trusting, warm relationships. Seek opportunities to show that students are accepted and part of the school community, regardless of their behavior (Wolpow, Johnson, Hertel, & Kincaid, 2011). For example, if a student lashes out and says, "I hate you," respond with, "I'm sorry you feel that way. I care about you and hope you feel better soon."

Empower students. Early trauma experiences can affect a child's sense of personal agency (Craig, 2016). Identify ways to empower students, such as offering opportunities for choice and preference. For example, have the class vote on the next book to read together or allow students to choose whether to submit a typed or handwritten report. In addition, providing opportunities for students to get involved in activities that benefit others can increase their sense of purpose and improve feelings of connectedness to the school community. For example, arrange for a student to assume a meaningful role in the school, act as a peer mentor for younger students, or volunteer to help out with a school event.

Focus on student strengths and foster resilience. Schools have a unique opportunity to foster resilience. Due to the brain's neuroplasticity, schools can help students recognize their strengths and assets, increase their connection to the school community and ability to meaningfully connect with others, and gain skills in self-management and awareness of their own behavior, needs, and goals (Greenberg, 2006). Trauma-affected individuals can sometimes use their trauma as a rationale for low expectations or failure to achieve success. To help combat this, praise effort, remind students that mistakes are OK, and support the belief that ability isn't fixed and can change over time (Dweck, 2007).

Introduce strategies for managing stress. As students become more aware of how their brain and body work together, help them learn to be more tolerant of uncomfortable sensations and situations. Encourage students to remind themselves that the discomfort won't last forever and to use self-soothing strategies, such as deep breathing, movement, or visualizing a peaceful, safe place.

Practice and encourage positive self-talk. Children who have experienced trauma often lack self-confidence and optimism, leading to a negativity bias that continues to affect their ability to achieve goals, maintain motivation, and persevere in the face of adversity (Ayoub et al., 2006). Patterns of self-talk (verbal statements and thoughts people have about themselves and others) can affect how a child thinks about achievements and setbacks. By working with the student to redirect verbalized statements in a more positive direction, you can help reframe the student's internal dialogue. Over time, practice in positive self-talk can help students overcome problems associated with negative thinking and self-criticism, leading to a healthier and more accurate self-image.

Help students develop an optimistic outlook on the present and future. Encourage gratitude and affirmations by displaying a wall for students to respond to prompts such as "I am thankful for . . ." and "I can . . . ," having students write thank-you notes to meaningful people in their lives, and regularly discussing the benefits of feeling and expressing gratitude for good things that happen in life.

Model effective problem-solving. Approach student problems with empathy and encouragement to find solutions. Introduce a framework for problem-solving, discuss alternative ways to interpret and resolve a problem, and verbalize your own personal problem-solving process. For example, if a highly anticipated guest speaker needs to cancel, you might say: "I know we were all looking forward to Ms. Santos coming today to talk to us about video game design. Although she isn't able to make it to our class today, we're going to work on scheduling another date later this month. Fortunately for us, we still have time reserved in the computer lab, so this is a perfect opportunity for us to work on our web design projects."

Help students become aware of the sources of support in their lives. Guide students in identifying trusted adults and peers they can call on for support. Reassure students that it's OK to seek out others for support, and teach them how to ask for help.

Intentionally collect and share data with students about their accomplishments and growth across nonacademic domains. This might include collecting data on a student's use of self-management skills, calming down when frustrated, participating in class, helping peers, and cooperating with adults. Celebrate progress regularly and share accomplishments with other students, staff, and families in the school community.

Anticipate and be sensitive to environmental cues that may cause a reaction to a traumatized child. For example, a fight response might be triggered by a teacher who is physically close and uses a loud voice to redirect a student. In this case, take care to remain calm, quiet, and provide ample personal space when interacting with the student. For a student who has experienced trauma related to natural disasters and has heightened levels of anxiety during a storm warning, respond with additional supports, comfort, and efforts to connect with the student.

Model emotional control. Your reaction to their behaviors will affect the relationship that you have with students. By developing self-awareness about your triggers, emotions, and tendencies, you will be better equipped to act consistently and stay calm in the face of stress. Further, by remaining in control of you own emotions, you will model appropriate ways to manage stress.

Prevent reenactments. Students with trauma histories are likely to mistrust adult authority figures. This mistrust can result in extreme reactions to reasonable adult directives and requests. A gentle correction, perceived lack of attention, or feeling of misunderstanding can set off such a student. Students with trauma histories may engage in repeated misbehavior or escalating interactions that are more "related to events that happened in the past rather than in the present" (Bloom & Farragher, 2013, p. 98). These "bids for reenactment" offer staff an opportunity to step in and interrupt this interactional cycle (Craig, 2016). Rather than react to the misbehavior itself, respond by offering assistance, by prompting the student to use self-soothing behaviors, or by redirecting the student toward another activity that is grounded in the present moment.

Have a plan for responding to escalating behavior. By recognizing a student's typical stress response, you can avoid power struggles and bids to reenact past traumas, and effectively redirect the student toward healthy ways of managing feelings and behaviors. Once you are aware of a student's escalating behavior patterns, develop a plan for anticipating and defusing these types of interactions.

Resources

Child Trauma Toolkit for Educators

This toolkit from the National Child Traumatic Stress Network offers valuable information for educators, parents, and caregivers on the psychological and behavioral impacts that trauma has on students of all ages. Learn more: nctsn.org/resources/child-trauma-toolkit-educators

Trauma-Sensitive Schools Training Package

This training package from the National Center on Safe Supportive Learning Environments is supported by a substantial body of research on childhood trauma and its effects, trauma-sensitive practices across youth-serving systems, and lessons from implementation science. Learn more: safesupportivelearning.ed.gov/trauma-sensitive-schools-training-package

References

American Psychiatric Association. (2013). *Diagnostic and statistical manual of mental disorders* (5th ed.). Washington, DC: Author.

American Psychological Association Zero Tolerance Task Force. (2008). Are zero tolerance policies effective in schools? An evidentiary review and recommendations. *American Psychologist, 63*, 852–862.

Ayoub, C. C., O'Connor, E., Rappolt-Schlichtmann, G., Fischer, K. W., Rogosch, F. A., Toth, S. L., & Cicchetti, D. (2006). Cognitive and emotional differences in young maltreated children: A translational application of dynamic skill theory. *Development and Psychopathology, 18*, 679–706.

Blaustein, M. (2013). Childhood trauma and a framework for intervention. In E. Rossen and R. Hull (Eds.). *Supporting and educating traumatized students: A guide for school-based professionals* (pp. 3–21). New York, NY: Oxford University Press.

Blodgett, C., & Lanigan, J. D. (2018). The association between adverse childhood experience (ACE) and school success in elementary school children. *School Psychology Quarterly, 33*(1), 137–146.

Bloom, S. L., & Farragher, B. (2013). *Restoring sanctuary: A new operating system for trauma-informed systems of care.* New York, NY: Oxford University Press.

Chafouleas, S. M., Johnson, A. H., Overstreet, S., & Santos, N. M. (2016). Toward a blueprint for trauma-informed service delivery in schools. *School Mental Health, 8*(1), 144–162.

Chartier, M. J., Walker, J. R., & Naimark, B. (2010). Separate and cumulative effects of adverse childhood experiences in predicting adult health and health care utilization. *Child Abuse & Neglect, 34*(6), 454–464.

Craig, S. E. (2015). *Trauma-sensitive schools: Learning communities transforming children's lives, K–5.* New York, NY: Teachers College Press.

Durlak, J. A., Weissberg, R. P., Dymnicki, A. B., Taylor, R. D., & Schellinger, K. B. (2011). The impact of enhancing students' social and emotional learning: A meta-analysis of school-based universal interventions. *Child Development, 82*, 405–432.

Dweck, C. S. (2007). The perils and promises of praise. *Kaleidoscope, Contemporary and Classic Readings in Education, 12*, 34–39.

Eklund, K., & Rossen, E. (2016). Guidance for trauma screening in schools. Delmar, NY: The National Center for Mental Health and Juvenile Justice. Retrieved from https://www.ncmhjj.com/resources/guidance-trauma-screening-schools/

Felitti, V. J., Anda, R. F., Nordenberg, D., Williamson, D. F., Spitz, A. M., Edwards, V., & Marks, J. S. (1998). Relationship of childhood abuse and household dysfunction to many of the leading causes of death in adults: The Adverse Childhood Experiences (ACE) Study. *American Journal of Preventive Medicine, 14*(4), 245–258.

Greenberg, M. T. (2006). Promoting resilience in children and youth: Preventive interventions and their interface with neuroscience. In B. M. Lester, A. S. Masten, & B. McEwen (Eds.), *Resilience in children* (pp. 139–150). Boston, MA: Blackwell.

Hamre, B. K., & Pianta, R. C. (2006). Student–teacher relationships. In G. G. Bear and K. M. Minke (Eds.), *Children's needs III: Development, prevention, and intervention* (pp. 59–71). Bethesda, MD: National Association of School Psychologists.

Ko, S. J., Kassam-Adams, N., Wilson, C., Ford, J. D., Berkowitz, S. J., & Wong, M. (2008). Creating trauma-informed systems: Child welfare, education, first responders, health care, juvenile justice. *Professional Psychology: Research and Practice, 39*(4), 396–404.

Kutash, K., Duchnowski, A. J., & Lynn, N. (2006). *School-based mental health: An empirical guide for decision-makers.* Tampa, FL: University of South Florida, The Louis de la Parte Florida Mental Health Institute, Department of Child & Family Studies., Research and Training Center for Children's Mental Health.

Lubit, R., Rovine, D., Defrancisci, L., & Eth, S. (2003). Impact of trauma on children. *Journal of Psychiatric Practice, 9*(2), 128–138.

Marsh, S., Dierkhising, C., Decker, K., & Rosiak, J. (2015). *Preparing for a trauma consultation in your juvenile and family court.* Reno, NV: National Council of Juveniile and Family Court Judges. Retrieved from https://www.ncjfcj.org/sites/default/files/NCJFCJ_Trauma_Manual_04.03.15.pdf

McInerney, M., & McKlindon, A. (2014). Unlocking the door to learning: Trauma-informed classrooms & transformational schools. *Education Law Center*, 1–24.

National Association of School Psychologists. (2015). *Creating trauma-sensitive schools: Supportive policies and practices for learning* [Research summary]. Bethesda, MD: Author.

National Child Traumatic Stress Network Schools Committee. (2008, October). *Child trauma toolkit for educators.* Los Angeles, CA and Durham, NC: National Center for Child Traumatic Stress.

Sacks, V., & Murphy, D. (2018) *The prevalence of adverse childhood experiences, nationally, by state, and by race or ethnicity.* Retrieved from https://www.childtrends.org/publications/prevalence-adverse-childhood-experiences-nationally-state-race-ethnicity

Streeck-Fischer, A., & van der Kolk, B. A. (2000). Down will come baby, cradle and all: Diagnostic and therapeutic implications of chronic trauma on child development. *Australian and New Zealand Journal of Psychiatry, 34*, 903–918.

Souers, K., & Hall, P. (2016). *Fostering resilient learners: Strategies for creating a trauma-sensitive classroom.* Alexandria, VA: Association for Supervision and Curriculum Development.

Substance Abuse and Mental Health Services Administration (2014). *SAMHSA's concept of trauma and guidance for a trauma-informed approach.* [HHS Publication No. (SMA) 14-4884]. Rockville, MD: Author.

Taylor, N., & Siegfried, C. B. (2005). *Helping children in the child welfare system heal from trauma: A systems integration approach.* Los Angeles, CA & Durham, NC: National Child Traumatic Stress Network, Systems Integration Working Group. Retrieved from http://www.nctsn.org/nctsn_assets/pdfs/promising_practices/A_Systems_Integration_Approach.pdf

Terr, L. (1990). *Too scared to cry: Psychic trauma in childhood.* New York, NY: Basic Books.

Terr, L. C. (1991). Childhood traumas: An outline and overview. *American Journal of Psychiatry, 148*(1), 10–20.

Van der Kolk, B. (2003). The neurobiology of childhood trauma and abuse. *Child and Adolescent Psychiatric Clinics of North America, 12*(2), 293–317.

Wolpow, R., Johnson, M. M., Hertel, R., & Kincaid, S. O. (2011). *The heart of learning and teaching: Compassion, resilience, and academic success.* Olympia, WA: State Office of Superintendent of Public Instruction.

Reinforcer Checklist
For Elementary and Secondary Students

Rewards and reinforcers need not be elaborate or expensive. Note that many of the items listed below are already available in the classroom or school environment. Other potential sources include:

- Donations from teachers and other school personnel (e.g., items, talents, and interests they could share with students)
- School bookstore
- Donations from community organizations
- Discount stores (e.g., Dollar Store)
- Novelty stores
- Local fast-food restaurants (e.g., McDonald's)
- Donors Choose (donorschoose.org), a website whose visitors can donate to fund projects posted by teachers
- Past school or district programs (t-shirts, pencils, etc.)
- Churches
- University Greek organizations
- Conferences (collect expo giveaways)
- Oriental Trading Company (orientaltrading.com)

The checklist below is split into elementary and secondary sections. Within each of those sections are lists for individual students, groups and classes, and schoolwide rewards. Many individual rewards could be adapted for use with a class or school, and vice versa. Likewise, depending on the maturity level of the student, some elementary reinforcers may be appealing to secondary students, and vice versa. Browse through the list and check those rewards that seem feasible for you to deliver. Then, whenever you implement a reinforcement system, pick rewards that address the function of the misbehavior and that the student finds desirable. For example, if the student bullies to gain access to a particular item, use that item as a reward for reducing bullying behavior or increasing appropriate behavior. You might observe the student to see what they like to do. You might ask the student, or create a checklist on which the student can rank the choices. The test of any reinforcer comes when you use it with the student—does the desired behavior increase? If not, reinforcement has not occurred.

Elementary Reinforcers

Individual

FOOD/DRINK

- [ ] Ice cream
- [ ] Cookie
- [ ] Pudding
- [ ] Lollipop/sucker
- [ ] Candy bar
- [ ] Soft drink or juice
- [ ] Slushie frozen drink (e.g., Slurpee)
- [ ] Popcorn
- [ ] Potato chips
- [ ] Chewing gum
- [ ] Picnic lunch outside the cafeteria

INTANGIBLES

- [ ] Verbal praise
- [ ] Thumbs-up from a teacher

MATERIALS

- [ ] Hand stamp
- [ ] Carnival prizes
- [ ] Jerseys/School spirit items
- [ ] Stickers
- [ ] Book
- [ ] Bookmark
- [ ] Bouncy ball
- [ ] Play dough/Modeling clay
- [ ] Bouncing putty (e.g., Silly Putty or Gak—recipe available online)
- [ ] Pencil/Giant pencil
- [ ] Erasers
- [ ] Notepads
- [ ] Crayons/Markers
- [ ] Poster
- [ ] Art supplies
- [ ] Interlocking plastic building blocks (e.g., LEGO bricks)
- [ ] Basketball
- [ ] Army parachute people
- [ ] Blocks
- [ ] Balloon
- [ ] Squirt gun
- [ ] Shoestrings
- [ ] Key chain
- [ ] Charm
- [ ] Ribbon
- [ ] Hair ornament
- [ ] Temporary tattoo
- [ ] Smiley bean (kidney bean)
- [ ] Rock Stars: rock painted with stars
- [ ] Socks
- [ ] Water bottle
- [ ] Comb
- [ ] Lip balm
- [ ] Lotion (free samples)
- [ ] Playing cards
- [ ] Trading cards of staff members dressed in goofy clothes
- [ ] Autographed item
- [ ] Hula Hoop
- [ ] Flying disc (e.g., Frisbee)
- [ ] Jump rope
- [ ] Superhero glasses (old frames without the lenses)
- [ ] Spirit stick
- [ ] American flag
- [ ] Sports trading card
- [ ] Gift card to download a song from a music website
- [ ] Wrist bands
- [ ] Bracelet that says, for example, "I am awesome."
- [ ] Marbles in a jar
- [ ] Fake money, with sayings such as "Thanks a million"
- [ ] Trophy or medal
- [ ] Small work kit (nuts, bolts, etc.)
- [ ] Seeds and a pot for growing
- [ ] Fun worksheet/Mad Libs
- [ ] "I'm a teacher's pet" shirt
- [ ] Coupon to the school store
- [ ] Flashcards (printed on computer)

Special Awards/Recognition

- [ ] Behavior certificate
- [ ] A note from teacher
- [ ] Sock it to Ya certificate or poster for best behavior in PE class
- [ ] Gold Record for best behavior in music

APPENDIX B: REINFORCER CHECKLIST

- ☐ Golden Spatula for best manners in the cafeteria
- ☐ Platinum awards for art, PE, music classes (household items painted silver)
- ☐ Picture on a school poster
- ☐ Name on the school marquee
- ☐ Brave Badge—other students salute when the student walks by
- ☐ Teacher's Assistant badge
- ☐ Caught You Doing Good wall
- ☐ Featured photo recognition board in classroom (Wall of Fame)
- ☐ Special mention in the school paper
- ☐ Special acknowledgment from principal
- ☐ Special mention in announcements
- ☐ A letter sent home
- ☐ Sing national anthem

Free Passes

- ☐ Free activity for the entire class
- ☐ Pass for recess
- ☐ Pass to help younger students
- ☐ Dress down (no-uniform)/out-of-uniform pass
- ☐ Ten minutes of computer time
- ☐ Basketball/football game or school dance passes
- ☐ Study time
- ☐ Field trip funds
- ☐ VIP area (punch, etc.) at school dance
- ☐ One free test
- ☐ One free test answer
- ☐ Skip one assignment
- ☐ Complete half of an assignment
- ☐ Recess pass
- ☐ IOU card that can be used for homework
- ☐ Homework pass
- ☐ Guaranteed A on a quiz
- ☐ No early morning work

ACTIVITIES

Adult Relationship

Be a helper for:

- ☐ Principal
- ☐ Custodian
- ☐ Library
- ☐ Lunchroom
- ☐ Specialist teacher (art, music, gym)
- ☐ Own classroom
- ☐ Another classroom
- ☐ Read to the principal
- ☐ Have lunch with a leader
- ☐ Spend extra time with teacher
- ☐ Spend extra time with leader (prep/helper/lunch)
- ☐ Visit with volunteer artists/local celebrities
- ☐ Time with teacher who shares a common interest
- ☐ Teacher shares a special skill (e.g., instrument)
- ☐ "Classroom scout" tells the specialist teacher the class is coming
- ☐ Work as principal's apprentice for 20 minutes
- ☐ Interview the principal
- ☐ Courier or messenger for office/teacher
- ☐ Time with an adult/mentor
- ☐ Breakfast club with teacher or principal
- ☐ Cocoa and cookies with a teacher/principal
- ☐ Lunch with the principal
- ☐ Pizza with the principal
- ☐ Lunch with a teacher in the staff room

Activities Outside of School

- ☐ Pass to a school game/event
- ☐ Tickets to a professional or college sporting event
- ☐ Ski pass
- ☐ Pass to the zoo, aquarium, museum
- ☐ Voucher for swimming at a local pool or waterpark
- ☐ Voucher for rock climbing wall
- ☐ Voucher for miniature golf
- ☐ Voucher for shoes and a game of bowling
- ☐ Video store or movie theater coupon
- ☐ Voucher for ice rink (group or individual)
- ☐ Earn opportunities for summer employment or internship
- ☐ Earn service learning opportunities

Activities in School

- ☐ Read morning announcements
- ☐ Read a book of student's choice
- ☐ Receive a "mystery pack"
- ☐ Draw from classroom prize box
- ☐ Have picture taken and distorted with a computer program
- ☐ Paint a ceiling tile
- ☐ Decorate a chair
- ☐ Blow bubbles
- ☐ Color
- ☐ Draw

INTERVENTIONS: SUPPORT FOR INDIVIDUAL STUDENTS WITH BEHAVIOR CHALLENGES

- ☐ Play video games
- ☐ Play computer games
- ☐ Record story on voice recorder
- ☐ Play with clay
- ☐ Read aloud to the class
- ☐ Help present a lesson to the class
- ☐ Select a learning activity for the class
- ☐ Post a drawing in the hallway
- ☐ Tell a joke to the class
- ☐ Operate PowerPoint slide controller for a lesson
- ☐ Create a PowerPoint presentation
- ☐ Teach a portion of a lesson
- ☐ Read morning announcements
- ☐ Lead a class game
- ☐ Choose music for class to hear
- ☐ Dance to favorite music in the classroom
- ☐ Email a parent: Good job!
- ☐ Phone call home: Good job!
- ☐ Perform for the class
- ☐ Share a hobby with the class
- ☐ Check out a book from the teacher's library
- ☐ Help raise the flag
- ☐ Watch video instead of recess
- ☐ Indoor recess with a friend
- ☐ Dictate a story (print and have student illustrate)
- ☐ Use a voice recorder
- ☐ Hangman game: Student earns letters to play/solve
- ☐ Earn puzzle pieces to solve a giant puzzle
- ☐ Decorate and wear a crown for the day
- ☐ Serve as class monitor
- ☐ Choose a movie for the class to watch
- ☐ Read under the desk ("cave reading" time)
- ☐ Bring a stuffed animal "buddy" to class for the day
- ☐ First choice of recess equipment
- ☐ Tend the garden
- ☐ Ride a fire truck to school
- ☐ Ride in a limo to school
- ☐ Lead vocabulary review
- ☐ Wear a hat to school
- ☐ Earn flashcards (printed on computer)
- ☐ Spend time with a therapy dog
- ☐ Wear flip-flops to school
- ☐ Learn how to draw something that looks hard but with help is easy
- ☐ Learn how to do something on the computer: graphics/sounds
- ☐ Add a fun message to the school's scrolling marquee
- ☐ Use colored chalk
- ☐ Dress-down/No-uniform day
- ☐ Serve as student ambassador for visitors in the school
- ☐ Paint nails—"spa day"
- ☐ Answer the office phone
- ☐ Record a message for school answering machine
- ☐ Record video greeting for the school's website
- ☐ Have silhouette made by the teacher
- ☐ Take apart a broken item such as a clock
- ☐ Water classroom plants
- ☐ Choose a study buddy
- ☐ Take a class game home for the night
- ☐ Use couch/beanbag for the day
- ☐ Choose center of your choice
- ☐ Play chess for 30 minutes
- ☐ Design "gotcha" certificates for other students to earn (for good behavior)
- ☐ Sit at teacher's desk for the day
- ☐ Special seat privilege
- ☐ Peer tutor
- ☐ "Caller" for class bingo
- ☐ Make up math problems
- ☐ Lead class game
- ☐ Earn time to swing your feet
- ☐ Earn privilege of taking shoes off in class
- ☐ Line captain
- ☐ Staple expert: Staples others' papers
- ☐ Take attendance for class
- ☐ Pass out papers to class
- ☐ Get a drink without permission
- ☐ Use the pencil sharpener anytime
- ☐ Lead school in Pledge of Allegiance
- ☐ Select paperback book to take home (from teacher's library)
- ☐ Early dismissal
- ☐ Sit in a reserved section of the lunchroom
- ☐ Write with a pen/marker for the day
- ☐ First choice in selecting work materials: crayons and scissors
- ☐ Earn time at dress-up center
- ☐ Choose any class job for the week
- ☐ Earn "bear hug" points—when you accrue enough, you can carry a teddy bear
- ☐ Class held outside
- ☐ Sit next to teacher during story time
- ☐ Take care of class animal

APPENDIX B: REINFORCER CHECKLIST

- [ ] Sit in teacher's chair
- [ ] Student in charge of recycling

Small Group or Class Reinforcers

FOOD/DRINK

- [ ] Class pizza party
- [ ] Smoothie party
- [ ] Make healthy snacks

MATERIAL

- [ ] Puzzles

Special Awards/Recognition

- [ ] Eat lunch on thrones at a specific table
- [ ] Golden Plunger for cleanest pod/table/classroom
- [ ] Flying fish: When a student shows expected behavior, teacher yells something like, "Flying fish to Jen for listening," and tosses the fish to the student
- [ ] Bench of honor at an assembly

ACTIVITIES

Special Days

- [ ] Pajama day
- [ ] Free dress day
- [ ] Dress of choice day
- [ ] Wear favorite jerseys/shirts to school
- [ ] Teacher wears funny clothes to school

Parties

- [ ] Class party
- [ ] Reading party
- [ ] Beach party
- [ ] Zero the Hero party (for zero office disciplinary referrals): Teacher dresses up in a Zorro-like costume and eats lunch with kids
- [ ] Silly String party

Activities Outside School

- [ ] Voucher for karate or dance lessons
- [ ] Voucher for ice rink (group or individual)
- [ ] Voucher for laser tag

Point Systems

- [ ] Earn raffle tickets
- [ ] Earn good behavior points
- [ ] Paper football field displayed—kids earn yards toward a goal for specified behaviors

Bonus Time

- [ ] Longer lunch
- [ ] Free time (game/art/creative)
- [ ] Computer time
- [ ] Extra PE time
- [ ] Extra recess time
- [ ] "Game" hour
- [ ] Chat break at the end of class
- [ ] Lunch 5 minutes early with a friend(s)
- [ ] Time to play with friends
- [ ] Story time
- [ ] Five minutes to run
- [ ] YouTube Friday (5 minutes watching funny/cute videos)
- [ ] Make armpit noises for 20 seconds
- [ ] Have a snowball fight with recycled paper for 20 seconds
- [ ] Tap their pencils on their desk for 20 seconds
- [ ] Make favorite animal sounds for 10 seconds
- [ ] Chat with a neighbor for 2 minutes
- [ ] Play air guitar for 40 seconds

Activities in School

- [ ] Play dodgeball
- [ ] Serve as door monitor
- [ ] Classroom jobs (in group or in classroom)
- [ ] First to shop at point store during group
- [ ] Help setting up
- [ ] Watch a movie
- [ ] Listen to music while working
- [ ] Draw on the chalkboard
- [ ] Participate in a play
- [ ] Play checkers
- [ ] Lunch bunch (eat lunch with the teacher)
- [ ] Campus improvement activity
- [ ] Art afternoon in the classroom
- [ ] Play card games
- [ ] Play board games
- [ ] Play charades
- [ ] Go to the library and choose books

- ☐ Choose study buddies
- ☐ Design bulletin board for the hall
- ☐ Lunch outside with the class
- ☐ Walking field trip
- ☐ Pick a game everyone plays, including the teacher
- ☐ Class show and tell
- ☐ Rearrange the classroom
- ☐ Invite a guest to class
- ☐ Invite parents to class to watch a special activity
- ☐ Sneak peak at spelling words
- ☐ Field trip
- ☐ Invite a local celebrity
- ☐ "Storage wars"—students bid on old stuff
- ☐ Water fight
- ☐ Do the conga twice around the room
- ☐ Finger knitting while the teacher reads
- ☐ Teacher plays class theme song
- ☐ Create group currency
- ☐ Class sings the national anthem
- ☐ Jeopardy review game
- ☐ Class plays "Minute to Win It" games (search on Internet to find games)

Whole School Reinforcers
ACTIVITIES

Special Awards/Recognition
- ☐ Call out student of the day
- ☐ School recognition board
- ☐ Invite a speaker to the school
- ☐ Principal grills food for students

Special Days
- ☐ Hat day
- ☐ Sunglasses/Funky apparel day
- ☐ Fun and Funky Field Day: different outside activities/obstacle courses for students to participate in
- ☐ Principal spends a day on the roof

Activities in School
- ☐ Help organize a school assembly
- ☐ School fundraising effort
- ☐ Lottery to pick student tour guides
- ☐ Create school announcements
- ☐ Principal wears a crazy tie—one student's name is drawn to cut it off in front of the whole school
- ☐ Principal/teacher has to kiss a pig in front of the school (specific goal/behavior)
- ☐ Buzz-cut a design into a male adult's hair at school assembly
- ☐ Duct tape principal/teacher to the wall (earn coupons for strips of tape)
- ☐ Give principal pink highlights
- ☐ Staff/students participate in a pie-eating contest
- ☐ Create school currency

Games/Puzzles
- ☐ Miniature brain teaser games/puzzles (e.g., Rubik's Cube)
- ☐ Specialized LEGO brick kits (e.g., Star Wars)
- ☐ Box of puzzles
- ☐ Set of playing cards
- ☐ Dominoes/Chess/Checkers set
- ☐ Favorite board game

APPENDIX B: REINFORCER CHECKLIST

Secondary Reinforcers

Individual

FOOD/DRINK

- [ ] Milk and doughnuts for breakfast
- [ ] Bag of candies
- [ ] Bag of chips
- [ ] Candy bar
- [ ] Ice cream bar
- [ ] Cookies
- [ ] Smoothie
- [ ] Personalized cake/cupcake
- [ ] Pizza at lunch
- [ ] Favorite meal at lunch
- [ ] Free drink from vending machine

Voucher for:

- [ ] Meal from cafeteria or food stand
- [ ] Food/Candy item from student store
- [ ] Chewing gum/eating in class
- [ ] Eating snacks in class
- [ ] Drinking soda in class
- [ ] Snack at school function or sporting event
- [ ] Off-campus breakfast at nearby eatery with a school escort
- [ ] Off-campus lunch at nearby eatery with a school escort

Lunch (catered or from the lunchroom):

- [ ] With teacher in classroom
- [ ] With teacher in faculty lounge
- [ ] With three friends in supervised classroom
- [ ] With three friends in faculty lounge

SENSORY

- [ ] Exercise ball to sit on in class
- [ ] Squeeze ball during class
- [ ] Pillow to sit on
- [ ] Modeling clay to play with
- [ ] Play with Silly String

Ten-minute break to:

- [ ] Wear headphones
- [ ] Jump on mini trampoline
- [ ] Hit punching bag/cushioned wall
- [ ] Snap rubber bands
- [ ] Jump in place
- [ ] Do jumping jacks

INTANGIBLES

Social Recognition

- [ ] Name announced over PA system
- [ ] Name announced at school function (assembly/rally)
- [ ] Name announced at school sports event
- [ ] Name listed on school marquee
- [ ] Name listed in school newsletter
- [ ] Named listed in local newspaper
- [ ] Name listed in Hall of Fame for a week
- [ ] Photo and story listed in local newspaper
- [ ] Photo and story listed in school newsletter
- [ ] Photo and story posted in Hall of Fame for a week
- [ ] Photo and story posted in classroom
- [ ] Phone call home from school to provide positive praise
- [ ] Letter home from school to provide positive praise
- [ ] Certificate/Award of recognition

MATERIALS

Gift card for:

- [ ] Cash
- [ ] Online store
- [ ] Online music store
- [ ] Clothing store
- [ ] Fast-food restaurant
- [ ] Local arcade
- [ ] Miniature golf course
- [ ] Comics store
- [ ] Nail salon
- [ ] Hair salon
- [ ] Minutes for mobile phone
- [ ] Gas (for students who drive)
- [ ] Bag of toiletries (hairbrush, comb, deodorant, lip balm, body spray, lotion)
- [ ] Bag of school supplies (pencils, pens, markers, erasers, highlighters)
- [ ] Bag of locker supplies (shelf, mirror, magnets)

INTERVENTIONS: SUPPORT FOR INDIVIDUAL STUDENTS WITH BEHAVIOR CHALLENGES

- ☐ Backpack/Book bag
- ☐ Cool book covers
- ☐ School apparel (e.g., hat, t-shirt, sweater, etc.)
- ☐ Choice of mystery bags
- ☐ Copy of favorite book
- ☐ Copy of favorite movie
- ☐ Music album of choice
- ☐ Favorite poster
- ☐ Water canteen/bottle
- ☐ T-shirt from favorite band
- ☐ Phone accessory (e.g., case, trinket)
- ☐ Movie tickets for two
- ☐ Paid mobile phone application
- ☐ Free car wash (for student drivers)
- ☐ School bucks to be used in school store

Games/Puzzles

- ☐ Miniature brain teaser games/puzzles (e.g., Rubik's Cube)
- ☐ Specialized LEGO brick kits (e.g., Star Wars)
- ☐ Box of puzzles
- ☐ Set of playing cards
- ☐ Dominoes/Chess/Checkers set
- ☐ Favorite board game

Voucher for Discounted or Free Item. Examples include:

- ☐ School store merchandise
- ☐ School portraits
- ☐ School yearbook
- ☐ College application
- ☐ College entrance exam (PSAT, SAT, ACT)
- ☐ Gym clothes
- ☐ Class textbook
- ☐ Sports uniforms (for student athletes)
- ☐ Class field trip
- ☐ Driver's education course
- ☐ City bus pass
- ☐ Class at local recreation center
- ☐ Haircut at local salon
- ☐ Shoes and play at bowling alley

Voucher or Pass for Free Admission for Two to:

- ☐ Local museum
- ☐ Local zoo
- ☐ Festival
- ☐ Local sports event
- ☐ Choice of school sports event
- ☐ Choice of school function (play, concert, dance)
- ☐ Homecoming game/dance
- ☐ Junior/Senior prom

Pass That Entitles Student to:

- ☐ Play video games in supervised classroom with two friends
- ☐ Wear no uniform for a day
- ☐ Wear flip-flops for a day
- ☐ Wear hat/hoodie in class
- ☐ Not participate in gym class
- ☐ Spend class period in supervised computer lab/library/media room
- ☐ Spend class period in another classroom
- ☐ Join school sports team to an away game
- ☐ Jump to front of lunch line
- ☐ Leave class 5 minutes early
- ☐ Be 5 minutes tardy to class
- ☐ Make up missing assignment
- ☐ Turn in assignment late
- ☐ Miss one assignment
- ☐ Skip one item on assignment
- ☐ Skip one quiz/test question

Pass for 10 Minutes to:

- ☐ Eat snack in class
- ☐ Rest head on desk
- ☐ Complete last night's homework
- ☐ Play with cell phone in class
- ☐ Play with computer or tablet
- ☐ Listen to personal music player (phone, iPod) during independent class work

Certificate for:

- ☐ Removal of tardy on attendance sheet
- ☐ Removal of absence on attendance record
- ☐ Extra points (specify number) on homework assignment
- ☐ Extra points (specify number) on in-class assignment
- ☐ Extra points (specify number) on quiz/test
- ☐ Extra time (specify) on homework assignment
- ☐ Extra time (specify) on in-class assignment
- ☐ Extra time (specify) on quiz/test
- ☐ Extra time (specify) on class project
- ☐ Extra help on class project
- ☐ One extra-credit assignment

APPENDIX B: REINFORCER CHECKLIST

ACTIVITIES

Special Privileges/Positions

- [ ] Special dinner banquet for recognized students
- [ ] Reserved prime parking spot for a day/week (for student drivers)
- [ ] Reserved table in lunchroom for a day/week
- [ ] Reserved seating for student and friends at school assembly/rally
- [ ] Reserved seating for student and friends at school function or sports event (play, basketball game, concert, etc.)
- [ ] Team captain during gym class
- [ ] Hall monitor for a day/week
- [ ] Air vortex cannon (e.g., Airzooka) holder for a day/week
- [ ] Student mentor for a period/day (attend a lower-grade class and tutor)
- [ ] Student representative at faculty meeting
- [ ] PA announcer for a day/week
- [ ] Swap seats with a peer for a day/week
- [ ] Sit in teacher's chair for day/week
- [ ] Receive copies of the day/week's lecture notes

Opportunity to Choose:

- [ ] Class activity or topic
- [ ] Peer buddy to work with on in-class assignment
- [ ] Peer buddy to work with on class project
- [ ] Music played for whole class during independent seatwork
- [ ] Movie for movie day
- [ ] YouTube video to show class
- [ ] Gym activity
- [ ] Locker location

Adult Relationship

- [ ] Teacher's assistant for a day/week (call roll, pass out papers)
- [ ] Principal's assistant for a day
- [ ] Office aide for a day/week (filing, greet visitors, make copies)
- [ ] Coach's assistant for a day/week
- [ ] Teacher for a day (run lesson plan)
- [ ] Gym teacher's assistant for a day/week (blow whistle, hand out equipment)
- [ ] Sports team assistant for a day/week (hand out water, take stats, sit on sidelines at game)

Activities in School

- [ ] Lead class discussion
- [ ] Prepare next day's lecture/curriculum
- [ ] Run through wall of paper or wall of streamers
- [ ] Pie a teacher/educator in the face
- [ ] Make online video
- [ ] Decorated desk for a week (balloons, streamers)
- [ ] Chauffeured golf cart rides to/from classes by campus officer for day/week
- [ ] Participate in student government meeting

Home Collaboration (prearranged with parents)

ACTIVITIES

- [ ] Sleepover with friends
- [ ] Have friends over for dinner
- [ ] Movie with friends
- [ ] Trip to the mall

TANGIBLES

- [ ] One new clothing item
- [ ] New cell phone

PRIVILEGES

- [ ] Sleep in for an extra hour
- [ ] Car for the afternoon (for student drivers)
- [ ] No chores for a day/week
- [ ] No babysitting younger siblings for a day/week
- [ ] Voucher to pass on one family event/function (birthday party, dinner at uncle's)
- [ ] Extra time watching television
- [ ] Extra time using the computer
- [ ] Extra time using the phone
- [ ] Extra allowance
- [ ] Increase in regular allowance
- [ ] Control of television remote for a night

Choice of:

- [ ] Television show to watch
- [ ] Meal for dinner
- [ ] Restaurant for breakfast/lunch/dinner
- [ ] Weekend family activity

INTERVENTIONS: SUPPORT FOR INDIVIDUAL STUDENTS WITH BEHAVIOR CHALLENGES

Whole Class/Small Group

FOOD/DRINK

- [ ] Catered breakfast in class
- [ ] Catered lunch in class

Special Days

- [ ] Snack day (snacks during class)
- [ ] Candy day (candies for all students)
- [ ] Food day (meals during class)
- [ ] Smoothie day (smoothies during class)
- [ ] Drinks day (juice/sodas during class)
- [ ] Gum day (gum allowed during class)

Class Party

- [ ] Pizza party
- [ ] BBQ party
- [ ] Ice cream party

INTANGIBLES

Recognition

- [ ] Reserved front rows for school assembly/rally
- [ ] Hall of Fame (picture and name of each student in school hallway)

MATERIALS (one per student)

- [ ] School gear (e.g., hat, t-shirt. mug, sticker, etc.)
- [ ] Bag of toiletries
- [ ] Bag of school supplies
- [ ] Mystery bag

Vouchers (one for each student)

- [ ] Soda from vending matching
- [ ] Lunch in lunchroom
- [ ] Snack from school store

ACTIVITIES

Special Days

- [ ] Free class day
- [ ] Movie day
- [ ] Carnival day (classroom carnival)
- [ ] Casino day (classroom games with fake money)
- [ ] Games day (board games in class)
- [ ] YouTube day (watch approved videos as a class)
- [ ] Field/Gym day (outdoor sports and activities)
- [ ] Library day
- [ ] Computer lab/media room day
- [ ] Music day (low-volume music played in background)
- [ ] Catch-up day (students can catch up on assignments in class)

Class Party

- [ ] Nerf gun party
- [ ] Water gun party
- [ ] Silly String party

Sports

- [ ] Dodgeball tournament
- [ ] Kickball tournament
- [ ] Softball tournament

Ten Minutes of Class Time to:

- [ ] Use phone/text
- [ ] Watch YouTube videos
- [ ] Spend as free time
- [ ] Review before a quiz/test
- [ ] Rest head on desks

Voucher (one for each student):

- [ ] Admission to school function
- [ ] Admission to school sports event
- [ ] Admission to local zoo
- [ ] Admission to local museum
- [ ] Admission to local festival

Field Trip to:

- [ ] Arcade
- [ ] Local zoo/museum
- [ ] Amusement park
- [ ] Bowling alley
- [ ] Movies
- [ ] Laser tag

Miscellaneous

- [ ] Photography session/shoot
- [ ] Graffiti wall (students paint designated wall, and it remains for a week before another group takes it on)
- [ ] Rearrange classroom for a week
- [ ] Outdoor lecture period
- [ ] Principal teaches class for a period

APPENDIX B: REINFORCER CHECKLIST

- ☐ Visit from a local celebrity
- ☐ Classroom mentors (visit a lower grade class and pair students to be mentors for a period)

ACADEMIC REWARDS

- ☐ Make extra credit assignment available for class
- ☐ Free choice in seating arrangement for a week
- ☐ Free choice in assignment (several assignments to complete same task)
- ☐ Free choice in partners for a project
- ☐ No homework night
- ☐ No in-class assignment day
- ☐ Extension on homework
- ☐ Extension on project assignment
- ☐ Opportunity to work in pairs/groups on an assignment
- ☐ Early dismissal from class to go to lockers/next class

Award each student:

- ☐ Extra point on homework
- ☐ Extra point on in-class assignment
- ☐ Extra point on quiz/test
- ☐ Extra time on in-class assignment
- ☐ Extra time on quiz/test
- ☐ Extra time past tardy bell
- ☐ Voucher for early dismissal from class for lunch (can be used if different class period before lunch)

Pass for each student to:

- ☐ Skip an item on an in-class assignment
- ☐ Skip an item on a homework assignment
- ☐ Skip a quiz/test question
- ☐ Skip a homework assignment
- ☐ Skip an in-class assignment

Schoolwide

FOOD/DRINK

Party

- ☐ Pizza
- ☐ Ice cream
- ☐ BBQ

ACTIVITIES

Special day

- ☐ Casino day
- ☐ Field day
- ☐ Carnival day
- ☐ Games day
- ☐ Western day
- ☐ Wacky water day (water activities)
- ☐ Staff-only dress-up day
- ☐ Staff pie-in-the-face day
- ☐ Themed days for Spirit Week
- ☐ No uniform day
- ☐ No homework day

Events

- ☐ Dance
- ☐ Concert
- ☐ Talent show
- ☐ Comedy show
- ☐ Staff-only talent show
- ☐ Pep rally
- ☐ Amusement park field trip

Activities in School

- ☐ Photo booth during lunch
- ☐ Stereo system set up and music played during lunch
- ☐ Local radio station/DJ visits and plays during lunch
- ☐ Movie afternoon (movie day in gym or assembly hall)
- ☐ Music played over PA system between class periods
- ☐ Visit from local celebrity
- ☐ Visit from local sports team
- ☐ Principal as lunch server for a day
- ☐ Principal as clown for a day
- ☐ Principal as janitor for a day
- ☐ Student concert
- ☐ Staff talent show

Activities Outside of School

- ☐ Movie night (movie in gym or assembly hall after school)
- ☐ Supervised overnight slumber party/movie night (gym or assembly hall)

- ☐ 24-hour relay event (camp out in back field and teams run relay)
- ☐ Amusement park field trip
- ☐ Schoolwide dance

Sports

- ☐ Dodgeball tournament
- ☐ Kickball tournament
- ☐ Students versus staff sports games
- ☐ Tailgate party before school sports event (hamburgers, hot dogs, etc.)
- ☐ Tailgate party before homecoming football game (hamburgers, hot dogs, etc.)

Miscellaneous

- ☐ Paint mural on school wall
- ☐ Graffiti wall/zone

Privileges

- ☐ Early dismissal/half day
- ☐ Late start day
- ☐ Extended lunch hour

STRATEGIES

Foundational Intervention Strategies

Antecedent strategies — 248
    A. Change assigned seating. — 248
    B. Change work requirements. — 249
    C. Provide breaks. — 249
    D. Change expectations or procedures. — 250
    E. Offer viable choices. — 250
    F. Use precorrections. — 250
    G. Increase opportunities to respond. — 251
    H. Increase monitoring and supervision. — 251

Teaching strategies — 252
    I. Re-teach classroom expectations. — 253
    J. Provide demonstrations and modeling. — 254
    K. Provide positive practice and feedback. — 254
    L. Provide opportunities for verbal practice. — 255

Positive consequence strategies — 257
    M. Deliver praise and specific feedback. — 257
    N. Offer rewards. — 258
    O. Send positive news home. — 258

Corrective consequence strategies — 261
    P. Ignore misbehavior. — 264
    Q. Reduce peer attention. — 266
    R. Use gentle verbal reprimands or warnings. — 266
    S. Assign time owed. — 267
    T. Assign in-class timeout. — 267
    U. Assign out-of-class timeout. — 268
    V. Revoke a privilege. — 270

Interactional strategies — 276
    W. Increase the frequency of noncontingent positive attention. — 282
    X. Assign a meaningful duty or responsibility at school. — 283
    Y. Encourage and facilitate the student's participation in clubs, after-school activities, and other school events. — 283
    Z. Connect the student with an adult or peer mentor at school. — 283

Specialized Intervention Strategies

    1. Behavioral Contracting — 322
    2. Structured Reinforcement — 344
    3. Self-Monitoring and Self-Evaluation — 373
    4. Behavior Emergency Planning — 406
    5. Managing Emotional Escalation — 433
    6. Supporting Students With Internalizing Challenges — 469

REPRODUCIBLE DOCUMENTS

Reproducibles of all tools and forms discussed in this book are available for download. Go to download.ancorapublishing.com and enter access code 978-1-59909-105-1

You can print the forms and fill them out by hand. Where appropriate, the forms can be filled out and saved electronically using Adobe Reader. See the "Using the Files" document in the download files for more details.

Reproduction of the downloadable materials is granted to a single school-based professional (principal, school psychologist, teacher, special education teacher, school counselor, or behavior specialist) to assist in designing behavior interventions for individual students. Except as expressly permitted above and under the United States Copyright Act of 1976, no materials in this work may be used, reproduced, or distributed in any form or by any means, electronic or mechanical, without the prior written permission of the publisher.